History
of
Philosophy

by

Julián Marías Aguilera

Translated from the Spanish by
Stanley Appelbaum
and
Clarence C. Strowbridge

Dover Publications, Inc.
New York

Library of Congress Catalog Card Number: 66-29156

Manufactured in the United States of America
Dover Publications, Inc.
180 Varick Street
New York, N.Y. 10014

To the memory of my teacher
MANUEL GARCÍA MORENTE
who was dean and guiding spirit of
that Faculty of Philosophy and Letters
where I was introduced to philosophy

19213

Preface to the English Edition

REFLECTIONS ON ONE OF MY BOOKS

As I take a fresh look at this book with the rather general title *History of Philosophy*, which, completed twenty-five years ago, is now to be published in New York in an English translation, I feel as if I were seeing a child of mine who has grown up and is about to set out on a long journey. It is the first of my books, and it has also been the most successful. Since its initial publication in Madrid in January, 1941, it has gone through twenty-two Spanish editions. It has become the standard text in the history of philosophy for numerous classes in Spanish and Latin American universities. In 1963 it was translated into Portuguese; now it makes its appearance in the English-speaking world. Is it not extraordinary that a Spanish book of philosophy should have met with such great success? How did it happen that, despite the enormous prestige then enjoyed by German philosophy in Spain and Latin America, this book by an unknown twenty-six-year-old Spaniard was able to supplant almost entirely the German works that had dominated the intellectual marketplace and universities of the Spanish-speaking world? And how was this possible when, from its opening page, the book recalled the intellectual tradition of the years from 1931 to 1936, which was then all but completely proscribed and condemned to ostracism and oblivion?

Perhaps an explanation can be found through an investigation of the roots of this *History of Philosophy*. I had been a student in the Faculty of Philosophy and Letters of the University of Madrid from 1931 to 1936. The intellectual excellence which that Faculty's courses had attained was so superior to all that had come before and, more-over, lasted such a short time that it scarcely seems possible today that it ever existed. The Department of Philosophy, especially, had acquired a brilliance and a precision unknown in Spain either before or after. It was inspired and animated by one of the greatest creative geniuses in the philosophy of our age, who was at the same time an outstanding teacher: Ortega. For him, philosophy was a personal matter; it was his very life. We Madrid students were then present at the spellbinding and almost unreal spectacle of a philosophy that was *being shaped* before our eyes. Those were the last years of one of the most brilliant and fruitful epochs of European thought, the years between Husserl and Heidegger, from Dilthey to Scheler, from Bergson to Unamuno. We were aware that philosophy was discovering new possibilities, that this was a germinal period. (I think it really was and that if its horizon seems less promising today, it is not because those possibilities were not real and are not still with us, but because there have been certain failures of the will, slothfulness and evil passions which perhaps afflict man in some eras.) There was a dawn-like atmosphere in the Madrid Faculty of Philosophy; we were con-firmed in this feeling as we saw a new philosophy of great import being constructed like a sailing vessel in a shipyard.

The image of the shipyard is not inappropriate, because that Faculty was beginning to be a *school*. Ortega's associates were Manuel García Morente, Xavier Zubiri and José Gaos, all pupils of his; these men, together with the older fellow professors, were all col-laborating on the same task. Without indulging in excessively wishful thinking, one could believe that perhaps the prime meridian of Euro-pean philosophy would some day pass through Madrid for the first time in history.

The Faculty of Philosophy was convinced that philosophy is inseparable from its history, that its immediate content is the achieve-ments of the philosophers of the past that are still valid today; in other words, that philosophy is historical and that the history of philosophy is strict philosophy: the creative interpretation of the philosophic past from the viewpoint of a thoroughly contemporary philosophy. Therefore, we studied the classic thinkers of Western culture without regard to epochs: Greeks, medieval writers and moderns, from the pre-Socratics to contemporaries, were read—almost always in their original languages—studied, commented on; all this without a trace of "nationalism" or "provincialism." Spain, which between 1650 and 1900 had remained isolated from Europe in many respects—although not so completely as is sometimes thought—

had become one of the countries in which there prevailed a less narrow view of the real horizon of culture. Spanish thought—philosophically very modest up to the present—was not given any special emphasis. In every course the classic writers were studied. Zubiri, in his lectures on the history of philosophy, introduced us to the pre-Socratics and Aristotle, to St. Augustine and Occam, to Hegel, Schelling and Schleiermacher, to Leibniz and the Stoics. Morente, who held the chair of ethics, expounded the ethical teachings of Aristotle, Spinoza, Kant, Mill, Brentano. The courses in logic and esthetics given by Gaos led us to Plato, to Husserl. Ortega, lecturing on metaphysics, commented on Descartes, Dilthey, Bergson and the French, English and German sociologists.

This was the atmosphere in which I received my education, these were the presuppositions of my view of philosophy; in short, these are the *intellectual* roots of this book. But I do not think they are sufficient to explain, first, how I came to do something which neither my teachers nor my classmates did: to write a *History of Philosophy*; and, secondly, how this book became the one which for a quarter of a century has introduced Spanish-speaking people to this discipline. To explain this I must relate what might be called the *personal* roots which made this book possible.

That admirable Faculty gave penetrating and illuminating courses on specific subjects, but there was no general survey course on the history of philosophy; there was not even a course that studied any large period as a whole. And yet all students, no matter what their field of specialization, had to pass an examination, then called the *examen intermedio* ("intermediate examination"), in which they were questioned on the entire history of philosophy and its major themes. Needless to say, this examination worried everyone, particularly those who had taken only introductory courses in philosophy and were obliged, in preparing for the examination, to read long and difficult books, almost always in foreign languages and not always very clear.

A group of women students, from eighteen to twenty years old, classmates and very close friends of mine, asked me to help them prepare for this examination. This was in October of 1933; I was nineteen years old and in my junior year of university studies, but I had followed my professors' lectures attentively and had voraciously read a large number of books on philosophy. We organized a small and unofficial course in one of the meeting halls of the women's dormitory, of which María de Maeztu was then the director. We held class whenever we could, frequently for two or three hours on Sunday mornings. The girls were quite successful in their examinations, to the rather great surprise of the professors. The following year some other girls, who were faced with the same examination, asked me to give the course again; but the girls who were most interested in such a class were those who had already passed the examination and wanted to continue to attend those classes in philosophy. At the end of each of the two courses, they showed their gratitude with a gift: Heidegger's *Sein und Zeit* and Nicolai Hartmann's *Ethik* in 1934, and two volumes of Dilthey's *Gesammelte Schriften* in 1935. I still have these four volumes, inscribed with the names of the girls; I also still have an indelible memory of those classes and a gratitude which they could not even have suspected. I have also kept up my friendship with almost all of them. The following academic year, 1935–1936, María de Maeztu entrusted me with a formal course in philosophy for the residents of the dormitory; and thus, during my three undergraduate years—I received my degree in philosophy in June, 1936, one month before the Civil War— I found myself transformed into a university professor.

Those philosophy courses were unique in many respects, but particularly in one: my students were my classmates, my friends, girls of my own age. Thus they did not automatically respect my opinion. This experience in what might be called "lectureship without respect" was invaluable to me. These young girls accepted nothing *in verba magistri*; they did not recognize the argument of authority. In those days a boundless esteem for clarity and intelligibility prevailed throughout the Faculty of Philosophy. Ortega often quoted Goethe's verses:

> Ich bekenne mich zu dem Geschlecht,
> das aus dem Dunkel ins Helle strebt.
>
> (I declare myself to be of those
> Who from the darkness to the light aspire.)

And time and time again he said: "In philosophy, clarity is courtesy." There was no satisfaction with what Ortega himself had once labeled "the luxury of intellectual obscurity." This means that my students insisted upon understanding everything I was teaching them, which was nothing less than the entire history of Western philosophy. They asked me to clarify everything, to justify everything; to show why every philosopher thought as he did and to show that his thought was coherent, or, if it was not, why not. But this means that I had to understand it myself, if not beforehand, then at least during the progress of the class. I have never had to work harder, or more rewardingly, than in front of that class of fourteen to sixteen young women; smiling girls, mocking at times, with minds as fresh as their complexions, fond of discussion, eager to see clearly, inexorable. No one else, not even my professors, taught me so much philosophy. To be perfectly fair, I ought to share the royalties from my books with them.

Actually, I am sharing the royalties with one of them. At the close of the Civil War in 1939, the job possibilities open to a man like me, who had remained in Spain and was resolved to be faithful to the spirit of that university and to what it represented in our national life, were extremely limited and uncertain. It was pointless to think about obtaining a teaching position in any of the Spanish universities or even of contributing articles to magazines and newspapers. I was forced to undertake unusually significant tasks because the lesser jobs were all closed to me. This is one of fate's many ironies. One of the girls who had taken the courses, and who two years later was to become my wife, urged me to write a *History of Philosophy*. When I pointed out to her the enormous difficulties of the enterprise, she presented me with a large stack of notebooks: they contained her admirable, clear and extremely accurate notes on my informal lectures. I began to work with them: they were the first draft of this book. I had to fill in many items; I had to rethink everything, find a written instead of oral expression for what was said there. In short, I had to write a book that would really be a book. After a while I became discouraged; I rallied and went back to work. In December of 1940 I wrote the last page. There was still time, while correcting the proof, to add a reference to Bergson's death, which occurred in the first days of January, 1941. I ought to mention that Ortega, who was consulted by his son about the advisability of publishing this book, which in every way represented a considerable risk, without having read it replied in the affirmative from his exile in Buenos Aires; and so the Revista de Occidente, the most respected publishing house in Spain, published a book by an author of whom the most they could hope for was that no one would know him. Zubiri, who had been my instructor in the history of philosophy for four years and who had taught me countless things—he was at this time a professor in Barcelona—wrote a preface to the book.* On the seventeenth of January I dedicated the first copy to that girl, whose name was Lolita Franco and who a few months later was to change her name to mine.

I have related these details about the manner in which this book came to be written because I think they are the real reasons for its

---

* Not included in the English edition.

extraordinary success. Its readers have received the same impression from it that my first students had: the intelligibility of philosophical doctrines, the history of Western man's efforts to throw light on the deepest layers of reality; a history in which even error is explained and becomes intelligible and, to that extent, justified.

One of Ortega's central concepts, which permeated philosophical instruction in Madrid during my student years, is that of *historical reason*. This book, inspired by that principle, takes into account the total setting of each philosopher, since ideas do not derive solely from other ideas, but also from the overall world situation in which each man must create his philosophy. Thus, a history of philosophy can be written only philosophically, only by reconstituting the entire series of past philosophies from the standpoint of a present philosophy that is capable of giving meaning to them, one that does not cast them aside as obsolete errors, but acknowledges them as its own roots.

Many years have passed by since 1941, and this book has been enlarged, kept up to date, polished and made more precise during the course of successive editions; but it is the same book that came into being in front of a handful of young girls in one of the purest and most intense experiences of that phenomenon: philosophic communication.

JULIÁN MARÍAS

Madrid
July, 1966.

Contents

CHRISTIANITY

MEDIEVAL PHILOSOPHY

History
of
Philosophy

Introduction

PHILOSOPHY. Philosophy has been understood to mean principally two things: *knowledge* and a *way of life*. The word "philosopher" contains the two different meanings of "the man who possesses a certain knowledge" and "the man who lives and acts in a particular way." Philosophy as knowledge and philosophy as a way of life—these are two ways of interpreting the word, and the two interpretations have alternated and at times even existed simultaneously. Ever since the first philosophical speculation in Greece, a certain *theoretic life* has been spoken of, and at the same time philosophy has meant knowledge, speculation. It is necessary to understand the word "philosophy" in such a way that in our idea of it there is room for both meanings *at the same time*. Both interpretations are valid, inasmuch as they have constituted philosophic reality itself. And one can discover the full meaning of the word and the reason for the duality only in the total comprehension of that philosophic reality, that is, in the history of philosophy.

There is an indubitable connection between the two ways of understanding philosophy. Although the problem of explaining this connection is in large part the problem of philosophy itself, we can understand that the two interpretations are intimately connected, and in fact have never been completely separated. *Philosophy is a way of life— an essential way—that consists precisely of living according to a certain knowledge; therefore, this way of life postulates and requires this certain knowledge. It is thus knowledge which determines the meaning of the philosophic life.*

But what kind of knowledge? What is the nature of philosophic knowledge? The individual sciences—mathematics, physics, history—afford us a certainty in regard to some things—a *partial* certainty, which does not exclude doubt outside the realm of its concern. Moreover, the various certainties afforded us by these individual sciences contradict one another and demand a higher authority to arbitrate among them. In order to know precisely what to rely on, man needs a fundamental and universal certainty, by means of which he can live and arrange the other partial certainties in a hierarchical perspective.

Religion, art and philosophy give man a total conviction regarding the whole of reality—but not without essential differences. Religion is a certainty which is *received* by man, given gratuitously by God: it is *revealed*. Man does not achieve this certainty by himself; he does not conquer it, and it is not of his own creation: rather, just the opposite is true. Art also indicates a certain conviction by means of which man finds himself, and from which he interprets the sum total of his life. But this belief—which is, of course, of human origin—does not justify itself; it cannot account for itself; it does not possess intrinsic evidence. It is, in short, *unable to answer for its own consequences*. Philosophy, on the other hand, is a fundamental, universal certainty which is also *autonomous*; that is, philosophy justifies itself; it constantly demonstrates and proves its own validity; it thrives exclusively on *evidence*. Philosophy is always renewing the reasons for its certainty (Ortega).

THE IDEA OF PHILOSOPHY. It is useful to direct our attention for a moment to a few historical high points in order to see how the interpretations of philosophy as knowledge and as a way of life have been expressed simultaneously. For Aristotle, philosophy is a rigorous science, *wisdom* or *knowledge* par excellence: the science of things as they are. However, when he speaks of the various ways of life, he includes among them, as an exemplary form, a *theoretic life* which is precisely the life of the philosopher. After Aristotle, in the Stoic and Epicurean schools and the like, that overrun Greece following the death of Alexander—and later the entire Roman Empire—philosophy empties itself of scientific content. More and more it is converted into a way of life—the life of the serene and imperturbable *wise man*, which is, in fact, the human ideal of the epoch.

Within the Christian era, philosophy is to St. Augustine a question of the even more profound contrast between a *vita theoretica* and a *vita beata*. And several centuries later, St. Thomas is concerned with a *scientia theologica* and a *scientia philosophica*; the duality has passed from the sphere of life itself to the sphere of the various forms of knowledge.

For Descartes, who lived at the beginning of the modern era, philosophy is no longer a question of knowledge, or at least not exclusively so; it might perhaps be called a knowledge *for* life. It is a question of living, of living in a certain way, knowing what one does and especially what one ought to do. Thus, philosophy appears as a way of life which postulates a science. But at the same time, the highest standards of intellectual precision and absolute certainty become a part of this science.

The history does not end here. At the moment of modern Europe's maturity, Kant speaks to us (in his *Logic* and at the end of the *Critique of Pure Reason*) of *scholastic* and *worldly* concepts of philosophy. According to his scholastic concept, philosophy is a *system* of all philosophic knowledge. But in its worldly sense (the more profound and fundamental interpretation) philosophy is the science of the relationship between all knowledge and the essential goals of human reason. The philosopher is no longer the artificer of reason, but rather the legislator of human reason. And in this sense, Kant says, one may be proud to call oneself a philosopher. The ultimate goal is moral destiny; therefore, the concept of the *moral person* is the culmination of Kantian metaphysics. Philosophy in its worldly sense—as an essential way of life of man—is what gives meaning to philosophy as a science.

Finally, in our day, while Husserl insists once more on presenting philosophy as a *strict and rigorous science* and Dilthey links it essentially to human life and history, Ortega's idea of *vital reason* restates the very nucleus of the question in a fundamental way and establishes an *intrinsic* and necessary relationship between rational knowledge and life itself.

THE ORIGIN OF PHILOSOPHY. Why did man begin to philosophize? Rarely has this question been raised and discussed adequately. Aristotle's treatment of it was such that it decisively influenced the entire subsequent development of philosophy. The opening section of his *Metaphysics* is an answer to that question: *All men desire naturally to know.* For Aristotle, the reason for man's desire to know is nothing less than that it is his nature. And the nature of a thing is its substance, that of which it really consists; therefore, knowledge seems to define man; man's very essence moves him to know. Here again we find a more evident link between knowledge and life, whose meaning will become more and more clear during the course of this book. But Aristotle says something else. A little further on in the *Metaphysics*, he writes: *It is because of awe that men begin to philosophize—now and in the beginning. At first, men were awed by strange things that were closer to hand; later, pushing forward little by little in this manner, men investigated the most important things, such as the movements of the moon, sun and stars and the generation of everything.* Thus we find the most concrete root of the process of philosophizing to be a human attitude—*awe*. First man *wonders* about nearby things, and then about the sum total of all that exists. Instead of circulating among *things*, using them, enjoying them or fearing them, man stands apart from them, *alienated* from them; he inquires with awe about these nearby, everyday things which now for the first time appear to be *opposite* him and therefore alone, isolated by the question: "What is this?" Philosophy begins at this moment.

This is a completely new human attitude, which Zubiri has called *theoretic* in contrast to *mythic* attitudes. This new human outlook appears in Greece one day for the first time in history, and from that moment there is something radically new in the world, something which makes philosophy possible. To mythic man, things are propitious or harmful *powers* which he lives with and which he uses or shuns. This is the pre-Hellenic attitude and one which the people to whom the brilliant Greek discovery has not penetrated continue to share. Theorizing consciousness, on the other hand, sees *things* where previously it saw only powers. This constitutes the great discovery of *things*, a discovery so profound that today it is difficult for us to realize that it actually was a discovery or to imagine that it could have happened any other way. In order to realize its significance, we must make use of forms of thought which, while differing from the modern Western attitude, retain a remote analogy with the mythic attitude: for example, that of the infantile consciousness, the attitude of the child who finds himself in a world full of benign or hostile powers or persons, but not, strictly speaking, of *things*. When man begins to theorize, instead of being *among* the things, he is *opposite* them, *alienated* from them, and thus they acquire a meaning of their own which previously they did not have. They seem to exist for themselves, apart from man, and to have a determined consistence: that is, they possess a number of *properties*, something of their own, something that belongs to them alone. Then the things are seen as realities that *exist*, that have a special content. And only in this sense can one speak of truth or falsity. Mythic man moves outside the realm of this discovery. Only as something *existing* can things be true or false. The oldest form of this *awakening* to the truth of the things is *awe*. And therefore it is the root of philosophy.

PHILOSOPHY AND ITS HISTORY. Philosophy's relationship to its history is unlike that of science, for example, to its own history. In the latter case, the two things are distinct: science, on the one hand, and on the other, what science *was*, that is, its history. The two are independent of one another, and science can exist and be understood and cultivated separate from the history of what it has been. Science is constructed from an object and from the knowledge which at a particular moment is available about that object. In philosophy, the problem is philosophy itself; moreover, in every instance this problem is stated according to the historical and personal situation in which the philosopher finds himself, and this situation is in turn determined in large measure by the philosophic tradition to which the particular philosopher belongs. The entire philosophic past is included in every act of philosophizing. In the third place, the philosopher must investigate the philosophic problem in its totality and, therefore, philosophy itself from its original root. He cannot start from and accept a ready-made (de facto) state of knowledge; rather, he must start at the beginning and *at the same time* from the historical situation in which he finds himself. That is, philosophy must establish and fulfill itself wholly in every philosopher, not in just any manner, but in every philosopher in a uniquely appropriate way: the way in which he has been conditioned by all previous philosophy. Therefore, all philosophizing includes the entire history of philosophy; if it did not, it would not be intelligible and, what is more, it could not exist. At the same time, philosophy possesses only that reality which it achieves historically in each philosopher.

There is, then, an inseparable connection between philosophy and the history of philosophy. Philosophy is historical, and its history is an essential part of it. Moreover, the history of philosophy is not a mere erudite account of the opinions of philosophers, but the true exposition of the real content of philosophy. Then it is, in all truth, philosophy. Philosophy does not exhaust itself in any one of its systems; rather, it consists of the *true history* of all philosophic systems. And, in their turn, none of these systems can exist independently, for each one requires and involves all previous systems. There is still another point: each system of philosophy achieves maximum reality, full *truth*, only outside of itself—that is, in the thought of those philosophers who are to succeed it. All philosophizing originates from the totality of the past and projects itself toward the future, thus advancing the history of philosophy. This is, briefly, what one means when one says that *philosophy is historical*.

TRUTH AND HISTORY. The foregoing account does not mean that *truth* is not of interest in philosophy, that philosophy is to be considered merely as a historical phenomenon unconcerned with truth and falsity. Every philosophic system claims to be true; on the other hand, contradictions between systems are evident and far from coincidental; but these contradictions do not by any means signify complete incompatibility. No system of philosophy can claim *absolute* and *exclusive* validity, because none *exhausts* reality; to the extent that any system claims to be the only true system, it is false. Every philosophic system apprehends a portion of reality—precisely that part which is accessible from its point of view or perspective. Nor does the truth of one system imply the falsity of other systems, except on points which are formally contradicted. A contradiction arises only when a philosopher affirms more than he actually sees. Thus all philosophic visions are true (I mean, of course, partially true) and in principle do not exclude one another. Moreover, every philosopher's point of view is conditioned by his *historical* situation, and therefore every system, if it is to be faithful to its own perspective, must include all previous systems as part of its own composition. Thus, the various *true* philosophies are not interchangeable; rather, they are rigorously determined according to their sequence in human history.*

* See my *Introducción a la Filosofía* [*Reason and Life*], ch. XII.

GREEK PHILOSOPHY

The Suppositions of Greek Philosophy

If we ignore the obscure problem of Oriental (Indian, Chinese) philosophy, in which what is most problematic is the meaning of the word "philosophy" itself, and focus our attention on what philosophy has been in the West, we will find that its first stage is the philosophy of the Greeks. This initial phase, which lasted for more than a millennium, differs from all later phases in that it does not have a philosophic tradition behind it; that is, Greek philosophy emerges from a concrete human situation—that of "ancient" man—which contains no philosophical element or ingredient. This circumstance has two important consequences: in the first place, the birth of philosophy in Greece has a purity and originality superior to all that is to come later; secondly, ancient man's vital and historical situation directly conditions Hellenic speculation to the point that the major theme of the history of Greek philosophy consists in determining why man, upon reaching a certain stage in his development, found himself compelled to fulfill a completely new and unknown need, which today we call philosophizing. We cannot discuss this problem here, but we must at least point out some of the historic suppositions which made philosophy possible and necessary in the Hellenic world. *

A way of life is defined above all by its repertory of *beliefs*. Naturally, beliefs change, as Ortega has shown, from generation to generation—this is what constitutes historical mutation. But a certain basic core of beliefs endures through several generations and gives them the higher

* Cf. my *Biografía de la Filosofía*, I. "La filosofía griega desde su origen hasta Platón." (Emecé, Buenos Aires, 1954). [*Obras*, vol. II.]

unity which we designate by such words as *epoch, era* or *age*. What are the basic beliefs held by Greek man which limit and give form to his philosophy?

Hellenic man finds himself in a *world* which has always existed and which is therefore never a problem; all questioning *presupposes* this world, takes it for granted. The world is interpreted as *nature* and, therefore, as an original *principle*, or as that from which all concrete reality emerges or issues. Thus the world appears to be endowed with *potentiality*, with productive capacity. But at the same time it is a *multiplicity*; the world contains many things which are capable of changing and are defined by opposites. Every one of these things has an independent consistency, but the things themselves are not permanent. They change, and their properties are understood in terms of opposites: cold is the opposite of warm, even the opposite of odd, and so on. This polarity is characteristic of the ancient mind. The properties inherent in the things permit them to be used in a technic basically different from magical procedures, in which things are treated as powers.

The Greek's world is *intelligible*. It can be understood, and comprehension consists in *seeing* or contemplating that reality and of *explaining* it. *Theory*, *lógos* and *being* are the three decisive terms of Hellenic thought, and they are rooted in this primary attitude toward the world. As a consequence, the world appears as something which is ordered and subjected to law: this is the notion of the *cosmos*. Reason is inserted into this lawful order of the world, which can be governed and directed, and the concrete form of this lawful order in human affairs is the political coexistence of men in cities. It is necessary to keep this basic outline of ancient beliefs in mind in order to understand the historical fact of Greek philosophy.

The Pre-Socratics

1. THE MILESIAN SCHOOL

The Greek philosophers prior to Socrates are called the *pre-Socratics*. This name has, to begin with, a chronological value: these are the thinkers who lived from the end of the seventh century to the close of the fifth century before Christ. However, the term also has a more profound meaning: the earliest beginnings of Greek philosophy can be considered true philosophy because after them there existed a full and indisputable philosophy. Examined in the light of mature philosophy—from Socrates onward—the first Hellenic speculations are seen to be philosophic, although not all of them would merit this designation were they not the beginning and promise of something to come later on. By being *pre-Socratics*, by announcing and preparing a philosophic maturity, the first thinkers of Ionia and Magna Graecia are themselves already philosophers. One must not forget that if it is true that the present depends on the past, then the present sometimes redounds on the past and colors it as well. Specific affirmations of the oldest Indian and Chinese thinkers are often similar to those of the Greeks; the major difference between these two philosophies is that after the pre-Socratics came Socrates, whereas the stammering Oriental speculation was not followed by a philosophic fullness in the sense which this phrase has taken on in the West. This explains the fundamental difference which we notice between the earliest thinking of the Hellenic people and that of the Orientals.

The last pre-Socratics do not predate Socrates; they are his contemporaries in the second half of the fifth century. However, they remain part of the group that antedates him because of the theme and character of their speculation. *Nature* (φύσις) is the subject of the entire first stage of philosophy. Aristotle calls these thinkers φυσιολόγοι, physicists; they create a physics by philosophic method. Confronted by nature, the pre-Socratic adopts an attitude that differs enormously from that of Hesiod, for example. The latter attempts to *narrate* how the world has been shaped and ordered, or supply the genealogy of the gods; he creates a *theogony*, relates a *myth*. Myth and philosophy are closely related, as Aristotle has observed, and this constitutes a serious problem; but myth and philosophy are two different things. The pre-Socratic philosopher confronts nature with a theoretical question; he attempts to tell *what it is*. Philosophy is chiefly defined by the question which motivates it: *What is all this*? This question cannot be answered with a myth, but only with a philosophy.

MOTION. What is it that makes the Greeks wonder about the nature of things? What is the root of the awe that first moved the Greeks to philosophize? In other words, what is it that alienates Hellenic man and makes him feel strange in the world in which he finds himself? Bear in mind first that the pre-Socratics' situation differs from that of all later philosophers. The later men, upon setting themselves a problem, found united with it a repertory of solutions already proposed and tried, whereas the pre-Socratics abandoned the answers given by tradition or myth for a new instrument of certainty—*reason*.

The Greek wonders at and is awed by *motion*. What does this mean? Motion (κίνησις) has a fuller meaning in Greek than in English or the Romance languages. What we call motion is only a particular form of *kinesis*, whereas in Greek "motion" means change or variation. The Greeks distinguished four types of motion: (1) local motion (φορά), change of place; (2) quantitative motion, that is, augmentation or diminution (αὔξησις καὶ φθίσις); (3) qualitative motion, or alteration (ἀλλοίωσις); and (4) substantial motion, that is, generation and decay (γένεσις καὶ φθορά). All these kinds of motion, and especially the last named, which is the most profound and radical, perturb and trouble Greek man because they make the existence of things problematic; they overwhelm him with uncertainty to the point that he does not know what to rely on in respect to them. If things change, what are they *really*? If a white object ceases to be white and becomes green, it is and it is not white; if something that is ceases to be, then the thing both *is* and *is not*. Multiplicity and contradiction permeate the very being of things; thus, the Greek wonders what the things *really* are, that is, what they are *permanently*, behind their many appearances. Confronted by the numerous aspects of the things, the Greek searches for their permanent and immutable roots, which are superior to this multiplicity and which can give it meaning. Therefore, what is truly interesting is the initial question of philosophy: What is all this really? Or: What is Nature, the source from which all things emerge? The history of Greek philosophy is made up of the various answers given to this question.

Greek philosophy has a very concrete and well-known origin. It begins on the Ionian coasts, in the Hellenic cities of Asia Minor in the first years of the sixth century before Christ—or perhaps at the end of the seventh century. The origin of philosophy can be said to be ex-centric, since it took place outside the center of the Greek world; it was not until much later (the fifth century B.C.) that philosophic speculation appeared in Greece proper. The cities on the eastern coast of the Aegean were richer and more prosperous than those of Hellas, and it was in the Aegean cities that an economic, technical and scientific awakening first developed. This awakening was promoted in part by contact with other cultures, especially with the Egyptian and Persian civilizations. It was in Miletus, the most important city in this region, that philosophy first appeared. There, a group of philosophers who were also men of great stature in the affairs of the country and who belonged to approximately three successive generations, attempted to supply answers to the question of what nature is. These first philosophers are usually referred to as the Ionian or Milesian school; the three principal and representative figures are Thales, Anaximander and Anaximenes, and their activity fills the sixth century.

THALES OF MILETUS. Thales lived from the last third of the seventh century to the middle of the sixth century. Ancient documents credit him with several occupations: those of engineer, astronomer, financier, politician; therefore, he is included among the Seven Wise Men of Greece. He may have been born in distant Phoenicia. Thales is thought to have traveled through Egypt, and is credited with having introduced into Greece Egyptian geometry (the calculation of distances and heights by means of the equality and similarity of triangles, but certainly by empirical methods). Thales also predicted an eclipse. He is, then, a great man of his time.

Aristotle is our major and most valuable source of information for what most interests us here, Thales' philosophy. In fact, Aristotle is our best authority on the interpretation of everything pre-Socratic. He says that according to Thales, the source or original principle (ἀρχή) of all things is water; that is, the moist state. The reason for this is probably that animals and plants have moist nutrition and seed.

The land floats on water; moreover, the world is full of spirits and souls and many demons. Or, as Aristotle says, "all things are full of gods."

This animation or vivification of matter is called *hylozoism*. But the truly significant thing about Thales is the fact that, for the first time in history, a man is questioning everything that exists, not because he is wondering about the mythic origin of the world, but because he wants to know what nature *really* is. Between theogony and Thales there is an abyss—the abyss which separates philosophy from all previous thinking.

ANAXIMANDER. Toward the middle of the sixth century, Anaximander succeeded Thales as the leader of the Milesian school. Hardly anything about his life is known with certainty. He wrote a work (which has been lost) known by the title later assigned to the greater part of pre-Socratic writings: *On Nature* (περὶ φύσεως). Various inventions of a mathematical and astronomical character are attributed to him; he is also credited—with greater likelihood—with drawing the first map of the world. To the question concerning the source of things, Anaximander answers that it is the *ápeiron*, τὸ ἄπειρον. This word means, literally, infinite, not in a mathematical sense, but rather in the sense of limitlessness or indeterminateness. It is convenient to understand it as something *grandiose* and unlimited in its magnificence, something which provokes awe. It is the marvelous totality of the world in which man is surprised to find himself. This nature is, furthermore, a source: from it all things spring forth. Starting from this ἀρχή, some things come to be, others cease to be, but the source endures because it is independent of and superior to these individual changes. Things are created through a process of separation; they separate from the mass of nature in a sieve-like movement—first cold and warm, and then the other things. This process of being created and dying is an injustice, an ἀδικία, an unjust predominance of one opposite over another (warm over cold, damp over dry, and so on). Individual things maintain their predominance by means of this injustice. However, there is a natural law which will make things return to an ultimate end that is without injustice, the immortal and incorruptible *ápeiron*, in which opposites do not predominate over one another. *Time* is the means by which this natural law must be realized. Time will make all things return to this unity, to the quietude and irresolution of the φύσις, from which they have unjustly departed.

Anaximander was also an astronomer, and made a considerable contribution to the development of this science, but we cannot here discuss his achievement in this field. As a philosopher he represents the step from the simple designation of a substance as a source of nature to a more acute and profound idea of nature, and one which already shows the features which will later characterize all pre-Socratic philosophy: a totality which is the source of everything, which is free from mutation and plurality and which is *set in opposition to the things*. We will see these features reappearing constantly in the very heart of Greek philosophical development.

ANAXIMENES. Anaximenes, who lived in the second half of the sixth century, was a pupil of Anaximander, and was also from Miletus. The final important Milesian, he adds two new concepts to the doctrine of his master. First, he supplies a concrete indication of what the source of nature is: *air*, which he relates to respiration or breathing. All things are created from air and return to it when they decay. This appears to be something of a return to Thales' point of view, except that water has been replaced by air; but Anaximenes adds a second stipulation: that the things are formed from air in a specific way—by condensation and rarefaction. This is of the greatest importance; we now have not only the designation of a primal substance but also the explanation of how all things are made from it. Rarefied air is fire; when air is more condensed, it becomes clouds, water, land, rocks, depending on the degree of density. To the first substance, which supports the changing variety of things, is added a source of motion. And it is at this moment that the Persian domination of Ionia impels philosophy toward the West.

2. THE PYTHAGOREANS

PYTHAGORAS. The Pythagoreans were the first philosophic group to appear after the Milesians. At the end of the sixth century, philosophy was transported from the Ionian coasts to the coasts of Magna Graecia, to southern Italy and to Sicily; there it formed what Aristotle called the *Italic school*. The Persian invasion of Asia Minor apparently forced certain Ionic groups to move toward the extreme western edge of the Hellenic world, and Pythagoreanism arose from this fertile emigration.

Pythagoreanism is one of the most obscure and complex chapters in Greek philosophic history. In the first place, everything relating to the history of the movement is problematic; in the second place, it is extremely difficult to interpret. We will have to limit ourselves here to pointing out its most important features, without discussing the serious questions it raises.

Pythagoras was the founder of this school, but he is little more than a name; we know hardly anything about him, and nothing at all with certainty. It appears that he came from the island of Samos and settled in Croton, in Magna Graecia. Several journeys are attributed to him, including one to Persia, where he is said to have met the Magus Zaratas, that is, Zoroaster or Zarathustra. He was probably not at all concerned with mathematics, although his school later became interested in this subject. Pythagoras' activity must have been principally religious in character, connected with the Orphic mysteries, which were, in turn, related to the cults of Dionysus. Aristotle speaks of the Pythagoreans in an impersonal manner, and underscores this vagueness with his favorite expression: *those called Pythagoreans.* . . .

THE PYTHAGOREAN SCHOOL. The Pythagoreans settled in a series of cities on the Italian mainland and in Sicily, and then continued into Greece proper. They formed a league or sect and submitted themselves to many strange rules and taboos: they did not eat meat or beans, they could not wear clothes made of wool, or pick up anything that had fallen, or stir a fire with an iron, and so on. It is difficult to see the reasons for these rules—if indeed there were any. Two groups of Pythagoreans, the *akousmatikoi* and the *mathematikoi*, are distinguished, according to the nature and degree of their initiation. The Pythagorean order tended to oppose the aristocracy, but it ended in forming one itself and in taking part in politics. As a result of this, there was a violent democratic reaction in Croton, and the Pythagoreans were persecuted. Many were killed and had their homes burned. The founder escaped and, according to legend, died shortly afterward. Later, the Pythagoreans achieved a new flowering, called neo-Pythagoreanism.

More interesting to us at this point, however, is the meaning of the Pythagorean order as such. It was a proper *school.* (The word "school" (σχολή) means, in Greek, *leisure*: it is useful to bear this in mind.) This school is defined by the way of life of its members—emigrants, expatriates—in short, foreigners. Following the example of the Olympic games, the Pythagoreans spoke of three ways of life: that of those who buy and sell, that of those who run in the stadium, and that of the spectators, who limit themselves to watching. The Pythagoreans, inquisitive foreigners in Magna Graecia, lived as spectators. This is what is called the βίος θεωρητικός, the theoretic or contemplative life. The main difficulty in leading this kind of life lies in the body, with its necessities which subdue man. It is necessary to free oneself from these necessities. The body is a tomb (σῶμα σῆμα), say the Pythagoreans; one must triumph over it, but one must not lose it. In order to accomplish this, the soul must first attain the state of *enthusiasm*—that is, *ecstasy*. Here the connection with the Orphics and their rites, founded on *manía* (madness) and on orgy, is evident. The Pythagorean school utilizes and transforms these rites. In this way one attains a self-sufficient, theoretic life, a life not tied to the necessities of the body, a divine life. The man who achieves this is a wise man, a σοφός. (It appears that the word *philosophía*, or love of wisdom, more modest than *sophía*, was first used in Pythagorean circles). The perfect *sophós* is at the same time the perfect citizen; because of this, Pythagoreanism creates an aristocracy and ends up by taking part in politics.

MATHEMATICS. Another important aspect of the activity of the Pythagoreans is their speculation in the field of mathematics. Greek and modern mathematics do not greatly resemble one another. The former was begun—almost as a mere operative technique—in the Milesian school, and inherited the knowledge of Egypt and Asia Minor. But it was not until the time of the Pythagoreans that mathematics was converted into an autonomous and rigorous *science*. Within the Pythagorean school—and especially in the so-called neo-Pythagorean period—the mathematical knowledge which was later to be continued in the schools of Athens and Cyzicus was developed. In the fourth century, the Platonic Academy and the school of Aristotle were to forge the major philosophical concepts which, in the Hellenistic period, beginning with the third century, would permit the elaboration and systemization of mathematics, as epitomized in the work of Euclid.

The Pythagoreans discovered a type of entity—numbers and geometric figures—which is not corporeal, but has reality and offers resistance to the mind; this discovery leads men to think that *being* cannot be identified baldly with corporal being, and this in turn necessitates a decisive amplification of the notion of entity. But the Pythagoreans, carried along by their own discovery, make a new identification, this time in reverse order: for them, being comes to mean the being of mathematical objects. Numbers and figures are the *essence* of things, and entities which exist are *imitations* of mathematical objects. In some texts it is affirmed that numbers are *the things themselves*. Pythagorean mathematics is not an operative technique; rather, it is the discovery and construction of new entities, which are changeless and eternal, as opposed to *things*, which are variable and transitory. This situation gives rise to the mystery surrounding the discoveries of this school—for instance, the discovery of regular polyhedrons. One tradition relates that Hippasus of Metapontum was drowned—or rather shipwrecked, punished by the gods—during a

sea voyage for having revealed the secret of the construction of the
dodecahedron.

Looking into another matter, we find that arithmetic and geometry are closely related: the number 1 stands for a point, 2 for a line,
3 for a surface, 4 for a solid; the number 10, the sum of the first four
numbers, is the famous *tetractys*, the major number. The Pythagoreans
speak geometrically of square, oblong, plane and cube numbers and
the like. There are mystical numbers, endowed with special properties.
The Pythagoreans establish a series of opposites, by means of which
qualities maintain strange interrelationships: the unlimited with the
limited, the even with the odd, the many with the one, and so forth.
The symbolism of these ideas is problematic and difficult to understand.

The Pythagoreans also created a mathematical theory of music.
They made use of the relationship between the lengths of the strings of
instruments and the corresponding notes to carry out a quantitative
study of everything musical; since the distances of the planets from the
earth correspond approximately to the musical intervals, it was
thought that every star emitted a note, and all the notes together comprised the so-called harmony of the spheres or *celestial music*, which we
do not hear because it is constant and without variation.

The Pythagoreans' contributions to the field of astronomy were
profound and penetrating. Ecphantus affirmed the rotation of the
earth, and Alcmaeon of Croton made penetrating studies in the fields
of biology and embryology. Archytas of Tarentum and Philolaus of
Croton were the two most important figures in the field of Pythagorean
mathematics.*

In the Pythagorean school we have a first clear example of philosophy understood as a way of life. The problem of the self-sufficient life
leads the people of this school to a special discipline consisting of contemplation. There appears in Greece with the Pythagoreans the
theme of *freedom*, the theme of the man who is self-reliant, which is to
become one of the permanent themes of Hellenic thought. This preoccupation with the soul leads the Pythagoreans to the doctrine of
transmigration or *metempsychosis*, which is related to the problem of
immortality. And the problem of immortality, which is intimately
related to age and time, is linked with speculation about numbers;
numbers are, above all, measures of time, the *ages of things*. We thus see

* Concerning the problem of Greek mathematics, see my *Biografía de la Filosofía*,
I, p. iii, and especially *Ensayos de teoría*, "El descubrimiento de los objetos mate-
máticos en la filosofía griega" [*Obras*, IV].

that the unifying base of the extremely complex Pythagorean movement is centered in the theme of the contemplative and *divine* life.

3. PARMENIDES AND THE ELEATIC SCHOOL

There is another philosophic budding in Magna Graecia besides
Pythagoreanism: the Eleatic school. Parmenides is the major figure in
this group, and Zeno and Melissus are his principal followers. This
philosophic group is of the greatest importance, for with these philosophers, philosophy acquired a level and rank it did not previously
possess. Parmenides' influence has had a decisive impact on the history
of philosophy up to the present day. It is convenient to mention at this
time a precursor of the Eleatic school—Xenophanes.

XENOPHANES. Xenophanes was from Colophon, in Asia Minor.
The exact dates of his birth and death are not known, but it has been
ascertained that he was at least ninety-two years old when he died and
that he came after Pythagoras and before Heraclitus. Therefore, he
lived in the second half of the sixth century B.C. and the first half of the
fifth. It is also known that he traveled throughout Hellas reciting
poetry, usually his own. Xenophanes' work was written in verse; it
comprises elegiac verse of a poetic and moral nature, in which are
intermingled conjectures on cosmological doctrine. The most significant things about Xenophanes are, in the first place, his criticism of
the Greek popular religion and, secondly, a certain "pantheism," an
anticipation of the doctrine of the oneness of being that was developed
in the Eleatic school.

Xenophanes felt pride in wisdom, which he believed to be superior
to brute force or physical skill. He thus thought the adulation accorded
the winners of the games, races, and the like, unmerited. Xenophanes
found the gods of Homer and Hesiod immoral and absurd; from them,
he said, one can learn only robbery, adultery and deception. At the
same time, he rejected the anthropomorphic concept of the gods,
saying that, just as the Ethiopians conceive of gods as being flat-nosed
and black, lions or oxen would—if they could—make their gods in the
image of lions or oxen. Confronted with this anthropomorphic outlook, Xenophanes spoke of a single god. Here are the four fragments
from his satires which refer to this (Diels, frag. 23–26): "A single god,
the greatest among gods and men, not similar to men either in form or
in thought. . . . He sees in his entirety, thinks in his entirety, hears in his
entirety. . . . But, without effort, he governs everything by the force of
his spirit. . . . And he dwells always in the same place, without moving
at all, nor does it suit him to displace himself from one side to the
other."

The meaning of these fragments is clear enough. There is a divine unity, and its divinity is strongly emphasized. And this single god is immovable and *all-inclusive*. It is for this reason that Aristotle said that Xenophanes was the first person who "one-ized" (ἐνίζειν) things; that is, that he was a partisan of the One. Therefore, even while ignoring the obscure problem of influences, we must consider Xenophanes as a precursor of the doctrine of the Eleatics.

PARMENIDES. Parmenides is the most significant of all the pre-Socratic philosophers. In the history of philosophy he represents a moment of major importance—the appearance of metaphysics. With Parmenides, philosophy acquires its true hierarchy and constitutes itself as a strict discipline. Up until his time, Greek speculation had been cosmological, physical, with a philosophic purpose and method. It is Parmenides who discovers the proper theme of philosophy and the method by which this theme can be approached. In his hands philosophy comes to be metaphysics and ontology. He is no longer simply going to discuss *things*; he is going to discuss things *for what they are*, that is, as *entities*. The Entity, the ἐόν, ὄν (*ón*), is Parmenides' great discovery. This is true to such a degree that philosophy *sensu stricto* begins with him, and metaphysical thought to our day retains the imprint of Parmenides' mind. And together with the object is the method which permits us to reach it, what the Greeks called νοῦς (*noûs*) and the ancient Romans translated as *mens*: mind, intelligence, or even in some cases perhaps, spirit. As we shall see, this *noûs* is essentially united with the *ón*. The interpretation of Parmenides' philosophy presents serious difficulties which we cannot discuss here; we will simply point out what was newest and most efficacious in his thought. The understanding of this Eleatic philosopher has been decisively advanced in recent years by the work of Karl Reinhardt and, especially, by my teacher, Xavier Zubiri.

Parmenides of Elea lived at the end of the sixth century and in the first half of the fifth: his dates cannot be determined with greater precision. Although Xenophanes indisputably influenced him, it is unlikely that the two men knew each other personally. Parmenides was also apparently influenced by the thinking of the Pythagoreans. Plato dedicated a dialogue to Parmenides, naming it after him; it is perhaps the most important of all the Platonic dialogues. Aristotle studied Parmenides' work very carefully. In addition, large fragments of a poem by Parmenides are preserved; the poem is written in hexameters and is known by the traditional title, *On Nature*.

PARMENIDES' "ON NATURE." This poem consisted of an introduction of great poetic power and two succeeding parts. The first part dealt with the *way of truth,* and the second with the *way of opinion.* More of the first part is preserved than of the second. We will limit ourselves to pointing out the most important passages of the poem.

In the introduction the poet is traveling the road of the *goddess* in a chariot drawn by spirited horses. The daughters of the *Sun* guide him; *they draw aside the veils from their faces* and leave the abode of night, which is guarded by Justice. The goddess greets Parmenides and tells him that it is necessary for him to learn everything, "the inviolable heart of well-rounded truth, as well as the opinions of mortals, who do not possess true certainty." She also informs him that one can speak of but one way of life. The introduction to the poem ends at this point. There is a clear allusion to the passage from mythical to theoretical consciousness: the daughters of the Sun have rescued Parmenides from darkness. The metaphor of the veils stands for truth, which was understood in Greece as an *unveiling* or discovering (ἀλήθεια).

In the first part of the body of the poem the goddess speaks of "two ways," but these are not the two aforementioned ways, the ways of truth and opinion, for the latter is, strictly speaking, a third way. The first two are ways which are possible *from the point of view of truth,* of the things as they *are*: first, the way of *what is* and *what could not possibly not be* (the way of persuasion and truth) and, secondly, the way of *what is not.* This latter way is impracticable, since what is not cannot be known or expressed. Here we see the intimate connection between the *noûs* and the *ón,* between the mind or spirit in truth and the Entity. Afterward there follows what we could call Parmenides' ontology; that is, the explication of the attributes of the Entity which he has just discovered. But this subject requires a detailed exposition.

The second part of the poem abandons the way of truth in order to enter upon the way of the opinion of mortals. The few extant fragments of this section deal with the interpretation of motion or change, not from the point of view of *noûs,* or, therefore, from the point of view of the Entity, but rather from that of *sensory perception* and of *things.* This discussion also includes a few cosmological statements.

The various ways can be shown schematically as follows:

method	object	way
noûs	the *Entity*	$\left\{\begin{array}{l}\text{of truth (way of "what is")}\\\text{of impasse (way of "what is not")}\end{array}\right.$
sensory perception	the *things*	of opinion (way of "what is and is not")

THE PREDICATES OF THE ENTITY. It is useful to enumerate and

explain briefly the predicates which according to Parmenides correspond to the ὄν, Entity.

1. The *ón* is *present*. The things, insofar as they are, are present to the
mind, the *noûs*. The Entity neither was nor will be; it *is* now, in the
present. *"Ον* (Latin, *ens*) is a present participle. The things can be far
away from or close to the senses, either present or absent, but as
Entities they are contiguous with the *noûs*. The mind possesses the
presence of the ὄν.

2. All things are Entities; that is, they *are*. They are enveloped by
being; they are united, *one*. The multiplicity of the things does not
affect the oneness of the Entity. The *ón* is one. Therefore, Parmenides
arrives at the statement that the Entity is a sphere without spaces of
non-being.

3. Furthermore, this Entity is *immovable*. Motion is understood as a
mode of being. Coming to be or ceasing to be implies a duality of
entities, and the Entity is one. For this reason, from its own point of
view, the Entity is *homogeneous* and *indivisible*: if I divide a thing into
two parts, the Entity remains as undivided as ever; it envelops the
two parts equally; the division does not affect it in the least.

4. The Entity is *full*; it has no empty spaces. (The problem of the
void is very important throughout Greek philosophy.) The Entity is
continuous and *all-inclusive*. If something happened to be outside of the
Entity, it would not exist, and if something *existed* outside of the
Entity, it *would be*—that is, it would be the *Entity*.

5. For the same reason, the Entity is *uncreated* and *imperishable*. The
contrary would imply a non-being, which is impossible.

These are the principal predicates of the Entity, not of the
things. These predicates are discovered by the first way, the way of
truth.

OPINION. Inasmuch as the second way, the way of *what is not*, is
impracticable, we will examine the third way, the way of δόξα, the
opinion of mortals. This third way moves within the sphere of truth,
and therefore can be truth or falsity. The extent to which one or the
other exists can only be decided on the basis of truth.

1. *Dóxa* relies on worldly information, information based on *things*.
This information is *manifold* and *capable of changing*. The things are
green, red, hard, cold, water, air, and so on. Moreover, the things
transform themselves from one thing to another and are in a constant
state of flux. However—

2. *Dóxa* understands this motion, this change, as a coming to be, and
this is where it is wrong. Being is not discovered by the senses, but by
noûs. And *dóxa*, which moves in the realm of sensory perception, which

is what it possesses, jumps directly to being without benefit of *noûs*, which it lacks. This is why it is unreliable.

3. *Δόξα*, besides being opinion, is *of mortals*. This is because its organ is sensory perception, *αἴσθησις*; sensory perception is composed of opposites and therefore is mortal, perishable, just as the things themselves are. Opinion does not have *noûs*, the only thing which is *divine*, immortal, as being is.

In this way Parmenides interprets motion as *light* and *darkness*, as an illuminating and a darkening. That is, coming to be is nothing more than a coming to be *apparent*. Things which seem to come to be already existed, but in darkness. Motion is change, not generation: therefore, from the point of view of being it does not exist. All motion or change is convention (*νόμος*); that is, names which men give to things.

ONTOLOGY AND METAPHYSICS. We can now ask ourselves the meaning of Parmenides' discovery. The things—in Greek *πράγματα*, *prágmata*—manifest multiple predicates or properties to the senses. Things are colored, warm or cold, hard or soft, large or small, animals, trees, rocks, stars, fire, boats made by man. But when they are considered with another organ, with the mind or *noûs*, the things manifest a property which is of the greatest importance and common to all: before being white, or red, or warm, the things *are*. The things simply are. Being is seen to be an essential property of things, what has since been called a *real predicate*, a quality which manifests itself only to *noûs*. The things are now *ὄντα*, entities. And the *ὄν* and *νοῦς* are seen to be essentially related, and the one does not occur without the other. Parmenides says that in this sense being and the *noeín* or *noûs* are the *same*. When seen through *noûs*, the Entity is *one* and *immovable*, in contrast to the *plurality* and *changeability* of the things perceived by the senses. In Parmenides' thinking we see already beginning the division between the two worlds, the world of truth and the world of appearances (opinion or *dóxa*); the latter world is false when it is taken as true reality. This division comes to be decisive in Greek thought.

Upon looking at things somewhat more closely, we can say that Parmenides, after thinking that the things have a *determined* consistency, realizes that this implies they have a determined *consistency*, with the word "consistency" now emphasized. The things consist of something; but now attention is not directed to that something but to their *previous* consistency, whatever it may be that they consist of. Things appear, above all, as *consistencies*; and this is precisely what the participle *eón*, *ón*, which is the core of Parmenidean philosophy, means. Things consist of this or that because they consist previously;

that is, they consist of being *what is consistent* (*tò ón*). Therefore, Parmenides' discovery might be expressed as follows: before all other determinations, the things *consist of consisting*.

With Parmenides, then, philosophy changes from physics to ontology—an ontology of the cosmic, physical Entity. And since the Entity is immovable, physics is impossible from the point of view of *being*, and, therefore, of philosophy. Physics is the science of nature, and nature is the principle of the motion of natural things. If motion *is not*, then physics as a philosophic science of nature is not possible. This is the serious problem that is to be debated by all the later pre-Socratics and that will only be adequately solved by Aristotle. If the Entity is one and immovable, there is no nature, and physics is impossible. If motion *is*, an idea of the Entity distinct from that of Parmenides is necessary. This new idea of the Entity is what Aristotle achieves, as we shall see later on. Before Aristotle, Greek philosophy is the effort to make motion possible within Parmenidean metaphysics, a fruitful effort which inspires philosophy and makes it restate the problem in a basic way—a struggle of giants over being, to quote Plato.

ZENO. Zeno, Parmenides' most important pupil, directly succeeded him as leader of the Eleatic school. From Elea also, Zeno seems to have been some forty years younger than Parmenides. His method, known as *dialectics*, is his most interesting discovery. This manner of argumentation consists of taking a thesis that has been accepted by the adversary or has been commonly admitted, and of showing that the consequences of this thesis contradict one another or contradict the thesis itself; in short, that according to the principle of contradiction, which Parmenides implicitly used, the thesis is impossible.

Parmenides' theses, especially those relative to the oneness of being and the possibility of motion, contradict general opinion. To support Parmenides' ideas, Zeno constructs several arguments which begin with the idea of motion and show that it is impossible. For example, one cannot traverse the distance *AB*, because in order to arrive at *B* it is necessary to pass first through a middle point *C*; in order to reach *C*, one most pass through point *D*, halfway between *A* and *C*, and so on, to infinity. Thus, one would have to pass through an infinite series of intermediate points, and motion would be impossible. To give another example, Achilles, who runs ten times faster than the tortoise, will never catch up with it if the tortoise has a certain head start. This is because while Achilles is running off this head start, the tortoise advances one-tenth of that distance; while Achilles runs off this new distance, the tortoise advances another one-tenth of the new distance, and so on, to infinity; therefore, Achilles never catches up with the tortoise. Zeno proposed several other *aporiai* (ἀπορίαι) or problems, but we need not go into detail about them here.

Naturally, the *aporiai* cited above do not mean that Zeno believed that things actually happen in this way. *Motion is demonstrated to be in the act of moving*; by *moving along* one gets from *A* to *B* and Achilles catches up with the tortoise. However, it is not a question of this, but rather of explaining motion. According to the ideas of the era, motion is impossible and Parmenides is right. In order for motion to be interpreted *ontologically*, a different idea of the Entity is necessary. If the Entity is the Entity of Parmenides, then motion *is not*. Zeno's *aporiai* reveal this fact very clearly. Aristotle's entire ontology will be necessary in order to answer adequately the problem posed by Parmenides. Motion cannot be *built up from parts*, any more than the continuum can be *composed* in this way. Aristotle will construct an idea of being which is essentially different from that of Parmenides, and only then will the *being* of motion be explained, and physics be possible.

MELISSUS. Melissus, the last important member of the Eleatic school, was not from Elea; he was Ionian, from Samos. He was an admiral of this island during the rebellion against Athens, and achieved a great naval victory in 442 B.C. Melissus represents the continuation of Parmenides' thought—with some individual characteristics. He denies multiplicity and the possibility of motion; he denies that knowledge of manifold things constitutes knowledge of truth. But, whereas Parmenides affirmed that the Entity is finite, Melissus says that it is infinite, because it has neither origin nor end, since these would be distinct from it. For the same reason he rejects the idea that the Entity is a sphere; a sphere might be interpreted as a limited part of the extension of the Entity.

PARMENIDES' INFLUENCE. It is useful to remember that Parmenides' most profound influence in philosophy is found not within his school— that is, expressed in the thought of the Eleatics—but outside of it. As is the case with all genuine philosophy, Parmenides' philosophy is effective because of the very problem which it poses, not because of scholastic or group action. His great discovery sets Greek philosophy earnestly developing along metaphysical lines; and the consequences of Parmenides' discovery are still felt today.

4. FROM HERACLITUS TO DEMOCRITUS

THE GENERAL PROBLEM. Parmenides succeeded in discovering *things* as Entities, as something that *is*; and as a consequence of this he had to attribute to the Entity a series of predicates that turned out to contradict the way in which things actually happened; this is how the problem arose. Actually, a problem is precisely this: the awareness of a contradiction. The classic example is that of the pole which is submerged in water. It is straight to the touch and bent to the sight; it is and is not straight; therefore, it is and is not. Likewise, the Entity is one and immovable, but actually things—which exist—move and are manifold. This is basically the same contradiction that Parmenides dealt with: the contradiction between being and non-being.

Parmenides discovered that when we say a thing is white, we have not only the thing and the whiteness, but also the *is*; this *is* penetrates the thing and the whiteness and makes the thing *be* white. The Entity is, as Plato says, a third thing, a certain third element, τρίτον τι.

This problem of the ὄν, the Entity, permeates all the concrete theorizing which arises after Parmenides in the field of philosophy; all questions resolve themselves into this antinomy of being and non-being, which is closely linked with the antinomy of oneness and multiplicity, and also with that of motion. Motion, in fact, is moving *from* a source *to* an end—it was understood as such in Greece. Therefore, it assumes at least a duality, something contrary to the uniqueness of the Entity, and also an inconsistency: motion is realized between opposites (the passage from white to black, from warm to cold, from being to non-being); and here we find ourselves again at the very center of the problem of being one. All Greek philosophy from Heraclitus to Democritus moves within the scope of Parmenides' idea of the Entity, and this gives a basic unity to the entire period. The philosophy of this era is a progressive splintering of Parmenides' idea of the Entity (his predicates are retained and the essence of the concept of the Entity is unaltered) in order to introduce multiplicity into this Entity and make possible motion and the solution of the other problems which had been posed.

But this is not enough. Parmenides' concept of the Entity does not allow multiplicity. We gain nothing by fragmenting it; the problem withdraws, but in the final instance it remains intact. This is what Zeno's arguments demonstrate to us. It will be necessary to investigate the *oneness*, the unity itself, and arrive at an idea of being which, without excluding unity, may make it compatible and coexistent with multiplicity. Thus it is necessary to alter radically the very idea of the Entity. A century and a half later, Aristotle will give us the idea of the ἕν, the one (which is essentially different from the Entity of Parmenides) and with this also an absolutely new concept of being. And in the light of this new concept of being, Parmenides' difficulties can be explained.

Aristotle will then be forced to say that *the Entity is expressed in many ways.* We will soon see why this is so.

At this time it is interesting to follow the first attempts to solve Parmenides' problem—attempts that remain within the philosophic limits which his brilliant discovery established.

Heraclitus

LIFE AND CHARACTER. Heraclitus, who was from Ephesus in Asia Minor, lived within the sixth and fifth centuries. It is said that he was from the royal family of Ephesus and in line to rule the city, but that he renounced this position and dedicated himself to philosophy. There are subtle problems of chronology as regards Xenophanes, Parmenides and Heraclitus; they are approximately contemporary, but Heraclitus moves within the Parmenidean dialectic of being and non-being and can therefore be considered as Parmenides' successor philosophically. Heraclitus despised the masses and condemned the cults and rites of the popular religion. Theophrastus calls him "melancholy." Because of his rather sibylline style, the Greeks gave him the nickname of "Heraclitus the Obscure." The Delphic Oracle used to say that it neither showed nor concealed its thought, but indicated it by signs. And this could also, perhaps, be said of Heraclitus' writings.

BECOMING. The important thing is to characterize Heraclitus' metaphysics and place it within the evolution of philosophy after Parmenides. Heraclitus affirms in a limited way the change or motion of things: πάντα ῥεῖ, everything runs, *everything flows.* No one can bathe twice in the same river; the river endures, but the water is no longer the same. Reality is changing, unstable. Therefore, the primordial substance is *fire,* the least consistent of all substances, the substance which most readily transforms itself. He adds, moreover, that *war* is the father of all things, πόλεμος πατὴρ πάντων. That is, discord, contrariety, is the origin of everything in the world. The world is an eternal fire which transforms itself. As, according to an old principle of knowledge, like is known by like, so the dry soul, the one which resembles fire, is the best soul and the one best at acquiring knowledge: the soul of the wise man. The damp soul, which is like mud, is inferior.

At first glance, it appears that Heraclitus' theories could not be in greater opposition to those of Parmenides. Heraclitus seems to invert the terms completely and to posit constitutional mobility in the things. Even if such were the case, one would still have to interpret Heraclitus' theories as being very closely related to those of Parmenides, since their opposition is too complete to be coincidental; but we must consider a few other points as well. In the first place, when Heraclitus speaks of multiplicity, he is speaking of the world, the cosmos, and Parmenides also recognized motion and multiplicity in the world: he simply denied that this motion and multiplicity in the things had anything to do with the Entity. But there are a number of fragments by Heraclitus in which his own emphasis is quite different.

First of all, Heraclitus says that it is judicious "to confess that all things are one." Moreover, *noûs* is common to all. These affirmations are very different from his statements about flux and multiplicity and contain clear overtones of Parmenides. And there is still another point to consider: Heraclitus introduces a new concept, for which he claims the traditional predicates of Parmenides' philosophy. This is the concept of the σοφόν (*sophón*).

Tὸ σοφόν. Heraclitus speaks of the *sophón*, which is the neuter form of the word "wise." It is neither the wise man nor wisdom. Heraclitus says of this *sophón* that it is, of course, *one*, and that it is *at all times*. Moreover, it is *separated from all things*, πάντων κεχωρισμένον. As we can see, the predicates of the *sophón* are the same as those of the Entity of Parmenides. Heraclitus advises us that we ought to be guided by *what is common to all men*, and this, according to what we have seen, is *noûs*. This becomes especially clear when we keep in mind the fragment which says: "Those who are awake have a common world, but each sleeping person returns to his individual world."

The meaning of these texts is evident. We see a new division of the two worlds: the waking man, who follows what is common to all, *noûs*, is the one who reaches the *sophón*, which is one and always. In contrast, there is the world of sleep, which is the individual world of every one of us—in short, of *opinion*. It is in this latter world that everything is change and becoming. There is a key to this duality in one of Heraclitus' most expressive sentences: φύσις κρύπτεσθαι φιλεῖ, "nature likes to obscure itself." The world obscures the *sophón*, which is what truly is, separated from everything. It is necessary to discover the *sophón*, to unveil it, and this is precisely ἀλήθεια, truth. When man discovers truth he finds Parmenides' predicates of the Entity.

Since man is a thing of the world, he is subject to becoming, but he possesses that something in common, especially if he has a dry soul, and then he inclines to the *sophón*, to the divine. He is not the *sophón*—that would mean becoming a god—but only a *philosopher*. Again man finds himself, like Parmenides, confronted by the old dilemma, the antinomy between his perishable being (the opinion of *mortals*, the condition in which "everything flows") and his eternal and immortal being (the *ón* and *noûs*, the *sophón*).

We now see the most general significance of Heraclitus' philosophy. It is an attempt to interpret motion by changing it fundamentally, by converting it entirely into continuous change, while taking great care to distinguish it from the σοφόν, which is *separated from everything*. Being is still separated from all motion and all multiplicity. Thus we remain within the limits of Parmenides' metaphysics.

Empedocles

LIFE. Empedocles was from Agrigentum in Sicily in Magna Graecia. Although he held a pre-eminent position, he was not content to be king; he wanted to be a god. Some people believed him to be a demigod; others thought him a charlatan. He traveled throughout Sicily and the Peloponnesus teaching and performing cures, and he was venerated by many people. The story is told that in order to have a death worthy of his divinity he threw himself into Mount Etna. Another legend claims that he was raised up to the skies—an end something like Elijah's. It appears more likely that he died in the Peloponnesus. Empedocles was an extraordinarily vital and interesting person. He wrote two poems—*On Nature* and *The Purifications*—which were imitated by Lucretius; the fragments of these that are preserved contain very interesting religious, cosmological and biological ideas and, above all, a doctrine which is truly philosophical in nature.

COSMOLOGY. We shall merely enumerate the most important points of Empedocles' cosmology. According to him, there are two suns: one authentic sun, fire; and another reflected sun, which is the one we see. It had been discovered that the light of the moon is reflected light, and man, as always, had drawn analogies from his discovery. Empedocles, who says that night is produced by the interposition of the earth between the sun and fire, was the one who discovered the true reason for eclipses. According to him the stars and the planets are authentic, not reflected, fire; the stars are fixed and the planets are free-moving. Empedocles believes light to be something that goes from one place to another in a very short interval of time.

BIOLOGY. Beings are mortal, but their origin is eternal. The first things that were, were trees; Empedocles has a vague suspicion that plants have sex. Heat is principally male. Human beings are produced by the chance aggregation of separate components and only those that are properly organized survive. He believes in the transmigration of the soul, and says of himself: "In another time, I have been boy and girl, a shrub and a bird, and a dumb fish in the sea." He also has an interesting theory of perception. There is a fixed relationship between sensory perception and the size of the pores: therefore, the organs for the different senses vary in size. Like things are known by like things: I know fire, if fire is found *in me*; and the same for water and the other things.

THE FOUR ROOTS. Let us examine the central question in Emped-ocles, the problem of the being of things. It is necessary to reconcile immovable being with the changeable multiplicity of things. Empedocles tries to solve this problem by means of the four elements: air, fire, water and earth. This marks the first formal appearance of the four traditional elements. Empedocles says that these elements, which are *the roots of all things*, ῥιζώματα πάντων, are opposites; they contain the contrarieties of dry and damp, of cold and warm.

These roots are *eternal*. Empedocles bases this affirmation on Parmenides' thinking, but he makes a new point: the Entity of Parmenides was a homogeneous sphere which could not change. It is also a sphere for Empedocles, but instead of being homogeneous, it is a *mixture*. All bodies are composed through the aggregation of elemental substances.

LOVE AND HATE. In order to explain motion—that is, how, deriving from the four roots, all things are engendered and perish—Empedocles introduces two more principles: φιλία καὶ νεῖκος (love and hate). Hate separates the different elements, and love tends to join them; this already constitutes motion. In a certain sense, it is hate which joins things, because the union takes place when the elements are separate, at which time similar elements unite with each other. Authentic love is the attraction of dissimilarities. There are four periods in the motion of the world:

1. The mixed sphere.
2. Hate, which gives rise to separation.
3. The domination of the *neíkos*; now hate has separated everything.
4. *Philía* (love) returns and the things begin to unite again.

This cycle is repeated over and over. In this manner things united in very different ways are formed—lions with the head of an ass, and so on—and only those which have a *lógos*, a *ratio*, an internal structure which permits them to continue to exist, survive and propagate.

Various cycles in which the things continue to change through the action of love and hate occur in this fashion, but the four roots remain invariable and eternal. And so we are again faced with being and non-being, the *cosmos* that does not really exist, and the *being* which really is. Multiplicity is introduced into Parmenides' Entity by dividing it into four elements, but this still does not explain motion from the point of view of being. The ontology of motion, physics as philosophy, continues to be impossible.

Anaxagoras

LIFE. Anaxagoras was from Clazomenae in Asia Minor and lived in the fifth century. Like Empedocles, he was from a noble family and was in line to rule. He renounced this position in order to dedicate himself to a *theoretic life*. Indeed, Anaxagoras was considered the man who lived this type of life in exemplary fashion. On the one hand, he seems to us to be linked with Empedocles as the second of the two important *physici recentiores*. But, on the other hand, he is linked in a different way with the Sophists and, especially, with Protagoras. Both Anaxagoras and Protagoras were teachers of Pericles. Anaxagoras was the first philosopher in Athens, even though he was not born in that city. Things did not go well for him there. The Athenians were not very tolerant at that time and there was little freedom of thought: Pericles (perhaps influenced by his mistress, Aspasia) wanted to bring the Ionian way of life to Athens and make the city more democratic. The Athenians made fun of Anaxagoras and called him " *Noûs.*" Later they made accusations against him, but it is not known exactly of what he was accused; nor can we be certain of the punishment to which he was sentenced—there are conflicting stories about all this. It appears that he was freed by Pericles and that because he could not remain in Athens, he set forth to Lampsacus, where he was very well received. Anaxagoras had a great influence on Athenian life, and beginning with his time Athens becomes the leading philosophical city in Greece. Philosophy, after having spread throughout the Orient and the Occident, through Asia Minor and Magna Graecia, belatedly settles in Greece proper, where it is to have its major center. Anaxagoras' influence was not extrinsic to his thought; rather, it was closely linked with his philosophy.

THE HOMOIOMEREIAI. For Anaxagoras, there are not four but an infinite number of elements. *There is everything in everything.* He calls the homogeneous parts, the minuscule particles of which things are made, *homoiomereiai* (ὁμοιομέρειαι). Anaxagoras says that if we take a thing, any thing, and divide it, we will never obtain the roots specified by Empedocles; what we will find are the homoiomereiai. In the smallest part of everything there are minute parts of all other things; this theory is called *panspermía*, the belief that every thing contains seeds of all other things.

How, then, does one explain the formation of the various things? By the union and separation of the homoiomereiai. We now witness one more step in the division of the Entity of Parmenides: first, the Entity was placed in relationship with fire, which moves and changes (Heraclitus); then, in order to explain the world and motion, it was divided into the four roots of Empedocles, and the world and motion were shown to derive from the roots; now Anaxagoras fragments it into the homoiomereiai. And this is not the final stage in the process. Parmenides' predicates of the Entity are preserved, and motion is explained by a process of union and separation.

Things differ because the homoiomereiai group themselves in various ways, according to the positions which they occupy. Anaxagoras discovers the importance of the form, of the *eîdos*; that is, of the arrangement of things. We can make an analogy to an important element in the Athenian life of that period—the theater—and say that what Anaxagoras contributed to philosophy was *perspective*; the fifth century in Athens is given over to the *eîdos*, to sculpture and the visual arts; it is a century of spectators.

"Noûs." *Noûs* is the cause of motion. For Anaxagoras, *noûs* is probably the subtlest form of matter, but it is not spiritual; the concept of spirit is foreign to the thought of this epoch. The other things are not found in the *noûs*, but some of these—the living things—have *noûs*. Therefore, *noûs* is unmixed.

Anaxagoras arrived at this doctrine of νοῦς through considerations of astronomy. *Noûs* is the ruling principle of the universe, and seems to be connected with the origin of Greek monotheism.* Anaxagoras' doctrine possesses a scope and dignity which surpass even his own development of it. Plato and Aristotle valued the concept of the *noûs* very highly, and reproached Anaxagoras for having made very restrained use of the theory; Anaxagoras had used νοῦς almost exclusively to explain motion, whereas it promised to be the explanation of the origin of the world. However, Anaxagorean *noûs*, separated from matter or at least at the margin of it, is, notwithstanding its being the orderer of cosmic motions, similar to an impersonal intelligence.

According to Anaxagoras, knowledge has certain limitations because the homoiomereiai cannot be perceived by the senses. His idea of perception is contrary to that of Empedocles: things are known by their opposites. These two ideas of perception are opposing theses which are contrasted in this period.

---

* Cf. W. Dilthey: *An Introduction to the Sciences of the Spirit.*

Democritus

THE ATOMISTS. The Atomists are the last pre-Socratics. They are approximately contemporary with Socrates, but follow the tradition of those preoccupied by φύσις and, above all, in the line of Eleatic philosophy. The two principal Atomists were Leucippus and Democritus. Both (or at least the latter) were from Abdera in Thrace. Almost nothing is known about Leucippus. His doctrine was basically the same as that of Democritus, who was a great intellectual figure in Greece and a great traveler and writer. As is the case with the rest of the works of the pre-Socratics, only fragments of Leucippus' work remain. We can, therefore, address ourselves principally to Democritus.

THE ATOMS. The Atomists make the final division of the Entity of Parmenides. They arrive at the atoms (ἄτομοι); that is, at "uncuttable," indivisible parts which cannot be broken down further. These atoms are distinguished from one another solely in that they have different forms, and their properties depend on their form. They move in whirlwinds and unite in various ways, and in this manner the things are produced. There are many worlds, some in the process of formation, some in the process of disintegration, and others in actual existence. Properties are based on the form and also on the degree of subtlety of the atoms. And every one of these atoms retains the fundamental attributes of Parmenides' Entity, which one might say here appears to be completely pulverized.

MATERIALISM. Democritus' ideas represent the first formal attempt to create a materialism. Everything, even the soul, is composed of atoms. This is the materialistic interpretation of the Entity. Therefore, motion comes to be, above all, local motion (φορά). And then the problem of location confronts the Atomists, the problem of the τόπος in which the atoms must be located. Indeed, the Atomists will say that the atoms are in the *void*. This is of great importance. Traditionally, the void was non-being, but now non-being is necessary as a place for the atoms. Democritus takes a very original step: he attributes a certain being to the void, and converts it into *space*. Instead of being considered absolute non-being (οὐκ ὄν), the void is interpreted as relative non-being (μὴ ὄν), in comparison to what is full, or to the atoms. The void has a *spatial* being. The problem of being and non-being is mitigated but not resolved by this atoms-space concept. This constitutes the final attempt to solve this question within the limits of Parmenides' concept of the Entity.

KNOWLEDGE. According to Democritus, perception is realized in the following manner: the things emit a kind of spectre or subtle image (εἴδωλον) which is composed of finer atoms. These finer atoms penetrate the sense organs, and thus the mind receives a copy or replica of the thing; this is what knowledge consists of. Therefore, Democritus' is a sensationalist doctrine.

Democritus' moral ideas already begin to delineate the figure of the "wise man," the σοφός, whose characteristics are imperturbability, serenity, control over himself.* However, Democritus' frame of reference is still physics, cosmology, speculation concerning the heavens and the world and the motion of the things as opposed to immovable being. But we are now in the time of Socrates.

* Concerning the idea of serenity, refer to my study "Ataraxía y alcionismo" ("Ataraxia and Halcyonism") in *El oficio del pensamiento*, 1958 [*Obras*, VI].

The Sophists and Socrates

Beginning with the fifth century a new phase of philosophy commences in Greece. This period is essentially characterized by the turning of man's attention to the study of himself. Preoccupation with the world is succeeded by concern with man. Such concern had not been lacking previously; we have seen the notion of the theoretic life, the doctrine of immortality or transmigration, and the like. But man now realizes that he must ask who he himself is. This trend of thought was influenced by some factors external to philosophy: the predominance of Athens after the Persian Wars, the triumph of democracy, and so forth. There appears in the forefront the figure of the man who can speak well, the citizen; and the Athenian's interest turns to political and civic realities, and thus to man himself.

The tenor of life in Greece in this period changes considerably. The perfect citizen, the πολίτης, replaces the former ideal of the καλὸς κἀγαθός, the man *comme il faut*, endowed with a handsome person and remarkable talents, what we would perhaps call the perfect gentleman. In the center of Greek thinking is no longer φύσις (the nature of the outside world), but εὐδαιμονία (happiness), in the sense of the development of the essence of the individual. And there appears, as the outstanding representative of this time, the *Sophist*.

1. THE SOPHISTS

The Sophist movement appears in Greece in the fifth century. At this moment, when philosophy is beginning to exert an influence on

35

Athenian life, there is a certain similarity between the Sophists and Anaxagoras. But the Sophists present essential differences. They are characterized outwardly by certain traits: they were itinerant teachers who went from town to town instructing the young men; and they taught for money, accepting a fee—a new situation in Greece, and one that occasioned no little surprise. Their éclat and social success were great; they were orators and rhetoricians, and basically educators. They claimed that they knew and could teach everything—in fact anything and its opposite, the thesis and the antithesis. They had great influence on Greek life and were important personalities; some were extremely intelligent. But what is of most consequence about the Sophists, the reason that they interest us here, is the manner in which the path of their movement crossed that of philosophy.

The word "Sophist" is a formation of the word *sophia* (wisdom) which appears in the word "philosophy." Philostratus says of the Sophists that they speak about the things that philosophers speak about. And Aristotle says: "Sophist thought is apparently wisdom, but really is not, and the Sophist is a man who practices what is apparently wisdom, but really is not." In these two very brief quotations the problem of the Sophist movement is characterized; it speaks of philosophic *themes* and *appears* to be wisdom, but really is not. The Sophist appears to be a philosopher, but really is not. He is a very strange man, says Plato, whose being consists in not being. It should be noted that this does not mean the Sophist is *not a philosopher*; that negative description fits the carpenter as well; but the carpenter does not consist in not being a philosopher, but in being a carpenter, while being a Sophist consists in *seeming* to be a philosopher and not being one. There are two problems: (1) the philosophy that may exist in the Sophist movement; (2) the philosophic problem of the reality of the Sophist.

Sophist thinking poses once more the problem of being and non-being, but apropos of itself and, thus, of man. The aristocracy's concept of what a man should be had been transformed in Greece. Now, instead of its being the well-formed, naturally gifted man who is admired—a good warrior, for example—it is the clever man, the man with *noûs*, who knows what should be said and done, the good citizen. When this new concept became current in Greece, the result (since every man has *noûs* and *noûs* is common to all) was a democracy. This *noûs* and being able to use it in speaking were what counted. So it was philosophy that made possible this situation and, therefore, the Sophist movement itself.

The Sophists move in a milieu of rhetoric. They are concerned with saying things in a convincing manner, "speaking well" ($\epsilon\tilde{v}$ $\lambda\acute{\epsilon}\gamma\epsilon\iota\nu$). Truth does not matter, and for this reason theirs is a false philosophy. In the face of this, Socrates and Plato will call for "thinking well," that is, for truth.

Further, the Sophist movement is public, that is, addressed to the *citizen*; it has, thus, a clear political tendency. And, lastly, it is a *paideía*, formal instruction, the first properly so-called to exist.

The positive dimension of the Sophists and their historical justification is that, in the face of a philosophy which based itself on the Entity and neglected the things (the Eleatic school), they signified the need to base philosophy on the things and to try to account for them. The serious flaw was that the Sophists proclaimed the *non-consistency* of things and abandoned the viewpoint of being and truth, which had to be readopted by Socrates and Plato, who thus at the same time gave the Sophists' demand for emphasis on the things its just due. Socrates and Plato had to investigate what *things are*, or, stated in other terms, the consistency of things.

There were many important Sophists. Several are known to us in a vivid and penetrating way through Plato's dialogues. The details of their activities and ideas are less interesting than the total significance of the movement. The most important were Hippias, Prodicus, Euthydemus and, above all, Protagoras and Gorgias.

PROTAGORAS. Protagoras, like Democritus, came from Abdera. He was very influential in Athens at the time of Pericles. He concerned himself with grammar and language, was a great rhetorician, and manifested a certain skepticism with regard to the possibility of knowledge, especially knowledge of the gods. But his greatest fame rests on a statement of his reported by several later philosophers: "Man is the measure of all things, of those that are, that they are; and of those that are not, that they are not." Numerous interpretations have been given for this sentence, ranging from relativism to subjectivism. We cannot go into this theme here; it is sufficient to point out Aristotle's remark that it would first be necessary to know whether man is there referred to as the arbiter of *real knowledge* or of *sensations*; that is, whether reference is made to the viewpoint of truth or simply of *dóxa*. Protagoras does not speak of the *ón* (being), but of things as opposed to being ($\chi\rho\acute{\eta}\mu\alpha\tau\alpha$), things that are handled, movable goods, and hence used in the sense of money (chrematistics). Thus, this is the world of *dóxa*, and the sentence is therefore understood within the framework of Parmenides' conceptual world. *Dóxa* is "the opinion of mortals," "names that men give to things," convention.

GORGIAS. Gorgias, from Leontini in Sicily, was one of the great

Greek orators. He wrote a book called *On Non-being*, in which the clear dependence of the Sophists on the Eleatics is once more apparent. He pointed out the difficulties of the Eleatics' doctrine of the Entity, and affirmed that there is no Entity, since if it existed it would not be knowable by man, and if man could know it he could not communicate this knowledge. Thus the Sophists lead us to a final dissolution of Parmenides' dialectic of being and non-being. Philosophy loses itself in rhetoric and in renunciation of truth. In order to restate the problem of metaphysics in a productive manner it will be necessary to place it on new bases. This is what Socrates will demand and initiate and what Plato and especially Aristotle will accomplish.

2. SOCRATES

THE LIFE OF SOCRATES. Socrates' life fills the second half of the fifth century in Athens; he died at the age of seventy in 399 B.C., at the beginning of the fourth century, the century which was to see Greece's greatest philosophical outpouring. He was the son of a sculptor and a midwife, and used to say that his art, like his mother's, was *maieutiké* (midwifery), the art of delivering children in the name of truth. Socrates is one of the most interesting and disturbing personalities in all of Greek history; he inflamed his contemporaries, so much so that it cost him his life, and his role in the life of Greece and in philosophy is not lacking in mystery. His activity as citizen and soldier was noble and courageous; but, above all, he was the man of the agora, the man of the street and town square who, talking, troubled all of Athens. At the outset Socrates seemed to be just one more Sophist. Only later was it seen that he was not; that, to the contrary, he had come to the world precisely to supersede the Sophists and to reestablish the meaning of truth in Greek thinking. He soon gained a circle of eager pupils and admiring followers; the cream of the youth of Athens, and even of other Greek cities, hung upon his every word; Alcibiades, Xenophon, above all Plato, were numbered among his enthusiastic listeners.

Socrates claimed to be accompanied by a "genius" or familiar spirit (δαιμόνιον) whose voice counseled him at the critical moments of his life. This *daimónion* never moved him to action, but would on occasion restrain him and dissuade him from an action. It was an inspiration within him that has at times been interpreted as something divine, as a voice of the Deity.

Socrates' attitude is exasperating. An oracle had said that no one was wiser than Socrates. He modestly claims that he will demonstrate the contrary; and to do this, he goes about the streets and squares asking his fellow citizens the meaning of things that he does not know; this is the well-known *Socratic irony*. The ruler, the cobbler, the soldier, the courtesan, the Sophist, all suffer the barbs of his questions. What is bravery? What is justice? What is friendship? What is true knowledge? It turns out that they do not know either; but, unlike Socrates, they are not even aware of their ignorance, and the upshot is that the oracle was right. This is supremely annoying for those being questioned, and this malaise becomes concentrated into hate, which terminates in an accusation against Socrates "for introducing new gods and corrupting the youth." The result is a ridiculous trial, which Socrates takes with composure and irony, and a death sentence, which he accepts calmly. Not wishing to violate the unjust laws by running away, although his friends propose a safe means of flight to him, he drinks the hemlock in the midst of a keen-edged discussion on immortality with his pupils.

SOCRATIC KNOWLEDGE. What meaning does knowledge have for Socrates? How does Socrates ask his questions, and why are people unable to answer him? He opposes, above all others, the Sophists, and directs his greatest efforts to proving the emptiness of their presumptive knowledge. To accomplish this, he confronts the rhetorical discourses of the Sophists with his own clipped dialogue of questions and answers. We may ask what, in short, is Socrates' contribution to philosophy; we find a passage in Aristotle in which that author states categorically that we owe two things to Socrates: "inductive reasoning and the universal definition." Both, Aristotle adds, are related to the very beginning of knowledge. When Socrates asks a question, he asks *what is*, for example, justice. He asks for a definition. To define a thing is to set limits to it, thereby stating what it is, its *essence*; definition leads to essence, and knowledge understood as simple discernment or distinction is succeeded, through the efforts of Socrates, by a new knowledge of how to define, which leads us to say what things are, to discover their essence (Zubiri). From this point originates all the fertility of Socrates' thinking, turned toward the quest of truth, centered once more in the viewpoint of being, from which the Sophists had turned away. In Socrates there is the attempt to say truly what things are. And this path of defined essence is the one that leads to the Platonic theory of the Ideas.

SOCRATES' ETHICAL TEACHING. Socrates is principally concerned with man. This is not new; we have seen it as a characteristic of the Sophists and of the whole era. But Socrates considers man from a different point of view: that of his inner life. "Know yourself" (γνῶθι σεαυτόν), says Socrates; bring your inner self to light. And this bears a new meaning in Greece; it means reflection, criticism, maturity that enrich the Greek even if costing him something of the frank and courageous impulsiveness with which the first centuries of Greek history had been lived. One cannot speak of *corruption*, but it is assuredly true that Socrates decisively changed the spirit of Athenian youth. (See Ortega's *Espíritu de la letra* [Spirit of the Letter].)

The core of Socrates' ethics is the concept of *areté*, virtue. This is not virtue in its usual sense, but more like what the word means when one speaks of the virtues of plants or of a violin *virtuoso*. Virtue is the deepest and most basic propensity of man, that for which he was actually born. And this virtue is *knowledge*. A bad man is bad through ignorance; the man who does not follow the good fails to do so because he does not recognize it. Thus, virtue can be taught (intellectualist ethics), and what is necessary is for everyone to know his own *areté*. This is the meaning of the Socratic imperative, "Know yourself." It is thus a moral imperative, whereby man may gain possession of himself and be his own master, through knowledge. Just as from the Socratic definition there arises the problem of essence and with it all the metaphysics of Plato and Aristotle, so from Socrates' ethics originate all the ethical schools that will fill Greece and the Roman Empire from that time on: first the Cynics and Cyrenaics, and then, especially, the Epicureans and the Stoics. All of Greek philosophy from the beginning of the fourth century on is rooted in Socrates; what is merely outlined or sketched in him was to be realized in the fruitful tradition based on his teachings.

Socrates' doctrinal contribution to philosophy was modest. He was probably not a man of many profound metaphysical ideas, as Plato and Aristotle were shortly to be. His role was to prepare for them and make them possible, placing philosophy for the second time on the *way of truth*—the only path it can follow—from which it had been diverted by the rhetoric of the Sophists and the apparent wisdom of "speaking well," which was incapable of being anything more than *opinion*.

THE TRANSMISSION OF SOCRATIC THOUGHT. Socrates never wrote anything. He has left us not a page, not a line of his own. We know his thought through references by other philosophers, especially by his pupils. Xenophon wrote the *Memorabilia*, devoted to reminiscences of his master, as well as a *Symposium*, or *Banquet*, and an *Apology of Socrates*. But it is Plato above all others who has preserved for us the thought and vivid figure of a Socrates differing considerably from Xenophon's. Plato's portrayal of Socrates is incomparably richer, more profound and more attractive than Xenophon's. But since Plato makes Socrates the principal character in his dialogues and puts his own philosophy into his teacher's mouth, it becomes difficult at times to determine where Socrates' authentic thinking ends and where Plato's original philosophy begins. Nevertheless, the situation is clear in the majority of cases. Another source of information on Socrates, no less valuable for being indirect, is Aristotle. Aristotle's brilliant penetration makes all his information priceless; in addition, his twenty years spent in Plato's company must have given him a great familiarity with Socrates' thinking. This third source is of especial value in determining the boundaries between the teachings of Socrates and those of Plato himself. And there is an almost symbolic value to the fact that Socrates' teaching is found in the works of other men, just as the greatest flowering of his philosophy was only to come through these other followers of his. *

* One should not forget the enormous historical value of the image of Socrates— distorted and hostile, but the reflection of an attitude of Athenian society—in *The Clouds* of Aristophanes.

Plato

LIFE. Plato was born in Athens in 427 and died in 347 B.C., while still wholly dedicated to his intellectual activities. He belonged to an old aristocratic family, who claimed descent from Codrus and Solon. His position by birth and his personal vocation were drawing him into political life when the attraction of Socrates led him to devote himself to philosophy. After two attempts at playing a role in Athenian public life, he was turned away from such a career by the death of Socrates. All that remained of this career was Plato's permanent interest in political themes, which made him give such a paramount position in his system to the theory of the State, and which made him several times —even at a grave risk—urge his pupil Dion to make the ideal Platonic state an actuality during the reign of Dion's brother-in-law Dionysius, the tyrant of Syracuse, and later in the reign of Dion's nephew, the younger Dionysius. These projects fell through, and Plato limited his activities to his brilliant philosophical meditations, his great labors of authorship, and his personal instruction in the school of philosophy he founded, around 387 B.C., on a piece of land very close to the Cephissus, on the road to Eleusis. This property included a grove dedicated to the hero Academus, and Plato's school thus became known as the Academy. It lasted, though with profound changes, until 529 A.D., the year in which the Emperor Justinian ordered it closed. Plato fulfilled the duties of master there until his death, in close and profound collaboration with his greatest pupil, Aristotle.

WRITINGS. The corpus of Plato's writings is almost completely preserved. Plato's works, together with those of Aristotle, form the

42

pinnacle of all of Greek philosophy and culture. In addition, their literary value is perhaps the highest among all Hellenic productions. Plato's philosophic genius combines with a miraculous gift of language which enables him to find the perfect expressions and metaphors for establishing a new way of thought. The Platonic contribution to the formation of philosophical terminology is incalculable. As the literary genre for expressing his thought, Plato chose the dialogue, which is intimately related to his doctrine of dialectic as a philosophic method. Many of these dialogues are of astonishing poetic beauty. The principal character is always Socrates, who bears the burden of the argument. The youthful dialogues, the *Apology*, the *Crito*, the *Euthyphro*, are strongly tinged with Socratic teachings. Among the most important dialogues of Plato's mature years are the *Protagoras*, the *Gorgias*, the *Euthydemus*, on the Sophists; the *Phaedo*, on the immortality of the soul; the *Symposium*, or *Banquet*, on love; the *Phaedrus*, which contains Plato's theory of the soul; and the *Republic*, on justice and the concept of the State. Lastly come the *Theaetetus*; the *Parmenides* (perhaps the most important of all the Platonic writings), the *Sophist* and the *Statesman*; and, in Plato's old age, the *Timaeus*, containing his references to Atlantis; the *Philebus*; and a notable work, the largest in volume, containing a second exposition of the theory of the State and including no mention of Socrates: the *Laws*. The authenticity of certain Platonic works, especially some of the letters ascribed to him (a few of which, like the seventh, are highly important) has been the subject of serious doubts and problems.

Plato's thinking shows an evolution; it takes its departure from the teaching of Socrates, arrives at the brilliant discovery of the Ideas, and culminates in the examination of the difficulties and problems posed by the theory of the Ideas, an examination assuredly prompted by personal discussions with Aristotle. We cannot follow here this development of Platonic metaphysics; we will confine ourselves to an exposition of the most stimulating and fruitful features of his mature philosophy, which contain all the problems that were to set in motion the further history of Greek thought.*

1. The Ideas

THE DISCOVERY. What problem must Plato come to grips with? With the problem that all Greek metaphysics since Parmenides had

* An examination as to origins of the teachings of Plato within Greek philosophy and history will be found in my *Biografía de la Filosofía* (Biography of Philosophy), cited above.

posed: the problem of being and non-being. For more than a century Hellenic philosophy had striven to solve the *aporia* (perplexing problem) of making *the Entity*—one, immovable and eternal—compatible with the *things*—manifold, variable and transitory. We have seen that pre-Socratic philosophy subsequent to Parmenides had been a series of attempts to solve this central problem, attempts which, strictly speaking, signified no progress beyond the level of understanding on which Parmenides had set the problem. Plato, on the other hand, gives a decisive direction to the question; he takes a step forward. The train of thought that he initiates is so new and brilliant that he is himself irresistibly drawn along with it, and from that time on he must make laborious efforts to cope with his own discovery, his doctrine, which becomes his most serious problem. Plato discovers nothing less than the *Idea*. What does this mean?

Plato is seeking the being of things. But in this search he runs into several difficulties of a varied nature which drive him, coincidentally, to a fundamental solution, one that appears paradoxical. In the first place, Plato finds that things themselves do not exist; if, for example, I examine a sheet of white paper, it turns out that actually it is not white; that is, it is not completely white, but has some gray or yellow in it; it is no more than almost white. The same must be said of its presumed rectangularity: its sides are not totally and absolutely straight, nor does it have perfect right angles. What is more, this sheet of paper has not existed always, but only since a certain time; within a few years it will no longer exist. Therefore, it is white and not white, it is rectangular and not rectangular, *it is and it is not*; or—what amounts to the same thing—it does not fully and truly exist.

But if, in the second place, we look at the other side of the question, we find that although the sheet of paper is not strictly white, it is *almost white*. What does this mean? When we say that something is *almost* white, we deny it absolute whiteness by comparing it to something that is unconditionally white; that is, in order to see that a thing is not truly white, I must know already what whiteness is. But since no visible thing—neither snow, nor clouds, nor foam—is absolutely white, I am referred to a reality that is distinct from all concrete things, the reality of total whiteness. Expressed in other terms, the fact that many things are *almost white* requires the existence of the truly white, which is not any thing, but which exists outside the realm of things. This true being, which is distinct from things, is what Plato calls an *Idea*.

In the third place, this problem comes into sharpest focus if we keep in mind Plato's point of departure in regard to the theory of knowledge. Plato is building upon concepts established by Socrates. Socrates—who, strictly speaking, does not engage in metaphysics but reestablishes the viewpoint of truth in philosophy—desires to know *what* things *are*; that is, he seeks *definitions*. Whereas Parmenides moves in a milieu of being and tries to distinguish that which has true being from what which merely appears to be, Socrates attempts to state *what* (τί) that-which-is is, in other words, to define, discover and firmly establish the *essences* of things. From this concrete standpoint Plato initiates his philosophy.

A definition is, to begin with, a *predication* of the form "A is B." In this predication I come across a problem of oneness and multiplicity. When I say, "Man is an animal that speaks," I identify "animal" with "man," I say that two things are one, that A is B. What makes it possible for me to make a true predication? We should note that in the statement "A is B," A fulfills two functions. First, it is the subject, when I say "A." But, in the second place, when I say that it is B, I am speaking not only of B, but am including A in that predicate as well. In other words, I am not merely mentioning A first and B next, with no further connection; B is the being B of A and, consequently, A has two functions. In the predication "A is B" it is presupposed that *A is A*, that is, that A is identical with itself. This concept in its turn is found to consist of these two presuppositions: (1) that A is one; (2) that A is permanent.

When I say, then, that man is a speaking animal, it is necessary that "man" be univocal and, in addition, that when identified as a speaking being, "man" should continue to be "man." Definition in the Socratic and Platonic sense originates in the supposition that entities are self-identical and permanent—a supposition that raises one of the weightiest possible problems. If I want to make a statement about the horse, it occurs to me, first of all, that there are many horses; in the second place, that these horses I now see are not permanent: they did not exist fifty years ago and will not exist fifty years from now. Finally, if I say that a horse is black, this is not strictly true, because the horse has some white or gray on it; the perfect horse, the unconditional horse, does not exist. It may be said that we *quasi*-predicate certain *quasi*-properties of certain *quasi*-things.

Plato, who realizes this (and it is here that his genius lies) supposes— and this is the matter of consequence—that this quasi-blackness is a defect in the horse, because the horse ought to be absolute and absolutely black. Confronted with this difficulty, he takes no more notice of the individual horse, which is and is not, which does not exist completely, and seeks the true horse; because, naturally, the fact that approximative horses exist presupposes the existence of a true horse. There are two things which Plato must do: find the absolute horse, and from it account for the approximative horses which gallop in the world. Plato transfers his attention from the world of things, which do not permit rigorous predications, to the world in which such predications are possible, to what he calls the world of *Ideas*. But what is meant by *Ideas*?

THE BEING OF THE IDEAS. The word "Idea" (ἰδέα)—sometimes *eídos* (εἶδος) is used—means "image, aspect": in short, that which is seen. It can also be translated, in certain contexts, as "form"; thus, in Aristotle it appears as a synonym of *morphé*, and elsewhere in his writings it is equivalent to "class, species." (In Latin, *species* is from the same root as the verb *spicio*, "see, look at," just as the Greek words εἶδος and ἰδέα are connected with the notion of seeing; and among the meanings of the Latin *species* is also found that of "beauty," which makes it equivalent to *forma*, from which *formosus*, "beautiful," is derived.) An "idea" is what I see when I see something. When I see a man, I see him as himself—that is, I see him as a man—because I already have the idea of man, because I see him as sharing in that idea. In the same way, when I say that a sheet of paper is not completely white, what permits me to view it as almost white is the idea of whiteness. When I read a written word, I see it immediately because I already possess the *idea* of it; if it happens to be a word in a foreign language I do not know at all, I do not see it directly as it is, but only as a group of letters—although, on the other hand, I possess the ideas of the individual letters. But if I turn to a word written in characters I am not familiar with, I do not, strictly speaking, *see* the letters, and I could not reproduce them without previously examining them in detail and reducing them to groups of familiar strokes. A man who does not merely not know how to read, but does not know what reading is, does not see a book, because he lacks the idea of one. The "Idea," therefore, is the basis for knowledge and for viewing things for what they are.

The discovery of the Ideas was already partially prepared for in the philosophy before Plato. First, let us recall the *perspective*, by means of which Anaxagoras' homoiomereiai could vary their positions and take on distinct forms; secondly let us recall the Socratic *definition*, which tells us not what each concrete thing is but rather all the things each concrete thing comprises; that is, its class. But there is a vast difference between these anticipations and Plato's doctrine.

True being, which philosophy had been seeking since Parmenides, does not reside in things, but outside of them: in the Ideas. These, therefore, are *metaphysical entities which contain the true being of things*;

they are that which authentically exists, what Plato calls ὄντως ὄν. The Ideas possess the predicates traditionally required of the Entity, which cannot be possessed by things as perceived by the senses; the Ideas are *one, changeless, eternal*; they contain no admixture of non-being; they are not subject to motion or decay; they absolutely and unconditionally *are*. The being of *things*, which is a subordinate and defective being, is founded on the being of the Ideas in which the things share. Plato originates the division of reality into two worlds, the world of things perceived by the senses, which he discredits, and the world of the Ideas, which is true and full being.

We see, therefore, the necessity for the Ideas: (1) in order to know things for what they are; (2) in order that these things, which are and are not (i.e., do not truly exist) may be; (3) in order to understand how it is possible for things to come to be and cease to be—in general, how they move or change—without contradicting the traditional predicates of the Entity; and (4) in order to make the oneness of the Entity compatible with the multiplicity of the things.

THEORY OF KNOWLEDGE. When Plato investigates the being of the things he comes across a rather paradoxical situation: that these things have no being and, therefore, cannot help him to discover being. Where then should he seek it? True being resides in the Ideas, but the Ideas are not directly accessible to my consciousness, they are not in the world. Nevertheless, I know them in some way, they are within me and thus permit me, as we have seen, to know the things. How is this possible? To solve this problem, Plato resorts to one of his characteristic procedures: he relates a myth. The myth in the *Phaedrus* simultaneously explains the origin of man, our knowledge of the Ideas, and the intellectual method of Platonism.

According to the now-famous myth which Socrates relates to Phaedrus on the bank of the Ilissus, the soul, in its original state, can be compared to a chariot drawn by two winged horses, one a docile thoroughbred, the other an ungovernable steed (the passions and sensual instincts). This chariot is driven by a charioteer (reason) who strives to guide it properly. In a region above heaven (τόπος ὑπερουράνιος) the chariot travels through the world of the Ideas, which the soul thus contemplates, although not without difficulty. Troubles arise in guiding the flight of the two horses, and the soul falls; the horses lose their wings and the soul becomes incarnated in a body. If the soul has seen the Ideas, even though only briefly, this body will be human and not bestial. Depending on the greater or lesser extent of their contemplation of the Ideas, souls are placed in a hierarchy of nine grades, ranging from the philosopher down to the tyrant. The origin of man as such, therefore, is the fall of a soul which has come from heaven and has there contemplated the Ideas. But the incarnated man does not remember them. Of his former wings there remain only aching stumps, which are stimulated when man sees things, because the things make him *remember* the Ideas which his soul saw in its earlier existence. This is the method of knowledge. Man starts with things—but not to remain at their level, not to find in them a being which they do not possess—but in order that they may excite his memory or reminiscence (*anámnesis*) of the Ideas he contemplated at an earlier time. Knowledge, therefore, is not *seeing* what is outside of us, but, on the contrary, *remembering* what is inside of us. Things are only a *stimulus* for us to abandon them and raise our thoughts to the Ideas.

Things, Plato says, with an expressive metaphor, are *shadows of the Ideas*. Shadows are signs of things and they can make one aware of the existence of things. The mutilated stumps of the former wings are agitated and long for regeneration; there is a feeling of restlessness, a painful itching: "The virtue of wings consists in lifting heavy things upward, bearing them through the air to the place where the race of the gods resides," says Plato. This is, as we shall see in detail, the cognitive meaning of the Platonic *éros*: love, starting with the contemplation of beautiful *things*, of beautiful bodies, ends by making us remember the Idea of beauty itself and leads us into the world of Ideas.

Man, who is for Plato a fallen being, is nevertheless distinguished as having seen the Ideas, the true being of things, and as sharing in truth; this is what defines man. One of the most profound arguments that Plato uses to prove the immortality of the soul is that, in order to know truth, the soul must have a certain affinity with it; we have already seen the connection between the Entity and *noûs* in Parmenides. An entire metaphysic is implicit in this argument. (In present-day philosophy the problem of the eternity of truths has been raised with acuteness, especially by Husserl and Heidegger. Opposed to the idea of the eternity of truths is that of a temporal link between truths and human existence. But this is an extremely complex question, which cannot be gone into here.)

2. THE STRUCTURE OF REALITY

THE MYTH OF THE CAVE. In the seventh book of the *Republic*, Plato relates a myth of astonishing power, in which he represents symbolically the situation of man in relation to philosophy, and, at the same time, the structure of reality. It is curious to note that immediately before this, at the end of the sixth book, Plato had expounded in the form of a thesis this same doctrine of reality and the methods of knowing it. This procedure of Plato's recalls—but with an essential change of sequence—his customary technique of making a truth comprehensible by means of a poetical representation that renders it clear and precise for the mind's grasping; but this inversion of terms reveals that this is no simple example in the form of a metaphor, but that the myth adds something to the exposition preceding it.

The content of the myth can be reduced in its essentials to the following: Plato pictures some men who have remained from their childhood in a cave which has an opening through which the light from outside enters. The men are bound in such a way that they cannot move or look in any other direction than at the back of the cave. Outside the cave, behind the men's backs, blazes the bright glow of a fire burning on a lofty place in the terrain, and between the fire and the chained men there is a road with a low wall along it. Down this road pass men carrying all sorts of objects and small statues that rise above the top of the wall; the chained men see the shadows of these things projected onto the back of the cave. When the passers-by speak, it seems to the prisoners that those voices proceed from the shadows they see—their only reality. One of the prisoners, freed from his chains, views the real world outside; the light makes his eyes ache and he can scarcely see; the sun dazzles him painfully and blinds him. Little by little he tries to grow accustomed to the light; first, he manages to see shadows; then, the images of things reflected in bodies of water; afterward, the things themselves. He sees the sky at night, the stars and the moon, and at dawn, the reflected image of the sun. Finally, after a long preparation (γυμνασία), he can look at the sun itself. Then he realizes that the world he lived in previously was unreal and contemptible. But when he speaks to his companions in that world of shadows and says that the shadows are not real, they will laugh at him; and when he tries to save them and bring them into the real world, they will kill him.

What is symbolized in this myth? The cave is the world perceived by the senses, and its shadows are the things of the world of the senses. The outside world is the true world, the world perceived by the mind, or the world of the Ideas. The objects of the outside world symbolize the Ideas; the sun symbolizes the Idea of the Good. Following Plato's own indications, we can represent graphically the structure of reality referred to in the myth of the cave.

THE DIAGRAM OF THE TWO WORLDS. Plato distinguishes two great regions of reality, the world of the senses (of things) and the world of the mind (of Ideas), which he symbolizes as two segments of a line. Each one of these two regions is divided into two parts, standing for two degrees of reality within each world. There is a correspondence between the first portions and between the second portions of the two segments. Finally, to each one of the four forms of reality there corresponds a way of knowledge; the two that pertain to the world of the senses constitute opinion, or *dóxa*; those of the world of the mind are manifestations of *noûs*. In this we notice echoes of Parmenides' teachings. Schematically, therefore, reality has the following structure:

WORLD OF THE SENSES (Apparent reality)		WORLD OF THE MIND (True reality)	
shadows	real things	mathematical entities	Ideas
conjecture	belief	reasoning	noetic vision (perception by the mind)
dóxa		*noûs*	

THE MEANING OF THE MYTH. The myth of the cave, narrated by Plato as a continuation of this schematic presentation, adds something to it. In concrete fashion, it symbolizes simultaneously the ontological structure of reality and the meaning of philosophy, and thus introduces the fundamental oneness of those two worlds. The two great regions of reality are united into *one* reality by virtue of the role played by man, who comes face to face with both of them. The visible world and the world of the mind now appear related to two essential human potentialities: seeing and understanding. The man who is at first in the cave and then in the light is the one who gives a unity to the two worlds; the world as a whole is a double world integrated by man's passage from darkness to light. (From another point of view, there is a second unifying link: the Good, the ontological basis of the being of both worlds.) What happens to the man in the cave is something that can be narrated, and it is of this narrative that the myth consists. The theme of the myth of the cave is, in its most profound dimension, the essence of philosophy; and this, as we see, is something more clearly arrived at in a narrative than in a definition. Even though Plato is the champion of the definition, philosophy in its essence cannot be defined; it must be set forth in a narrative, or relation. What happens to the philosopher, the drama of philosophy, is what makes clear the structure of reality: this is the double substance of the myth of the cave.

Let us not forget, however, that the journey of the man in the myth includes a return trip: the prisoner, once he has viewed the world of light and freedom, goes back to the cave; that is, he intends to explain the shadows on the basis of the visible things, and the reality perceived by the senses on the basis of the Ideas. We see prefigured here the philosophy of Plato, and at the same time we notice that Plato's philosophy is not carried to its conclusion, because Plato should have returned to the cave in order to explain the being of things on the basis of the theory of Ideas. Strictly speaking, as we shall see, he did not do this, but remained in the world of the mind, dazzled and detained by his inner problems. And the tragic ending of the myth reflects the form in which the philosopher's life was lived in Plato's age: the memory of the death of Socrates is latent in the killing of the philosopher by his companions in the cave.

3. Problems Raised by the Theory of Ideas

Being and entity. We have seen that Plato was inquiring into the being of things. But he learned that they do not have a being of their own; they have a *share* of being, which they receive from another reality that is outside of the things. And Plato at that point discovered the Ideas.

It is necessary to pause for a moment to consider what this discovery means. To begin with, it was the discovery of the mode of being of things, the discovery of what makes things be, and therefore at the same time the discovery of what can be known about things, that is, what they are. The problem of the theory of knowledge is inseparably linked to the problem of being and is thus strictly metaphysical. It is not possible to discover one individual thing and see it without seeing the Idea of it; without seeing the Idea of man, it is impossible to see *a* man. An animal, as we have seen, cannot see a book because it has no "idea" of the book, and the reality "book" does not exist for the animal. What, then, has Plato discovered? What actually is the Idea?

In reality, Plato has discovered the being of things. Being is what makes things be, what makes them *entities*. Being is the being of the entity, and at the same time, to know a thing is to know what that thing is: to understand the being of that entity. Let us suppose that I have a thing with which I am going to become acquainted. This thing is an entity; but when I have come to know it, I do not have the thing itself in my consciousness. What do I have, then? I have the being of the thing, what that thing is—what Plato would call "its Idea." Plato would describe the process of knowing as seeing a thing in its Idea.

In short, we find that Plato has discovered being, rather than the Entity. Parmenides had discovered the Entity, things for what they are. Plato discovers being, that which makes things be, and he finds that this being is not to be confused with the things. But in addition to making a distinction between them, he *separates* them: the Ideas are something separate from things, something absolute. Now he runs into a most serious difficulty: he was inquiring into the being of things, and has now found being; but he does not know yet what the things are. Plato remains at the level of the Ideas, the being he has discovered. What is lacking in his system is nothing less than the ability to explain the *being of things* on the basis of the Ideas (Ortega).

This is what happens when a man makes a brilliant discovery such as the discovery of the Ideas: Plato stops short at that point, and never succeeds in explaining the things; he stops short without creating his metaphysics. (See Ortega, *Filosofía pura* [Pure Philosophy].) Such a task is precisely what Aristotle will accomplish. He reproaches Plato with having used these myths, not because they are myths, but because they are not supported by a metaphysics. The concept of "participating" or "sharing" (μέθεξις) is completely insufficient. For Plato, μέθεξις is the type of relationship that exists between the Ideas and the things. Things share in the Ideas. The Ideas, Plato says, are like a veil that covers various things, which share in it. The Idea of man is like a common veil covering all men. Aristotle will say that all this is nothing but metaphor. What is this "sharing," ontologically speaking? It means that the Ideas are present in the things. But how is this sharing ontologically possible? What is the mode of this presence?

THE "COMMUNICATION" OF THE IDEAS. Within the world of Ideas itself Plato also runs into problems. Let us consider the Idea of man. Man is a living rational creature. The being of man is the Idea of man. Does this man I have here before me share in the Idea of "living" or the Idea of "rational"? Within the very world of Ideas I have the problem of the one and the many. How is Plato going to solve this problem of the *koinonía*, the "communication," of the Ideas? He will use a notion similar to that of sharing. The Idea of man is in *communication* with the Idea of living, the Idea of rational, and so forth.

By these paths Plato arrives at two important concepts: the Idea of being as the highest genus and the Idea of the Good as the Idea of the Ideas, or, as he says in a final metaphor, as the "sun of the Ideas."

THE GOOD. What is the Good? What is the Idea of the Good? Before all else, it is an Idea. This Idea is placed at the pinnacle of a hierarchy in which all the Ideas are found: because the Ideas are ranged and organized in a hierarchy—this is what makes their κοινωνία, or communication, possible. Plato tells us that the Idea of the Good is the worthiest and highest Idea; that it is, I repeat, the sun of the Ideas, and, above all, that it is the Idea of the Ideas. This should not be understood as a mere hyperbole, but in a much stricter sense: the "Idea of the Ideas" is the Idea which makes all the others *be* Ideas, which confers upon them their character as Ideas. But the Ideas are the true entities and thus, if the Idea of the Good gives the rest of the Ideas their character, it gives them their *being*. But what can make them be? Naturally, being. It is being that makes each individual entity be an entity; being is present in all entities, giving them their character as entities. This being is what Plato calls the Good; but in Greece "the Good" is understood in a sense closer to that of our plural "goods," that is, wealth. This permits us to see clearly the link between being and the Good. The "good" of each thing is what that thing is, what it is useful for; conversely, when we say a thing is good we mean that it is what it is. A good knife is one which is fully—truly— a knife; and a good statesman is one who is fully—truly—a statesman. Naturally, this concept is close to that interrelationship of being, the Good, and the One (those aspects that the medieval Scholastics will call the *transcendentals*) which we will find in Aristotle.

In a certain sense, Plato's doctrine of the Good is his theology. The Good appears in many Platonic texts (although not always with sufficient clarity) in such a way that we are led to understand it as God. Plato's teaching was interpreted in this way, first by the Neoplatonists and then by St. Augustine; in this form it became a motive force in the entire medieval Christian tradition.

THE ENTITY AS A GENUS. A second important point remains to be considered: the Idea of the Entity as a *genus*. For Plato, it is the highest genus. All other things are successive species of this unique genus. Thus the Entity could be divided into genera and species; this would be a hierarchical division, with successive differentiations being added on. Aristotle resolutely opposes this point of view also, for profound reasons which we will examine later. In his criticism of Plato's theory of Ideas, Aristotle will make several major affirmations: (1) that the Ideas are not separate from the things; (2) that the Entity is not a genus, but the highest universal; (3) that the Entity, the Good, and the One are mutually associated; finally (4) that being is expressed in many ways and that these expressions of being are expressions by *analogy*. Although the form Aristotle gives them is new, these last two notions are not alien to Plato's system of thought.

4. MAN AND THE CITY

In Plato, the Idea of the Good appears simultaneously as the Divinity and the Artificer or *Demiurge* of the world. Plato imagines the creation of a "world soul," halfway between the Ideas and the things. This soul animates the world. The human soul, too, as we have seen, is something intermediate. On the one hand, it has fallen from heaven, it has been incarnated in a body, it is in bondage to the world of the senses, it is changeable and subject to decay. On the other hand, it has seen the Ideas and has a special connection with them; through them it shares in that world of the Ideas which is eternal and perceived by the mind.

DOCTRINE OF THE SOUL. We have already seen, in the *Phaedrus*, Plato's account of the mythical origin of man. Plato particularly insists on the immortality of the soul. In doing this, he adopts a deep-seated element of Greek religion and of all Greek thinking. Belief in the immortality of the soul had been a cardinal point of the Dionysiac and Orphic mysteries and of Pythagoreanism. The Pythagoreans had a profound influence on Plato, in this area as well as that of their mathematical teachings. His principal proofs of the immortality of the soul are based on the soul's uncomplicated form, its immateriality and its analogy to the eternal Ideas and to truth, which is known through the soul. These proofs have traditionally been used in Greek and Christian philosophy.

The soul has three parts: an "appetitive" or sensual part, the part most closely related to the needs of the body; a second, "spirited" part, corresponding to the drives and emotions; and, finally, a rational part, by means of which knowledge of the Ideas and volition in the deliberative sense—following the dictates of reason—are possible. This outline of psychology is developed further in Aristotle's thinking.

ETHICS. Plato's ethics shows a strict parallelism with his theory of the soul. The parts of the human psyche correspond rigorously to ethical requirements. Each part must be governed in a certain way, must possess a particular *virtue*, the quality that makes possible its perfect functioning. The sensual part requires moderation, what is traditionally called temperance (*sophrosýne*). To the emotional part corresponds fortitude, or *andría*. The rational part must be endowed with wisdom or prudence, *phrónesis*. But there is also a fourth virtue; the parts of the soul are elements of a unity, and are thus interrelated; a good relationship among its parts constitutes the most important requirement of the soul and, consequently, its highest virtue: justice, or *dikaiosýne*. These are the four virtues that were handed down as the cardinal virtues; they passed even into Christian doctrine, where they are usually termed prudence, justice, fortitude and temperance.

THE CITY. Individual morality is transferred almost exactly into the theory of the civil constitution, or *politeía*, as Plato expounds it in the *Republic* and, later, in an attenuated, more easily realized form, in the *Laws*. The city, like the soul, can be considered as a whole composed of three parts, which correspond to the three parts of the soul. These parts are the three great social classes recognized by Plato: the mass of citizens, including the tradesmen, artisans and farmers; the guardians; and the philosophers. There is a close correlation between these classes and the faculties of the human soul, so that each of these social groups is particularly associated with one of the virtues. The proper virtue of the producing class is temperance; the virtue of the guardians, or warriors, is fortitude; and the virtue of the philosophers is wisdom, *phrónesis* or *sophía*. Here, too, the prime virtue is justice, which in this case is understood even more rigorously: it consists here in the equilibrium and proper relationship of the individuals among themselves and with the State, and of the different classes among themselves and with the social community. Thus justice governs and determines the life of the body politic, which is the city. The Platonic state is the traditional Greek *pólis*, of small dimensions and scanty population; Plato never imagines any other type of political unit.

The philosophers are the "archons," or board of governors, charged with the supreme direction of the State, with legislation and with the education of all the classes. The guardians have a military function: the defense of the State and the established social and political order against their enemies within and without. The third class, the producing class, has a more passive role and is subservient to the two higher classes, which it must sustain economically. In exchange it receives from them direction, education and protection.

In the two higher classes Plato establishes a communistic government, which involves community ownership not only of property, but also of wives and children, all of whom belong to the State. Only the lowest class is allowed private property and private families. The governing classes must have no private interests, but must subordinate all their interests to the highest service of the *pólis*.

Education, which is similar for women and for men, is administered in stages; it constitutes the selective process among the townspeople, determining the class that each citizen is to belong to, according to his aptitudes and merits. Those with the fewest natural gifts receive elementary instruction and go to make up the producing class of society; those who are more apt continue their education, until a new selection separates those who are to remain among the guardians from those who, after further preparation, enter the class of philosophers and are thus called upon to bear the burden of government. In Plato's system of education physical exercises alternate with intellectual disciplines; the role of each citizen is rigorously determined according to his age. Procreation and the relationship between the sexes are strictly dependent on the interests of the State, which regulates these matters for its own convenience. Plato's entire conception of the *pólis* reveals a thoroughgoing subordination of the individual to the interests of the community. Authority is exercised vigorously, and the primary condition for the functioning of the political life of the city is that the city be ruled by justice.

5. PHILOSOPHY

Let us now see what philosophy means to Plato. What is understood by "philosophy" and "philosophizing" at this point, when Hellenic thought has reached its first stage of full maturity?

At the beginning of the seventh book of the *Republic*, as we have seen, Plato relates the *myth of the cave*, which symbolizes, on the one hand, the differences between everyday life and the life of the philosopher and, on the other, the various strata of reality within the Platonic metaphysical system.

Moreover, Plato says in the *Symposium*: "None of the gods philosophizes or wishes to become wise, because the gods already are so; nor does any wise man philosophize, either. Nor do the ignorant philosophize or desire to become wise." And he adds further on: "Who, then, are those who philosophize, if they are neither the wise nor the ignorant? Clearly, those who are intermediate ($\mu\epsilon\tau\alpha\xi\acute{u}$) between these two groups."

This is definitive. In Plato's mind, neither the wise man nor the ignorant man philosophizes. The ignorant man does not have knowledge, and that is that. The intermediate man does not have knowledge either, but he realizes that this is so; he knows that he does not know, and therefore he wants to know: he *feels the lack* of that knowledge. Strictly speaking, neither the wise man nor the ignorant man feels the want of knowledge. I do not have branches, but I do not feel the lack of them. Only that man philosophizes who feels that knowledge is lacking. This leads us to two important matters which emanate, as it were, from Plato's thought: the relationships philosophy can have with *love*, on the one hand, and *Divinity*, on the other.

In the *Symposium*, the theme is discourse "on love," and also the eulogy of the god Eros, who is closely related to philosophy. For Plato, love is the feeling that something is lacking, a search for what one does not have, for what is missing. According to the myth, Love, who is the son of Porus ("means," plenty) and Penia (poverty), possesses all sorts of wealth, but at the same time is needy. Love, as well as the lover, the *erastés*, seeks that which is lacking, especially beauty. Socrates in the *Symposium* scandalizes everyone when he says that if Love seeks beauty, Love must feel the lack of beauty and therefore cannot be a god. What is Love, then? A great "demon" or "genius," a *metaxý*, something halfway between men and the gods. And this is the very thing that happens to the philosopher, who is also *metaxý*, halfway between the wise man and the ignorant man. Wisdom is knowledge of the most beautiful things, and love is love of the beautiful; therefore, Love must be a philosopher. Through the beautiful one arrives at the true, and thus philosophers are "lovers of the vision of truth." There is an essential association between beauty and truth. Immediately below the Idea of the Good and of truth, the object of philosophy, Plato places the Idea of the beautiful. And beauty, for Plato, is more easily visible than truth; it can be better seen, is brighter, is more vividly and immediately in evidence. Beauty can lead us to truth: therefore the philosopher is a *lover*, and from the contemplation of the beauty of a body he raises his mind to the beauty of bodies in general, then to the beauty of souls and, finally, to the beauty of the Ideas themselves. And that is when he *knows*, when he truly has *sophía*.

Let us recall that "beauty" in Latin is *forma*, and that which is beautiful, *formosus*. Beauty is also one of the meanings of *species*; and *species*, like the Greek *eîdos* or *idéa*, is that which is seen. That which is seen can be *beauty* and the *Idea*; and the same applies to *forma*, which is what constitutes the essence of a thing, its "good" in the Greek sense.

We see that the notion of love appears in Plato as an essential element in philosophy. But the matter is not so simple, because there are many words for love in Greek. The three principal words are ἔρως, φιλία and ἀγάπη. *Éros*, as we have seen, is primarily a desire for something that one does not have and misses, basically a longing for beauty. *Philía* is to be found at the very root of the word "philosophy." It is a type of friendship: concern and familiar companionship. Aristotle chose *philía* for speaking about philosophy. *Agápe* was a rather marginal word; it signified a type of *dilectio*, reciprocal esteem and warmth. This concept is essentially modified by Christianity and becomes *caritas* (charity) in the Latin translations of St. John and St. Paul (Zubiri). And St. Augustine utters this simple sentence, which limits and defines the word: *Non intratur in veritatem nisi per caritatem* ("One does not enter truth except through charity").

Thus, in three philosophical systems as great as those of Plato, Aristotle and St. Augustine, philosophy uses as a method, as a way of access to truth, the three forms of love in Greek. For Plato, one cannot gain access to philosophy except through *éros*; for Aristotle, through a certain *philía*; for St. Augustine, through *caritas* (*agápe*). And again, twelve centuries later, Spinoza will define philosophy as *amor Dei intellectualis* (the intellectual love of God), and in our own century Ortega will define it as "the general science of love."

Aristotle

With Aristotle, Greek philosophy achieves full and perfect maturity. This is true to such an extent that philosophy begins to decline after his time, and does not again reach a similar height; in fact, the Greeks are not even capable of maintaining the level of Aristotle's metaphysics, because they lack the ability to grasp the philosophic problems in the profound dimension in which Aristotle had stated them. Thus, Hellenic thought becomes trivial in the hands of the schools of moralists which, after Aristotle's time, fill the Hellenic cities and later the cities of the Roman Empire.

Aristotle, together with Plato, is the greatest figure in Greek philosophy, and even, perhaps, in all philosophy. In greater degree than any other thinker, he determined the paths which philosophy after his time was to follow. He was the discoverer of a deep stratum of metaphysical questions; the shaper of many of the most important concepts which for many long centuries the human mind has used in order to reflect on the being of things; the creator of logic as a discipline, which has been maintained until this day practically within the limits which Aristotle set for it, modified by only two or three brilliant endeavors over the entire course of the history of philosophy; in short, the man who possessed all the wisdom of his time. Wherever he placed his hand he has left the imprint of his unique genius. Aristotle has, thus, influenced all philosophy in an incalculable manner, and because of this he is, perhaps, our first problem, the problem which present-day thinking must most earnestly confront if it wishes to understand itself and root itself in its own era and in the true problem of philosophy.

LIFE. Aristotle was not strictly Greek; he was a Macedonian, but he was certainly greatly influenced by Greek civilization. He was born in Stagira, on the Chalcidic peninsula, in the year 384 B.C. His father, Nicomachus, was a physician and a friend of Amyntas II, king of Macedonia. It is possible—as Ross points out—that this background influenced Aristotle's interest in physical and biological questions. When he was eighteen years old he entered Plato's school in Athens; he remained there nineteen years—until the master's death—in the capacity of student and also of teacher, all the while very closely related to and at the same time in profound disagreement with Plato. Aristotle, the only authentic Platonist, shows how in one sense only one true disciple of a philosopher is possible. When Plato died, Speusippus took over the administration of the Academy, and at this time Aristotle left the school and Athens. He went to Mysia, where he remained three years and where he married. Later, his first wife having died, he lived with another woman, who became the mother of his son, Nicomachus. Aristotle also spent some time in Mytilene, on the island of Lesbos.

About the year 343, Philip of Macedonia invited Aristotle to take charge of the education of his son Alexander, who was then thirteen years old. Aristotle accepted the position and proceeded to Macedonia. His influence on Alexander must have been very great. It is known that they disagreed on the question of the fusion of Greek culture with that of the Orient, Aristotle not believing this plan to be advisable. In 334 Aristotle returned to Athens and founded his own school. In the suburbs of the city, in a grove that was consecrated to Apollo Lyceus and the Muses, he rented some houses which were to constitute the Lyceum. There, *while strolling*, he discussed the most profound philosophic questions with his best students; therefore, the members of this school were called the *Peripatetics*. In the afternoons he used to expound on more accessible topics—rhetoric, sophistry or politics—to a larger audience.

Aristotle's intellectual activity was enormous. Almost all of his works date from the period 334 to 323 B.C. He assembled an incalculable body of scientific data which permitted him to advance the knowledge of his time prodigiously. At the death of Alexander, in 323, an anti-Macedonian movement broke out in Athens, and this hostility also came to be directed against Aristotle. He was accused of the crime of impiety. Saying that he did not want Athens to be responsible for a third sin against philosophy (he was referring to the persecution of Anaxagoras and to Socrates' death), he moved to Chalcis, on the island of Euboea, where Macedonian influence was strong. He died there in the year 322.

WORKS. Aristotle wrote two types of books. Some were intended for a wide audience; these, called the *exoteric* works, were, in general, in the form of dialogues; they were greatly admired for their elegant style and literary value. His other books are the philosophical or *acroamatic* works, that is, his *esoteric* writings; these dealt with the more profound questions and were directed solely to the superior students at the Lyceum; the esoteric writings were, as a rule, in the form of *textbooks* or *lectures*, and a few are preserved in rough-draft form, without elaboration—that is, as mere notes. All the dialogues have been lost; only fragments of them remain. In contrast, the greater part of Aristotle's scientific writings is preserved. Naturally, one must bear in mind that there are spurious pieces among the writings attributed to Aristotle, and that many treatises were written by him in collaboration with students, or were composed by students from their classroom notes and papers.

Aristotle divides the sciences into three groups: Theoretical or Speculative Science, Practical Science and Poetical Science. This division must be explained. *Poíesis*, which is connected etymologically with our word "poetry," means, in Greek, "production, manufacture"; the characteristic of this activity is that it has an end or goal distinct from itself. For example, in the manufacture of an armoire, the armoire is the goal, and in the composition of an ode, the ode is the goal. *Práxis* or Practical Science is an *action*, an activity, whose goal is the action itself, not something external to the performance of the activity. *Práxis* is superior to *poíesis* because it is its own goal; therefore, it is self-sufficient—it is the *autarchía* which the Greeks so greatly admired. Politics is an example. One should not forget that *theoría* or contemplation is a type of *práxis*. *Theoría* is also Practical Science; Theoretical and Practical Science differ only in that Theoretical Science is the highest *práxis*, in contrast to something that is *only* practical and does not succeed in being theoretical. Contemplation is an action which is its own goal, but which also contains its object within itself. In order to be able to act, the statesman, for example, requires—in addition to himself—a city. But the man who practices Theoretical Science needs nothing but his own mind; this man is thus the most self-sufficient of all men, and therefore the superior man.

This distinction between the sciences results in three ways of life and three modes of knowledge.

But first we must mention one science that does not enter into the discussion of the others because it is previous to them all. This is the science of *logic*. It is called the *Organon*, or instrument—the title given to it—and it serves all the sciences. Aristotle's *Organon* is composed of various treatises: the *Categories*, *De Interpretatione*, the *Prior* and *Posterior Analytics*, the *Topics*, *Sophistical Refutations* and other brief works on logic.

The Theoretical Sciences are mathematics, physics and metaphysics. The principal works pertaining to this group of sciences are the *Physics*, the book *De Caelo* (On the Heavens), the *De Mundo* (On the World), the *De Anima* (On the Soul), a whole series of treatises on physical and biological questions and, especially, the fourteen books of the *Metaphysics* or *First Philosophy*.

The Practical Sciences are ethics, politics and economics; that is, those sciences which are concerned with man's private and social life. Aristotle's principal works in this area are the three *Ethics*: *Nicomachean Ethics*, *Eudemian Ethics* and *Magna Moralia*. (The last is the least important of the three and is not authentic.) This group of writings also includes the *Politics* and the *Economics*, but these are of inferior interest and are certainly spurious.

The major poetical works are the *Poetics*, which has wielded an extraordinary influence, and the *Rhetoric*.

To complete the list of the most important works by Aristotle that have come down to us, one must add a great number of brief treatises on every subject in the Aristotelian scientific corpus, and also a repertory of questions on many things; this collection, which is probably of later composition, is called the *Problems*.

1. THE LEVELS OF KNOWLEDGE

At the beginning of his *Metaphysics*, Aristotle raises the problem of knowledge par excellence, which is precisely what he called "first philosophy" and which, since the edition of his works prepared by Andronicus of Rhodes, has traditionally been called *metaphysics*. (The texts on "first philosophy" were grouped *after* those of physics, and were called *tà metà tà physiká*; this purely editorial designation was later interpreted to mean something which was *beyond* physics, a "*transphysics*," and, as is well known, the name for the highest philosophic science came about through this chance circumstance.)

The first sentence in the *Metaphysics* says, "All men desire naturally to know." Aristotle is quick to add that the pleasure which we derive from our senses, and especially from the sense of sight, is an indication that this is so. He distinguishes the use we make of senses for their value in accomplishing things, from the enjoyment that we also derive from them when we are not going to do anything. But these senses, which presuppose a lowest level of knowledge, are not exclusively man's;

animals also have them, and some animals even have memory, which, by providing for the retention of knowledge, permits learning.

Man, on the other hand, has other, higher modes of knowledge. He has, especially, experience, *empeiría*, in the sense of one's "experience of things." This is an intimate knowledge of things—of particular things—in an immediate and concrete way, something which gives us information only about the particular things. Therefore, *empeiría* cannot be taught; one can only place another person in the circumstances under which he may acquire it. There is another, higher mode of knowledge—art or technique, τέχνη; that is, art in its traditional meaning, as when one speaks of the art of healing, which is the example to which Aristotle most closely refers. *Tékhne* is a "know-how." The *tekhnítes*, the artisan or technician, is the man who knows how to do things, knows what means to use in order to obtain the desired results. But art does not give us an understanding of individual things; rather, it provides a certain universal, an idea of things. Since one can discuss what is universal, art can be taught, whereas what is individual can only be seen or shown. Thus *tékhne* is superior to *empeiría*; but the latter is also necessary—for example, in order to heal, since the doctor does not have to heal man in general, but Socrates (that is, an individual who is a man); therefore, the doctor heals Socrates directly, and man only in an indirect way.

This *tékhne* gives us the *what* of things, and even their *why*; but we know a thing completely only when we know it in its causes and first principles; only wisdom, *sophía*, can give us this type of knowledge. This highest mode of knowledge must tell what things are and why they are; that is, it must *demonstrate* these things on the basis of their *principles*. Science, demonstrative knowledge, is called *epistéme* in Greek; this is the true science, the science which Aristotle seeks, ζητουμένη ἐπιστήμη. But principles cannot be demonstrated—that is why they are principles; they do not derive from anything. Therefore, an intuitive knowledge of principles is necessary, and this is what *noûs* is; it is another essential ingredient which, together with *epistéme*, comprises true *wisdom*. And with this we reach the highest level of knowledge, which has for its object the Entity for what it is, things for what they are, understood in their causes and principles. All the sciences, Aristotle says, are more necessary than this one, but none is superior to it.

And man reached this knowledge—which is, in short, philosophy—because of awe; awe is always—today as in the beginning—the root of philosophy.

2. METAPHYSICS

In his *Metaphysics* (IV, 1) Aristotle defines "first philosophy" as the science that considers *the Entity as such* in a universal manner; that is, the totality of things for what they are. The other sciences study a portion of the things according to a determined, arbitrary arrangement; for example, botany is the study of plants as vegetable organisms; mathematics is the study of figures and numbers from the point of view of measure. Metaphysics, on the other hand, has as an object the totality of things, but for what they *are*, the Entity as an Entity, τὸ ὄν ἦ ὄν. Moreover, Aristotle says that in two senses metaphysics is a divine science: in the sense that if God possessed any science, it would be the science of metaphysics, and also, in the sense that God is the subject of metaphysics. Thus metaphysics is also called the *theological* science, or theology, θεολογικὴ ἐπιστήμη. And, finally, Aristotle defines metaphysics in other places as the science of substance, περὶ τῆς οὐσίας. What does this mean? Are there three sciences, or is there but one? This question concerns Aristotle deeply; he returns to it time and again, and then affirms the oneness of first philosophy. Metaphysics is a single science, and is at the same time the science of the Entity for what it is, the science of God and the science of substance. We will attempt to show the internal connection among these three aspects, and by doing this also show the unity of Aristotelian metaphysics.

THE ENTITY AS SUCH. There are different types of entities. In the first place, there are *natural things*, physical objects. For Aristotle, nature is the principle of the motion of things (ἀρχὴ τῆς κινήσεως); something is natural if it contains within itself the principle of its motion. For example, a tree or a horse is a natural thing, but a table is not. (The concept of motion here includes repose as well, if repose is the *natural* state of a thing; thus, a stone is also a natural thing.) Natural things are, then, true things; but they move, they come to be and cease to be, and to this extent they are not fully entities. *Mathematical objects* are another kind of entity, and they do not move; it would seem that the science which concerned itself with these objects would be a higher science. But mathematical objects have one very serious drawback: they are not things; they exist in the mind, but not outside of it, not *separately*. If mathematical objects have greater dignity as entities because they are immovable, they have less stature as entities because they do not exist as things.

But what must an entity be like if it is to unite the two conditions? It would have to be immovable but also separate—a thing. If such an entity existed, it would be self-sufficient; it would be the highest entity, the one which would completely merit the name of *Entity*.

GOD. Aristotle says that this highest entity is divine; he says that it is god, θεός. And the highest science, the one which deals with this Entity, is a *theological* science. For Aristotle, God is the aggregate of metaphysical conditions which makes an entity be fully an entity. The science of the Entity for what it is and the science of God, the Entity par excellence, are one and the same science.

Provisionally, this Entity is *alive*, because living beings exist more completely than inert beings. But, in addition, this Entity must be self-sufficient. We should remember that there are several different types of action; there are, for instance, *poíesis* and *prâxis*. The former is essentially insufficient, since its goal is outside itself, a *product*. If God's activity were a *poíesis*, he would require those products in order to exist; he would not be self-sufficient, and thus would not be God. In *prâxis*, on the other hand, the goal is not the product, the *érgon*, but the very process of acting, the activity or *enérgeia*. For example, political *prâxis* has two drawbacks. In the first place, it requires a city in which it can be exercised, and to this extent is not self-sufficient, though as an activity in itself it might be considered to be self-sufficient. In the second place, political knowledge always refers to a specific opportunity, a specific moment—it is knowledge dependent upon opportunity.

However, as we have seen, there is another kind of *prâxis*—*theoría*, the theoretic life. This form of *prâxis* deals with seeing and discerning the being of things in their totality. This is the highest way of life; therefore, God must lead a theoretic life, for it is the supreme mode of being. But this is not enough, because in order to lead a theoretic life man requires the Entity; he needs the things in order to know them, and thus is not absolutely self-sufficient. Only if this *theoría* were concerned with itself would it be self-sufficient. Therefore, God is the *thought of the thought*, νόησις νοήσεως. God's activity is the highest knowledge, and metaphysics is divine because it is the science of God. This is so in two ways, since God is the object of metaphysics and at the same time its pre-eminent subject.

Theoría is no mere contemplation; rather, it is taking care to see that things are what they are, placing them *in the light* (ἐν φωτί). This is *sophía*, wisdom, and in a strict sense, only God has it. Only at certain moments can man have it. What man can possess is a *philosophía*, a love for *sophía*. Aristotle says that if a man is to be a philosopher, it is not enough for him to have a momentary vision of *sophía*; he needs a ἕξις, a *habit*, a way of living. And according to Zubiri, this is what is truly problematic.

SUBSTANCE. Thirdly, metaphysics is the science of substance; it is necessary to show that that science is one with the science of the Entity as an Entity and the science of God. Aristotle says (*Metaphysics*, IV, 2) that while the Entity is expressed in many ways, it is not expressed ambiguously; but it is expressed analogously; that is, with relation to a single principle which gives a unity to its many meanings. Therefore, the Entity is *one* and *manifold* at the same time. As we shall see more clearly later, *substance* is the basic meaning of being. The other modes of being depend on this one, because all are either substances or "affections" (attributes) of substance. Color is color *of* a substance, and if we say "three," we are referring to three substances. Even the concept of want or deprivation contains this reference to substance.

In order for there to be a science, there must be a unity, a certain Nature in terms of which all other things are expressed. This unity is that of substance, which is the principal expression of being, the basis of the analogy. Substance is present in all forms of being and, therefore, it is not distinct from the Entity as an Entity and from God; rather, the Entity as an Entity finds its unity in substance. What we have, then, is a single first philosophy or metaphysics with a three-part root.

We began by seeking the same science which Aristotle sought, and discovered the characteristics of *sophía*. We saw that it is the science of God and the science of the Entity as an Entity, because God is the whole complex of the ontological conditions of the entity. We then saw that this science is also a divine science, because in it man resembles God. Finally, we saw that this science is the science of substance, which is present in all the modes of the Entity. The θεός is nothing but the Entity as an Entity, the plenary form of substance; and the essential unity of the science we sought is based on this conclusion.

3. The Modes of Being

THE ANALOGICAL NATURE OF THE ENTITY. A term is univocal when it has a single meaning; for example, man. A term is ambiguous when it has two or more independent meanings which have no other similarity than that they are both expressed with the same word; for example, the word "chest," which designates a part of the body or a piece of furniture. We saw that the word "being" is not ambiguous in spite of its many meanings, because its various meanings have a connection or unity in themselves; that is, they are not entirely dissimilar. "Being" is an *analogous* or *analogical* word, as is the word "healthy" in the phrases "a healthy man," "a healthy appetite," "a healthy influence." In each case something different is meant: the man possesses health, the appetite indicates health, the influence promotes health. These are different meanings, but they involve a common reference to well-being. It is well-being, then, that creates the analogous unity. As we have seen, a similar thing happens with being, which has its unity in substance, because in a broad sense all the forms of the Entity are substances or attributes of it.

But this concept must be stated even more precisely. When I say that being is expressed in many ways, I do not mean only that there are many entities, or just that there are many kinds of entities, but that the word "being" means something different when I say that something *is* a man, or *is* green, or that objects *are* three, or that a coin *is* counterfeit. It is not that the objects named are distinguished from one another, but rather that the word "is" means a different thing in each case, even though it always involves an allusion—direct or indirect—to substance.

THE FOUR MODES OF BEING. Aristotle says concretely that being is expressed in four ways. The four modes of being are the following: (1) being *per se* (καθ᾽ αὑτό) or *per accidens* (κατὰ συμβεβηκός); that is, by essence or by accident; (2) according to the categories; (3) true being and false being; and (4) according to the potential and the actual. Let us briefly examine the meaning of these four modes of being.

"PER SE" AND "PER ACCIDENS." If we say, for instance, that man is musical, we are pointing out something that is in man by accident or chance. Musicality is accidental in man; it is simply something that comes about in a man but is not part of his essence. If we say that the just man is musical, we are again pointing out something that is *per accidens*, because the two qualities, "just" and "musical," belong to the subject, "man," by accident. Being *per se* is expressed essentially. Man is living, for example, not by accident, but by essence. This essential being is expressed with different meanings, and these are the modes according to which being can be predicated. These modes are the so-called *predications* or *categories*.

CATEGORIES. The categories are the various modes in which being can be predicated. They are, thus, the inflections or *grammatical "cases" of being*, πτώσεις τοῦ ὄντος. Aristotle gives several lists of these predications, and the longest list consists of ten: Substance (for example, man), Quantity (two cubits in height), Quality (white), Relation (double), Place (in the Lyceum), Time (yesterday), Position (seated), State (wearing shoes), Action (cutting) and Passivity (being cut). It is not a question of the differences between these things, but rather that being itself is inflected in each of these modes and means

something different in each of the categories. Therefore, if to the
question, "What is this?" one answers, "Seven," there is, apart from
the truth or falsity of the statement, an *incongruence*, because the *is* of
the question moves in the category of substance, and the answer moves
in the category of quantity. These categories have a unity, which is
precisely substance, because all the other categories refer to it: this is
the clearest instance of the analogous nature of oneness. Substance is
present in all the other categories, and in the final analysis, all the
other categories refer to substance and have meaning only when it is
presupposed.

THE TRUE AND THE FALSE. Truth and falsity occur primarily in
judgments. The statement "A is B," which unites two terms, necessarily embraces truth or falsity, depending on whether it unites what in
reality is united or unites what in reality is separated—or, negatively,
whether it separates that which is really united or that which is
separated. But there is a more fundamental meaning of truth and
falsity, which is the truth or falsity of things, of being. Thus we say,
"This coin is false," or "This coffee is real." Here truth or falsity
refers to the thing itself. And when we say that two and two are four,
the meaning of the verb "to be" is *to be truly*. Something is true
(ἀληθές) when it shows the being which it has, and false (ψεῦδος) when
it shows a being other than its own, when it presents one being for
another, as when a mere lead disk has the appearance of a coin. The
lead disk *as such* is perfectly true, but it is false *as a coin*; that is, when it
pretends to be a coin and is not a coin, when it shows an apparent
being, a being which it does not really have. This demonstrates the
fundamental meaning of truth, ἀλήθεια, in Greek. To be true means
to be uncovered, patent, and there is falsity when what is uncovered is
not the being which a thing has, but an apparent being; that is, falsity
is a *concealment* of being, the revelation of a fraudulent being where a
true being should be, as when the true being of lead is concealed behind
the deceitful appearance of money.

THE POTENTIAL AND THE ACTUAL. Finally, being is divided according to the potential (δύναμις) and the actual (ἐνέργεια). An entity can
exist in actuality, or only as a possibility. A tree can be an actual tree or
a potential tree, a tree in the realm of possibility, that is to say, a seed.
The seed is a tree, but only in the realm of potentiality, just as a child
is a potential man, and what is small is potentially large. But one must
keep two things in mind: in the first place, potentiality does not exist
in the abstract; potentiality is always potentiality for a specific actuality. That is, a certain seed has the potential to be an oak tree, but not to
be a horse, or even a pine tree. This means—as Aristotle affirms—that

the actual is prior (ontologically) to the potential, since the potential is potential *for* a specific actuality. The actuality is already present in the potentiality itself. The oak tree is present in the acorn, and the hen in the egg—for the simple reason that there are no simple, abstract *eggs*; an egg is, for instance, *a hen's egg*. Then the chicken is already implicit in the egg and is what gives the egg its potentiality. In the second place, in order to exist, potential beings must have a certain actual existence, although not as potentialities. That is, a seed, which is a potential oak tree, is an actual acorn, and an egg, which is a potential chicken, is a very real and actual egg. The same entity has, then, an actual being and the potential being of another entity. This concept is of the greatest importance to the metaphysical interpretation of motion.

Aristotle uses two different words to express the idea of actuality: *enérgeia* (ἐνέργεια) and entelechy (ἐντελέχεια). Even though these words are sometimes used as synonyms, they are not equivalent because *enérgeia* indicates simple actuality whereas entelechy means "that which has arrived at its end," its *télos*, and therefore supposes an *actualization*. It is possible to say that God—who is pure actuality and who, as we shall see, does not have either potentiality or motion; who is, then, *actual*, but not *actualized*—is *enérgeia*, but one cannot say strictly that God is entelechy.

We now see that the four modes of being have a fundamental analogous unity, which is that of substance. It is for this reason that Aristotle says that the major question of metaphysics is, "What is being?" He clarifies this by adding, "That is, what is substance?" We must now investigate Aristotle's ontological analysis of substance.

4. SUBSTANCE

In Greek, "substance" is οὐσία, *ousía*. In the everyday language, this word means holdings, property, goods, that which is possessed. It is the whole complex of available components of a thing, those parts which can be utilized. We find a similar meaning in English when we say that something has substance—a substantial dinner, for example. We also use this word somewhat differently, as when we say that evidence is insubstantial. The word "substance" itself points out another train of thought: something that is *sub-stantia* is underneath, subject, in the literal meaning of *sub-jectum*, which is not the translation of οὐσία, but of another Greek word, ὑποκείμενον, which means substratum or subject. This is a decisive point: substance is the support or substratum for its "accidents"; red, hard, square, and so on, are supported by the substance "table." On the other hand, "accidents" are predicated of other things, subjects, whereas substance is not predicated of any other thing. The table is a table in itself, whereas the red is the red *of* the table. But we must not forget that the primary meaning of substance is not this concept of substratum, but that of *ousía*, and that precisely because substance is a thing in itself, it can be a subject of which "accidents" are predicated. Therefore, substance is, above all, a *thing*, something separate, independent, something that exists in itself and not in something else. And the fundamental mode of substance is nature (φύσις), because, as we have seen, substance consists of the principle of motion, of what constitutes the individual possibilities of each thing.

But there are various classes of substances. First of all, we have concrete, individual things: this man, this tree, this stone. These are substances in the strictest sense, what Aristotle calls primary substances. But we have another kind of entity—universals, genera and species, *man* or *tree* (that is, the counterpart of the Platonic Ideas). These things are evidently not substances in the strict sense of separate things; Aristotle sees that they are not, but asks to what other category can they correspond? It is clear that they can correspond to no other category than the category of substance; then Aristotle must distinguish them from primary substances by calling them secondary substances. What does this mean? What is the ontological structure of substance? In order to explain this, Aristotle expounds his brilliant theory of matter and form.

MATTER AND FORM. Substance is interpreted as a composite of two elements: matter and form. This is not a question of two real parts that unite to form substance, but of two *ontological moments or ingredients* which can be distinguished in *ousía* by analysis. Matter is that *of which* a thing is made; form is what makes a thing be what it is. For example, the matter of a table is wood, and its form, that of table. Matter (ὕλη) and form (μορφή, εἶδος) cannot exist separately; matter is always found determined by form, and form is always found determining matter. And form should not be understood in an exclusively geometrical sense, which is a secondary meaning, but as that which confers being; that is, wood or meat have, respectively, the form of wood or meat, but another form can be superimposed on this form. For example, the form of table can be superimposed on wood. In such a case wood, which could itself be form, functions as matter in relation to the form of table.

The concrete Entity is a *hylomorphic* compound (from *hýle* and *morphé*), and is also called σύνολον, *sýnolon*. The universal is form, but—

unlike the Platonic Ideas—it is not separated from the things but present in them, determining them. That is, man, the species man, is not separated from each individual man; rather it is present in each man as the human form. This explains for the first time the problem that Plato attempted in vain to clarify with the insufficient concept of sharing—the problem of the relation of Ideas or species to individual things. Universals are substances, but abstract substances, abstract ingredients of each individual thing, and for this reason they are called secondary substances.

There is a close connection between matter and form and the potential and the actual. Matter is simply possibility; it is potential that actuates itself by shaping itself; thus, it does not have reality in itself. For this reason, God, who is pure actual reality, cannot be matter, because God is not a mixture of the potential and the actual; God is *pure actuality*. This theory permits the problem of motion to be solved for the first time since Parmenides.

MOTION. Let us recall that there were two serious problems that were debated in early Greek philosophy, and that these two problems were intimately connected: the problem of the oneness of being and the multiplicity of things, and the problem of motion. The two problems were merged in the momentous question of being and non-being. We have seen that the first part of the problem finds its solution in Aristotle's assertion that the Entity is one and, at the same time, by means of analogy, multiple; this reconciles and resolves the *aporia*. Let us now examine something that refers more concretely to motion.

Moving or changing is a coming to be and a ceasing to be. All motion presupposes two limits: a principle and an end. If the Entity is one, this duality is ontologically impossible. So, within Aristotelian metaphysics, this duality does not exist. What is motion for Aristotle? The apparently obscure definition which he gives for it is at bottom extremely clear: *the realization of the possible in so far as it is possible*. We have already indicated the suppositions necessary for understanding this. We have seen that a potential entity, such as an egg or a seed, also has a certain actuality, to wit, that which makes it possible for us to eat an egg or to trade in wheat; this involves dealing with realities, not with pure possibilities. He who eats an egg eats an *actual egg*, not a potential chicken; when that potential, instead of remaining as a possibility, actualizes itself, there is motion, which is, concretely, generation. Then, what has been called the step from the potential to the actual is verified; this has been referred to more precisely as the step from the potential entity to the actual entity. Motion had been impossible since Parmenides, because it had been understood as a step from non-being to being, or vice versa. The theory of the analogous nature of the Entity shows that it is a question of passing from one *mode* of being to another; that is, of remaining always within the realm of the one and multiple being. With this discovery, the crucial problem of motion finds its mature solution within Hellenic philosophy; physics as a philosophic discipline becomes possible, because one can speak of *nature* from the point of view of being.

THE CAUSES. For Aristotle knowledge—which is concerned with universals (because what is individual has an infinity of attributes and cannot be exhausted in knowledge) and which is not by accident but by essence—is, above all, demonstrative knowledge, which makes things known by their causes and principles. Knowledge is no longer a discerning, as with the pre-Socratics, nor is it even a defining, as with Socrates and Plato; it is rather a demonstrating, a knowing *why*. (Cf. Zubiri: *Filosofía y metafísica*.) The principles are, at one and the same time, principles of being and of knowing; in Aristotle, as in all authentic philosophy, the theory of knowledge is essentially linked to metaphysics. The causes are the possible senses in which "why?" can be asked. In the first book of his *Metaphysics*, Aristotle reviews the doctrines of his predecessors in order to show that they contain in a stammering fashion his own theory of the causes. These causes are four in number: material cause, formal cause, efficient cause and final cause.

The material cause is matter, that *of which* something is made. The formal cause or form is what determines an entity and makes it be what it is. The efficient cause is the first principle of motion or change; it is what *makes* the thing that is caused. Lastly, the final cause is the end, the answer to the question, *for what purpose*. If we take a statue, as an example, the material cause is the bronze of which it is made; the formal cause is the model or shape; the efficient cause is the sculptor who has made it; and the final cause is the reason why it has been sculptured—for example, as an adornment or to commemorate something. The formal cause and final cause frequently coincide.*

GOD. We now command the elements necessary for understanding Aristotle's theory of God, which he expounds principally in the twelfth book of his *Metaphysics*. God is the *unmoved prime mover*. What does this mean? Every moving body requires a mover. A is moved by B; B is moved by C, and so on. How far back does this process go? It would have to go back to infinity, εἰς ἄπειρον, but this is impossible. It is

---

* On the internal difficulties of the Aristotelian theory of substance and its interpretation from the standpoint of matter and form, potentiality and actuality, see my *Biografía de la Filosofía*, App. 11 [*Obras*, II, pp. 487–494].

necessary that the series of movers end sometime, that there be a prime mover. And this mover must be unmoved, so that, in turn, another mover would not be necessary, and so forth, to infinity. This unmoved mover, like the object of love and desire, that moves without being moved, is God. The Aristotelian θεός is the end, the *télos* of all motions, and he himself does not move. Therefore, he must be pure actuality, with no mixture of the potential; God is, then, form without matter. It follows that God is the sum of reality, the Entity whose possibilities are all real: the plenary substance, the Entity as such.

The God of Aristotle is *the absolute moment of the world*. His mission is to make motion possible and, even more, to make possible the oneness of motion; it is he, then, who makes there be a *Universe*. But God is not a creator; this idea, which will mark the deep difference between Hellenic and Christian thinking, is foreign to Greek thought. The God of Aristotle exists separately and consists of pure *theoría*, in thought of thought or vision of vision, νόησις νοήσεως. Strictly speaking, contemplation as something that is possessed in a permanent way occurs only in God. The Aristotelian God is the absolutely self-sufficient Entity and, therefore, the highest Entity. All of Aristotle's philosophy culminates in this theory.

THE ENTITY AS A TRANSCENDENTAL. In order to complete this brief investigation of Aristotelian metaphysics, it remains for us to touch upon an especially important and difficult point. As we saw, Plato considered the Entity as the *highest genus*. This genus could be divided into species, which would be the different classes of entities. Aristotle categorically denies that the Entity is a genus. The reason he gives is the following: In order for it to be possible to divide a genus into species, it is necessary for a *specific difference* to be added to the genus; thus, to the genus *animal*, the difference *rational* is added in order to obtain the species *man*; but this is not possible with being, for the difference must be distinct from the genus; if the difference is distinct from being, it does not exist. Therefore, there can be no specific difference to be added to being, and therefore being is not a genus.

Aristotle's reasoning is incontestable. However, even after recognizing its indisputability, we are left with a certain uneasiness, because we see with equal clarity the possibility of dividing the Entity. One thinks of the different classes of entities that exist, and sees that division is, in fact, possible. Naturally, Aristotle would not deny this; he himself makes several divisions. Then what does all this mean? Something very simple: one must not confuse the division of genus and species with simple division. The Entity can be divided, but not in such a simple fashion. There is a much more complex ontological connection, which is precisely the *analogous nature of the Entity*. There are many modes of being, but they are not species; rather, they are, for example, categories, *inflections of the Entity*, and being is present in all these modes without intermingling with any of them. Aristotle says that the Entity is the most universal of all things, καθόλου μάλιστα πάντων, and that it envelops and permeates all things, without intermingling with any of them. Being is one of the medieval philosophers' three principal *transcendentals*: the Entity, the One and the Good. They are not things, but they permeate all things, and—Aristotle says—always occur together. An entity is one, and its being is its good in the Aristotelian sense. This is the triple unity of the ὄν, the ἕν and the ἀγαθόν.

Essence. Aristotle distinguishes between the word "substance" and "essence." Essence is expressed in Greek by a strange expression, τὸ τί ἦν εἶναι, which has been translated into Latin as: *quod quid erat esse*, literally, *what being was*. The interesting thing about this expression is that it employs the past tense. Essence is, therefore, prior to being; it is what makes it possible, what makes it be. Essence cannot be understood as a complex of especially important attributes of an entity; rather, it expresses that which makes an entity be what it is. If we say that man is a rational animal, or an animal that has *lógos*, that talks, it is not that we take two major attributes of man, his animal nature and his rationality, and unite them, but that this animal nature and rationality, *essentially* united, are what make a specific entity be a man. Therefore, when it is said that *lógos* gives the essence of a thing, it does not simply mean that *lógos* enunciates its major attributes, but that it manifests or makes patent in truth the hidden being of which the thing consists, that which makes it be. Essence always has a strict ontological significance, and it cannot be understood as a mere correlative of a definition.

5. Logic

As we have already seen, Aristotle's treatises on logic are grouped together under the general title of *Organon*, or "instrument," the title given to them by Alexander of Aphrodisias. The *Organon* is the first work in which the problems of logic are studied directly and systematically; in it logic itself is established as a discipline. Aristotle accomplished this so well that the entire corpus of his logical writings has endured almost unaltered to the present day; only at rare moments in history have new viewpoints been introduced. All subsequent studies of logic have felt the weight of this work's perfection; this has not been without its disadvantages and has perhaps hindered the development of the discipline. But it should not be forgotten that the logic traditionally used and called Aristotelian has to a great extent been further systematized and rendered trivial; the fecundity of the *Organon* in its original form has not yet been exhausted, not by far. Before all else, let us look at the significance of this discipline within the totality of Aristotle's work and the relationship in which *lógos* stands to being and truth.

"Lógos." The word *lógos* (λόγος) in Greek means "word." Its Latin translation is *verbum*, as in the opening of the Gospel of Saint John: *In principio erat Verbum* ("In the beginning was the Word"). But in Greek *lógos* also means "proportion" or "ratio" in the mathematical sense and, therefore, "meaning"; and, finally, "reason" in its fullest significance. (The English word "reason" is also derived from the Latin *ratio*, which numbered "ratio" and "reason" among its meanings.) But it should be remembered that the primary meaning of *lógos* is derived from the verb *légein*, "to join together" or "gather" and also "to say." *Lógos* is "saying," that is, a "meaningful word."

Lógos tells us what things *are*, and is closely related to being. The principles of logic—for example, the principles of identity or contradiction—are ontological principles that refer to the behavior of entities. I cannot say or think that A is and at the same time is not B, because A cannot *be and not be* B. Logic is nothing but metaphysics. Now, we have seen that being is *expressed* in many ways. What mode of being is *lógos* concerned with? Evidently, with being as seen from the viewpoint of truth or falsity.

We have observed that the notion of "true" and "false" is based on the way in which the being of things is made patent or manifest. Truth and falsity exist only within the realm of truth in the broad sense, understood as *alétheia*, as discovery, unveiling or openness. And things are especially revealed in speech, when it is said what they are, when their being is declared. Thus Aristotle says that our judgment is the natural seat of truth. When I say *A is B*, I am of necessity declaring a truth or a falsehood; this does not occur with other verbal moods, in a wish, for example ("Long live the Queen!"), or with interjections ("Ah!"). A declarative statement places things in the realm of truth. But, naturally, the possibility of doing this depends on the potentiality for truth which each thing has, on the potentiality for openness of each thing's being.

Truth shows the being of a thing, while falsity substitutes something else for it. In a true affirmative judgment, I unite those things that in truth are united; in a true negative judgment I separate those things that in truth are separated. In a false judgment I do the opposite in each case.

Man is the animal that has *lógos* and is therefore the instrument of truth. He is the entity through which the truth of things flows; he discovers the things and places them in their truth (Zubiri). Aristotle says that the human soul is thus in a certain sense all things. There is an essential relationship between being and the man who knows it and expresses it. The basis for this relationship is knowledge, *sophía*, philosophy. In philosophy being attains its veritable reality, in the light of truth.

THE CONTENT OF THE "ORGANON." The treatise on the *Categories*, with which Aristotle's work on logic opens, studies the *terms* of logic first and distinguishes the isolated use of the terms—out of combination, ἄνευ συμπλοκῆς—from the connected use—in combination, κατὰ συμπλοκήν. This leads him to the doctrine of the categories (or "predications"), which by themselves neither affirm nor negate anything and therefore are neither true nor false until they enter into a combination to form propositions or judgments.

The treatise *On Interpretation*, or *Hermeneutics* (Περὶ ἑρμηνείας), distinguishes, first of all, between two classes of words: the noun (ὄνομα) and the verb (ῥῆμα). The noun is a φωνὴ σημαντική, a word that by convention is meaningful, and makes no reference to time; none of its separate parts has a meaning of its own. The verb has, in addition to its particular meaning, a reference to time, or tense. It is the sign of something that is being said about another thing; that is, the verb operates within speech or discourse (λόγος). *Lógos* is a meaningful enunciation, the independent parts of which have meaning. But not every *lógos* is a declaration, only that *lógos* in which truth or falsity resides; that is, affirmation (κατάφασις) and negation (ἀπόφασις) are the two species into which declaration (ἀπόφανσις, or *lógos apophantikós*) is divided. With these basic assumptions, Aristotle studies the relationships among propositions.

The *Prior Analytics* contains Aristotle's theory of the syllogism, which constitutes a central chapter of logic and is elaborated in all but definitive fashion by Aristotle. The syllogism (συλλογισμός) is opposed in a certain sense to induction (ἐπαγωγή); even though induction appears at times to be a reasoning process, reducible to a syllogism (this would be complete induction), it has the character of a direct intuition which progresses from consideration of particular, concrete cases to that of principles; the things *induce* us to look for the universal principles.

The *Posterior Analytics* concentrates on the problem of true knowledge, and thus on the problem of demonstration (ἀπόδειξις). Demonstration leads to the definition, which is related to the *essence* of things. Furthermore, demonstration is based on first principles, which are per se indemonstrable and can only be apprehended directly and immediately by the *noûs*. The highest knowledge, as we have seen elsewhere, is demonstrative, but its ultimate basis is the noetic vision of the principles.

This is the culmination of Aristotelian logic. The last two treatises, the *Topics* and the *Sophistical Refutations*, are of secondary importance; they are concerned, respectively, with the commonplaces of dialectics that are used in arguing from probability, and with the analysis and refutation of Sophistic arguments.*

6. PHYSICS

PHYSICAL SCIENCE. Physics has for its object the study of moving entities. If metaphysics is "first philosophy," then physics is *second philosophy*. In theme it agrees with the content of Greek philosophical speculation of the pre-Socratic era. For this reason, Aristotle, in the first book of his *Physics*, must deal with the opinions of his predecessors, and especially the Eleatics, who deny the existence of nature and thus the very possibility of physics. For the Eleatics, motion does not exist; that is, motion *is* not, it does not have being, and consequently there can be no *science* of nature. In the face of this thesis, Aristotle must restore the reality of motion; he establishes as a principle and assumption that all, or at least some, natural entities move. This, he adds, is evident from experience or induction (*Physics*, I, 2). From this point of departure, Aristotle must arrive at the principles, causes and elements of natural phenomena. Science must begin with phenomena that are intrinsically less knowable in the final sense, but easier for us to "know" in the everyday sense and accessible to our senses—concrete, mixed things. From them science will arrive at the principles and elements, which are further removed from us, but clearer and intrinsically knowable. This is the method of that concrete form of analysis of nature which Aristotle established as his physics.

NATURE. Aristotle makes a distinction between entities which exist by nature (φύσει) and those which exist from other causes, for example artificial beings (ἀπὸ τέχνης). Among the natural entities are animals

---

* On the problem of Aristotelian logic, and its traditional interpretations, see my *Introducción a la Filosofía*, p. 61 [*Obras*, II] [Eng. trans. *Reason and Life*, pp. 268–281]. Cf. also *Ensayos de teoría* (Essays on Theory) [*Obras*, IV, pp. 414–419] and *La filosofía del Padre Gratry* (The Philosophy of Father Gratry) [*Obras*, IV, pp. 274–277 and 312–314].

and their parts, plants, and the simple bodies such as earth, fire, water, air; on the other hand, a bed or a cloak is artificial. Natural entities are those that have a nature; and by nature (φύσις) Aristotle understands the *principle of motion or rest*, which is inherent in the things themselves. In this sense, nature is substance, that which a thing can make use of for its inner transformations.

Given these assumptions, Aristotle must establish his theory of the four causes and, above all, must pose the problem of *motion*, following the thread of the doctrine of potentiality and actuality. Motion, as a *realization of the possible in so far as it is possible*, consists in a mode of being which determines the step from potential being to actual being, in virtue of Aristotle's discovery that the Entity is not univocal but analogical, and is expressed in many ways (πολλαχῶς).

Afterward, Aristotle must study the physical problems of location (τόπος), of the void (τὸ κενόν) and, above all, of time (χρόνος), which he defines as "the number of motion according to before and after." Aristotle's detailed study of the problems of motion leads him to infer the unmoved prime mover (God), which, because it is unmoved, is not a part of nature, although it is the key to nature. Thus the study of the prime mover does not come under physics (although it has its place in the problems of this discipline), but under first philosophy, or metaphysics, which, as we have seen, is the theological science.

7. The Theory of the Soul

Aristotle deals with the problem of the soul in his book entitled Περὶ ψυχῆς, usually called by its Latin name *De Anima*. First of all, one must keep in mind that *De Anima* is a book on physics, one of the treatises concerned with natural things. Aristotle made the first systematic elaboration of the problem of the *psyche*, and this falls within the sphere of biology.

THE ESSENCE OF THE SOUL. The soul (ψυχή) is the principle of life; living entities are *animate*, in contrast to inanimate entities, like stones. For Aristotle, the life of an entity consists of its nourishment, growth and self-consumption. Thus the soul is the *form* or realization of a living body. The soul "informs," or gives form to, the matter of a living thing, giving it its corporal being and making it a live body; that is, it is not a question of the soul's being superimposed on the body or added to it; rather, the body is a living body because it has a soul. According to Aristotle's definition (*De Anima*, II, 1), the soul is the realization or first entelechy of a natural organic body. If the eye were a living creature, Aristotle says, its soul would be its sight. The eye is the matter of sight, and if sight is lacking there is no eye; and just as the eye, strictly speaking, is the physical eye united with the power of sight, so the soul and the body make up the living thing.

It is "living" that defines the animate entity; but "living" is spoken of in many senses, and thus there are different classes of souls. Aristotle distinguishes three: the vegetative soul, the only type of soul possessed by plants but one also found among animals and men; the sensitive soul, which plants lack; and the rational soul, which man alone possesses. Let it be understood, however, that each living thing has only one soul; man, concretely, has a rational soul, which is the form of his body, and that soul includes the other elementary functions.

Man possesses sensory perception ($\alpha \check{\iota} \sigma \theta \eta \sigma \iota s$), which provides a direct contact with individual things, and, as we have already seen, constitutes the lowest stratum of knowledge. Man's imagination, through the agency of his memory, makes generalizations possible. The third level is the *noûs*, or intelligence, man's highest mental faculty. Aristotle rejects Plato's doctrine of innate Ideas and reminiscence, or *anámnesis*; in place of this metaphor he uses another, that of the *tabula rasa*, the wax tablet on which impressions are engraved; the *noûs* is passive. But alongside this passive intelligence Aristotle introduces the so-called *noûs poietikós*, or active intelligence, the role of which remains rather obscure; this *noûs poietikós* constituted one of the favorite themes of the medieval Scholastics in their disputes with the philosophy of Averroës. In a famous and obscure passage (*De Anima*, III, 5) Aristotle says that this *noûs* "is such that it becomes all things and is such that it makes all things, according to its habit or pattern, as light does; since in a certain sense light, too, turns potential colors into actual colors. This intelligence," he adds, "is separable, impassive and without mixture, since it is essentially an activity. . . . Only after it has been separated is it truly what it is, and only this is immortal and eternal." This is the primary reference in Aristotle to the immortality of the soul or a part of it; but the sense in which this immortality should be understood has been interpreted at length from the time of the ancient commentaries up to the modern age.

Since knowledge and sensory perception are, in a certain sense, that which is known or sensed through their agency, Aristotle can say that in a certain manner the soul is *all things*. Using a felicitous metaphor, he adds that the soul is like the hand, since like the hand it is the instrument of the instruments—that which gives the instrument, or tool, its actual being as an instrument. Intelligence is the form of the forms, and the senses are the form of the sensible things. As we have already seen, it is through being known that things acquire their true being, their openness, their ἀλήθεια; in a certain manner, they come to exist within the soul, while nevertheless remaining outside it. The stone is not in the soul, Aristotle says, but only the form of the stone.

ESTHETICS. Aristotle's esthetic teachings, which we cannot examine in detail here, are closely connected to his theory of the soul. Our principal source for these teachings is the *Poetics*, in which Aristotle studies tragedy. He makes a distinction between poetry and history, not because poetry uses verse and history uses prose—this is merely incidental—but because history recounts what has actually happened and poetry speaks of what *could* happen. Poetry, Aristotle says, is more philosophical and more important than history, because poetry speaks more of the universal, whereas history concentrates on the particular occurrence. History states that someone *really* said or did something; poetry, on the other hand, determines what a certain type of man would probably or necessarily say or do in a certain situation. Here Aristotle points to a certain *comprehension* of reality and human life which is essential to poetry if it is to have meaning.

In the masterly study that Aristotle devotes to tragedy, he considers this art form as an imitation of a serious action that arouses *fear and pity* and causes a *catharsis*, or purification, of those emotions. These are painful emotions, and yet tragedy, by its artistic nature, becomes an esthetic pleasure. The art of the tragic author frees these experiences from their disagreeable associations and occasions an emotional release, by virtue of which the soul is soothed and purified.

8. ETHICS

Aristotle's ethics is his ontology of man. We have already indicated, in speaking of possible types of lives, the most profound aspects of the problem of ethics. Here we shall merely review these ideas briefly and complete them.

THE HIGHEST GOOD. The fundamental exposition of Aristotle's ethics is found in the *Nicomachean Ethics*, probably edited by his son Nicomachus and taking its name from him. In this work Aristotle poses the question of the good (ἀγαθόν), which is the ultimate goal of things and thus of human actions. The highest good is happiness (εὐδαιμονία). But even more clearly than in Socrates, a distinction is made between *eudaimonia* and pleasure, or *hedoné*. Pleasure is simply "a supervening end," something that cannot be desired and sought directly, but is only an accompaniment to the fruition of a way of life. In his *De vita beata* (On the Happy Life), Seneca, who adopted Aristotle's ethical teachings, compared pleasure to the poppies that grow in a field of grain and embellish it, as an addition, without having been planted or sought for.

HAPPINESS. Happiness is the fruition of a man's way of life, in the truly human aspect of that way of life. The good of each thing is its own function, its way of being, which is at the same time its realization; thus, vision is the good of the eye and walking is the good of the foot. It is clear that there is an activity proper to the carpenter or the cobbler; but Aristotle asks what is the activity proper to *man* as man, without further qualifications. He examines the hypothesis that it is "living," but finds that life is common to plants and animals as well; he continues to seek that which is peculiar to man. He decides it is "a certain active life proper to rational man"; this is human happiness. This form of life is the contemplative or *theoretic* life, which, it goes without saying, is superior to the life of pleasures, but is also superior to the life governed by *poïesis*, or production, and the merely practical life—for example, the political life. But Aristotle points out that in order for this "theoretic" way of living to be happiness, it must truly occupy one's life, "because one swallow does not make a summer, nor does one day, and therefore, neither does one day or a brief time make man fortunate and happy."

THE CONTEMPLATIVE LIFE. The contemplative way of life is, in the first place, the most excellent from two points of view: because our intelligence is our most excellent faculty, and because the things known through the agency of our intelligence are the most excellent among knowable things. In the second place, the contemplative life is the most continuous way of life, since it does not cease when its goal is obtained; vision or intellection of an object persists even after the object has been seen or thought. In the third place, this type of life is accompanied by pure and stable pleasures, which are necessary to happiness, although they are not to be confused with it. In the fourth place, the contemplative life is the most self-sufficient form of life, because every man has need of things necessary for life, but the just man, or the brave man, needs other people in order to exercise his justice, or bravery, while the wise man can exercise his contemplation even in complete solitude. Finally, the contemplative life is the only way of life that is sought after and loved for its own sake, since it has no result outside of contemplation, whereas in an active life we seek something that is outside of our activity itself.

This "theoretic" form of life is, in a certain sense, higher than the human condition, and is only possible in so far as there is something *divine* in man. Even if we are men and mortal, Aristotle says, we do not necessarily have to have human and mortal feelings; it is necessary to immortalize ourselves as much as we can and live in accordance with the best that is in us, even if it is only a tiny part of our reality. The best that is in anything is what is most characteristic of it, or proper to it; and "it would be absurd," Aristotle concludes, "not to choose our own life, but someone else's" (*Nicomachean Ethics*, X, 7).

THE VIRTUES. Aristotle divides the virtues into two classes: the dianoetic, or intellectual (virtues of the *diánoia*, or of the *noûs*), and the ethical, or more strictly moral virtues. And he states that the character of virtue consists in the mean (μεσότης) between two opposed human tendencies; for example, bravery is the true mean between cowardice and rashness; generosity is the mean between avarice and profligacy, and so on. (It would take us too far afield to investigate the deeper meaning of this theory of the *mesótes*, or mean. I shall merely indicate, for purposes of orientation, that it is related to the idea of measure, *métron*, and that measure is related to the *One*, which in turn refers directly to the Entity, since the One and the Entity are mutually associated as transcendentals.)

Aside from this, the content of Aristotelian ethics is primarily a *study of character*: an exposition and evaluation of human modes of being, of the different types of souls and their virtues and vices. It is to Aristotle that we owe the subtle descriptions of the soul that have enriched the language of the Western world with such precise and expressive terms as "magnanimity," "pusillanimity," and so forth.

9. POLITICS

In the eight books of his *Politics* Aristotle was deeply concerned with the problems of society and the State. In addition, he was extraordinarily well versed on the subject of the constitutions of the Greek cities; but of the 158 studies known to have been in his school's collection, only one, the *Constitution of Athens*, has been preserved. He combined with this information a profound knowledge of economic matters.

SOCIETY. Aristotle disagrees with the Sophists and Cynics, who for various reasons interpreted the city, the *pólis*, as *nómos*, law or convention. Aristotle, differing from them, includes society within nature. His guiding idea is that social organization is a natural state and not convention; thus, society is inherent in man, not merely something statutory. In accordance with the principles of Aristotelian ethics, every activity, or *prâxis*, is carried on with some *good* in view; this good is thus the goal of the activity and gives it its meaning. It is on this assumption, and on the assumption that every community (*koinonía*) or society strives for some good, that Aristotle bases his interpretation of the being of the *pólis*.

Aristotle meditates on the origin of society. For him, the elementary, primary form of society is the household or family (οἰκία), the result of the union of man and woman for the perpetuation of the species. To this primary sexual function is added the function of command, represented by the master-slave relationship; the goal of this second relationship is the attainment of economic stability within the *oikía*. Therefore, as Hesiod says, among the poor the ox takes the place of the slave. The grouping of several families into a higher social unit produces the village, or *kóme*. The union of several villages forms the city, or *pólis*—for Aristotle the highest type of society. The unifying bond in the village is the family relationship, the community of "blood": children and children's children. The *pólis* is a "perfect community," self-sufficient and meeting all its own needs, in contrast to villages, which are not self-sufficient, but mutually dependent.

The goal of the family, or *oikía*, is merely *to live* (τὸ ζῆν); the goal of the village, or *kóme*, is more complex: *to live well*, that is, in comfort (τὸ εὖ ζῆν). Since the perfect form of each thing is its natural state, and the *pólis* is the most perfect of all communities, the *pólis*, too, is a natural state. Consequently, man is by nature a "political animal"— an animal who lives in a *pólis*—a social creature (ζῷον πολιτικόν). Whoever—by nature and not by some chance—lives without a city is either lower or higher than man; whoever cannot live in a society, or needs nothing because he is sufficient unto himself, is not a man, but a beast or a god.

LANGUAGE. The social nature of man is made manifest in his language, in his speech, or *lógos*. Animals also have a voice (φωνή), which expresses pleasure and pain; but words (λόγος) are meant to indicate the useful and the harmful, the just and the unjust. Knowledge of such things is the characteristic of man and the basis of communities. Thus, justice is essential to the city—as Plato had said; it is the order of the *pólis*. Man can function as a *thing*—as is the case with women and slaves—or as a man; he can function as a man only within the community. Man is a speaking animal (ζῷον λόγον ἔχον) and speaking is a social function; it is telling *someone* what *things are*—for example, whether they are just or unjust. Therefore, man needs a community in which to live, and his political being is based on his being articulate, his power of speech. This is precisely what is not the case with God— especially the Aristotelian god; this god can ignore the world and be merely *nóesis noéseos*, thought of thought, vision of vision. Whereas man needs some other entity on which to fix his contemplation, and a neighbor or *fellow man* to whom he can tell what he has seen, God is completely self-sufficient and contemplates himself.

SOCIETY AND THE STATE. Aristotle grants an important role to free will in social matters, and does not distinguish "natural" societies, like the family, of which one is a member involuntarily, from associations created by a voluntary act, like a club, to which one belongs or ceases to belong at will. Furthermore, he emphasizes the voluntary and sometimes even unjust character of the constitutions of various villages and cities, but says that these communities exist *by nature*: we would not say this today. Such passages show that Aristotle liked to use the concept of nature in the sense of the nature of each individual thing, rather than in the broad sense of nature in general. These two senses of the word intermingle constantly from the time of the pre-Socratics on. Therefore, since society and the culmination or perfection of society—the *pólis*—are natural, society and the State are identical: social has the same meaning as political, and the *pólis* indicates society interpreted in terms of the State.

Aristotle does not realize that society is not the same as the State, that in his day the two coincide because of historical circumstances; thus he calls the *pólis*—the city-state—the perfect society. After the creation of Alexander's empire, when the old boundaries of Hellenic life are broken, ancient man is disoriented with respect to the real limits of communities. This disorientation culminates in the cosmopolitanism of the Stoics.

THE ORGANIZATION OF THE STATE. The hierarchy of the city dwellers is in accordance with the possible types of lives. Menial labors with a purely economic aim are the responsibility of slaves, at least in part. Aristotle upheld the idea of slavery in accordance with the old Hellenic conviction that the barbarians ought to serve the Greeks. On this point Aristotle differed from the policy which Alexander followed and which led to the formation of the Hellenistic cultures.

Economics, says Aristotle, should tend toward self-sufficiency, so that the city can provide for its own needs as much as possible. Here, projected into the political community, we find once again the Greek ideal of self-sufficiency. Therefore Aristotle is more favorably inclined toward an agricultural city than toward an industrial one.

In regard to the form of the government, or constitution, Aristotle does not believe that there must of necessity be only one kind. He considers three pure forms possible, governed in accordance with the interests of the community. These three forms degenerate if the rulers begin to act for their own personal interests. The government may be a monarchy, an aristocracy or a democracy, depending on whether the sovereignty resides in a single individual, in a minority made up of the best citizens or in the community as a whole. The respective degenerate forms are tyranny, oligarchy (almost always based on plutocracy) and demagogy. Aristotle particularly dwells on the advantages offered by a "mixed government," or republic (*politeía*), a mixture or combination of the pure forms, since he considers this to afford the greatest stability and security (*aspháleia*), and security is the basic theme of his *Politics.* * We must keep in mind that Aristotle, like Plato, is thinking always of the city-state, without imagining other, broader types of political units as desirable forms. This is all the more surprising in Aristotle (although it can be understood after thorough consideration), since he was then witnessing the transformation of the Hellenic world. In his own day and by the agency of his pupil Alexander, the multitude of independent cities was being unified into a great territorial empire. This ephemeral Macedonian Empire was soon to break up into the kingdoms of the Diadochi, but the idea of a monarchy of vast extent was to linger on from that time, and there was to be no return to the fragmentation into city-states.

Aristotle's philosophy cannot be compressed into an exposition such as the present one or even a much longer one, and much less so a discussion of the fundamental problems his philosophy raises, which are, in a way, the problems philosophy has faced ever since and the ones we must solve today. His philosophy is a whole world of ideas: the most brilliant attempt in history to systematize the problems of metaphysics in their most profound strata. Therefore, more than anyone else, Aristotle determined the subsequent course of the history of philosophy, and from this point on we will find him everywhere.

It has been necessary in this discussion to omit many important and even essential matters. Faced with this necessity, I chose from the start to leave out almost all the *specific information* and scholarly details of Aristotle's teachings, and to give instead the central problems of his metaphysics, presenting them with some degree of precision and without falsification. I believe it is not so serious a thing for one to be ignorant of the greater part of what Aristotle actually said, but one must have a clear awareness of the problems that motivated him and of the brilliant originality of his solutions. In this way we see how Hellenic philosophy reaches its maturity in Aristotle's *Metaphysics* and how he marks the effective conclusion of one stage of philosophy. For long centuries philosophy will of necessity run in the channels which Aristotle's thinking marked out for it. †

* Cf. my Introduction to the *Politics* of Aristotle (Madrid, 1950).
† See my Introduction to the *Nicomachean Ethics* (Madrid, 1960).

The Ideal of the Wise Man

After Aristotle, Greek philosophy loses the character with which he and Plato had endowed it. It ceases to be *explicitly* metaphysics and becomes mere ethical speculation. It does not really cease to be ontology, but it is no longer concerned formally and thematically with the major problems of metaphysics. After an era of extraordinary activity in this realm, there comes a long hiatus in philosophy, one of those that appear repeatedly in the history of human thought. In a sense, the history of philosophy is essentially discontinuous. This does not mean that philosophy is absent during this long period, but that it ceases to be authentically original and creative philosophy and becomes in large part a labor of exegesis, or commentary. At the same time, as always in such periods, man appears as almost the exclusive theme of philosophy. Philosophy then becomes principally ethics. Moral questions are paramount, and especially what has been called the ideal of the wise man, or *sophós*.

If we disregard the obvious differences, we could say that something similar occurred in the Renaissance, in the age of the Enlightenment and in the nineteenth century. The study of man, in different forms ranging from humanism to "Kultur," made its appearance at those times when metaphysical tension had given way. It would seem that mankind cannot sustain metaphysical thought for any long time. Historically, philosophy appears concentrated at certain periods of time, after which it seems to slacken and lose its vitality and precision for long years. This discontinuous structure of philosophy will become more and more evident in the course of this book.

The stage of Greek philosophy we now come to is usually designated as post-Aristotelian philosophy. I have rejected this name for two reasons: first, because a prior philosophic current, originating in Socrates, is closely related to the philosophic movements of this period —the earlier current including the Cynics and Cyrenaics; and secondly, because Neoplatonism is also later than Aristotle, but Neoplatonism returns to metaphysics and differs profoundly from the ethical philosophy we are discussing. And there is also a third reason, perhaps the most serious: even though the name "post-Aristotelian" is in itself purely chronological, it nevertheless seems to imply an affiliation; whereas the philosophy of the period under consideration derives only in very small measure from Aristotle, or at least from his truly living and efficacious thought. Doubtless, this new philosophy is closely related to the schools founded by Plato and Aristotle; but it is clear that after the death of these two great figures both the Academy and the Lyceum have rather little to do with the real philosophical significance of their founders.

We shall, then, consider here a philosophic current lasting several centuries, from Socrates in the fourth century B.C. to the apogee of the Roman Empire, that is, at least up to the end of the second century A.D. and perhaps even later. This movement, initiating in the Socratic tradition, proliferates enormously in the Hellenistic age, and even more in the Roman period.

Its general character is as we have already noted: lack of concern with metaphysics as such; an attention directed primarily to questions of ethics; a conception of philosophy as a way of life, together with a neglect of its theoretic value; in short, a new loss of the meaning of truth, although this deviation from truth is of a quite different aspect from that of the Sophists. All this is summed up in the problem of the wise man, in the discovery of those traits that define the independent, self-sufficient man, the man who lives as is needful, in complete serenity and balance, the man who embodies the philosopher's way of life—which now is not precisely Aristotle's *theoretic life*.

But the most serious problem raised by these Hellenistic philosophies is this: from the point of view of *knowledge*, all of them—even the worthiest, Stoicism—are clumsy, almost completely lacking in intellectual precision and extremely limited in their flights of imagination. There is no comparison possible between these schools and the marvelous speculation of Plato and Aristotle with its miraculous acumen and metaphysical profundity. Nevertheless, it is an overwhelmingly evident historical fact that immediately after the death of Aristotle these schools displace his philosophy and flourish uninterruptedly for five centuries. How is this possible?*

During these centuries there is a substantial change in the meaning the Greeks attach to the word *philosophy*. In Plato and Aristotle it is a "*science*," a *knowledge* of what things *are*; the character of this knowledge is determined by the necessity of living in the realm of *truth*, and the origin of this knowledge is *awe*. But in the later schools philosophy comes to connote something very different. For Epicurus, "philosophy is an activity that attains the happy life by means of discourse and reasoning." According to the Stoics, philosophy is the *practice* of an *art*, the aim of which is the proper governing of one's life. Thus, the meaning of philosophy changes. It is not that the teachings of the Stoa or of Epicurus replace the teachings of Aristotle. Rather, the man of the late fourth and early third centuries B.C. abandons philosophy-as-knowledge and seeks a basis for his life in another activity. This new activity is given the name of philosophy—not without a certain ambiguity—and has in common with philosophy a number of ideas and problems.

The deepest reason for this change is the historical *crisis* of the ancient world. At the moment when his situation becomes critical, the Hellene returns to philosophy, the highest creation of his culture; but he no longer makes the same requests of it. Instead, he wants it to be a substitute for the religious, political and social convictions—in short, the *moral* convictions—which have by now become dubious. Philosophy, once more diverted from the *way of truth*, becomes a sort of "occasional" religiosity, suitable for the masses. Therefore, the intellectual inferiority of the philosophies of this period is precisely one of the conditions for their enormous success. Using them, ancient man in his critical hour acquires a minimal morality for hard times, a morality of resistance, until the crisis is overcome in radical fashion by Christianity, which signifies the advent of the *new man*.

We shall now attempt to sketch briefly the traits of the various schools in this group.

1. ETHICAL PHILOSOPHIES IN THE SOCRATIC TRADITION

We have already seen the most fruitful and brilliant moments of the Socratic tradition: Plato and, through him, Aristotle. Nevertheless, it will be remembered that what Platonism adopted from Socrates was principally the necessity of knowledge as a definition of the universal;

---

* For a more detailed analysis of this problem see my study "La filosofía estoica" (Stoic Philosophy) in *Biografía de la Filosofía* (Biography of Philosophy).

this led Plato to his theory of the Ideas. Yet Socrates' own concern was largely ethical. This other direction of his thought is the one that is continued in two branches of Hellenic philosophy of purely secondary importance: the Cynics and the Cyrenaics.

The Cynics

The founder of the Cynic school was Antisthenes, a pupil of Socrates, who founded a gymnasium in the square of Cynosarges ("Nimble Dog"); hence the name Cynics (dogs or, rather, doglike) that was given to the followers of this sect, and which they accepted with a certain pride. The best known among the Cynics is Antisthenes' successor, Diogenes of Sinope, who lived in the fourth century B.C. Diogenes is famous for his eccentric life and certain displays of wit.

The Cynics exaggerate and push to extremes Socrates' doctrine of *eudaimonia*, or happiness, and give it, in addition, a negative sense. In the first place, they identify happiness with *autarchia*, or self-sufficiency; in the second place, they find that the way to attain happiness is to suppress all necessities. This entails a negative attitude toward life as a whole, from material pleasures up to the life of the State. The only desirable value that remains is independence, the absence of necessities, tranquillity. Naturally, the result of this is a beggar's existence. The standard of living is lowered, all refinements are lost, as are all bonds with the city and civilization. Indeed, Greece became full of these beggars with more or less philosophical pretensions who traversed the land as vagabonds, sober and disheveled, pronouncing moral discourses and frequently resorting to charlatanism.

Cynic doctrine, if it exists, is quite scanty: it is rather the renunciation of all theorizing, a disdain for truth. All that matters is the necessities of life—life, naturally, in the Cynic manner. The good of man consists merely in *living in society with oneself*. Everything else— comfort, riches, honors and their opposites—does not count. The pleasures of the senses and love are the worst things of all and are most to be shunned. Work, exercise, ascetic practices: these are the only things desirable. Since the Cynic despises all that is *convention* and not *nature*, he is unconcerned with family and country, and feels himself to be a *kosmopolites*, a citizen of the world. This is the first important appearance of that cosmopolitanism which was to have such weighty consequences in the Hellenistic and Roman world.

The Cyrenaics

The Cyrenaic school, founded by Aristippus of Cyrene, a Sophist who later joined the Socratic circle, is extremely similar to the Cynic school, despite the great differences and even apparent contradictions between them. For Aristippus, the highest good is pleasure. Subjective impressions are our value criteria, and pleasure is whatever impression is agreeable. The problem in this conception is that pleasure must not dominate us; rather, we must dominate our pleasure. This is important. The wise man must be master of himself; therefore he must not give vent to his passions. Moreover, pleasure easily becomes disgust when it dominates us and upsets us. The wise man must be master of all circumstances, must always rise above them, must adapt himself to all situations, to wealth and to poverty, to prosperity and to ill fortune. At the same time, the Cyrenaic must select his pleasures in such a way that they are moderate, lasting and not likely to get the better of him. In short, the supposed hedonism of the Cyrenaics is extraordinarily similar to the asceticism of the Cynics, although the point of departure is very different. It should not be forgotten that what is important for the ethical philosophers in the Socratic tradition, as for the Stoics and Epicureans later on, is the independence and imperturbability of the wise man; the manner in which these desirable qualities are attained is secondary. It may be through asceticism and virtue or through the moderate, peaceful pleasures of day-to-day life.

Cosmopolitanism is a trait of the Cyrenaics, too. In addition, this school presents marked Hellenistic features; it merely emphasizes and exaggerates another aspect of Socrates' thought—that crossroads from which the various directions of the Greek mentality take their departure.

2. Stoicism

The philosophers of the Stoic school are intrinsically related to the earlier ethical philosophers in the Socratic tradition, especially to the Cynics. In the final analysis, Stoicism revives the attitude of these earlier schools toward life and philosophy, although Stoicism produced men of superior intellectual attainments and presented a more fully worked out theoretic system.

THE STAGES OF STOICISM. Within the history of Stoicism, three periods are distinguished: the Early Stoa, the Middle Stoa and the Late Stoa. The school's entire history extends from about 300 B.C. to the second century A.D., that is, half a millennium. Zeno of Citium founded the Stoic school in Athens, in the so-called Painted Portico (*Stoà poikíle*), a public hall decorated with paintings by Polygnotus. The group took its name from this meeting site. The principal figures of the Early Stoa, apart from Zeno, were Cleanthes of Assos, a former boxer whose mind was dull and anything but theoretic, and, above all, the third leader of the school, Chrysippus, the true founder of Stoicism as a doctrine. Only titles and fragments of his numerous writings have come down to us. The leaders of the so-called Middle Stoa were Panaetius of Rhodes (180–110) and the Syrian Posidonius (175–90). Panaetius was influenced by the teachings of the Academy; it was he, the friend of Scipio and Laelius, who introduced Stoicism to Rome. Posidonius, Cicero's teacher in Rhodes, was one of the finest thinkers of the ancient world. In the late period, which was almost exclusively Roman, the outstanding and most influential Stoic was Seneca (4 B.C.–65 A.D.), who was born in Cordova. Seneca was the tutor of Nero, and it was by Nero's order that he finally opened his veins in his bath. Aside from his tragedies, Seneca wrote philosophical works which included *De ira* (On Anger), *De providentia* (On Providence), *De beneficiis* (On Benefits), *De constantia sapientis* (On the Constancy of the Wise Man), *De brevitate vitae* (On the Brevity of Life), *De tranquillitate animi* (On Serenity of Mind), *De clementia* (On Clemency), *De vita beata* (On the Happy Life), *Naturales quaestiones* (Investigations of Nature) and the *Epistulae ad Lucilium* (Epistles to Lucilius). After Seneca come two other important Stoic thinkers: Epictetus (50–120 A.D.), a Phrygian slave, later a freedman, author of the *Diatribes*, or *Dissertations*, and of a brief *Enchiridion*, or *Manual*, written in Greek; and the emperor Marcus Aurelius (121–180 A.D.), of the Antonine succession, who wrote, also in Greek, the famous *Meditations*, the title of which is literally *To Himself* (Εἰς ἑαυτόν).

STOIC DOCTRINE. The center of Stoic concern is once again man, the wise man. Stoic philosophy is divided into three parts—logic, physics and ethics—but the true interest of Stoicism is only in questions of morality. In epistemology, the Stoics are sensationalists. For them, it is sensory perceptions that leave their trace in the human soul and form its ideas. The Stoics' principal concept is the φαντασία καταληπτική ("the imagination that conveys direct apprehension")—a highly difficult concept to grasp. The mind makes use of association and comparison in order to arrive at this "imagination." The Stoics spoke of certain κοιναὶ ἔννοιαι, *notiones communes* (common ideas), that are present in everyone and determine a universal consensus. Later on, Stoic opinion as to the origin of these common ideas changed, and they were thought to be innate. Absolute certainty was derivable from these ideas. This theory has influenced very profoundly all the modern theories which claim that ideas are innate. The repercussions of Stoicism in logic as well as in ethics have been much more extensive and persistent than is generally thought; in the Renaissance especially,

Stoic philosophy was perhaps the most influential of all the ancient
systems that were rediscovered.

Stoic physics is based on materialism or, more precisely, on the concept of corporeality. This physics establishes two principles, an active
and a passive; that is, *matter*, and *reason* residing in matter. This reason
is called *God*. This is a corporeal principle, which mingles with matter
in the form of a generative fluid, or *seminal reason* (λόγος σπερματικός).
Aside from the two *principles*, the Stoics distinguish the four *elements*:
fire, water, air, earth. But the active principle is identified with fire,
following the inspiration of Heraclitus. Nature is conceived of as if it
were a craft (τέχνη), and fire is thus called the craftsman or *artificer*
(πῦρ τεχνικόν). History repeats itself in cycles; when the stars regain
their original positions, a *great year* has ended and the world is destroyed in a conflagration. After the world has thus returned to the
primordial fire, the cycle is repeated. This doctrine is clearly a forerunner of Nietzsche's concept of the *eternal return*.

Stoicism identifies God with the world; God is the ruler of the world,
but he is in turn substance, and the whole world is the substance of
God. Nature, which is governed by the principle of reason, is identified
with the Deity. The divine principle binds all things together by
means of a *law*, which is identified with universal reason; this
inexorable enchainment is destiny, or fate (εἱμαρμένη). This doctrine
makes divination possible and leads to a *determinism*. But, on the other
hand, the Stoics believe that a certain element of chance and of human
freedom are included in the general plan of destiny, which appears at
the same time to be *providence*. All things serve the perfection of the
whole; the only criterion for valuation is the universal divine law
which holds everything in its bonds, and which we call *Nature*. Nature
is the culmination of Stoic physics and the foundation of the school's
ethical teachings.

Stoic ethics is also based on the idea of *autarchia*, or self-sufficiency.
Man, especially the wise man, must be self-sufficient. The connections
of Stoic ethics with the ethics of the Cynics are very profound and
complete. The highest good is *happiness*—which has nothing to do with
pleasure; happiness consists of virtue. Virtue, in turn, consists in
living in accordance with one's true nature: *vivere secundum naturam*,
κατὰ φύσιν ζῆν. Man's nature is *rational*, and the life demanded by Stoic
ethics is the rational life. Human reason is a portion of universal
reason, and thus our nature puts us in accord with the entire universe,
that is, with *Nature*. The wise man accepts Nature just as it is, and
molds himself completely to the will of destiny: *parere Deo libertas est*,
obedience to God is freedom. This acceptance of destiny is charac-

teristic of Stoic ethics. The Fates, said the Stoics, guide the man who wishes to be guided; the man who does not wish to be guided they drag along with them. Thus, resistance is useless. The wise man achieves independence and bears up under all events, like a rock that defies all the assaults of the waves. At the same time, the wise man attains self-sufficiency by reducing his needs: *sustine et abstine*, bear up and do without. The wise man must shed all his passions in order to acquire imperturbability, *apathía, ataraxía*. The wise man is master of himself, he lets nothing overwhelm him, he is not at the mercy of external events; he can be happy in the midst of the severest pains and ills. The good things of life may be, at the most, desirable and worthy to be sought after, but they do not have true value and importance—only virtue has these qualities. Virtue consists in rational conformity with the order of things, in *right reason*. Strictly speaking, the concept of duty, of what one "ought" to do, does not exist in ancient ethics. The ancient words for that which "ought" to be done—καθῆκον in Greek and *officium* in Latin—connote, rather, what is "fitting," or "decent" (that is, what is suitable, *id quod decet*), what is "right" almost in an esthetic sense. That which is "right" (Latin *rectum*) is primarily that which is "correct" (κατόρθωμα), that which is in accord with reason.

ANCIENT COSMOPOLITANISM. The Stoics do not feel as isolated from society as the Cynics; they are much more interested in the community. Marcus Aurelius describes his own nature as rational and social, λογική καὶ πολιτική. But the city is also a convention, *nómos*, and not a natural state. Man is not a citizen of this or that country but of the world: a cosmopolite. The role that cosmopolitanism plays in the ancient world is of the highest importance. It is apparently similar to the unity of mankind proclaimed by Christianity, but they are two totally different things. Christianity proclaims that men are brothers and makes no distinction between Greek and Roman, Jew and Scythian, slave and free man. But this brotherhood has a basis, a principle; it is based on the belief that all men have a common Father. In Christianity men are brothers because they are—all of them—sons of God, and for no other reason. Thus it is seen that what is involved is not a historical fact, but the supernatural truth of man. Men are brothers because God is their common Father; they are fellow men, that is, neighbors, even though they are in separate places within the world, because they are united by being sons of the divine Father. We are all one in God. Therefore the Christian bond between men is not a bond of country, race or society, but *charity*, the love of God, and therefore the love for men *in God*, that is, as our "fellow men," our neighbors. Thus, there is no question of anything historical, of the social

coexistence of men in cities, nations or any other form of community:
"*My kingdom is not of this world.*"

This unifying principle is fundamentally missing in Stoicism. It
makes its appeal only to the nature of man, but this is not a sufficient
basis for a society. Mere similarity of nature does not presuppose a
common concern that can group all men together in one community.
If cosmopolitanism is based only on this, it is false. But there is another
set of reasons—historical reasons—that lead the Stoics to this idea:
the replacement of the city as a political unit. Over a long period,
starting with Alexander the Great and culminating in the Roman
Empire, the *pólis* loses its vitality. Ancient man feels that the city is *no
longer* the limit of society; his problem is in seeing what the new limit is.
But this is difficult to see; what is obvious is the insufficiency of the old
idea. Therefore, ancient man tends to exaggerate the situation,
believing that the limit can only be reached by including the whole
world—whereas the truth is that the political unit of the age is only the
Empire. This lack of historical awareness, the brusque jump from the
city to the world, which kept ancient man from a sufficiently precise
and profound study of the character and needs of the Empire, was one
of the principal causes of the decline of the Roman Empire, which
never attained its full and perfect form. The Stoics, and especially the
Emperor Marcus Aurelius, felt that they were citizens of Rome or of
the world; they did not know enough to be what it was then necessary
for them to be: citizens of the Empire. Thus the Empire fell.

3. EPICUREANISM

Just as the Stoics correspond to the Cynics within the framework of
post-Aristotelian philosophy, so the Epicureans display a marked
parallelism with the Cyrenaics; and just as there was a fundamental
identity between the two earlier schools in the Socratic tradition, so is
there a kinship between Stoicism and Epicureanism. Epicurus was an
Athenian citizen but was born in Samos, to which his father had
emigrated. He came to Athens at the end of the fourth century, and in
306 B.C. he founded his school, or community, in a garden there. He
seems to have been a remarkable figure, with extraordinary influence
upon his followers. In Epicureanism it is clear that the Greeks no
longer understand philosophy as knowledge, but as a special way of
life. A few women also belonged to Epicurus' garden. The school
acquired—especially after the founder's death—an almost religious
character, and was extremely influential in Greece and the Roman
world. Epicureanism maintained its activity and influence until the

fourth century A.D. The most important exposition of the teachings of Epicurus is to be found in the poem by Titus Lucretius Carus (97–55 B.C.) entitled *De rerum natura* (On the Nature of Things).

Epicurean philosophy is based on a materialistic physics; essentially, it revives Democritus' philosophy, with its theory of the atoms. Everything is corporeal and formed by the aggregation of various atoms. The universe is purely mechanical: it has no teleological end, and the gods take no part in its operation. The gods, like men, are material, but they are made of finer, shining atoms and, in addition, are immortal. Sensory perception is also explained by the atomistic theory of the *eídola*, or images, of the things, which penetrate the sensory organs.

But the Epicureans, too, are lacking in the feeling for philosophical speculation. When they discuss physics, they are not interested in discovering the truth concerning nature, but merely in calming themselves. For example, they give not one, but several different physical explanations for thunder and lightning; they are not really concerned about the true explanation, but only about knowing that explanations are possible. They want to show that lightning is a natural phenomenon and not a display of divine wrath; they wish to make it possible for man to live in serenity without fear of the gods. All the teachings of the Epicureans are directed toward ethics, the type of life that the wise man should live.

Epicurus considers pleasure to be the true good; in addition, he says it is pleasure that shows us what suits our nature and what is repugnant to it. He thus corrects the notions of unnatural hostility toward pleasure that were invading large areas of Greek philosophy.

At first sight, Epicureanism and Stoicism appear to be at opposite poles; but the similarities between them go deeper than the differences. In the first place, Epicurus makes very definite demands of pleasure: pleasure must be pure, unmixed with pain or discontent; it must be lasting and stable; finally, it must leave man master of himself, free, imperturbable. This eliminates sensual pleasures almost completely, and opens the way for other, more subtle and spiritual pleasures—above all, for friendship and the joys of human companionship. Violent passions are excluded from Epicurean ethics because they overcome man. The ideal of the wise man is thus that of the serene man, moderate in everything, governed by temperance, free from worries, maintaining a perfect balance in all circumstances. Neither adversity nor physical pain nor death disturbs the Epicurean. It is well known with what kind and cheerful resignation Epicurus bore up under his extremely painful illness and his death. Thus, this is an ideal of great asceticism which, in its deepest roots, coincides with the Stoic ideal. The withdrawal from public office, the isolation from the community, is even stronger in Epicureanism than in Stoic circles. The two schools have a different point of departure: in one case, virtue is to be attained; in the other case, pleasure is sought. But in this twilight period of the ancient world the type of life that results in the two schools is the same, and is defined by two traits indicative of human weariness: self-sufficiency and imperturbability, being sufficient unto oneself and being disturbed by nothing.

4. Skepticism and Eclecticism

The lack of interest in truth which dominates the eras in which theoretic tension is absent, is normally associated in such eras with the lack of confidence in truth, or *skepticism*. Man has no trust; there arise suspicious and distrustful generations, which doubt that man can attain truth. This is what occurs in the ancient world, and the process of the decline of theoretic speculation, which begins with the death of Aristotle, is contemporaneous with the formation of the Skeptic schools. One of the roots of such skepticism is generally to be found in a multiplicity of opinions: upon becoming aware that there have been many different beliefs about each issue, the Skeptic loses all confidence that any of the answers may be true or that some new answer may be true. This is the famous argument of the διαφωνία τῶν δοξῶν (discrepancy among opinions). Nevertheless, a distinction must be made between skepticism as a philosophical thesis and skepticism as an attitude in life. As a philosophical thesis, it is a contradictory one, since it affirms the impossibility of knowing truth, although this affirmation itself claims to be true. Thus, skepticism as a thesis refutes itself in the very act of being formulated. The other aspect is different: this is the abstention from all judgments (ἐποχή), skepticism in life, which neither affirms nor denies. This skepticism appears in history time and again, although here, too, it is doubtful whether human life can remain floating in this abstention without taking root in convictions.

The first and most famous of the Greek Skeptics, if we disregard his forerunners among the Sophists, is Pyrrho, at the beginning of the third century B.C. Other Skeptics are Timon, Arcesilaus and Carneades, who lived in the third and second centuries B.C. Later, beginning with the first century A.D., a new Skeptic current appears with Aenesidemus and the famous Sextus Empiricus, who lived in the second century and wrote the *Outlines of Pyrrhonism* (Πυρρώνειοι ὑποτυπώσεις). Skepticism completely invaded the Academy, which since the death of Plato had moved further and further away from the metaphysical stamp given it by its founder. The Academy was the home of Skepticism until its closing in 529 A.D. by order of Justinian. The Skeptics we have named belonged to the Middle Academy and New Academy, so called to distinguish them from the Old, or original, Academy. For centuries the term "Academic" meant skeptic.

Eclecticism is another phenomenon of eras of philosophic decline. At such times the spirit of compromise and conciliation appears, borrowing ideas from various sources and building systems that will bridge the deepest discrepancies. In general, this procedure tends to make philosophy trivial; this was especially true of Roman culture, which used the results of philosophical thought only as material for erudition and moralizing, keeping always at a distance from true philosophic problems.

The most important of the Roman eclectics is Cicero (106–43 B.C.). The life of this major figure is very well known. His philosophical writings are not original, but are valuable as a copious repository of references to Greek philosophy. At the same time, Cicero was extraordinarily gifted in philology, and the terminology he coined to translate the expressions of Greek philosophy has had a great influence on modern languages and on all European philosophy, even though his translations were not always perfect. Other interesting figures are Plutarch, who lived in the first and second centuries A.D. and wrote, in addition to his famous *Lives*, a *Moralia* with an ethical content; and Philo of Alexandria, a Hellenized Jew who lived in the first century A.D. Philo tried to find Biblical correspondences in Hellenic philosophy, above all for the philosophy of Plato. The Jewish character of his doctrine is revealed especially in the important role played in it by God, and in Philo's effort to reconcile Greek ideas with the Old Testament. Included among his works are a study on the Creation (known by the Latin title *De opificio mundi*) and others on the immutability of God and on the contemplative life.

Neoplatonism

Metaphysics, which, strictly speaking, had been absent from Greek philosophy since Aristotle, reappears once again in the last great system of the Hellenic world—*Neoplatonism*. For the last time the great metaphysical problem is stated in Greek terms; the frame of reference is still Greek, even though it shows definite Christian influences as well as the influences of the whole group of Oriental religions which enter the Greco-Roman world in the first centuries of the Christian era. This is a crucial moment, in which philosophy is split into the only two truly discontinuous phases in its history; there is, on the one hand, ancient philosophy, and, on the other, modern philosophy, or, what is the same thing, Greek and Christian philosophy: the two basic types of authentically philosophic thought that have appeared in the world to date.

PLOTINUS. Neoplatonism was founded in the third century A.D. by Plotinus (204–270). Born in Egypt, he started for the Orient, going to Persia and India with the Emperor Gordian III; later he settled principally in Rome. He was a very important person in his day and attracted the devoted and fervent attention of many pupils. Plotinus led a life of strange asceticism and mystery, and he claimed to have had several mystical experiences. His writings were collected by his pupil, Porphyry, in six groups of nine books each, which were consequently called the *Enneads*. This work is of profound interest and contains an original philosophy which was enormously influential on later Christian thought. Its influence was felt throughout the Middle Ages but particularly during the first centuries of that epoch; in the thir-
98

teenth century it was superseded by the writings of Aristotle, which had just become known in the West.

Plotinus' system is governed by two principal features: its pantheism and its opposition to materialism. The principle of its ontological hierarchy is the One, which is at the same time being, the Good and the Deity. All things *emanate* from the One: first, *noûs*, the world of the spirit, of the Ideas. *Noûs* presupposes a recollection of itself, a reflection, and, therefore, a dualism. Secondly, the soul, the reflection of *noûs*; Plotinus speaks of a "world soul," the vivifier and animator of the entire world and of the individual souls, which retain a trace of the oneness of the world soul, which is, as it were, their source. These souls occupy an intermediate position in the world, a position halfway between *noûs* and the bodies they inform. The lowest level of being is matter, which is almost non-being: that which is multiple, which barely exists or exists only in the furthest reaches of the emanation. The soul must liberate itself from matter, into which it periodically relapses through the reincarnations which are a part of the theory of transmigration. There is the possibility of frequent *ecstasies*; that is, states of *being outside* (or *beside*) *oneself*. In such a state the soul frees itself from matter entirely and unites with the Deity, the One, to become the One itself. Making use of one of Plato's concepts, Plotinus assigns great importance to beauty: beautiful things are the most accurate visual representations of the Ideas, and by means of them the suprasensible world is manifested in sensible form.

Neoplatonism is pantheistic. It does not distinguish between God and the world; the world proceeds from the One, not by the process of creation (an idea foreign to Greek thought), but by that of emanation. The One's *very being* diffuses and manifests itself, makes itself explicit in the entire world, from *noûs* down to matter. Plotinus employs strikingly beautiful and significant metaphors to explain this emanation. For example, he compares the Universe to a tree with a single root, from which the trunk, the branches and even the leaves spring. In a yet more acute and profound metaphor he compares it to a light, a powerful beam which spreads and diffuses through space; during the fight against darkness it grows progressively dimmer and is gradually extinguished. The last glow, just before the light is extinguished and darkness reigns, is matter. The light is always the same in that it comes from the same powerful source, but it passes through a series of degrees of strength ranging from plenary being down to nothingness, to become ever weaker and more diminished. One sees similarities between Neoplatonic doctrine and several Christian themes (perhaps due to the influence of Plotinus' teacher, Ammonius Saccas) and this

explains Neoplatonism's great influence on the Fathers of the Church
and on medieval thinkers, particularly the mystics. Many of the
writings of the mystics are of Neoplatonic inspiration, and pantheism
has been a great danger which Christian mysticism has constantly had
to skirt.

Strictly speaking, Plotinus represents the first Greek who—doubtless influenced by Christian doctrines—dares to conceive of the world
as something that is actually *produced*, instead of as something that is
merely "manufactured" or "ordered." The world's being is received;
it is a product of the Deity, the One. However, Hellenic thought is not
capable of coming to grips with the problem of *the void*, and so the
world is seen to have been produced by the One, not *from nothingness*,
but *from itself*. In the final analysis, divine being and that of the world
are identical. This theory gives rise to the concept of *emanation*, the
concrete form of Neoplatonic pantheism, which actually amounts to
an attempt to conceive of the creation without acknowledging the
void. This is the characteristic reaction of the Greek mind when confronted with the idea of creation, which was introduced by Judaeo-
Christian thought.

Man occupies an intermediate position in Plotinus' system. His
place is between that of the gods and that of the animals, and according
to Plotinus man can incline toward the one or the other. There is a link
between man and what is superior to him, and he can raise himself up
to the highest level. Plotinus adds, "Man is a beautiful creature, the
most beautiful creature possible, and his fate in the plot of the universe
is superior to that of any other animal on earth."

NEOPLATONIC PHILOSOPHERS. Neoplatonism flourished without
interruption until the sixth century—that is, until the end of the
ancient world. Its influence permeated the thought of the Fathers of
the Church and later that of the medieval Scholastics. One sees
references to the Platonic sources of the first centuries of Scholasticism,
but one must realize that these are largely Neoplatonic influences,
which have constituted an exceptionally active element in all later
philosophy.

Porphyry (232–304 A.D.), Plotinus' closest pupil, wrote the school's
most influential books; he condensed his master's doctrines into a brief
treatise entitled 'Αφορμαὶ πρὸς τὰ νοητά (Aids to the Study of the
Intelligibles). He also wrote an *Eisagogé*, or Introduction to the Categories of Aristotle, which is also called *On the Five Terms* (genus and
species, difference, property and accident), a work of great renown
in the Middle Ages. Iamblichus, a Syrian who died around the year
330, was a pupil of Porphyry; he was primarily concerned with the

religious aspect of Neoplatonism, and became very famous. The emperor Julian the Apostate was also a Neoplatonist. The last important philosopher of the school was Proclus (420–485), from Constantinople. Proclus was an active writer and teacher, and dealt with all the philosophical themes of the epoch. He wrote a rather unoriginal general study, a systematization of Neoplatonic thinking entitled the Στοιχείωσις θεολογική (*Elementatio theologica*, as it was called in Latin). He also wrote lengthy commentaries on Plato and on the first book of Euclid's *Elements*; the latter commentaries are of great interest in the history of Hellenic mathematics, and the prologue which accompanies them is considered a major text for this history. We must also include among the Neoplatonic thinkers the anonymous fifth-century author who until the fifteenth century was thought to be Dionysius the Areopagite, the first bishop of Athens; he is now generally referred to as Pseudo-Dionysius. His works—*The Celestial Hierarchy, The Ecclesiastical Hierarchy, The Divine Names* and *Mystical Theology*—were translated into Latin several times, and wielded immense authority and influence during the Middle Ages.

Greek philosophy ends with Neoplatonism. Afterward there comes a new philosophic stage, in which the Christian mind ponders the metaphysical problem. Greek philosophy was the earliest philosophy; this fact is essential, since philosophy received its fundamental character and methods at the hands of the Greeks. All later philosophy passes through the channels which the Greek mind opened. The imprint of Hellenic philsophy is therefore—as the Greeks wished it to be—*for always, ἐς ἀεί.* Western man's very modes of thought are in essence derived from the Greeks. This is true to such a degree that philosophers who have had to conceive of kinds of objects or even realities other than those that were discussed in Greece have had to struggle with the problem of freeing themselves from the Hellenic molds of Western mentality.

Thus, Greek philosophy enjoys an active existence as an integral part of present-day philosophy.

CHRISTIANITY

Christianity and Philosophy

Christianity marks the most profound division in the history of philosophy; it separates the two great phases of Western thought. However, it would be wrong to think of Christianity as a philosophy; it is something quite different—a religion. Nor can one speak precisely of "Christian philosophy," if the adjective "Christian" is meant to define the character of the philosophy. The only philosophy that we can call Christian philosophy is the *philosophy of Christians as Christians*; that is, that philosophy which is shaped by the Christian situation from which a particular philosopher begins to philosophize. In this sense Christianity has played a decisive role in the history of metaphysics, because it has essentially altered the presuppositions upon which man bases his thought and actions and, therefore, the situation from which he must philosophize. The Christian is *different* and therefore his philosophy is also different; for example, different from Greek philosophy.*

Christianity introduces an entirely new idea to interpret the existence of the world and man: the idea of the Creation. *In principio creavit Deus caelum et terram*: modern philosophy derives from this first sentence of Genesis. We saw that the Greek's problem concerned motion: things are problematic because they move, because they change, because they come to be and cease to be what they are. Being is opposed by *non-being*, by something's not being what it is. Beginning with the Christian era it is *nothingness*, the void, that menaces being.

* See my study "La escolástica en su mundo y en el nuestro" in *Biografía de la Filosofía*.

The Greek did not question the existence of all things, whereas this is exactly what the Christian finds strange and in need of explanation. It is possible that things might not have existed; and so their very existence—and not what they are—requires justification. "The Greek is alienated by the world because of its *changeability*. The European of the Christian era is alienated by its nullity or, better yet, its *nihility*. . . . For the Greek, the world is *something* that changes; for the man of the Christian era it is a *nothingness* that seems to be or exist. . . . With this change of perspective *being* comes to mean something *toto caelo* different from what it meant in Greece: for a Greek, being means to be there, at hand; for the Western European, being means, first of all, *not being nothingness*. . . . In a certain sense, then, the Greek still philosophizes *from the point of reference of being*, and the Western European philosophizes *from the point of reference of nothingness*." (Zubiri: *Sobre el problema de la filosofía*.)

This basic difference separates the two great phases of philosophy. The problem is stated in two essentially different ways: it becomes a *new* problem. And, just as in the life of the Christian there are two worlds—this world and the other—there must be two different meanings for the word "being" if it is to apply in both instances; that is, to God's being and to the world's being. The concept of the *Creation* allows the being of the world to be interpreted *through the being of God*. On one hand we have God, the true being, the Creator; on the other hand we have the created being, God's creature, whose being is received. The *religious* truth of the Creation requires the interpretation of this being, and poses the *philosophic* problem of the creative and created being; that is, God's being and that of His creature. Thus Christianity, which is not philosophy, affects philosophy in a decisive way; and the philosophy that arises from the basic situation of the Christian is what may with precision be called *Christian philosophy*. This term involves neither Christianity's consecrating a philosophy nor the necessity of making an untenable attribution of the Christian religion to some philosophy; rather, it describes the philosophy which emerges out of the major problem confronting Christianity—that of its own reality before God. In a broad sense, this takes place in all European philosophy after the Greek era, and particularly in the first centuries of the Christian era and in medieval philosophy.

Patristic Speculation

The thought of the Fathers of the Church in the first centuries of the Christian era is called Patristic speculation. The Christians' purpose is neither intellectual nor theoretical. In spite of the extraordinary profundity of their writings, St. John and St. Paul do not intend to create a philosophy; it is another matter that philosophy must inevitably concern itself with them. But, little by little, speculative themes acquire a place in Christianity. This is brought about particularly by two stimuli of a polemical nature: heresies and the intellectual reaction of paganism. Religious truths are interpreted, elaborated on, and formulated into dogma. The first centuries of the Christian era are those of the establishment of Christian dogma. Orthodox interpretation is accompanied by many heresies, which call for greater conceptual precision if the Church is to discuss them, repel them and convince the faithful of the authentic truth. Dogma is formulated all during the struggle against the numerous heretical movements. On the other hand, the pagans pay belated attention to the religion of Christ. At first it seemed to them to be a strange and absurd sect, one which they did not clearly distinguish from Judaism; they considered it a religion made up by men who were almost insane, who worshipped a dead—and crucified—God, a religion of people who related the most surprising and disagreeable stories. When St. Paul speaks on the Areopagus to the refined and curious Athenians of the first century, who are only interested in saying or hearing something new, they listen attentively and courteously while he speaks of the *unknown God* whom he has come to announce; but when he mentions the resurrection of the dead, some laugh and others say that they will listen to him speak of that some other time, and almost all of them leave him. The almost total ignorance of Christianity on the part of even such a man as Tacitus is well known. Later, Christianity acquires greater influence; it reaches the higher classes, and paganism begins to take notice of it. Then the intellectual attacks begin, and the new religion must defend itself from them in like manner; to effect this it must make use of the intellectual instruments which it has at its command: the Greek philosophical concepts. In this way Christianity, which shows a total hostility toward reason in many of its earliest figures (the most famous example is Tertullian), ends by assimilating Greek philosophy in order to use it, in Apologist writings, in defending itself against attacks based on the point of view of Greek philosophy.

Thus, Christianity sees itself committed, first, to the intellectual formulation of dogma and, secondly, to a rational discussion with its heretical or pagan enemies. This is the origin of Patristic speculation, the purpose of which, I repeat, is not philosophical, and which can be considered philosophical only in a limited sense.

THE PHILOSOPHICAL SOURCES OF PATRISTIC SPECULATION. The Fathers of the Church do not have a definite and precise system. They take from Hellenic thought the elements which they need at that particular moment. One must also bear in mind that their knowledge of Greek philosophy is very incomplete and faulty. In general, they are eclectics: they select from all the pagan schools what seems to them most useful in obtaining their goals. We find a formal declaration of eclecticism in the writings of Clement of Alexandria (*Stromateîs* [Miscellanies], I, 7). But the major philosophic source which nourishes the Fathers is, of course, Neoplatonism, which is to influence the Middle Ages so greatly, especially until the thirteenth century, when its influence will pale before Aristotle's prestige. The Fathers come to know Plato (in a rather imprecise way) through the Neoplatonic philosophers (Plotinus, Porphyry, etc.), and they look for analogies to Christianity in Platonic thought. They do not know very much about Aristotle; the Roman philosophers—Seneca, Cicero—are better known to them, and in these figures they find a repertory of ideas which stems from the whole range of Greek philosophy.

THE PROBLEMS. The questions which most concern the Fathers of the Church are the most important problems created by dogma. As a general rule, philosophic problems are created by religious, revealed truths which require rational interpretation, and this is the case in the Middle Ages. Thus, reason is used to clarify and formulate dogma, or to defend it. The Creation, God's relationship with the world, evil, the soul, the meaning of life and of redemption—these are the major problems with which the early Fathers of the Church concern themselves. And alongside these problems we find strictly theological questions, such as those that refer to the essence of God, the Trinity of divine persons, and so on. Thirdly and finally, there appear the Christian moralists who are to establish the bases of a new ethics which, although it makes use of Hellenic concepts, is essentially founded on the idea of sin, on grace and on man's relationship with his Creator, and which culminates in an idea which is foreign to Greek thought—the concept of *salvation*.

These problems are dealt with by a whole series of thinkers who are frequently of the first rank but who do not always remain orthodox; they sometimes fall into heresies. We will briefly consider the most important moments in the evolution which culminates in the brilliant thought of St. Augustine: the Gnostics, the Apologists, St. Justin Martyr and Tertullian, the Alexandrians (Clement and Origen), the Cappadocian Fathers, and so forth.

THE GNOSTICS. The principal heretical movement of the first centuries is Gnosticism. It is related to Greek philosophy of the final epoch, particularly to Neoplatonic ideas, and also to the thought of Philo, the Hellenized Jew who interpreted the Bible allegorically. Gnosticism, a Christian heresy, is also closely linked with all the syncretism of the Oriental religions which was so complex and intricate at the beginning of the Christian era. The Gnostic problem concerns the reality of the world and, more particularly, of evil; it is a dualism between good (God) and evil (matter). By the process of emanation the divine being produces a series of *eons* whose perfection gradually decreases; the world is an intermediate stage between what is divine and what is material. This system allows the essential features of Christianity—such as the creation of the world and the redemption of man—to acquire a natural character, as simple moments of the great struggle between the elements of the dualism, between what is divine and what is material. A fundamental Gnostic idea is that of the ἀποκατάστασις πάντων, the *restitution* or restoration of all things to their proper places. Gnostic knowledge is not knowledge in the usual sense of the word, nor is it revelation; it is a special, superior illumination or intelligence, the so-called *gnôsis* (γνῶσις). Obviously, these ideas can be reconciled with the sacred Christian texts only by resorting to very forced allegorical interpretations, and the Gnostics therefore become heretics. Closely related to them is a movement that has been called Christian gnosis, which opposes the Gnostics with great acuity. The importance of Gnosticism, which almost became a marginal, heterodox church, was very great, especially until the First Council of Nicaea in the year 325.

THE APOLOGISTS. Faced with divergences within the Christian world and, above all, with the attacks of the pagans, the Apologists carry on a strong defense of Christianity. The two most important Apologists are Justin, who suffered martyrdom and was canonized, and Tertullian. Later and less important Apologists are St. Cyprian, Arnobius and Lactantius, who lived in the third to fourth centuries. Justin wrote in Greek; Tertullian wrote in the Latin of Carthage, in Romanized north Africa, as did St. Augustine later. There is a profound difference between Justin and Tertullian in their attitude toward Greek culture and, especially, philosophy.

Justin came out of that culture; he knew it and studied it before his conversion to Christianity. He uses this background in his exposition of the truth of Christianity, making constant reference to Hellenic ideas; he tries to show that these ideas are in agreement with Christian revelation. Therefore there is evident in Justin's writings an acceptance of the pagans' rational methods of thought which contrasts with Tertullian's hostility to those methods.

Tertullian (*c.* 160–220 A.D.) wrote various important books: *Apologeticus, De idolatria, De anima.* He was a passionate enemy of Gnosticism and the entire pagan culture, including the very concept of rational knowledge. In his attacks on the Gnostics, who resorted to philosophic methods, he attacks philosophy itself. There is a whole group of famous sayings of Tertullian that affirm the certainty of revelation on the very basis of its incomprehensibility, its rational impossibility. Outstanding among these sayings is an expression traditionally attributed to him, although not found in his writings: *Credo quia absurdum* (I believe because it is absurd). But this opinion, strictly examined, is inadmissible in Christian thinking, and the doctrines of Tertullian—a fiery, severe and eloquent Apologist—are not always irreproachable. This is true, for example, of his *traducian* doctrines concerning the soul, which he believed to be inherited through procreation from one's parents, like physical traits. This doctrine was particularly intended to explain the transmission of original sin from one generation to the next. All things considered, despite Tertullian's vehement opposition to Hellenic speculation, he is greatly indebted to it, and his writings are permeated by the influence of the Greek philosophers.

THE GREEK FATHERS. Gnosticism was combated in an especially intelligent manner by a series of Church Fathers of Greek background and language, from St. Irenaeus (second century A.D.) until the end of the fourth century. St. Irenaeus, one of the earliest formulators of dogma in the East, uses faith, *pistis*, to oppose the special illumination, *gnôsis*, of the Gnostics. This is a highly significant moment: the return to the security of revealed tradition, to the continuity of the Church, which had been menaced by the Gnostic movement.

Clement of Alexandria, who died at the beginning of the third century, wrote the *Stromateîs* (Miscellanies), an eclectic book full of Greek philosophic ideas. He places an immense value on reason and philosophy, aiming to achieve a comprehension, a true albeit a Christian gnosis, which will be subordinate to revealed faith. Such a gnosis would be the supreme criterion of truth, and philosophy a preliminary stage for arriving at that unsurpassable knowledge.

Origen, a pupil of Clement who lived from 185 to 254 A.D., wrote a work of capital importance, $\Pi\epsilon\rho\grave{\iota}\ \grave{\alpha}\rho\chi\hat{\omega}\nu$, *De principiis*. Origen, too, is greatly influenced by Greek thinking, even more so than his teacher. He gathers together the whole world of ideas that were in ferment in third-century Alexandria. Aristotle, Plato and the Stoics, especially as transmitted by Philo and the Neoplatonists, are Origen's sources. The doctrine of *Creation* has a particular significance in his writings. This doctrine, decisive for all later philosophy, interprets the Creation rigorously as the production of the world *from nothingness* by an act of free will of God. Creation is thereby clearly contrasted with every type of generation or emanation, and the separation between Greek and Christian thinking is sharply demarcated. But not even Origen was completely free from heterodoxy, which was a constant menace in those first centuries of Christianity when dogma was not yet sufficiently precise and when the Church did not yet possess the mature body of doctrine that began to exist only with the theology of St. Augustine.

After Alexandria, Antioch and Cappadocia were the centers in which Eastern theology most flourished. A series of heresies, primarily Arianism, Nestorianism and Pelagianism, occasioned a series of controversies—Trinitarian, Christological and anthropological, respectively. Arianism was combated by St. Athanasius, bishop of Alexandria (fourth century), and by the three Cappadocian Fathers, St. Gregory of Nyssa, his brother St. Basil the Great and St. Gregory of Nazianzus, who were of extraordinary importance in the formation of Christian dogma and ethics. In the West, Arianism was combated by St. Ambrose, the famous bishop of Milan.

Patristic thought attains its full maturity in the fourth century, at the moment when the heretical attacks become most acute. The three heresies mentioned above, together with the great Manichaean movement extending from East to West, are, on the one hand, threatening the Church. On the other hand, Christian thought has acquired profundity and clarity, as well as social validity within the Roman Empire. The ancient world is in its last stage. For some time the barbarians have been clamoring at all the gates of the Empire. All along the Empire's frontiers is felt the pressure of the Germanic tribes, who continue to infiltrate slowly before accomplishing their great break-through in the fifth century. Above all, paganism has ceased to exist. Roman culture wears itself out in labors of commentary, and goes on deriving its nourishment, after so many centuries, from a philosophy—Greek philosophy—that is incapable of renewal. At this point St. Augustine appears, the culmination of Patristic thought. In his immense personality he combines the ancient world, to which he still belongs, and the modern age, which he heralds and for which he himself is the point of departure. The work of St. Augustine sums up this decisive step from one world to another.

St. Augustine

1. LIFE AND CHARACTER

St. Augustine is one of the most interesting figures of his time, of Christianity and of philosophy. His highly original and many-faceted personality leaves a profound imprint on everything to which he turns his hand. Medieval philosophy and theology, what has been called Scholasticism; all of Christian dogma; entire disciplines, such as the philosophy of the spirit and the philosophy of history, show the unmistakable mark he set on them. But there is more: the spirit of Christianity and of the modern age have been decisively influenced by St. Augustine, and the Reformation as well as the Counter-Reformation had recourse to his writings as a particular source of doctrine.

St. Augustine was from Africa. This must not be forgotten. He was, like Tertullian, from Africa, a son of that Romanized and Christianized Africa of the fourth century which was a hotbed of heresies, where varied religious forces coexisted, all animated by an extraordinary vehemence. He was born at Tagaste in Numidia, near Carthage, in 354. In his family background two quite different influences met: the influence of his father, Patricius, a pagan magistrate who was baptized only when dying, a violent and wrathful man of fiery sensuality (that sensuality which was later to trouble Augustine so greatly); and the influence of his mother, Monica, later canonized by the Church, a woman of great virtue and a deeply Christian spirit. Augustine, who loved his mother devotedly, was faced with inward struggles between the conflicting impulses of his double inheritance.

Aurelius Augustinus pursued his studies at a very early age in Tagaste, in Madaurus, and then, when he was seventeen, in Carthage. At this time he fell in love with a woman, who bore him a son, Adeodatus. It was also in this period that Augustine first felt the power of philosophic revelation, when he read the *Hortensius* of Cicero, which made a very strong impression on him. From that time on he acquired an awareness of the problem of philosophy, and his longing for truth was never to leave him until his death. He examined the Scriptures, but they seemed childish to him, and his pride frustrated this first contact with Christianity. He then began to seek truth in the Manichaean sect.

Manes was born in Babylonia at the beginning of the third century, and preached his doctrines in Persia and much of Asia, even reaching India and China. Returning to Persia, he was arrested and crucified. His influence extended throughout the West also, and was a serious problem to Christianity well into the medieval period. Manichaeism contained many elements of Christianity and of various heresies, reminiscences of Buddhism, Gnostic influences and, especially, the fundamental concepts of Mazdaism, the Persian religion of Zoroaster. The point of departure of Manichaeism is the irreducible dualism of good and evil, light and darkness—in short, of God and the devil. All of life was held to be a struggle between the two irreconcilable principles. St. Augustine came to Manichaeism full of enthusiasm.

In Carthage Augustine taught rhetoric and oratory and devoted himself to astrology and philosophy. Then he traveled to Rome, and from Rome to Milan, to which city his mother followed him. There he met the great bishop St. Ambrose, theologian and orator, whose sermons he attended faithfully and who contributed greatly to his conversion. Augustine discovered at that time the superiority of the Scriptures and, not yet a Catholic, became alienated from the sect of Manes. Finally he entered the Church as a catechumen. From that time on he moved closer and closer to Christianity, studying St. Paul and the Neoplatonists. The year 386 was a decisive one for him. In a garden in Milan he was seized by a fit of weeping and discontent with himself, of remorse and anxiety, until he heard a child's voice ordering him to "take and read" ("*Tolle, lege*"). Augustine opened his New Testament and read a verse of the Epistle to the Romans which refers to the life of Christ as contrasted with the appetites of the flesh. He felt transformed and free, full of light; the obstacle of his sensual nature disappeared. Augustine was now fully a Christian.

From that moment on his life was different, dedicated entirely to

God and to religious and theological activities. The story of his life becomes the story of his works and his evangelical efforts. For a while he retired to a friend's country house with his mother, his son and a few pupils; from this sojourn came some of his most interesting writings. Then he was baptized by St. Ambrose and decided to return to Africa. Before leaving Italy he lost his mother, whom he mourned fervently; two years later, in Carthage, his son died. He was then ordained as a priest in Hippo in north Africa and later consecrated as bishop of the same city. His activity was extraordinary, and as the fervor of his soul became more and more a model for Christians, so did his writings continue to increase. In August of the year 430 St. Augustine died in Hippo.

WORKS. St. Augustine's output was copious, but uneven in scope and value. His most important works are those concerned with dogma and theology and those which expound his philosophic thought. The most valuable are the following:

The thirteen books of the *Confessions*, an autobiographical work in which St. Augustine, with an intimacy unknown in the ancient world, relates his life up to the year 387, at the same time indicating his intellectual development and the stages through which his soul passed before arriving at the truth of Christianity; in the light of this truth his whole life is illuminated as he confesses it all before God. This is a book without a counterpart in world literature, a work of the highest philosophical interest.

The other major work of St. Augustine is entitled *De civitate Dei* (The City of God). This is the first philosophy of history, and its influence lasted to the time of Bossuet and, later, Hegel.

We may include alongside these two books the three dialogues that St. Augustine wrote shortly after his conversion: *De beata vita, Contra Academicos* and *De ordine*. We might also name, among others, the *Soliloquia* and the *De Trinitate*.

St. Augustine adopts a number of Hellenic doctrines, especially those of the Neoplatonists Plotinus and Porphyry. His knowledge of Plato and Aristotle is very limited and indirect; he knows much more of the Stoics, Epicureans and Academicians and, above all, Cicero. This invaluable stock of Greek philosophy passes into Christianity and the Middle Ages through St. Augustine. But he generally adapts the contributions of the Greeks to the philosophic necessities of Christian dogma; this is the earliest instance in which Greek philosophy as such comes into contact with Christianity. Thanks to these efforts, the stabilization of dogma takes a vast step forward and St. Augustine becomes the most important of the Latin Church Fathers. His philosophical work is one of the major sources that later metaphysics drew upon. We will examine this philosophy in special detail.

2. PHILOSOPHY

POSING THE PROBLEM. The content of St. Augustine's philosophy is expressed most fundamentally in the *Soliloquies* in the statement: *Deum et animam scire cupio. Nihilne plus? Nihil omnino.* (I desire to know God and the soul. Nothing more? Nothing at all.) That is, there are only two themes in St. Augustine's philosophy: God and the soul. The central point of his speculation will be God—hence his metaphysical and theological efforts; secondly, St. Augustine, the man of intimacy and confession, will bequeath to us the philosophy of the spirit; and lastly, the relationship of this spirit, which lives in the world, to God will lead St. Augustine to the idea of the *civitas Dei* and thus to the philosophy of history. These are St. Augustine's three great contributions to philosophy, and they form the three-part root of his thinking.

GOD. This element of St. Augustine's thought has weighty consequences. One of them is the placing of love, charity, in the forefront of man's *intellectual* life. Knowledge is not to be had without love. *Si sapientia Deus est* (he writes in the *De civitate Dei*), *verus philosophus est amator Dei* (If God is wisdom, then the true philosopher is a lover of God). And with even greater clarity he states: *Non intratur in veritatem nisi per caritatem* (One cannot enter truth except through charity). Thus religion is at the very root of his thinking and sets his philosophy in motion. It is from St. Augustine that are ultimately derived the concept of the *fides quaerens intellectum* (faith seeking understanding) and the principle *credo ut intelligam* (I believe in order to understand)— a concept and a principle that are to have profound repercussions in Scholasticism, especially in St. Anselm and St. Thomas. The problems of the relationship between faith and knowledge, between religion and theology, are already posed in St. Augustine's work.

St. Augustine adopts the philosophy of Plato, but with important changes. In Plato, the point of departure consists of *things*; St. Augustine, on the other hand, bases his philosophy above all on the *soul* as the innermost reality, on what he calls the *inner man* (or the *interior of man*). Therefore, St. Augustine's dialectic in his search for God is *confession*. St. Augustine relates his own life. The soul is raised from the body to the contemplation of itself, then to reason, and finally to the light which illuminates it, God Himself. To arrive at God, one begins with the reality of God's creation, and especially with the inner nature of man.

Since man is the image of God, he finds God, as in a mirror, in the intimacy of his own soul. To turn away from God is the same as to rip out one's own vitals, to empty oneself and to wane constantly. On the other hand, when man enters within himself, he discovers the Deity. But man can know God directly only by means of a *supernatural* illumination.

God, according to St. Augustine's doctrine, created the world from nothingness (not, that is, from His own being) and of His free will. St. Augustine also adopts Plato's theory of the *Ideas*, but in Augustine's system the Ideas are located in the Divine mind: they are the exemplary models according to which God created the things by virtue of a decision of His will.

THE SOUL. The soul plays an important part in St. Augustine's philosophy. What interests us most is not his specific theory about the soul, but, above all, the fact that he makes us aware of the peculiar reality of the soul in a way in which no one had done previously. The intimate analysis of his own soul which constitutes the theme of the *Confessions* is enormously valuable for the inner knowledge of man. For example, there is St. Augustine's contribution to the problem of experiencing death.

The soul is spiritual. The character of the spiritual is not merely negative, that is, not mere immateriality, but something positive, to wit, the faculty of *entering within oneself.* The spirit has a *within*, a *chez soi*, in which it can seclude itself—a privilege which it shares with no other reality. St. Augustine is the philosopher of the inner man: *Noli foras ire, in te redi, in interiore homine habitat veritas*, he writes in *De vera religione.* (Do not go outside, return within yourself; truth dwells in the interior of man.)

Man, who is at one and the same time rational—like an angel—and mortal—like an animal—has an intermediate position. But he is, above all, the image of God, *imago Dei*, because he is a mind, a spirit. In the triple division of the faculties of the soul—memory, intelligence and will or love—St. Augustine discovers a trace of the Trinity. The unifying factor in the person—who *possesses* these three intimately interconnected faculties, but who is not any one of them—is the single *ego*, which remembers, understands and loves, making a perfect distinction among these faculties, and yet preserving the oneness of life, mind and essence.

Using formulas analogous to Descartes' *cogito*, but different from Descartes' formula in their deep meaning and philosophic scope, St. Augustine affirms the internal evidence for the existence of the ego, which is exempt from any possible doubt, in contradistinction to the

dubious testimony concerning the existence of things furnished by the
bodily senses and rational thought. "In these truths," he says (*De
civitate Dei*, XI, 26), "there is no need to fear the arguments of the
Academicians, who say 'What if you are mistaken?' Because if I am
mistaken, I exist. Because the man who does not exist, truly, cannot be
mistaken, either; and therefore, I exist if I am mistaken. And granting
that I exist if I am mistaken, how can I be mistaken about my existence, when it is certain that I exist if I am mistaken? And thus, since
I, the mistaken one, would exist even if I were mistaken, without a
doubt I am not mistaken in knowing that I exist."

The soul, which by its natural reason, or *ratio inferior*, knows the
things, itself and, indirectly, God, Who is reflected in His creation, can
receive a supernatural illumination from God, and by means of this
ratio superior can raise itself to the knowledge of eternal things.

What is the origin of the soul? St. Augustine is somewhat perplexed
in the face of this question. He falters—and along with him so do all
the other Fathers and all the early medieval philosophers—between
generationism or traduciansim, and creationism. Is the soul engendered like the body from the souls of one's parents, or is it created by
God on the occasion of the procreation of the body? The doctrine of
original sin, which seems more comprehensible to St. Augustine if the
soul of the child, like its body, proceeds directly from its parents, leads
him to favor generationism; but at the same time he realizes the weakness of that theory, and does not reject the solution provided by
creationism.

MAN IN THE WORLD. In the writings of St. Augustine, the moral
problem is seen to be intimately connected with the theological questions of nature and grace, predestination and man's free will, and sin
and redemption; but we cannot discuss these relationships in detail
here. However, we must point out that this whole complex of theological problems has had a great influence on the later development
of Christian ethics. Moreover, St. Augustine's writings—exaggerated
and altered from their true meaning—were widely used in the sixteenth century by the leaders of the Reformation (remember that
Luther was an Augustinian monk), and in this way an Augustinian
root persists in modern Protestant ethics.

For St. Augustine, in the same way that man has a natural light
which makes it possible for him to know, man has a *moral conscience*.
The divine *eternal law* to which everything answers illumines our intelligence, and its imperatives constitute *natural law*. It might be likened
to a transcription of divine law in our souls. Everything ought to be
subject to a perfect *order*: *ut omnia sint ordinatissima*. But it is not enough

for man *to know the law*; he must also *love* it. This is where the problem of free will arises.

The soul possesses a weight which moves and transports it, and this weight is love: *pondus meum amor meus* (my weight is my love). Love is active, and it is love which actually determines and qualifies free will: *recta itaque voluntas est bonus amor et voluntas perversa malus amor* (and so a proper will is good love and a perverse will is bad love). Good love—that is, charity in the strict sense of the word—is the central point of Augustinian ethics. Therefore, its most significant and concise expression is the famous imperative *Love and do what you will* (*Dilige, et quod vis fac*).

In St. Augustine's writings, the philosophy of the State and the philosophy of history depend on God, just as ethics does. Augustine lived in days that were crucial for the Empire. The political structure of the ancient world was rapidly changing, to make way for a new order. The barbarians were pressing harder every day. Alaric succeeded in occupying Rome. Christianity had already deeply penetrated Roman society, and the pagans blamed the misfortunes that were happening on the abandonment of the gods and on Christianity. Tertullian had already had to confront these accusations, and to answer them St. Augustine embarked on an enormous work of an apologist nature in which he expounds the full meaning of history: *The City of God*.

The central idea of this work is that all human history is a struggle between two kingdoms: the kingdom of God and the kingdom of the World; that is, between the *civitas Dei* and the *civitas terrena*. The State, which has its roots in profound principles of human nature, is charged with overseeing temporal things: well-being, peace, justice. This gives it a divine significance as well. Following St. Paul's example, St. Augustine teaches that all power comes from God. Therefore, religious values are not foreign to the State, and the State must become saturated with Christian principles. At the same time, the State must lend its power to support the Church, so that the Church can fully realize its mission. St. Augustine believes that politics can no more be separated from the consciousness that man's ultimate goal is not worldly than can ethics. Man's goal is to discover God in the truth that resides in the interior of the human creature.

3. THE SIGNIFICANCE OF ST. AUGUSTINE

It has been said that St. Augustine is the last ancient man and the first modern man. He is a son of Romanized Africa, which had been

permeated with Greco-Roman culture and converted, a long time
before, into an Imperial province. Augustine's century witnesses a
world in crisis, threatened on all sides but still subsisting. The social
and political horizon that he finds is the Roman Empire, the grandest
creation in ancient history. The intellectual sources from which he
draws sustenance are largely of Hellenic origin. Thus St. Augustine's
thinking is nourished by antiquity.

This influence, furthermore, is the more profound because St.
Augustine is not a Christian from the outset; his first vision of philosophy comes to him from sources which are clearly pagan, such as
Cicero, one of the chief representatives of ancient man's way of life.
Christianity takes a long time to conquer Augustine: *Sero te amavi,
pulchritudo tam antiqua et tam nova!* (I came to love you late, you beauty
at the same time so ancient and so new!), St. Augustine exclaims in
the *Confessions.*

Ortega writes: "St. Augustine, who had remained immersed in
paganism for a long time, who had for long seen the world through
'ancient' eyes, could not help but esteem the animal values of Greece
and Rome. And in the light of his new faith, such an existence without
God was bound to seem null and empty. Nevertheless, the evidence
with which the vital grace of paganism asserted itself to his intuition
was such that he used to express his esteem with an ambiguous statement: *Virtutes ethnicorum splendida vitia* (The pagans' virtues are splendid vices). Vices? Then they are negative values. Splendid? Then
they are positive values. "*

This is the situation in which St. Augustine finds himself. He sees the
world through pagan eyes, and he fully understands the marvel of the
ancient world. But from the standpoint of Christianity, all this—
without God—seems to him to be pure nothingness and evil. The
world—and with it, classical culture—has an enormous value; but
one must understand and live it from the realization of God. Only then
is it estimable in the eyes of the Christian.

St. Augustine, a frontiersman who lives on the boundary between
two different cultures, not only knows and embraces the two, but also
reaches what is most profound and original in both. He is, perhaps, the
ancient thinker who best understands the overall significance of the
Empire and Roman history. On the other hand, St. Augustine represents one of the most perfect realizations of the idea of Christianity,
one of the three or four highest modes in which the new type of man

* Ortega adds the following note: "As is well known, this statement, which has
always been attributed to St. Augustine, is not to be found in his works; but all his
work paraphrases it. Cf. Mausbach: *Die Ethik Augustinus.*"

has been expressed. Notwithstanding Scholasticism's great achievements, it derives essentially from St. Augustine. The last ancient man represents the beginning of the great medieval stage of Europe's history.

St. Augustine's thought contains something characteristic not only of Christianity but also of the modern epoch: intimacy. We have seen how he bases his philosophy on the inner man. He asks man to enter the interior of his own soul in order to find himself, and with himself, God. This is the great lesson which St. Anselm will learn first, and through him all of Western mysticism. In contrast to the flights into the external world that characterized ancient man, the man of the agora and forum, St. Augustine finds himself in the calm interior of his own ego. This leads him to affirm the ego as the highest criterion of certainty, in a statement which although reached by means of different suppositions, is similar to Descartes' *cogito: Omnis qui se dubitantem intelligit, verum intelligit, et de hac re quam intelligit, certus est* (Every man who understands himself to be doubting, understands truly, and is certain of this thing which he understands).

More than anyone else in his time, St. Augustine achieved what was to constitute the very essence of another mode of being; his incomparable fecundity derives from this fact. The *Confessions* represents man's first attempt to approach himself. Until the advent of idealism— that is, until the seventeenth century—no one will achieve anything comparable. And when modern man, guided by Descartes, returns to himself and remains alone with his own ego, St. Augustine will again acquire profound influence.

St. Augustine determined one of the two great aspects of Christianity, that of interiority, and made it possible for that aspect to achieve full development. The other element remained in the hands of the Greek theologians, and therefore in the Eastern Church. This situation has in large measure determined European history, which since its birth shows the imprint of Augustinian thought.

MEDIEVAL PHILOSOPHY

Scholasticism

1. The Era of Transition

The ancient world ends approximately in the fifth century A.D.; if we focus our attention on the history of thought, we can consider 430, the year of St. Augustine's death, as the cut-off date. The Middle Ages extends midway into the fifteenth century, and 1453, the year in which the Byzantine Empire fell into Turkish hands, is frequently taken as its limit. This means we are dealing with ten centuries of history, too long a period to be studied as a *single* epoch. In such a long interval of time there are bound to be great changes, and a unitary exposition of medieval philosophy would necessarily have to pass over large differences.

There is, in the first place, a long gap of four centuries, from the fifth to the ninth, in which actually there is no philosophy. The world is essentially changed with the fall of the Roman Empire. The great political unity of antiquity is replaced by fractionization; waves of barbarians surge over Europe and cover it almost completely; they form barbaric kingdoms in the various regions of the Empire, and classical culture is overwhelmed. One important consequence of the Germanic invasions is often not sufficiently noted: the isolation. The social and political unity of the different peoples of the Empire is now replaced by the separativeness of the barbaric states. Visigoths, Swabians, Ostrogoths, Franks form various unconnected political communities, which are a long time in establishing ties with their neighbors; and when these ties are finally established they do not result in the reëstablishment of the Western Empire, as was expected at the time, but in an entirely new community—Europe. Thus the elements of the ancient culture are all but lost and, above all, *dispersed*. The culture itself is not destroyed to the extent usually believed, and the proof of this is that later, little by little, it reappears. But very little of it remains *in any one place*. And so a new problem arises: to save what is found, to preserve the remains of the shipwrecked culture. This is the mission of the intellectuals of these four centuries; their labor is not—nor can it be—creative; it is only a process of compilation. In Spain, France, Italy, Germany, England, a few men, working along parallel lines, carefully collect everything that is known about antiquity and gather it in books of an encyclopedic nature. These books were not at all original; they were mere repositories of Greco-Roman knowledge. Nevertheless, these men save the continuity of Western history, and with their patient labor fill the hollow of those centuries of historic fermentation, in order that the new European community may arise later on.

A major figure of this time is St. Isidore of Seville, who lived in the sixth and seventh centuries (approximately from 570 to 646). Besides other theological and historical works of secondary interest, he compiled the twenty volumes of the *Etymologiae*, or *Origins*, a true encyclopedia of his time; it does not limit itself to the seven liberal arts, but includes all the religious, historical, scientific, medical and technical knowledge and practical information that he could unearth. The contribution to the common base of medieval knowledge made by this great personality of Visigothic Spain is one of the most significant of his time.

In Italy, the most important thinker of this period is Boethius, counselor to the Ostrogothic king Theodoric, who finally imprisoned him and ordered him beheaded in the year 524 or 525. While in prison Boethius composed a very famous book in prose and verse entitled *De consolatione philosophiae*. In addition, he translated into Latin Porphyry's *Eisagogé* as well as some of Aristotle's treatises on logic, and wrote monographs on logic, mathematics and music, and several theological treatises (*De Trinitate, De duabus naturis in Christo, De hebdomadibus*), the principal interest of which consists in their definitions, which were utilized by philosophers and theologians for centuries. Martianus Capella, who lived in the fifth century, was from Carthage but settled in Rome. He wrote a treatise entitled *The Marriage of Mercury and Philology*, an odd encyclopedia in which the studies which were to become dominant in the Middle Ages are systematized: the *trivium* (grammar, rhetoric and dialectic) and the *quadrivium* (arithmetic, geometry, astronomy and music). Together these subjects comprised the seven liberal arts. Cassiodorus, who, like Boethius, was a minister to Theodoric, is also important.

The British Isles were affected by the barbaric invasions to a lesser degree than the rest of Europe, and so in England we find important groups of scholars guarding the legacy of classical culture. In Ireland especially, there were monasteries in which the knowledge of Greek endured, something that was all but lost in the West. The most important figure in these circles was the Venerable Bede (now St. Bede), a monk from Jarrow (Northumberland), who lived from 673 to 735—that is, one century after St. Isidore. The Venerable Bede's most important work, which marks the beginning of English history, is the *Historia ecclesiastica gentis Anglorum*, known in English as the *Ecclesiastical History of the English People*. He also wrote other treatises, notably the *De natura rerum*, which was inspired by St. Isidore's work. Alcuin (739–804, approximately) was from the school of York, in England. He taught at Charlemagne's court for several years and was one of the moving spirits of the Carolingian intellectual renaissance, which was principally of English origin.

Alcuin's most important pupil was Rabanus Maurus, who established the school at Fulda, in Germany, where other intellectual centers were set up at Münster, Salzburg, and so forth.

Throughout this era of transition, the ancient wisdom of the pagan writers and that of the Fathers of the Church is preserved in disorganized fashion and without intellectual precision. No distinction is made as to disciplines of knowledge, and a systematic and congruent body of doctrines is of course completely lacking. This phase is concerned only with the accumulation of knowledge, but it prepares the way for the prodigious speculative labor of the following centuries.

2. THE NATURE OF SCHOLASTICISM

Beginning with the ninth century there appear, as a consequence of the Carolingian Renaissance, the *schools*, and with them *Scholasticism*, a special knowledge cultivated in the schools. In contrast to the seven liberal arts of the *trivium* and *quadrivium*, this knowledge is principally theological and philosophical. The school's work is of a collective nature; it is a cooperative labor and is closely connected with the ecclesiastical organization, which assures an unusual continuity of thought. In Scholasticism there exists—particularly from the eleventh to the fifteenth centuries—a unitary body of doctrine which is preserved as a *common property*: a body of doctrine which the various individual thinkers collaborate on and which they all use. In Scholasticism, as in all spheres of medieval life, the personality of the individual is not emphasized. Just as the cathedrals are immense anonymous works—or almost such, the results of entire generations' long collective labor—so medieval thought is continued uninterruptedly over a common base until the end of the Middle Ages. Therefore, the modern meaning of the word "originality" does not have application to Scholasticism. Frequently a writer in this period uses in the most natural way borrowed material which cannot be attributed to him lightly without danger of error. But it does not by any means follow that Scholasticism is homogeneous, or that it lacks eminent personalities. On the contrary: in the Middle Ages we find some of the most profound and perspicacious minds in all of the history of philosophy; and medieval thought, which is of a surprising richness and variety, experiences during the course of this epoch a definite and basic evolution which we will attempt to trace with some degree of precision. The volume of Scholastic writings is so great that we will of necessity have to limit ourselves to pointing out the major phases of the problems involved and to outlining briefly the significance of the medieval philosophers who most deeply influenced philosophy.

THE EXTERNAL FORM OF SCHOLASTIC WRITINGS. The Scholastic literary forms correspond to the circumstances in which they were developed; they maintain a close relationship with educational life, at first with the life of the schools and later with that of the universities. Scholastic teaching is first developed on the basis of texts that are read and commented on; it is for this reason that we speak of *lectiones* (lectures); sometimes these texts are from the Scriptures themselves, but frequently they are works of the Fathers of the Church, of theologians or of ancient or medieval philosophers. The *Liber sententiarum* of Peter Lombard (twelfth century) was read and commented on constantly. At the same time, the daily give and take of academic life leads to the *disputationes*, in which important questions (and, at the end of the Middle Ages, unimportant questions as well) are debated, and by means of which the participants become skillful in argumentation and in establishing proof.

The literary forms spring from this activity. First of all there are the commentaries (*Commentaria*) on the various books studied. Secondly, there are the *Quaestiones*, huge repertories of problems which had been discussed, together with their authorities, arguments and solutions (*Quaestiones disputatae, Quaestiones quodlibetales*); when the problems are dealt with individually in brief, independent studies, the works are called *Opuscula*. Finally, there are the great doctrinal syntheses of the

Middle Ages in which the general content of Scholasticism is summarized, the *Summae*. Outstanding among the *Summae* are those of St. Thomas, particularly his *Summa theologiae*. These are the principal forms in which the thought of the Scholastics is set forth.

PHILOSOPHY AND THEOLOGY. What is the content of Scholasticism? Is it philosophy? Is it theology? Is it both, or something different still? The answers to these questions are not immediately clear. Of course, Scholasticism is theology; there can be no doubt about that. But it is no less true that if there is any philosophy in the Middle Ages, it is especially to be found in the works of the Scholastic writers. The next logical thought would be that theology and philosophy coexist in this period, that alongside Scholastic theology there is a *Scholastic philosophy*. At once there arises the problem of the relationship between theology and philosophy. An attempt is usually made to resolve this problem by resorting to the idea of subordination and recalling the old phrase *philosophia ancilla theologiae* (philosophy, the handmaiden of theology); from this viewpoint, philosophy is an auxiliary, subordinate discipline, which theology makes use of for its own ends. This conception is simple and apparently satisfactory, but only apparently. Philosophy is not and cannot be a subordinate science, used as a means to something else. As Aristotle already knew, philosophy is not useful for anything, and all the other sciences are more necessary than philosophy, though none is superior to it (*Metaphysics*, I, 2). On the other hand, judging from the facts, it is not certain that in the Middle Ages there was any philosophy separate from theology for theology to make use of. The truth of the matter is something quite different.

The problems of Scholasticism, like the problems of Patristic thought which preceded them, are primarily theological problems— one might say merely dogmatic problems, involving the formulation and interpretation of dogma, and at times involving rational explanation or even demonstration. These *theological* problems call forth new questions, and these are *philosophic* questions. Let us take as an example the dogma of the Eucharist. This is a religious matter which in itself has nothing to do with philosophy. But if we wish to understand it in some fashion, we must have recourse to the concept of transubstantiation, a strictly philosophic concept. This idea leads us into a different world, the world of Aristotelian metaphysics; the question of how the transubstantiation of which the Eucharist consists is possible, is stated in terms of the philosophic theory of substance. Similarly, the dogma of the Creation compels us to consider the problem of being, bringing us back to the realm of metaphysics. It is the same with all the other dogmas. Thus Scholasticism deals with philosophic problems that arise *in connection* with religious and theological questions. But philosophy is not used as a tool in these cases; rather, the framework within which the philosophic problems are considered is rigorously determined by the actual situation from which they arise. Medieval philosophy is essentially different from that of the Greeks, principally because its questions are different and are based on different suppositions. The outstanding example of this difference is the problem of the Creation, which radically transforms the great ontological problem; as a result of this, Christian philosophy comprises a new period in the history of philosophy quite separate from the ancient period. At all times in our consideration of Scholasticism we shall be viewing it as a complex of theology *and* philosophy united by a special tie corresponding to the attitude toward life which gives rise to the speculation of the Christian theorist. It is St. Anselm's lemma *fides quaerens intellectum* (faith seeking understanding)—in which equal stress must be given to *fides* and *intellectus*, within the fundamental unity of the *quaerere*. The two poles between which medieval Scholasticism will move are joined together in this *quaerere*, this quest. *

We shall examine briefly the three major problems of medieval philosophy: those of the Creation, the universals and reason. In the evolution of these three problems, which have a parallel development, we will find concentrated the entire history of medieval thought and of the era as a whole.

* See my above-mentioned study, "La escolástica en su mundo y en el nuestro."

The Great Themes of the Middle Ages

I. THE CREATION

We have already seen that the Christian point of departure is essentially different from the Greek's; that is, the Christian begins with the *nihility of the world*. In other words, the world is contingent, not necessary. It does not contain within itself its reason for being, but receives it from another, from God. The world is an *ens ab alio* (entity which derives its being from another), as distinguished from the Deity, who is the *ens a se* (entity which derives its being from itself). God is the Creator and the world is His creation: two profoundly different, perhaps irreducible modes of being. Thus, the Creation appears as the first metaphysical problem of the Middle Ages, from which, in fact, all the others are derived.

The Creation must not be confused with what the Greeks called genesis or generation. Generation is a type of motion, substantial motion. It presupposes a subject, an entity that moves, passing *from* a beginning *to* an end. The carpenter who makes a table makes it of wood, and the wood is the subject of the motion. This does not occur in the Creation; there is no subject. God does not manufacture or make the world out of a previously existing material, but *creates* it, sets it in existence. The Creation is a creation *from nothingness*—in Scholastic terminology, *creatio ex nihilo*, or more explicitly, *ex nihilo sui et subjecti*. But it is a principle of medieval philosophy that *ex nihilo nihil fit*, nothing can be made from nothing. This would seem to indicate that the Creation is impossible, that being cannot result from nothingness;

this principle would be the formula of pantheism. But the sense in which this phrase is used in the Middle Ages is that nothing can be made from nothing *without the intervention of God*, that is, precisely *without the Creation*.

This concept opens up between God and the world a metaphysical gulf which was unknown to the Greeks. Consequently, there now appears a new question, which affects being itself: can the one word "being" be applied to God and to His creatures? Is it not an equivocation? At most, one might speak of a new analogical conception of the Entity, in a sense much more profound even than Aristotle's. It was even denied that being can be applied to God at all; being is a created thing, distinct from its Creator, who is beyond being. *Prima rerum creatarum est esse* (Being is the first of the created things), said the medieval Platonists (see Zubiri, "En torno al problema de Dios"). Thus we see that the idea of the Creation, religious in origin, profoundly affects medieval *ontology*.

This Creation could be *ab aeterno* or within time. The opinions of the Scholastics are divided. They are not so much divided with regard to the dogmatic truth that the Creation did occur within time, as with regard to the possibility of demonstrating this rationally. St. Thomas considered that the Creation was demonstrable, but not its temporality, which could be known only through revelation. Moreover, the idea of a Creation dating from eternity is not contradictory, since being created means only receiving being from God, that is, *ab alio*, and this is independent of time relationships.

But a new question arises: the relationship of God to the world which has been created. The world is not sufficient unto itself for its existence; it does not have sufficient reason for being. It is maintained in its existence by God so that it does not lapse into nothingness. Thus, aside from the Creation, there is a need for *preservation*. God's action upon the world is constant; He must keep on causing it to exist at each moment. This is tantamount to a *continuing creation*. Thus, the world always has need of God and is constitutionally needy and insufficient. The early Scholastics believed it was so. The ontological basis of the world is found in God, not only at the origin of the world, but also at the present time, at all times. But in the nominalism of the fourteenth and fifteenth centuries this conviction wavers. The nominalists think that continuing creation is not necessary, that the world does not need to be maintained. The world is still understood to be an *ens ab alio* which is not self-sufficient and which has received its existence at the hands of its Creator, but the nominalists believe that the being which God gave the world when He created it is sufficient for its subsistence.

The world is an entity with the capacity to *go on* existing by itself; God's participation in its existence, after His act of creation, consists merely of not annihilating it, of allowing it to exist. In this manner, the idea of continuing creation is succeeded by the idea of the relative self-sufficiency and autonomy of the world *as a creature.* The world, once it is created, can exist without further aid; it can be left to operate in accordance with its own laws, without the direct and constant intervention of the Deity.

We see that in the development of the problem of the Creation in the Middle Ages philosophers are led to grant the creature greater independence with regard to the Creator; this contributes to an estrangement from God. Following separate paths, all the great problems of medieval metaphysics lead man to a single situation at the close of the medieval period.

2. THE UNIVERSALS

The question of the universals is omnipresent in the Middle Ages. It has even been said that the entire history of Scholasticism is the history of the dispute over the universals. This is not true, but it is true that this problem is present in all the other problems and its development is closely connected with that of all the others. The universals are the genera and species, in contradistinction to individual things. The question is one of knowing what type of reality these universals possess. The objects which present themselves to our senses are individuals: this thing, that thing. On the other hand, the concepts by means of which we imagine these same objects are universals: man, tree. The things we see before us are conceived of through their species and genera. What relationship do these universals have with the things? In other words, in what measure do our perceptions correspond to reality? In this way there arises the question of knowing whether or not the universals are things, and in what sense. The idea we are to have of both the being of things and the nature of knowledge is dependent upon the solution to this problem. At the same time, a multitude of highly serious metaphysical and theological problems are connected with this question.

The medieval period begins with an extreme position, *realism,* and ends with the opposite extreme solution, *nominalism.* Of course, nominalism has origins almost as ancient as those of realism, and the history of both has many complications and various gradations. But the general line of historic development is the one that has just been indicated. Realism, which is the generally accepted position until the twelfth century, maintains that the universals are *res*, things. The adherents of the extreme form of realism believe that the universals are present in all the individuals that fall under their headings (for instance, the universal "man" would be present in each individual man) and that, consequently, there is no essential difference between individuals, there are only accidental differences. The universals are prior to the individual things (*ante rem*). In essence there would thus be only one man, and the distinction between individual men would be purely accidental. This is tantamount to a denial of individual existence and comes dangerously close to pantheism. On the other hand, the realist solution had great simplicity, and was, moreover, adaptable to the interpretation of various dogmas—for example, that of original sin. If in essence there is only one man, Adam's sin naturally affects the essence of humanity, and thus all later men. Realism is represented by St. Anselm and, in its extreme form, by William of Champeaux (eleventh and twelfth centuries).

But adversaries of the realist thesis soon arise. Beginning in the eleventh century there appears what has been called nominalism, starting principally with Roscellinus of Compiègne. According to nominalism, it is the individuals that exist. There is nothing in nature that is universal. The universals exist only in the mind, as something posterior to the things (*post rem*), and they are expressed in words. Roscellinus arrives at a purely verbalistic interpretation of the universals; they are no more than exhalations of the voice, *flatus vocis*. But this theory, too, is very dangerous. If realism, exaggerated, threatens to lead to pantheism, nominalism, when applied to the Trinity, leads us to tritheism: if there are three persons, there are three Gods. Moreover, the Incarnation is very difficult to conceive of within the framework of Roscellinus' ideas. Thus, the first two solutions are imperfect and do not solve the problem. A long and painstaking mental effort, a large share of which falls to the Jews and Arabs, leads to more mature and subtle formulas in the thirteenth century, especially in the writings of St. Thomas.

The thirteenth century contributes solutions of its own to the problem of the universals: these consist of a *moderate realism*. The adherents of this philosophy recognize that the true substance is the individual thing, as was maintained by Aristotle, whose authority St. Albertus Magnus and St. Thomas invoke. The individual is the first substance, *próte ousía*. But this philosophy is not a form of nominalism; the individual is a true reality, but is an individual *of a species*, and is obtained from the species by individuation. Thus, in order to explain the individual reality, there is need of a principle of individuation, *principium individuationis.* St. Thomas says that *formaliter* the universals are products of the spirit, but that *fundamentaliter* they are based on the reality outside the mind. The universals, considered formally—that is, as such—are products of the mind. They do not have an independent existence, but are formed by the mind. They do, however, have a basis *in re*, in reality. The universal has an existence, not as a *separate thing*, but as an ingredient *of the things*. It is not a *res*, as the extreme realists claimed, but neither is it merely a word. It is *in re*.

Now it is necessary to find a principle of individuation. That is, what is it that makes this entity be *this one* and not *this other one*? St. Thomas says that an individual is nothing but *materia signata quantitate*. Thus, quantified matter is the principle of individuation. A certain quantity of matter is what individuates the universal form that shapes the matter. But it should not be forgotten that there is a hierarchy of entities ranging from primal matter to pure actuality (God). Primal matter cannot exist actually, because it is pure possibility. But "informed" matter may be form or matter, depending on how it is considered. For example, wood is itself a form, but it is the matter of a table. Thus, there is a series of hierarchic forms within a single entity, and there are essential forms and accidental forms. This principle of individuation raises a serious problem for St. Thomas: What about the angels? The angels have no matter; how is individuation possible among them? According to the Thomist solution, it is in no way possible. St. Thomas says that the angels are not individuals, but species. The unit among angels is not the individual, but the species, and each species is exhausted in each angel.

In the final period of the Middle Ages, the problem of the universals undergoes a profound development. By the time of John Duns Scotus, the great British Franciscan, and especially in the thought of William of Occam, there is a return to the nominalist formulation of the question. Scotus makes many distinctions; the *distinctio realis*, the *distinctio formalis* and the *distinctio formalis a parte rei*. The first or real distinction is the one that exists between one type of thing and another: for example, between an elephant and a table. The rational or formal distinction is the one that is made when considering one thing in its various aspects; it can be an actual or a purely nominal distinction. It is actual if, for example, we distinguish a vase as a recipient for water from a vase as a decorative object. A nominal distinction does not correspond to the reality of the thing, but merely to its designation. The *distinctio formalis a parte rei*, finally, is also a formal distinction, but rather than being *a parte intellectus*, it is *a parte rei*. That is, here also it is a question of things not numerically distinct, but in this case it is not the mind that makes the distinction; the distinction is present in the thing itself. Thus, according to Scotus, a man has various *forms*: he has a human form, or *humanitas*, but he also has a form which distinguishes him from all other men. This is a formal distinction *a parte rei*, what Scotus, using an original term, calls *haecceitas*, or "thisness." *Haecceitas* consists in being *haec res*, this thing. Peter and Paul both contain full human essence, but Peter possesses an additional *formalitas*, which is "Peterness," and Paul possesses "Paulness." This is Scotus' principle of individuation, which is not only material, as in Thomist metaphysics, but also formal.

Scotus' position opens the way for nominalism. From his time on, and especially in the fourteenth century, the distinctions multiply and the existence of the individuals is increasingly proclaimed. Even in Scotus' conception, there are multiple *formalitates*, without excluding the *forma* of the species. Occam goes one step further and absolutely denies the existence of the universals in nature. They are exclusively creations of the spirit, of the mind. They are *terms* (hence the name *terminism* which is also given to this direction of thought). And the terms are merely *signs* for things; they are mental substitutes for the multiplicity of the things. They are not conventions, but *natural signs*. Things are known through our concepts of them, and these concepts are universal. In order to know an individual we must have recourse to knowledge of the universal, the Idea; if, with Occam, we understand the universals to be mere signs, knowledge becomes *symbolic*. Occam is the artificer of a great renunciation: man will renounce the possession of the things and will resign himself to remain only with the symbols of things. This is what will make possible mathematical knowledge, based on the use of symbols, and modern physics, which derives from the nominalist schools, especially that of Paris. Aristotelian and medieval physics desired to understand motion, the causes themselves; modern physics is content with the mathematical signs for all of that. According to Galileo, nature's book is written in mathematical signs; we thus have a physics that measures variations in motion, but no longer seeks the knowledge of what motion is. We see that, just as in the case of the problem of the Creation, the internal dialectics of the problem of the universals leads the man of the fifteenth century to turn his eyes toward the world and formulate a science of nature. The third great question of medieval philosophy, the problem of reason, will definitively center man's attention on the new theme of the world.

3. REASON

Lógos has been an essential theme in Christian thought from the very beginning. The first sentence of the Gospel According to St. John says literally that in the beginning was the word, the *lógos*, and that God is *lógos*. This means that provisionally God is the word and, in addition, *reason*. Several especially important problems arise as a result of this situation, and in particular the problem of man's situation in the universe.

What is man? He is a finite entity, a creature, an *ens creatum*, one thing among the other things; like the world, man is finite and contingent. But at the same time man is *lógos*; according to all Hellenic tradition, man is an animal which possesses *lógos*. On the one hand, man is just one more thing in the world, but on the other hand, man, like God, is cognizant of the whole world and, again like God, possesses *lógos*. What is the nature of man's relationship with God and the world? It is an essentially ambiguous relationship; man is an entity which partakes of being in the sense that all creatures do, but man is also a spirit capable of knowing what the world is; that is, an entity which is *lógos*. The philosophers of the Middle Ages will say that man is a creature which exists halfway between nothingness and God: *medium quid inter nihilum et Deum*. Moreover, man's special situation was already pointed out in Genesis: *Faciamus hominem ad imaginem et similitudinem nostram*. Man is made in the image and likeness of God. That is, the Idea of man, the exemplary model according to which man is created, is God himself. It is for this reason that Meister Eckhart said that in man there is something—a spark, *scintilla*, *Funken*—that is uncreated and uncreatable. This statement was condemned as pantheistic because it was interpreted to mean that man was not created. However, as Zubiri has clearly shown, its correct meaning is that man has a *scintilla*—that is, his very Idea—that is uncreated and uncreatable; and this concept is completely orthodox.

In what ways is Christian thought to influence philosophy? In order to know truth, one must enter oneself, one must turn one's attention within oneself, as we have already learned when discussing St. Augustine's contribution to philosophy. *Intra in cubiculum mentis tuae* (Enter into the chamber of your mind), St. Anselm too will say. Accordingly, if man wants to learn, the worst thing he can do is to begin to observe the things of the world, because truth is not in the things but in God; and man finds God in himself. Since truth is God, it can only be arrived at through *caritas*: we reach God only through love, and only God is truth. This is the precise meaning of St. Anselm's phrase, *fides quaerens intellectum* (faith seeking understanding). St. Bonaventure will call philosophy the journey of the mind toward God (*Itinerarium mentis in Deum*), and will say that this journey begins with faith. This concludes the outline of the state of early medieval philosophy.

In St. Thomas, theory is rational, speculative knowledge. Theology rests on faith in so far as it is based on revealed, supernatural information; but man scrutinizes this information with his reason in order to interpret it and arrive at theological knowledge. Therefore, complete accord between God and human reason is assumed. If God is *lógos*, as St. John says, and if man is also defined by *lógos*, there is accord between the two and knowledge of the divine essence is possible. Theology can be rational even though based on revealed information. But if theology and philosophy both deal with God, how do they differ? St. Thomas says that the *material* object of theology and philosophy can be the same when both speak of God, but that their formal objects are different. Theology and philosophy approach the divine Entity by different paths, and therefore theology and philosophy have different formal objects, even though that Entity may be numerically the same.

We pass from this state of equilibrium in St. Thomas to a very different situation in Duns Scotus and Occam. For Scotus, theological knowledge is no longer speculative, but practical, moralistic. Man is a rationalizing animal and thus will create a rational philosophy, because this is a matter of *lógos*. But on the other hand, theology is supernatural; reason has little to do with it; it is, above all, *práxis*.

Occam exaggerates Scotus' ideas. For Occam, reason comes to be an exclusively human concern. Reason is, indeed, characteristic of man, but not of God. God is omnipotent and cannot be subject to any law, not even to the law of reason; Occam says that if it were otherwise, the divine will would be inadmissibly limited. Things are as they are—true, good, and the like—*because God wills them so*; the followers of Occam will say that if God wanted the act of murder to be good, or two and two to be nineteen, they would be so. Occam is a voluntarist and believes very strongly in the priority of the divine will; he does not admit of anything superior to God's will, not even reason. "One might say that, beginning with this moment, metaphysical speculation hurls itself into a vertiginous race in which *lógos*, which begins as the essence of God, ends up as merely the essence of man. At this moment in the fourteenth century Occam declares textually and in so many words that the essence of the Deity is arbitrariness, free will, omnipotence, and that therefore the need to rationalize is a property which is peculiar to human thought. . . . At this moment when Occam's nominalism reduces reason to a matter of *doors within* man, to a purely human quality instead of the essence of the Deity, the human spirit also becomes separated from the Deity. Alone, alienated from the world and from God, the human spirit begins to feel insecure in the universe." (Zubiri: *Hegel y el problema metafísico*.)

If God is not reason, then human reason cannot concern itself with God. At the end of the Middle Ages, the Deity ceases to be man's great theoretic subject, and this separates man from God. Reason concerns itself again with those objects to which it is appropriate, to a realm wherein it can be fruitful. What are these objects? Above all, man himself. Secondly, the world, whose marvelous order is just then being discovered; it is found to possess a mathematical as well as rational order. Symbolic knowledge, to which nominalism had led us, is adapted to the mathematical character of nature. And this world which is independent of God—who set it in motion by His act of Creation but who does not have to sustain it—becomes the other great object of concern to human reason when the Deity becomes inaccessible to reason. Man and the world are the two principal themes of the age; therefore, humanism and modern physics, the science of nature, come to be the two chief concerns of Renaissance man, who finds himself alienated from God.

We now see how the three deepest questions of medieval philosophy —the problems of the Creation, the universals and reason—combine to lead to this new situation in which we find modern metaphysics.

The Medieval Philosophers

Medieval philosophy proper begins in the ninth century. As we have seen, the intellectual activity prior to this time consisted merely of a labor of compilation and preservation of classical culture and Patristic speculation; it was without originality, and did not possess great inherent possibilities. Furthermore, the organization necessary to philosophic study was completely lacking and was only to appear in the *schools*, which arise at the beginning of the ninth century; these flourish particularly in France, around the court of Charlemagne, and constitute what is known as the Carolingian Renaissance. From these schools, led by teachers from all the European countries, and particularly by Frenchmen, Englishmen and Italians, there arises in the reign of Charles the Bald the first important budding of philosophy in the Middle Ages; this new activity is centered around the figure of the English thinker John Scotus Erigena or Eriugena.

1. SCOTUS ERIGENA

John Scotus Erigena was born in the British Isles, probably in Ireland, where more than in any other region the knowledge of classical culture and even of the Greek language had been preserved. However, Erigena carried out his intellectual activity principally in France, at the court of Charles the Bald, which he reached toward the middle of the ninth century. Erigena represents the first example of English influence on European culture. It is quite true that many European intellectual movements and ideas have originated in England; however, as a rule these ideas have not been developed in their country of origin, but on the Continent, and later have passed from Europe back to Great Britain, which has again undergone their influence. This is what happens with Scholasticism, and happened later with the natural sciences, which were begun by Roger Bacon and developed in France and Italy, only to return and flourish once more in England in the seventeenth century. Something similar occurs later: the Enlightenment was also of British inspiration, but it was developed in France and in the German states, undergoing the sensationalist empiricism and deism of the English philosophers. Finally, the diffusion of romanticism presents an analogous phenomenon: it was born in the British Isles toward the end of the eighteenth century, but flowered in Germany and in the rest of the Continent, and later was reborn in England.

Scotus Erigena is greatly influenced by Neoplatonic mysticism and particularly by the anonymous writer once known as Dionysius the Areopagite, and now known as Pseudo-Dionysius. Scotus Erigena translated his works from Greek to Latin, and with this effort assured their fame and enormous influence on medieval thought. Erigena was himself very successful. He was persuaded to write a treatise against the idea of predestination which some heresies were then making very fashionable; his treatise, *De praedestinatione*, was considered excessively daring and was condemned. His major work was another treatise, *De divisione naturae*.

Scotus Erigena's purpose is always strictly orthodox; he does not even imagine that there can be a discrepancy between true philosophy and revealed religion; reason is merely the instrument which interprets the sacred texts for us, nothing more. When both philosophy and religion are true, they are identical: *veram esse philosophiam veram religionem, conversimque veram religionem esse veram philosophiam*. In the first rank Scotus places revelation, strictly understood—that is, the authority of God. However, there are other sources of authority—the Fathers of the Church and the earlier commentators on sacred texts—and *this* type of authority must be subordinated to reason, which occupies the second rank, the rank below the divine word.

Scotus Erigena's metaphysics is expounded in his *De divisione naturae*. This division assumes a series of emanations or acts of sharing by means of which all things are born from the single true Entity which is God. There are four stages in this process:

(1) Nature which is creative and not created (*natura creans nec creata*); that is, God in his first reality. He is unknowable, and can be dealt with only by means of the negative theology which Pseudo-Dionysius had made so popular.

(2) Nature which is creative and created (*natura creans creata*); that is, God in so far as He contains the first causes of the entities. Upon knowing these causes in Himself, God creates and manifests Himself in His *theophanies*.

(3) Nature which is created and not creative (*natura creata nec creans*); the corporeal or spiritual beings created in time which are mere manifestations or theophanies of God. Scotus Erigena, who is an extreme realist, affirms the priority of the genus with respect to the species, and of the species with respect to the individual.

(4) Nature which is neither created nor creative (*natura nec creata nec creans*); that is, God as the end of the entire universe. All motion ends where it began; God returns to Himself, and the things become deified, they resolve themselves in the divine all (θέωσις).

John Scotus Erigena presents an interesting metaphysics which touches acutely upon several major problems in the Middle Ages and constitutes the earliest phase of Scholasticism. However, his doctrine is dangerous and naturally inclined toward pantheism. Both well- and ill-founded accusations of pantheism are leveled against numerous thinkers during the Middle Ages, the majority of whom, we must remember, did not by any means deliberately profess pantheism; but their doctrines—or sometimes only their professions of faith—inclined toward it. As a consequence of this extreme form of realism, Scotus Erigena comes to believe in a single soul for all mankind—another of the various dangers which are to menace Scholasticism. Thus, in the first important medieval thinker we find the features which are to characterize the epoch as well as the difficulties with which the era must come to terms.

FROM SCOTUS ERIGENA TO ST. ANSELM. For Western Europe, the tenth century is a terrible century: there are battles and invasions everywhere; the Normans attack, devastate and sack; the Carolingian Renaissance and all the intellectual awakening of the ninth century disappears, and the schools find themselves in a difficult situation. Medieval thought shuts itself up in the cloisters and from this time begins to acquire the monastic nature which is to weigh upon it for a long time; the Benedictine Order becomes the principal repository of theological and philosophical knowledge. Great personalities are rare; the one of greatest interest is the monk Gerbert.

Gerbert of Aurillac obtained an exceptionally complete education, principally in Spain, where he had contact with the Arabic schools. Later, after teaching in Rheims and in Paris, he was made an abbot, then an archbishop and finally pope, under the name of Sylvester II. He died in 1003. Gerbert was not an original thinker; he was most concerned with logic and ethics and is important mainly because he was the center of an intellectual nucleus which achieved further development in the eleventh century.

In this century the extreme realism we have mentioned is in vogue; it has a notable representative in Odon, of Tournai, where there was a very popular school. Odon applied his realism principally to the problems of the meaning of original sin and the creation of the souls of children; according to him, the latter question involved only the appearance of new individual, accidental qualities of the single human substance.

This realism is opposed by the opinion of the *nominales* (nominalists), the *sententia vocum*, which declares that the universals are *voces* (terms), not *res* (real things). The leader of this group is Roscellinus of Compiègne, who taught in France, England and Rome toward the end of the eleventh century. This budding nominalism scarcely outlived Roscellinus; it reappears only in the last centuries of the Middle Ages, and then it is based on different suppositions.

2. St. Anselm

LIFE AND WORKS. St. Anselm was born in 1033 and died in 1109. He was from Aosta, in Piedmont. As a member of the medieval Christian community and of the European community which·had begun to take shape, he did not restrict his life and activity to the country of his origin, but lived principally in France and England. He went first to the abbey of Bec, in Normandy, where he spent many years, the best and most important of his life. He was prior and then abbot of Bec, and ultimately was named Archbishop of Canterbury, in 1093; he remained in that office until his death. St. Anselm's entire life was devoted to study and religious activity, and in his last years he was concerned with upholding the Church's rights as a spiritual power, which were then being seriously threatened.

St. Anselm is the second great medieval philosopher, Scotus Erigena being the first. Strictly speaking, St. Anselm was the founder of Scholasticism, for it is only with him that this movement acquires its definite character. On the other hand, he is immersed in the Patristic tradition of Augustinian and Platonic (or, more precisely, Neoplatonic) origin. The intellectual influences which differ from those of Patristic speculation and later strongly affect the character of Scholasticism are not yet evident in him: the influences of the Arabs and, through them, Aristotle. St. Anselm is a faithful Augustinian; in the preface to his *Monologium* he writes: *Nihil potui invenire me dixisse quod*

non catholicorum Patrum et maxime beati Augustini scriptis cohaereat. He is
aware of his constant conformity with the Fathers of the Church and
particularly with St. Augustine. Nevertheless, we already detect in
Anselm the great lines which are to define Scholasticism, and in fact
his work constitutes a first synthesis of it. Thus, medieval philosophy
and theology are profoundly influenced by his thought.

St. Anselm wrote several books. Many are of predominantly theological interest; there are numerous letters full of doctrinal substance.
The most important philosophical works—all short pieces—are contained in the *Monologium* (*Exemplum meditandi de ratione fidei*—A Model
for Meditation on the Reason of Faith) and the *Proslogium*, which
carries as a motto the phrase which summarizes the meaning of all his
philosophy: *Fides quaerens intellectum* (Faith seeking understanding).
He also wrote the reply to Gaunilo's book on the fool, the *De veritate*
and the *Cur Deus homo?*

FAITH AND REASON. St. Anselm's theological—and philosophical—
work is primarily concerned with proofs of the existence of God. This is
the topic which receives most discussion in his writing and the one
most closely associated with his name. However, these proofs cannot
be properly understood unless one is aware of the whole range of St.
Anselm's thought.

St. Anselm begins with faith; the proofs are not meant to lend
support to faith, but are themselves supported by faith. His principle
is *credo ut intelligam* (I believe in order to understand). In the *Proslogium*,
his major work, he writes: *neque enim quaero intelligere ut credam, sed credo
ut intelligam* (For I do not wish to understand in order to believe; rather,
I believe in order to understand). However, this is not a question of
something distinct from faith; faith itself desires to know, seeks intellection, and this desire for knowledge arises from the internal character
of faith. St. Anselm distinguishes between living faith, which is actually
operative, and dead faith, which is useless; living faith is founded on
dilectio, love, and this is what gives it life. This love makes man, who is
separated from the face of God by sin, anxious to *return* to God's
presence. Living faith wants to contemplate the face of God; it wants
God to *reveal* Himself in the light, in truth. Therefore, living faith
seeks the *true God*, and this is *intelligere*, understanding. "If I did not
believe, I would not understand," adds St. Anselm; that is, without
faith, or rather, *dilectio*, love, he could not attain God's truth. This
is a clear echo of St. Augustine's statement, *non intratur in veritatem
nisi per caritatem*, which in turn is perhaps fully understood only in the
light of St. Anselm's work.

Thus we see that theology relates in a special way to St. Anselm's religion; however, the *result* of theology does not so relate. In his writings St. Anselm says that "The Christian should approach understanding through faith; he should not approach faith through understanding, or withdraw from faith if he cannot understand. When he *can* reach intelligence, he will be contented; and if he cannot understand, he should worship" (Epistle XLI). This statement is a clear definition of the intellectual basis for all of St. Anselm's philosophy.

THE ONTOLOGICAL ARGUMENT. In his *Monologium*, St. Anselm gives various proofs of the existence of God, but the most important proof is the one he expounds in the *Proslogium*, and which, since the time of Kant, has generally been referred to as the ontological argument. This proof of the existence of God has had enormous repercussions in the entire history of philosophy. Even during St. Anselm's lifetime a monk named Gaunilo attacked the proof, and St. Anselm himself replied to Gaunilo's objections. Later on, opinion was divided and interpretations of the argument differed. St. Bonaventure took a position close to that of St. Anselm; St. Thomas rejected the proof; Duns Scotus accepted it with modifications; Descartes and Leibniz made use of it, with certain alterations; then Kant, in his *Critique of Pure Reason*, established its impossibility in an apparently definitive way. Yet Hegel afterward restated the proof in different terms, and still later, in the nineteenth century, it was studied in depth by Brentano and especially by Father Gratry. Up to the present day the ontological argument is a central theme of philosophy, because it involves not only mere logical argumentation, but also a question that concerns all of metaphysics. This is the reason for the singular renown of St. Anselm's proof.

We cannot here enter into details of the interpretation of the argument.* It will be sufficient to indicate briefly its essential meaning. St. Anselm's point of departure is God, a hidden God who does not manifest Himself to man in his fallen state. This is a religious point of departure: the faith of man, who was made in order to see God but has not seen Him. This faith seeks to understand, to practice theology: it is a *fides quaerens intellectum*. But there does not yet appear the necessity or the possibility of *demonstrating* the existence of God. St. Anselm cites the thirteenth† psalm: *Dixit insipiens in corde suo : non est Deus* (The fool hath said in his heart, There is no God). This denial calls the existence of God into question for the first time and gives St. Anselm's proof a meaning it lacks without the fool's statement. St. Anselm formulates his famous proof in these terms: When the fool says that there is no

---

* See my book *San Anselmo y el insensato* [*Obras*, IV].
† [Psalm 13 in the Vulgate, Psalm 14 in the King James Version.—TRANS.]

God, he understands what he is saying. If we say that God is that entity such that no greater entity can be imagined, the fool will understand this as well. Therefore, God is in his understanding; what he denies is that God is also *in re*, that is, that He really exists. But if God exists only in the imagination we are able to imagine that He could also exist in reality, and this conception of Him is greater than the earlier one. Therefore, we are able to imagine something greater than God if He does not exist. But this contradicts our premise that God is such that nothing greater than He can be imagined. Then God, who exists in the understanding, must also exist in reality. That is, if He exists only in the understanding, He does not fulfill the necessary condition; therefore, it would not be God of whom we were speaking.

As a matter of fact, St. Anselm's proof shows that the existence of God cannot be denied. It consists of confronting the *fool's* denial with the *meaning* of what he is saying. The fool does not understand the full implication of what he is saying, and for this very reason he is a fool. He is not thinking of God, and his denial is an error. His folly consists of this: *he does not know what he is saying.* If, instead, we imagine God as fully as possible, we see that it is impossible that He should not exist. Therefore, St. Anselm confronts folly with the doctrine of intimacy, the return to oneself, following the example of St. Augustine. When man enters within himself and finds himself, he also finds God, in whose image and likeness he is made. Thus, the ontological argument is an appeal to the sense of intimacy, to the depths of the personality, and is based concretely on the refutation of the fool.

This meeting with God in the intimacy of the mind opens a clear path to St. Anselm's speculation. This is the course that medieval thought will follow in the subsequent period.

3. The Twelfth Century

After the work of St. Anselm, Scholasticism is established. There is a framework of problems within which Scholasticism can move forward, and that body of doctrine appears which could be called the "common property" of the Middle Ages, or the "Scholastic synthesis." This body of doctrine prepares the way for the great general works of the thirteenth century, especially St. Thomas' *Summa theologiae*. At the same time the world of ideas of Western Europe acquires stability; the historical groups that are to compose Europe attain consistency. During the entire twelfth century the social organization of the Middle Ages progresses toward consolidation, which it will achieve in the following century. The schools become important intellectual centers which will soon lead to the creation of the universities. The principal home of philosophy in this period is France, especially the schools of Chartres and Paris. Later, the foundation of the University of Paris, the most important intellectual focal point of the entire medieval era, will definitively establish Paris as the capital of Scholasticism.

In the twelfth century, the question of the universals is thoroughly discussed. In general, realism prevails, but there is a series of attempts to oppose the extremes of realism, and these attempts come close to the moderate solution that St. Thomas will impose. Arabic and Jewish influences are brought to bear intensively on Scholasticism and, with them, the influence of Aristotle, whose original works were almost unknown until then. This intellectual fermentation also gives rise to heterodox theological movements, especially pantheistic movements, and there is a resurgence of dualism in the Albigensian and Catharist heresies. Lastly, mysticism of a speculative nature enjoys a great flowering. All these tendencies, coming to the fullness of their development, will produce the culminating period in medieval philosophy, which includes Roger Bacon, Meister Eckhart, St. Bonaventure and St. Thomas Aquinas.

THE SCHOOL OF CHARTRES. The school of Chartres was founded by Fulbert, bishop of Chartres, who died at the beginning of the eleventh century; but only in the twelfth century did the school acquire its true importance as a center of Platonist and realist thought. Among the most interesting thinkers in this group are the brothers Bernard and Thierry (Theodoric) of Chartres, who were chancellors of the school. Their teachings are principally known through the works of their English pupil John of Salisbury. They believed that only the universal realities deserved the name of entities; that the individual sensibles were no more than shadows. Bernard distinguished three types of realities: God; matter, which was brought out of nothingness by the Creation; and the Ideas, exemplary forms through which the possibles and the existents are present in the mind of God. The union of the Ideas with matter produces the sensible world. A strong Platonic influence is visible in this extreme form of realism.

Gilbert de la Porrée (Gilbertus Porretanus), who became bishop of Poitiers, was a pupil of Bernard and chancellor of the school of Chartres after Bernard and before Thierry. Gilbert opposed the realism of the school of Chartres. He avoided all danger of pantheism by distinguishing the divine Ideas from their copies, which are the innate forms inherent in the sensible things. The universals are not the Ideas, but *images* of the Ideas. The mind compares similar essences and unites them mentally; this common form is the universal, genus or species.

Thus, Gilbert de la Porrée is the author of the first sketchy outline of the thirteenth-century solution to the problem of universals.

Other important thinkers related to the school of Chartres are William of Conches and the above-mentioned John of Salisbury, a keen and interesting philosopher who wrote two major works, the *Metalogicus* and the *Polycraticus*. Separate from this group, but related to it and engaging in polemics with it, are various adversaries of the extreme realist positions. These men fashion several theories to solve the problem of the universals, taking as their point of departure the existence of the individuals and considering the genera and species as different *aspects* of the individuals. Especially noteworthy among these philosophers are the Englishman Adelard (Æthelard) of Bath and the Fleming Walter (Gautier) of Mortagne, authors of the theory of the *respectus* (the aspects of the individuals), the *status* and, lastly, the *collectio*. In the theory of the *status*, or states, essences remain unchanged in themselves, but change their "state" according to the bodies with which they are united. In the theory of the *collectio*, a group of individuals taken collectively is accorded a universality that is denied to the individuals taken separately.

ABELARD. The figure of Abelard, the belligerent and passionate dialectician, together with the story of his affair with Héloïse, his castration and the restless nature of his entire life, are all too well known. There have even been attempts to construct on the basis of these established facts an image of Abelard as a freethinker and anti-scholastic, but modern research has proved this image to be false. Abelard was born near Nantes in 1079 into a family of soldiers who liked to spend a few years studying before taking up their military profession. Abelard was destined to do the same, but he was won over by the academic life and remained in it always. His pugnacious spirit led him into involvement in dialectics and polemics with his successive teachers. He attended the school of Roscellinus, then the school of William of Champeaux. Afterward, he founded a school at Melun, which was later transferred to Corbeil. Years later, he returned to Paris, studied theology with Anselm of Laon, and taught with enormous success. According to a letter written by a contemporary, his pupils came from all over France, Flanders, England and Swabia. After this period of glory came his misfortunes. Then Peter Abelard became a monk, leading his restless life and bearing his teachings from monastery to monastery until his death in 1142.

Abelard was a passionate and refined spirit. He was a highly cultured man, and it has been said that in him and in the entire twelfth century there is a partial anticipation of the Renaissance. His writings include a large theological work, from which an *Introductio ad theologiam* is preserved; his famous book *Sic et non*, in which he unites apparently contradictory theological and Biblical authorities in an effort of conciliation; a philosophical work, *Scito te ipsum, seu Ethica*; a *Dialectica*; and various other works.

Peter Abelard establishes firm relationships between philosophy and religion. The Christian mysteries, according to him, cannot be demonstrated and known experimentally; they can only be understood or believed by means of analogies or similitudes. In spite of this formulation, Abelard tended in practice to interpret various dogmas —that of the Trinity, for example—and lapsed into errors that were condemned. With regard to the question of the universals, he first criticized Roscellinus' "nominalism," but later especially attacked William of Champeaux because of his extreme realist doctrines. According to Abelard, the intellect apprehends the similarities between individuals by means of abstraction. The result of this abstraction—which is always based on the imagination, because knowledge begins with the individual and the sensible—is the universal. The universal cannot be a thing (*res*), because things are not predicated of subjects, whereas universals are so predicated. But the universal is not merely a *vox* (a mere term) either; it is a *sermo*, a word as used in *discourse*, which is related to the real content; it is a true *nomen* (noun) in the strict sense that is equivalent to *vox significativa* (a meaningful word). The theory of the *sermones* comes close to what will later be formulated as conceptualism.

Therefore, although Abelard does not have a doctrinal importance comparable to that of Scotus Erigena or St. Anselm, he exercised an extraordinary personal influence in the schools and made keen contributions to many important questions. His activity prepared the way for the apogee of Paris as a Scholastic center and for the philosophical and theological fulfillment of the thirteenth century.

THE VICTORINES. The Augustine Abbey of St. Victor in Paris becomes in the twelfth century one of the most important intellectual centers of Christendom. Above all, it is a center of mysticism, but of a mysticism which does not exclude rational knowledge or even the profane sciences, which it actually encourages energetically. The Abbey of St. Victor indulges intensively in philosophy and theology; the Victorines' profound religious spirituality is sustained by a precise and wide-ranging knowledge. In the work of the philosophers of St. Victor, especially Hugh and Richard, the systematization of Scholasticism takes a step forward.

Hugh of St. Victor, the major figure among them, is the author of a comprehensive synoptic work entitled *De sacramentis*, which is already a *Summa theologiae*, more complete and perfect than Abelard's attempt. Hugh recommends learning all the sciences, sacred and profane; he believes that they mutually support and strengthen one another and that they are all useful. He distinguishes four sciences: theoretic science, which investigates truth; practical science, or ethics; mechanical science, the study of human activities; and logic, the science of expression and discussion. Hugh especially recommends the study of the seven liberal arts, the *trivium* and the *quadrivium*, which he considers to be inseparable.

In discussing the problem of the universals and knowledge, Hugh of St. Victor also uses the theory of abstraction, Aristotelian in origin, in advance of the great influence of Aristotle in the thirteenth century. He considers the history of the world to be ordered about two principal moments: the Creation of the world and its restoration through Christ Incarnate and the sacraments. The work of restoration is the primary object of the Scriptures, but the Creation is studied by the profane sciences. In this way the two classes of sciences are united in Hugh's thought. Hugh's philosophy is strongly tinged with Augustinianism; he affirms that man's first knowledge is of his own existence and of the soul, which is distinct from the body. This is another philosophy of intimacy, and this, too, is a facet of Hugh's orthodox mystical orientation.

Richard of St. Victor, a pupil of Hugh, restated his master's thought and continued it with original elements. Richard wrote a *Liber excerptionum* and the *De Trinitate*. Concerned with the proofs of the existence of God, he rejected the a priori proofs and especially emphasized the validity of sensory perception and observation. Richard's work, too, contains the close union between mysticism and rational argument that was to culminate in the speculative mysticism of Meister Eckhart.

The knowledge of God and of man illuminate each other. We know man through experience, and what we find in him serves as a basis for inferring—*mutatis mutandis*—some of the properties of the divine Entity. Conversely, the information which rational argument gives us concerning the Deity can be applied toward a knowledge of man, the image of God, in his most profound being. Perhaps Richard of St. Victor is the philosopher who made the most technical and acute use of that intellectual method which consists in contemplating the reality of God and His human image alternately with the various suitable means for doing so. Therefore, his *De Trinitate* is one of the most interesting medieval contributions to theology and anthropology at one and the same time.

The great twelfth-century Christian figure St. Bernard of Clairvaux is also closely related to mysticism. It was St. Bernard who vivified and inspired the Cistercian Order, which had been founded at the end of the preceding century in order to make religious practice at Cluny more rigorous and ascetic. The Cistercian spirit was one of extreme austerity, as was St. Bernard's own life. His spirit of ardent religiosity and his capabilities as a leader of men are well known. He grants philosophy its due, but mysticism is dominant in his thought; indeed, St. Bernard is one of the principal representatives of mysticism in the Middle Ages.

Among the theologians who use philosophy only as a tool, the most interesting is Peter Lombard, called the *magister sententiarum* (master of the sentences, or maxims) par excellence. He was bishop of Paris, and died in 1164. Throughout the Middle Ages his *Libri IV sententiarum* were a repository of theology, commented on numberless times in the entire Scholastic age that followed.

THE HERESIES OF THE TWELFTH CENTURY. This century, so full of intellectual activity, could not keep itself free from heterodox currents in theology. These currents were related to philosophic orientations marginal to the general development of Scholasticism. In this sense it can be stated, along with Maurice de Wulf, that these philosophies are "antischolastic"; but it should not be forgotten that they have in common the same set of problems as Scholasticism and that it is for this reason that the solutions of the two groups appear divergent and that the polemics are kept alive throughout the Middle Ages. These heresies are principally concerned with a few points that received special discussion: atheism (infrequent in its strict form), pantheism, materialism, the eternity of the world. These are the most disputed points, those to which Arabic philosophy will later contribute, and which will have heterodox repercussions until the end of the Middle Ages.

There appear in the twelfth century, especially in France and some places in Italy, two different but interrelated heretical movements: the Albigenses (from Albi in southern France) and the Cathari. The violent struggles which these heresies aroused are well known, as is the intense activity of theologians and preachers which they produced, an activity that culminated in the foundation of the Dominican Order by St. Dominic (Domingo de Guzmán). These heresies professed a dualism of good and evil; evil, opposed to God, had an independent nature. This was tantamount to a denial of Christian monotheism and, in addition, the heresy had moral consequences. *Cathari* means *the pure*; among the Cathari, the *perfect* led a particularly austere life and constituted a special clergy. This contrast between a model difficult to follow and a great majority incapable of such perfection led to serious immorality. The suppression of the Albigensian movement, at the beginning of the thirteenth century, was extremely severe and ended after several "crusades," with the consequent devastation of the regions affected by the struggle. The heresy of the Cathari was particularly dangerous, because their materialism, which denied the spirituality and the immortality of the soul, contradicted the Catholic dogmas and, at the same time, the very foundation of Christian ethics.

In another direction, there was a series of movements that more or less approximated *pantheism*. The Neoplatonic concepts of monism and emanation were in vogue. One such philosopher was Bernard of Tours, author of a book called *De mundi universitate*. The sect led by Amalric of Bena was more important. According to Amalric, everything is one because everything is God: *omnia unum, quia quidquid est est Deus*. The being of all things is based on the being of God; thus, there is an immanence of the Deity in the world. Man is a manifestation or apparition of God, as is Christ Himself. These ideas stirred up much controversy, had many repercussions (for example, in the work of Joachim of Flora) and encountered lively opposition. Another representative of the pantheistic tendencies was David of Dinant, who made a distinction between God, souls and matter, but believed that they were one in number and that God was identical with matter. In 1215, the Cardinal Robert de Courçon forbade the reading in the University of Paris of the physical and metaphysical works of Aristotle, which had just become known, together with the writings of David of Dinant, Amalric and a certain Maurice of Spain (Mauritius Hispanus). In this condemnation of Aristotle along with the representatives of the pantheistic tendencies, which were so foreign to his thought, can be seen the confusion of Aristotelian doctrines, still little known, with those of certain Arabic commentators. The influence of Averroës, especially, will later produce an unorthodox movement known by the name of Latin Averroism.

4. EASTERN PHILOSOPHIES

At the same time that philosophy was developing in the West, a similar movement had originated among the peoples of the East, especially the Arabs and Jews. In no case is this an original, autonomous Arabic or Hebrew philosophy. Nor is it an isolated speculation, without contact with the Christians. In the first place, the impulse comes particularly from the Greeks, principally Aristotle and some of the Neoplatonists. In the second place, Christianity has a decisive influence on Moslem and Jewish thought. In the case of Mohammedanism, the influence extends to the religion itself. Strictly speaking, Islam might be considered a Judaeo-Christian heresy that appears by virtue of Mohammed's connections with Jews and Christians. The Moslem dogmas are formulated negatively, with a polemic air, against the doctrine of the Trinity, the influence of which, for example, they denounce: "There is no God but Allah; he is not the son or the father, nor does he have a partner." Here may be noted a polemic against the primitive polytheism of the Arabs as well as against the Trinitarian dogma. Conversely, the philosophy of the Arabs and Jews is known to the Christian Scholastics and influences them strongly. In addition, acquaintance with the works of Aristotle gave Eastern philosophy a head start with respect to Christian philosophy, and in the twelfth century Eastern thought had already reached maturity, whereas this was not to occur in Europe until the following century. But, above all, the great role of the Arabs and Jews was as the transmitters of Aristotelian thought. It was especially the Spanish Arabs who brought the texts of the great Greek philosopher to the countries of the West, and this contribution marks the period of Scholasticism's maturity. From the point of view of this transmission as well as from the point of view of philosophic activity, Arabic Spain merits first place in the world of medieval Eastern philosophy.

Arabic Philosophy

CHARACTER. In the seventh century, during the Abbasid Empire, the Syrians introduce Aristotle's thought to the Arabs in rather indirect fashion. The Aristotelian texts are translated—not always accurately—from Greek to Syriac, from Syriac to Arabic, and sometimes also pass through the Hebrew language. These extremely indirect Arabic translations are in turn translated into Latin and then come to the attention of the Scholastics. Sometimes Aristotle's works are translated first into Spanish and then into Latin; on the other hand, a Greek version is occasionally available, and then the Latin translation is made directly from the original. Moreover, the Aristotle to which the Arabs are introduced has frequently been disfigured by the Neoplatonic commentators. Nevertheless, a considerable Aristotelian element enters into what has been called *Arabic syncretism*. The Arabs—especially Averroës—were the great commentators on Aristotle in the Middle Ages.

Arabic philosophy is also a *Moslem Scholasticism*. Its principal topic is the rational interpretation of the Koran, and the relationships between religion and philosophy parallel those in the West. The same thing happens with Jewish philosophy; in this way, around the three religions, three scholastic movements of unequal importance are created, and all three influence one another.

ARAB PHILOSOPHERS IN THE EAST. Arabic philosophic speculation begins around the intellectual center of Baghdad. A first great figure appears in the ninth century; this is Alkindi, a contemporary of John Scotus Erigena. Another, more important, thinker lives in the following century: Alfarabi, who died around 950. Alfarabi does not limit himself to translating; instead he devotes himself principally to commenting on Aristotle and introduces the concept of the "active intellect" as a separate form of matter, a theory which came to have great importance in Moslem philosophy. He also introduces the distinction between essence and existence. Later we have Avicenna (Ibn Sina), who lived from 980 to 1037. He was a philosopher, theologian and one of the most famous physicians of the Islamic world and of the whole medieval period. He was singularly precocious, and his life was disturbed and occupied by pleasures and public duties, but in spite of this he left a large body of work. His most important work, *Al-Shifa* (The Book of Recovery), is the *Summa* of his philosophy and shows strong Aristotelian influences. Avicenna also wrote *Al-Nadjat* (The Book of Salvation), as well as many other treatises. In the Middle Ages, the so-called *Avicennae metaphysices compendium* was very influential, and a large share of the ideas of the Christian Scholastics derives from it. Avicenna accepted the distinction between essence and existence, and in his hands it acquired great importance. He also introduced the concept of intentionality, which is so fruitful in our day, and left a profound imprint on all later philosophy, particularly on that of St. Thomas.

In opposition to this group of philosophers there appears among the Arabs an orthodox theological movement that is linked with the mysticism of *Sufism*, which was greatly influenced by Christianity (cf. Asín: *El Islam cristianizado*) and by Indian Neoplatonic currents. The most important of these theologians is Al-Gazel, author of two books entitled *The Destruction of the Philosophers* and *The Restoration of the Sciences of Religion.* Unlike other Arabs who accepted the theories of emanation, Al-Gazel was an orthodox mystic, not a pantheist.

THE SPANISH ARAB PHILOSOPHERS. From the tenth to the thirteenth centuries, Arabic Spain is an extremely important intellectual center. Cordova is the nucleus of this flowering. In the East philosophy begins to decline, but in Spain it is at an apogee, and the Spanish branch of philosophy represents a continuation of the speculation which culminated in Avicenna's work. Beginning at the end of the eleventh century and all during the twelfth century, several great Moslem thinkers make their appearance in the Western world: Avempace (Ibn Bajja), who died in 1138; Ibn Tufail (1100–1185), and most notably Averroës.

Averroës (Ibn Rushd) was born in Cordova in 1126 and died in 1198. He was a physician, mathematician, lawyer, theologian and philosopher; he held the position of judge and was in and out of favor depending on the times. During the entire Middle Ages Averroës is considered the commentator par excellence: *Averois, che'l gran comento feo* (Averroës, who made the great commentary), Dante remarks in the *Divine Comedy*. Averroës also wrote original treatises, and in the following centuries his thinking greatly influenced the treatment of several philosophical topics.

First among these topics is the eternity of the world, and therefore of matter and motion. Matter is a universal potentiality, and the prime mover extracts the active forces from matter; this process is repeated eternally and is the cause of the sensible, material world. Secondly, Averroës believes that the human intellect is an immaterial, eternal and single form; it is the last of the planetary intelligences and there is only one for the entire species; it is therefore impersonal. The different ways in which man is united with the universal intellect determine the various classes of knowledge, ranging from the sensible to the illuminating wisdom of mysticism and prophecy. For this reason individual consciousness is lost, and only the consciousness of the species endures; Averroës denies personal immortality; only the one intellect of the species lasts forever. The eternity of motion and the oneness of human intellect are the two areas in which Latin Averroism appears at the heart of Western philosophy. Finally, Averroës establishes a system of relationships between faith and knowledge. He distinguishes three classes of spirits: men of proof; men of dialectics, who are content with probable reasonings; and men of exhortation, who are satisfied with oratory and images. The Koran's meaning varies depending on how profoundly it is interpreted, and therefore it is useful to everyone. This idea gives rise to the famous theory of the *double truth* which was dominant in Latin Averroism; according to this theory a thing can be theologically true and philosophically false, and vice versa.

Jewish Philosophy
In the Middle Ages, particularly in Spain, Jewish philosophy develops under the influence of the Arabs. The eleventh and twelfth

centuries are the centuries of greatest activity, just as they are for Arabic philosophy. Jewish philosophy is similar in character to Arabic philosophy, from which indeed it derives, but is also influenced by Neoplatonic and mystic elements of the Cabbala. Just as the Arabs attempt to establish a Moslem Scholasticism, so the Jews try to create a Hebrew Scholasticism, and their philosophy is inseparably linked with theological questions.

One of the most important Spanish Jewish philosophers is Avicebron (Ibn Gabirol), who lived in the first half of the eleventh century and who was very well known among Christians for his *Fons vitae* (The Well of Life). Avicebron's most famous thesis is that the soul is composed of potentiality and actuality and therefore is material, although not necessarily corporeal. Avicebron was greatly influenced by Neoplatonism. Other interesting thinkers are Ibn Zaddik of Cordova and Judah Halevy, author of the *Sefer ha-Kuzari*, a book of Jewish apologetics. However, the principal figure of Jewish philosophy is Maimonides.

Moses ben Maimon or Moses Maimonides (1135–1204) was born in Cordova, as was Averroës, his Moslem contemporary, and his principal work is the *Guide for the Perplexed* (*Dux perplexorum*); this title used to be incorrectly interpreted as a guide for the *strayed* or *misled*. It was written in Arabic, in Hebrew characters, under the title of *Dalalat al-Hairin,* and later translated into Hebrew with the title *Moreh Nebuchim.* The book's purpose is to reconcile Aristotelian philosophy with Judaic religion. It is a true *Summa* of Jewish Scholasticism, the most complex and perfect example of this type of work in Eastern philosophy. The supreme object of religion and philosophy is the knowledge of God; it is necessary to find agreement between the principles and results of both. Maimonides' treatise is directed at men who, possessing this knowledge, are uncertain or perplexed about how to make the two things compatible; it is a question of indecision, not of straying from the path.

Maimonides' thinking is similar to that of Averroës, but the two men disagree on several points. Maimonides does not completely accept the allegorical interpretation of the Bible; however, he admits that it is necessary to keep in mind the undeniable results of philosophy when interpreting the Bible, and to avoid letting oneself be dominated by literalism. In spite of its conservative character, Maimonides' philosophy seemed suspect to the Jewish theologians and encountered considerable opposition. His is a negative philosophy; one can say what God is not, but not what He is. God's essence is not accessible, but His effects are. There is a hierarchy of spheres between God and the entities of the world; in the form of Providence God concerns Himself with the totality of the things. The human intellect is single and separate, just as Averroës says. An individual man possesses passive intellect, but through the workings of the active intellect an *acquired intellect* develops in him, and this acquired intellect is destined to unite with the active intellect after death. This unification which philosophy effects thus provides man with the possibility of perpetuating a part of himself. These ideas influenced the thought of Spinoza, who, being a Jew, takes Maimonides' work into account.

The importance of Arabic and Jewish philosophy—particularly that of their principal representatives, Avicenna, Averroës and Maimonides—is great; however, this is due more to their influences on Christian Scholasticism than to their inherent interest. The Arabic and Jewish achievements in the fields of metaphysics and theology cannot be compared with those of the great medieval Christians. Yet the Arabic and Jewish thinkers had one great advantage which allowed them to gain a century on the Christians: their knowledge of Aristotle's work. Until the thirteenth century they possessed philosophical material enormously superior to that of their contemporary Christian thinkers. In this book, whose subject is Western philosophy, we cannot deal with the particulars of Arabic and Jewish thought, but only with their ties with philosophy in the West: their Greek inspiration, contribution to Scholasticism and influence on subsequent Western philosophy. A later figure of decisive importance was the Arabic philosopher Ibn Khaldun. Of Spanish ancestry, he was born in Tunis in 1332 and died in Cairo in 1406. His major contribution to philosophy is the *Muqaddimah*, the introduction to his *Universal History*, a brilliant philosophy of society and history.*

5. THE SPIRITUAL WORLD OF THE THIRTEENTH CENTURY

THE REAPPEARANCE OF ARISTOTLE. The thirteenth century marks a new phase of philosophy. In its early stages Christianity had to confront Greek thought, and this necessity arises once again under somewhat different circumstances in the Middle Ages. Up until this time Christian philosophy had been constructed on the basis of a few Greek writings of Platonic or Neoplatonic character; in the thirteenth century the thought of the greatest of the Greek philosophers bursts forth in the West, and Scholasticism has to take into account this marvelously profound and acute philosophy which comes to it by way of the Arabs

* Cf. Miguel Cruz Hernández: *La filosofía árabe*, Madrid, 1963.

and which is different from anything in its own philosophic tradition. Christian philosophy passes through a stage in which Aristotelian thought is assimilated; this task is accomplished primarily by St. Albertus Magnus and St. Thomas Aquinas. This effort enormously enriches the possibilities of Scholasticism, but at the same time it leads Christian philosophy away from paths down which its original nature might have taken it. In any case, Aristotle's appearance signals the arrival of a new and extremely fruitful era.

A large and important role in this labor of assimilation falls to Spain. Ever since the twelfth century there had been intense activity in Spain in the field of translation; the school of translators in Toledo which was founded by the Archbishop Don Raimundo deserves special mention because it was one of the most active centers in all of Europe. Arabic and Jewish books were translated: the works of Alfarabi, Al-Gazel, Avicenna, Avicebron; later, the Arabs bring to the West their translations of Aristotle, which are translated into Castilian and then into Latin or else directly into Latin. The most important of these translators was Gundisalvus, or Dominicus Gundisalvus, sometimes mistakenly called Gundissalinus, the author of a philosophical encyclopedia of Aristotelian character entitled *De divisione philosophiae* and a treatise called *De immortalitate animae*. Gerard of Cremona and Johannes Hispanus were also important. A few translations directly from the Greek are also made in Europe, and these are much superior to the indirect translations; among the best are those of Robert Grosseteste, bishop of Lincoln, and, most notably, those of William of Moerbeke, the great Dominican translator who undertook the retranslation and revision of Aristotle's works at the request of St. Thomas.

All of Aristotle's philosophy but particularly his *Metaphysics* and his books on natural science was suspect. His thought was seen to consist of a great number of important doctrines mixed in with the rather unorthodox theories of the Arabic commentators. In 1210 a provincial council in Paris forbade all persons to read and comment on Aristotle's works on natural philosophy; in 1215 the legate Robert de Courçon renewed the prohibition but authorized the reading of Aristotle's works on logic and ethics in the newly founded University of Paris. On the other hand, the reading of all of Aristotle's work continued to be authorized in Toulouse. A little later, Pope Gregory IX ordered a revision of Aristotle's work, so that after it was corrected he could allow it to be read. Aristotle's fame increased steadily, to such a point that in 1366 Pope Urban V's legates made the reading of Aristotle a requirement for the degree in arts. It was the immense labor of St. Thomas more than anything else that effected the incorporation of Aristotelian philosophy into Christian thought.

From this time, Scholasticism's destiny is decided. To the Platonic-Augustinian influences is added the even more important influence of Aristotle's thought. The Christian thinkers now possess immeasurably superior intellectual material and achieve maturity. The thirteenth century also witnesses the simultaneous appearance of the most important universities—most notably those of Paris and Oxford—and of the two great mendicant orders, the Franciscans and the Dominicans. Together these elements produce the great classical century of the Middle Ages.

THE FOUNDING OF THE UNIVERSITIES. The University of Paris, one of the greatest spiritual powers of the Middle Ages, is created at the beginning of the thirteenth century. A university was then neither a building nor a single center of learning, but a large gathering of teachers and pupils from the schools (*universitas magistrorum et scholarium*), all subject to the authority of a chancellor. University life prospers in Paris; little by little it becomes organized and is finally divided into four faculties: theology, arts (philosophy), law and medicine. Most numerous are the students and teachers of the faculty of arts, and these are divided according to *nations* (those from Picardy, from Gaul, from Normandy, from England, and the like); their leader is the rector, who ends up by replacing the chancellor in the direction of the university. The degrees awarded by the university are the baccalaureate, the licentiate and the doctorate, the rank of *doctor* or *magister*. The University of Paris was subject to two protective influences: that of the king of France and that of the pope. Both realized the immense importance of this intellectual center, an influence that has even been compared with that of the Empire and the papacy. Pope Innocent III was the great protector and inspirer of the University of Paris in its first years.

A little later the University of Oxford is founded, and it too acquires great importance. Thus an English intellectual center distinct from the one in France is created in which the Platonic and Augustinian traditions are kept very much alive. Aristotelianism is also cultivated in the English university, but there the emphasis is on the empirical and scientific aspects of Aristotle's system. Instead of underscoring the logical and metaphysical aspects and subordinating the theological aspect, Oxford makes use of the mathematics and physics of Aristotle and the Arabs and prepares the way for Occam's nominalism and the English empiricism of the modern era. The University of Cambridge dates from somewhat later, but was fully organized in the fourteenth

century. The University of Bologna is as old as that of Paris, but in the
thirteenth century it was important as a center for legal rather than
philosophical studies. Later, the universities of Padua, Salamanca,
Toulouse and Montpellier were founded; then, in the fourteenth century, those of Prague, Vienna, Heidelberg, Cologne and, in Spain, the
University of Valladolid.

THE MENDICANT ORDERS. At the beginning of the thirteenth century the two great mendicant orders—the Franciscan and the Dominican—are formed; in a certain sense these replace the Benedictine
Order as the focal point of intellectual life. St. Francis of Assisi founds
the Order of the Friars Minor, and St. Dominic (Domingo de Guzmán) founds the Order of Preachers. In principle, the functions of
these orders are different: *devotion* appertains more to the Franciscans
and *preaching* appertains more to the Dominicans. The latter order,
which was formed to combat the Albigensian heresy, was charged with
the defense of orthodoxy, and therefore the Inquisition was entrusted
to it. But the Franciscans also quickly display great theological and
philosophical activity of comparable volume and quality. The Franciscans preserve the earlier Platonic-Augustinian influences, particularly in the branch which St. Bonaventure represents; but after
Duns Scotus the Franciscans, like the Dominicans, partake of Aristotelianism.

The mendicant orders quickly penetrate the University of Paris, but
not without great polemics with the laymen. Finally the presence of the
Franciscan and Dominican Orders is accepted, and then they attain
such influence that the University comes under their control. The first
Dominican teacher was Roland of Cremona and the first Franciscan
was Alexander of Hales. From that time forward the greatest figures of
medieval philosophy belong to these orders: St. Albertus Magnus, St.
Thomas Aquinas and Meister Eckhart are Dominicans; St. Bonaventure, Roger Bacon, Duns Scotus and William of Occam are Franciscans. Thus the Friars Minor and the Preachers both maintain
themselves at the level of true philosophic creativity. If St. Thomas
systematized Scholasticism and incorporated Aristotle into Christian
thought better than anyone else, then, to compensate, the English
Franciscans established the basis for nominalist physics and prepared
the way for the modern natural science of Galileo and Newton, on the
one hand, and, on the other, for the philosophy that was to culminate
in the period of idealism from Descartes to Leibniz.

6. ST. BONAVENTURE

LIFE AND WORKS. St. Bonaventure (John of Fidanza) was born at

Bagnorea in Tuscany in 1221. He entered the Franciscan Order, and studied in Paris as a pupil of Alexander of Hales, an interesting thinker who has left us an important *Summa theologiae*. St. Bonaventure taught in Paris as Alexander's successor during the polemics against the mendicant orders, and was a good friend of St. Thomas. In 1257 he was named General of the Order and gave up teaching. He died while taking part in the Council of Lyons in 1274. The Church has given him the name of *Doctor seraphicus*.

St. Bonaventure's principal works are the *Commentaries on the Sentences* [of Peter Lombard], the *Quaestiones disputatae*, the *De reductione artium ad theologiam*, the *Breviloquium* and, above all, the *Itinerarium mentis in Deum*.

What St. Bonaventure represents in the thirteenth century is the *spirit of continuity*; thanks to him the general lines of traditional Scholastic ideology are maintained. In his *Commentaries on the Sentences* he writes explicitly: *Non enim intendo novas opiniones adversare, sed communes et approbatas retexere* (For I do not intend to put forth new opinions, but to renew commonly held and approved ones). His personal character, as well as the influences of St. Augustine, St. Bernard and the Victorines on the development of his thought, lead him to continue these major currents of twelfth-century speculative mysticism. He emphasizes the more practical and emotional sides of theology rather than the purely theoretic side, thus becoming an unmistakable forerunner of the nominalists of the next two centuries. St. Bonaventure, full of religious ardor, is imbued with a tenderness that is typical of his authentically Franciscan lineage. For St. Bonaventure, natural things, created after the semblance of the Deity, retain a trace of Him; love of the things is also love of God, of whom they bear this trace. It should not be forgotten that these tender feelings of the Franciscans toward nature are in no way alien to the splendid growth of mathematical physics in the Renaissance, although this may seem strange to some.

DOCTRINE. The goal of human knowledge is God. This knowledge is gained in different ways and on different levels and culminates in the mystic union. The influence of St. Augustine is evident in St. Bonaventure's writings. For St. Bonaventure, philosophy is in reality *itinerarium mentis in Deum* (the journey of the mind toward God). Knowledge of God can be obtained from nature, since natural things bear a trace of Him. God can be known in a more direct way in His own image, which is our soul—a reappearance of St. Augustine's and St. Anselm's theme of the inner man. When divine grace communicates the three theological virtues, God is seen *in imagine*, within ourselves. Lastly, God can be known directly, in His being, in His goodness, in the very mystery of the Trinity and, as a culminating experience in ecstatic contemplation, in the *apex of the mind* (*apex mentis*), to use St. Bonaventure's expression.

St. Bonaventure believes in the possibility of demonstrating the existence of God, and accepts St. Anselm's ontological proof. The *proper* understanding of the divine essence makes us see the necessity for His existence. With regard to God and the soul, St. Bonaventure does not believe that they are known by means of the senses, as the other things are, but directly; God is light, and this knowledge is gained by means of the uncreated light. *Necessario enim oportet ponere quod anima novit Deum et se ipsam et quae sunt in se ipsa sine adminiculo sensuum exteriorum* (For it must of necessity be posited that the soul knows God, itself, and that which is in itself without the aid of the external senses). Moreover, St. Bonaventure, rejecting the Averroist doctrine of the oneness of the intellect of mankind, insists with special emphasis that man is the efficient cause of his own mental actions.

St. Bonaventure affirms the plurality of the substantial forms; besides the *forma completiva*, he recognizes other subsidiary forms. This theory was generally professed by the Franciscans, from Alexander of Hales to the end of the Middle Ages. The world was created within time; this dogmatic truth is denied by no one except the heterodox Averroists. But in addition St. Bonaventure believes that this truth is known not only through revelation but also rationally, and that the Creation *ab aeterno*, which St. Thomas considers possible, is contradictory. This problem of the eternity of the world is one of the central questions of the period, aroused by study of Aristotle and by the Arabic commentators. St. Bonaventure and St. Thomas, who are in agreement in regard to the temporality of the Creation, differ concerning the origin of the knowledge of this truth. The Franciscan assigns this knowledge to reason, whereas the Dominican refers it to faith.

From the work of St. Bonaventure is derived an entire current of medieval speculation, one which will be extremely fruitful. The controversy between this direction of thought and the Thomist position animates the philosophy of the Middle Ages. And if it is true on the one hand that Thomism dominated Scholasticism in greater measure, on the other hand the orientation of the Franciscan thinkers has exerted a greater influence on modern philosophy, which represents the most authentic and fruitful continuation of medieval Christian thought.

FOLLOWERS OF ST. BONAVENTURE. The great Franciscan master's activity as a teacher was continued by a long succession of pupils and followers. In the first line is Matthew of Aquasparta, who taught in Paris and Bologna, and was General of the Order, as well as a cardinal and bishop of Oporto. Another personal pupil of St. Bonaventure was John Peckham, who was a master at Oxford and later Archbishop of Canterbury. Later, less direct, followers were Petrus Johannis Olivi (Pierre Olieu) and, above all, Richard of Middleton, known as Ricardus de Mediavilla.

The influence of these Franciscan masters was very great; they preserved the general lines of St. Bonaventure's thought in the face of the prevailing Thomism. Nevertheless, at the end of the thirteenth century, there appeared once more within the Order of the Friars Minor a figure who was to play a leading role in philosophy, John Duns Scotus. From that moment on, the Franciscan movement was embodied in Scotism, and the *direct* influence of St. Bonaventure was diminished. But it should not be forgotten that in reality his influence endures efficaciously, in the most interesting way possible in philosophy: not in a close and unchanging teacher-pupil relationship, but as the inspiration of a metaphysical renewal. The role of an authentic philosopher is not to perpetuate himself within any one "ism," but to be effectually present in the thought of other philosophers who have their own, different, names, and thus to activate the inexorable advance of the history of philosophy.

7. ARISTOTELICO-SCHOLASTIC PHILOSOPHY

As we have seen, the thirteenth century is faced with the enormous problem of coming to grips with Aristotle, with a philosophy of a depth and importance which strike one immediately upon first contact. In Aristotle's system there are mental tools which make great progress possible, but they must now be applied to themes very different from those for which they were originally invented. The intimate union of theology and philosophy known as Scholasticism is something completely different from the realm of ideas in which Aristotle's thought operated. How can Aristotle's thought be applied to the problems of the Middle Ages? And there is a still more serious obstacle. Aristotle's system does not merely comprise the extremely perfect logic of the *Organon*; nor is it merely an arsenal of concepts—matter, form, substance, accident, categories, and the like—which are useful as tools. Before all else, it is *a philosophy*, a metaphysics, conceived in the Greek language, based on radically different, non-Christian, suppositions, but a philosophy which nevertheless in many senses seems to be *truth*. What is to be made of this? Aristotle speaks of God and says extremely acute and interesting things about Him; he speaks of the world and of motion, and accounts for their existence with an enlightening penetration as yet unknown in the Middle Ages. But this God is not the Christian God; He is not the Creator, He does not have three persons, His relations with the world are different. Nor is the Aristotelian world the one which came forth from the hands of God according to the book of Genesis.

This is a very serious problem. Scholasticism cannot renounce Aristotle; it cannot ignore him. The Stagirite's philosophy commands attention through its overwhelming superiority and the truth which it so obviously contains. But it is necessary to adapt it to the new situation, to the problems that concern men of the thirteenth century. Aristotle's thought must be assimilated into Christian philosophy. What consequences will this have for Christian thinking? That is another question. Perhaps the compelling brilliance of the Aristotelian system was too great to be adopted without risk. Perhaps Aristotle's influence obliged Christian philosophy to become something different from itself, and frustrated certain original potentialities that might have come to maturity if another path had been followed. This is still an open question.

The influence of Aristotle is already evident in the works of St. Bonaventure, but only marginally, in a secondary way; the Peripatetic system did not affect the central core of St. Bonaventure's philosophy, which remained essentially under the influence of Plato and St. Augustine. This was not enough. It was necessary to confront resolutely the gigantic mass of Aristotelian philosophy, to investigate it all, try to understand it and incorporate it into the ideological system of the Middle Ages. This is the extraordinary task that was undertaken and achieved in the thirteenth century by two Dominicans, master and pupil, both canonized by the Church: Albert of Bollstädt (known in his own day as Albert of Cologne and today as St. Albertus Magnus) and St. Thomas Aquinas.

St. Albertus Magnus

LIFE AND WRITINGS. St. Albert was probably born in 1193—the date is not certain; others say 1206 or 1207. He died in Cologne in 1280. He entered the Dominican Order and worked and traveled a great deal, teaching at Cologne, Hildesheim, Freiburg, Ratisbon and Strassburg. He returned to Cologne, where he was the teacher of St. Thomas Aquinas, and from there moved on to Paris, the center of Scholasticism. Afterward he was bishop of Ratisbon. He finally settled in Cologne, where he followed a normal course of life and instruction. St. Albert's activity as teacher and cleric was extraordinary.

His writings are voluminous. The authority he acquired was so enormous that he was quoted alongside such great men of the past as Aristotle, Averroës or Avicenna, according to Roger Bacon's emphatic statement, or alongside the Church Fathers. His ample and rich works are principally paraphrases of the greater part of Aristotle's books, but he also produced original treatises on philosophy and theology, and a vast accumulation of erudition which also includes the work of the Arabs and Jews and which made possible the brilliant synthesis of his pupil, St. Thomas.

THE WORK OF ST. ALBERTUS MAGNUS. St. Albert's purpose was to interpret and assimilate all of Aristotle's philosophical disciplines: *nostra intentio est omnes dictas partes facere Latinis intelligibiles* ("our intention is to make all the aforementioned parts intelligible to those who read Latin"). Thus, he *paraphrased* the works of Aristotle, explaining them at length, in order to make them more easily understood, and augmenting them with commentaries borrowed from the Arabs and the Jews as well as some of his own. This attempt at popularization met with great difficulties, which caused numerous defects in St. Albert's writings. These writings suffer from a frequent lack of clarity; the sense of perspective is often lost; there is no rigorous and precise mental architecture, such as St. Thomas will later supply. Furthermore, the assimilation which is sought for is often not attained. St. Albertus Magnus was too much the prisoner of the traditional thought-structure of Scholasticism. He poured forth his immense knowledge of Aristotle into these Scholastic molds, but did not succeed in uniting the Hellenic thinker's philosophy and Christian mentality into a congruent and harmonious synthesis.

What he did accomplish was to put into circulation an incalculable number of ideas, which had now become the common property of the thinkers of the period. Henceforth Aristotle's philosophy is readily available, something that can be easily studied and utilized. The difficult task of assimilation has already been attempted; the materials are already at hand: St. Thomas will find the most painful and least profound part of the labor already accomplished by his teacher, and will be able to devote himself to the higher task and achieve it. Seen from another viewpoint, St. Albertus Magnus—in this a true follower of Aristotle—was also a man of encyclopedic knowledge. Roger Bacon in England and St. Albert in Germany are the two great figures of thirteenth-century science. St. Albert was acquainted with and practiced all the sciences, from astronomy to medicine, and advanced them all. The feeling for observation and experiment, which was in no way alien to the Middle Ages, guided his copious labors in this area.

Finally, in addition to his more strictly philosophical works, St. Albertus Magnus applied himself to theology as well, and here, too, made use of the intellectual framework of Aristotelian thought, thus anticipating the mature achievement of St. Thomas.

St. Thomas Aquinas

LIFE AND WORKS. St. Thomas, born at Roccasecca about 1225, was of the family of the Counts of Aquino. His first studies were in the monastery of Monte Cassino. In 1239 he went to Naples to take up the seven liberal arts; there he studied the *trivium* (grammar, rhetoric and dialectic) with Peter Martin and the *quadrivium* (arithmetic, geometry, astronomy and music) with Peter of Ibernia. He also studied in the faculty of arts at the University of Naples, and it was in Naples in 1244 that he donned the Dominican habit. Shortly afterward he started out for Paris with the Master-General of the Order, but his brothers, angry over his becoming a monk, kidnapped him en route and carried him off to Roccasecca. The following year he went to Paris, where he met St. Albertus Magnus, under whom he studied there and, later, in Cologne. In 1252 St. Thomas returned to Paris, where he became a master in theology and where he lived and worked for some years. From 1259 to 1269 he taught in various cities in Italy (Agnani, Orvieto, Rome, Viterbo). He then returned to Paris, his true center of activity. Afterward he resided in Naples; he set out from Naples in 1274, answering the summons of Gregory X to attend the Second Council of Lyons. But his health could not support the overwhelming intellectual labor to which he was committed: he fell ill on the journey and died at Fossanova on March 7, 1274.

St. Thomas was a man of pure spirituality. His whole life was dedicated to philosophical and theological labors and inspired by religion. He was a man of singularly simple and kindly ways, devoted heart and soul to the great intellectual task which he fully accomplished. Testimonials by those nearest to him tell of the profound affection which he inspired in his closest friends. These included his teacher, St. Albertus Magnus, who at a very advanced age set out for Paris to defend his pupil's doctrines, which had been condemned by Bishop Tempier, and who in the latter years of his life deeply mourned the death of St. Thomas; St. Thomas' biographer, William of Tocco; and, above all, his fellow Dominican and faithful friend, Brother Reginald of Piperno. The Church canonized Thomas, acknowledging, along with his sainthood, his great importance in Scholasticism. St. Thomas has been given the name of *Doctor angelicus*.

The works of St. Thomas are very numerous. Some are of interest more as apologist writings or as exegeses of sacred texts, for instance, the *Catena aurea super quattuor Evangelia* (The Golden Chain on the Four Gospels). Others are strictly theological, dogmatical or juridical. Here we are especially interested in his works on philosophy and the systematization of theology, in which Thomist philosophy is most particularly expounded. In first place come his *Commentaries on Aristotle*, a long series of writings in which he studies and analyzes the thought of the Stagirite. In second place are the *Opuscula*, short treatises on philosophy or theology, rich in doctrine, among which are the works *De ente et essentia* (On Being and Essence), *De unitate intellectus* (On the Oneness of the Intellect), *De principio individuationis* (On the Principle of Individuation), and so forth. In third place are the *Quaestiones quodlibetales* (Miscellaneous Questions) and the *Quaestiones disputatae* (Disputed Questions)—*De veritate* (On Truth), *De potentia* (On Potentiality), *De anima* (On the Soul), and so forth. Lastly, there are the theological treatises, especially the *Summa contra Gentiles* (The Summa Against Non-Believers), the *Compendium theologiae ad Reginaldum* (Compendium of Theology Addressed to Reginald) and, above all, St. Thomas' most important work, the great systematic exposition of his own thought and, indeed, of Scholasticism in its entirety: the *Summa theologiae*. These are the Thomist writings that must be borne in mind if St. Thomas is to be studied from the viewpoint of the history of philosophy. Beginning in the thirteenth century itself, these became the major texts of Scholasticism, and a large part of the subsequent productions of Scholasticism consisted of commentaries on books by St. Thomas, especially on the various parts of the *Summa theologiae*.

RELATIONSHIP WITH ARISTOTLE. St. Thomas accomplished the adaptation of Aristotle's Greek philosophy to the Christian thought of Scholasticism. The general content of his thought, therefore, derived from Christian dogma, the Church Fathers, the earlier medieval tradition and, above all, Aristotle. St. Thomas labored extensively over the Peripatetic writings, using principally William of Moerbeke's direct translations from the Greek. Instead of St. Albertus Magnus' long and involved paraphrases, which were imprecise and full of unresolved difficulties, St. Thomas wrote commentaries in which he followed Aristotle's text closely and tried to explain it fully. There is undoubtedly a close affinity between the minds of St. Thomas and Aristotle; Brentano, using a felicitous word, speaks of a *congeniality*. Because of this, the exposition of St. Thomas' doctrines is equivalent in many points to that of Aristotle's; this occurs in the area of logic, in the general lines of their physics and metaphysics, and in the outline of their psychology and their ethics. But it should not be forgotten that St. Thomas, at a distance of sixteen centuries, utilizes these same Aristotelian ideas with very different ends in mind, and, above all, that he and Aristotle are separated by the development of Christianity. Moreover, St. Thomas was too brilliant a philosopher simply to submit to the Aristotelian system, and the general meaning of his own system is profoundly different. One need only remember that all of St. Thomas' intellectual activity was directed toward the establishment of *Christian theology*, which is based on suppositions completely alien to the Hellenic mind.

Aristotle's great problem concerned the modes of being; he was attempting to solve the question that had painfully racked Greek philosophy since the times of Parmenides. His principal solution of this problem was the elaboration of the theory of substance, which was closely related to the Entity as such and to God understood as the prime mover: that is, the establishment of metaphysics, the "sought-after knowledge," and the complete systematization of the problem of knowledge. In addition, Aristotle's doctrine of the oneness and change-lessness of the Entity achieved the restoration of physics, which had been called into question by the Eleatics. The problems that concern St. Thomas are very different: above all, the demonstration of the existence of God and the explanation, in so far as possible, of His essence; the rational interpretation of the dogmas or the isolation of the core of their suprarational, but not antirational, mystery (for example, the Trinity, the Creation of the world, the Eucharist); in another direction, the doctrine of the spiritual and immortal human soul; ethics, oriented toward the supernatural life; the problem of the universals; and many others.

Thus, two quite different things are involved, and the very common expressions, *Aristotelico-Scholastic philosophy* or *Aristotelico-Thomist philosophy*, are misleading. They are meaningful only if applied to these medieval systems which we are studying; here they signify the assimilation of the Aristotelian system into Scholasticism. But they cannot be understood as names for *a single philosophy* comprising the systems of Aristotle and of St. Thomas. Thus, strictly speaking, the two above-mentioned terms are not equivalent, and the second one is inexact: there is no Aristotelico-Thomist philosophy, but a *Thomist* philosophy pure and simple, and Thomism is *Aristotelico-Scholastic* in the sense which has just been indicated.

PHILOSOPHY AND THEOLOGY. For St. Thomas, there is a clear distinction between philosophy and theology: they are two sciences, two different kinds of knowledge. Theology is based on divine revelation, philosophy on the exercise of human reason. It has been said, and rightly, that strictly speaking, theology is not practiced by man, but by God, when He reveals Himself. Philosophy and theology must be true; God is truth itself and it is impossible to doubt revelation, whereas reason, properly used, also leads us to truth. Therefore, there can be no conflict between philosophy and theology, since this would be a discord within the realm of truth.

Thus, these are two independent sciences, but with a common area of investigation. The difference between them arises, above all, from the viewpoint of their *formal objects*, though their *material objects* partially coincide. There are revealed dogmas which can be known through reason—for example, as St. Thomas will point out, the existence of God and many of His attributes, the Creation, and so on. Nevertheless, the revelation of these dogmas is not superfluous, because if reason alone were used, very few people would know these truths. In the cases where rational *understanding* is possible, this is preferable to pure belief. Here we encounter a softened allusion to the *fides quaerens intellectum*; St. Thomas now believes that it is only partially possible to try to understand the object of faith rationally. The application of reason to themes which are also topics for faith and theology is the so-called *natural theology*; there is thus a natural theology alongside the *theologia fidei*. This natural theology is what St. Thomas considers philosophy, and the most important aspect of philosophy; strictly speaking, it is *Thomist philosophy*.

Revelation is the criterion of truth. In the case of a contradiction between revelation and philosophy, the error can never be on the part of revelation. Therefore, the disagreement of a philosophic doctrine with a revealed dogma is a sign that the doctrine is false, that reason has gone astray and has not arrived at truth; it thus jars against truth. In this sense philosophy is subordinated, not exactly to theology as a science, but to revelation. But this does not operate as a hindrance or imposition; on the contrary, philosophy sets up as its norm that which is most proper to it; that is, truth. Revelation keeps philosophy on its guard, but it is philosophic reason itself that will have to seek out true knowledge.

THE DIVISION OF PHILOSOPHY. For St. Thomas, as for the Greeks, the origin of philosophy is awe; the desire to know is satisfied only when things are known in their causes. St. Thomas is a good Aristotelian; but inasmuch as the first cause is God, only knowledge of God can suffice for the human intellect and satisfy philosophy. The goal of this philosophy is that there be depicted in the soul the entire order of the universe and its causes; *ut in ea describatur totus ordo universi et causarum ejus.* The human soul (which in Aristotle's work had already been compared with the hand, because, just as in a certain sense the hand is all the instruments, so the soul is in a certain way all the things) envelops the totality of the universe with its knowledge, and thus rises above its position as a mere creature in order to share in the character of the spirit, in the image of the Deity.

This order of the universe is threefold. In the first place, there is an order which the human intellect finds as already existing: the order of the things, of nature, of true being. This type of order is the concern of natural *philosophy* in a strict sense, or physics, whose object is the *ens mobile*; it is also the concern of mathematics, but especially of metaphysics, which, according to the Aristotelian definition, studies the *ens in quantum ens* (the entity as an entity) and culminates in knowledge of God. Secondly, there is the order of understanding, which is the object of rational philosophy or logic. Thirdly, the order of the acts of will, an order produced by man; this is the moral order, and it is the object of moral philosophy or ethics; in its collective dimensions this order includes the sciences of the State—economics and politics. This is an outline of the Thomist philosophic disciplines. We cannot here enter into a detailed discussion of this division of philosophy, for this would take us too far afield; it will suffice to explain briefly the most interesting features, those that are responsible for this scheme's position of esteem and influence in the history of philosophy.

METAPHYSICS. According to St. Thomas, who adopts the Aristotelian doctrines, being is the most universal of all concepts. *Illud quod primo cadit sub apprehensione est ens, cujus intellectus includitur in omnibus, quaecumque quis apprehendit* (that which first comes under one's apprehension is the Entity, the understanding of which is included in all things, whatever one apprehends). But, as Aristotle had earlier shown when confronting Platonic doctrine, this universality is not that of the genus; the Entity is one of the *transcendentals*, which are present in all the things without intermingling with any. These transcendentals are *ens, res, aliquid, unum et bonum.* And as special forms of the *bonum* referring to understanding and desire, we have the *verum* and the *pulchrum*, truth and beauty.

The two principal meanings of the word "being" are essence and existence; the Scholastics had long debated the difference between these terms. St. Thomas affirms the actual difference between the essence and existence of creatures, which are contingent entities. However, there is no such difference between the essence and existence of God. God's existence follows necessarily from His essence. This is the concept of *aseity* or *self-existence*, to be an *ens a se*; it plays an essential role in the proof of the existence of God and in all of theology.

St. Thomas rejects St. Anselm's ontological proof and gives five methods of proving God's existence; these are the famous *five ways*. (1) By motion: motion exists; everything that moves is moved by another mover; if this mover moves, it will require another mover in turn, and so on to infinity; this is impossible, because there would be no mover if there were not a first, and this first mover is God. (2) By the efficient cause: there is a series of efficient causes; there must be a first cause, because otherwise there would be no effect; and that *first cause* is God. (3) By the possible and necessary: generation and decay show that there are entities which can be or not be; at one time these entities did not exist, and there must have been a time in which nothing existed and in which nothing came to be; there must be an Entity which is necessary in itself, and it is called God. (4) By the degrees of perfection: there are various degrees of all the perfections which more or less approximate the absolute perfections, and therefore they are degrees of the absolute perfections. Thus, there is an Entity which is completely perfect, the highest Entity; this Entity is the cause of all perfection and all being and is called God. (5) By the ordering of the world: intelligent entities tend toward a goal and an order, not by chance but because of the intelligence which directs them; there is an intelligent Entity which orders nature and which impels it toward its goal, and this Entity is God.

These are the five ways, briefly stated. The fundamental idea which inspires them is that God, who is invisible and infinite, is demonstrable by means of His visible and finite effects. Thus, *that God is*, is known, but not *what He is*. But it is possible to learn something about God by observing His creatures, and this is effected in three ways: by means of causality, by means of excellence and by means of negation. St. Thomas distinguishes at least two possible modes of seeing: one mode is by means of mere natural reason, and the other is by means of a supernatural light. Some see the light, he says, but they are not in the light: *quidam vident lumen, sed non sunt in lumine*.

The world has been created by God; we have already seen that the Creation consists of placing the world in existence by means of a voluntary and free act of God; revelation adds that this occurs in time, but according to St. Thomas this is not rationally demonstrable. God is the cause of the world in a double sense: He is the efficient cause and also the exemplary cause; moreover, He is the final cause, since all goals direct themselves to God.

With respect to the universals, St. Thomas' doctrine is one of *moderate realism*, as has already been pointed out. The universals are real, but exist only in abstract form; the species appears only in an individual state, and the principle of individuation is the *materia signata* (signate matter). This gives rise to the theory that each angel is a species rather than an individual, since the angels are immaterial.

THE SOUL. Thomist doctrine regarding the soul differs from the traditional Scholastic doctrine, which was of Platonic-Augustinian origin, and approximates Aristotle's theory, which it adapts to the Christian viewpoint. In accordance with Aristotelian psychology, St. Thomas interprets the soul as a *substantial form* of the human body, the first principle of its life. The soul is what makes the body be a body—that is, a living body. There are as many souls or substantial forms as there are human bodies; St. Thomas rejects the theory that there is a single soul for all mankind, which was of Arabic origin and which reappears with force in Latin Averroism. He also denies that the body and the soul are two complete substances, and that the soul gives the body life but not corporeality. St. Thomas believes that the soul and the body form a *substantial union*; that is, the soul and the body together, and without the help of any other form, constitute the complete and single substance which is man. The Council of Vienna (1311–12) described the rational soul as the intrinsic and essential form of the human body.

On the other hand, the *human* soul—in contrast to the animal soul—is a *subsistent form*; that is, the intellect or understanding has an operation of its own in which the body does not essentially participate; therefore, the intellect can subsist and exercise that operation even though it is separated from its corporeal substratum. Thus the soul is incorporeal and is not composed of matter and form; and it is spiritual, since it possesses reason and is a *mens*. Therefore, the human soul is incorruptible and immortal; its immateriality and simplicity preclude decomposition and decay; its spirituality and consequent subsistence prevent it from accidentally destroying itself when the human body decays. Thus the human soul is immortal, and would perish only if God were to annihilate it. St. Thomas finds further proof of personal immortality in man's desire to continue to live; and, he adds, since this natural desire cannot be in vain, all intellectual substance is incorruptible.

ETHICS. Thomist ethics is based on the framework of Aristotelian ethics, but it keeps the Christian point of departure constantly in mind. Ethics is *motus rationalis creaturae ad Deum*, movement by the rational creature toward God. The goal of this movement is bliss, which consists in the direct vision of God. Therefore, man's ultimate goal is God, and this goal is achieved through knowledge, through contemplation; St. Thomas' ethics has a clear intellectualist nuance. The first law of the human will is *lex aeterna, quae est quasi ratio Dei* (the eternal law, which is, as it were, the reasoning of God).

St. Thomas' philosophy of the State is subordinated to Aristotle's philosophy of politics. Man is by nature an *animal sociale* or *politicum*, and society exists for the benefit of the individual, and not vice versa. Power derives from God. St. Thomas studies the possible kinds of government, and considers monarchy tempered by full participation on the part of the people to be the best form and tyranny to be the worst. In any event, the highest power is that of the Church.

THE RESPONSE TO THOMISM. St. Thomas' system represented a radical innovation within Scholasticism. Its opposition to many Platonic-Augustinian doctrines and clear preference for Aristotelianism made the Franciscans hostile to it. Even a few Dominicans opposed Thomism.

First Thomism elicited written challenges; the principal attacks were the work of William de la Mare and Ricardus de Mediavilla and were primarily in reference to the theory of the oneness of the substantial forms. Later it attracted official condemnations. The first (1277) was that of Étienne Tempier, the bishop of Paris, and was aimed at certain Thomist propositions. This condemnation was at first restricted to the diocese of Paris, but later was extended to Oxford by the action of two Archbishops of Canterbury, Robert Kilwardby, a Dominican, and John Peckham, a Franciscan.

But simultaneously and with greater strength Thomism was welcomed triumphally; this occurred first in the Order of Preachers, immediately thereafter at the University of Paris, and soon in all the schools. In 1323 St. Thomas was canonized, and from that time until this the Church has particularly insisted on the high value of the Thomist system.

NEO-THOMISM. St. Thomas' influence on theology and philosophy has continued without interruption; since his death, the number of commentaries on his *Summa theologiae* and other works has been multiplying. Theology in particular has drawn new life from the immense Thomist contribution, which gave it a precise and rigorous structure. However, after the Middle Ages and the transitory splendor of Spanish Scholasticism in the sixteenth century, Thomist thought lost fecundity. In the second half of the nineteenth century intense intellectual movement was initiated which was enthusiastically supported by the Church and especially by Pope Leo XIII in his encyclical *Aeterni Patris*

(1879). In Italy it was fostered by Gaetano Sanseverino, S. Tongiorgi and Luigi Taparelli. This movement attempted to restore Thomism and to approach theological and philosophical problems through general suppositions. The most fruitful consequence of this movement has been the University of Louvain, which was inspired and made intellectually energetic by Cardinal Mercier. Among the principal Neo-Thomist thinkers we should include Jacques Maritain and Father Maréchal and, in Germany, Georg von Hertling and Clemens Bäumker, who contributed so much to the study of medieval philosophy; also, A. Dyroff, Victor Cathrein, who was dedicated to moral philosophy, the psychologist J. Fröbes, and Étienne Gilson, the historian of philosophy.

8. ROGER BACON

The thirteenth century is almost completely filled by Aristotle's influence and by the great Thomist systematization. Nevertheless, there are a few very interesting independent philosophic activities which deviate from the central current of Scholasticism. One such activity is the above-mentioned *Latin Averroism*, the principal representative of which was Siger of Brabant. Latin Averroism revived the Arabic doctrines of the eternity of the world and the oneness of the human intellect and, most important, placed in the forefront the famous theory of the double truth. In contrast to this movement there was a branch of English Scholasticism which was of the Platonic-Augustinian tradition but which was also dedicated in a new and intense way to the cultivation of the experimental sciences. This British current formed ties with an Anglo-French group established at Chartres in the twelfth century and thereafter enjoyed a higher level of development in Oxford. Here, languages, mathematics and the natural sciences were studied along with the traditional disciplines of philosophy and theology; Aristotle's other great aspect, which had been neglected on the Continent, was developed in England and later flourished in the European Renaissance. This group's first important figure was Robert Grosseteste, bishop of Lincoln, but Roger Bacon was its outstanding member.

LIFE AND WORKS. Roger Bacon was a singular and fertile thinker— certainly more so than was Francis Bacon, who lived three centuries later. Roger was born around 1210–14; he studied in Oxford and in Paris, entered the Franciscan Order and passionately dedicated himself to the study of philosophy, languages and the sciences. Within the Order he was the object of constant persecutions and suspicions on the part of his superiors; he enjoyed only a brief respite during the pontificate of Clement IV (1265-1268), his friend Guy Foulques, who protected him and prompted him to compose his major works: the *Opus majus*, the *Opus minus* and the *Opus tertium*. He wrote until 1277; around that time several of his ideas were condemned by Tempier, and the following year Bacon was imprisoned. It is not known how long he remained in prison, nor has the exact date of his death been ascertained; it is believed that he died around 1292-94.

Roger Bacon dedicated himself to the study of all the sciences that were known in his day, and his knowledge of them was superior to that of any of his contemporaries. He was a genuine investigator and experimenter. He applied mathematics to physics, manufactured optical instruments, was an alchemist, astronomer and linguist. He also studied medieval thought, and in his *Opus majus* one finds what might be called an attempt at writing a history of philosophy.

DOCTRINE. For Bacon, philosophy and the sciences have no meaning other than to explain the truth revealed in the Scriptures: *Una est tantum sapientia perfecta quae in sacra scriptura totaliter continetur.* God taught men to philosophize, for men would not have been able to do this by themselves; but human evil prevented God from manifesting the truths fully, and so they became mixed with error. That is why true wisdom is to be found in the early times, and for this reason it is necessary to look for it in the works of the ancient philosophers. From this situation there arises the need for history, languages and mathematics in order to interpret nature. Thus Bacon represents what has been called *scientific traditionalism*, a designation in which it is important to emphasize both terms equally.

Bacon recognizes three modes of knowledge: authority, reason and experience. Authority by itself does not suffice; it requires reasoning. But reasoning is not certain unless it is confirmed by experience, the chief source of certainty. Experience is twofold: external and internal. The first is *per sensus exteriores*, whereas the second is a true *scientia interior*, founded on divine inspiration. The enlightenment of God, which culminates in *raptus* (rapture), plays an important role. At one extreme Bacon's experimentation is related to the supernatural intuition of mysticism.

Actually, in the fields of philosophy and theology Bacon represents a less advanced point than, for example, St. Thomas; but his work contains a new germ—interest in nature. By means of the Franciscan physicists of the fourteenth and fifteenth centuries and the school of Paris, this germ develops into modern natural science.

9. CHRISTIAN PHILOSOPHY IN SPAIN

Apart from the aforementioned Arabs and Jews, philosophy does not present great personalities in the Middle Ages in Spain. For reasons that require lengthy explanation, Christian Spain is at the periphery of the formation of Scholasticism. It plays an extremely interesting but secondary role in this development, a role that consists principally in the transmission of thought, as at the school of translators in Toledo, of which Dominicus Gundisalvus, who has already been mentioned, was the outstanding figure. Nevertheless, given these limitations, we find in Spain several inherently interesting philosophers who wielded influence in their own time; and at least a few of these men influenced thought over a period of many centuries.

Petrus Hispanus, who was born in Portugal, was extremely active in the thirteenth century. He was a bishop, archbishop, cardinal and finally, pope, with the name of John XXI. He studied medicine, theology and philosophy and wrote several *Summulae logicales* which enjoyed extraordinary fame in their time; they were actually used as textbooks. He was the author of the mnemonic verses of syllogistic and of the names for the valid modes of the syllogism, *Barbara, Celarent,* and so forth.

Arnaldo de Vilanova, a Valencian physician and theologian, is also of interest, as is Raimundus Lullus, of whom it will be necessary to speak in some detail. In the fifteenth century there lived another Catalan theologian and physician, Raimundo de Sabunde (Sabiuda, called Raymond Sebond by Montaigne), whom Montaigne treated at length; he was the author of a *Theologia naturalis seu Liber de creaturis* (Natural Theology, or the Book of the Creatures), which was inspired by the work of Lullus.

RAIMUNDUS LULLUS. Raimundus Lullus (Ramón Llull in its un-latinized Catalan form, often Raymond Lully or Lull in English) was born in Mallorca, apparently about 1233, and died around 1315; it has not been established whether he was killed by the Saracens. In his youth he was a courtier of "scandalous gallantry," but the vision of Christ crucified appeared to him several times, and he abandoned his family, estate and country and dedicated himself to preaching among the infidels. His life was as full of adventure as a novel. He made numerous trips through Italy and France, and traversed large parts of Africa and Asia. He sailed the entire Mediterranean, was shipwrecked, taken prisoner and stoned. It is said that he traveled as far as Abyssinia and Tartary. His life was animated by apostolic zeal and exalted fervor.

In order to be able to convert the infidels, Raimundus Lullus learned Arabic and studied logic. He investigated the sciences, and was also a mystic and poet. He wrote a long series of books in Catalan, Latin and Arabic. His chief works are *Libre de contemplació en Dèu, Art abreujada d'atrobar veritat (Ars compendiosa inveniendi veritatem seu Ars magna et major), Liber de ascensu et descensu intellectus, Ars generalis ultima,* and the mystical book entitled *Libre de amic e amat* which forms part of his philosophic novel *Blanquerna.*

This Mallorcan thinker believed that the conversion of the infidels required rational proof of the Christian truth; he thought that reason could and ought to prove everything, and in his hands philosophy becomes apologetics. Raimundus Lullus proposed a process for finding and automatically proving truth: this is the so-called *Ars magna.* It consists of a complex combination of ideas which have special reference to God and the soul and which form tables capable of being manipulated like a mathematical symbolism in order to find and prove God's attributes, and the like. These tables operate in a fashion that is very difficult to understand and become more and more numerous and complicated. This idea of constructing philosophy in a deductive and almost mathematical manner by means of a general combinatory system later exerted a strong attraction on other thinkers, particularly on Leibniz; however, the philosophic value of these attempts is more than questionable.

Lullus' most interesting feature is his singular and forceful personality; he was called the *Doctor illuminatus,* and inspired great admiration. His intellectual background was clearly Franciscan; it was built on a Platonic and Augustinian base and culminated in mysticism. The spiritual relationship between Roger Bacon and Raimundus Lullus has been properly pointed out. The two cultivate the sciences and Oriental languages with the same goals of evangelizing and reforming Christianity. In both there is a clear priority of theological—even mystical—knowledge over all other knowledge, and in the work of each the two themes of Franciscan thought—the subordination of all knowledge to theology and the progress of the individual intellect toward God—are taken up. These two themes are summarized in the titles to two works by St. Bonaventure: *De reductione artium ad theologiam* and *Itinerarium mentis in Deum.*

10. Duns Scotus and Occam

The period from the end of the thirteenth century through the fourteenth century represents a new phase of Scholasticism, a phase which continues in decadent fashion in the fifteenth century. The fullness of

Thomist philosophy is followed by a philosophic current of Franciscan character which, like St. Thomas, incorporates Aristotelian philosophy; however, the new current acquires more and more pronounced voluntarist and nominalist characteristics. With these thinkers we come to the extremes of the dialectical evolution of the great problems of medieval philosophy. We have already seen, above, the positions which they take in regard to the three questions of the Creation, the universals and *lógos*. We shall now point out the most important features of the philosophy of the two great English Franciscans, John Duns Scotus and William of Occam.

Scotus

LIFE AND WORKS. Scotus was born somewhere in the British Isles either in 1266 or in 1274. He entered the Franciscan Order, and studied and taught at Oxford. In 1304 he went to Paris, and in 1308 to Cologne, where he died that same year, still very young. Scotus is one of the few precocious philosophers in history, he and Schelling being among the few exceptions to the general rule that great philosophers are of necessity fully mature men. Duns Scotus displayed brilliance in philosophy from a very early age; his keen and penetrating mind won him the sobriquet of *Doctor subtilis*. He was a champion of the now official dogma of the Immaculate Conception of the Virgin.

Several of the works traditionally attributed to Scotus are not authentic. Among those that are certainly his, the most important are the *Opus oxoniense*, especially, and the treatise *De primo rerum omnium principio*.

PHILOSOPHY AND THEOLOGY. The equilibrium in which the two disciplines of philosophy and theology appear in the works of St. Thomas will soon be upset. The distance between the two is much greater in Scotus' writings, and will be even greater in those of Occam. They now differ not only in their *formal* object, but also in their *material* object. Theology is reduced to that which is given to us through revelation, by *supernatural* means; on the other hand, everything within the *natural* scope of reason is a topic for philosophy. The history of the late Middle Ages and the modern period will be the progressive dissociation between the world of nature and the world of grace, and the old principle *gratia naturam non tollit, sed perficit* (grace does not take away nature, but perfects it) will be forgotten. Theology in this period is no longer speculative, but practical. More and more, *theologia rationis* will disappear, leaving the field to *theologia fidei* alone. Soon *ratio*, or *lógos*, will become completely separated from *theós*.

Nevertheless, this attitude should not be confused with the theory of the double truth derived from Averroës, since the revealed truth of theology remains in first place and offers a supernatural certitude. It is the impossibility of penetrating the mystery of God rationally that separates philosophy from knowledge concerning the Deity.

SCOTIST METAPHYSICS. Scotus, whose distinctions are always innumerable and subtle, distinguishes three classes of prime matter: *materia primo prima*, which is indeterminate, but has a certain reality, like something created; *materia secundo prima*, which possesses the attributes of quantity and already presupposes shaping by a corporeal "form"; and, lastly, *materia tertio prima*, which is matter available for the modifications of already corporeal entities.

Moreover, there are several *forms*, also, and Scotus makes a distinction between the *res* and the *formalitates* which constitute it. We have already seen the role played by these *formalitates*, especially *haecceitas* ("thisness"), and by the formal distinction *a parte rei* in the interpretation of the problem of the universals.

Duns Scotus accepts St. Anselm's ontological argument for the demonstration of the existence of God, adding a few modifications which were later adopted by Leibniz. If God is possible, then He exists; it is first necessary to demonstrate His possibility. Scotus proves this—as Leibniz will—on the basis of the impossibility of God's contradicting Himself, since in God there is nothing negative. God, as an *ens a se*, is necessary, and His essence coincides with His existence; therefore, His possibility implies His reality. This is what Scotus called *colorari ista ratio Anselmi de summo cogitabile* ("lending color to that proof of Anselm's on the highest imaginable Being").

Scotus, in contrast to St. Thomas, is a voluntarist. He affirms the priority of the will over the intellect in all fields. The will is not passive, but *active*; it is not determined by necessity: *voluntas nihil de necessitate vult* (the will has nothing to do with necessity). The ethical importance of the will is greater, and therefore love is superior to faith. It is better to love God than to know Him; conversely, the perversion of the will is more serious than the perversion of the intellect. All these Scotist tendencies will acquire their maximum force in the following centuries and will determine the passage from the Middle Ages to the Renaissance. We shall continually encounter in the following pages the consequences of Scotus' thought.

Occam

LIFE AND WORKS. William of Occam (Ockham) was so called from the town of Ockham in England, where he was born at the end of the thirteenth century. He, too, was a Franciscan who studied at Oxford and was a professor there and later in Paris. After his important scientific activities, he took part in political and religious controversies, and some of his propositions were condemned. In the fourteenth century the great medieval social structure was beginning to dissolve; the struggle between the pontificate and the Holy Roman Empire was raging once more. Occam sided with the emperor and was excommunicated by Pope John XXII because of his stand on the question of temporal rights. Occam took refuge at the court of the Emperor Ludwig of Bavaria, to whom he addressed the famous line: *Tu me defendas gladio, ego te defendam calamo* (Defend me with the sword, I shall defend you with the pen). Occam died in Munich about 1350.

Aside from his political and ecclesiastical works (*Quaestiones octo de auctoritate summi pontificis, Compendium errorum Joannis papae XXII, Breviloquium de potestate papae*, and so forth), Occam wrote *Super IV Libros sententiarum, Quodlibeta septem*, the *Centiloquium theologicum, De sacramento altaris, Summa totius logicae* and commentaries on Aristotle.

OCCAM'S PHILOSOPHY. All the tendencies that are outlined in Scotus' writings are carried to extremes in Occam's. What Scotus presented as the germ of an idea, Occam develops to its ultimate consequences. In the first place, he puts the greatest possible distance between theology and physics. Theology receives an even greater scope than it had, but not as a rational science; the truths of faith are inaccessible to reason, and philosophy has nothing to do with them. Science is *cognitio vera sed dubitabilis nata fieri evidens per discursum* (a true knowledge, but one it is doubtful can be made evident through discourse). God is not reason; reason is something that only has the value of "doors within" man. God is omnipotence, free will, will without hindrances, not even the hindrances of reason. Scotus' voluntarism is converted into this attitude which separates reason from the Deity and thus removes the Deity from the field of man's rational speculation. God disappears from the intellectual horizon and ceases to be a proper object for the mind, as He has been in the Middle Ages up to this time. At this point begins the process which may be called the *loss of God*, the stages of this process being the stages of modern history.

With regard to the question of the universals, Occam, as we have seen previously, is a *nominalist*. For him, the universals have reality neither in the things nor in the mind of God as eternal exemplars of the things; they are abstractions of the human mind—concepts or terms: *conceptus mentis significans univoce plura singularia* (a concept of the mind designating several things or single things by one and the same term). Science is related to the universals and therefore *is not a science of things*, but only of signs or symbols. This prepares the way for the apogee of mathematical thought in the Renaissance.

Thus, Occam represents the extreme development of the Franciscan tendencies in medieval philosophy. Man, who had been cut off from the world since the inception of Christianity, is now left without God. "Alone, alienated from the world and from God," writes Zubiri, "the human spirit begins to feel insecure in the universe." From this time on and through all the centuries of the modern age, man will seek in philosophy *security* first of all. Modern philosophy will be inspired by caution, by wariness, more by the fear of error than by the yearning for truth.

11. MEISTER ECKHART

The great figure of Meister Eckhart is little known and studied. He is one of the most brilliant personalities in medieval philosophy, but the difficulties in the interpretation of his writings are very great. We cannot here go deeply into the study of his thought, but shall merely point out the role he played and observe that his work is an essential element for the comprehension of medieval philosophy and the transition to modern philosophy.

Eckhart was born in 1260, probably in Gotha. He was a Dominican, perhaps a personal pupil of St. Albertus Magnus. He taught theology in Paris at the same time as Scotus, at the beginning of the fourteenth century. Later he held various offices in the Dominican Order and was an important preacher. The Franciscans instigated a trial against him, and he was accused of pantheism and Averroism. In 1329, two years before his death, several of his propositions were condemned. "But," writes Zubiri, "nothing could be further from Eckhart than the pantheism that was ascribed to him with unbelievable haste." Eckhart left many sermons in German and various works in Latin. His speculative mysticism had a profound influence on the entire development of German mysticism, as well as on the Flemish and French mysticism of the fifteenth century. It also had a direct influence on the great Spanish mystics of the sixteenth century.

We have already seen the meaning of Eckhart's doctrine of the *scintilla animae*, the spark of the soul, uncreated and uncreatable; we have seen that there is no pantheism in this affirmation, but rather the strictly orthodox conviction that the *Idea* of man, his exemplary model, of which he is the image, is God Himself. God is beyond being; Eckhart even says that God is *a pure nothingness*, thus denoting His fundamental infiniteness and superiority to all essences. The road that leads to God is the soul itself, and Eckhart seeks solitude and with-drawal from society.

To quote Zubiri: "Without Eckhart the origin of modern philoso-phy would be completely inexplicable. It is easy, but inexact, to say that it derives from Cusa or Occam. Despite all appearances, Occam's nominalism, with its prevailing negativity, would be incapable of germinating the positive principle that Nicholas of Cusa was to extract. . . . And the difficulty of understanding Eckhart is more serious than it might seem at first sight, not only because not all his Latin writings are yet known, but because an honest appraisal of the problem would oblige us to go back and review completely our inter-pretation of medieval metaphysics. . . . Then we would see in Eckhart a brilliant thinker who does not succeed in expressing in Scholastic concepts and terms his new metaphysical intuitions, which are in many senses antipodal to Augustinian thought and the Reformation. For St. Augustine, the problem is the world, because he came to believe that he knew what God is. For Eckhart, the problem is God, perhaps because he believed he already knew what the world is. On the other hand, whereas the Reformation makes its appeal to the indi-vidual, Eckhart has recourse to withdrawal into the inner life, an attitude which is probably miles away from every Lutheran tendency. Only in this way will we know what is speculation and what is mysti-cism in Eckhart, and wherein the fundamental tie between the two consists."

12. THE LAST PHASE OF MEDIEVAL PHILOSOPHY

After Occam and Eckhart, medieval philosophy enters into a rapid decline, which is dominated by the growing complication of its *distinc-tiones* and by an excessive branching out into secondary questions. But it would be wrong to think that it is all over in the middle of the four-teenth century, or that the speculation of the late fourteenth century and fifteenth century contained no fruitful elements that were to figure later in modern philosophy. Without entering into the complex prob-lems raised by this period, it will be interesting to point out at least the major elements and figures of this final stage, the crisis of Scholas-ticism.

THE OCCAMISTS. In England and France especially, Occamism spreads rapidly and is fostered by a series of keen minds. Among these are the English Dominican Robert Holkot, a contemporary of Occam, and above all, the Parisian master Nicolas d'Autrecourt, who lived slightly later, a critical mind who at times comes close to Latin

Averroism. Then, too, there is Nicolas' pupil, Cardinal Pierre d'Ailly (1350–1420), who was versed in cosmography, and whose *Imago mundi* decisively influenced Columbus' ideas on the sphericity of the earth, the ideas which led him to the discovery of the New World. A pupil of the cardinal and his successor as chancellor of the University of Paris was Jean Gerson (1363–1429), one of the most important figures of the fifteenth century; Gerson finally turned toward mysticism.

In another direction, the French nominalists practice the natural sciences with great intensity and, strictly speaking, anticipate many of the discoveries of the Renaissance physicists. Jean Buridan, who lived in the first half of the fifteenth century; Albert of Saxony, who died in 1390; and especially Nicholas Oresmus, who died in 1382, are the principal "scientific Occamists," as they are called by Gilson. Nicholas Oresmus, bishop of Lisieux, who wrote in both Latin and French— in this a forerunner of Descartes—was a thinker of great importance who appreciably advanced physics and astronomy. He wrote the treatise *De difformitate qualitatum*, the *Traité de la sphère* and commentaries on the physical works of Aristotle.

AVERROISM. The philosophical movement called Latin Averroism began in the thirteenth century, continued to the end of the Middle Ages, and still had repercussions in the Renaissance. It can be said to have constituted a philosophical current independent of Scholasticism, although closely related to its problems. The most important figure of Latin Averroism is Siger of Brabant, who lived in the thirteenth century and based his thought on the teachings of Aristotle as interpreted by Averroës. Siger of Brabant, many of whose propositions were condemned, taught the eternity of the world and the oneness of human intellect; in his view, there is a single intellect for the entire human species, and belief in the immortality of the individual man disappears. Also of Latin Averroist origin is the aforementioned doctrine of the *double truth*, according to which a single proposition may be true in theology and false in philosophy, or vice versa.

In the fourteenth century, Jean of Jandun (*d.* 1328) continues the Averroist tendency, carrying it to even greater extremes and emphasizing its dependence on the Cordovan philosopher. Jean of Jandun makes philosophy the superior discipline and ascribes truth primarily to it.

SPECULATIVE MYSTICISM. The influence of Meister Eckhart extends to several important mystics of the fourteenth century, particularly in Germany and the Netherlands, who maintain relations with the French mystics, such as the above-mentioned Gerson and Denys the Carthusian. These mystics, who more or less directly inspire the religious renewal of the fifteenth century, especially the so-called *devotio moderna*, an anticipation of the Renaissance, are principally Johannes Tauler (1300–1361), Heinrich Suso (1300–1365), Jan van Ruysbroeck (1293–1381) and the author of the *Theologia deutsch*, which had such great influence on Luther. From these religious groups arise the stimuli that will inspire the spiritual life of the sixteenth century, among the Protestants as well as in the Counter-Reformation.

THE FIFTEENTH CENTURY. In the last century of the Middle Ages the decline of Scholasticism is accentuated. The principal schools—Thomist, Scotist, Occamist—persist, but their activity becomes a sterile formalism. There are a few important commentators, like Cardinal Cajetan, the commentator of St. Thomas, and the Scotists Peter Tartaretus, famous for his commentaries on Aristotle, and the Belgian Peter Crockaert, later a Dominican and a Thomist, who was the teacher of Francisco de Vitoria. Scotism lasted until the seventeenth century, with representatives like Luke Wadding, the famous editor of Scotus' work, and Juan de Merinero, a professor at Alcalá. But the last important Scholastic whose efforts did not merely consist of exegesis or instruction was the Occamist Gabriel Biel (1425–1495). The resurgence of Scholasticism in Spain in the sixteenth century is different in character and is openly influenced by the Renaissance.

We have seen the paths that medieval philosophy followed. We have glanced briefly at its immense wealth of thought, but closely enough to understand the fundamental problems it raised and the exemplary profundity with which it was able to attack those problems. On the other hand, we have seen in the last few pages that medieval philosophy is not fully exhausted—what, after all, would that mean? —and that its final phase points to something new. It is an ending because it is a beginning at the same time, and it will continue to be operative in the period that now opens.

Modern philosophy does not arise from nothingness. Nor, as the humanists so superficially thought, did it arise as a reaction to Scholasticism and a return to the Greeks and Romans, especially Plato and the Stoics. In fact, it was just the opposite. The thought of the Greek philosophers—there is little to be said for the Romans—gained new efficacy in the Scholastic era, and the humanists' presumptive restoration was a hindrance and a retrogression which lasted until the authentic modern philosophy, from Descartes to Leibniz, could open up a path for itself. It is in this modern philosophy, rather than in any "renascence," that Scholasticism, and with it, the living thought of the Greeks, find their true continuation.

From Plato and Aristotle (or even Parmenides) to Descartes and Leibniz and then to Kant and Hegel and even after, there is a line uninterrupted as regards problems and truth, although interrupted perhaps as regards time; and this line is precisely the line of the history of philosophy.

MODERN PHILOSOPHY

THE RENAISSANCE

The Renaissance World

1. THE SPIRITUAL CIRCUMSTANCES

By the end of the Middle Ages, man's religious situation had become problematic. Theology was in a state of profound crisis; its supernatural aspect was becoming more and more pronounced, and thus it was changing into mysticism. Moreover, the entire medieval organization—both Church and Empire—was in equally critical condition. The Empire's power—which was almost more spiritual than temporal—had been broken, and nations were beginning to take shape. Now preoccupation with the State begins; during the course of the Renaissance there appear all the political theorists of varied tradition —from Machiavelli to Hobbes. In general, the problem of the dissolution of the old organization is approached by means of the rationalism that comes into being, that new use of reason as applied to man and nature, the two topics to which reason is directed after God is renounced. And rationalism is antihistorical; throughout the modern epoch, antihistoricalism has been the fundamental vice of the philosophy of society and the State, which are historical realities. Attempts are made to solve the problem schematically: *De optimo reipublicae statu, deque nova insula Utopia*, by Thomas More; the *Civitas Solis*, by Campanella; later, the *Leviathan*, by Hobbes.

Mysticism flourishes in Flanders and later in France and the rest of Europe. People live in communities that cultivate a new religiosity. They are averse to theology. It is not important to know, but to feel and to act: "It is better to feel compunction than to be able to define it." In Flanders, in art as well as in all other fields, the end of the Middle Ages is already the Renaissance: this is the case, for example, with the brothers van Eyck. And in the realm of mysticism there is Jan van Ruysbroeck. Mysticism is represented in France by Denys the Carthusian and Jean Gerson; in Germany by Heinrich Suso, Johannes Tauler and Thomas à Kempis.

People of this time, obviously inspired by the Franciscans, begin to discover nature. Everything, from St. Francis of Assisi's love of natural objects to the Franciscan philosophers' nominalism, which produced mathematical thought, leads to an interest in nature. Petrarch is characteristic: he ascends a mountain in order to contemplate on the summit; but once there he does not yet know enough to look around, and instead reads St. Augustine.

A few expressive book titles illustrate the dividing line between the two epochs: *De contemptu mundi* (On Contempt for the World), by Petrarch (and many others); *De incertitudine et vanitate scientiarum* (On the Uncertainty and Vanity of the Sciences), by Agrippa; *De docta ignorantia* (On Instructed Ignorance), by Nicholas of Cusa. A little later Francis Bacon writes the *Novum Organum*, a title which points to a new dawn, in contrast to the other titles, which represent the setting of the sun. *De dignitate et augmentis scientiarum* (The Advancement of Learning), also by Bacon, is in reply to Agrippa's title. But the most exultant and significant title is *De interpretatione naturae et regno hominis* (On the Interpretation of Nature and the Reign of Man). The era quickly loses its autumnal character and, in contrast, becomes aware of the emerging consciousness of the "Renaissance."

Humanism appears and quickly spreads far and wide. Greek and Latin books reach the West; the worship of antiquity is carried to great lengths, but people lack discernment and do not value things according to their true worth. Scholasticism is attacked. Aware that a reform is necessary, humanism establishes ties with the new religiosity; at first this idea of a reform is orthodox, but soon it becomes the Lutheran Reformation.

Interest in nature transcends its own sphere. Man is no longer content to concern himself wholeheartedly with natural objects; he tries to impose a natural character on everything. There is to be not only a natural science, but also a natural law, a natural religion, a natural ethics, and human naturalism. What does "natural religion" mean? It is what remains of religion after everything supernatural—revelation, dogma, history, and the like—has been withdrawn from it. Natural religion is what man feels "by" his own nature: a God; not the personal God of Christian dogma, but an idea of God. Natural law and natural ethics are the disciplines that appertain to man simply because he is man. It is a matter of something outside of history and, especially, outside of grace.

Thus, in the Renaissance many things are accomplished. There are discoveries that extend the world, notably those by the Spanish and Portuguese; inventions, such as the printing press, firearms and a series of techniques superior to those of the Middle Ages; realistic politics of the new nations, such as that of Ferdinand the Catholic or Louis XI, and theories of the State; humanistic literature in good Latin and in the vernacular; ethics; mysticism; an art that abandons the Gothic and revives ancient styles. Something called philosophy is also cultivated to some extent, and it is worthwhile to examine this topic in some detail.

We must distinguish two different aspects in Renaissance philosophy: one of these aspects is the body of thought of the fifteenth and sixteenth centuries which displays the two principal characteristics of the "Renaissance"—opposition to the Middle Ages and the restoration, *rebirth*, of antiquity; the other current—less visible, perhaps, but more profound—is that which continues the authentic philosophy of the Middle Ages and achieves full maturity in Descartes. Here, naturally, there is no break, but rather a carrying of the internal dialectics of the medieval philosophic problems to their ultimate consequences.

The humanists—the thinkers of the Platonic Academy of Florence which was founded in 1440; those of the Roman Academy; all those saturated with the wealth of classical learning which proceeded chiefly from the ruined Byzantine Empire, from Lorenzo Valla to Luis Vives—propose as a primary goal the deprecation of Scholasticism and the renewal of the philosophy of the ancients. However, they forget that Scholasticism was founded in large part on Platonic and Neoplatonic writings and especially on Aristotle, himself an ancient philosopher. What does this mean? The truth of the matter is that the Aristotle of Scholasticism was not very interesting. He had been Latinized—in impure, medieval Latin—and moreover had been handed down through theology. He was full of syllogisms and distinctions, the number of which had been increased by the medieval monks. This was not what was interesting about the ancient world. Of greater interest was Plato, who permitted one to speak of the soul and of love, and who wrote in such beautiful Greek. But there was something still more interesting: Stoicism. The Stoics had all the advantages: they preferred to concern themselves with man—and this conformed with the interests of humanism and the general preoccupation of the

Renaissance—in writings that were full of dignity and nobility; they offered examples of a quiet and serene life that was full of moderation and removed from the frenzy of the close of the Middle Ages; and, most important, they made their whole philosophy revolve around the concept that was most in vogue: nature. To live according to nature—this is what was necessary. It mattered little that the Stoic idea of nature, the *phýsis*, resembled very slightly the Renaissance idea of nature; nor was it important that for a long time the word *nature* had been equated with the word *grace*. It was not necessary to take such subtle distinctions into account.

Renaissance philosophy is characterized by a considerable lack of precision and intellectual discipline. If we compare it with the best moments of Scholasticism, its inferiority becomes evident; in fact, it would not be going too far to say that the Renaissance was a period of negligible activity *from the viewpoint of philosophy*. The Renaissance interpretation of the ancients is superficial and false beyond measure. Cicero and Quintilian are cited as great philosophers and are put on a level with Plato. The Renaissance ideas of Platonism (fundamentally Neoplatonic) and Aristotle lack philosophical and historical significance. The Renaissance is certainly not a period of creative metaphysics. Its philosophers have not yet fully pondered the ontological situation which the Middle Ages bequeathed: a world inhabited by rational man and alienated from God. Man has not seriously questioned his new intellectual position. This questioning, which continues the apparently interrupted metaphysical tradition, begins in the first decades of the seventeenth century, in the work of Descartes. In Cartesianism the modern age ponders metaphysically its own suppositions.

2. HUMANIST THOUGHT

ITALY. The Renaissance begins in Italy. Some persons, at the risk of having this concept lose all precise significance, have wished to date it from the end of the thirteenth century so as to include Dante. This view is exaggerated, but Petrarch (1304–1374) can be considered an early example of Renaissance man. In the fifteenth century a center of great activity—more literary than philosophic—arises at the court of Cosimo de' Medici in Florence, and the Platonic Academy appears, with such humanist personalities as the Greek Cardinal Bessarion, Marsilio Ficino, Pico della Mirandola, and so on. There are also "Aristotelians" in Italy, who champion a badly disfigured Aristotle; among these are such men as Ermolao Barbaro and Pietro Pomponazzi.

The theoreticians of politics and the State form a separate group, but one which is closely connected with the aforementioned humanists. In first rank is the clever Florentine secretary Niccolò Machiavelli (1469–1527), who in his *Prince* expounded the theory of a State which is not subordinated to any higher authority, either religious or moral. There is also Tommaso Campanella (1568–1639), a Calabrian monk; he wrote of the *Civitas Solis*, a utopia of communistic tendencies inspired, like all works of this type, by Plato's *Republic*. However, Campanella's State is a universal monarchy of a theocratic character in which papal authority is supreme.

Among the first rank of Italian Renaissance thinkers oriented toward nature we find the great artist and physicist, Leonardo da Vinci (1452–1519), and Bernardino Telesio (1508–1588), who dedicated himself to the study of the natural sciences and founded a theory of vitalism on a physical basis. The way is prepared for the foundation of modern natural science, which in Italy is to produce the brilliant figure of Galileo.

FRANCE. The Renaissance in France has a pronounced skeptic tendency. There is Michel de Montaigne, author of the *Essais*, which were more notable for their perspicacity and literary value than for their philosophic profundity. Montaigne's mocking and penetrating but offhand criticism had great influence up until the Enlightenment. The skeptic par excellence is Pierre Charron. As for the movement that was anti-Aristotelian and in opposition to Scholasticism, its chief figure in France is Pierre de la Ramée, called Petrus Ramus, who violently attacked Aristotelian philosophy and ended up embracing Calvinism. Humanism was quick to establish ties with the Reformation; so was the great Hellenist Henri Estienne (Stephanus) and, in Spain, Juan de Valdés.

SPAIN. Apart from purely literary activity, the Renaissance in Spain has representatives who are characteristic of the times, and even among the most important figures. Although the fact has sometimes been questioned, Spanish culture was affected by Renaissance currents; there is in Spain as in all of Europe a preoccupation with esthetics, an interest in the vernacular (Valdés) and in classical languages and literatures (the Complutensian University [of Alcalá de Henares], Cisneros, Nebrija, Fray Luis de León, Arias Montano). In Spain the Renaissance was certainly less at odds with medieval tradition than it was in other countries, and for this reason it was less noticeable. Nevertheless, in reference to philosophic thought, the skeptic current is seen to be represented by the Portuguese Francisco Sánchez, author of the famous book *Quod nihil scitur*. And anti-Scholastic but orthodox

Catholic humanism, faithful to the principal elements of the medieval world but at the same time full of the spirit of the times, produces in Spain the great figure of Luis Vives (1492–1540), who was born in Valencia, lived in Louvain, Paris and England, and died in Bruges. Vives, a friend of the most eminent men of his time—a citizen of Europe if ever there was one—is an unassuming thinker; the historical nucleus to which he belonged did not contain a full-fledged philosophy, but he was undeniably sagacious and is of considerable interest today. Vives wrote a great deal on questions of ethics and education, and his treatise *De anima et vita* is one of the most vigorous and penetrating books that the humanist movement produced.

Sebastián Fox Morcillo also wrote philosophical treatises which were independent in spirit from Scholasticism, as did the physicians Vallés and, especially, Gómez Pereira, the author of the *Antoniana Margarita*, published in 1554, in which scholars have claimed to find ideas analogous with some of Descartes'.

But what is most important in Spanish thought in the sixteenth and seventeenth centuries is not to be found here, but in the splendid though ephemeral flowering of Scholasticism arising out of the Council of Trent; it philosophically and theologically directs the entire Counter-Reformation, which is further animated by the work of the great mystics, especially St. Teresa and St. John of the Cross, whose intellectual interest is very high, although not strictly philosophical.

ENGLAND. The most interesting figure in English humanism is Thomas More, who was chancellor to Henry VIII and was beheaded because of his opposition to the king's refusal to obey the pope; he has recently been canonized by the Church. More wrote the *Utopia* (*De optimo reipublicae statu, deque nova insula Utopia*), about another ideal State. The most famous of such treatises published in the Renaissance, it was also communistic in nature and full of Platonic echoes.

HOLLAND. The greatest of the European humanists, the one who most fully embodied its characteristics and at the same time achieved the greatest fame and wielded the most extensive influence was Erasmus of Rotterdam. Possessed of a great talent for writing in Latin, he composed his works in a precise and elegant style that found enthusiastic imitators and admirers throughout Europe. Erasmus wrote several books that were widely read in all countries, in particular *The Praise of Folly* (*Encomium moriae*), the *Manual of the Christian Knight* (*Enchiridion militis christiani*) and the *Colloquies* (*Colloquia*). In spite of his contact with the reformers, Erasmus kept within the bounds of dogma, but his Catholicism was unenthusiastic and always mixed with irony and criticism of the Church. Erasmus, himself a canon and close to the cardinalate, did not cease to be a Christian; his faith was perhaps not as deep as that of medieval man, but his spirit was open and comprehensive. In spite of all his limitations and undeniable liberties, Erasmus, who represents the spirit of concord in a hard and violent epoch, is the most perfect example of Renaissance man.

GERMANY. The Renaissance in Germany is of great importance. There it presents a character different from that shown in other countries, and it perhaps has more philosophic fecundity. Instead of displaying a predominantly humanistic nature with pronounced literary tendencies, German thought at the end of the fifteenth and in the sixteenth century is closely connected to speculative mysticism. Heinrich Suso; Johannes Tauler; Angelus Silesius (Johannes Scheffler); the author of the *Theologia deutsch*, all derive from Meister Eckhart's speculative mysticism; the Protestant mystics are also linked to this tradition. The German Renaissance makes equal use of alchemy, astrology and even magic. In this way mystical speculation becomes involved in the development of the natural sciences.

This complex mixture of science and mysticism, together with the rejection of rational and rigorous philosophy, is found in Agrippa von Nettesheim, the author of the book entitled *De incertitudine et vanitate scientiarum*, which has already been mentioned. Philippus Aureolus Paracelsus (Theophrastus von Hohenheim), a physician and eccentric philosopher, employed these ideas in the study of the physical world and man, whom he considered a mirror of the universe. In spite of his extravagant theories, some advances in the field of the natural sciences must be credited to Paracelsus.

Religious and mystical thought is of great interest in Germany, and in particular, of course, the theology of the Reformers, especially that of Luther and, to a lesser degree, that of the Swiss Zwingli; but this subject goes beyond the scope of our discussion. The Reformation is linked with the German humanism of Philip Melanchthon and Johann Reuchlin on the one hand and, on the other, with Protestant mysticism. The principal Protestant mystics are Sebastian Franck, Valentin Weigel and, most important, Jakob Böhme (1575–1624). Böhme was a cobbler who led a retiring and simple life dedicated to meditation. His chief work is a book known as *Aurora*, which shows the influence of Paracelsus and of Nicholas of Cusa; from the latter it derives its interpretation of God as the unity of opposites. Böhme was a pantheist; in his work God and the world are synonymous. His influence on German thought has been long-lasting.

The Beginning of Modern Philosophy

We must now study the most fertile moments in the thought of the fifteenth and sixteenth centuries, those events that actually prepared the way for the great modern metaphysical systems beginning with Descartes. There is a discontinuous and hidden line of thinkers who keep the authentic philosophical problem alive or create the necessary bases on which to state the essential questions of the new European metaphysics in an original and sufficient way. The two major themes are the continuity of the medieval and Greek tradition on the one hand and the new idea of nature on the other. It is for this reason that elements which are apparently disparate and usually studied separately are included together in this chapter: first, Nicholas of Cusa and Giordano Bruno; secondly, the modern physicists; thirdly, the Spanish Scholastics of the sixteenth century. At first glance it appears that the first two figures are part of so-called Renaissance philosophy, whereas the physicists are outside the realm of philosophy and the Spaniards represent a movement back toward the "superseded" Middle Ages. Actually, the physicists think in terms of the modern idea of nature, founded on medieval nominalism, and their suppositions, if not their science, are strictly philosophical; moreover, the idealist metaphysics of the seventeenth century cannot be properly understood unless the role played by the new physics is taken into account. As for the Spaniards, except for a few who have proper claims to places in the history of philosophy, they are principally theologians. The Spanish Scholastic has the clear purpose of gathering all medieval philosophy and synthesizing it from the higher perspective of the new age; this is the case with Suárez, in particular. It is not a question of merely commenting on St. Thomas or Duns Scotus, but of an attempt by men who are no longer of the thirteenth century, who are motivated by modern ideas, to state the problems in an original way. If there were any need to prove this, it would suffice to point out a few very obvious facts: this Scholasticism gives rise to something as *modern* as international law, the principal nucleus of which is established by Jesuits, men of their own time if ever there were such. Above all, these thoughts center about the Council of Trent; that is, they are situated at the crucial point of the modern age, in the struggle between the Reformation and the Counter-Reformation. We must bear in mind the deep and more or less explicit influence of Suárez on Descartes and Leibniz and on all German philosophy up to Hegel—his actual presence, therefore, in all modern philosophy.

1. NICHOLAS OF CUSA

CHARACTER. Nicholas Chrypffs (Krebs) was born in Cusa (Kues) in 1401; from his native city he received the name by which he is known: Nicolaus Cusanus, or Nicholas of Cusa. He studied at Padua, held high offices in the Church and became a cardinal and bishop of Brixen. He died in 1464. Nicholas of Cusa wrote several philosophical works, the most important of which are *De docta ignorantia*, *Apologia doctae ignorantiae* and *De conjecturis*; the first-named is the most significant, his masterwork.

Nicholas of Cusa is one of the most interesting philosophers of his time. In one way, he is in the line of development of Scholasticism, but at the same time, he touches on themes that mark the transition to modern philosophy. Occam and Descartes are separated by nearly three hundred years, a period which represents a significant lack of continuity, an extremely long gap between two moments of metaphysical maturity. In this interval are to be found a few thinkers who keep alive the authentic spirit of philosophy and achieve the intermediate stages: Cardinal Cusanus is one of these men.

PHILOSOPHY. Nicholas of Cusa's starting point is mysticism, particularly that of Eckhart; that is, speculative mysticism. He combines with this an unusual interest in the world and a facility in handling metaphysical concepts. This is the path by which modern philosophy is reached. The outline of Cusanus' system is the following: God, or the infinite; the world and man, or the finite; God the Redeemer, who is the union of the finite and the infinite. This theme of the union of the two is the central point of his philosophy. There are different kinds of knowledge: in the first place, knowledge derived through the senses (*sensus*); this kind of knowledge does not furnish us with a sufficient truth, but only with images. Secondly, there is *ratio* (which a German idealist would have translated as *Verstand*, or understanding); the *ratio*, in an abstract and fragmentary way, comprehends these sensory images in their diversity. Thirdly, there is the *intellectus* (this, in turn, would correspond to the German idealist's *Vernunft*, or reason); the *intellectus*, aided by supernatural grace, leads us to the truth of God. But this truth makes us comprehend that the infinite is impenetrable, and then we learn of our ignorance; this is true philosophy, the *docta ignorantia* (instructed ignorance) of which the highest knowledge consists. And this is related to the idea of *negative theology* and to the general situation of the period.

Ratio does not take us past the diversity of opposites; on the other hand, *intellectus* leads us to intuit the oneness of God. The Deity appears in Nicholas of Cusa's writings as *coincidentia oppositorum*, the coincidence of opposites. In this higher unity, contradiction is overcome: in the infinite all different factors coincide. This idea has had its most profound repercussion in Hegel. Nicholas employs mathematical ideas to make this understandable: for example, a straight line and the circumference of a circle tend more and more to coincide as the radius of the circle is continually increased; they do coincide at the limit, if the radius approaches infinity. If, conversely, the radius becomes infinitely small, the circumference coincides with the center of the circle. A straight line will finally coincide with a triangle if one of the angles is continually increased.

Nicholas of Cusa compares the mind of God with the mind of man, and at the same time draws a sharp distinction between them. "If all things are present as precise and proper truths in the mind of God," he writes, "they are all present in our mind as images or likenesses of proper truth; that is, notionally. Indeed, knowledge is gained through likenesses. All things are present in God, but there they are the exemplars of the things; they are all present in our mind, but here they are likenesses of the things." The way in which the things relate to their exemplary Ideas in the mind of God can be compared with the way in which human ideas relate to the things. Knowledge, for Cusanus, is based on *likenesses*; this is a serious asseveration, since it implies a change in the Scholastic interpretation of knowledge and truth as *adaequatio intellectus et rei* (making the mind and the thing equal). For Cusanus, to know is no longer to gain possession of the thing itself, but of something *similar* to it. And Cardinal Cusanus adds: "Between the mind of God and our mind there is the same difference as between doing and seeing. When the mind of God conceives, it creates; when our mind conceives, it assimilates, that is, likens notions, or when it acts, it assimilates intellectual visions. The mind of God is an entifying, or entity-creating force; our mind is an assimilating force."

The seeing activity of man corresponds to the creative activity of God. *Assimilare* is to make like, to obtain a *similitudo*, a likeness of the thing which God created. When God creates the things, he gives them their character as *entities*; man obtains a precipitate which is the *assimilation*. There is no *adaequatio*, but merely *assimilatio*. The truth of the human mind is an *image and likeness* of the truth of the mind of God.

Nicholas of Cusa is very much concerned with the world; he is greatly interested in setting it in harmony with God and reconciling opposites. Medieval man is interested in the being of the world because it was created by God and helps man discover God; Nicholas is interested in God in order to understand the world. And the world, according to Cusanus, is *explicatio Dei*. The oneness of the infinite is explained and manifested in the multiplicity and variety of the world. All things are present in God, but conversely God is present in all things and *explains* or explicates them. The world is a manifestation of God, a *theophany*. Each thing, says Cusanus, is *quasi infinitas finita aut deus creatus*, a finite infinity, as it were, or a created God. He goes so far as to say that the universe is *Deus sensibilis* (God apparent to the senses) and that man is a *deus occasionatus* (a circumstanced god).

These expressions provoked an accusation of pantheism against Cardinal Cusanus similar to the one brought against Meister Eckhart. Again like Eckhart, Nicholas combated this accusation forcefully. According to Nicholas, the presence of God in the world and the interpretation of the world as *explicatio Dei* do not imply a denial of the duality of God and the world or of the idea of the Creation; but we have seen that at the close of the Middle Ages there is an emphasis on the independence of the *created* world with respect to its Creator.

Cusanus' world is the best of worlds; this idea was to be adopted by Leibniz in his metaphysical optimism. Moreover, his world is order and reason; this principle will also be professed by Hegel. In addition, it is infinite in space and time—not like God, who has positive and total infinity and eternity, but with a sort of indeterminateness or limitlessness. In this, the modern position with regard to infinity is neatly defined. For a Greek, to be infinite was a defect in a thing; it was, precisely, a lack of limits. To have limits, to be something determined, was a positive quality. On the other hand, Christianity attributes infinity to God as the highest value; finiteness is felt to be a limitation, something negative; but the finitude of created being, man and the world, is always emphasized. Now, Nicholas of Cusa extends this "near-infinity" to the world in a physical and mathematical sense. This position concerning infinity prevails throughout modern metaphysics, from Giordano Bruno to the German idealists. Nicholas' influence on Spinoza is very strong.

Lastly, Cardinal Cusanus proclaims a principle of individuality within the world. Each thing is an individual concentration of the cosmos, a unit which, like a mirror, reflects the universe. This is especially true of man; each man reflects the world in a different way, and men are true *microcosms*. There is an absolute variety in these units because God never repeats Himself. This is a first sketch of Leibniz' theory of the *monads*.

The mind is "a living measure which achieves its full capacity by measuring other things." *Mens* is here interpreted as *mensura*. Knowledge of the measurable world gives us as a necessary consequence a knowledge of man. Here we find the seeds of physics and of humanism, which are born together. And if the mind is a mirror, it is a *living* mirror which consists in activity. If the mind of God is a *vis entificativa*, the human mind is a *vis assimilativa*; it is only a step from this to Leibniz' "force of representation."

Thus, at the beginning of the fifteenth century, within the direct tradition of the nominalist philosophers and the speculative mystics, there appear one after another the major themes of modern metaphysics. In the work of Nicholas of Cusa we have, in embryo, all the philosophy that is to develop in Europe, from Giordano Bruno's imprecise and confused attempts up to the splendid maturity of Hegel. But this philosophy begins to have true reality only in the seventeenth century, in the thought of Descartes. This fully justifies the present interpretation of the Renaissance.

2. GIORDANO BRUNO

LIFE. Giordano Bruno is the most important Italian philosopher of the Renaissance. He was born in Nola in 1548. He entered the Dominican Order, but later, accused of heresy, abandoned the Order and traveled through several European countries: Switzerland, France, England and Germany. Afterward, he returned to Italy. The Roman Inquisition imprisoned him in 1592, and in 1600 he was burned for refusing to retract his heterodox doctrines. His tragic death and the impassioned brilliance of his writings won him great fame, and this helped increase his subsequent influence.

The influences of Bruno's time are prominent in his work, which reveals ties with Raimundus Lullus, with the practitioners of natural philosophy (Copernicus particularly), and especially with Nicholas of Cusa. For Bruno, too, the world is the matter of chief concern, and he speaks of it with poetic exaltation and enthusiasm for its infinity. Giordano Bruno's principal works were *De la causa, principio ed uno, De l'infinito, universo e dei mondi* and *Degli eroici furori*, in Italian; and, in Latin, *De triplici minimo et mensura, De monade, numero et figura* and *De immenso et innumerabilibus*.

DOCTRINE. Bruno is a pantheist. His major thesis is the immanence of God in the world. As in Cusa's writings, God is *complicatio omnium* (the taking together of all things), *coincidentia oppositorum*; but Bruno goes even further. God is, in addition, the soul of the world, *causa immanens*. This was interpreted as pantheism, as equating the world with God, even though Giordano Bruno did not consider himself a pantheist and made reference to the concept of *natura naturans*, creative nature, the divine soul of the world, as contrasted to *natura naturata*, the world of produced things. But this does not succeed in clarifying the decisive problem of the transcendence of God. For Bruno, the transcendent God is only an object of prayer and worship, but the philosophic God is the immanent cause and harmony of the universe; from this arises Bruno's tendency to revive the Averroist doctrine of the double truth.

This universe is infinite, even spatially. It is full of life and beauty, since everything is a factor in the divine life. Everything is richness and multiplicity. Bruno has an esthetic enthusiasm for nature which is the key to the Renaissance attitude.

Bruno also adopts Nicholas of Cusa's theory of the monads. The individual units of life are indivisible and indestructible, and their infinite combinations produce universal harmony. The soul of the world is the basic monad, *monas monadum* (the monad of monads). Substance is all one, and individual things are no more than particularizations—*circonstanzie*, Bruno calls them—of the divine substance. Bruno's theory of individuals relapses once more into pantheism. Its influence reappears in Leibniz and especially in Spinoza and in Schelling.

3. MODERN PHYSICS

THE FOUNDERS OF THE NEW SCIENCE OF NATURE. With nominalist metaphysics as its starting point, a natural science is established in the sixteenth and seventeenth centuries which differs essentially from that of Aristotle and the Middle Ages in two decisive points: the idea of nature and the physical method. Scientists from Copernicus to Newton fashioned this new physics, which was handed down as a remarkable and respected body of knowledge to our own day, when it underwent another radical transformation at the hands of Einstein, who formulated his theory of relativity; Planck, who founded quantum mechanics; and the physicists who established the bases of wave mechanics (Heisenberg, Schrödinger, de Broglie, Dirac) and nuclear physics (Hahn, Fermi, Oppenheimer, and so forth).

Nicholas Copernicus, a Polish canon, lived from 1473 to 1543. He studied mathematics, astronomy and medicine, and in the last year of his life published his work *De revolutionibus orbium caelestium*, in which he declared that the sun is the center of our celestial system and that the earth and the other planets revolve around it. This idea, which adopted very ancient Greek suppositions, was received with hostility in many areas of opinion because it contradicted all the customary conceptions. In Spain the Copernican system was accepted and taught very quickly. From this time on, the activity of applying mathematical thought to physics becomes very intense.

Johann Kepler (1571–1630), a German astronomer, adopted Copernicus' ideas and in 1609 published the *Physica caelestis*. Kepler supplied rigorous mathematical expressions for Nicholas Copernicus' discoveries, which he formulated in the famous three laws of planetary orbits. In these laws he established that the orbits of planets are ellipses (not circles, which had been considered a more perfect form), that the radius vectors of the planets sweep out equal areas in equal intervals of time, and that the squares of the periodic times of the planets are proportional to the cubes of their mean distances from the sun. Kepler was an extremely energetic champion of the role of mathematics in science: "Man can know nothing perfectly except magnitudes or by means of magnitudes," he wrote. Nevertheless, Kepler did not yet know the general principles of the new physics, nor was he fully master of the modern idea of nature.

Galileo Galilei (1564–1642), born in Pisa, Italy, is the true founder of modern physics. His principal works are *Il Saggiatore*, the *Dialogo dei massimi sistemi* and the *Discorsi e dimostrazioni matematiche intorno a due nuove scienze*. A professor at Padua, he discovered the satellites of Jupiter and declared himself a follower of Copernicus. He was tried by the Roman Inquisition and forced to retract; the traditional tale, not proved, is that on this occasion he uttered his famous phrase, *eppur si muove*. Subsequently the Church recognized the great value and orthodoxy of his thought. It is in Galileo's work that we find stated clearly the idea of nature that is to characterize the modern age, and the full use of the scientific method. We shall presently examine these ideas, which appear completely matured in his writings.

After Galileo there is a long series of physicists who complete and further develop his science: Torricelli, his pupil, who invented the barometer; the Frenchman Gassendi, who remodeled the atomic theory; the Englishman Robert Boyle, who gave chemistry its scientific character; the Hollander Huygens, who discovered important laws of mechanics and originated the wave theory of light; Snellius, who did important work in optics; Descartes, who invented analytical geometry; Leibniz, who invented the infinitesimal calculus; and, above all, the Englishman Newton, who invented it simultaneously and who made the general formulation of the principles of modern physics.

Isaac Newton (1642–1727) was a professor at Cambridge, a philosopher, mathematician, physicist and theologian. In 1687 he published one of the most important books in history: *Philosophiae naturalis principia mathematica*. Newton formulated the law of universal gravitation and interpreted the totality of mechanics as a function of the attractions between masses, expressible mathematically. In his work modern physics attains its purest form and comes to be based on a unitary principle of maximum generality. With the two great mathematical instruments of the seventeenth century, analytical geometry and the infinitesimal calculus, physics can now follow along its path, the "sure path of science" of which Kant will speak a century later.

NATURE. Aristotle understood nature to be the *principle of motion*; an entity is natural if it contains within itself the principle of its movement and, thus, its own ontological possibilities. Aristotle's concept of nature is closely related to his idea of substance. Thus, a dog is a natural entity, whereas a table is artificial, a product of art, and has no principle of motion within itself. The physics of Aristotle and the Middle Ages is the science of nature, the science which is concerned with discovering the *principle* or the *causes* of motion.

Beginning with Occamism, knowledge is conceived of as a knowledge not of *things*, but of *symbols*. This leads us to mathematical thinking, and Galileo will say literally that the great book of nature is written in mathematical characters. Aristotelian motion was a coming to be or ceasing to be; it was thus understood in an ontological way, from the viewpoint of the being of things. Beginning with Galileo, motion is considered as a variation of phenomena: something quantitative, capable of being *measured* and expressed mathematically. Physics will be not a *science of things*, but a science of *variations of phenomena*. Faced with the problem of motion, the physics of Aristotle and the Middle Ages sought its *principle*, and therefore a real affirmation concerning things; modern physics *renounces* principles and seeks only a mathematically determined *law* of phenomena. The physicist renounces the quest for the knowledge of causes and contents himself with an equation which will permit him to measure the course of phenomena. This renunciation, so fertile in its results, separates physics from that which is not physics—philosophy, for example—and establishes it as a *positive* science; thus modern physics is created. (Cf. Zubiri: *La nueva física.*)

METHOD. For a long time it was thought that the characteristic feature of the new physics was the use of experiments. Thus, in contrast to rational Scholastic physics, Galileo's was said to be experimental and empirical, springing from the observation of nature. This is not true; what distinguishes modern physics is what is called the *analysis of nature*. The physicist's starting point is a *hypothesis*, that is, a mathematical type of a priori construction. Before performing his experiment, Galileo knows what will happen; the experiment is merely an a posteriori confirmation of that a priori knowledge. The physicist examines nature with an already existing outline or questionnaire, which is his mathematical hypothesis, his mental construction; *mente concipio*, I conceive with my mind, Galileo said. And with his instruments, with his experiment, the physicist puts his question to nature and compels her to answer, to confirm or refute the hypothesis. "Thus," Ortega writes, "physics is an a priori knowledge confirmed by an a posteriori knowledge." Physics is a science, and therefore an a priori construction; it is not, however, an ideal science, like mathematics, but a science of reality, and therefore requires experimental confirmation. But the decisive trait of Galileo and of the entire *nuova scienza* is the former factor, the a priori character of physics. Moreover, experiments never confirm the hypothesis *exactly*, because the real conditions do not coincide with those of the ideal case in the a priori mental construction, and the Scholastic physicists *based their statements on experiments* in their disputes with the moderns. Thus, a ball rolling down an inclined surface will never satisfy the law of the inclined plane, because the imperfection of the plane and of the sphere and the resistance of the air introduce disturbing friction. Nevertheless, the physical law does not refer to real balls that roll down planes that exist in reality, but to non-existent perfect spheres and perfect planes in frictionless space. (Cf. Ortega y Gasset: *La "Filosofía de la Historia" de Hegel y la historiología.*)

The *inductive* method—here the word "inductive" has a much broader meaning than that which Francis Bacon gives it—is the method that modern physics has used effectively since Kepler, who made use of it to determine the elliptical form of the planetary orbits. Newton—who called it *analysis*, in contrast to *synthesis*—brought great precision to this method and believed it capable of the greatest achievements. The analytical method begins with phenomena and experimentation and works up to universal laws. *In hac philosophia* [*experimentali*], Newton writes, *propositiones deducuntur ex phaenomenis, et redduntur generales per inductionem.* The basis of this inductive method is the very idea of *nature* as the permanent mode of the being and behavior of reality. *Given* the existence of nature, the individual things *induce* us to raise ourselves to general propositions. A single fact reveals a natural determination by virtue of nature's permanent concord with itself; nature is *sibi semper consona.* And, Newton adds, this is the basis of all philosophy: *Et hoc est fundamentum philosophiae totius.* *

This new idea of nature comes about for philosophical reasons and is based on metaphysical *suppositions*, which are foreign to the *positiveness* of science. Therefore, the *principles* of natural science do not belong in the domain of natural science and constitute a problem for philosophy.

4. SPANISH SCHOLASTICISM

In the sixteenth century there is an extraordinary flowering of Scholasticism; it has its center in Spain and culminates in the Council of Trent. The great theologians confront the problems which the Reformation has created; in addition, though faced with Renaissance criticism, they reaffirm their belief in the Scholastic tradition. These philosophers turn again to Thomism and the great systematic works of the Middle Ages, not to repeat them, but to comment on and clarify them—actually, to perform an original and fruitful labor. Moreover, the Spanish Scholastics investigate a series of political and social problems which the Renaissance had questioned; thus, international law is an important topic to them, and ties in with the problem of the condition of the Indians in the recently discovered New World. The two intellectual centers of this movement are Salamanca and Alcalá, but the movement has direct repercussions in Coimbra and also in Rome. Almost all of these Spanish Scholastics acquired their education in Paris, which continued to be an extremely important intellectual focal point.

However, this flowering was short-lived. It remained isolated in Spain and Portugal, and in 1617, after the death of Suárez, it entered into a period of decline. The predominance of theology over philo-

* See my essay "Física y metafísica en Newton" in *San Anselmo y el insensato* [*Obras*, IV].

sophical interest, an orientation determined by the Counter-Reformation, prevented the Spanish Scholastics from establishing sufficient contact with the philosophy and natural sciences of modern Europe, and so this vigorous movement did not become incorporated into the new metaphysics. If things had not occurred in this way, the destiny of Spain and that of Europe would probably have been different. Naturally, the doctrinal contribution to Catholic theology and dogma in the Council of Trent is what has had the greatest importance and most lasting effect.

THE THEOLOGIANS. This restorative labor is carried on by two great Orders, both founded by Spanish saints: the Order of Preachers, founded by St. Dominic Guzmán, and the Society of Jesus, founded by St. Ignatius of Loyola. Both of these Orders included Spanish and French elements and had widespread significance from the very beginning. If the Dominican Order represents the organization of the Church in the thirteenth century, the Society of Jesus stands for the defense of Catholicism in the sixteenth century.

First come the Dominicans. Among them we find Francisco de Vitoria (1480–1546), who studied in Paris and was a professor at Salamanca. He wrote some important commentaries on the *Summa theologiae*, and his lections or *relections*—especially *De justitia* and *De Indis et jure belli*—are a valuable contribution to international law, and one which considerably predates Grotius' *De jure belli ac pacis* (1625).

Vitoria was surrounded by several significant Dominican pupils: Domingo de Soto (1494–1560), who was also a professor at Salamanca; Melchor Cano (1509–1560), who taught at Alcalá and later at Salamanca, was bishop of the Canary Islands and wrote an important work, *De locis theologicis*. Later there was Carranza, and notably, Domingo Báñez (1528–1604), who wrote commentaries on the *Summa* and carried theology to new extremes of acuity in his theory of *physical premotion*.

Toward the middle of the sixteenth century Jesuit theologians begin to appear in Spain. The most important were Alfonso Salmerón, a professor at Ingolstadt and a theologian at the Council of Trent; Luis de Molina (1533–1600), the author of the famous treatise *De liberi arbitrii cum gratiae donis concordia*, in which he expounds his theory of the *middle science*, a doctrine which had a great influence on theology and shaped the movement known as Molinism; the Portuguese thinker Fonseca, a great commentator on Aristotle; and, most important, Francisco Suárez, who was an original philosopher as well as a theologian.

The last important thinker of this group was the Portuguese João de

São Tomé (1589–1644), the author of a *Cursus philosophicus* and a *Cursus theologicus*, both still of great interest.

FRANCISCO SUÁREZ. Francisco Suárez was born in Granada in 1548 and died in Lisbon in 1617. He was born in the same year as Giordano Bruno, and his dates of birth and death are just one year later than those of Cervantes. Suárez joined the Society of Jesus in 1564, after having once been rejected because he was judged not sufficiently bright. He was a professor at Segovia, Ávila, Valladolid, Rome, Alcalá, Salamanca, and finally, from 1597, at the University of Coimbra. He was called *Doctor eximius* and was quick to achieve widespread respect.

After completing several theological treatises, Suárez published, in the same year in which he began his professorship at Coimbra, his philosophical work: the two great volumes of his *Disputationes metaphysicae*. His complete works, which comprise twenty-six folio volumes, include the treatise *De Deo uno et trino*, his great legal opus *De legibus ac Deo legislatore*, the *Defensio fidei adversus Anglicanae sectae errores*—against King James I of England—and the treatise *De Anima*.

Suárez, the only great Scholastic philosopher after Occam, encounters a centuries-old theological and philosophical tradition which had been overwhelmed by a multitude of opinions and commentaries and been handed down in routine fashion. Above all, therefore, it is necessary for Suárez to understand that past, to explain it; in short, *to reconsider tradition in terms of present-day knowledge*. In order to do this he separates metaphysics from theology for the first time in the history of Scholasticism, and creates a systematic construction of first philosophy, based on Aristotle but independent of him, that keeps in mind all the doctrines of the Greek and medieval commentators and the work of the Scholastics—especially that of St. Thomas—in order to determine the "true judgment." Thus, in the fifty-four *Disputationes metaphysicae* he studies the problem of being with clarity and precision, divorcing it from theological questions; however, he does not lose sight of the fact that his metaphysics is oriented to theology, which serves as a prior foundation. Zubiri has written, "Suárez represents the first attempt after Aristotle to make metaphysics an independent body of philosophic doctrine. With Suárez, metaphysics is elevated to the level of an autonomous and systematic discipline."

Suárez' work is not merely a commentary. It is an original philosophy that remains relatively faithful to Thomism, but that maintains the same independence toward it that we saw in Duns Scotus and other great medieval thinkers. He disagrees with St. Thomas on many problems, even on some important ones; however, in Suárez' work these problems are thought out and resolved from his own situation and from a different perspective, one that includes a consideration of the entire doctrinal content of Scholasticism.

For these reasons, Suárez is a real and effective philosopher who should be included in a modern history of philosophy; he has influenced modern thinking more than is generally believed. We are not discussing here an "unknown genius," an unpublished "great thinker" without influence or consequence, for throughout the seventeenth and eighteenth centuries the *Disputations* was used as a textbook in many European universities and even in some Protestant schools. Descartes, Leibniz, Grotius and the German idealists knew and made use of this work. It can be truthfully said that for two centuries Europe learned metaphysics from Suárez, even though his own metaphysics was *utilized* in order to create a different metaphysics, rather than *continued* along the lines of its original inspiration. The most fruitful aspects of the wealth of Scholastic learning passed into modern philosophy by way of Suárez, and in this way Scholasticism was incorporated into a new metaphysics created from a new point of view and by a different method.

Suárez' metaphysics studies the major points of Scholastic philosophy with astuteness and precision. As we have seen, he endeavors to remain as faithful as possible to Thomism, but he does not hesitate to deviate from this doctrine where he thinks it necessary to do so. Sometimes he adopts the view of pre-Thomist philosophers; at other times he comes closer to Duns Scotus and the nominalists; at still other times he expounds new solutions of his own. The Thomist doctrine of the real *distinction* between essence and existence seems false to him; he believes that the distinction consists in a mere intellectual abstraction, and that in an existing complex entity the existence of each one of the metaphysical elements is implied in its essence. Existence, as well as essence, involves composition of partial elements; to be specific, prime matter possesses an existence of its own which is free from the actuality that determines form, and therefore God could maintain it separately.

With regard to the problem of the universals, Suárez, who pays particular attention to the problem of individuation in relation to *persons* and to immaterial entities, does not accept *materia signata quantitate* as being the principle of individuation. The decisive thing about individuals is their *incommunicability*; Suárez affirms that the constituent elements of each substance are principles of individuation: the modal unity of these elements constitutes the individuality of the compound. Suárez' profound investigations into the nature of personality are of Trinitarian and anthropological interest.

Suárez affirms the analogous nature of being, which is predicated of God in a proper and absolute way, and of the things only as things *created* in reference to the Deity. His denial of the real distinction between essence and existence does not imply an identification between divine being and created being, since these are, respectively, *a se* and *ab alio*—the first necessary and the second, contingent. For Suárez, the only incontrovertible arguments for demonstrating the existence of God are *metaphysical* arguments, and he affirms the impossibility of seeing and knowing God naturally; God is seen and known only indirectly, that is, as He is reflected in His creatures.

In his *Treatise on the Laws*, Suárez takes a position on the question of the source of authority. He rejects the theory of the divine right of kings, which the Protestants had made use of and according to which a king derives his authority directly from God, and instead affirms the thesis of popular sovereignty. True authority is based on the consent of the people; the people actually possess the power derived from God, and they have the right to dismiss sovereigns who are unfit to govern.*

An English philosophical current begins in the sixteenth century— with Bacon and Hobbes—which antedates Descartes and Continental idealism; however, we will discuss Cartesianism and idealism first, because the British current is the source of the English empiricism of the following two centuries and forms a separate chapter in modern European philosophy.

* See "Suárez en la perspectiva de la razón histórica" in *Ensayos de teoría* [*Obras*, IV].

SEVENTEENTH-CENTURY IDEALISM

Descartes

Modern philosophy is formed in the seventeenth century. After attempts to restore antiquity and refute Scholasticism, the discontinuous line of thinkers who kept alive the meaning of metaphysics enters into a phase of splendid philosophic maturity. Earlier, I alluded to the discontinuous structure of philosophy; we have witnessed long periods of time that were like great gaps in philosophic speculation, epochs in which man is reduced to commenting on or interpreting earlier works or to a trivial meditation on himself. In contrast, there are other periods in which several brilliant thinkers appear in close succession. This is what happens in the fifth and fourth centuries before Christ in Greece, where, after the great figure of Parmenides and the later pre-Socratics, we find, in a direct teacher-pupil relationship to one another, Socrates, Plato and Aristotle. Then comes a long period of decline. There is an analogous situation in the Middle Ages: the thirteenth century and the first half of the fourteenth century witness a procession made up of the great personalities of medieval thought: St. Bonaventure, St. Thomas, Duns Scotus, Roger Bacon, Eckhart, Occam; and then there is a new falling off, until the seventeenth century. At that time such thinkers as Descartes, Malebranche, Spinoza, Leibniz—not to mention Bossuet, Fénelon and Pascal, who are on the borderline between philosophy and religious thought—appear in close succession. There are also the Englishmen, from Francis Bacon to Hume. Then metaphysics declines once again, until German idealism—from Kant to Hegel—achieves a new splendid outburst; this is soon followed by the somber positivist and naturalistic period of the nineteenth century. And today we are witnessing a latest mighty renaissance of metaphysical thought.

It is in the first decades of the seventeenth century that the philosophic problem is first stated by the modern age. This is the work of Descartes.*

LIFE AND CHARACTER. René Descartes is the decisive figure in the transition from one era to another. His generation marks the passage from the medieval world to the mature modern spirit. Ortega has called Descartes *the first modern man*.

Descartes was born of a noble family in La Haye, Touraine, in 1596. As he was sickly in childhood he required special care, but his cheerful disposition later caused his health to improve. When he was eight years old he went to study at the Jesuit school in La Flèche. This school was extremely important in French intellectual life at that time and had a particular interest in classical languages and literatures, and these Descartes studied intensely. Afterward he began to study philosophy, but a philosophy that was limited by the molds of traditional Scholasticism and that did not refer to or take into consideration the discoveries of modern natural science. Mathematics appealed to him, but he found it lacked application to physics; this is something which he himself was one of the first to establish, in brilliant fashion.

In 1614 he quit La Flèche to go to Paris and lead a life of pleasure. At this time he became a complete skeptic. The knowledge that he had learned in La Flèche seemed to him to be inconsistent, doubtful; only logic and mathematics appeared to contain self-evidence and certainty; but on the other hand, they were of no help in the quest for knowledge of reality. In order to see the world, Descartes took up military life in Holland in 1618 under the command of Prince Maurice of Nassau. There he became familiar with mathematics and the natural sciences. As Goethe remarked, Descartes took advantage of every opportunity to observe everything, to immerse himself in the contemplation of reality, without considering effort, expense or danger.

Later, at the beginning of the Thirty Years' War, he entered the imperial army of Maximilian of Bavaria. Maximilian was fighting the Bohemians, who were led by Frederick V; it was with Frederick's daughter, the Princess Palatine Elizabeth, that Descartes enjoyed a deep and noble friendship. Descartes traveled through Germany, Austria, Hungary, Switzerland and Italy on various campaigns.

---

* The reader will find a more detailed account of the historical origins and the structure of the philosophy of this time in "La metafísica moderna" (in *Biografía de la Filosofía*) [*Obras*, II].

While in winter quarters in Neuburg on November 10, 1619, he made the sensational discovery of his *method*. Later he went to Loretto in order to fulfill a vow of gratitude to the Virgin for this discovery, and in 1625 he again settled in Paris.

From 1629 on, he lived in Holland. This country's tranquillity, liberal atmosphere and independence appealed to him. This was Descartes' most fruitful period, in which he wrote and published his most important works. He established contact with European philosophers and men of science and at the same time was deeply hurt by attacks on his doctrines; these attacks were led principally by the Jesuits, in spite of his still being a Catholic. At this time a few of his pupils deceived and disappointed him, and as a result of this he cultivated his epistolary friendship with the Princess Elizabeth with greater intensity than ever. When Descartes met her in 1643, he realized that Elizabeth, a pretty girl of twenty-five years, had studied his works with interest and intelligence; he mentions this fact with emotion in the dedication to his *Principles of Philosophy*. After this, the friendship became even more profound and intellectually rewarding.

Descartes left Holland only to make short trips, one of them to Denmark. Later he made more frequent excursions into France, where he had become famous. In 1646 he began corresponding with Queen Christina of Sweden, who later invited him to come to Stockholm; Descartes accepted and arrived in the Swedish capital in October of 1649. In spite of his friendship and admiration for Christina, whose conversion to Catholicism his conversations helped to effect, Descartes did not feel at ease in her court. A few months later, in February, 1650, the cold Stockholm winter brought on an attack of pneumonia, and Descartes died that very month. Thus ended this exemplary life of a searcher after truth.

WORKS. Descartes' literary work is quite extensive. His writings are not restricted to philosophical works, but also comprise basic books in the fields of mathematics, biology and physics, and an extensive correspondence. His principal works are *Discours de la méthode*, published in 1637, together with the *Dioptrique*, the *Météores* and the *Géométrie*; the *Meditations on First Philosophy* (1641), together with the *Objections* by Arnauld, Gassendi, Hobbes and others, and Descartes' *Replies* to them; the *Principia philosophiae* (1644); the *Traité des passions de l'âme* (1649), and the *Regulae ad directionem ingenii* (*Rules for the Direction of the Mind*), published after his death, in 1701. Among his not strictly philosophical works are the above-mentioned *Géométrie analytique* and the *Traité de l'homme*. Descartes wrote in Latin, as did practically all the thinkers of his day—but also in French; he was one of the first French prose writers and one of the first to discuss philosophy in the vernacular.

1. THE CARTESIAN PROBLEM

DOUBT. In his development as a philosopher, Descartes realizes that he is deeply insecure. Nothing seems trustworthy to him. The past history of philosophy is completely contradictory; men have championed the most diametrically opposed theses. This multiplicity of opinions gives rise to skepticism (the so-called *historical Pyrrhonism*). Our senses often deceive us and we are also subject to dreams and hallucinations. Our thought processes are untrustworthy because we formulate paralogisms and frequently fall into error. The only sciences that seem to have a secure basis, mathematics and logic, are not real sciences; they do not aid us to know reality. What are we to do in this situation? Descartes wishes to construct—if this is possible—a completely certain philosophy, one which cannot be doubted, and he finds himself totally overwhelmed by doubt. Thus it is precisely his doubt which must be the foundation on which to build; on beginning to philosophize, Descartes starts with the only thing he possesses: his own doubt, his profound uncertainty. It is necessary to cast doubt on all things at least once in one's lifetime, Descartes says. He must not accept a single "truth" that is open to doubt. It is not sufficient that he does not actually doubt that "truth"; there must not be room even for the possibility of a doubt. Therefore Descartes makes doubt the very method of his philosophy.

Only if he finds some principle which it is impossible to doubt will he accept it for his philosophy. It should be kept in mind that he has rejected the presumptive evidence of the senses, the reliability of the thought processes and, of course, traditional and received knowledge. Therefore, Descartes attempts first of all to remain completely alone; this is, in effect, the situation in which man finds himself at the close of the Middle Ages. Starting with this solitude, Descartes must try to reconstruct certainty, a security that is unassailable by doubt. As a primary goal, Descartes attempts *not to err*. This is the beginning of the philosophy of caution.

And, as we shall see, there arise the three great questions of medieval philosophy—and perhaps of all philosophy: the world, man and God. The only thing that has changed is their order and the role each one plays.

THEOLOGY. With regard to theology, which had always afforded a greater certainty, Descartes begins by affirming that separation of philosophy from theology which he found before him. One should not

Descartes

concern oneself with theology, highly respectable though it may be—precisely because it is too respectable and lofty. The reasons he gives are symptomatic of the entire way of thought of the close of the Scholastic era.

"I revered our theology and hoped as much as anyone else to attain heaven; but having learned, as a very sure fact, that the road to heaven is no less open to the most ignorant than to the most learned, and that the revealed truths which lead us there are above the level of our intelligence, I would not dare to submit these truths to my weak powers of reasoning, and I thought that in order to try to examine them and succeed one would need to have some extraordinary assistance from heaven and to be more than man" (*Discourse on Method*, Part I).

Descartes emphasizes the practical, devout side of theology. What is involved is to attain heaven; but it happens that this can be done without knowing anything about theology, and this makes its uselessness manifest. It should be observed that Descartes does not present this as a discovery of his own, but just the opposite: it is something he has learned. Therefore, it is a fact already known, handed down and, in addition, perfectly certain; it is thus *current opinion*. Secondly, this is a matter of revelation which is beyond the level of human intelligence. Reason can accomplish nothing with the great topic of God; it would be necessary to be *more than man*. It is clearly a question of jurisdiction: on one side, man with his reason; on the other, God—omnipotent, inaccessible, higher than all reason—who occasionally deigns to reveal himself to man. It is not man who practices theology, but God; man has nothing to do with this matter: God is too exalted.

2. MAN

THE "COGITO." With the first steps he takes, Descartes must renounce the world. Nature, which showed itself so joyously to Renaissance man through the agency of his senses, is something completely uncertain. Hallucinations, the deceitfulness of our senses, our errors in judgment—all of these make it impossible to find the least certainty in the world. Descartes prepares himself to think that everything is false, but he finds that there is one thing which cannot be false: his own existence. "While I wished to think thus, that everything was false, it necessarily had to be true that I, who was thinking this, was something; and, observing that this truth—*I think, therefore I am*—was so firm and so sure that all the most extravagant suppositions of the skeptics were incapable of shaking it, I judged that I could accept it without a scruple as the first principle of the philosophy I was seeking" (*Discourse on Method*, Part IV).

In effect, if I am in error, it is *I* who am in error; if I am mistaken, if I feel a doubt, *I* am the mistaken one, *I* am the doubter. In order to be wrong in declaring that *I am*, I would need first of all to *be*; that is, I *cannot* be wrong about this. This first truth of my existence, the *cogito, ergo sum* of the *Meditations*, is the first indubitable truth, which I cannot doubt even if I wish to.

There is nothing certain except myself. And I am nothing more than *a thing that thinks*: *mens, cogitatio. Ego sum res cogitans*, Descartes says textually: *je ne suis qu'une chose qui pense*. Therefore, I am not even a bodily man, I am only *reason*. From what we have seen, it is impossible to hold onto the world: it slips away; nor is it possible to retain the body; the only thing that is secure and certain is the thinking subject. Man is left alone with his thoughts. Philosophy is to be based on "me" as a consciousness, as reason; beginning now and for centuries to come, philosophy will be *idealism*—Descartes' great discovery and great error.

This solution is consistent. God had been left out because He was no longer an object of reason; this was the decisive factor. Thus, it is not surprising that reason is found to be the only solid point on which to base philosophy. Despite all appearances, this is nothing new; what occurs now is that reason is a human matter; therefore, philosophy is not merely *rationalism*, but *idealism* as well. There will be an attempt to base all metaphysics on man, or rather on the ego; the history of this attempt is the history of modern philosophy.

THE CRITERION FOR TRUTH. The world did not withstand Descartes' doubt; on its first contact with this doubt, the world was lost and only the ego stood firm. But Descartes has only just begun his philosophy, setting his foot on solid ground. Descartes is interested in the world; he is interested in the things and in that nature which is the concern of the science of his day. But he is a prisoner of his own consciousness, locked up in his thinking ego, and he is unable to take the step which will lead him to the things. How can he emerge from this subjectivity? Now that he has found his indubitable principle, how can he continue his philosophy? Before seeking a second truth, Descartes lingers over the first. It is a very humble truth, but it will help him see what a truth is like. That is, before undertaking the quest for new truths, Descartes examines the only one he possesses in order to see what its truthfulness consists of, what there is about it that makes him know it is true. He thus seeks a *criterion for certainty* in order to recognize the truths he may come across (Ortega). He finds that the truth of the *cogito* consists in his being unable to doubt it; and he cannot doubt it because he sees that it must be so, because it is *self-evident*. This self-evidence consists in the absolute *clearness and distinctness* which this idea possesses. That is the criterion for truth: self-evidence. In possession of a firm truth and a sure criterion, Descartes prepares himself for the reconquest of the world. But to accomplish this he must take a long, circuitous route. And, strange to say, Descartes' roundabout path for getting from the ego to the world passes through God. How is this possible?

3. GOD

THE "MALIGNANT GENIUS." We have seen that Descartes abandons theology, that God is incomprehensible; and now, surprisingly, the Deity interposes itself between man and the world, and Descartes has to concern himself with it. It is necessary to explain this. Descartes knows that he himself exists, and he knows it because he clearly and distinctly perceives the truth of it. It is a truth which justifies itself; whenever he comes across something similar, he will of necessity have to accept it as truth—unless he is in a situation where he is being deceived, unless he is the victim of an illusion, unless there is someone who makes him see as self-evident that which could not be more false. In that case self-evidence would be of no use at all, and he could not affirm any truth other than that he himself existed; this would still be possible because, naturally, if someone deceives me, I am the deceived or, what amounts to the same thing, *I, the deceived, am.* In this situation man would definitely remain a prisoner within himself, and could not with certainty know anything other than his own existence. Who would be able to deceive me in such a way? God, if He exists; we do not know that He does exist, but neither do we know that He does not. (It is understood that this argument is based on the viewpoint of rational philosophic knowledge, and is considered apart from revelation, which Descartes excludes from the realm of doubt.) But if God were to deceive me in this way, making me believe in something that does not exist, plunging me into error, not because of my weakness or because of my rashness, but because of my own feeling of self-evidence, He would not be God; the mind shrinks from imagining such deceitfulness on the part of the Deity. I do not know that God exists, but if He exists, He cannot deceive me. One who could do this would be some powerful *malignant genius.* In order to be sure of the self-evident, in order to be able to trust in the truth which presents itself as truth accompanied by clear and distinct proofs, we would have to demonstrate the existence of God. Otherwise, we cannot take another step in philosophy or seek any truth other than that the ego exists.

THE DEMONSTRATION OF THE EXISTENCE OF GOD. In effect, Descartes proves the existence of God. He does this in several ways, with arguments very different in scope. On the one hand, Descartes says, I find within my mind the idea of God, that is, of an entity which is infinite, completely perfect, omnipotent, all-knowing and so on. Now, this idea cannot come from nothingness, nor can it originate within myself. I am finite, imperfect, weak and full of doubt and ignorance, and if the idea originated within me, the effect would be superior to the cause. This is impossible. Consequently, the idea of God must have been placed within me by some higher entity which attains the perfection of that idea; that is, by God Himself. This proves His existence.

The other demonstration is the one which since Kant is generally known as the *ontological* proof, that is, the argument used by St. Anselm in his *Proslogium* (see above). Nevertheless, there are profound differences between the meaning of St. Anselm's argument and Descartes' proof. Descartes says: I possess the idea of a completely perfect entity, which is God; now, *existence* is an element of perfection, and I find that existence is included essentially in the concept of this entity; thus, it is necessary for God to exist. The two Cartesian proofs, which are closely related to each other, have a factor in common: *I possess the idea of a perfect entity, therefore it exists.* The difference between the two proofs is in the *reasons* Descartes gives, that is, in the manner in which the concept proves existence: the first proof declares that only God can place the idea of Himself within me; the second proof shows that this idea of God which I possess implies His existence. Therefore, the two proofs mutually require and support each other.

Strictly speaking, the point of departure for Descartes' demonstration is the reality of the ego, taken together with a clear and distinct concept of the Deity. My finiteness and imperfection are contrasted with the infinity and perfection of God, the idea of whom I find within myself. By raising to the infinite what is positive in me and removing all limits, I raise myself intellectually to God. In other words, man has within him the *image* of God, which permits him to arrive at the knowledge of God. "This idea [of God]," Descartes says at the end of his third *Meditation*, "was born and produced together with me at the moment of my creation, just as the idea I have of myself was. And in truth it should not be a cause for surprise if God, when creating me, placed that idea within me so that it might be like the *artisan's mark stamped on his product*; nor is it necessary for this mark to be something different from the product itself; on the contrary, by the very fact that God created me, it is easy to believe that in a certain manner He produced me in His *image and likeness*, and that I conceive this likeness, in which the idea of God is contained, by means of the same faculty with which I conceive of myself; that is, that when I reflect upon myself, I not only know that I am an *imperfect* thing, one that is incomplete and dependent upon something else and that unceasingly *reaches and aspires* toward something better and greater than what I am, but I also know at the same time that that upon which I am dependent possesses within itself all those great things to which I *aspire, the ideas of which I find within myself,* and possesses them not in an indefinite manner or only in potentiality, but enjoys them effectually, *actually and unlimitedly,* and that therefore it is God. And the entire force of the argument which I have used here to prove the existence of God consists in my recognizing that it would not be possible for my nature to be the way it is, that is, for me to possess within myself the idea of a God, if God did not truly exist."

But the key to Descartes' proof is the significance which he and, together with him, almost all seventeenth-century philosophers, give to the word "idea." An idea is not merely something which occurs to man; nor is it something which man thinks and which must *coincide* with reality. It is reality itself, *seen. L'idée est la chose même conçue,* Descartes says textually. This is the decisive point, the basis of his two-fold proof; at the same time, it is the most questionable part of the proof, but this is not the place for an extended investigation of the problem involved.

We have seen the necessity for God and the reasons which Descartes adduces to prove His existence, and now one may well ask what is the ontological meaning of that strange argument about the "malignant genius."

THE COMMUNICATION BETWEEN THE SUBSTANCES. If we are deceived by some perverse power, if our strongest self-evidence is merely error, this means that my ideas have no truth, that they are merely "ideas," corresponding to nothing outside of themselves. Then I would be a prisoner within myself, a thinking substance which could not reach the other things—specifically, the extended substance which is the world. This problem of truth and knowledge, stated in Cartesian terms, is the problem of the communication between the substances, which proves to be so difficult when the starting point is my ego, a thinking thing which is absolutely heterogeneous and different from every extended thing, even from the extremely close reality of my own body.

"From this I knew that I was a substance the entire essence or nature of which is merely to think and which in order to exist has no need of any place nor is dependent upon any material thing; so that this ego, that is, the soul, through which I am what I am, is completely distinct from the body" (*Discourse on Method*, Part IV).

REASON AND BEING. Descartes has taken such great care to emphasize the separateness or independence of his reasoning soul that now he cannot emerge into the world. Despite all their self-evidence, the ideas of the *res cogitans* may be pure chimeras, lacking the least connection with the *res extensa*, which is separated from them by a metaphysical gulf: they may be clear and distinct fantasies. But, serious as this may be, it is not the most serious problem. This impossibility of the ego's truly knowing the world has an effect not only on this knowledge of the world but also on the very nature of the *res cogitans*. Reason is not the faculty for producing ideas without truth and without reality; if it is incapable of gaining possession of the world, if it does not permit the ego to envelop the entire extension of the things through that strange process called "knowing" and to possess the truth of the things, it does not deserve to be called *reason*. Therefore, if man is to be in reality what he is for Descartes—a thinking thing, a rational entity—he must achieve a knowledge of the things, he must transcend himself and be capable of truth. And it is God who furnishes the certainty that this is so; He does not deceive man; that is, He causes man's clear and distinct ideas to be true. In other words, God brings it about that when man's ideas are completely clear and distinct, they are *more than ideas* and reflect the reality of the things.

God is the infinite substance which is the basis for the being of the extended substance and the thinking substance. The two are separate and heterogeneous, but they have something in common: they both have being, in the same basic sense of *created being*. And this common root which the two finite substances find in God is the basis for the possibility of their coinciding, and, in short, for the possibility of truth. God, the ontological basis of the ego and of the things, makes it possible for man to know the world.

Only from this point of view do Descartes' proofs acquire their full meaning. The ideas which I possess of the things, he says, may very well be no more than something I have produced, something dependent upon my nature as a thinker, and nothing more; and therefore, these ideas may be true or false. Nothing assures me that what they signify really exists, that they correspond to anything outside of my subjectivity, which is thinking them. On the other hand, the idea of God is one of such perfection and so foreign to my nature and my possibilities that it cannot originate within me; I receive it from without, and therefore from another thing which is not I, viewing a reality which is different from myself. Therefore, the idea of God exerts a

liberating action upon man and makes him emerge from his own self
and come face to face with the actual reality of that which is not
himself.

THE PROBLEM OF SUBSTANCE. Here, however, there arises an
extremely serious question which affects Descartes' ontology at its
root. The ego and the world are two created, finite substances, and
their ontological basis is God, the infinite substance; but now one must
ask: What is *res*, what is *substance*? *Per substantiam*, Descartes says (*Principia*, I, 51), *nihil aliud intelligere possumus, quam rem quae ita existit, ut
nulla alia re indigeat ad existendum* (By substance we can understand
nothing other than a thing which exists in such a manner that it has
need of no other thing for its existence). Thus, substance is defined by
independence; to be a substance means *not* to need another thing in order
to exist; this involves a negative determination which does not tell us
positively what it is *to be a substance*.

On the other hand, Descartes observes that, strictly speaking, the
only independent entity is God, since the created entities have need of
Him, and the word "substance" is not applied to God and to the
created entities univocally, but only *analogically*. It is precisely here,
however, that the difficulty begins. The mind and the world are called
substances because they need *only* God in order to exist, Descartes says;
thus, they possess a relative, attenuated independence. But Descartes
adds that we cannot know substance *alone*, as pure substance, because
it does not affect us, and that we apprehend it only by means of some
attribute, such as extension or thought. Then we must ask again:
What is there in common between God and the created entities that
permits us to call them both substances?

Descartes explains that they are so called merely by analogy; but,
as Aristotle showed in the past, an analogy requires a *basis* that must,
naturally, be *univocal*. What can be the common basis for Descartes'
analogical conception of substance? According to Descartes, the only
defining trait of substance is independence. But *this is also an analogical
conception*, since the independence of the created substances is only
relative. The basis of the presumptive analogy is in turn analogical;
this amounts to saying that for Descartes the notion of substance is
ambiguous. Actually, Descartes does not have a sufficiently strict conception of *being*; he considers it something so obvious that he believes
he can neglect to define it precisely and can concern himself directly
with *entities*. This is the basic defect of Descartes' metaphysics, the consequences of which affect all the thought of the modern age.

From the foregoing we see that before Descartes can concern himself with the world, he must first consider God, and that even though he has renounced theology, there comes a time when he must concern himself intellectually with God. But it is certainly not necessary for him to construct a theology; he need only prove the existence of God, and this he does by means of the ontological proof. The ontological argument allows the idealist, who had lost God and then also the world, to recover the one and, consequently, the other. Cartesian philosophy and, as we shall see, all of idealism up to Leibniz are based on the ontological argument.

4. THE WORLD

THE "RES EXTENSA." In Descartes, the physical world is determined by extension. The *res infinita*, which is God, is accompanied by two finite substances: the thinking substance (man) and the extended substance (the world). These two spheres of reality do not have any contact with each other and are completely dissimilar. This situation gives rise to the problem of the communication between them; this dilemma, which is a consequence of idealism, becomes the chief problem of the seventeenth century. The very fact of knowledge or of man's being already poses this question. How can I come to know the world? How can that which is extended penetrate to me, who am unextended and non-spatial? What is more, if my body and I are two different realities without any possible interaction, how can I govern my body and make it move? It must be God, the ontological basis of the two finite substances, who effects this impossible communication between the substances. The problem which Descartes poses has three possible solutions; these are given by Descartes himself (and more clearly by Malebranche) and by Spinoza and Leibniz.

The world is pure extension. Energy is not a clear idea to Descartes and so he does not consider it. Cartesian physics is geometry; Leibniz will correct this notion by placing the concept of energy in the foreground and by changing static physics into dynamics. Descartes' and Leibniz' two great mathematical discoveries—analytical geometry and the infinitesimal calculus—correspond to these two conceptions. Analytical geometry consists of the application of analysis, of operational calculus, to geometry—and, therefore, in Descartes, to physical reality itself; the infinitesimal calculus makes possible the calculation of variations and the development of dynamics. Matter and space are one and the same; spatiality is the principal quality of matter. The world could be explained by means of a series of whirlwind motions, and after being created could develop in a purely mechanical fashion.

This is an echo of the theory that God's maintenance of the world—
continuous creation—is unnecessary, and that, once created, the
world is self-sufficient.

BIOLOGY. Descartes applies this mechanistic theory to all of physics,
to his studies in the fields of optics and meteorology, and even to
biology. For him, animals are simply automatic machines, *res extensa*.
Since they are the work of God's hands, they are, of course, absolutely
perfect machines, but they have nothing in common with the spiritual
and thinking substance which is man. In man, the pineal body—the
only organ in the area of the brain which occurs singly and furthermore one whose function is unknown—is the point at which the soul
and the body can affect one another. From the pineal body the soul
directs the activity of the *animal spirits*, and vice versa. Later Descartes
realized the impossibility of explaining the communication which
obviously takes place. In his *Treatise on the Passions* Descartes begins a
series of attempts to explain the mechanism of the human psyche by
means of a combination of a few fundamental operations of the mind.
This concludes a basic sketch of Descartes' theory of the world.

5. RATIONALISM AND IDEALISM

Descartes bases his speculation on the criterion of self-evidence.
This self-evidence does not relate either to perception or to the senses
which frequently deceive us, but to the clearness and distinctness of
ideas; it is the self-evidence of reason. Therefore, Descartes' method is
rationalism. Man's only valid criterion is reason, which is common to
all men. Man is a thinking substance, *raison*; and reason is one of the
roots of the a priori science of the seventeenth century. Cartesian
rationalism is also the cause of the equally a priori and antihistorical
spirit that shapes the entire following century and culminates in
dramatic fashion in the French Revolution.

On the other hand, Descartes' method is also *idealist*. How can this
be? The thesis of idealism is in direct opposition to metaphysical
realism. As represented in ancient Greece and the Middle Ages,
realism is the belief that the things have a being of their own, that the
ego exists merely as one thing among others, and that true reality
consists of the things, *res*. To be means *to be* (or exist) *separately, to have a
being that is independent of me*. Idealism, on the contrary, is the belief that
the ego has no sure knowledge of anything other than itself (the *cogito*);
that I know the things only while I am seeing them, touching them,
thinking of them, desiring them, and so forth. (The word *cogitatio* does
not mean only *thought*; it also includes all mental processes.) In other

words, I know the things only while I have dealings with them and witness them. I do not and cannot know what the things are like when they are apart from me—not even if they exist in me, since I know nothing of them without being present. That is, the things appear as existing or being *for me*; thus, they are provisionally *ideas* of mine and the reality that corresponds to them is an ideal reality. The being of things is based on the ego, and resembles ideas on the part of the ego: this is idealism.

Since in Descartes' thought reason is of course no longer the point in which man links himself with the supreme reality of God but rather something exclusively man's own, something restricted to his subjectivity, rationalism is necessarily changed into idealism; thus later on it becomes necessary for God to save this subjectivism and assure the transcendency of the thinking subject.

Descartes bases his philosophy on these two principles of rationalism and idealism, and with rare exceptions, from his time until our own, philosophy is both of these things. Only in recent years has metaphysics reached conclusions which, although deriving from the great partial truths that the two Cartesian principles contain, correct the element of error that affects them. Recent metaphysics on the one hand points out that the ego is in turn essentially dependent on the things it encounters constantly during its life; and on the other hand transforms the exclusively speculative and mathematical conception of reason. Ortega took a decisive step in this direction with his metaphysics of vital reason.*

* Cf. "Los dos cartesianismos" in *Ensayos de teoría* [*Obras*, IV].

Cartesianism in France

Descartes shapes all the philosophy of the seventeenth century on the Continent. His influence is seen not only in his pupils and immediate followers, but also in the independent thinkers and even the theologians Pascal, Fénelon and Bossuet. In France it is especially apparent in Malebranche, and outside of France in the great figures of Spinoza and Leibniz. Let us see how this philosophy develops.

1. MALEBRANCHE

Nicolas de Malebranche was born of a prominent family in Paris in 1638 and died in 1715. As he was always in very poor health he endured great suffering and had to be extremely cautious. He studied philosophy at the Collège de la Marche, but felt deceived, just as Descartes had at La Flèche; later he studied theology at the Sorbonne, but the intellectual methods there did not satisfy him either. In 1660 he joined the Congregation of the Oratory, an organization that has given France a great many men of superior mentality, from Malebranche himself to Father Gratry in the nineteenth century. Fontenelle remarked that Malebranche had been raised to the priesthood "by nature and grace." The members of the Congregation had great intellectual restlessness and studied Plato and St. Augustine at the same time that they investigated Descartes' philosophy. In 1664, Malebranche bought a copy of Descartes' *Traité de l'homme* in a bookstore; it made a tremendous impression on him and he discovered in it the method which he had always secretly looked and longed for. From that time on his predilection for philosophy was decided, and he began to study Descartes' philosophy seriously. He completed his education by studying the work of St. Augustine in particular and also that of Arnold Geulincx, a thinker from the Netherlands as well as that of others who were concerned with advancing the progress of natural science: Francis Bacon, Hobbes, Gassendi, and so on. Ten years later Malebranche began his literary production. At the same time he established cordial and/or dissentious relationships with most of the great contemporary figures: Arnauld, Fénelon, Bossuet, Leibniz, Locke, Berkeley. Malebranche was very much drawn to the quiet life and to solitary meditation, and his life in the bosom of the community of the Oratory was as retiring and silent as he could make it. He died at the age of seventy-seven, full of tranquillity and profound religious feeling.

WORKS. Malebranche's principal work is the *Recherche de la vérité*. Afterward he published the *Conversations chrétiennes*, and later the *Méditations chrétiennes*. Still later he wrote the *Traité de la nature et de la grâce*, a work that occasioned a violent controversy and was included in the Index by the Roman Inquisition. He also wrote a very important dialogue called *Entretiens sur la métaphysique et sur la religion*, and a *Traité de morale*. These are the most important items of Malebranche's philosophic production.

OCCASIONALISM. The core of Malebranche's philosophy is his theory of occasionalism, which had been begun by Arnold Geulincx, a professor at Louvain and later, after his conversion to Calvinism, at Leiden. Malebranche's problem, which arises from the Cartesian situation, is that of the transcendency of the thinking subject and, in general, of communication between the substances. Descartes had already attempted to make allowance of a sort for the interaction between the substances by reducing it to the tiny motions and changes of the pineal body. Malebranche affirms textually that there is not, nor can there be, any communication between the mind and corporeal bodies. "It is self-evident that bodies are not visible in themselves, that they cannot act upon our spirit or manifest themselves to it" (*Recherche de la vérité*, explanation X). Direct knowledge of the world is therefore absolutely impossible; however, there is something that makes knowledge of the world possible: God has within Himself the ideas of all the created entities; this is part of the explanation; furthermore, "God is very closely united to our souls by His presence, so that it can be said that He is the site of spirits, just as space is in a sense the site of bodies. Given these two things, it is certain that the spirit can see what there is in God that manifests the created beings, since this is very spiritual, very intelligible and very much present to the spirit." And a few pages further on, Malebranche adds: "If we did not see God in some manner, we would not see anything" (Recherche de la vérité, book III, part 2, chapter VI).

The difficulty is found in the phrase "in some manner." God is known indirectly; He is reflected in the created things, as in a mirror; according to the text of St. Paul (Romans 1:20): Invisibilia Dei . . . per ea quae facta sunt intellecta conspiciuntur (The invisible things of him . . . are clearly seen, being understood by the things that are made). Malebranche strives to retain a correct and admissible interpretation of the vision of God, but he does not succeed in avoiding error. He frequently inverts the terms of the Paulist formula and affirms the direct knowledge of God and of the things in Him. This error has had repercussions, especially on Antonio Rosmini-Serbati and Vincenzo Gioberti, Italian "ontologists" of the nineteenth century.

It is God who makes it possible for me to know the inaccessible things. His spirituality carries within it the ideas of the corporeal things created by Him. All things have in common the fact that they are created beings. Being is present in the things and in a sense unifies them, in spite of their basic diversity. This complete ontological link is what permits us to speak meaningfully of reason. From the condition of a subjectivity without reference to reality, one would not be able to say that reality existed. The things are extended and corporeal, foreign to my spirit; but God's ideas, the models according to which the things are created—a union of Augustinianism and Cartesianism—are spiritual, adapted to the thinking being, and God is the site of the spirits. Man partakes of God, and through Him of the things, and thus the metaphysical gulf is bridged. There is no direct interaction between the substances; the harmony between them is achieved by God; this is the theory of the occasional causes: I do not perceive the things; rather, on the occasion of a movement of the res externa, God arouses in me a certain idea; on the occasion of a volition on my part, God moves the extended body that is my arm. What is decisive is the human spirit's relationship with God, and with the things only through him. Malebranche is fully aware of this: "There is no one who does not agree that all men are capable of knowing truth; and even the least enlightened philosophers agree that man partakes of a certain reason which they do not specify. Therefore, they define man as animal RATIONIS particeps: for there is no one who does not know, at least confusedly, that the essential characteristic of man consists in the necessary union that he has with universal reason" (Recherche de la vérité, explanation X).

Malebranche's words are so clear and meaningful that I prefer to quote them textually, rather than comment upon them. In God we see all the things; this is the necessary condition for all knowledge and all truth. Malebranche takes literally and strictly St. John's words in the fourth Gospel: God is *lux vera quae illuminat omnem hominem venientem in hunc mundum* (the True Light, which lighteth every man that cometh into the world). Therefore, God is absolutely necessary; although the totality of the essence of God is not known, it is necessary to know at least that He exists. Malebranche's philosophy also requires proof of the existence of God, and finds its basis in this. Malebranche carries Cartesianism to its ultimate consequences in the direction indicated by its founder. Other philosophers will begin at the same point but will follow different paths.

2. THE RELIGIOUS THINKERS

In the seventeenth century and in the first years of the eighteenth there is in France a series of Catholic thinkers, mostly theologians and even mystics, who are profoundly influenced by Cartesian philosophy. There thus originates an extremely fruitful intellectual current that characterizes French spiritual life for a century and conditions the subsequent destiny of French philosophy. In other countries theological thought remains attached to the mental and even expository forms of Scholasticism, while modern philosophy follows a separate course without even touching them. The French religious thinkers follow in the medieval tradition, which is composed of two principal parts—the philosophy of St. Augustine and that of St. Thomas; but they are influenced by Cartesianism, especially in regard to Descartes' method, and from this synthesis there arises a new form of thought which could perhaps be called "Cartesian theology" or even *modern* theology. The general architecture of Thomism is maintained over a base of Augustinian presuppositions but, at the same time, Descartes' philosophic discoveries are utilized, as are his methods of investigation and literary exposition. In this way the Hellenic and medieval traditions are salvaged and are studied in the light of modern thought; thus in France Catholic thought retains a vitality that it soon loses in other places. On the other hand, these theologians constantly touch on philosophic problems, and frequently they bring to bear on philosophy the precision and high standards which theology has always contributed to metaphysical thought.

THE JANSENISTS. Cornelis Jansen or Jansenius, bishop of Ypres, who was closely connected with the Abbé de Saint-Cyran, tried to create a theological interpretation of human nature and grace based on the thought of St. Augustine and the Fathers of the Church. In 1640, shortly after the author's death, Jansen's *Augustinus* was published; it was condemned three years later. The Jansenist spirit infiltrated in particular the abbey of Port-Royal, which was run by Mother Angélique Arnauld. In France, the condemnation of the *Augustinus* and the condensation of Jansenist doctrine into five propositions, which were also condemned, led to a long and lively controversy, the details of which do not pertain to this discussion. In brief, the Jansenists opposed the moral casuistry of the Jesuits, whom they accused of laxity. The most important thinkers of the Port-Royal group were Antoine Arnauld (1612–1694) and Pierre Nicole (1625–1695). Apart from their theological works, they are together the authors of the famous book entitled *La logique ou l'art de penser*, known by the title of *Logic of Port-Royal*.

PASCAL. Blaise Pascal (1623–1662), a brilliant mathematician of exceptional precocity and a mystic and polemicist with a profound and passionately religious spirit, maintained close ties with the recluses of Port-Royal. Apart from his physical and mathematical treatises, Pascal wrote the *Lettres à un Provincial* or *Lettres provinciales*, by means of which he took part in the anti-Jesuit polemics, and above all, his *Pensées sur la religion*, a fragmentary work of extraordinary religious and philosophic interest; actually it consists of only random notes for a book that was never written.

Seemingly, Pascal is opposed to Cartesianism, to its confidence in reason, and is almost a skeptic. But in reality Pascal is in large measure Cartesian, even when he opposes Descartes. Primarily he is rigorously motivated by Christian presuppositions, and his thought evolves from them. If on the one hand Pascal, like Descartes, apprehends man in his thinking dimension, on the other hand he is acutely aware of man's frailty, dependence and misery: man is a thinking reed (*un roseau pensant*). And one rises from this misery of man separated from God to the greatness of man together with God, who is great because he recognizes his dependence and can have knowledge of the Deity. Pascal's anthropology is of very great interest.

With regard to the problem of Pascal's attitude toward reason, it is necessary to emphasize that he distinguishes between what he calls *raison*—which is generally understood to mean reasoning power or syllogism—and what he calls *cœur*, heart. "The heart," he says, "has its reasons of which reason knows nothing." And he adds, "We know truth not only through reason, but also through the heart; we know the first principles by the latter way, and in vain does reasoning, which does not partake of them, try to discredit them. . . . Our knowledge of the first principles is as firm as any knowledge that reasoning furnishes us. And it is on knowledge obtained through the heart and the instinct that reason must depend and on which it must base all its discourse." *Cœur* has nothing to do with sentiment; rather, for Pascal it is a faculty for obtaining knowledge of the principal truths which are the basis for reasoning.

Pascal seeks God, but since he is basically a religious man, he wants to seek God in Christ, and not only in mere reason; he writes these words, which echo Augustinian thought: "Truth itself is made an idol. But truth separated from charity is not God; it is His image, an idol which one need not love or worship." And he sums up his whole philosophic attitude in a phrase which illuminates its true meaning: "Two excesses: to exclude reason; to admit nothing but reason."

BOSSUET. One of the major figures of that theological current influenced by Descartes' philosophy was Jacques Bénigne Bossuet (1627–1704), bishop of Meaux. Bossuet was an important personality of his day, and the soul of the Church in France for half a century. He was a great religious orator, historian, theologian and philosopher. In association with Leibniz, he was very active in the *irenic* negotiations aimed at reconciling the Protestant and Catholic Churches; in this connection, he wrote his *History of the Variations in the Protestant Churches*. His most significant philosophical works are the treatise *De la connaissance de Dieu et de soi-même* and the *Discours sur l'histoire universelle*, a true philosophy of history which relates to St. Augustine's *City of God* and which, in a certain manner, prepares the way for the work of Vico, Herder and especially Hegel.

FÉNELON. Another great ecclesiastical figure in France is Fénelon (1651–1715), the Archbishop of Cambrai. Fénelon engaged in a controversy with Bossuet over quietism, the heresy which was introduced by the Spaniard Miguel de Molinos, author of the *Guia espiritual*, and was spread abroad in France by Madame Guyon. Certain propositions in Fénelon's *Histoire des maximes des saints* were condemned; as a faithful Christian, he retracted his error. His most interesting philosophical work is the *Traité de l'existence de Dieu*.

In a certain sense, Fénelon represents a continuation of Bossuet's thought, but he carries it even further. Not only does he adopt a series of Descartes' discoveries, such as his dualism and the conception of man as a thinking entity; he also makes Descartes' method his own: universal doubt. Starting with the indubitable self-evidence of the ego, he attempts to reconstruct reality and to arrive at God. The second part of his treatise is unadulterated Cartesianism. But whereas Descartes is purely and simply a philosopher, Fénelon is above all a theologian; in the last analysis, therefore, the orientation of his thought is very different.

Spinoza

LIFE AND WORKS. Baruch de Spinoza was born in Amsterdam in 1632. He came from a family of Spanish Jews who years before had emigrated to Portugal and afterward to the Netherlands. His religious opinions caused his expulsion from the synagogue, and from that time on he was more closely associated with Christian circles, although he did not profess Christianity. He Latinized his given name Baruch (blessed), using the form Benedictus. His life was spent in Holland, especially in the city of his birth and in The Hague; he was always poor and withdrawn, and he earned his living by polishing lenses. Spinoza (or perhaps he might be called by the Spanish form of his name, Espinosa, which his family probably used originally) was always sickly and felt a great need of independence. When offered a professorship at the University of Heidelberg, he refused in order not to compromise his freedom. Spinoza was a loyal friend of Jan de Witt. He was still young when he died in 1677.

His writings, with the exception of a few works in Dutch, are almost all in Latin. The most important works are the *Tractatus de intellectus emendatione*, the *Brief Treatise on God, Man and His Happiness* (in Dutch), the *Tractatus theologico-politicus*, the *Tractatus politicus* (an exposition of Descartes' *Principia*), the *Cogitata metaphysica* and, above all, his master-work, published after his death: the *Ethica ordine geometrico demonstrata*. This work follows the manner of exposition customary in books on mathematics, with axioms, definitions, propositions with their proofs, scholia and corollaries. It is an example of the rationalistic and mathematical tendencies carried to their extreme and by this time affecting even the external form of philosophy.

1. METAPHYSICS

THE POINT OF DEPARTURE. Spinoza appears as the heir of several philosophical traditions. First of all and most directly, he follows in the path recently established by Descartes; in addition, he has ties with Scholasticism, particularly with Scotism and Occamism; he has studied the work of Suárez. He also has contact with Jewish sources: first, with the Bible and the Talmud; secondly, with medieval Jewish philosophers, principally Maimonides and those of the Cabbala. Another influence should be noted: the Greek tradition, especially Stoicism. And, of course, there is the influence of the natural science of Spinoza's day and the philosophy of Giordano Bruno, as well as Hobbes' theories of the State and politics. These are the principal roots of Spinoza's thought; from them he derives his unique philosophical personality within seventeenth-century metaphysics.

SUBSTANCE. Spinoza adopts Descartes' situation as his starting point. For Descartes, substance was understood as that which has need of nothing else in order to exist; strictly speaking, only God could be substance. Afterward Descartes came across other substances which did not need other *creatures* in order to exist, although they did need God; these were the *res cogitans* and the *res extensa*. Spinoza accepts this quite rigorously, and defines substance in this way: *Per substantiam intelligo id quod in se est et per se concipitur ; hoc est, id cujus conceptus non indiget conceptu alterius rei, a quo formari debeat* ("By substance I understand that which exists in itself and is conceived through itself; that is, that thing the concept of which does not have need of the concept of any other thing, by which it must be formed"). Therefore, Spinoza will only recognize a single substance. What, then, are all the other things? They are not substances, but *attributes*; an attribute is that which the mind perceives in substance as a constituent of its essence. There are an infinite number of attributes, but the intellect knows only two: *cogitatio* and *extensio*, thought and extension, that is, Descartes' *res cogitans* and *res extensa*, now demoted in the ontological hierarchy; they are no longer substances, but merely attributes of the one substance.

The *individual things*—which Descartes had already deprived of their traditional nature as part of substance, reserving the name of substance for his two *res*—are *modes* of substance, that is, affections of substance; they are that which exists in some other thing and is conceived through some other thing. These modes affect substance according to its different attributes.

GOD. Spinoza defines God as the *absolutely infinite* entity, that is, the substance which consists of infinite attributes, each one of which expresses an eternal and infinite essence. This entity coincides with the single possible substance. God is the necessary entity, the entity *a se*, and is synonymous with substance; the attributes of substance are the infinite attributes of God. And this God of Spinoza's, who is equated with substance, is *nature*. *Deus sive natura* (God, or nature), Spinoza says. Substance—or God—is *everything that exists*, and all the things are affections of Him. Therefore, He is nature in a double sense. In one sense, all things proceed from God and God is the origin of all things; this is what Spinoza calls *natura naturans*. But, on the other hand, God does not create anything which is different from Himself, so that He is nature in another sense: He is the emerging, budding things themselves; this is what Spinoza calls *natura naturata*. Thus, Spinoza's system is pantheistic.

Spinoza's God is expressed through the individual things in the two basic attributes which man knows: thought and extension. Thus, this is a reappearance of Descartes' outline, but with an essential change: of Descartes' three substances, one infinite and two finite, only the first is still characterized as substance, while the other two are now attributes of substance.

COMMUNICATION BETWEEN THE SUBSTANCES. We have seen how the problem of the communication between the substances made its appearance within Descartes' metaphysics, and we have observed the first solution to it as provided by occasionalism. Malebranche denies that there is any actual communication between the substances. Spinoza's doctrine is much more radical: he frankly and openly denies all plurality of substance. There is only *one* substance, with two attributes; there can be no *communication*, but only *correspondence*. There is a strict parallelism between the two attributes of the single substance which man knows, extension and thought, and therefore, between the mind and corporeal things: *Ordo et connexio idearum idem est, ac ordo et connexio rerum* (The order and connection of ideas are the same as the order and connection of the things). And it is precisely by his depriving extension and thought (in short, the *world* in its broadest sense) of their standing as substances, which they still retained for Descartes, and reducing them to mere attributes of the single substance, that Spinoza is compelled to identify substance with God, on the one hand, and with nature, on the other: *Deus sive substantia sive natura* (God, or substance, or nature). It is at this point that Spinoza's pantheism arises. His philosophy is scarcely concerned with anything else but God, but although this would seem to be a new theology, it is only the metaphysical study of substance and, at the same time, the rational

consideration of nature, understood as Descartes understood it, geometrically.

In Spinoza's system, as in all other seventeenth-century systems, it
is necessary to establish the existence of God, but here in a perhaps
even more extreme sense, since it is necessary to attribute to nature
itself not only the standing of substance but godhood as well. For
Spinoza, *being* does not mean *being that is created by God*, but simply
God's being.

2. ETHICS

THE PLAN OF THE "ETHICS." Spinoza's metaphysics culminates in
his ethics. Therefore, his major work, in which he expounds the
general content of his philosophy, bears that title. The *Ethics* (*Ethica
ordine geometrico demonstrata*) is divided into five parts: I. Of God;
II. Of the Nature and Origin of the Mind; III. Of the Origin and
Nature of the Passions; IV. Of Human Bondage, or Of the Force of
the Passions; and V. Of the Power of the Intellect, or Of Human
Freedom. First of all, therefore, he expounds his ontology: the theory
of God, or substance. Secondly, he studies the structure of the mind
and takes up the problem of knowledge. Then he enumerates and
defines the passions, which he interprets in a naturalistic and geometrical fashion: he wishes to speak about human actions and drives "as if
discussing lines, planes or solid bodies." Lastly, he expounds his
theory of human slavery or freedom, depending on whether man's
passions or his reason prevail; it is in these final sections, in which he
states his ethical problem proper, that the meaning of his whole philosophy is summed up.

MAN. For Spinoza, everything is nature; it makes no sense to contrast something else, such as *spirit*, with nature. Man is *cogitatio*,
thought, but this thought is just as much nature as a stone is. Man is a
mode of substance, a mere modification of God in the two attributes of
extension and thought; in this consists the unique standing of man,
who has a body and a soul; the soul is the idea of the body. And just
as there is an exact correspondence between ideas and things, so there
is a strict parallelism between the soul and the body. Everything that
happens to or affects man, and especially his own passions, is natural
and follows the necessary course of nature. For Spinoza, "that thing is
called free which exists only by necessity of its nature and determines
its actions by itself"; this is a concept of freedom which allows freedom
only to God. Spinoza is a determinist: "Man cannot be considered as
an empire within another empire." Therefore, man is not free and the
world does not have a teleological end; everything is necessary and

causally determined. Man is a slave because he believes he is free while being drawn along by necessity. Only one type of freedom remains open: knowledge. When man knows what he is, he knows that he is not free and does not feel constrained or coerced, but determined according to his essence; therefore, reason is freedom. The being of man, who is a mode of substance, a *mens* and a *corpus*, consists in not being free and knowing it, in living within nature, in God. This is an echo of the Stoic principle: *parere Deo libertas est*, obedience to God is freedom.

Philosophy, the knowledge concerning being and substance, is a knowledge of God. And this highest type of knowledge, in which freedom and happiness reside, is *amor Dei intellectualis*, the intellectual love of God, which for Spinoza represents the culmination of both philosophy and human life.

3. Being as a Desire to Survive

In the third part of his *Ethics*, Spinoza expounds a conception of being as a longing to go on living forever; it is important to touch on this conception, if only very briefly. Every thing, says Spinoza, in so far as it exists in itself, tends to persevere in its being, and this desire is nothing more than the actual essence of the thing; it is a desire involving a limitless, infinite time; it is a longing to continue to exist forever. The human mind wishes to endure without limitation in time and is aware of this desire, which, when referring to the mind alone, is called the *will*, and when referring to the mind and the body together, is called an *urge*. This urge to live is nothing other than the very essence of man: his *wish* is the awareness of his urge.

We do not seek after things, Spinoza says, we do not want or long for something because we believe it is good, but just the reverse: we think something is good because we seek it, want it, long for it or desire it. This *cupiditas* (longing) is man's principal emotion; there are two other major emotions, joy and sadness, which correspond to an increase or a diminution, respectively, of being and perfection. All the other emotions are derived from these three, as is man's entire psychic life: love, hate, and so forth.

Therefore, what constitutes the being of things for Spinoza is a *desire*, a striving, and this desire is a yearning to live forever. Thus, for Spinoza, *to be* means *to want to be forever*, to have a *longing for eternity* or at least for a lasting existence. The essence of man is wishing: man consists in the wish to live forever and the knowledge that he wishes it. This is the deep-rooted form in which the problems of being and immortality are linked together in Spinoza's philosophy.

Leibniz

LIFE AND CHARACTER. Gottfried Wilhelm Leibniz was born in Leipzig in 1646 and died in Hanover in 1716. His family was Protestant, and many of his forebears had practiced law. Leibniz devoted himself to intensive study from a very early age. He learned the classical languages, Greek and Latin; the literatures of antiquity; Scholastic philosophy, of which he acquired a very good knowledge; and, afterward, modern philosophy—Francis Bacon, Campanella, Descartes, Hobbes. He became acquainted with the mathematics and physics of his day, and studied the works of Kepler and Galileo. In addition, he seriously pondered questions of law and history, took up the study of alchemy and felt a boundless curiosity for all forms of knowledge.

Leibniz soon began to participate in the life of his age. He sent papers to the European learned societies; he went to France as part of a diplomatic mission, and made the acquaintance of the greatest intellectuals of that time; he also visited London. Later, in 1676, he invented the infinitesimal calculus, *le calcul des infiniment petits*, at the same time that Newton invented the same discipline, although Newton developed it in a different form and called it the *method of fluxions*. A great controversy raged between the partisans of both men—greater than that between the two originators themselves—but it appears that each one developed the calculus independently, without reciprocal influences.

When Leibniz returned to Germany, the Duke of Brunswick appointed him librarian of the ducal library at Hanover, where he lived almost constantly from that time on, except when he was trav-

236

eling. At Hanover he was engaged in intense intellectual, diplomatic and political activities; he also busied himself as a historian, compiling the *Annales Brunswicenses*. On his own initiative he founded the Berlin Academy of Sciences in 1700, modeling it on those of Paris and London; he was its first president. An important figure of his time, he also traveled in Italy, Austria and Holland. He was actively concerned with his plan to unify the Catholic and Protestant Churches. Leibniz was very much attracted to Catholicism, but did not wish to renounce his background and be converted; he wished instead to reconcile the two creeds. Despite his efforts and those of Bossuet and Rojas Spínola, the project failed. Leibniz died in obscurity, almost totally neglected after an intense life full of marvelous intellectual achievement.

WORKS. Leibniz wrote numerous books on mathematics, physics, history and especially philosophy. Nearly all his works are written in French or in Latin, and only a very few, secondary ones in German. No one had yet cultivated German as a language suitable for philosophy; it was Leibniz' pupil Wolff who first did this. Leibniz' entire personality reveals a strong French influence, and alongside the international language—Latin—he preferred to use French, the civilized language of the era. Leibniz' principal *philosophical* works are two long books, the *Nouveaux essais sur l'entendement humain* and the *Théodicée*. The first of these, directed against the English philosopher Locke's *Essay Concerning Human Understanding*, was not published during Leibniz' lifetime, because Locke died while it was being prepared for publication. The *Theodicy* poses the problem of the *justification of God's ways*, that is, the problem of reconciling God's goodness and omnipotence with the existence of evil and with human freedom. In addition, Leibniz produced several brief writings, in particular the *Discours de métaphysique*, perhaps his most systematic and interesting philosophical exposition; the *Système nouveau de la nature*; the *Principes de la nature et de la grâce, fondés en raison*; and the *Monadologie*, written for Prince Eugene of Savoy. Besides these, Leibniz left a great deal of correspondence on intellectual matters with Arnauld, Clarke and others; most of this is still unpublished.

1. LEIBNIZ' PHILOSOPHIC SITUATION

Leibniz represents the end of the period of philosophy which began with Descartes and which more or less corresponds to the Baroque age. This means that Leibniz appears at the end of a seldom equaled epoch of intense metaphysical speculation; indeed, when Leibniz reached his intellectual maturity this metaphysical outburst had already been going on for sixty years. The rationalist systems had succeeded one another rapidly—those of Descartes, Malebranche, Spinoza, the thinkers of Port-Royal, the Jansenists. This era had also witnessed a great outburst of theological speculation: Spanish Scholasticism, which included Suárez, Melchor Cano, Báñez, Molina and all the speculation centered on the Council of Trent. Leibniz is aware of this double current made up of rationalism, on one hand, and Scholasticism—particularly Spanish Scholasticism—on the other. His pages are sprinkled with Spanish names, precisely the names of those individuals who possessed true intellectual worth and command places in the living history of thought, those who have affected philosophy and been intellectually precise; this is comforting to anyone who keeps the meaning of truth alive and does not delight in easy praise wherein all clarity and critical judgment are lost. Leibniz rose completely above that disdain of Scholasticism which characterized the superficial thinkers of the Renaissance and which the earliest rationalists retained, at least externally; he once more explicitly makes use of Aristotelian ideas, as well as numerous medieval ideas and many of the acute theological concepts put forth at Trent. In addition, he devotes himself intensely to mathematics and the new natural science, and advances both to an extraordinary degree. In this way he unites and completely dominates all philosophic, theological and scientific traditions. Leibniz is the epitome of the entire age.

The specific background against which Leibniz moves is the philosophic situation bequeathed by Descartes and Spinoza. Leibniz is perhaps the first idealist in the strict sense of the word; in Descartes, idealism is still weighed down with realism and Scholastic ideas, and Spinoza is not really an idealist with regard to what is most characteristic or personal in his thought, although perhaps the ideological tenor of his time, within which he stated his problems, was idealistic. Leibniz will see himself obliged to set forth with precision the great questions of the epoch, and he will have to alter essentially the conception of physics and the very idea of substance, in which philosophy since Aristotle has always been centered.

2. LEIBNIZ' METAPHYSICS

DYNAMISM. For Descartes, being was either *res cogitans* or *res extensa*. The physical world was extension, something at rest. The concept of force was foreign to him; he found it confusing and obscure, and did not see how it could be translated into geometrical concepts. Descartes understood motion as a change of position of a moving body in respect to a point of reference; the two points are interchangeable: to say that

A moves in respect to *B* is the same as saying that *B* moves in respect to *A*; physics is interested only in change of position. Descartes believed that the quantity of motion in the universe (mv) remains constant. Leibniz shows that what is constant is the kinetic energy, *vis viva* $(\frac{1}{2}mv^2)$. Descartes' static, geometrical concept of physics seems absurd to Leibniz. Motion is not mere change of position, but something *real*, something produced by a *force*. If one billiard ball collides with another, the latter is sent off; this is so because there is a force, a *vis*, which sets the second billiard ball in motion. This concept of force, *vis*, *impetus*, *conatus*, is the basis of Leibniz' physics—and his metaphysics as well. Descartes'notion of static and inert nature is replaced by a *dynamic* concept of nature; a physics based on energy is set up in opposition to a physics based on extension—in short, a physical rather than a geometrical concept of nature. One must not forget that since the days of Greece nature was the *principle of motion*. Now Leibniz must arrive at a new idea of substance.

THE MONADS. For Leibniz, the metaphysical structure of the world consists of the *monads*. Monad (in Greek, μονάς) means *unity*. The monads are basic substances, substances without component parts, which group to form complex things; they are the elements of the things. Since they are not made up of parts, they are strictly indivisible —atoms—and therefore unextended, for atoms cannot have extension, inasmuch as extension is always divisible. A "material atom" is a contradictory expression: the monad is a *formal atom*. These elemental monads cannot decay or perish through disintegration, nor can they be built up from parts. Therefore a monad comes to be only through creation and ceases to be only through annihilation. Thus a monad comes into being *tout d'un coup* and not by a process of generation. Leibniz says that these monads are "windowless"; that is, that nothing can issue from one monad and pass on and affect another. The monads possess qualities and are different from one another; moreover, they change continually. However, this changing is not extrinsic; rather it is the unfolding of the monad's internal possibilities.

The monad is *vis*, force; a *vis repraesentativa*, or force of representation. Every monad *actively* represents or reflects the entire universe *from its own perspective*. Therefore, the monads are irreplaceable, since each one reflects the universe in its own special way. Leibniz' metaphysics shows that he is a *pluralist* and that he believes the things actually exist, even when no perceiver is present. The monads are not all of equal rank; they reflect the universe with varying degrees of clarity. Furthermore, not all monads are conscious of their power of reflection. When monads have this consciousness and also memory, it is possible to speak not only of *perception* but also of *apperception*: such is the case with the human monads. And this representation of the universe is active: it is the monads' purpose, tendency—a *desire* that arises from the monad's ontological basis itself, from its own reality. Everything that happens to a monad arises from its own being, from its internal possibilities; the monads are completely insensitive to external influences.

Thus Leibniz does just the opposite of Spinoza; Spinoza reduces substance to a single entity—nature or God—whereas Leibniz restores to substance the character of an *individual thing* which it had had since Aristotle. In a certain sense this represents a return to the interpretation of the concept of substance as a thing's *property* or *goods* (οὐσία, in Greek), instead of stressing the significance of the *independence*—as did Descartes and, even more so, Spinoza—which in Greek metaphysics was always a consequence of the character of substance in the sense of *ousía*. Aristotle said that substance is *what is peculiar to each thing*. Leibniz, when faced with the Cartesian dualism of the *res extensa* and the *res cogitans* governed by the *res infinita*, which is God, returns to the idea of an absolute multiplicity of substantial monads which contain strictly within themselves all their ontological possibilities. Substance or nature is again the principle of motion in the things themselves, as in Aristotle. In spite of his apparent close relationship with Plato because of the theory of innate ideas, Leibniz is the most Aristotelian of the rationalist metaphysicians; from this he derives in part his incomparable fecundity, a quality which philosophy has always possessed when in *live* contact with Aristotle.

PRE-ESTABLISHED HARMONY. Since the manifold monads that make up the world are windowless, the problem of the impossibility of communication between the substances no longer involves only the source of knowledge, but above all, the very order and congruency of the world as a whole. Happenings in the universe can be explained only by starting with the supposition that everything emerges from the depths of all the individual monads. How does it happen, then, that the monads form a world that is full of coherent relationships, that it is possible to know the things, and that everything happens in the world as if there existed that chimerical communication between the substances which we find it necessary to reject? One must acknowledge for each monad a previously established order that sees to it that as it unfolds its possibilities, it coincides with all the other monads, so that they all find themselves in harmony with one another, thus constituting a world in spite of their essential solitariness and independence.

And this order can only have been made by God in his grand design when creating the monads, which are at once solitary and united. "Thus it is necessary to say that God first created the soul, or some other real unity, in such a way that everything would evolve from its own depths with perfect spontaneity with respect to itself, and nevertheless in perfect conformity with the things outside itself" (*Système nouveau*, 14). This is what Leibniz called *pre-established harmony*.

Thus there are three possible solutions to the idealist problem of the communication between the substances: occasionalism, monism and pre-established harmony. According to the famous comparison, the problem is equivalent to that of synchronizing several clocks. In Descartes' and Malebranche's solution, the clockmaker (God) constantly synchronizes the two clocks (thought and extension) which have no direct relationship whatsoever. Spinoza denies the problem; that is, in his philosophy there are not two clocks, but only one with two faces: two aspects of the same reality, two attributes of the same substance, which is synonymous with God. In Leibniz, there are not two clocks, but many; they do not have any interrelationship either, nor does the clockmaker constantly synchronize them: this would be a perpetual miracle and it seems absurd to Leibniz; however, the clockmaker has constructed the clocks in such a way that they keep perfect time without affecting one another and without His touching them; independently, and by virtue of their previous construction, the clocks keep time with one another, remain harmonious. This constitutes pre-established harmony.

THE ROLE OF GOD. If we turn our attention to the problem of knowledge, we find that in Leibniz, too, God assures the correspondence between my ideas and the reality of the things when He makes the development of my thinking monad coincide with all the universe. If in Malebranche all the things are seen and known *in* God, it can properly be said that in Leibniz they are known only *through* God. Leibniz expresses this in extremely clear terms: "According to strict metaphysical truth, there is no external cause that actuates us but God alone, and He communicates with us directly only by virtue of our continuous dependency on Him. From this it follows that there is no other external object that touches our soul and directly stimulates our perception. Thus, we have the ideas of all the things in our soul only by virtue of God's continual action on us . . ." (*Discours de métaphysique*, 28). In other words, the monads do in fact have windows, but instead of putting the monads in communication with one another, these windows all open out onto the Deity.

Thus in the midst of Leibniz' mature philosophy we see once again the necessity for establishing the existence of God. God is a basic supposition in all Leibniz' metaphysics, since it is He who makes possible the existence of the monads, understood as that autonomous and spontaneous force of representation which mirrors the universe from the infinite plurality of the monads' individual perspectives. Thus Leibniz must philosophically prove the existence of God, and to do this he too employs as a tool the often used ontological argument. He modifies it, and then it becomes a major tenet of all rationalist metaphysics of the seventeenth century. According to Leibniz, it is necessary to prove the *possibility of God*, and only then is His existence assured by virtue of the ontological proof, since God is the *ens a se*. If God is possible, He exists. Leibniz says that the Divine Essence is possible because, since God does not contain any negation, He cannot contain any contradiction whatsoever; therefore, God exists (cf. *Discours de métaphysique*, 23, and *Monadologie*, 45).

Now Leibniz goes further: he also attempts an a posteriori and experimental proof. If the *ens a se* is impossible, so also are all the entities *ab alio*, since these exist only through this *aliud* which is, precisely, the *ens a se*; therefore, in such a case nothing would exist. If the necessary entity does not exist, there are no possible entities; however, these exist, since we see them; therefore, the *ens a se* exists. These two propositions *taken together* comprise Leibniz' proof of the *existence of God. If the necessary entity is possible, it exists; if the necessary entity does not exist, there are no possible entities.* This reasoning is based on the existence (known a posteriori) of the possible and contingent entities. The simplest expression of this argument would be: *Something exists, therefore God exists.* *

3. Theory of Knowledge

Perception and apperception. The monads have perceptions. However, these perceptions are not always the same; they can be clear or obscure, distinct or confused. Things have insensible perceptions, perceptions without consciousness, and man also has such perceptions, in varying degrees. A sensation is a confused idea. When perceptions have clarity and consciousness and are accompanied by memory, they are apperceptions, and these are peculiar to souls. There is a hierarchy among souls, and human souls come to know universal and necessary truths; then it is possible to speak of reason, and the soul is *spirit*. At the

---

* For an analysis of the problems posed by this proof, see my essay "El problema de Dios en la filosofía de nuestro tiempo" in *San Anselmo y el insensato* [*Obras*, IV].

summit of the hierarchy of the monads is God, who is pure actuality. TRUTHS OF REASON AND TRUTHS OF FACT. Leibniz distinguishes between what he calls *vérités de raison* and *vérités de fait*. The truths of reason are necessary; it is inconceivable that they do not exist; that is, they are based on the principle of contradiction. Therefore they are evident from a priori knowledge, apart from all experience. Truths of fact, on the contrary, cannot justify themselves on a priori knowledge alone. They cannot be based solely on the principles of identity and contradiction; rather, they require the principle of sufficient reason. Two and two are four; this is a truth of reason, and is based on what two is and what four is; two and two *cannot* not be four. Columbus discovered America; this is a truth of fact, and requires experimental confirmation; it is conceivable that it is not true; that is, it is not self-contradictory that Columbus did not discover America.

THE INDIVIDUAL NOTION. However, this idea is not as simple as it appears. We must not forget that the monad contains within itself all its reality, and that nothing outside it can influence it; therefore, everything that happens to it is included in its essence and, consequently, in its complete notion. Columbus discovered America because the act of discovering America was included in Columbus' being, in the complete notion of Columbus. In a famous example Leibniz says that if Caesar had not crossed the Rubicon he would not have been Caesar. Therefore, if we could know the complete individual notions we would see that truths of fact are included in the essence of the monad, and that their absence is self-contradictory. Then all truths are *vérités de raison*, that is, necessary and a priori. But who possesses the complete notion of the monads? Only God; therefore, this distinction between truths of reason and truths of fact disappears only for Him, and still exists for man.

Strictly speaking, then, Leibniz does not allow accidental occurrences; he says that every true predication is based on the nature of things. Thus all judgments are *analytic* judgments: they only make explicit the notion of the subject. Later Kant, using metaphysical suppositions different from those of Leibniz, will point out the important distinction between analytic and synthetic judgments.

INNATISM. In Leibniz, all ideas proceed from the internal activity of the monads; nothing is received from outside. Leibniz is a hundred leagues removed from every type of empiricism, which is formally impossible in his metaphysics. Thus the ideas are *innate* in this concrete sense. It is more a metaphysical than a psychological problem. The ideas have their origin—which is active—in the mind itself, in the *vis repraesentativa* that produces them. Thus Leibniz is completely opposed to Locke and all the British empiricism that influences the Continent greatly and comes to dominate the eighteenth century. Leibniz amends the traditional principle that there is nothing in the understanding that has not been previously in the senses by excepting from this statement the understanding itself: *Nihil est in intellectu quod prius non fuerit in sensu . . . nisi intellectus ipse.*

LOGIC. Traditional, demonstrative logic does not satisfy Leibniz. He thinks it is useful only in proving already known truths, and of no use in discovering new truths. This objection, as well as the tendency toward innatism, appeared as far back as Descartes, and in Leibniz both ideas find their fullest expression. Leibniz wanted to create a true *ars inveniendi*, a logic that would be useful in discovering truths, a *universal combinatory system* that would study the possible combinations of concepts. Such a system could investigate truth as if it were a mathematical problem, and could supply an a priori and certain knowledge. This is the famous *Ars magna combinatoria*, inspired in part by Raimundus Lullus' work; from it is derived the idea of the *mathesis universalis*, which has recently demonstrated its fecundity in the fields of phenomenology and mathematical logic.

4. THEODICY

Leibniz' *Theodicy* carries as a subtitle "Essays on the Goodness of God, the Freedom of Man and the Origin of Evil," thus revealing the meaning and scope of this "justification of God." On one hand, God is defined as omnipotent and infinitely good, but evil exists in the world. On the other hand, it is said that man is free and responsible, but Leibniz on the contrary points out that everything that occurs is previously included in the monad. The problem is, how can these ideas be made compatible?

METAPHYSICAL OPTIMISM. Evil can be metaphysical (the imperfection and finiteness of the world and man), physical (pain, misfortune, and the like) or moral (wickedness, sin, and so on). Metaphysical evil derives from the impossibility of the world's being infinite like its Creator. Physical evil has its justification in that it gives rise to higher values (for example, adversity gives rise to the opportunity for such virtues as fortitude, heroism and self-sacrifice to appear); furthermore, Leibniz believes that life as a whole is not evil, and that pleasure is more prevalent than pain. Finally, moral evil, which is what constitutes the most serious problem, is actually a *deficiency*, something negative. God does not desire moral evil; he simply permits it to exist because it is a condition for other, greater good. Facts cannot be judged singly, for we do not know God's total plan; in order to be understood, facts would have to be viewed with knowledge of God's complete design. Since God is omnipotent and good we can rest assured that the world is *the best of all possible worlds*: that is, that it contains the maximum good and the minimum evil proper for the good of the whole. This is called the *principe du meilleur*, and is connected with arguments used by Scotus to prove the Immaculate Conception. God does everything for the best because He can and because He is good; if He could not, He would not be God, since He would not be omnipotent; if He could but did not wish to, He would also not be God, since He would not be infinitely good. "He could do it, it was fitting to do it, and so He did it," Scotus concluded. In an analogous way Leibniz bases his metaphysical optimism on the affirmation that the world is the best of all possible worlds.

FREEDOM. All the monads are *spontaneous* because nothing outside them can coerce or compel them at all; but this is not enough to make them *free*. In addition to spontaneity, freedom requires deliberation and decision. Man is free because he chooses between possibilities after deliberating on them. But the Divine Prescience introduces itself as a difficulty; God sees the being of the monads from the beginning, and the monads contain within themselves all that is to happen to them and everything that they are to do. Then how is freedom possible?

In order to interpret God's knowledge, Leibniz makes use of certain subtle distinctions of Catholic theology, especially some points advanced by the Spaniard Molina. God has three kinds of knowledge: (1) knowledge of pure intellection, (2) knowledge of vision, (3) middle knowledge. By the first kind God knows all possible things; by knowledge of vision He knows all real or future things; by middle knowledge He knows the "futuribles," that is, the conditioned future, the things that will come to be if certain conditions arise, although it is not determined that such conditions shall arise. God knows how free will would act, without its being determined that it must act in this way and therefore that these must be future events, just as Christ knew that if miracles had been performed in Tyre and Sidon the people would have repented (Matthew 11:21). Contingent things are not necessary; necessity accrues to them only in an a posteriori way, following a decision of the Divine Will, subsequent to knowledge of simple intellection and middle knowledge.

God creates men and He creates them free. This means that they determine their own actions freely, although God has determined that they should *exist*. God wishes man to be free, and He allows him to sin because the freedom to sin is preferable to the lack of such freedom. Thus sin is a possible evil that permits a higher good: to wit, human freedom.

GOD IN SEVENTEENTH-CENTURY PHILOSOPHY. We have seen that despite the separation of theology from philosophy in this period, God was not lost. All rationalistic and idealistic philosophy from Descartes to Leibniz can be established because God is there—at a distance, it is true, but surely there. Perhaps reason cannot gain knowledge of God's essence and is not able to practice theology, but it does know with certainty that God exists. The philosophers of this period, I repeat, possess a God who is somewhat remote, somewhat inaccessible and without direct effect on intellectual activity, but who nevertheless surely exists. God provides these philosophers with a sure footing, even though He is not a prospect on which their eyes rest with steady interest. He ceases to be the ever-visible *horizon* and becomes the *solid ground* beneath eighteenth-century European philosophic speculation.

This is what gives the period of the history of philosophy which runs from Descartes to Leibniz its essential unity. This group of philosophic systems appears as if enveloped in a common atmosphere, which reveals a similar interrelationship of ideas. A basic coherence can be observed among all the philosophic constructions that are clustered together in these few decades. And taken as a group, these systems will appear as if in contraposition to another group of lofty metaphysical edifices: the so-called German idealism which originates in Kant and culminates in Hegel. The philosophers of the Romantic age will hurl a reproach at the metaphysics of the entire Baroque era. In this objection the seventeenth-century systems will be grouped together into one complex and will not be treated separately as individual constructions. It is interesting to note the significance of qualifying them as a single complex. This Baroque philosophy is called *dogmatic*. What does this mean? For an answer we shall have to see what the fate of the problem of God will be at the hands of the German idealists. This problem will be summed up in the question of the ontological argument and will reveal to us the metaphysical situation of the new stage in modern philosophy.*

* See my essay "La pérdida de Dios" in *San Anselmo y el insensato* [*Obras*, IV].

EMPIRICISM

British Philosophy

From the sixteenth to the eighteenth centuries, running parallel with Continental rationalistic idealism, a philosophy with clearly developed characteristics of its own develops in Britain. Between Francis Bacon and David Hume there extends a series of thinkers who in a certain measure oppose the philosophers we have just studied, the group from Descartes to Leibniz. British philosophy presents two features which distinguish it from Continental thought: a lesser concern with strictly metaphysical questions, accompanied by a greater concern with theory of knowledge (which, naturally, always presupposes a metaphysics) and the philosophy of the State; and, as regards method, a *sensationalist empiricism* as contrasted with an a priori, mathematically inclined rationalism. British philosophy has a tendency to become psychology and to grant first place to sensory experience as a source of knowledge.

This British philosophy of the modern age is undeniably important, but perhaps more because of its influence and historical consequences than in consideration of its strictly philosophical significance. Despite their great renown and the widespread influence which they exerted, the British philosophers of these three centuries do not have the significance of those extraordinary British thinkers of the Middle Ages, Roger Bacon, Duns Scotus and William of Occam, not to mention others who are somewhat less important than these but whose importance is still very great. Britain's great contribution to philosophy must therefore be sought in the medieval period, at least as much as in the modern age.

And yet it was the British thinkers of the sixteenth to eighteenth
centuries who furnished the ideas which perhaps most intensely influenced the transformation of European society: sensationalism; the
critique of the cognitive faculty, which in some cases arrived at skepticism; the ideas of tolerance; liberal principles; the spirit of the
Enlightenment; deism, or natural religion; and finally, as a practical-
minded reaction to metaphysical skepticism, the philosophy of common sense, utilitarian ethics and pragmatism. All these elements, of
extraordinary influence on the structure of Europe in the eighteenth
and nineteenth centuries, have their origin in the ideological systems
which were dominant in Britain in the preceding centuries. These
systems have profound repercussions in the nations of the Continent,
especially in France and Germany.

1. Francis Bacon

LIFE AND WORKS. Bacon was born in 1561 and died in 1626. He is
thus a couple of generations earlier than Descartes. He was Lord
Chancellor of England and was ennobled as Baron Verulam; he was a
great political figure in Elizabethan and Jacobean England. Later he
was shorn of his offices and in his retirement devoted himself to intellectual labors. The attribution to Bacon of the works of Shakespeare is
highly improbable.

Bacon's major work is the *Novum Organum*, which presents an inductive logic, as opposed to Aristotle's deductive and syllogistic logic. He
also wrote, all under the general title of *Instauratio magna* (The Great
Renewal), the treatise *De dignitate et augmentis scientiarum* (The Advancement of Learning) and numerous essays on different subjects: *Filum
Labyrinthi* (The Thread Through the Labyrinth), *De interpretatione
naturae et regno hominis* (On the Interpretation of Nature and the Reign
of Man), *Temporis partus masculus sive instauratio magna imperii humani in
universum* (The Male Child of Time, or the Great Renewal of Man's
Empire in the Universe), *Cogitata et visa* (Things Thought and Seen),
and so on. We note that all these titles are positive in outlook and
herald the triumphant beginning of a new science.

DOCTRINE. Bacon's fame has been greater than his true merit. For
a long time he was considered the renewer of modern philosophy,
equal or superior to Descartes. This view has little foundation, and it
has been necessary to limit Bacon's achievement to the introduction of
empiricism and the inductive method. But even here it is not possible
to forget the role played by his fellow countryman and namesake of

three centuries earlier, Roger Bacon, who was more original than the Renaissance chancellor and who to a great extent prepared the way for him, even though the consequences of Roger Bacon's work were incomparably less noticeable.

Francis Bacon represents the culmination of the Renaissance, which in philosophy is nothing more than the long stage of indecision reaching from the last of the original and lively Scholastic systems—Occamism —up to the first mature and clear formulation of the thought of modern times—Cartesianism. Bacon combines speculative with technical concerns: knowledge is power. From the very outset of his *Novum Organum*, he places on the same plane *doing* and *understanding*, the hand and the mind; hence the vital new meaning which he gives to Aristotle's metaphor of the *órganon*, or tool, as a designation of logic. Neither the bare hand nor the isolated and unaided mind can dominate the things; material and mental tools together lend hand and mind their true efficacy. And just as the craftsman does, so the thinker must submit to the exigencies of reality: *natura non nisi parendo vincitur*, it is possible to conquer nature only by obeying her.

Bacon believes that philosophic investigation requires a previous examination of the prejudices (idols) which can conceal truth. As in Cartesianism, so here concern with criticism and fear of error make their appearance. Bacon speaks of four idols: 1. *Idola tribus*. These are the prejudices of the *tribe*, the human species, and are inherent in the nature of man: illusions of the senses, the tendency to personify inanimate objects, and so forth. 2. *Idola specus*. These are the prejudices of the *cave* in which each man finds himself (an allusion to the Platonic myth): individual tendencies and predispositions which may lead men into error. 3. *Idola fori*. These are the idols of the marketplace, of human society and of the very speech which we use. 4. *Idola theatri*. These are the prejudices of authority, based on the prestige which a few men enjoy on the *stage* of public life; these prejudices may hinder men's direct and personal vision of the things and lead their opinions off the true path.

In addition, Bacon criticizes the syllogistic method. The presumptive logical rigor which gives the syllogism its demonstrative value is nullified because the *major premise* of a syllogism is a universal principle which is not itself obtained syllogistically, but frequently by means of an inexact and superficial apprehension of things. The rigor and certainty of *inference* are purely formal and have no pertinence if the major premise is not certain. This leads Bacon to establish his theory of *induction*: from a series of *individual facts*, grouped in a suitable systematic way, one obtains by abstraction, after following a rigorous experimental and logical procedure, the general concepts of the things and the laws of nature.

This induction of Bacon's, which is also called *incomplete* induction in contrast to induction based on *all* the pertinent individual cases, does not afford an absolute certainty, but it does provide sufficient certainty for the purposes of science when carried out scrupulously. In a certain sense, this method is opposed to the method of philosophic rationalism and even to the method of modern mathematical physics which began with Galileo. Bacon was not clearly aware of the value of mathematics and a priori reasoning, and his empiricism was much less fruitful than the *nuova scienza* of the Renaissance physicists or the rationalism of the philosophers who based their systems on that of Descartes.

2. HOBBES

Thomas Hobbes (1588–1679) is another interesting English thinker. He enjoyed a long life and outlived even Spinoza, but, as can be seen from the date of his birth, actually belonged to the generation before Descartes. Hobbes maintained close contact with France, and there he became acquainted with Descartes and imbued with the method of the mathematical and physical sciences. For several years in his youth he was secretary to Bacon, and he shares Bacon's concerns; but Hobbes applies the naturalistic method of modern physics to the study of mankind. Man as an individual and in society, and thus psychology, anthropology, politics, the science of the State and society: these are Hobbes' themes. He wrote in Latin and English; his principal works are *De corpore, De homine, De cive* and *Leviathan*, which contains his theory of the State and is named after the beast mentioned in the Book of Job.

Hobbes, too, is an empiricist. For him, knowledge is based on experience, and his concern is to instruct men for practical purposes. On the other hand, he is a nominalist, and thus a continuer of the medieval Oxford tradition. The universals exist neither outside the mind nor even within it, because our representations are individual; the universals are merely *names*, *signs* for the things, and thought is a symbolic operation, a sort of calculus, closely linked to speech.

Hobbes' metaphysics is naturalistic. He seeks causal explanations, but eliminates final causes and wishes to explain phenomena mechanically, on the basis of motions. Descartes, too, admitted mechanical explanations with regard to the *res extensa*, but contrasted with this the immaterial world of thought. Hobbes believes that the processes of the soul and the mind have a material and corporeal basis; according to him, the soul cannot be immaterial. Hobbes is a materialist and denies the freedom of the will. A natural determinism prevails in everything that happens.

THE DOCTRINE OF THE STATE. Hobbes' theory of the State presupposes the equality of all men. He believes that all men aspire toward the same goal and that when they fail to achieve it, enmity and hate spring up. Whoever does not obtain his desire distrusts the man who has met with success and, in order to ward off a possible attack, attacks him. Hence arises Hobbes' pessimistic conception of mankind: *homo homini lupus*, man is a wolf to man. Men have no direct interest in the company of their fellows, except to the extent that they can reduce them to submission. The three motives of discord among human beings are competition, which provokes aggression with gain as an object; mistrust, which makes men attack each other in order to achieve security; and vanity, which creates enmity between rivals for fame.

This *natural* situation defines a state of perpetual struggle, of a war of all against all (*bellum omnium contra omnes*), to use Hobbes' awesome phrase. This does not mean isolated outbursts of warfare, but a state of war—a *time* of war, Hobbes calls it—in which mankind exists, a permanent condition in which no one can be sure of peace.

Man is endowed with a power which he uses as he sees fit; he has certain passions and desires which cause him to seek for things and want to acquire them for himself at everyone else's expense. Since everyone is aware of this attitude, men distrust one another; man's natural state is one of aggression. But man realizes that this situation of insecurity is untenable; his life is wretched in this state of struggle and he is compelled to seek peace. Hobbes distinguishes between *jus*, or right, which he interprets as freedom, and *lex*, or law, which signifies obligation. Man has the freedom—that is, the right—to do anything he can or desires to do; but three things can be done with a right: it may be exercised, renounced or transferred. The mutual transfer of a right is called a pact, contract or *covenant*. This leads to the idea of a political community.

In order to gain security, man tries to substitute a *status civilis* for the *status naturae* through a covenant by which each man transfers his rights to the State. Strictly speaking, this is not a covenant with the person or persons charged with the administration of the State, but of each man with every other man. The sovereign merely represents the force established by the covenant; all the other men are his subjects. Now, the State as thus constituted is *absolute*: just as formerly the power of the individual knew no restriction, so it is now with the authority of the State—*it is coextensive with its might.* When the State strips the individual men of their power, it assumes all of it itself and governs without limitations. The State is a mighty machine, a monster which devours the individuals, and from which they cannot appeal to any higher authority. Hobbes finds no more suitable name for this monster than that of the great beast of the Bible: *Leviathan*; this is the State, superior to all else, a mortal God, as it were.

Hobbes' State decides upon *everything*, not only politics, but also morality and religion; if religion is not recognized by the State, it is merely *superstition*. This system, acute and profound in many points, represents the authoritarian and absolutist conception of the State, based simultaneously on the principle of equality and on a thoroughly pessimistic view of human nature. Although Hobbes speaks of God at times, the outlook of his work is basically atheistic. In contrast to the ideas of spirituality and freedom, Hobbes' political system is dominated by naturalistic mechanics and the affirmation of the universal power of the State.

This doctrine, which was extremely influential in the eighteenth century and had long-ranging historical consequences which are still felt today, aroused two kinds of reaction in its own day. One type of reaction was that of Sir Robert Filmer, author of *The Patriarch*, who tried to salvage the absolute monarchy of the Stuarts by means of the theory of the divine right of kings; the basis of this theory is that man is not born free, but is subject to his father's authority, from which is derived the legitimacy of the paternal and patriarchal rule of kings. The other type of reaction, which was opposed to Filmer as well as to Hobbes, was that of Locke, who upheld the principles of liberty and parliamentarianism, that is, the principles of the second English revolution, that of 1688.

3. Deism

NATURAL RELIGION. The naturalism of the modern age leads as a matter of course to the concept of *natural religion*. This is also called *deism*, as distinguished from *theism*. Theism is the belief in God, that is, in the supernatural God of religion who is known through revelation. Deism, on the other hand, arises as a reaction to the atheism that creeps into English philosophy, but it remains within the realm of the strictly natural. God is known by means of reason, without any supernatural aid. Natural religion is merely what our reason tells us about God and our relationship with Him. Therefore, it is a religion without revelation, without dogmas, without churches and without formal worship. The entire eighteenth-century Enlightenment, with its idea of the " Supreme Being, " is dominated by deism.

Deism thus appears in the writings of the English thinker Edward Herbert of Cherbury (1581–1648), whose major works are *De veritate, prout distinguitur a revelatione, a verisimile, a possibili, et a falso* (On Truth, as Distinguished from Revelation, Probability, Possibility and Falsity) and *De religione gentilium, errorumque apud eos causis* (On the Religion of the Heathens, and the Causes of Their Errors). The content of natural religion—a very scanty content—is universally admitted by all men, because it proceeds solely from natural reason. This content can be reduced to the belief in the existence of a " Supreme Being, " to whom we owe a veneration consisting of virtue and piety, the belief that man must repent for his sins and, lastly, the belief in a life to come in which man's conduct will receive its just reward or just punishment. The revealed religions, according to Herbert, have a historical origin and are derived from poetical imaginings, philosophical ideologies or the interests of priestly classes. According to him, Christianity, especially in its primitive form, is the purest revealed religion and the closest to natural religion.

Herbert's argument, of course, loses sight of many things. The universal agreement as to the content of natural religion is not so assured as he claims, nor did religions really originate in the way he states. Besides, he overlooks the authentic content of religion, *religio*, the *bond* between God and man.

NATURAL MORALITY. In a movement that parallels deism, the English moralists of the seventeenth century attempt to base morality on nature and to make it independent of all religious or theological content. This attempt is made by the bishop Richard Cumberland (1622–1718), author of the book *De legibus naturae*, in which he asserts that mankind has a peaceful and benevolent social instinct, just the opposite of Hobbes' conception. According to Cumberland, morality is based on the experience of nature and human behavior; the good is that which proves to be useful for the community. Thus, there appears here an early manifestation of the social utilitarianism which is to culminate in the nineteenth century in the work of Jeremy Bentham and John Stuart Mill.

Other British moralists find the basis for morality, not in experience, but in the direct, a priori self-evidence of reason. Morality consists in adjusting oneself to the true nature of the things and relating oneself to them according to their manner of being; direct intuition shows us this nature of the things. This movement is chiefly represented by Ralph Cudworth (1617–1688) and Samuel Clarke (1675–1729). Cudworth wrote *The True Intellectual System of the Universe* and *A Treatise Concerning Eternal and Immutable Morality*. Clarke was also a notable metaphysician, who meditated profoundly on the problem of the Deity and carried on a discerning correspondence with Leibniz. His most interesting work is *A Discourse Concerning the Being and Attributes of God*.

But the most interesting and characteristic form of British moral philosophy is that of Shaftesbury (Anthony Ashley Cooper, third earl of Shaftesbury, 1671–1713), author of *Characteristics of Men, Manners, Opinions, and Times*. His is the ethics of the *moral sense*: man has an innate faculty for judging behavior and personality (and this judgment is valid) and for deciding on their moral qualifications, approving or rejecting them. It is this direct moral sense which influences men's decisions and guides them, especially in evaluating a type of personality in its totality, a beautiful and harmonious form of human soul. Shaftesbury is influenced by Greek and Renaissance ideas, and his ethics is deeply tinged with estheticism. Shaftesbury's influence in art and literature was very widespread in Britain, among the thinkers of the French Enlightenment and among the German classicists from Herder to Goethe.

4. LOCKE

LIFE AND WORKS. John Locke was born in 1632 and died in 1704. At Oxford he studied philosophy, medicine and the natural sciences; later and with greater interest he studied Descartes and Bacon; he also established contact with Robert Boyle, the great English physicist and chemist, and with Thomas Sydenham, the physician. In the household of the first earl of Shaftesbury (the grandfather of the above-mentioned moralist) he held the position of counselor, physician and tutor of the earl's son and grandson. This connection led Locke into politics. He emigrated during the reign of James II and later took part in the second English revolution of 1688. He lived in Holland and France for a number of years. Locke's influence has been extremely important, greater than that of any other English philosopher. Through his leadership, empiricism, which found in him its most able and fortunate expounder, came to dominate eighteenth-century thought.

Locke's most important work is the *Essay Concerning Human Understanding*, published in 1690. He also wrote political works—*Two Treatises on Government*—and the *Letters on Toleration*, which defined his position on religious matters.

THE IDEAS. Locke, also, is an empiricist: the origin of knowledge is experience. As is customary with English thinkers, he uses the word "idea" in a very broad sense: it includes everything that one thinks or perceives, the whole content of consciousness; understood in this way, it comes close to the meaning of the Cartesian *cogitatio*, to what today we would call representation or, better yet, *percepts*. According to Locke, ideas are not innate, as Continental rationalism had thought. The soul is *tamquam tabula rasa*, like a clean slate on which nothing has been written. The ideas come from experience, which can be of two classes: external perception obtained by means of the senses, or *sensation*; and internal perception of psychical states, or *reflection*. In either case reflection operates on material introduced by sensation.

There are two kinds of ideas: simple ideas and complex ideas. The former result directly from a single sense or from several senses simultaneously, from reflection, or, finally, from a combination of sensation and reflection. Complex ideas are the result of the activity of the mind, which combines or *associates* simple ideas.

Locke distinguishes among simple ideas those which have objective validity (primary qualities) from those which have only subjective validity (secondary qualities). The primary qualities (number, figure, extension, motion, solidity, and so on) belong to the bodies and cannot be separated from them; the secondary qualities (color, odor, taste, temperature, and the like) are subjective sensations of the man who perceives them. This distinction is not original with Locke—it dates from ancient philosophy, figuring in philosophic thought from the time of the Greek atomists to that of Descartes—but in Locke's philosophy it plays an important role.

Memory is the basis on which complex ideas are formed. Simple ideas are not instantaneous; rather, they leave an impression in the mind; thus they can be combined or associated with other ideas. This concept of *association* is of great importance in English psychology. The modes, the notions of substance and relation are complex ideas and result from the associative activity of the mind. Thus, in the final instance all these ideas, including the ideas of substance and the very idea of God, proceed from experience, by means of successive abstractions, generalizations and associations.

Locke's empiricism limits the possibility of knowledge, especially in regard to the great traditional themes of metaphysics. With him there begins the distrust of the cognitive faculty that is to culminate in Hume's skepticism and which will oblige Kant to formulate the crux of the problem of the validity and possibility of rational knowledge.

ETHICS AND THE STATE. Locke's ethics presents certain inconsistencies. In general, he is a determinist, and does not grant that human will is free; however, he admits a certain freedom of indifference which allows man to decide. Morality, independent of religion, consists of accommodating oneself to a norm, which can be divine law, the law of the State, or the norm of common social opinion.

With respect to the State, Locke is the typical representative of liberal ideology. He returned to England from Holland on the same boat with William of Orange—the king of the limited monarchy accompanied by the theoretician of the limited monarchy. Locke rejects Filmer's advocacy of a patriarchal institution and his doctrine of the divine right and absolute power of kings. Locke's point of departure is analogous to that of Hobbes: the natural state. For Locke, however, this term (which he considers to include equality and liberty, since all men have the same experience of birth and possess the same faculties) does not have an aggressive tinge. Obligation is born out of liberty; there is a master and lord of all things, who is God, and He imposes a *natural law*. In Hobbes, equality gave rise to a fierce and aggressive independence, whereas in Locke it promotes love for one's fellow man; men ought never to break this natural law. Strictly speaking, men are not born *in* a state of liberty (therefore the parents who have to raise them exercise a legitimate jurisdiction over them), but are indeed born *for* liberty. And so the king does not have absolute authority; rather, he receives his authority from the people. Thus the proper form of the State is that of a constitutional and representative monarchy, independent of the Church, tolerant on matters of religion. Such is Locke's thought, which corresponds to the form of government adopted in England as a result of the revolution of 1688, which eliminated civil wars and revolutions from the previously turbulent English history and established a period of internal peace that has already lasted for more than a quarter of a millennium. Using Ortega's terminology, we could say that a skinlike State replaced one that had been in the nature of an orthopedic apparatus.

5. BERKELEY

LIFE AND WORKS. George Berkeley was born in Ireland in 1685. He studied at Trinity College in Dublin, and later became dean of Dromore and of Derry. Still later he went off to America with visions of founding a great missionary college in the Bermudas. After returning to Ireland he was named Anglican bishop of Cloyne. Toward the end of his life he moved to Oxford, where he died in 1753. Berkeley was full of a religious spirit that profoundly influenced both his philosophy and his life. His philosophic formation depends on Locke especially; he is an actual continuer of Locke's thought even though he presents a much more intense and direct preoccupation with metaphysical questions than does his predecessor. Berkeley was very greatly influenced by the Platonism that was traditional in England; his spiritualist philosophy was shaped by his religious convictions, which he attempts to defend against attacks by skeptics, materialists and atheists. Thus he arrives at one of the most extreme forms of idealism ever known.

His principal works are *Essay Towards a New Theory of Vision*; *Three Dialogues between Hylas and Philonous*; *Principles of Human Knowledge*; *Alciphron, or the Minute Philosopher*, and the *Siris*, in which along with metaphysical and medical reflections he expounds the virtues of pine tar.

METAPHYSICS. Locke's theory of ideas leads Berkeley into the realm of metaphysics. Berkeley is a nominalist; he does not believe that *general ideas* exist; for example, there cannot be a general idea of a triangle, because any triangle imagined is necessarily either equilateral, isosceles or scalene, whereas the general idea of the triangle does not involve such distinctions. Berkeley refers to the *intuition* of the triangle, but he does not believe in the *concept* or thought of the triangle, which is truly universal.

Berkeley professes an extreme form of spiritualism and idealism. For him, matter does not exist. Primary qualities are just as subjective as secondary qualities; extension or solidity are *ideas*, just as color is an idea; they are all the content of my perception; there is no material substance behind the ideas. Their being is exhausted in being perceived: *esse est percipi*; this is Berkeley's basic principle.

The entire material world is but a representation or perception of mine. The only thing that exists is the spiritual Self, of which we have an intuitive certainty. Therefore it is senseless to speak of causes of physical phenomena and to give real meaning to that expression; there are only concordances, relations between ideas. Physical science establishes these *laws* or connections between phenomena, which are understood as ideas.

These ideas proceed from God; He puts them in our spirit: the regularity of these ideas, which is based on God's will, causes to exist for us what we call a corporeal world. Once again and under very different circumstances we find God as the basis of the world in this new form of idealism. According to Malebranche or Leibniz, we can see and know the things only in or through God; according to Berkeley, there are only the spirits and God, who is the One who acts upon the spirits and creates a "material" world for them. We do not only see the things in God; rather, literally, "we live, move and exist in God."

6. HUME

LIFE AND WORKS. David Hume is the philosopher who carries to its ultimate consequences the empiricist direction initiated by Bacon. Hume was born in Scotland in 1711 and died in 1776. He studied law and philosophy; at various times he lived in France for a number of years, and he had a great influence on the Encyclopedists and Enlightenment circles. He was secretary to the English embassy, and his fame spread quickly throughout England, France and Germany.

His most important work is the *Treatise on Human Nature*. He also wrote several recastings of different parts of this work, such as *An Inquiry Concerning Human Understanding, An Inquiry Concerning the Principles of Morals* and the *Dialogues Concerning Natural Religion*. In addition to his philosophical work, Hume was extremely productive in the field of historiography, the most important work in this field being his great *History of England*.

SENSATIONALISM. In Hume empiricism reaches an extreme and becomes sensationalism. According to him, ideas are necessarily based on intuitive *impressions*. Ideas are pale and lifeless copies of direct impressions; the belief in the continuity of reality is based on this capacity to reproduce experienced impressions and to create a world of representations.

Berkeley had made a general critique of the concept of substance, but he had restricted it to material and corporeal substance. The "things" have a being that is exhausted in being perceived; but the spiritual reality of the Self that does the perceiving remains firm. Hume makes a new critique of the idea of substance. According to his theory, perception and reflection provide us with a number of elements which we attribute to substance, which acts as a basis or support for them; but nowhere do we find the impression of substance. I encounter impressions of color, consistency, taste, odor, extension, roundness, smoothness, all of which I refer to an unknown something that I call an apple, a substance. Sensible impressions have more vitality than imagined impressions, and this causes us to believe in the reality of what is represented. Thus, Hume explains the notion of substance as the result of an associative process, without observing that actually the opposite is true: my direct and immediate perception is of the apple, and the sensations are abstract elements which appear only as I complete my perception of the *thing*.

There is another aspect to this problem. Hume does not limit his criticism to material substances, but extends it to the ego itself. The ego is also a bundle or *collection* of perceptions or contents of consciousness that succeed one another continually. Thus the ego does not have substantial reality; it is a result of the imagination. Hume forgets that it is *I* who have the perceptions, that it is *I* who find myself facing them and that therefore I am distinct from them. Who unites this *collection* of states of consciousness and makes them constitute a *soul*? When formulating his sensationalist criticism, Hume does not even touch upon the problem of the ego; apart from the problem of its nature, substantial or not, the ego is something basically distinct from *its* representations.

Together with the critique of the concepts of substance and the soul, Hume makes a critique of the concept of *cause*. According to him, the causal connection signifies only a relationship of *coexistence and succession*. When a phenomenon repeatedly coincides with another or succeeds it in time, by virtue of an *association of ideas* we call the first "cause" and the second "effect," and we say that the latter occurs *because* the former takes place. No matter how many times this succession is repeated, it does not afford us the certainty of its indefinite reiteration, and it does not allow us to affirm a causal link in the sense of a *necessary condition*.

SKEPTICISM. In Hume, empiricism reaches its ultimate consequences and becomes *skepticism*. Knowledge cannot achieve metaphysical truth. The intimate and immediate convictions by which man lives cannot be proved or refuted. The reason for this is that, as nominalism long ago pointed out, in this instance knowledge is not knowledge of the things. As a result, reality becomes perception, experience, *idea*. The contemplation of these ideas, which do not succeed in being things, which are nothing but subjective impressions, is skepticism. We see what happens to idealism when God is not present to assure transcendency, to save the world and make the ideas be ideas *of the things* and cause there to be something that merits the name of *reason*. Kant, following in Hume's footsteps, will have to investigate this problem from its roots; and his philosophy will consist of precisely a *Critique of Pure Reason*.

7. THE SCOTTISH SCHOOL

Within the scope of British philosophy, and more precisely in Scotland, there arises in the eighteenth century and at the beginning of the nineteenth a reaction to Hume's skepticism. This movement constitutes the so-called "Scottish School," which had considerable influence on the Continent.

The chief thinkers of this school are Thomas Reid (1710–1796) and Dugald Stewart (1753–1828). Reid wrote *An Inquiry into the Human*

Mind on the Principles of Common Sense, Essays on the Intellectual Powers of Man, Essays on the Active Powers of Man; Stewart wrote *Elements of the Philosophy of the Human Mind, Outlines of Moral Philosophy, The Philosophy of the Active and Moral Powers*. Their point of departure is always empirical; experience is the origin of knowledge. But this experience is understood as something direct and immediate that gives us the reality of the things as they are understood by *sane reason*. The philosophy of the Scottish School consists of an appeal to common sense. Common sense is the maximum source of certainty; all criticism leaves its immediate self-evidence beyond doubt. This acceptation places us directly in the midst of the things, and again anchors us in their reality. But the philosophical insufficiency of the Scottish School did not permit it to solve, or even to state in a mature manner, the problem with which it was concerned.

In spite of this, the Scottish School exercised prolonged influence in France (Pierre Paul Royer-Collard, and so on) and in Spain, especially in Catalonia, where its imprint is seen in Jaime Luciano Balmes and in Marcelino Menéndez y Pelayo.

The Enlightenment

The complex intellectual movement called the Enlightenment cannot be considered a mere manifestation of empiricism. It is made up of various other elements—many of which derive from idealist rationalism and, in the final analysis, from Cartesianism. However, there are two reasons for our including the thought of the Enlightenment in the current of empiricism: in the first place, as we have seen, British empiricism depends in large part on Continental rationalism, and does not exclude (but, on the contrary, presupposes) the influence of this school of thought; secondly, the Enlightenment, in the scant measure in which it is philosophy, is more concerned with the problems of knowledge than with metaphysical questions, and follows empirical paths, carrying them to the extreme of absolute sensationalism. On the other hand, the most important elements of the Enlightenment—deism, political ideology championing freedom and representative government, tolerance, the economic doctrines, and the like—have their origin in the empirical thought of the sixteenth to eighteenth centuries.

The epoch of the Enlightenment, the eighteenth century, represents the end of the metaphysical speculation of the seventeenth century. After almost a century of intense and profound philosophical activity, we encounter a new hiatus in which philosophic thought loses momentum and becomes trivial. This is an epoch in which the ideas of the preceding period are disseminated. And dissemination always has the following consequence: in order to act upon the masses, in order to transform the face of history, ideas must necessarily become trivial, lose their precision and difficulty, become superficial images of themselves. Then, in return for ceasing to be what they really are, they are spread about and the general public shares them. In the eighteenth century, a group of able and ingenious writers who with as much insistence as impropriety call themselves "philosophers" expound, interpret and popularize a series of ideas conceived—in a different form and a different scope—by the great European minds of the seventeenth century. After a few years these ideas permeate the atmosphere, become part of the air one breathes, suppositions which everyone takes for granted, and then we find ourselves in a different world. Europe has changed completely in a rapid, almost brusque, *revolutionary* manner. And this transformation of popular thought will soon shape the radical alteration of history that we know as the French Revolution.

1. THE ENLIGHTENMENT IN FRANCE

In the last years of the seventeenth century and throughout the eighteenth, France underwent a change in ideas and convictions which altered the character of its politics, social organization and spiritual life. The most substantial changes took place between 1680 and 1715; all that followed was a process of dissemination and propagation of the new ideas, but by that time the outline of French history had already changed. There was a transition from the notions of discipline, hierarchy, authority and dogma to those of independence, equality and natural religion, even a decided opposition to Christianity. It was the transition from the mentality of Bossuet to that of Voltaire: the critique of all traditional convictions, from the Christian faith to absolute monarchy, by means of a review of history and social norms. It was, in effect, a revolution in the intellectual presuppositions of France and, since France was then the guiding nation in the European community, of all Europe. (See Paul Hazard's magnificent book, *The European Mind, 1680–1715*.)

The Encyclopedia

PIERRE BAYLE. The Enlightenment wishes to gather together all *scientific* knowledge and make it available to a wide public. Strictly philosophical problems, not to mention theological ones, are relegated to a secondary level. "Philosophy" at this time refers principally to the findings of natural science and the empirical and deistic doctrines of the British; it is a popularization of the less metaphysical portions of Cartesianism and, at the same time, of British thought. Following the

Cartesian tradition, the thought of the Enlightenment is rationalistic and, consequently, revolutionary: it attempts to state and solve problems once and for all, mathematically, without taking historical circumstances into account. Following the British tradition, the prevailing theory of knowledge is sensationalist empiricism. These two philosophic currents, the Continental and the British, converge in the Enlightenment.

The suitable organ for this popularization of philosophy and science is the "encyclopedia," and, in fact, the first typical representative of this movement, Pierre Bayle (1647–1706), did write one, the *Dictionnaire historique et critique*. Bayle subjected numerous questions to keen negative criticism. Although he did not deny the truths of religion, he made them completely independent of reason, and even contrary to reason. He was a skeptic who believed that reason can comprehend nothing of dogma. In an age that doted on *reason*, this viewpoint had to end in a complete estrangement from religion; abstention becomes resolute denial, and the enemies of Christianity later make copious use of Bayle's ideas.

THE ENCYCLOPEDISTS. Much more important than Bayle's work, however, was the so-called *Encyclopedia, or Rational Dictionary of Sciences, Arts and Trades (Encyclopédie, ou Dictionnaire raisonné des sciences, des arts et des métiers)*, issued from 1750 to 1780, despite attempts to prevent its publication. The general editors of the *Encyclopedia* were Denis Diderot and Jean Le Rond d'Alembert; the contributors included the greatest figures of the time: Voltaire, Montesquieu, Rousseau, Anne Robert Jacques Turgot, Paul-Henri Holbach and many others. The *Encyclopedia*, which at first glance seemed nothing more than a dictionary, was the greatest vehicle for Enlightenment ideas. With considerable circumspection and skill, it interpolated critical thoughts and attacked the Church and most prevailing convictions. D'Alembert was a great mathematician; besides his scientific contributions to the *Encyclopedia*, he wrote its *Preliminary Discourse (Discours préliminaire)*, which is an attempt to classify the sciences. Diderot was a prolific writer, a novelist, playwright and essayist, whose mature orientation was almost totally materialistic and atheistic.

SENSATIONALISM AND MATERIALISM. This trend in the Enlightenment originates with a Catholic priest, the Abbé Étienne de Condillac, who was born in 1715 and died in 1780. His major work is the *Traité des sensations*, in which he expounds a purely sensationalistic theory. Condillac imagines a statue which would be endowed, one by one, with all the senses, from the sense of smell to that of touch. When the statue possessed all the senses, it would have full human consciousness and, therefore, full cognitive powers. Condillac, who was a Christian, excludes from his sensationalism the era previous to the fall of Adam, as well as the life beyond the grave, and speaks of God and of the simple soul as a unit of consciousness. But later this exclusion is not maintained. Whereas the so-called *idéologues*, especially the Count Destutt de Tracy (1754–1836), indulge according to their methods in psychology or logic, Condillac's sensationalism is continued by the most extreme group among the Encyclopedists, who turn it into a mere atheistic materialism.

The principal thinkers of this group are the physician Julien de La Mettrie (1709–1751), author of a book with a very eloquent title: *L'homme machine*; Claude-Adrien Helvétius (1715–1771), who wrote *De l'Esprit*; and, in particular, a German who resided in Paris, Baron Paul-Henri Holbach (1723–1789), author of the *Système de la nature* and *La morale universelle*. All these writers believe that the only means of knowledge is sensory perception; that everything in nature is matter, including the foundation of psychical life; that religions are a deception and that, naturally, it is impossible to speak of the existence of God or the immortality of the human soul. The philosophical value of their rather unoriginal works is very slight. Much greater interest attaches to those Enlightenment thinkers who are oriented toward history and the theory of society and the State, especially Voltaire, Montesquieu and Rousseau, and also Turgot and Antoine-Nicolas de Condorcet, the theorists of the idea of progress.

VOLTAIRE. François Arouet de Voltaire (1694–1778) was a great figure of his age. His fame was extraordinary and won him the friendship of Frederick the Great of Prussia and Catherine the Great of Russia. His success and influence were unmatched in the eighteenth century. No other writer was so widely read, commented on, discussed, or admired. Voltaire's actual value does not measure up to his renown. In considering his work we must distinguish three aspects: its relation to literature, to philosophy and to history.

Voltaire is an excellent stylist. In his works French prose reached one of its peaks; he is enormously keen, witty and amusing. His short stories and novels, especially, reveal a splendid literary talent. His philosophical merit is something quite different. He is neither an original nor a profound thinker. His *Dictionnaire philosophique* is saturated with the philosophic ideas of the seventeenth century, which he adopts in their most superficial guise: empiricism, deism and a popularization of the physical image of the world. Thus Voltaire has no real philosophical interest. His antireligious ideas, which were devastating in his own age, appear ingenuous and harmless to us today. He had a complete lack of comprehension for religion and Christianity, and in his hostility he reveals most clearly the inconsistency of his thought. It is not merely that he attacks Christianity, but that he does it in so supremely superficial a way, taking an anticlerical position without even an awareness of the real issue.

Voltaire's most interesting and profound contribution to the development of thought is his historical work. He wrote a book on the great age prior to his own, called *Le siècle de Louis XIV*. But his principal historical production is the *Essai sur les mœurs et l'esprit des nations*. In this work there appears for the first time a new conception of history. History is no longer a chronicle, a mere narration of deeds or events; instead, its object becomes the *customs* and *spirit* of *nations*. Thus the nations appear as historical units, each with its own spirit and customs: the German concept of *Volksgeist*, "national spirit," is, as Ortega has shown, merely a translation of this *esprit des nations*. Voltaire finds a new object for history, and in his hands it takes the first step toward becoming an authentic science, although it does not succeed in overcoming naturalism.

MONTESQUIEU. Baron Montesquieu (Charles de Secondat, 1689–1755) made a different sort of contribution to the thought of the Enlightenment. He, too, is a witty writer; this is most evident in his *Lettres persanes*, a graceful and ironic critique of French society of his day. But, above all, he is a political and historical writer. His major work is *L'esprit des lois* (The Spirit of the Laws). His thesis is that the laws of each country are a reflection of the people who live by them; the naturalism of the age causes Montesquieu to emphasize especially the influence of climate. Montesquieu recognizes three types of constitutions which are repeated in history. First of all, there is despotism, with no place for anything but fearful obedience; then there are two types of States in whose history he discovers a *guiding motive*, different for each. In a monarchy the principal motive is *honor*; in a republic, *virtue*. When these qualities are lacking in their respective forms of government, a nation does not function as it should. With this theory Montesquieu furnishes a decisive complement to Voltaire's idea of history: a dynamic element which explains historical events. (Cf. Ortega: *Guillermo Dilthey y la idea de la vida* [Wilhelm Dilthey and the Idea of Life].)

Rousseau

Despite his connections with the Encyclopedists, Rousseau merits a place of his own in the history of thought. Jean-Jacques Rousseau was born in Geneva in 1712, the son of a Protestant watchmaker. His childhood was one of precocious intellectual stimulation; his later life was that of an unhappy wanderer, and frequently revealed traces of abnormality. His *Confessions*, a book in which he romantically exhibits his inmost feelings, is the best account of his life. He won a prize offered by the Academy of Dijon with his *Discours sur les sciences et les arts*, in which he denied that the sciences and arts had contributed toward the purification of manners. This study made him famous. Rousseau believes that man is good by nature, and that it is civilization which ruins him. His imperative is the *return to nature*. This is Rousseau's famous *naturalism*, which is based on religious ideas proceeding from his original Calvinism. Rousseau denies original sin and affirms the natural goodness of man, to which man ought to return. These ideas inspired another work of his, the *Discours sur l'origine de l'inégalité parmi les hommes* (Discourse on the Origin of Inequality among Men); he applied his ideas to the field of education in his famous book *Émile*. Rousseau represents a strong sentimental reaction against the chilly rationalistic aridity of the *Encyclopedia*; he wrote a passionate, tearful novel which was immensely successful: *Julie, ou la Nouvelle Héloïse*. This naturalism is linked with the idea of religion. Rousseau converted to Catholicism, then back to Calvinism and ended up a deist; his religion is sentimental; he finds God in nature, for which he feels a deep admiration.

But it is Rousseau's social philosophy that has had the most important consequences. His work on this subject is the *Contrat social*. Men, in their state of nature, make a *tacit* contract. This is the origin of society and the State, which, according to Rousseau, are thus based on a voluntary agreement; the individual is prior to society. It is man's will that determines the State; but, aside from the will of the individual, Rousseau distinguishes between two collective wills: the *volonté générale* and the *volonté de tous*. The latter is the sum of the wills of all the individuals, and is almost never unanimous; the *volonté générale* is the one which has political importance: it is the will of the majority, *which is the will of the State*. This is the important element. The will of the majority, just because it is the will of the majority, is the will of the community as such, that is, even of those who disagree; for such people, it is their will not as individuals, but as members of the State. This is the principle of democracy and of universal suffrage. What is significant here is, on the one hand, respect for minorities, who have the right to attempt to make their will prevail, and, at the same time, acceptance by the minorities of the general will as an expression of the will of the political community. The consequences of these ideas were profound. Rousseau died in 1778, before the beginning of the French Revolution, but his ideas were an essential element in the background of the Revolution and influenced European political history for a long time.

2. THE "AUFKLÄRUNG" IN GERMANY

Corresponding to the Enlightenment in France there was a similar, but not identical movement in Germany, which is also called an "enlightenment" or "illumination": *Aufklärung*. Here, too, it consisted of a popularization of philosophy, especially that of Leibniz, as well as of British thought. But in Germany this spirit of enlightenment is less revolutionary and less inimical to religion; the Reformation had already achieved the transformation of the content of German religion, and the *Aufklärung* does not come face to face with a Catholic tradition of long standing, as did the Enlightenment in France. Otherwise, the same rationalistic and scientific spirit prevails in Germany, and the Prussian court of Frederick the Great, along with the Berlin Academy of Sciences, is a great center of Enlightenment ideology.

WOLFF. The popularizer of Leibniz' philosophy was Christian Wolff (1679–1759), a professor at Halle. Afterward, expelled from the University of Halle, he taught at Marburg, but was later reinstated at Halle with great honors by Frederick. Wolff, a rather unoriginal thinker, wrote many works in Latin and even more in German; the general title of these works is frequently *Rational Thoughts on*.... Wolff introduced the German language into the universities and into philosophic writings. His thought consisted of the popularization and dissemination of Leibniz' philosophy, especially its less profound aspects. Following the precedents set by Johann Clauberg and Jean Leclerc at the end of the seventeenth century, he introduced the division of metaphysics into ontology (or general metaphysics), rational theology, rational psychology and rational cosmology (that is, the ontology of God, man and the world). The philosophy studied as a matter of course in Germany in the eighteenth century was that of Wolff; it is thus Wolff's philosophy that Kant will have to deal with most directly in his *Critique of Pure Reason*.

ESTHETICS. A philosophical discipline which is established independently in the German Enlightenment is esthetics, the science of beauty, which is here treated autonomously for the first time. The founder of esthetics was a pupil of Wolff, Alexander Baumgarten (1714–1762), whose *Aesthetica* was published in 1750. Also related to these problems is the historical activity of Johann Joachim Winckelmann, a contemporary of Baumgarten, who wrote the famous *History of the Art of*

Antiquity, which is so important for the study of the art and culture of Greece.

LESSING. The writer who most clearly represents the spirit of the *Aufklärung* is Gotthold Ephraim Lessing (1729–1781). He was a great literary figure, a poet, dramatist and essayist. He was deeply concerned with philosophic questions, especially with the meaning of history and the quest for knowledge. Lessing is the author of the famous saying that if God were to show him truth in one hand and in the other the path that leads to truth, he would choose the second. His study of the Laocoön sculpture is another important step toward the understanding of Greek art. Lessing's rationalism—with Spinozistic tendencies—is tolerant, not aggressive like Voltaire's, and does not include Voltaire's hostility toward the Christian religion.

THE TRANSITION TO GERMAN IDEALISM. The German religious currents of the eighteenth century—specifically the Pietism founded by Philipp Jakob Spener and August Hermann Francke—and the interest in history lead the German Enlightenment onto different paths. Great value is once more attached to sentiment—a phenomenon which appears in France with Rousseau; there is an attempt to find the meaning of the great stages of history; there is a renewed admiration for the Middle Ages and German culture, as a reaction to the *Aufklärung*, with its cold rationalism. There appears the movement called *Sturm und Drang*. Herder is perhaps the bridge between the two trends. Later there appears a group of writers who prepare the way for or accompany German idealism, the great phase of philosophy which extends from Kant to Hegel.

3. VICO'S DOCTRINE OF HISTORY

An outline of the intellectual panorama of the eighteenth century should not omit the figure of the Neapolitan philosopher Giambattista Vico (1668–1744), who stands somewhat apart from the rest. Although, strictly speaking, his thought does not fit exactly into the forms and suppositions of the Enlightenment, his historical position is determined by similar conditions, and his philosophy is frequently related to that of the founders of that intellectual movement.

Vico was born during the period when Naples was a Spanish viceroyalty. He was a jurist and a philologist. He was the first to cast doubt on the existence of Homer (formerly there had merely been controversies over the place of his birth). For Vico, Homer, Zoroaster and Hercules are not persons, but personified epochs or cultural cycles. After publishing several works in Latin—*De antiquissima Italorum sapientia ex linguae Latinae originibus eruenda* (On the Most Ancient Wisdom of the Italians as Discovered in the Origins of the Latin Language), *De uno universi juris principio et fine uno* (On the One Principle and the One End of Universal Law), *De constantia jurisprudentis* (On the Constancy of the Jurist)—Vico wrote his famous *Scienza nuova*, the full title of which is *Principii di scienza nuova d'intorno alla comune natura delle nazioni* (Principles of a New Science Concerning the Common Nature of the Nations); the first edition of this work dates from 1730, and the definitive edition (called the *Scienza nuova seconda*) from 1744.

Vico's philosophy—one of great complexity and confused structure —considers a series of *nations* as the protagonists of universal history. Vico establishes a series of prior axioms *(degnità)* and remarks that, whereas philosophy studies man as he ought to be, law considers him as he is. Legislators take man's vices and transform them into useful activities: from savagery is derived the military; from avarice, commerce; from ambition, the life of the courtier. We are halfway between the idea of nature and the idea of history. Human customs have a certain nature, a structure which is manifested in language (therefore he calls history "philology") and especially in proverbs.

The historical evolution of the nations, which are the subjects of history, occurs in accordance with an alternate rhythm of *corsi* and *ricorsi* ("cycles" and "re-cycles"). The *corso* consists of three phases: (*a*) The first phase, characterized by the dominance of the *imagination* over the reasoning faculty; this imagination is *creative*. Vico calls it *divine*, because it creates gods. Men are savage, but they revere the gods they have created; it is the era of *theocracy*. (*b*) The *heroic* age: there is a belief in heroes or demigods of divine origin; the form of government is *aristocracy*. (*c*) The *human* age: people are kind, intelligent, modest and reasonable; government is based on equality, and appears in the form of *monarchy*. The men of the first of these ages are religious and pious; those of the second are litigious and irascible; those of the third are accommodating and diligent, their manners having been formed by civic duties. To these three stages correspond three languages: one for silent religious acts (mental language), another for the exercise of arms (language of words of command), a third for conversing (language for understanding one another). Vico's ideas present an outline of a theory of the functions of speech.

When a nation has passed through the three stages, the cycle begins anew; this is the *ricorso*. It is a period not of decadence, but of rebarbarization. These ideas are echoed in Comte's theory of the three states, but in Comte's theory the positive state is the *definitive* one, in contrast to what happens with the human age in Vico's outline.

4. SPANISH PHILOSOPHERS OF THE ENLIGHTENMENT

In Spain the Enlightenment had characteristics of its own: its principal accomplishment was to bring Spain up to the level of the era by introducing the science and philosophy that had been developed elsewhere since the seventeenth century; in other words, to *Europeanize* Spain (despite the opposition of the partisans of national purity). The men of the Spanish Enlightenment were not irreligious, but they combated the abuses of the Church and the lack of freedom, while remaining loyal to their faith. They were champions of political and social reform, but not revolutionaries; the great majority of them were dismayed by the violence and suppression of freedom during the French Revolution. The reigns of Fernando VI (1746–1759) and Carlos III (1759–1788), especially, represent an intelligent transformation of Spanish society. This social progress was partially undone during the reign of Carlos IV, in which a strong reaction set in, and finally destroyed by the Napoleonic invasion with its political struggles and by the absolutism of Fernando VII (1814–1833).

The Spanish Enlightenment was a time of assimilation of ideas rather than of creativity, and thus is not of great philosophical importance; it merely signifies the incorporation of modern thought at a time when Scholasticism had become least productive. A leading figure was the Benedictine Benito Jerónimo Feijoo (1676–1764), a Galician, who was a professor at Oviedo and the author of the *Teatro crítico universal* in eight volumes and the *Cartas eruditas y curiosas*, in five volumes. A great essayist whose works were widely read, he was understanding and tolerant and concerned with rooting out mistaken beliefs and superstitions. Other important thinkers were Feijoo's friend and collaborator, Father Martín Sarmiento (1695–1771); the philosopher and physician Andrés Piquer (1711–1772), author of *Lógica moderna* and *Filosofía moral para la juventud española*; the doctor Martín Martínez, who wrote *Filosofía escéptica*; and Antonio Xavier Pérez y López, author of *Principios del orden esencial de la naturaleza*. Another interesting personality was the Jesuit Juan Andrés, author of *Origen, progreso y estado actual de toda la literatura*, a ten-volume work that perfectly reflects the temper and accomplishments of the era. Two other Jesuit writers were Esteban de Arteaga (*La belleza ideal*) and Lorenzo Hervás y Panduro (*Historia de la vida* *del hombre, Catálogo de las lenguas de las naciones conocidas*). The greatest thinker of the century was Gaspar Melchor de Jovellanos (1744–1811), author of innumerable essays and monographs. His most brilliant insights are contained in his *Diarios* (Journals).*

* See my books *Los Españoles* (1962) and *La España posible en tiempo de Carlos III* (1963) [*Obras*, VII].

The Formation of the Modern Epoch

1. Philosophy and History

Ideas are conceived in the realm of philosophy but end up having historical consequences. Concepts become generalized and are slowly converted into an activating force that reaches down to the masses. This phenomenon has always taken place, but occurs to a greater degree than ever in the epoch which we are now considering. The entire eighteenth century, all that we know as the Enlightenment, consisted of a process in which ideas conceived in previous centuries acquired influence and social reality. And this circumstance is not coincidental. To a certain extent, all eras exist on ideas; however, it is not necessary for ideas to show themselves as ideas, as theories; in fact, ideas generally obtain force by disguising themselves—for example, as traditional forms. But in the eighteenth century ideas have importance precisely because they are ideas; people endeavor to live according to those ideas, according to *raison*. The ideas do not have to disguise themselves, and thus acquire maximum force.

Precisely the same thing happens in regard to the metaphysical ideas, and the religious and theological ideas related to them, that I have attempted to set forth in the preceding chapters. The ideas gradually spread to and exercise influence over wider and wider circles. Slowly, everyday life and the sciences become shaped by the results which philosophy obtained for them previously. And in this fashion the face of the world is changed. The deep-rooted reasons for the change are prior and remain hidden; what manifests itself is the complete alteration of the surface of life. But this change can only be understood properly and in its entirety if one recognizes the subterranean forces that are in operation. We must investigate philosophy's place in history after this change, and see how its character is shaped by its very situation.

2. THE RATIONALIST STATE

The epoch subsequent to the Renaissance is characterized by the discovery of mathematical reason—rationalism. It was during the sixteenth and seventeenth centuries that the great rational systems of physics and philosophy were constructed: those of Galileo, Newton, Descartes, Spinoza, Leibniz. This rationalism has obvious historical consequences.

ABSOLUTISM. From the very beginning of the modern State, the absolute State, people commence to discuss reason, the reason of the State: Machiavelli's *ragione di Stato*. The State now has a personality, and also its reasons; therefore, it operates like a mind. This rationalist personification of the State makes its appearance at the same time as the modern nations.

Descartes mentions politics only in passing; he says that things are better made when they are made according to reason and by only one person, rather than by several. This is the rational justification of absolute monarchy, and from this same principle there emerges, later on, the revolutionary spirit. The States created during the Renaissance become powerful units of absolute power.

DIPLOMACY. At this moment, a new concept of diplomacy makes itself evident. It amounts to nothing more than the substitution of an abstract personal relationship for the direct relationship between States; this diplomacy results from the unification that the nations have achieved; previously it existed only in the medieval Italian States—precisely those states which most resembled nations in the modern sense of the word. (This may be the reason why it took Italy so long to become a unified country.) Thanks to diplomacy, a consequence of unification, the unity itself becomes accentuated. France as France begins to exist for Frenchmen and for people of other countries when they see it represented and personified, carrying on relations with other countries. The change can be demonstrated by comparing the consciousness of Spanishness of a subject of the Catholic Kings with that of a subject of Philip II. At Isabella's death, Ferdinand of Aragon can still "return to his States"; in the time of Philip II this would no longer have been possible. A nation is personified by its absolute king; relations between nations are carried out and personalized in the conversation of a few men. The various States begin to be factors in the consciousness of all individuals.

3. THE REFORMATION

The Reformation has a strictly religious dimension, the origin of which could easily be traced through the Middle Ages to Luther. However, we are not going to consider this aspect, but the vital and historical dimension of the Reformation—that is, the spiritual situation that made it possible and the new situation that it created.

FREEDOM OF INTERPRETATION. This most important element in the Reformation is the concept of freedom of individual interpretation of religious texts. This concept assumes that, instead of there being a Church authority to interpret the sacred texts, each individual must interpret them for himself. This is pure rationalism; there is a presentiment here of Descartes' statement, "Good sense is the most widely distributed thing in the world." But Luther is the least rational man in the world, an enemy of reason and of philosophy. What does this mean? It is one more proof that, in spite of his own individual ideas, a man is oriented by the beliefs of the epoch into which he is born, and that the prevailing suppositions of the epoch influence him much more than his own ideas do (Ortega).

The destruction of the Church is the necessary consequence of this spirit of free interpretation; as soon as one says, "man and God alone," the Church becomes an obstacle placed between man and God. The Church has always kept very close watch over mystical positions because they skirt this danger. A Catholic mystic's awesome statement is well known: "God and I, and no world at all." Man is alone with God. Protestant fractionization is the result of this concept; plurality is of the essence of Protestantism. Let us investigate two aspects of the reformed church—the "national" Church (for example, the Anglican) and that characterized by the Augsburg Confession—in order to see how they contain within themselves the seed of their own dissolution.

The national church revolves around the person of the king. The king of England or some German prince is the head of the Church, which is national, political. A fundamental link between religion and politics, between the Church and the State, is thus created. The State becomes a religious state, but something quite different from what a religious state was in the Middle Ages. The medieval State assumes and accepts the Church's religious principles; now, rather the opposite occurs—religion is affected by national principles; the *cujus regio,*

ejus religio formula is established. To a certain extent, this spirit penetrates the Catholic countries also, and in Protestant and Catholic
countries alike people speak of the "alliance between the throne and
the altar," forgetting those extremely clear words in the Gospels: *My
kingdom is not of this world.* The various modern inquisitions—so unlike
the medieval Inquisition—are really instruments of the State rather
than organs of the Church. This nationalization of the Church leads to
the loss of its religious content and its absorption with temporal
interests. Our era is not witnessing the disappearance of Protestantism,
but it does indeed witness frequent shortcomings of the "national
churches."

On the other hand, the Augsburg Confession, for example, assumes
an *agreement* on matters of faith. People subscribe to it because they are
in agreement with its dogmatic content. It is an association of isolated
individuals; the individuals *constitute* a Church, but they are not *within
a Church*, as Catholics are; the distinction is obvious. However, a community founded on concordant opinion is subject to change. Governed
by the spirit of individual interpretation, opinion evolves in many
ways and becomes divided; the single Confession is succeeded by
various sects; these in turn splinter even more, and thus we arrive at
the individual creed. So-called liberal Protestantism consists of the
suppression of almost all dogmatic content, to such a degree that the
word "Christianity" is practically a mere anachronism when applied
to it.

THE PROBLEM OF THE REFORMATION. The Catholic countries undertake the Counter-Reformation, that is, a Reformation in reverse. In
this way a schism is created between the Protestant and Catholic
countries, and Europe, which was handed down to us as a unit,
appears to be split in two. Contemplating these two halves into which
Europe has been divided, we can believe (1) that unity is maintained
by Catholicism, and that the Reformation is a transitory and unadulterated error; (2) that Protestantism represents Europe's destiny, and
that the Catholic populations are reactionaries (Hegel and François
Guizot hint at this, and it is France that precludes them from accepting
this historical interpretation); or (3) that both will subsist and that
Europe's unity is a dialectical unity, a tense, dynamic unity made up
of those two halves. Observe that this latter position does not touch
upon the question of the inherent truth of Catholicism; the Christian
mind finds itself facing the fact that God *has allowed the Reformation to
take place*, just as, on the other hand, He has allowed more than two
religions to coexist. One cannot ignore the fact of the Reformation, and
the Church has not ignored it; note that the Church does not take the

same position when faced with the break with the Orthodox Eastern Church and when faced with the Protestant movement: in the first instance, the Church loses the obedience of all the Eastern countries and remains unchanged; in the second instance, it *conducts a Counter-Reformation*: the existence of the Counter-Reformation demands the existence of the Reformation, no mere schism, which provoked the Counter-Reformation.

This position creates a new problem for us: What is the nature of the interaction between the Catholic and Protestant worlds? What is the nature of the unity that these two worlds establish? And, finally, what must the synthesis be like that resolves this antinomy? We could think —and this idea, welcome to a Catholic mind, is seen not to be contradicted by the evidence of our age—that the synthesis might consist of the ultimate reabsorption of Protestantism by Catholicism after the former comes to the end of what is erroneous in its path and reaches its ultimate consequences. Perhaps Protestantism will refute itself historically and find itself in a superior truth. The resultant unity of the Catholic Church would not by any means be the same as that unity which it had prior to the Reformation; it would not be as though the Reformation had never taken place. Rather, it would be preserved in this concrete form of its absorption.

4. MODERN SOCIETY

We have seen the roles played by two major elements of the modern age: rationalism and the Reformation. Now we must see how these elements influence the era's social structure, how, by virtue of philosophy and theology, all modern life—from the intellectual to the social and political—acquires a new air that culminates in the eighteenth century with the two great historical facts of the Enlightenment and the French Revolution.

Intellectual Life

THE CHARACTER OF THE INTELLECTUAL. What kinds of intellectuals do these centuries produce? What characterizes an intellectual man of this period, and to what purpose is his labor? What does being an intellectual in the seventeenth century involve, and how does it differ from being an intellectual in the Middle Ages, in the Renaissance or in the eighteenth century?

During the Middle Ages, the true intellectual is the cleric, especially the monk. The work of Scholasticism, with its connotation of a *school*, a collaboration, is carried out by men working jointly within the

Order or the University. The philosopher of this period is a man of the monastery, of the community, or rather a *magister*. He is the Scholastic —*scholasticus*—who collaborates on the great collective work.

During the Renaissance, the intellectual is a *humanist*. He is a man of the world, a layman, who cultivates his personality, chiefly in the dimensions of art and literature, both of which are saturated with the essence of classical culture. The Renaissance intellectual had a certain freshness in his manner of viewing nature and the world. Pietro Bembo is typical, in spite of his cardinal's hat, and so also are Thomas More, Erasmus, Guillaume Budé (Budaeus) and Vives.

Now we find a different type of intellectual: Galileo, Descartes, Spinoza. The intellectual of this epoch, as Ortega has pointed out, is the man of method. He does nothing but seek for methods, open new roads that allow him to reach the things, new things, new regions. He is the man who, using the essential imperative of rationality, constructs his science. The man of the seventeenth century has an effective and precise awareness of modernity. It was Renaissance man who had symptoms, signs of modernity, who went about finding ancient things, which seemed new precisely because they were so old. If the Renaissance is seen in detail, it becomes clear that in many ways it was a negative movement. The things that the modern age accomplishes are anchored more in the Middle Ages—in Occam, Eckhart, the school of Paris—than in the Renaissance. The Renaissance is dazzling, but it has little intellectual profundity. Renaissance men such as Vives and Ramus turn their backs on the Middle Ages—and their attitude endures: a century later, while people's very lives derive from medieval roots, the Middle Ages and Scholasticism are still thought to be completely false. Leibniz is the first man to possess a sense of history and recognize Scholasticism's value as well as the value of the new science.

THE THEME OF NATURE. The Reformation split Europe into two halves—not one reformed and one unreformed, but both reformed, although in different senses. There is one exception: France, which is not a country of the Reformation, but neither, perhaps, of the Counter-Reformation. France does combat the Calvinists, and even goes to the extreme of St. Bartholomew's Eve, but it also indulges in politics contrary to that of Austria and, during the Thirty Years' War, makes political alliances without regard for religious ties. Furthermore, France promulgates the Edict of Nantes and establishes the Gallican Church, still Roman Catholic, still subordinate to the Pope in religious matters, but with a strong nationalistic tinge. It is perhaps for this reason that Leibniz, when attempting to reunite the Catholic and Protestant Churches, approached neither the hierarchs of the Spanish

Church (except the bishop Rojas Spínola) nor Rome directly, but instead, Bossuet in particular—the spokesman of the Gallican Church.

We find a very important difference between those European countries which live under the Counter-Reformation and the rest of Europe: in the Counter-Reformation lands there are practically no investigators of natural science, except for the Italian physicists, the chief of whom, Galileo, became embroiled with the ecclesiastical authorities. The Counter-Reformation countries do cultivate another discipline which is very important: *jus naturae*. Instead of physics, they practice natural law, a juridical science of man. But there is a similarity underlying the differences: the law that is studied is *natural* law, and the theme of nature reappears here, too. This theory of law, as developed by the Spanish theologians, is still based on God; but at the hands of the Dutch and English—Hugo Grotius, Shaftesbury, Hutcheson—it becomes strictly natural law, a theory of law of human nature. Philosophers speak of natural religion, or deism, and of a natural God. This is all part of the naturalistic movement that culminates in Rousseau.

The Counter-Reformation ran a strange course: it remained intellectually self-contained and isolated, and did not form ties with the new philosophy and the new science. Descartes and Leibniz are acquainted with the Spanish theologians, but the Spanish themselves do not establish connections with the modern philosophers; they are interested only in their own kind of philosophy. They remain outside the new European intellectual community, and thus the splendid Spanish flowering is soon cut off and does not have *direct* fruitful consequences. But it must be noted that the work of the Spanish thinkers from Vitoria to Suárez was not sterile; it is just that its effectiveness became evident at a far remove from what was seemingly its *continuation*.

THE INTELLECTUAL UNITY OF EUROPE. In the seventeenth century there is a spiritual community in Europe which is guided by philosophy and natural science and even by theology. One element of this community has disappeared today, but possibly it will reappear before long, after these years of crisis: the intellectuals of the seventeenth century used to write each other long letters. A considerable part of the works of Galileo, Descartes, Spinoza, Leibniz, Arnauld, Clarke and all the representative men of the age consists of their scientific correspondence. This means that they were interested in each other's endeavors and, what is more, corrected each other; this exchange of objections gave an enormous precision to the works of the period. It is the age in which men publish brief pamphlets which transform philosophy with fifty lucidly written pages: *Discours de la méthode, Discours de la métaphysique, Monadologie.*

Social Transformation

THE NEW CLASSES. The profession of "intellectual" did not yet exist as such in the seventeenth century. Descartes, much to the chagrin of his family, did not choose a profession—the military, law or the Church: *gens de robe et gens d'épée*—but shut himself up with his work and studies. He was a man of independent means and good social standing, *un homme de bonne compagnie*, and devoted himself to intellectual pursuits without becoming a cleric or a professor. As the seventeenth century proceeds, the type of man which Descartes inaugurated becomes more prevalent.

On the one hand, the intellectual clears a path for himself, while, on the other, the nobility become dependents of the royal palace. Even at the end of the eighteenth century the intellectual class has not yet become completely established. Stendhal quotes a nobleman's remark about Rousseau: *Cela veut raisonner de tout et n'a pas quarante mille livres de rente* (That fellow wants to philosophize about everything and his income isn't even forty thousand livres). But at the same time a middle class is in formation; this bourgeoisie will have a share in intellectual pursuits, because one of its higher strata is composed of men of science.

The traces of feudalism die out and the independence of the nobility comes to an end. The final active manifestations of feudalism are the Fronde in Mazarin's France and, in Spain, the rising of Andalusia under the Duke of Medina Sidonia during the reign of Philip IV. The nobles have to form ties with the other two forces, the third estate and the monarchy. They become courtiers of the king, while at the same time establishing contact with the bourgeoisie. The nobility is supported by these two social elements, and its situation is very difficult after the French Revolution. The bourgeoisie, on the other hand, becomes stronger little by little.

The monarchy has reached its absolute culmination—regalism—and has achieved a complete organization of the State, which begins to be a perfect machine. Automatically, a series of matters which had been considered individual and private concerns become concerns of the State. The State furnishes more and more services, takes more problems on its shoulders and also makes its weight felt more and more. This is what is known as interventionism of the State; this process expands constantly and today the State enters into every part of our lives.

NATURE AND GRACE. We have seen how Reformation thought and rationalism involve an interest in nature, apart from God. In the Middle Ages, the two concepts of nature and grace were contraposed, and in the Renaissance, man flung himself into the pursuit of nature, neglecting grace and forgetting the old Christian principle: *gratia naturam non tollit, sed perficit* (grace does not remove nature, but perfects it). Nineteenth-century philosophers so completely forget that grace was once the companion of nature that they only contrast *culture* with *nature*, and this effectively transforms the idea of nature. Today philosophers prefer to speak of *spirit*—a word rich in meaning, but also in ambiguity—and, from another point of view, of *history*.

With the Renaissance the *natural* mode of thought triumphs. The *world* ceases to be Christian, although individual people still are—something very different. Man is now a mere natural entity. Protestantism started out with a completely pessimistic conception of man: it considered him a fallen being whose nature was essentially corrupted by original sin and whose justification could be achieved only *through faith*, by the application of the merits of Christ; works are inoperative: man is incapable of earning his own salvation. In the face of this view, the Council of the Counter-Reformation at Trent proclaims as its theme *faith and works*.

In the Renaissance, man becomes progressively more estranged from God as a consequence of God's inaccessibility to reason. For the Protestant, God's works have nothing to do with grace; they are merely works of nature, which dominate the world in accordance with physical laws; thus, man drifts away from God and from grace. The consequence of this is that when man remains alone with the world, accomplishing great things with it, and loses interest in the problem of grace, *he no longer considers himself evil*. Pessimism was based on the viewpoint of grace, but if man is a *natural entity* and is enjoying great success with his rationalistic physics, why should the old outlook continue? Protestant pessimism, finding itself in the realm of mere nature, becomes the optimism of Rousseau. Man forgets about original sin and considers himself to be *naturally good*.

THE FRENCH REVOLUTION. What results will this situation have in the eighteenth century? The eighteenth century is the era which makes use of the thought of the seventeenth. In history there are periods of intense creativity and others which make use of what has gone before them, which do not themselves grapple with important original problems, but only apply and put into effect prior discoveries. Everything is on a lower level. Thus, in place of the seventeenth-century intellectual there is the Encyclopedist, who is essentially a manifestation of journalism, but for whom science is still a living thing, even though, in general, it has been previously worked out. These men disseminate the thought of the seventeenth century, on which the following century lives. If an idea is to form the basis for living, it is necessary for time to elapse and for the masses to receive the idea, not as some individual's conviction, but as a prevailing belief. This is a slow process; as Ortega points out, the tempo of the life of a community is much slower than that of the life of an individual. Thus, in the eighteenth century, the ladies of Versailles discuss the themes which in the seventeenth had been the private domain of the most acute thinkers: Newton's physics and Monsieur Descartes' whirlwinds, which Voltaire had made accessible to the Court.

All this leads to the French Revolution. The Renaissance brought us two things: rationalism and the Reformation. These had two results: naturalism and optimism. We have seen that rationalism produces absolute monarchy in a very direct manner; but absolute monarchy is a phase in a process that began in the Middle Ages. The medieval period created a military spirit—knighthood—and the monarch is a leader with pronounced military traits. During the entire course of the seventeenth century, preparations are made for a struggle between two forces, the military and the intellectual. The concept of military command becomes more adapted to civilian political life; it becomes intellectualized. And since reason is essentially *one* and the same, and since what reason arranges is therefore that which *ought to be forever*, a *revolutionary* state of mind is engendered.

Men who are *rational* and *naturally good* find themselves in a society which was created historically, little by little, in an imperfect fashion, and which is based on a monarchic concept that is no longer alive and on a religious tradition that has lost social validity. These men decide to tear down the entire system in order to create a better one rationally, perfectly, once and for all: thus, they demand the "rights of man and of the citizen" and make no concessions to history. We find ourselves in the French Revolution. The world is to be organized in a definitive, geometrical way. *Raison* is to govern from now on.

5. THE LOSS OF GOD

I do not wish to imply that the evolution of the problem of God, which I have studied in detail in the preceding pages, was the only intellectual cause of all the changes in Europe at this time. That would be an exaggeration; but it is true that a very important group of these changes consists of the transition from a situation based on Christianity, with the idea of God as the foundation of all the sciences and with a divine law and religious morality based on dogma and theology, to another totally different situation, in which God is replaced by human reason and nature.

There is a factor which accelerates the triumph and dissemination of these ideas which do away with God and drive Him out of the sciences and intellectual researches. It is the primacy which the modern age grants to negative concepts. Indeed, in the modern period, the starting hypothesis is that it is necessary to justify a positive outlook, whereas a negative outlook is valid from the outset. Thus, one must make an effort to demonstrate freedom as opposed to determinism, or the existence of the external world or the possibility of knowledge. I do not mean to say that it is not really necessary to prove these things; I am referring to the tendency, the attitude which is today's point of departure. Fontenelle has a particularly expressive passage in this connection: "The testimony of those who believe an established thing carries no weight as a support of their belief; but the testimony of those who do not believe it is strong enough to destroy it—since those who believe it may not be informed about the reasons for not believing it, but it is not possible that those who do not believe it are not informed about the reasons for believing it."

Thus, by virtue of this supremacy of the negative, the progressive secularization of sciences acquires more strength. This explains why, just as in the past particular reasons were not given for each of those sciences to justify their being based on the Deity, so now sufficient proofs are not given to explain the exclusion of God from intellectual disciplines. Our age, with its imperative of starting out from neither one of these two attitudes and of justifying things, will have to come to a decision on such a serious question.

I have tried to show to what *unknown and impenetrable skies*, in Paul Hazard's phrase, God has been relegated. But we have also seen that, despite everything, God remained secure and firm in seventeenth-century philosophy. How did people forget this dimension and concern themselves only with the other, which separates us from the Deity?

I said above that God ceases to be the horizon of the thinkers and becomes the ground beneath their feet. In fact, He is no longer the divine object of speculation and science, but only their presupposition. Man goes to God, not because God interests him, but because the world concerns him. God is only the necessary condition for the reconquest of the world. Once the world is securely in man's grasp, God has no further importance. Nothing is of less interest to man than the ground beneath him; precisely because it is solid and secure, he neglects it and gives his attention to other things. Thus, modern man forgets God and gives his attention to nature. In the transition from the Middle Ages to modern times we see an outstanding example of that historical dynamism which, in alternation, converts what was formerly man's horizon into a presupposition with a quite different role.

But, above all, there is another, much more decisive reason. The process which we have briefly witnessed does not end here. The metaphysics of the period from Descartes to Leibniz is only a first stage in the process. We have yet to see how German idealism, in the philosophy of Kant, completes the loss of God in speculative reason by declaring the ontological proof impossible. Therefore, this expulsion of God, who is lost to theoretic reason, is in the making from Occam to German idealism. By the time of Leibniz we are only halfway along the path. What is then in the forefront, what is carried on most vigorously, what is being effected, is the banishment of God; the ontological bridge which still joins us to Him is only a vestige which defines a phase. This is what gives the years of change which we have been considering their *fundamental* unity and makes them, in spite of their extreme complexity, constitute a real stage in history.

GERMAN IDEALISM

Kant

We have seen what happens in the seventeenth and eighteenth centuries, the fundamental situation which faces man as a consequence of rationalism. The explanations set forth in the preceding section had a double purpose: first, they were an attempt to explain the historical reality of those two centuries; secondly, they represented an endeavor to establish rather precisely the intellectual environment in which Kant and the other German idealists are to move. It is useful to emphasize two important aspects of the thought of those two centuries: one is the physical image of the world which modern physics—more specifically, Newton—has given us; the other is the subjective and psychological critique which Locke, Berkeley and Hume—particularly Hume—have made. With these elements in view, we can undertake an explanation of Kantianism, one of the most difficult things one can attempt to do. It will be necessary to give a preliminary brief and simple exposition of the content of this philosophy, so that later we can discuss the significance of the Kantian problem.

Kantian Doctrine

KANT'S LIFE AND WORKS. Immanuel Kant was born in Königsberg in 1724; he died in the same city in 1804 after having passed his entire long life there. Kant was always a sedentary person; he never traveled beyond the boundaries of East Prussia and rarely went outside Königsberg itself. Kant's father was a master saddler; the family was of modest means, and Kant grew up in an atmosphere of honest artisanship and deep Pietistic religiosity. He studied at the university

284

in his natal city, gave private lessons and later taught at the university; however, not until 1770 was he named *Privatdozent* of logic and metaphysics, a position he held until 1797 when, seven years before his death, he abandoned it because of age and weakness. Kant's health was always very delicate, but in spite of this he attained the age of eighty and led a life of extraordinary exertion. He was punctual, methodical, serene and uncommonly kind. His whole life was a quiet but passionate quest for truth.

We can distinguish two epochs in Kant's work, and also in his philosophy: that which is called the *pre-critical* period—prior to the publication of the *Critique of Pure Reason*—and the later, *critical* period. The most important works of the earlier phase are *Allgemeine Naturgeschichte und Theorie des Himmels* (General Natural History and Theory of the Heavens) and *Der einzig mögliche Beweisgrund zu einer Demonstration des Daseins Gottes* (Only Possible Ground of Proof for the Existence of God) (1763). In 1770 Kant published his Latin dissertation, *De mundi sensibilis atque intelligibilis causa et principiis* (On the Form and Principles of the Sensible and Intelligible World), a work which marks the transition to the critical period. It was followed by a long silence lasting ten years, at the end of which, in 1781, there appeared the first edition of *Kritik der reinen Vernunft* (Critique of Pure Reason). Later, in 1783, Kant published the *Prolegomena zu einer jeden künftigen Metaphysik, die als Wissenschaft wird auftreten können* (Prolegomena to any Future Metaphysics Which Will Be Able to Come Forth as Science), in 1785 the *Grundlegung zur Metaphysik der Sitten* (Fundamental Principles of the Metaphysics of Ethics), and in 1788 the work that completes his ethics, the *Kritik der praktischen Vernunft* (Critique of Practical Reason). Finally, in 1790, he published his third book of criticism, the *Kritik der Urteilskraft* (Critique of Judgment). Kant's most important works are grouped in a space of ten years. Also of great importance are *Die Metaphysik der Sitten* (1797), *Die Religion innerhalb der Grenzen der blossen Vernunft* (Religion within the Boundaries of Pure Reason), the *Anthropologie in pragmatischer Hinsicht* and the *Lectures on Logic*, which were edited by Gottlob Benjamin Jäsche in 1800. Kant's works also include many more or less brief writings of extraordinary interest and some others published after his death (see *Kants Opus postumum*, edited by Erich Adickes and later by Artur Buchenau) that are essential for the interpretation of his thought.

1. Transcendental Idealism

KANT'S SOURCES. The principal source of Kantian philosophy is to be found in Cartesian philosophy and, consequently, in rationalism up to Leibniz and Wolff. On the other hand, Kant says that Hume's criticisms awakened him from his dogmatic slumbers. (We shall presently see what this adjective means.) In Descartes the *res cogitans* and the *res extensa* have something in common: *being*. As we have seen, this being which is based on God is what creates the unity between the two *res*, and what makes knowledge possible.

In Parmenides, who represents the beginning of metaphysics, being is a *real* quality of the things, something that is *in them*, as a color can be, but in such a way that it is prior to all other possible qualities. In short, in Parmenides the things are *real*. In idealist philosophy, the case is different. Being is not real, but *transcendental*. "Immanent" means what remains in, *immanet, manet in*. "Transcendent" refers to what exceeds or transcends something. "Transcendental" means neither transcendent nor immanent. A table has the quality of being, but all the table's other qualities also have being; the quality of being permeates and envelops all the rest but does not become intermingled with any of them. All the things are rooted in being, and therefore being serves as a bridge between the things. *This is transcendental being*.

TRANSCENDENTAL KNOWLEDGE. This concept, however, does not satisfy Kant. Knowledge cannot be explained simply by interpreting being as transcendental; it is necessary to create a transcendental theory of knowledge, and this knowledge is to be the bridge between the ego and the things. According to the realist, knowledge is knowledge of the things, and the things transcend me. According to the idealist (Berkeley), who says that for me there is nothing but my ideas, the things are immanent, and knowledge is knowledge of my own ideas. But the situation is very different if I believe that my ideas are *of the things*. The things do not then appear to me as objects that are independent of me; the things occur to me *in my ideas*; but these ideas are not only mine, they are *ideas of the things*. They are things that appear to me, phenomena in the literal sense of the word.

If knowledge were transcendent, it would know external things. If it were immanent, it would know only ideas; that is, what is in me. But knowledge is transcendental: it knows the phenomena, that is, the *things in me* (emphasizing equally both parts of this expression). Here there arises the Kantian distinction between the phenomenon and the thing-in-itself.

The things-*in-themselves* are inaccessible; I cannot know them because in so far as I know them they are *in me*, affected by my subjectivity; the things-in-themselves (*noumena*) are neither spatial nor temporal, and I cannot conceive of anything that is outside of time and space. The things in the form in which they manifest themselves to me, as they appear to me, are *phenomena*.

Kant distinguishes two elements of knowledge: what is given and what is posited by the thinking subject. Something occurs to me (a chaos of sensations) and I posit something (the space-time reference, the categories), and from the combination of these two elements there arises the *known thing* or *phenomenon*. Thus, when thought orders the chaos of sensations it *makes the things*; consequently Kant says that thought does not adapt itself to the things, but the other way around, and that his philosophy represents a "Copernican revolution." But thought does not create the things all by itself; it makes use of given material. Thus, the *things*, which are distinct from the unknowable things-in-themselves, arise out of the act of transcendental knowledge.

PURE REASON. Kant distinguishes three modes of knowledge: sensibility (*Sinnlichkeit*), reflective understanding (*Verstand*) and reason (*Vernunft*). To the noun "reason" Kant adds the adjective "pure." Pure reason is based on a priori principles; it is independent of experience. In Kant, "pure" means a priori, but not only that: *pure reason* is not the reason of any one man, nor even human reason, but simply that of the *rational being*. Pure reason is equivalent to *the rational conditions of rational beings in general*.

However, the titles of Kant's works can be misleading. He calls one the *Critique of Pure Reason* and the other the *Critique of Practical Reason*. *Practical* seems to be in opposition to *pure*, but this is not so. Practical reason is also pure, and is the opposite of speculative or theoretic reason. Thus the full expression would be *speculative* (or *theoretic*) *pure reason* and *practical* pure reason. But since in the first *Critique* Kant studies the general conditions of pure reason and in the second the practical aspect of the same reason, he adopts an abbreviated form in his titles.

Speculative reason refers to a *theory*, to a pure knowledge of the things; in contrast, practical reason refers to action, to a doing, in a sense close to the Greek *prâxis*, and is the focal point of Kantian ethics.

2. THE "CRITIQUE OF PURE REASON"

Kant writes his *Critique* as a propaedeutic to or preparation for metaphysics, which is understood as a priori philosophical knowledge. He must determine the possibilities of knowledge and the basis of its validity. This is the general problem. The *Critique* was published in 1781, and Kant altered it significantly in the second edition of 1787;

both editions are of great interest in the history of philosophy. The following is an outline of the *Critique of Pure Reason*:

Judgments

Knowledge can be either a priori or a posteriori. The former is knowledge whose validity is not based on experience; the latter is knowledge whose validity derives from experience. A posteriori knowledge cannot be universal or necessary; therefore, science requires a priori knowledge, that is, knowledge that is not limited by the contingencies of experience in the *here* and *now*. Kant finds several kinds of a priori knowledge: mathematics; physics; traditional metaphysics, which claims to know its three objects—man, the world and God. These objects are beyond experience because they are "infinite syntheses." I cannot have an intuition of the world, for example, because I am part of it and it does not appear to me as a *thing*. Kant wonders if metaphysics is possible; he finds that the other sciences (mathematics and physics) travel along a *sure path*, but it seems to him that metaphysics does not. So Kant formulates his three major questions: How is mathematics possible? (Transcendental esthetics) How is pure physics possible? (Transcendental analytics) Is metaphysics possible? (Transcendental dialectics). Observe that the third question differs in form from the other two; Kant does not assume the possibility of metaphysics. (*Esthetics* does not here refer to what is beautiful, but to sensibility, in its Greek sense of *aisthesis*.)

Truth and knowledge, therefore, occur in judgments. A science is a systematic complex of judgments. Kant must first of all establish a logical theory of judgment.

ANALYTIC JUDGMENTS AND SYNTHETIC JUDGMENTS. An *analytic* judgment is one whose predicate is contained in the notion of the subject. A *synthetic* judgment, on the contrary, is one whose predicate is not included in the notion of the subject but is *joined* or added to it. For example: bodies have extension, a sphere is round; but on the contrary, a table is wooden, lead is heavy. Extension is included in the notion of a body and roundness in that of a sphere; but woodenness is not included in the notion of a table, nor is heaviness included in that of lead. (One should observe that in Leibniz' philosophy all judgments are analytic judgments, since all the determinations of a thing are necessarily included in the complete notion of the thing; however, only God possesses the complete notion of a thing.)

Analytic judgments *explicate* the concept of the subject, whereas synthetic judgments *amplify* it. Thus synthetic judgments augment our knowledge and are the ones that have value for science.

A PRIORI AND A POSTERIORI JUDGMENTS. We have already alluded to another distinction, one which deals with a priori judgments and judgments based on *experience*. At first glance it seems that analytic judgments are a priori judgments, that they are obtained purely by analysis of the concept of the subject, and that synthetic judgments are a posteriori judgments. The first statement is true, and in general a posteriori judgments are synthetic judgments; however, the converse is not true; there are *a priori synthetic judgments*, even though this may seem to be a contradiction in terms, and these are the judgments that are of interest to science because they fulfill the two required conditions: they are on one hand a priori, that is, universal and necessary, and on the other, synthetic, that is, they effectively augment our knowledge. The equation $2 + 2 = 4$, the statement that the sum of the three angles of a triangle is equal to two right angles—these are a priori synthetic judgments; their predicates are not contained in the subjects, and the judgments are not based on experience. We find a priori synthetic judgments outside of mathematics also, in physics and metaphysics: "every phenomenon has its cause," "man is free," "God exists." Thus, the question of the possibility of these sciences is reduced to this other question: How are a priori synthetic judgments possible —if indeed they are possible—in each one of these sciences?

Space and Time

PURE INTUITIONS. Everything I know is made up of two elements: that which is given and that which I posit. That which is given is a chaos of sensations, and chaos is precisely the opposite of knowledge. I do something with that chaos of sensations. What do I do? I *order* it— first, in space and time, then, as we shall presently see, according to the categories. Then, utilizing the chaos of sensations, I make *things*—not things-in-themselves, but *phenomena*, things subject to space and time. Now, are space and time things-in-themselves? No, they are not. Then what are they?

Kant says that they are *pure intuitions*. They are the *a priori forms of sensibility*. Sensibility is not only receptive, but also active; it leaves its imprint on everything that it apprehends; and it possesses its forms in an a priori way. Space and time are forms which sensibility gives to the things which occur to it from outside; these forms are necessary conditions if I am to perceive; and I posit these conditions. I have a priori knowledge of space and time; I do not know them from experience, but rather just the opposite: they are indispensable conditions to my having experience. It is in these forms that my perception resides. Thus they are prior to the things and belong to the realm of pure subjectivity.

MATHEMATICS. I know space and time in an absolutely a priori way. Thus judgments that relate to the forms of sensibility are a priori judgments, even though they may be synthetic judgments as well. Therefore such judgments are possible in mathematics, a science that is based on *constructions of concepts*. The validity of mathematics is based on the a priori intuition of relationships between *spatial* figures and numbers which are based on the *temporal* succession of units. Consequently, space and time constitute the logical—not psychological— basis of mathematics, and synthetic a priori judgments are possible. Transcendental esthetics solves the first part of the problem.

The Categories

Space and time separate us from the reality of the things-in-themselves. Sensibility presents to our understanding only phenomena, things which it has already "deformed" or operated on. As Ortega has shown so well, thinking is *essentially* a process of transforming. But the understanding, like sensibility, also possesses a priori forms by means of which it apprehends and understands the things: these forms are the *categories*.

In Aristotle, the categories were modes or inflections of being to which the mind adapted itself. In Kant, conversely, the mind already contains the categories, and the things conform to the mind; this is the concept Kant referred to as a *"Copernican revolution."* The categories are in our understanding and not directly in the being of the things. No longer are we separated from reality *in itself* only by space and time; now there is a second "deforming" factor, the categories.

THE JUDGMENTS AND THE CATEGORIES. Kant begins with the logical classification of the judgments, as modified by him, in accordance with four points of view: quantity, quality, relation and modality.

1.
Quantity
Universal
Particular
Singular

2.
Quality
Affirmative
Negative
Infinite

3.
Relation
Categorical
Hypothetical
Disjunctive

4.
Modality
Problematical
Assertory
Apodictic

From these judgments, each one of which is a mode of synthesis, the categories are derived. Since the subdivision of the judgments is completely a priori, the categories derived from them are modes of pure a priori synthesis, the modalities of the concept of an object in general. In this way we get the following table of *pure concepts of the understanding*, or *categories*:

1.
Quantity
Unity
Plurality
Totality

2.
Quality
Reality
Negation
Limitation

3.
Relation
Substance
Causality
Community or
reciprocal action

4.
Modality
Possibility
Existence
Necessity

The close relation between the classes of judgments and the categories is evident. The categories are relationships among objects, corresponding to those among the judgments.

PURE PHYSICS. Using space, time and the categories, the understanding fashions the objects of pure physics; the category of substance
applied to space gives us the concept of *matter*; the category of causality
taken together with the form of time gives us the physical concept of
cause and effect, and so forth. Since we always remain entirely within
the realm of a priori thought, in which experience plays no part, the
validity of pure physics does not depend on experience, and a priori
synthetic judgments are possible within the domain of pure physics.
This is the result of transcendental analytics.

The Critique of Traditional Metaphysics

Traditional metaphysics, in its medieval forms and especially in the
generalized formulation of Wolff in the eighteenth century, consisted
of two parts: a *metaphysica generalis*, or ontology, and a *metaphysica
specialis*, which was concerned with the three great areas of being:
man, the world and God; this gives us three disciplines: rational
psychology, rational cosmology and rational theology. Kant is faced
with these sciences and their repertory of problems (the immortality of
the soul, freedom, the finiteness or infiniteness of the world, the
existence of God, and so on), and in his transcendental dialectics
attacks the problem of *whether* this metaphysics—which does not seem
to have set out upon the *sure path of science*—is possible.

METAPHYSICS. For Kant, metaphysics is identical with pure, a
priori knowledge. But real knowledge is possible only when sensory
perception or experience is added to the formal principles. Now, the
principles we have obtained are formal and a priori; in order to have
knowledge of reality, it would be necessary to supplement them with a
posteriori elements, with experience. Traditional speculative metaphysics is the attempt to acquire, by a priori thought, a real knowledge
of objects—the soul, the world, God—which are beyond any possible
experience. Therefore, it is a vain attempt. These three objects are
"infinite syntheses," and one cannot posit the necessary conditions for
intuiting them; therefore, it is impossible to acquire this knowledge.
Kant examines in turn the paralogisms contained in the demon-
strations of rational psychology, the antinomies of rational cosmology
and the arguments of rational theology (the ontological proof, the
cosmological proof and the physico-theological proof of the existence
of God), and concludes that these disciplines are invalid. We cannot
go into the details of this critique, since this would take us too far afield.
All that is of interest here is to indicate the basis of Kant's critique of
the ontological argument, since this critique is the key to his whole
philosophy.

THE ONTOLOGICAL ARGUMENT. Kant shows that the argument that originates with St. Anselm is based on a notion of being which he rejects: the notion of being as a *real predicate*. This is more true of Descartes' form of the proof, which is the form Kant is concerned with. This proof understands existence to be a *perfection* that cannot be lacking in the most perfect Entity. That is, existence is interpreted as something that is *in a thing*. But Kant declares that being is not a real predicate: *Sein ist kein reales Prädikat*. The thing which exists contains nothing that the thing which is only thought of does not contain: if it were otherwise, the concept in question would not be of that thing. A hundred real crowns (coins), Kant says in his famous comparison, contain nothing that is not contained in a hundred possible crowns. Nevertheless, he adds, it makes a difference to me whether I have a hundred possible or a hundred real crowns; of what does the difference consist? The actual crowns are connected with sensory perception; they are present, along with all the other things, in the totality of experience. That is, existence is not a property of the things, but their relationship with all the other things, the positive *position* of the object. Being is not a real, but a *transcendental* predicate. Seventeenth-century metaphysics understood it to be real, and therefore accepted the onto-logical proof; this is the meaning of the epithet which Kant applies to Baroque thought: *dogmatism*, ignorance of the transcendental nature of being.

THE IDEAS. The three disciplines of traditional metaphysics are, according to Kant, not valid. Metaphysics is not possible *as a specu-lative science*. Its themes have nothing to do with science, but remain as objects of faith, and as such cannot be refuted. "I had to suppress knowledge," Kant says, "in order to make way for belief."

But metaphysics continues to exist as a *natural predisposition* of man toward the absolute. And the objects of metaphysics are those which Kant calls *Ideas*; they are like new, higher categories corresponding to the syntheses of judgments in pure reasoning. Since these Ideas are not open to intuition, they can only have a *regulative* use. Man ought to behave *as if* his soul were immortal, *as if* he were free, *as if* God existed, even though theoretic reason cannot prove all this. But this is not the only role of the Ideas. Along with this hypothetical validity for speculative reason, the transcendental Ideas also possess another validity of a different kind, one which is absolute and unconditional; they reappear in the deepest layer of Kantian philosophy as *postulates of practical reason*.

3. PRACTICAL REASON

NATURE AND FREEDOM. Kant distinguishes between two worlds: the world of nature and the world of freedom. The former is determined by natural causality, but alongside this, Kant allows the existence of a *causality through freedom*, which governs the other domain. On the one hand, man is a psychophysical subject, ruled by the physical and psychical laws of nature; this is what Kant calls the *empirical ego*. Just as the body obeys the law of gravity, the will is shaped by stimuli, and in this empirical sense it is not free. But to this empirical ego Kant contraposes a *pure ego*, which is not determined naturally, but only by the laws of freedom. Man, as a *rational person*, belongs to this world of freedom. But we have already seen that theoretic reason does not extend this far; within its own field it is incapable of knowing freedom. Where do we encounter freedom? Only in the *fact of morality*; here there appears *practical reason*, which is not concerned with *being* but with *how one ought to be*; here it is not a question of speculative knowledge but of moral knowledge. And just as Kant studied the possibilities of the former in the *Critique of Pure Reason* (theoretic reason), he must now write a *Critique of Practical Reason*.

THE "FACTUM" OF MORALITY. In discussing practical reason, Kant accepts *postulates* which are not demonstrable with theoretic reason, but which possess a direct and absolute self-evidence for the thinking subject. Therefore, they are postulates and their acceptance is required and unconditionally imposed, although not speculatively. Kant is faced with a fact, a *factum*, which is the point of departure for his ethics: morality, the consciousness of duty. Man has a feeling of responsibility, of duty. This is a pure fact, indisputable and self-evident. Now, duty and the consciousness of responsibility presuppose the *freedom* of man. But freedom is not demonstrable by theoretic reason; from the speculative point of view, it is merely a *regulative Idea*: one ought to act *as if* one were free. On the other hand, freedom now appears as something absolutely certain and required by the consciousness of duty, even though theoretic reason does not tell us how it is possible. Man, in so far as he is a *moral person*, is free, and his freedom is a postulate of practical reason.

THE OBJECTS OF METAPHYSICS. Analogously, the immortality of the soul and the existence of God, which it was not possible to prove in the *Critique of Pure Reason*, reappear as postulates in the other *Critique*. The objects of traditional metaphysics are valid in a double sense: as regulative Ideas in the realm of theoretic reason, and as postulates with absolute validity in the realm of practical reason. This is to be the basis of Kant's ethics.

THE CATEGORICAL IMPERATIVE. In the *Fundamental Principles of the Metaphysics of Morals*, Kant formulates the problem of ethics as the question of the *highest good*. Good things may be good for something else or good in themselves. Kant says that the only thing that is good in itself, with no restrictions, is a *good will*. The problem of morality is thus brought into relation not with actions, but with the will which motivates them.

Kant wishes to create an ethics that will state how man *ought to be*. This ethics must also be imperative, obligatory. Thus Kant seeks an *imperative*. But the majority of imperatives are not suitable as a basis for ethics, because they are *hypothetical*, that is, they depend upon a condition. If I say: *nourish yourself*, a condition is understood: *if you want to live*; but for a man who wants to die, such an imperative has no validity. Kant has need of a *categorical* imperative which will be unconditionally and absolutely authoritative. The categorical imperative's obligatory power must be found within itself. Since the highest good is a good will, the moral evaluation of an action is based on the will that motivated the action, not on the action itself. And a good will is one which wills what it wills *purely out of regard to duty*. If I perform a good action because it pleases me to do so, or out of sentiment, fear, and the like, *it has no moral value*. (Here Kant raises the thorny problem of whether regard to duty is not itself a sentiment.) The categorical imperative is expressed in different ways; its basic meaning is the following: *Act in such a way that you can will what you are doing to be a universal law of nature.*

In effect, the man who commits a wrong action does it as a *mistake*, as an *exception*, and is affirming the universal moral law at the very moment when he is infringing it. If I lie, I cannot will that lying should be a universal law, since this would destroy the meaningfulness of what people say, and would even make impossible the effect of my own lie; lying presupposes, precisely, that the universal law is to tell the truth. And a similar thing occurs with every other instance of wrongdoing.

THE MORAL PERSON. Kantian ethics is *autonomous*, not *heteronomous*; that is, its laws are dictated by the moral conscience itself, not by an authority outside the ego. The ego is a *legislator in the kingdom of ends*, in the world of moral freedom. From another viewpoint, this ethics is *formal*, not *material*, because it prescribes nothing concrete, no action that is determined as to content; it prescribes only the *form* of action: keep duty in mind, whatever you do; act out of regard to duty, do what you *will*.

Strictly speaking, the last-mentioned expression is accurate: you ought to do what you *will*; not what you desire, long for or find suitable, but what your rational will is able to *will*. Kant asks man to be free, to be autonomous, not to let himself be determined by any motive alien to his will, which makes its own laws.

In this way, Kantian ethics culminates in the concept of the *moral person*. An ethics is always an ontology of man. Kant asks man to realize his essence, to be what he truly is, a *rational* being—because Kantian ethics is not concerned with the empirical ego, or even with the human condition, but with a pure ego, a purely rational being. On the one hand man, as an empirical ego, is subject to natural causality; but on the other hand he belongs to the kingdom of ends.

Kant says that *each and every man is an end in himself.* Immorality consists in treating a man—one's own self or one's fellow—as a *means* for something else, whereas man actually is an end in himself.

The moral laws—the categorical imperative—are derived from the legislation of one's own will. Therefore, the imperative and morality are of interest to us, because they are a thing of our own making.

THE PRIMACY OF PRACTICAL REASON. Practical reason, as contrasted with theoretic reason, possesses direct validity only for the ego, and consists in determining one's own actions. But Kant affirms the primacy of practical over speculative reason, that is, its priority and superiority. The primary aspect of human life is not *theoria*, but *prâxis*, *action*. Kant's philosophy culminates in the concept of the moral person, understood as a free person. Kant was not able to perfect his metaphysics fully, and left only an outline of it, because his whole life was taken up by the task of criticism which had to be completed first. But it is necessary to take as a point of departure the primacy of practical reason and of these notions of *freedom* and action, if one is to understand the philosophy of German idealism, which is born in Kant and ends in Hegel.

TELEOLOGY AND ESTHETICS. For our present purpose, we can omit an exposition of the content of the *Critique of Judgment*, which is concerned with problems of teleology in the biological organism and in the field of esthetics.

Kant's definition of the beautiful is well known; he calls it a *finality without end*, that is, something which contains a finality within itself, but which is not subordinated to any end alien to esthetic pleasure. Kant also distinguishes between the *beautiful*, which produces a pleasant feeling and is accompanied by the consciousness of limitation, and the *sublime*, which causes a pleasure that is mingled with horror and admiration—a storm, a lofty mountain or a tragedy is sublime—because the sublime is accompanied by the impression of infinity or limitlessness. These Kantian ideas had important repercussions in nineteenth-century thought.

The Problem of Kantian Philosophy

1. The Interpretations of Kant's Philosophy

METAPHYSICS. Kant is an unusual philosopher, because he represents an essential revolution in philosophic thought. He himself uses an expressive metaphor in presenting his philosophy: he says that it is like a *Copernican revolution*. Therefore, it is something essentially new, which opens different paths. This would be sufficient to explain the difficulty of Kant's thought. But in addition it so happens that Kant did not achieve the creation of a complete system, the full realization of his system. We need only observe the titles of his basic works: they are *Critiques*, something by means of which he sets certain limits to reason and delimits its objects; but it seems that after these critiques was to come his positive doctrine—which never came. There are only fragments which point in this direction. This is true, but only half true. It would not be proper to state bluntly that Kant did not create his metaphysics, because a metaphysics is contained in his *Critiques*, even (in fact, especially) in the *Critique of Pure Reason*. And here the difficulty begins: since this metaphysics was not created as such—indeed, it is negated—it is very easy to overlook it or to misunderstand it.

The case of Kant, as Ortega has very rightly observed, is similar to that of Plato. The problems which the things created for Plato led him to the discovery of the Ideas; and when a man has discovered the Ideas, he has already done quite a bit. Plato remained in the realm of the Ideas, amidst the difficulties that they caused him, and had no time left to return to the things. In his old age he longed to solve these difficulties—as in his dialogue *Parmenides*—and to return to the things, to create his metaphysics.

Something similar occurs with Kant. He was a slow man, not at all precocious—hardly anyone in the history of philosophy was—and when he arrived at old age, he had yet to accomplish the constructive part of his work; but his metaphysics was already created in its essentials: the *Critique of Pure Reason* is already metaphysics (see Ortega: *Filosofía pura* and, from another standpoint, Heidegger: *Kant und das Problem der Metaphysik*). But this is already an interpretation: Kant himself nowhere states that it is metaphysics; instead, he says that metaphysics is not possible. Therefore, to say that it is ontology requires some justification. This has not always been affirmed. We can consider three major phases of Kant's influence on subsequent philosophy: German idealism, neo-Kantianism and the philosophy of the present time.

THE PHILOSOPHIC PAST. Before I begin this discussion, I must make a preliminary remark. Some people may think that the ideas people have had of Kant are not important to us, and that the only thing that matters is what Kant's philosophy means today. This viewpoint is wrong. When I speak of Kant's philosophy, I claim to speak of something that has reality. A thing is real when it affects me, when I must take account of it. When I speak of Kantianism, I speak of something that *is* real: I am using the present indicative of the verb *to be*. To be real means to be real *now*. I take the past into account, for example, in so far as I am remembering it now, at the present time. Remembrance consists of the *presence* of the past as the past. Likewise, the hope of a future consists of the presence of the future as the future. Thus we see that the present lends reality to both the past and the future. If I ignore the present, the past no longer exists and the future does not yet exist. Furthermore, when we say that the past was, we mean that it once was the present; and when we say that the future will be, we mean that the future will be the present. What does all this signify? That the past as the past does not exist except in a present that gives it reality and in relation to which it is the past.

Let us keep these ideas clearly in mind and return to the case of Kantianism. Kantianism has reality; but Kantianism as it was thought of back in the eighteenth century is now a thing of the past. Therefore it receives reality only from the present—for example, when I think of it now.

Thus we find that what is the present today was not the present thirty years ago. Therefore, the reality of Kantianism is given by *each* present in which Kantianism is actualized, and we see that, far from its being unimportant to us, what interests us is what Kantianism has been in each moment. An appeal to Kantianism as such, divorced from what it meant to Kant's followers, is basically false, because it is based on a pure illusion, namely, that I can return to Kantianism *in itself*, when actually the most I can do is reactualize Kantianism in *my* present, not in that of Kant. I actualize it in *a* present, and I also take that present to be Kant's present; here lies the error.

Kantianism is Kantianism as it has been active in the various philosophies—and nothing else; it is Kantianism in the form in which I find it in me as the past—and nothing else. This does not mean that I cannot discover new and unrealized elements in it, but only that such elements have had no actual reality until now.

This discussion might be applied to the entire history of philosophy. What justifies its being raised in connection with Kant is that Kantianism has been a changing concept and has had very different interpretations; there have been several different Kantianisms, all more or less authentic. Let us now consider the three principal interpretations of Kant's philosophy.

1. GERMAN IDEALISM. Kant is recognized as the father of a splendid philosophical movement: German idealism. This is true to such a degree that the idealists begin by presenting their own philosophies as interpretations of Kant's. Fichte actually says: "Kant has not been properly understood; I understand him, perhaps better than he understood himself." While trying to explain Kant, Fichte adopts a point of view that differs from Kant's, and then he and the other idealists create their own philosophies. Actually, they create their own philosophies along Kantian lines and, starting from Kant's work, complete what Kant left undone. Expressed in general terms, the three great idealists—Fichte, Schelling and Hegel—attempt to create the metaphysics that Kant never got around to creating. We will presently see the extent to which this is true.

2. NEO-KANTIANISM. Let us consider the second manifestation of Kantianism. It is helpful to fix our attention on the name itself—*neo-Kantianism*. This movement is an express actualization of the past, for these men are not Kantians, but *neo*-Kantians. Therefore, Kantianism is not something that is in the present, but something that needs to be renewed, actualized. The neo-Kantians become the exegetes of Kantianism: Hermann Cohen and Paul Natorp, especially. They do not claim to present Kant, but a *neo*-Kant. Their position in relation to that of the German idealists is: Kant's philosophy is not as you have presented it; it is something different, which we will now expound.

Neo-Kantianism is not merely Kantianism, and so something must have taken place somewhere along the line to justify the prefix. What can have happened? Positivism (from 1835–40 to 1880, approximately). The neo-Kantians are positivists who cease to be positivists, who derive from positivism; this is what determines the character of neo-Kantian philosophy.

Kantianism has the following characteristics: (1) the denial of metaphysics in any form; (2) a very pronounced tendency to become a theory of knowledge; (3) a great interest in the *positive* sciences and (4) the tendency to understand philosophy as a theory of positive science. As for the *Critique of Pure Reason*, (1) it attempts to determine the possibilities of knowledge; (2) it attempts to establish a philosophic theory of the science of its day—mathematics and Newtonian physics; (3) it comes to reject traditional metaphysics as impossible. All this is part of the *Critique of Pure Reason*, and this is what the positivists see in Kant; but the *Critique* contains a great deal more, and much material of greater importance. Neo-Kantianism is colored by positivism and tends to become a theory of science, a philosophic reflection on knowledge and the positive sciences. Therefore, it is something very different from German idealism.

3. PRESENT-DAY PHILOSOPHY. We now come down to the present time. Kant's work can mean something quite different to us because many very significant events separate us from the neo-Kantians: (1) the elaboration of a philosophy of life of a metaphysical character, which began with Kierkegaard, Nietzsche, Dilthey and Bergson; (2) the establishment of Husserl's phenomenology, for which Brentano prepared the way, and (3) most recently, the development of a metaphysics of human life or rather of vital reason (Ortega), or an ontology of existence (Heidegger). We have therefore returned to metaphysics. It has once again been clearly perceived that philosophy is metaphysics and nothing else, and that theory of knowledge is metaphysics and cannot be considered an autonomous and prior discipline. Thus, the neo-Kantian interpretation of Kant seems to us to be incomplete— that is, false—because it emphasizes only what is least important. For us, Kant is first of all a metaphysician, one who did not elaborate his philosophy systematically but who nevertheless left it to us—in the pages which the neo-Kantians found of least interest. And Kant's metaphysics has to be such that it makes clear how the other metaphysical systems of German idealism arose out of it. (For further discussion of all these questions, see the above-mentioned essay by Ortega: *Filosofía pura*.)

2. THEORY OF KNOWLEDGE

Let us attempt an interpretation of Kant's contribution by considering two aspects of his work: the doctrine of being and the doctrine of knowledge. These two aspects, which are intimately interconnected, can lead us to an understanding of Kant's basic concept, that of the moral person and practical reason. When we achieve that understanding we will find ourselves at a high point of Kantian philosophy, and from there we will be able to view subsequent developments. The two aspects of the problem are inseparable.

Kant radically alters the concept of knowledge. This subject is what is known as *criticism* and what interested the neo-Kantians. We are going to emphasize a different aspect in our discussion, one which will reveal Kant's idea of being. Let us keep in mind the Kantian doctrine of the phenomenon and the thing-in-itself. Of this, what now interests us is the following: Knowledge is an active function of the thinking subject; it does not consist of receiving something that happens to be at hand, but of creating something that is known; in Kantian terms, the subject *posits* something. Kant says that we know of the things only what we have posited in them; thus, for Kant the things are not at hand; rather, the thinking subject creates them upon knowing them. This must be understood literally, for otherwise it might be thought that the only thing that exists in itself is the ego, that the only thing-in-itself is the ego, and that the other things are *in me*. But this is not so; I am not in myself a thing-in-itself because I am a thing to myself only in so far as I know myself.

We are going to emphasize the opposite aspect: the objective aspect. One must avoid possible subjectivist interpretations of Kantianism. I neither create nor invent the things; instead, there is something that is essentially *given* to me, and upon this I posit the a priori forms of sensibility and the categories. Only after I have applied these forms to what is given is it meaningful to speak of known things or of the being of the things. However, the situation is not such that there is on one hand what is given, what Kant calls the chaos of sensations, and on the other the ego with its subjective determinations. This would mean that there were two things-in-themselves and that knowledge arose from their union or contact; the truth is that the chaos of sensations can occur only in my subjectivity, because in order to exist it must occur in space and time and, therefore, in me; and, conversely, the ego exists only in relation to what is given. Thus it happens that knowledge, far from being the result of the contact or union of what is given and what is posited, is rather the superior fact on which is based the very possibility of speaking of what is given and what is posited.

3. BEING

We have seen that Kant's idea of knowledge is radically new; it constitutes a "Copernican revolution" because it is accomplished by a new idea of being. Ortega has seen this with extraordinary clarity.

BEING AND ENTITY.   Man has always asked himself *what is being*; this question embodies two meanings. We must distinguish between two essentially different things: *being* and *entity*. These terms are generally used as synonyms, and there are languages such as French in which there is but one word to convey both meanings: *l'être* (the word *étant* has recently been introduced in order to preserve the distinction when translating German expressions). In scholastic Latin we have *esse* and *ens*; in Greek, εἶναι and ὄν; in Spanish, *ser* and *ente*; in German, *das Sein* and *das Seiende*. It is not an accident that these words have been generally confused, because it has not been realized that they deal with two different things.

Being is something that belongs to the things that exist, or something that happens to them and that allows it to be said of them that they are *entities*. Apart from the question of what—or rather *who*—is the entity, of what things are, there exists the further and more profound question of what we mean when we say that things are. Aristotle, who in his *Metaphysics* studied the entity *as an entity*, at least glimpsed this fundamental problem.

The entity has been spoken of almost always, and it has been understood as substance, subsistence; thus, when Descartes affirms his idealist thesis, he affirms the ego, but the ego as an entity, as a prime substance: *ego sum* RES *cogitans*. And so idealism does not touch upon the question of what is meant by substance, of what substance (and therefore being) is. As long as idealism is nothing but idealism, it does not come to grips with the basic problem of philosophy; it merely deals with the relative rank of substances. The *próte ousía* becomes the ego. What the ego does is *cogitare*; thus, what actually exists and is the basis for the being of the other things is the *cogitatio* or idea. This, therefore, is *idealism*. In realism, it is the *res* that principally exists, whereas in idealism it is the *idea*; however, the idea is also *res, res cogitans*.

The Cartesian concept of substance is based on the notion of independence which had been traditional since Aristotle. This independence, this self-sufficiency, this subsistence, is *in se*. Let us recall the difference between being *in se* and being *a se*. Being *in se* is this independence of the substance; only God is a being *a se*. An entity can be *in se* or *in alio* and, on the other hand, *a se* or *ab alio*. The independence of a color, a horse and a God, for example, are very different.

One cannot conceive of a color by itself, alone; not to be independent, to be in association with extension—this is part of the essence of color; color is *ab alio*, but it is also *in alio*. A horse does not need anything else in order to be a horse; it is independent *in se*. This is in reference to its essence—but what about its existence? In order to exist it needs to be somewhere, for this is the meaning of the word "exist." Even if we ignore the question of the Creation, a horse or a stone or any finite entity cannot be said to exist independently, because of the very significance of the verb "to exist." To exist is *ex-sistere*; in German, *da-sein*. Both words contain an obvious reference to place: *ex*, *da*, to be there, outside something. Actually, it is not a question of place. Let us recall Kant's explanation of the difference between one hundred possible crowns and one hundred real crowns; there is no difference in the concept of them, but the one hundred real crowns exist not only in my thought, as do the possible crowns, but also outside it, among the things. Therefore, they have need of the existence of other things; there must at least exist something *in* which the crowns can exist. What is required is a world in which crowns and horses and stones can exist. Thus, even if we ignore the question of whether or not these things are independent of God, they are still dependent on the world. The horse and the stone are independent as regards essence, but dependent as regards existence; they are *in se*, but *ab alio*. Only God, whose essence contains His existence, is an *ens a se*.

TRANSCENDENTAL BEING. It is here that we find Kant's metaphysics. Its originality derives from this radical intuition: *being is not a real predicate*. A real predicate would be something that the things possessed in themselves; that is, the one hundred crowns would have something in themselves that would make them be real; Kant sees that they do not have anything in themselves that makes them different from the one hundred possible crowns. The difference is one of *position*, in that the real crowns are out there; they are *placed* among the things and are in association with the totality of experience. (In Kant, this continuous connection with experience is also a sign of reality as opposed to dreams.) The character of that which exists is not an intrinsic character; it is a transcendental character: it consists of a *being in*; it is something that transcends each thing and is based on each thing's relation to all the other things.

At this point there enters into play Kant's extremely important distinction between thinking and knowing. Knowledge is knowledge of something, knowledge of things; thus it is not limited to my ideas, but involves a true reference to the things. But one must distinguish between this idea of knowing and the one which a realist would have. A realist would say that my knowledge knows things, but things that are there, things-in-themselves. For Kant, this is not the case; it is not that there are two things-in-themselves—the ego and the known thing—and that the ego knows the things, but that it is precisely in the knowing that the things are things and the ego is the ego. It is not that the things simply transcend me, for without me there are no *things*; rather, knowledge is the basis for the being of the known things and of the ego that knows them. Knowledge is not something that intervenes between the things and the ego, but neither are the things ideas of mine; knowledge makes the things be things while they are known to the ego, and the ego be the ego while it knows the things. In this way, knowledge gives the things and the ego their respective being, but does not become intermingled with either. But this is nothing more than what we have called *transcendental*; we have thus explained why knowledge and being are both called transcendental.

GOD. The foregoing section explains Kant's position regarding the ontological argument. This proof presupposed that being was a real predicate and existence an *intrinsic perfection* which God had to possess. But if being is transcendental, merely to possess the idea of God is not sufficient proof that He exists; the existence of God would only be assured by His *position*. And since God, by His very nature as an infinite Entity, does not furnish me with the possibility of positing the conditions necessary to intuit Him, the result is that God remains beyond any possible experience. Since real things are distinguished from possible things precisely by their occurring to me in connection with experience, neither the existence nor the non-existence of God can be demonstrated.

This refutation of the ontological argument shows that it is not just any argument whatever, that it is not a piece of reasoning of the sort in which one must observe whether or not it is conclusive, but that it is a thesis which involves an idea of being, and thus a metaphysics; it is possible to raise objections to it only by starting out with a different idea of being. And any objection raised against this critique of Kant's must necessarily be raised against Kantian metaphysics as a whole.

Now we can understand in its entirety the problem of God in the philosophy of idealism. In Kant, speculative reason must renounce the intellectual possession of God, and can no longer use Him as a basis. As a result of this, metaphysics is radically changed. The metaphysics just before this, seventeenth-century rationalism, was based on the presupposition of the certainty of God's existence. This is now impossible. Being is interpreted in a different sense, and in contrast to the *dogmatic* idealism, from which Kant, according to his famous phrase, had awakened, philosophy becomes a *transcendental* idealism. This changes the situation of God vis-à-vis the mind, the entire problem of being and, with it, philosophy. This change is also occasioned by the fact that the ontological argument is no longer considered valid and conclusive. Thus begins the last stage of idealism; the bond which has until now continued to unite God with theoretic reason is broken, and the metaphysical process which began at the close of medieval Scholasticism is completed. In this last stage, God reappears in a new guise in the realm of practical reason, and in a different form in all metaphysics subsequent to Kant, especially that of Hegel. At that point the ontological argument acquires new philosophical validity.

4. PHILOSOPHY

Kantian metaphysics reaches its culmination in the concept of the moral person and in the theory of practical reason. We have seen that Kant found metaphysics to be impossible as a science; but two indubitable facts imposed themselves on Kant: the fact of metaphysics as a *natural predisposition* of man and the fact of morality.

Kant asked himself whether metaphysics was possible as a science, but not whether it was possible as a yearning, as a natural predisposition, because it has existed as such for centuries and centuries. It is necessary to take literally the expression *natural predisposition* (*Naturanlage*), something which is in nature. This means that man has in his very nature the predisposition to practice metaphysics.

WORLDLY CONCEPT OF PHILOSOPHY. Kant gives certain reasons to explain why man philosophizes; he is not content merely to say that it is a natural predisposition. True philosophy is not philosophy in a scholastic sense (*Schulbegriff*), but in a worldly sense (*Weltbegriff*). In this sense, philosophy is the system of the ultimate ends of reason; by means of philosophy man *chooses* the ultimate ends.

The ultimate problems of worldly philosophy are four in number:

(1) What can I know? (Metaphysics)
(2) What ought I to do? (Ethics)
(3) What may I hope for? (Religion)
(4) What is man? (Anthropology)

"But basically," Kant says, "all of this can be left to anthropology, because the first three questions all refer to the last." Philosophy becomes *anthropology*. The ultimate end of philosophy is that man should know himself. The highest object of metaphysics is the human person.

It happens that the knowledge of what a human person is involves many questions: What is the world in which this person is located? What is a person? What may he hope for and, thus, what can he know about God? This brings us back to the three themes of classical metaphysics. What does this mean? How is Kant able to return to these inaccessible objects?

Here they do not appear as objects of theoretic, but of practical reason. These objects are not attained by means of speculative knowledge; rather, man apprehends himself as a *moral person* in a way which is not open to proof but which is directly self-evident to the subject. And this *factum* of morality requires an explanation. What are the things which make it possible for man to be a moral person? They are the freedom of the will, immortality and the existence of God. Practical reason places us in extremely close, unconditional and absolute contact with these things, which are its postulates. Practical reason consists in the absolute self-determination of the moral subject. This is the fundamental meaning of Kant's *pure reason*.

Fichte

LIFE AND WORKS. Johann Gottlieb Fichte was born at Rammenau in 1762. He was of humble origin, the son of a weaver. By chance, a local nobleman recognized Fichte's extraordinary capabilities when he was little more than a child, and enabled him to pursue his studies. Despite great economic difficulties Fichte studied theology at the University of Jena, and then devoted himself to private tutoring. In 1791 he met Kant, who was already an old man, and the next year, through the good offices of the great philosopher, he published his *Versuch einer Kritik aller Offenbarung* (Essay towards a Critique of All Revelation), which appeared without his name and was attributed to Kant. When the true author became known, the attention aroused by the book was directed toward Fichte and quickly made him famous. From 1794 to 1799 he was a professor at Jena, where his activity as a writer was also great. He had a clash with the government concerning an article published in his review though not written by him, which was accused of atheism; the philosopher's arrogance caused him to lose his position. He moved on to Berlin, where he became a member of the Romantic circles, at the same time giving private classes with great success. When the French under Napoleon invaded Germany, Fichte was active in the campaign to arouse the German spirit; in the years 1807 and 1808 he delivered his famous *Addresses to the German Nation* (*Reden an die deutsche Nation*), which were one of the decisive contributions toward the formation of Germany's national consciousness. In 1811 he was rector of the University of Berlin, which had been founded just the year before. In 1813 he took part in the Napoleonic campaign as an orator, while his wife worked as a nurse in the hospitals of Berlin. An infection which his wife contracted and which Fichte caught caused his death in January, 1814.

Fichte's output is extensive. His principal works are a series of elaborations, each more mature than the last, of one major work titled *Wissenschaftslehre* (Theory of Science). In addition, he wrote *Die Bestimmung des Menschen* (The Vocation of Man), *Die Bestimmung des Gelehrten* (The Vocation of the Scholar), the *First* and *Second Introduction to the Theory of Science*—four books which are useful as an introduction to Fichte's difficult philosophy—as well as the *Anweisung zum seligen Leben* (Way to a Blessed Life) and, aside from the above-mentioned *Addresses*, several lectures on the philosophy of history titled *Die Grundzüge des gegenwärtigen Zeitalters* (The Characteristics of the Present Age).

Fichte was a personality of exceptional vividness. He always had a leaning toward public and oratorical activity, and his contribution to the formation of the German nation was very great. Fichte's literary style is energetic, lively and expressive.

1. Fichte's Metaphysics

KANT AND FICHTE. Fichte's philosophy is directly derived from Kant's. At the beginning, he presents his philosophy as a mature and profound exposition of Kantianism. But it is difficult to see this philosophical genesis if we adhere to the popular image of Kant handed down to us by the nineteenth century. It is necessary to return to the point at which Kant summed up the meaning of his philosophy.

The culmination of Kantian philosophy was practical reason. Kant ended by affirming the primacy of practical over theoretic reason, and the moral person, Kant's *pure ego*, determined himself practically and unconditionally. The self-determination of the ego by practical reason is very clearly seen in the form that could be given to the categorical imperative: *do what you will*, emphasizing the *will*; do what you are able to will. For Fichte, the moral imperative consists in saying: *become the man you are* (*werde, der du bist*), and in this sense Fichte's imperative is not far removed from Kant's, because when Kant says, "Do what you will" or "Be free," he asks man to act in accordance with what he ultimately is, to determine himself, with freedom. In this way the empirical ego, which is determined by many things, ought to act, according to Kant, as if it were free, or, expressed differently, the empirical ego ought to aim to be the pure ego that it is essentially. Thus Fichte tells man: "Be the man you are," aim to be the man you are essentially. In Fichte (as in Kant, when all is summed up) morality consists in adjusting to what one truly is, in not falsifying oneself.

The two positions have a presupposition in common: that human matters can have varying degrees of reality. To say, "Become the man you are," is to maintain the weighty hypothesis that human material admits of degrees of reality, that it is possible to be man in varying degrees of greater or lesser imperfection.

THE EGO. It was not an arbitrary choice to begin this very brief exposition of Fichte's thought with his ethical doctrine. The point of departure of his metaphysics—and at the same time the point at which it is affiliated with Kantianism—is this self-determination of the ego. At the same time we see with clarity that ethics is nothing other than metaphysics, a major aspect of all of metaphysics and even, perhaps, its culmination.

The *ego* is the basis of Fichte's philosophy. We must direct our attention for a moment to this concept, which we have been encountering with increasing frequency and which has been becoming more and more central to philosophy.

Ortega liked to relate the marvelous story of the *ego*. At the outset, in Greece, the ego was practically non-existent or else was a secondary thing. For a Greek, the ego was a thing; it had certain individual traits, but it was after all just another thing. When the Greeks—men of involved and tortuous mentality, who carried their urbanity even into metaphysics—had to speak of the ego, they used the plural and said "we," ἡμεῖς.

After the Greeks, the ego acquires a new and extraordinary rank. In the Christian Middle Ages, it becomes the subject of a mission, of a destiny; the ego is a creature, but one created in the image and likeness of God, and the subject of a destiny, of a personal mission. Later, after the Renaissance, in the Baroque age, the ego's career is in the ascendant. "As in Oriental tales, the man who was a beggar awakens as a prince. Leibniz is so bold as to call man *un petit Dieu*. Kant makes the ego the supreme legislator of nature. Fichte, immoderate in this as in all else, will not be content with less than saying: the Ego is everything" (Ortega: *Las dos grandes metáforas* [The Two Great Metaphors]).

It is necessary to add that the idea of *man* has undergone very profound changes. In antiquity, man is a distinctive entity who possesses the strange property of knowing the other things, and since he is one thing among the others, in a certain sense he envelops them all. In the Middle Ages, man is a creature made in the image and likeness of God; as a result of this, God is involved in the problem of man (this, let it be said in passing, shows the impossibility of understanding Christian ethics as *heteronomous*, since God is never something alien to man but, on the contrary, his exemplary Idea). But in Greece there had already occurred something analogous, although very different: the "divine something" which man possesses in Aristotle's philosophy. In the modern age, something totally new occurs. Up to now philosophers have spoken of man, but in the modern age it seems that man himself vanishes, leaving a *token* of himself in his place; in effect, we see that people speak about the ego, the will, reason, natural light and so forth, but not about man. When Descartes says *ego sum res cogitans*, he does not say *man is*, but *I am*; therefore, it is meaningless to raise objections to Descartes from the standpoint of Aristotle, or vice versa, because Descartes and Kant speak about the ego whereas Aristotle speaks about man. Naturally, man contains an element of *egoity*, but man and the ego are not *identical*. Nor is the fullness of human life exhausted in the ego. *

This digression allows us to understand the basis of Fichte's philosophy. Fichte says that *the ego posits itself and in so doing posits the non-ego*. What does this mean? In the first place, the *non-ego* is simply everything that is not the ego, everything that the ego encounters. Fichte returns energetically to Kant's concept of *position*. The ego posits itself; this means that it posits itself as existing, that it affirms itself as existing. The ego posits itself in an action, and in every action there is implicit the position of the ego which executes it.

Let us approach this from the other direction. In Kant, *position* was the positing or placing of oneself among the things. Thus, in Fichte, when the ego posits itself, it posits that which is other than the ego, in contrast to which it posits itself. The position of the ego cannot occur in isolation; it must be a position *along with* the "other."

Beginning with Brentano, philosophers have once again defined human actions as *intentional* actions; that is, an action is always directed toward an object, the object of that action. An action presupposes the following: a subject to execute it, the action itself and the object toward which the action is directed. This idea of the fundamental intentionality of man has shaped all of present-day philosophy. And it is not strange that this philosophy has looked back to Fichte as a classic forerunner of its position.

REALITY. The position of the ego and the non-ego—that is, *everything*—results, according to Fichte, in an *action*. Reality is thus pure

---

*See my anthology of philosophical writings, *El tema del hombre*, particularly the Introduction (Madrid, Revista de Occidente, 1943).

activity, liveliness, not substance or a thing. This is decisive, and constitutes the most profound and original aspect of Fichte's metaphysics. And since this reality is based on an action of the *ego*, Fichte's philosophy is also idealism. For Fichte, this transcendental idealism is the only philosophy proper to free man, and he says in a famous sentence: "The type of philosophy one chooses depends on the type of man one is."

2. FICHTE'S IDEALISM

"TATHANDLUNG." We have seen that for Fichte the position of the ego and the non-ego is reduced to pure action, pure activity; true reality is far from being substance; it is *Tathandlung*, which means activity, liveliness, deed. Reality loses its character as a substance and becomes pure dynamism. This is the profound intuition of Fichte's thought, as Ortega has seen.

INTUITION AND CONCEPT. Intuition, however, is one thing, and concept or thought another. Kant said that thought without intuition was blind, but that intuition without thought was not science. Intuition must raise itself to concepts. However, Fichte is not able to express his intuition conceptually and adequately because he is a prisoner of the Kantianism which he strives to continue. This makes him rather uneasy, and thus his entire work is a series of re-elaborations of his basic book. The word "intuition" comes from *intueri*, to see, and "concept" comes from *concipere, capere cum*, to grasp with. Fichte does not have the intellectual tools with which to grasp what he has seen, and he does not succeed in taking possession of it. Therefore he carries on within the limits of Kantian philosophy, and his metaphysics is idealist. Of what does Fichte's idealism consist?

IDEALISM. To begin with, the primary reality is the ego. Fichte does not say that there is a reality one of whose elements is the ego, and that the ego is necessarily opposed by the non-ego (this expresses his profound intuition); instead he says that the ego posits itself and upon doing so posits the non-ego. That is, the non-ego necessarily accompanies the ego, but this non-ego is not original; rather, it is posited only in so far as the ego posits it. Therefore, the non-ego is rooted in the ego, and it is the ego that posits the non-ego.

What is important and positive in Fichte is that this position is not secondary; *in order to be the ego*, the ego must *co-posit* or *compose* the non-ego. However, the ego is the basis for the non-ego, and it has a basic priority. And this is still idealism.

The non-ego's function is to limit the ego; upon limiting it, it gives the ego its true reality. A pure ego, one that exists unconditionally and separately, would be indefinite and unreal. The ego affirms itself as the ego in contrast to the non-ego in a position which is pure activity, and which consists of *actively doing*. (In this exposition of the problem of Fichte's idealism I have followed, in general, the interpretation of my teacher, Ortega.)

KNOWLEDGE. The ego posits itself—it affirms itself as *ego*—as identical to itself. Its position is that A = A, ego = ego. This is not just a tautology; rather, it expresses the formal character of the ego: the *ego* recognizes *itself*. Man can enter into himself and recognize himself as something which is not identical with the non-ego. The synthesis of the thesis "ego = ego" and the antithesis "non-ego ≠ ego" is *measure*. Here Fichte is in the most classical tradition, one that dates from Greece. Measure, the *one*, is what makes the things be. The synthesis of the *ego* and the *non-ego* is effected by *knowledge*. Knowledge is the *transcendental unity of the ego and the non-ego*. And Fichte says: "We do not possess knowledge, rather knowledge possesses us. Knowledge is not in us, rather we are in knowledge." This is the precise meaning of the expression *to be in truth*.

Schelling

LIFE AND WORKS. Friedrich Wilhelm Joseph von Schelling was born in Württemberg in 1775 and died in 1854. He was one of the very few philosophers who were extraordinarily precocious. He studied theology at Tübingen with Hölderlin and Hegel, who were friends of his. Schelling also devoted himself intensely to studies in philosophy, and in 1795, when he was twenty years old, he published his book *Vom Ich als Prinzip der Philosophie* (On the Ego as a Principle of Philosophy), a work which was greatly influenced by Fichte. Two years later Schelling wrote the *Ideen zu einer Philosophie der Natur* (Ideas for a Natural Philosophy), and the following year he was appointed a professor at Jena. There he established ties with the Romantic circles (Ludwig Tieck, the historian of Spanish literature; Novalis, the brothers Schlegel). Later he married Caroline Schlegel, an interesting personality within the Romantic movement and the former wife of August Wilhelm Schlegel. At Jena Schelling wrote one of his major works, *System des transzendentalen Idealismus* (System of Transcendental Idealism), the *Bruno* and the *Darstellung meines Systems der Philosophie* (Exposition of My System of Philosophy). Then he went to Würzburg and, in 1806, to the Academy of Sciences in Munich. He was a professor at Erlangen from 1820 to 1827 and at Munich from 1827 to 1841. From 1841 he was a professor at the University of Berlin. To complete the list of his most important works we must add his investigations *Über das Wesen der menschlichen Freiheit* (On the Nature of Human Freedom) (1809). In the final period of his life he wrote principally on the philosophy of religion:

Philosophie der Mythologie und Offenbarung (Philosophy of Mythology and Revelation).

Schelling, who had a very acute understanding of the natural sciences and, at the same time, of beauty and art, is a representative figure of the Romantic age. His influence on the science of esthetics has been profound. He also devoted much attention to problems of religion and history.

THE PHASES OF SCHELLING'S PHILOSOPHY

PHILOSOPHIC PERSONALITY. There have been very few precocious philosophers, and Schelling is the most spectacular example. By the time he was twenty he had worked out a system of philosophy; however, since he lived to be almost eighty, he made up four distinct systems. All four systems are in reality but the internal evolution of a single system which develops and matures over this period of time; but the phases differ from one another enough so that one can speak of four different systems: those of the *philosophy of nature and spirit*, of *identity*, of *freedom*, and of *positive religious philosophy*.

Philosophically, Schelling derives from Kant and Fichte, and from the latter in very direct fashion. Hegel, who was a friend of his, represents a later moment in metaphysics, a moment of full maturity, even though Schelling was somewhat the younger of the two. German idealism culminates in Hegel, and achieves its plenitude at the time of his death. Actually, Schelling's longevity represents nothing but mere survival.

NATURE AND SPIRIT. We saw that Fichte began with the position of the ego, which established the basic dualism of the ego and the non-ego. In German idealism this division gives rise to the problem of the distinction between the kingdom of nature and the kingdom of freedom. The idealists must establish a relationship between these two very different modes of being: nature and spirit. This is the problem with which Schelling is concerned, and it culminates in Hegelian philosophy.

The first phase of Schelling's thought makes considerable use of the natural science of that day, especially of chemistry and biology, which Schelling frequently interprets with too much freedom and imagination. Electricity had only just been discovered—the disproportionate use of the adjective "electric" in the literary works of this era is well known—and in this way Newtonian mechanics had been completed. On the other hand, evolutionary ideas were making themselves felt in the field of biology. Schelling's philosophy of nature, which sometimes abandons itself to pure imaginative speculation without contact with reality, greatly influenced psychology and also, in particular, medicine in the Romantic age. Nature is intelligence in the process of "becoming," Schelling says—spirit which is coming to be. Actually, it occurs as a slow awakening of the spirit. This explains the connection between nature and spirit which is especially manifested in the living organism or in works of art, each one in its respective sphere. The absolute which is at the base of both is revealed in history, art and religion. We see in these ideas embryonic forms of elements that will appear fully developed in Schelling's later systems.

IDENTITY. The second system, that of identity, consists in establishing a bridge between nature and spirit by means of something that may be both spirit and nature, a moment at which nature and spirit are *identical*. In the previous system, spirit is the ultimate phase of the evolution of nature. Here there is a common, identical zone in which nature is spirit and spirit, nature. This identity, Schelling says, cannot be expressed conceptually; it can only be known by *intellectual intuition* (*intellektuelle Anschauung*). Hegel said that this was "like a pistol shot"; and that identity, which according to Schelling is an *indifference*, was like the night "wherein all cats are gray."

This system of identity is *pantheistic*. As Hegel demonstrated, any system affirming that being is always being and nothingness always nothingness is pantheistic, because in such systems the principle *ex nihilo nihil fit* is interpreted in an absolute way, and the Creation is impossible. In this phase of Schelling's thought being is identical with itself and nothingness is also identical with itself.

THE METAPHYSICS OF FREEDOM. In his third system, Schelling renounces the system of identity. He explains reality as an unfolding, an evolution by means of which it develops by degrees and manifests itself in successive stages. It changes from inorganic nature into organic nature, and from organic nature into spirit. This theory is connected to the movement of the natural sciences (especially biology) in the direction of evolutionary ideas at the beginning of the nineteenth century. According to Schelling, reality evolves until it reaches the highest form, human freedom. Nature awakens and raises itself by degrees until it reaches freedom. This idea had great beauty and a powerful esthetic effect which was gratifying to the Romantic spirit; however, it exasperated Hegel's rigorously logical and metaphysical mind.

POSITIVE RELIGION. The last phase of Schelling's thought denotes an approximation of positive Christian religion, although it does not achieve orthodoxy. Schelling creates a *theistic* metaphysics based on the idea of human freedom; its activity is oriented in particular toward the theological interpretation of religion. At that moment speculative theology was being cultivated intensely in Germany, among the Hegelians just as much as among the followers of Schleiermacher. Schelling devoted particular attention to the study of mythology. In his last years he was summoned to Berlin to combat "Hegelian pantheism," but as we have seen Hegel's pantheism was never as complete and real as that of Schelling in an earlier period. This final stage of Schelling's philosophy was regarded with sympathy by orthodox Protestants and even, in a certain light, by his Catholic contemporaries.

Hegel

LIFE AND WORKS. Georg Wilhelm Friedrich Hegel, a Swabian, was born in Stuttgart in 1770. He came from a middle-class Protestant family. Hegel was a serious student at the *Gymnasium* in Stuttgart and then studied theology and philosophy at Tübingen. There he was an intimate friend of Schelling and Hölderlin; his friendship with the latter was the longer-lasting, because Hegel and Schelling clashed on the question of greatest importance to them both: philosophy. Afterward, from 1793 to 1800, Hegel was a private tutor, and lived in Bern and in Frankfurt am Main. In 1801 he was a *Privatdozent* at Jena, but there his scant gifts as an orator and the difficulty of his classes failed to win him very many students. He was already fully mature when in 1807 he published his first major writing, one which contains a personal philosophy and not just a program: the *Phänomenologie des Geistes* (Phenomenology of the Spirit). Germany's economic situation was at that time affected by war, and this circumstance obliged Hegel to accept a position as editor of a newspaper published in Bamberg in order to live; however, he considered this a temporary and painful task. Two years later he was named dean of the *Gymnasium* at Nuremberg, and he remained there until 1816, when he obtained a university chair at Heidelberg. Hegel's stay in Nuremberg was very fruitful and busy; he married there in 1811, and from 1812 to 1816 he published his major work, *Wissenschaft der Logik* (Science of Logic). In 1818 he was called to the University of Berlin; he was a professor there until his death, and in his last years he was also dean. While in Berlin he published the *Enzyklopädie der philosophischen Wissenschaften* (Encyclopedia

317

of the Philosophical Sciences) and gave enormously successful lectures which made him the major figure in German philosophy and even in all philosophy at that time. He died on November 14, 1831, during a cholera epidemic which ravaged Berlin. This date marks the end of a brilliant stage of philosophy and perhaps also of an epoch of history.

Besides the above-mentioned works, we must mention several very important ones which were published as his course *lectures*. These include the *Philosophy of Right*, the *Philosophy of Universal History* (*Vorlesungen über die Philosophie der Weltgeschichte*), the *Philosophy of Religion* and the *History of Philosophy*, the first exposition of this subject from a strictly philosophical point of view.

Hegel was in essence a philosopher. His entire life was consecrated to a meditation that left a profound stamp of wear on his face. "He was what his philosophy was," Zubiri writes. "And his life was the history of his philosophy; everything else was for him his counterlife. For him, nothing had personal meaning unless it could acquire meaning by being relived philosophically. The *Phenomenology* did and does represent his awakening to philosophy—philosophy itself, the intellectual reliving of his existence as a manifestation of what he called absolute spirit. The human element in Hegel, which is so quiet and foreign to philosophy on the one hand, acquires, on the other hand, the rank of philosophy by raising itself to the highest celebration of what is conceived. And, reciprocally, his conceptual thought occurs in the individual who was Hegel with a force conferred on it by the absolute essence of spirit and the intellectual sediment of all history. Therefore, in a certain sense Hegel represents Europe's maturity."

Hegel's thought is as difficult as it is important. It is the culmination of all German idealism in its most rigorous and mature form. One of the most fertile attempts to understand and interpret Hegel's philosophy has been made by my teacher, Zubiri, whom I have quoted above. The stamp of his interpretation is evident in the discussion that follows.

1. THE OUTLINE OF HEGEL'S PHILOSOPHY

For Hegel philosophy is a problem and therefore he feels that it must justify itself. Hegel found himself in the midst of a philosophy and a theology which sought "not so much for self-evidence as for edification." Philosophy had become more and more colored by vague generalities and sterile profundities until it had turned into a mere hazy enthusiasm. This seemed intolerable to Hegel: not the leaning toward an indeterminate enthusiasm, a vague *sentiment of God*, but the wish to make this into philosophy or, since this is of course impossible, to make it pass for philosophy. "Philosophy must avoid the desire to be edifying." In discussing the thinkers to whom he refers, Hegel says that "they believe they are among the elect to whom God grants wisdom while they slumber, but what they actually conceive and give birth to thus in their slumbers are nonetheless only dream fantasies." But Hegel is not content with mere reproaches. These words are followed by the hundreds of pages of the *Phenomenology of the Spirit.* Hegel explains his purpose: "The true form in which truth exists can only be the scientific system of truth. To contribute toward making philosophy approximate the form of science—toward enabling it to shed its name 'love of knowledge' and be a real knowledge—this is what I propose to do."

In the *Phenomenology of the Spirit* Hegel expounds the stages of the mind up to its attainment of absolute knowledge and the practice of philosophy. Only from this point on can a philosophy be created. Then he writes the *Science of Logic,* and later the *Encyclopedia of the Philosophical Sciences,* in which we find this outline: Logic, Philosophy of Nature, Philosophy of the Spirit. Philosophy of the Spirit includes in turn the phenomenology of the spirit, which we saw at the outset. What meaning does this have? Two very different viewpoints are involved: the *Phenomenology* contains the exposition of the successive stages of the spirit up to its attainment of absolute knowledge; but once philosophy has been practiced, this absolute knowledge embraces and comprehends everything, and the human spirit with all its stages becomes part of it. The spirit appears as an element of philosophy.

For Hegel, reality is the *absolute,* which exists in a dialectical evolution that is logical and rational in character. According to his famous statement, everything that is real is rational and everything that is rational is real. Everything that exists is an *element* of this absolute, a stage in the dialectical evolution which culminates in philosophy, where the *absolute spirit* possesses itself in knowledge.

2. THE "PHENOMENOLOGY OF THE SPIRIT"

ABSOLUTE KNOWLEDGE. In the *Phenomenology of the Spirit* Hegel explains the internal dialectic of the spirit up to its arrival at the beginning of philosophy. Hegel re-examines the modes of knowledge. (Thinking is different from knowing. To know is to know what the things are; knowing has an essential element which refers to the things; we have already seen that this was what Kant called "transcendental knowledge.") Hegel distinguishes mere information (history) from conceptual knowledge, in which I possess the concepts of the things (this would be the situation in the sciences in which there is a real knowledge). But an *absolute knowledge* is still required.

Absolute knowledge is an all-inclusive knowledge. If it is to be absolute, it cannot leave anything outside itself, not even *error*. It includes error as error. History must be this way: it must include all the elements of the human spirit, even the elements of error, which appear as such from the standpoint of truth.

DIALECTICS. This dialectic of the spirit in Hegel is *logical*, it is a *dialectic of pure reason*. This is what casts doubt today on Hegel's philosophy of history. The spirit passes through a series of stages before it reaches absolute knowledge. At the outset of philosophy is *being*. Philosophy begins here. Thus, philosophy begins with being.

3. THE "LOGIC"

THE MEANING OF THE "LOGIC." The problem "What is dialectic?" is ancient and complex; this question, which has been a concern of philosophy from the time of Plato, reaches its greatest urgency in Hegel, since it constitutes the core of his system. Dialectic is not a passage of the mind through various stages, but a *movement of being*. There is a necessary transition from one stage to another, and each stage contains the *truth* of the one before. (One should remember the significance of "truth" in Greek—*alétheia*—patency.) In each stage, the previous one is manifested and made evident, and this is its truth. Each stage includes the one before it, which is *absorbed* within it, that is, *preserved and superseded* at the same time.

Hegel's *Logic* is thus a dialectic of being, a *lógos* of the *ón*, of the entity; thus, *onto-logy*. Hegel's logic is *metaphysical*.

THE STAGES OF HEGELIAN THOUGHT. Summing up what we have said about Hegel's conception of knowledge, we find that it fits into the following outline; it should be noted that this is not a *division* but, once again, a movement of being.

Knowledge
- Phenomenology of the spirit (beginning of philosophy)
- Philosophy (the Encyclopedia)
  - Science of logic
  - Philosophy of the spirit
  - Philosophy of nature

Logic
- Doctrine of *being*
- Doctrine of *science*
- Doctrine of *concept*

Within *being* we distinguish the following three elements:

Being
{
1. Determinateness (quality)
2. Quantity
3. Measure
}

Within *quality*—to follow the example of Hegelian dialectic—we distinguish three stages:

{
1. Being (*Sein*)
2. Existence (*Dasein*)
3. Being for oneself (*Fürsichsein*)
}

Within the first of these three—this *being without quality*—we distinguish:

{
1. Being (*Sein*)
2. Nothingness (*Nichts*)
3. Becoming (*Werden*)
}

All this, I repeat, is not a *logical division*, but the movement of the absolute itself. Hegel's *Logic* will have to pass through these stages in reverse; that is, it will begin with simple being without quality and will ascend to each higher viewpoint. Thus we see that Hegel's dialectic has a ternary structure, in which the *thesis* is opposed by the *antithesis* and both are united in the *synthesis*. The synthesis, however, is not a mere *conciliation*; rather, the thesis leads necessarily to the antithesis, and vice versa, and this *movement of being* leads inexorably to the synthesis, in which the thesis and the antithesis are *preserved and superseded—aufgehoben*, that is, *absorbed*, according to the translation proposed by Ortega. Each stage finds its *truth* in the one that follows. This is the nature of the dialectical process. We shall attempt to explain the principles of the first elements of this dialectical movement of being.

THE PROGRESS OF DIALECTICS. At the end of the *phenomenology of the spirit* we arrive at the absolute beginning of philosophy—being. This being is pure being, absolute being. Being is indefinable because in this case the term to be defined would have to enter into the definition; but it is possible to make some statements about it. According to Hegel, being is the *indeterminate immediate* (*das unbestimmte Unmittelbare*). It is free from all determinateness as regards essence; it simply *is*; it is not *this* or *the other*.

This being has nothing to differentiate it from what is not itself, since it has no determinateness; it is pure *indeterminateness* and *emptiness*. If we try to intuit or think of being, we intuit nothing; if it were otherwise, we would intuit *something* (*Etwas*) and this would not be pure being. When I try to think of being, what I think of is *nothingness*. Thus, from being we pass to nothingness. But naturally, it is being itself that makes the transition, and not the ego. Being, the indeterminate immediate, is in fact *nothingness*, nothing more or less than nothing.

We have seen in *being* these two characteristics which Hegel gives us at the outset: *immediacy* and *indeterminateness*. The characteristic of indeterminateness is being *nothing*; that of immediacy is being *first*. From being we were hurled into nothingness. But what is nothingness? It is perfect emptiness, the absence of determinateness and content, the incapacity to be separate from itself. To think of or to intuit nothingness is just this: to intuit nothingness; this is pure intuition, *pure thought*. Thus we see that to intuit nothingness is the same as to intuit being. Pure being and pure nothingness are *one and the same thing*. Being, through its internal movement, has hurled us into nothingness, and nothingness into being, and we cannot remain stationary in either of the two. What does this mean?

We were inquiring after truth. Truth is patency, the state of being uncovered, exhibited. We have seen that the manner of being which "being" has is that of ceasing to be "being" and coming to be "nothingness"; and that the manner of being which "nothingness" has is, likewise, that of inability to remain within itself and coming to be "being." The truth is that being has passed into nothingness and nothingness has passed into being. This is *becoming* (*Werden, fieri, γίγνεσθαι*).

In this dialectic, I repeat, each stage contains the truth of the one before and finds its own truth in the one that follows. Thus, the truth of being was in nothingness, and that of nothingness in becoming. The truth of becoming will not be patent within itself, either; and the movement of being, following its inexorable ontological necessity, continues in this way in the further stages of the dialectic.

THE PROBLEM OF PANTHEISM. Hegel recalls three earlier elements in the history of philosophy: the philosopher Parmenides, who makes *being* the absolute, the only truth, in contrast to the Oriental systems (Buddhism), which take nothingness as their principle; Heraclitus, who contraposes to this abstraction the total concept of becoming; and the principle of medieval metaphysics, *ex nihilo nihil fit*. Hegel distinguishes between two meanings of this statement: one which is a pure tautology, and another which presupposes the identity of being with itself and of nothingness with itself. If being is always being and nothingness is always nothingness, there is no becoming; this is the system of identity (an allusion to Schelling). This identity, Hegel says, is the essence of pantheism. We thus see that Hegel is opposed to this pantheism because of the way in which he understands the dialectical movement of being.

Being had passed into nothingness, and vice versa. As a result of this there appears the problem of *oppositeness*. Hegel speaks of a certain *disappearance* of being into nothingness and of nothingness into being. But since these are two *opposites*, the mode of being which each one has is the exclusion of the other, the *removal* of the other. The German word *aufheben*, like the Latin word *tollere*, has as one of its meanings *to raise up*; to be raised up as an opposite of something else is a higher mode of being. When two things are necessary, they exclude each other; but they exclude each other within a unity, in a genus. Oppositeness occurs within a unity, Aristotle said. This manner of excluding one another which being and nothingness have is a mode of being preserved and raised up into the higher unity of *becoming*, where they exist in a state of mutual exclusion.

But although Hegel rejects the pantheism of identity and affirms the transition from nothingness to being, in another sense he is not exempt from pantheism. Hegel does not believe that the reality of the world is divine, that this *pân* is *theós*; but from another viewpoint we see that Hegel's God, the absolute, exists only in a state of *becoming*. According to Hegel's own expression, He is a God who becomes (*Gott im Werden*). The finite entities are not strictly different from God, but are *aspects* of this absolute, stages in its dialectical movement. Lastly, the Hegelian *Creation* is not so much the placing into existence of an entity different from God through a free act of the divine will, as it is a necessary production within the dialectic of the absolute.

HEGELIAN ONTOLOGY. We thus see that Hegel's *Logic*, which starts out with being, with the absolute beginning of philosophy, is true ontology. The logic must be understood, Hegel says, as the *system of pure reason*, as the reign of pure thought. This reign is *truth*. Therefore, Hegel concludes, it can be said that the content of the *Logic* is the *exposition of God as He is in His eternal essence, before the Creation of nature and any finite spirit*. This first stage will thus be followed by the other two parts of the philosophy: the *Philosophy of Nature* and the *Philosophy of the Spirit*.

4. THE PHILOSOPHY OF NATURE

NATURE. Greek philosophy understood nature to be the sum total of all existing things, with a principle or source (*arkhé*) and an end or goal (*télos*). Aristotle defines nature as the principle of motion. *Phýsis* is thus a coming to be. Something is called natural if it moves itself. Those things are natural, Aristotle says, which contain within themselves the principle of their own motion. In contrast to Plato, who affirmed nature to be an *Idea*, Aristotle says that the nature of each thing is its *ousía*, its *arkhé*, the internal principle of its transformations.

In Hegel, nature has a clearly determined character as an aspect of the absolute. This aspect of the absolute—nature—is characterized as a *being for another*, a *being there*. Nature is what is *other*, what is not *oneself*.

THE STAGES. This nature is an aspect of the Idea, which has different stages:

1. *Mechanics*. This, in turn, has three aspects:
   (*A*) *Space* and *time*: the abstract aspect of *being outside*.
   (*B*) *Matter* and *motion*: *finite mechanics*.
   (*C*) *Free matter*: *absolute mechanics*.
2. *Physics*. This, too, has three aspects:
   (*A*) Physics of *general individuality*.
   (*B*) Physics of *particular individuality*.
   (*C*) Physics of *total individuality*.
3. *Organic physics*, also with three aspects:
   (*A*) *Geological* nature.
   (*B*) *Vegetable* nature.
   (*C*) The *animal* organism.

This is the end of the evolution of the stages of nature.

5. THE PHILOSOPHY OF THE SPIRIT

SPIRIT IN HEGEL. We have already discussed the significance of the word *phýsis* in Greece. Greek philosophy asked itself: "What is that which is?" This is the same as asking, "What is nature?" The Greeks did not ask about the spirit. The notion of spirit first appears persistently outside the realm of philosophy, in the writings of St. Paul (πνεῦμα), and then somewhat later in St. Augustine's thought: *spiritus sive animus*.

In Hegel, *spirit* is *being for itself*, self-identity. Spirit is a moment in the evolution of the absolute, and it is defined as the *entrance into oneself*, *self-identity*, *being for itself*. Hegel makes a new outline of spirit.

STAGES OF THE SPIRIT. Let us point out the dialectical articulation of the stages of spirit, so that later we can briefly examine the most important moments in this process.

1. *Subjective spirit*.
   (*A*) Anthropology: the soul.
   (*B*) Phenomenology of the spirit: consciousness.
   (*C*) Psychology: the spirit.
2. *Objective spirit*.
   (*A*) Right.
   (*B*) Morality.
   (*C*) Social ethics.

3. *Absolute spirit.*
   (*A*) Art.
   (*B*) Revealed religion.
   (*C*) Philosophy.

Subjective Spirit

"Subjective spirit" strikes us as being a fairly easy-to-understand term. It is spirit and it is subjective; therefore, it is a subject, a subject that knows itself, that is *itself*, that has *interiority* and *intimacy*. Subjective spirit can be perceived in so far as it is united with a body in a vital unity, in so far as it is a *soul*. At such a moment spirit is *soul* and constitutes the subject of the science of *anthropology*. But subjective spirit is not only soul; rather, it *knows itself* and, by passing through all levels of *consciousness*, reaches absolute knowledge; it becomes spirit in so far as it knows itself. This is the way in which the *phenomenology of the spirit* develops; it is the study of the consciousness, and it prevails until being, or absolute knowledge, is attained. Lastly, spirit is not only consciousness; it *knows* and *desires*. Hegel calls this moment *spirit*, and it is the subject of *psychology*. The foregoing constitutes an overall description of subjective spirit.

Objective Spirit

A new and more serious difficulty arises from the very concept of objective spirit: it is *spirit* (being for itself, self-identity), but at the same time it is *objective*, a spirit which *exists out there*, a spirit without a subject. It is not nature, but it has nature's characteristic of "being at hand." Not to have a subject seems to be contradictory to the very concept of spirit.

Objective spirit is comprised of three forms, each one superior to the previous: *right, morality* and *social ethics* (objective ethics or *Sittlichkeit*, as opposed to *Moralität*).

RIGHT. Right is based on the idea of the *person*. A person is a rational entity, an entity with free will. Right is the most elementary form of relationships among persons. Anything that is not a person is the property of a person. This is the character of the form of right; the concept of the State does not enter into it at all. There can be infractions of right which do not involve persons as persons but as things; for example, slaves were once considered things, not persons. Kant had already said, "All men are ends in themselves." Man can never be a means to anything, a *thing*: he is an end in himself. Therefore, Hegel proposes that transgressions of lawful order be punished, and his *punishment* consists of nothing but a return to the previous state of right. In Hegel, to punish a person is to treat him once more as a person. In short, the punished person is one who has a right to punishment. The criminal has the right to be castigated, to be treated according to right and thus as a person.

MORALITY. There is a second stage, morality. In Hegel, morality is based on intentions or *purposes*. An individual's purpose determines the morality of his action. Thus, morality is subjectivized, made completely non-objective, and so the development of the idea passes from the stage of morality to the stage of social or objective ethics. In this latter stage the development of the moral idea is seen in the various institutions of social life: the family, society and, above all, the State.

SOCIAL ETHICS. Social ethics is the realization of objective spirit, the *truth* of subjective and objective spirit. The *family* is the immediate or *natural* phase of the ethical substance; *society* is everything pertaining to relationships between individuals as independent persons; and the *State* is spirit developed in an organic reality. The latter phase is the one which interests us the most.

THE STATE. The State is the final form of objective spirit. Hegel constructed what was perhaps the first ontology of the State. The State is a rational creation and the highest form in which the idea of morality is developed. Hegel does not view the State in the rather disinterested way in which Rousseau views it. It is an objective reality; it is a construction, and has the highest rank in the ontological hierarchy. However, the idea of the State is not fully realized in any actual state. The idea of the State can only be realized in the total development of universal history. *Universal history* is the unfolding of the internal dialectic of the idea of the State.

UNIVERSAL HISTORY. Certain characteristics of Hegel's thought are more clearly seen in his *Lectures on the Philosophy of Universal History*, one of the most brilliant books ever produced in Europe, than in any other portion of his work. His systemization is strict and complete. In Hegel, *system* has a very concrete meaning: it is the way in which *truth* exists: there are no independent truths, and nothing is true by itself, alone; rather, every truth is sustained by and based on all other truths. This is what constitutes the systematic structure of philosophy, in contrast to what might be called the *linear* structure—of mathematics, for example. This systemization leads Hegel to overlook certain facts and occasionally to misrepresent reality.

Hegel tries to explain the dialectical evolution of mankind. History is the realization of the divine plan, a revelation of God. *Weltgeschichte*, *Weltgericht*: universal history is universal judgment. For Hegel, everything that is real is rational and everything that is rational is real. Therefore, his dialectic is *logic*. Human history is *reason*, pure reason. Thus Hegel's philosophy of history becomes an attempt to explain all history as an absolute knowledge that does not omit anything, that even includes error as error.

Hegel distinguishes four moments in the historical evolution of peoples, and he compares these moments to the stages of human life: the Orient (childhood), in which government is in the form of a paternal relationship; Greece (adolescence), or the realm of "beautiful freedom"; Rome (manhood), the phase of universality, of the Roman Empire; and the Roman-Germanic peoples (old age), in which there is a contraposition of a *profane* and a *spiritual* empire. In history Hegel sees the progress of freedom: in the Orient there is but *one* free man, the despot; in Greece and Rome there are *several* free men (the citizens); and in the modern Christian world *all* men are free.

Hegel made grandiose syntheses of universal history: India, or the realm of the dreaming absolute spirit; Greece, or the realm of grace; Rome, or the realm of power, and so forth. Hegel's work represents the principal attempt thus far to make a philosophy of history. Following beginnings by St. Augustine (*De civitate Dei*), Bossuet (*Discours sur l'histoire universelle*) and Vico (*La scienza nuova*), Hegel, in his *Philosophy of History*, grapples with the theme of history brilliantly and on a grand scale. However, our own era must seriously question two problematical points in Hegel's thought. One of these points involves the denomination of *objective spirit*, applied to the State, to history, and so on. Spirit is the entrance into oneself, but then we also find spirit without a subject. Something similar occurs in connection with *social life*; it is not the life of any particular person, but life is characterized by being *my* life or the life *of someone*. We glimpse a contradiction in this. The second troubling point is Hegel's interpretation of the historical evolution of mankind as *pure reason*, as a *logical* dialectic. To what extent is this so? (See Ortega y Gasset: *La "Filosofía de la historia" de Hegel y la historiología.*)

Absolute Spirit

Absolute spirit is a synthesis of subjective and objective spirit, and also of nature and spirit. For Hegel, the identity between nature and spirit is not a void, an indifference, as it is for Schelling; rather, Hegel says that nature and spirit require a *common base*. Their common base is the base of everything else, of the *absolute*, which is *in itself* and *for itself*. Hegel calls this *absolute spirit*.

We have seen that this identity involves searching for a common base which can make things be either nature or spirit. Such a base would be the *fundamental reality*. However, it is not clear why this is to be called spirit, for spirits are traditionally entities which enter into themselves. This absolute is systematic thought in which each thing is true only as a function of the system. Now we can fully understand that system is the articulation of each thing's being within the absolute spirit. We are not concerned with an *absolute thing*, but with *the absolute*, that which is the base of the other things. The absolute is not an aggregate, any more than the world is the aggregate of the things; rather, the absolute is *where* the things occur (and this "where" is not primarily spatial).

THE ABSOLUTE AND THOUGHT. The absolute is *present* to itself; and this being present to itself is *thought*. "Being present to itself" means being patent, *alétheia*. It is not a question of starting with thought and then coming to possess the absolute. Rather, the absolute is patent to itself, and its immediacy to itself is thought. While I am not thinking *this*, it is not a being. Thought constitutes the actual being of the things. Being is not latent being, but patent being, *alétheia*, truth.

All attempts to define the absolute fall short of the mark; one must find oneself directly in the absolute; it is pure being. As we have seen, when I think of pure being it becomes *absolute negation*. *Becoming* represents the absolute's attempt to avoid nothingness and to maintain itself in being. The absolute can exist only in *becoming*. By becoming, the absolute spirit comes to be *something*. In Greece this was called "being in itself."

Nothing is self-sufficient; rather, to be something is *to become* something, and this presupposes a beginning. The truth of a thing consists in its being in itself what it already was in its absolute beginning. This is what has been called *essence*. Essence is what makes it possible for a thing to be. And absolute self-understanding is absolute being, *concept*. The absolute, which is the source of all action, becomes by itself; therefore, the Idea is *freedom*. Lastly, philosophy is *the absolute's knowledge of itself*. Philosophy is not thought about the absolute; rather, it is *the absolute in so far as it knows itself* (cf. Zubiri: *Hegel y el problema metafísico*).

THE STAGES OF ABSOLUTE SPIRIT. As we have seen, the three stages of absolute spirit are art, revealed religion and philosophy. Art involves the *sensible* manifestation of the absolute; here the absolute idea is *intuited*. In *religion*, on the other hand, the absolute idea is *represented*. Hegel's philosophy of religion is enormously important, but we cannot discuss it in detail here. Hegel is opposed to Schleiermacher's religion of feeling, and his thought gives rise to an important trend which dominates theology and the history of religion in the nineteenth century. Hegel makes a new interpretation of the ontological argument, and thus restores to it the validity which Kant's criticism has taken from it. For our purposes it is sufficient to point out that Hegel distinguishes between the viewpoint of *understanding*—the viewpoint from which Kant's criticism would be valid—and the viewpoint of reason. The relationship between thought and the absolute allows Hegel to give new meaning to the ontological proof, which is thus able to reassume its role in the history of philosophy.

The final stage of absolute spirit is philosophy. Here the absolute idea is no longer either intuited or represented, but *conceived*, raised to a concept. Philosophy is the absolute's knowledge of itself; it is not thought *about* the absolute; rather, it *is* the explicit form of the absolute itself. It is for this reason that the history of philosophy is an essential part of philosophy itself (Zubiri).

Hegel was the first person to make an actual *History of Philosophy*. He interprets the subject in a dialectical manner, as a series of moments which preserve and supersede one another. Hegel believes that philosophy reaches its *maturity* and attains its final form in his work, that his philosophy is the completion of philosophy. He is acutely aware that he represents the culmination and close of an epoch, the Modern Era. Therefore, at the end of his *History of Philosophy* he is able to make a sweeping evaluation and write a *Conclusion* of incomparable grandeur. "Philosophy is the true theodicy," he says. And he adds these words, which throb with all the majestic gravity of the history of philosophy and express it better than it has ever been expressed, either before or after his time: "The universal spirit has come this far. The most recent philosophy is the outcome of all previous philosophies; nothing has been lost, all the principles have been retained. This concrete idea is the consequence of the *spirit's efforts* during almost 2500 years [Thales was born in 640 B.C.], of the *spirit's most earnest labor* to make itself objective to itself, to know itself:

'Tantae molis erat, se ipsam cognoscere mentem.' "

The Thought of the Romantic Age

There is an intense intellectual activity in Germany from the time of Kant until the first half of the nineteenth century; we have already studied the most profoundly philosophical stratum of this thought: Kant, Fichte, Schelling and Hegel. However, there are at the same time other philosophers of somewhat lesser stature who nevertheless are of the greatest interest to philosophy and to other disciplines; it is important to note briefly the character of this group of thinkers.

First of all, we must take notice of two movements which arise in the eighteenth century and which emphasize sentiment and the life based on the emotions. One of these movements is primarily literary, the so-called *Sturm und Drang* (Storm and Stress), and the other is primarily religious, *Pietism*. Another movement, *Romanticism*, appears at the end of the eighteenth and the beginning of the nineteenth century; it derives principally from the *Sturm und Drang* movement. At the same time there is an extraordinary flowering of studies in history, and this leads to the formation of the circle known as the "German school of history." Natural science becomes definitely established with the discovery of electricity (Luigi Galvani and Alessandro Volta in Italy; Michael Faraday in England) and the development of biology (Georges Buffon, Étienne Bonnot de Condillac and Jean Baptiste Lamarck in France). Lastly, in the field of philosophy we find alongside the great figures we have already studied the names of Friedrich Schleiermacher and Arthur Schopenhauer, especially, but also Franz von Baader, Friedrich Jacobi and Karl Krause. We shall now try to sketch these various currents of thought.

330

1. The Literary Movements

As a reaction against the cold rationalist spirit of the *Aufklärung*, Germany produces a new literature whose greatest figures are not lacking in philosophic ideas and a deep interest in idealism. Chief of these is Johann Wolfgang von Goethe (1749–1832), who lived long enough to participate in every movement from Classicism to Romanticism; his incomparable literary brilliance was combined with a remarkable fertility in scientific and esthetic thought. Others were Friedrich Schiller, Friedrich Hölderlin, Novalis (Friedrich von Hardenberg), Johann Gottfried von Herder and the Romantic writers properly so-called: Ludwig Tieck, the two brothers Schlegel (Friedrich and August Wilhelm), the brothers Humboldt (Alexander and Wilhelm), and Heine as well.

Romanticism, as we have seen, signifies an esthetic of feeling. But in addition it involves a particular emotion for the past. Just as the Enlightenment, when thinking of the past, returned to the classical world, to Greece and Rome, the Romantics have an obvious preference for the Middle Ages. This leads many of them to a primarily artistic and historical appreciation of Catholicism that brings them close to the Roman Church. In many cases there takes place, in addition, an actual religious *rapprochement*; but there is always at least an admiration for the Catholic form of worship, for the continuity of the Pontificate and for the splendid historical reality which the Church is—even though it is so only secondarily. This interest in the medieval past leads the Romantics to cultivate the study of history also.

2. The School of History

We have already seen that in the eighteenth century in France (Voltaire and Montesquieu, following Bossuet's precedent) historical studies took a decisive step forward. The results of the French movement are adopted along with the contributions of certain Englishmen (Hume, Gibbon) by the German *school of history*. A distinction is made between nature and spirit, as we saw, and spirit is interpreted *historically*. General history, the history of law, the history of religions, linguistics, Classical philology, Romance philology, and the like, are cultivated intensively by a group of productive scholars. Friedrich Karl von Savigny, Leopold von Ranke, Franz Bopp, Barthold Georg Niebuhr and, later, Theodor Mommsen engage in a labor of great importance and volume. The school of history invents the technique of historical research, critical documentation and the study of primary sources, but it soon shows a lack of adequate intellectual constructiveness and tends to go no further than the accumulation of data. The example of Classical philology, which amassed an enormous amount of scholarly material but was unable to furnish an adequate picture of Greece, is especially clear. Hegel reacted energetically to this tendency, although perhaps he sinned in the direction of an excessively logical construction of history.

3. SCHLEIERMACHER AND THE PHILOSOPHY OF RELIGION

SCHLEIERMACHER'S LIFE AND WORKS. Friedrich Daniel Schleiermacher was born in 1768 and died in 1834. He was educated in the schools of the Moravian brotherhood, and his principal activity throughout his life was preaching and the study of religion and the philosophy of religion. For several years he was the pastor of the Charité Hospital in Berlin; afterward he taught at Halle, and later, until his death, at the University of Berlin. His most important works are *Grundlinien einer Kritik der bisherigen Sittenlehre* (Basis of a Critique of Ethics to the Present Time), *Ethik, Der christliche Glaube nach den Grundsätzen der Evangelischen Kirche* (Christian Dogma According to the Fundamental Principles of the Evangelical Church), *Hermeneutik* and the *Reden über die Religion* (Addresses on Religion). In addition, he made a splendid translation of Plato.

RELIGION. For several years Schleiermacher was the outstanding figure in German Protestant theology. Hegel opposed Schleiermacher's interpretation of religion, and from that time on the philosophy of religion was strongly influenced by the conceptions of both men.

Schleiermacher considers possible neither a rational theology nor a revealed theology nor even a moral theology like Kant's, which was based on the postulates of practical reason. The object of Schleiermacher's speculation is not so much *God* as *religion*; rather than theology, it is philosophy of religion that he practices. He interprets this religion as a *feeling*. His is the philosophy of *religious feeling*. Of what does this feeling consist? It is the feeling of *absolute dependence*. Man feels needy, insufficient, dependent. This state of subjection gives rise to man's awareness of being a creature. Thus in Schleiermacher's work the dogmatic content of religion is, in effect, deprived of its force and relegated to a lower plane; religion becomes purely a matter of feeling. Schleiermacher forgets the fundamental meaning of *religio* as *religatio*, and thus changes its *basic* significance.

LATER THEOLOGIANS. Throughout the nineteenth century Germany is the scene of intensive theological activity, partially influenced by Schleiermacher, but chiefly following in the steps of Hegel; outstanding in this respect is the so-called Tübingen school. One of the most important theologians of this period is Christian Baur; despite his greater superficiality, David Strauss also acquired much fame. On the other hand, Catholic theology was represented in Germany by the great figure of Mathias Josef Scheeben (died 1888), whose major work *Die Mysterien des Christentums* (The Mysteries of Christianity) was an extraordinary contribution to speculative theology.

4. DERIVATIONS OF IDEALISM

In the last third of the eighteenth century and the first half of the nineteenth several interesting thinkers flourished; their fame has been somewhat obscured by the great philosophers of German idealism, by whom they were influenced to a greater or lesser extent, and whom they in turn influenced. Some of these men opposed idealism, but they all moved within the milieu of its problems and were conditioned by the philosophic position of the age. Let us consider briefly the most important of these men.

HERDER. Johann Gottfried von Herder (1744–1803), who is to be considered partially within the framework of the *Aufklärung* but was already on the way toward Romantic thought, is one of the thinkers who initiate the understanding of historical reality in the eighteenth century. Herder takes into account the differences between nations and the influence of geographical factors, but he considers mankind as a totality subject to evolution; his desideratum was a "history of the human soul, by epochs and by peoples." His principal writings are *Auch eine Philosophie der Geschichte zur Bildung der Menschheit* (Another Philosophy of History for the Education of Humanity), which appeared in 1774, and the *Ideen zur Philosophie der Geschichte der Menschheit* (Ideas on the Philosophy of the History of Mankind), 1784–91.

JACOBI. Friedrich Heinrich Jacobi (1743–1819), a friend of Goethe in his youth and a representative of the principle of religious feeling, opposed rationalism in religion (Moses Mendelssohn) and appealed to faith, which he likened to society: man was born within and must remain within the one and the other. Jacobi produced a critique of Kantianism and of certain points in Schelling's philosophy. His most important writings are *David Hume über den Glauben, oder Idealismus und Realismus* (David Hume on Faith, or Idealism and Realism) and *Von den göttlichen Dingen und ihrer Offenbarung* (On Divine Things and Their Revelation).

HERBART. Johann Friedrich Herbart (1776–1841), a contemporary of the great figures of German idealism and imbued despite himself with their spirit, opposed the prevailing tendency of his age and, drawing on eighteenth-century thought and ultimately on Leibniz, created a personal philosophy—less brilliant than that of his contemporaries Fichte, Schelling and Hegel—which claimed to be *realism*. Herbart wrote the *Lehrbuch zur Einleitung in die Philosophie* (Introductory Manual of Philosophy), *Hauptpunkte der Logik* (Principal Points of Logic), *Hauptpunkte der Metaphysik* (Principal Points of Metaphysics), *Allgemeine Metaphysik* (General Metaphysics), *Theoriae de attractione elementorum principia metaphysica* (Metaphysical Principles of the Theory of Attraction of the Elements), *Lehrbuch zur Psychologie* (Manual of Psychology), *Psychologie als Wissenschaft* (Psychology as a Science), *Allgemeine praktische Philosophie* (General Practical Philosophy) and *Allgemeine Pädagogik* (General Pedagogy).

For Herbart, philosophy is the elaboration of concepts; it acts upon a primary knowledge, which is experience; it must therefore start out with what is "given," what is impressed upon us, whether matter or form. The material and formal aspects of experience pose problems: the given is only a starting point, necessary to make the problems real, and it obliges us to philosophize in order to make experience comprehensible; experience alone is not comprehensible. *Metaphysica est ars experientiam recte intelligendi* (Metaphysics is the art of understanding experience correctly). One must make the transition from a problem concept to a solution concept, and for this purpose there come into play certain contingent modes of considering the things which Herbart calls *zufällige Ansichten* (contingent views) or *modi res considerandi* (modes of considering the things); thus one arrives at the method of "integration of the concepts."

Herbart distinguishes that which is from being itself, the *quale* which is being. The latter is understood as absolute position, independent of us; Herbart calls this the "Real," that is, the entity—hence his attempted return to realism. The doctrine of the Reals is based on Leibniz' theory of the monads. Of the Real as an absolute, one can know only that it exists, that it is simple, that it is not quantity and that multiplicity of being (although not within being) is possible; that is, that there can be one or more Reals. But viewed in the light of our forms of thought, it becomes an *image* with contingent traits which do not contradict those essential characteristics: what the Real is for us. In short, Herbart relapses into idealism. The ego is one of the Reals; following up this idea, Herbart develops his psychology, which like his pedagogy is intellectualistic: the only original function of the soul is representation. Lastly, ethics is interpreted as a *Geschmackslehre*, a theory of taste or science of estimative sensibility; the good is the quality of that which compels our approval, just as evil compels our disapproval. Herbart here comes very close to the idea of value which was to attain maturity a century later. The good cannot be defined or discovered: one recognizes it, accepts it, esteems or approves it; ethics appears within an esthetic milieu; it is related to a moral beauty which is distinct from the beauty of music or the visual arts. The *practical ideas* are the fundamental relations that are worthy of esteem, the exemplary valuations; these are the idea of internal freedom, the idea of perfection, the idea of benevolence, the idea of right and the idea of retribution or equity (cf. Ortega: *Obras Completas*, VI, 265–291).

KRAUSE. Karl Christian Friedrich Krause (1781–1832) belongs to the group of younger idealist thinkers; strongly rooted in religion and ethics, he achieves a certain originality in his efforts to reconcile theism with the prevalent pantheistic tendencies of his age. His panentheism declares that all things are *in God*. Krause affirms the existence of destiny and the value of the person, understood in a moral sense, and from this viewpoint he interprets law and society; mankind is a federation of autonomous associations with universal or private goals. Krause's principal works are *Entwurf des Systems der Philosophie* (Sketch of the System of Philosophy), *Das Urbild der Menschheit* (The Ideal of Mankind), *System der Sittenlehre* (System of Ethics), *Vorlesungen über das System der Philosophie* (Lectures on the System of Philosophy) and *Vorlesungen über die Grundwahrheiten der Wissenschaften* (Lectures on the Fundamental Truths of the Sciences). Krause left behind many unpublished works, some of which have since been published. Despite the confused and somewhat vague style of his writings, he exerted a considerable influence. His system was developed by some of his German pupils, like Röder and Leonhardi, but even more so in Belgium by Heinrich Ahrens and Tiberghien and in Spain, where Krause's philosophy enjoyed an unexpected vitality which it is of interest to examine.

SANZ DEL RIO. Julián Sanz del Río (1814–1869) was the founder and principal figure in the Spanish Krausian school. Jaime Luciano Balmes and he—contemporaries even though Sanz del Río outlived Balmes by twenty-one years—are the two most important names in nineteenth-century Spanish philosophy. In 1843 Sanz del Río was appointed professor of the history of philosophy at the University of Madrid and was sent to study in Germany. At Heidelberg he was a pupil of Leonhardi and Röder and lived at the home of his history professor Georg Weber, where he was a companion of Henri

Frédéric Amiel. On his return to Spain he inspired the creation of a philosophical circle of great vitality which influenced intellectual and political life for a long time, almost throughout the entire century. Despite this, his philosophical value is scanty; at the moment of coming into contact with German philosophy, these Spanish thinkers chose in Krause a secondary thinker, one much less fruitful than the great figures of the age. Perhaps Sanz del Río's predilection for Krause was influenced by the religious and moral character of the latter's philosophy. The best historian of the Spanish Krausian movement, Pierre Jobit,* interprets it as a *premodernist* movement, an anticipation in the nineteenth century of the heterodox trend that arose in certain Catholic groups around 1900. Sanz del Río's writings were hardly circulated beyond the entourage of his pupils, partly because of his obscure and unpleasant style, but also because of the real difficulties of his thought, which signifies a considerable philosophic effort within the potentialities of the Spain of his time. Sanz del Río's principal works, which he presented as expositions of Krause, are *Ideal de la Humanidad para la vida* (Mankind's Ideal of Life); *Lecciones sobre el Sistema de filosofía analítica de Krause* (Lectures on Krause's System of Analytical Philosophy); *Sistema de la Filosofía: Metafísica: Primera parte, Análisis* and *Segunda parte, Síntesis*; *Análisis del pensamiento racional* (Analysis of Rational Thought); *Filosofía de la muerte* (Philosophy of Death); and *El idealismo absoluto* (Absolute Idealism).

SOCIALISM. The influence of the German idealists, especially Hegel, and also that of Ludwig Andreas Feuerbach (1804–1872), a Hegelian critic of theology in the direction of an atheistic anthropologism, and David Friedrich Strauss, combined with that of Charles Darwin, were exerted on the theoreticians of German socialism. (One should not forget the different roots that the contemporary or slightly earlier French socialism had.) The most important German socialists were Karl Marx (1818–1883), Friedrich Engels (1820—1895) and Ferdinand Lassalle (1825–1864). In 1848 Marx and Engels published the *Communist Manifesto*; they were the founders of the International. Marx won his doctorate with a dissertation on Democritus and Epicurus, and later published *Thesen über Feuerbach* (Theses on Feuerbach), *Die heilige Familie* (The Holy Family), *La misère de la philosophie* (in answer to Pierre Joseph Proudhon's *La philosophie de la misère*), *Zur Kritik der politischen Ökonomie* (Toward a Critique of Political Economy) and his major work, *Das Kapital*.

Les Krausistes by the Abbé Pierre Jobit (Paris-Bordeaux, 1936). Cf. my essay "El pensador de Illescas" in *Ensayos de teoría* [*Obras*, IV]. See also *El krausismo español* by Juan López-Morillas (Mexico, 1950).

Lassalle wrote *Die Philosophie des Herakleitos des Dunklen von Ephesos* (The Philosophy of Heraclitus the Obscure of Ephesus) and the *System der erworbenen Rechte* (System of Acquired Rights).

The point of departure of these thinkers is the idea of *dialectics*, derived from Hegel. This dialectics was "speculative," idealistic; it started out from pure thought, Engels says, and was to come from the most stubborn facts (*von den hartnäckigsten Tatsachen*). There was no place here for a method that "went from nothing through nothing to nothing" (*von nichts durch nichts zu nichts kam*), as Engels remarked ironically, quoting Hegel's *Logic*. It was necessary to subject this dialectics to a penetrating analysis, but Marx and Engels recognized "the enormous historical significance" on which it was based. This grandiose and epoch-making conception of history "was the direct theoretic presupposition of the new materialistic intuition."

In their hands Hegel's idealist dialectic becomes a materialist dialectic which leads these men to what is called—somewhat improperly—a materialistic interpretation of history; it is actually an economic interpretation of history. Political economy thus becomes the basic discipline; Engels, for his part, made a searching commentary on Marx's treatise *Zur Kritik der politischen Ökonomie*. Political economy begins with commodities (*Ware*), at the moment when products are exchanged. The product involved in the exchange is a commodity. And it is a commodity simply because the *thing*, the product, creates a *relationship* between two persons or communities, that is, between the producer and the consumer, who are no longer the same person.

This is the crux of Marx's conception: "Economy does not deal with things, but with relationships between persons and, in the final analysis, between classes; however, these relationships are always *bound to things* and *appear as things*." Here we see how a thought which formerly stressed personal relationships comes, without clear justification, to emphasize the things. Marx insisted on the importance of the economic factor in history with great insight and indisputable genius, but then wished to base history completely on this economic factor and, by means of an untenable arbitrary construction, to consider everything else as a *superstructure* of economics. Culture, religion, philosophy, man's entire life, would be explained by the economic component of life—a real but partial component; one not to be overlooked, but secondary in a complete perspective.

On the other hand, the political ideology associated with this philosophical doctrine led to a substantiation of the idea of social "classes," to the fixing of the two types "bourgeois" and "proletarian" as standard concepts. These terms were relatively useful in explaining the social situation in Europe at the beginning of the industrial age, but are absolutely inadequate when applied to other eras or other countries; in such cases they violently distort reality, which cannot be adapted to the framework they impose on it.

Marx was a very important economist, but is even more important as a political theorist, the founder of one of the greatest mass movements in history. However, this does not signify philosophical importance. The so-called "Marxist thought" of later times has been restricted by a very narrow discipline, to the extent that it constitutes a form of Scholasticism in which the most frequently quoted *philosophical* authorities, along with Marx and (secondarily) Engels, have been Lenin and Stalin (the authority of the latter was quickly cancelled after his death). Today the most interesting Marxist thinkers are the Hungarian György Lukács (*b.* 1885), author of *Die Theorie des Romans* (Theory of the Novel), *Geschichte und Klassenbewusstsein* (History and Class Consciousness), *Essays über den Realismus, Die Zerstörung der Vernunft* (The Destruction of Reason); and the German Ernst Bloch, at present a professor in West Germany, who has written *Das Prinzip Hoffnung* (The Principle of Hope) and *Naturrecht und menschliche Würde* (Natural Law and Human Dignity).

The dogmatic materialism and atheism professed as principles by Marxism have given this movement an extremely rigid character. Its quasi-religious features have very little to do with the original core of Marx's thinking, especially that of his youth, which is today studied with greater interest and academic freedom than the forms dictated by an inflexible organization alien to the attitude of perennial restlessness, quest and justification proper to philosophy.

5. SCHOPENHAUER

LIFE AND WORKS. Arthur Schopenhauer was born in Danzig in 1788 and died in Frankfurt am Main in 1860. His father was a wealthy businessman and his mother an intelligent, cultured novelist. After an introduction into the business world, he studied philosophy in Göttingen and Berlin. His doctoral thesis was his book *Über die vierfache Wurzel des Satzes vom zureichenden Grunde* (On the Fourfold Root of the Principle of Sufficient Reason). In 1818 he finished his major work, *Die Welt als Wille und Vorstellung* (The World as Will and Representation), which did not receive much notice. After 1820 he was *Privatdozent* in Berlin, but he had scarcely any students in his classes, which were announced at the same time as Hegel's. When the cholera epidemic struck Berlin in 1831, Schopenhauer fled the city and settled for good in Frankfurt; thus he escaped the epidemic which killed Hegel. Schopenhauer's later books were more successful: *Über den Willen in der Natur* (On Will in Nature), *Die beiden Grundprobleme der Ethik* (The Two Fundamental Problems of Ethics), *Aphorismen zur Lebensweisheit* (Aphorisms on the Wisdom of Life), and *Parerga und Paralipomena.*

Throughout his life, Schopenhauer was bitterly hostile to the post-Kantian idealist philosophers, especially Hegel, whom he disparaged, sometimes with wit, but often with little justification and poor insight. His failure to achieve success and fame as a professor and writer accentuated the biting and aggressive pessimism that characterizes his philosophy. Schopenhauer was keenly interested in art, music and literature. He was an admirer and translator of Baltasar Gracián, whose sententious and aphoristic style appealed to him. The strongest influences on Schopenhauer were Plato, Kant, the post-Kantian idealists—even though he disagreed with them—and on the other hand, Indian thought and Buddhism. Ever since the last years of Schopenhauer's life, and particularly since his death, his thought has been very influential, though its effect has been felt more in the realms of literature, theosophy, and the like, than in the realm of philosophy itself.

THE WORLD AS WILL AND REPRESENTATION. The title of Schopenhauer's masterwork contains the central thesis of his philosophy. The world is a "phenomenon," a representation or *idea*; Schopenhauer makes no distinction between a phenomenon and an appearance; he says that the two are identical. The world as we know it is an appearance or deception. Space, time and causality are the forms which change this world into a world of objects; they order and arrange the sensations. The Kantian roots in this theory are evident.

However, there is an aspect of the world which we do not apprehend as pure phenomenon; this is the ego, which is apprehended in a more profound and direct manner. On the one hand, the ego can be perceived as a body; but it can also be perceived as something non-spatial and beyond time and, what is more, as something free, and this is called the *will*. In his deepest level, man apprehends himself as *the will to live*. Every object in the world manifests itself as a longing or will to be; this is as true with respect to inorganic things as with respect to organic things and in the realm of consciousness. Thus, reality is will. However, inasmuch as desire presupposes *insatiability*, the will is constant pain. Pleasure, which can only be transitory, consists of a cessation of pain; fundamentally, life consists of pain. Thus, Schopenhauer's philosophy is rigorously pessimistic. The never-quenched will to live is an evil; and, therefore, the world and man's life are also evils. Schopenhauer's ethics derives from this idea. The moral emotions are *compassion* and the desire to alleviate the pain which other beings feel. Knowledge, art and especially music also tend to do this, but they are fleeting remedies. The only permanent salvation consists in *conquering the will to live*. When this will is subdued, one enters *nirvana*; and this, which appears to be mere annihilation, is actually the greatest good, the true salvation, the only thing which can end the pain and discontent of the never-satisfied desire to live.

Schopenhauer's ethics also has a deterministic feature, in that man is good or bad essentially and for always; there is, for example, no possibility of a bad man's changing for the good. Schopenhauer opposes Socrates' doctrine and believes that virtue cannot be taught; rather, a person is good or bad *a radice*.

Schopenhauer's philosophy is perspicacious, ingenious and frequently profound; it is expressed with much literary skill and is animated by his strong and fertile personality. However, it does not have a solid basis in metaphysics and it has led many thinkers to lose themselves in a trivial *dilettantism* impregnated with theosophy, literature and Indian "philosophy," in which the meaning of philosophy is actually lost.

We have seen that the period of German idealism really ends with Hegel; the subsequent thinkers represent the consequences of this idealism in that they give themselves up to a speculation which loses contact with the authentic problems of metaphysics. The vagueness, haziness and fantastic constructions which Hegel pointed out in his own time reappear with greater force after his death. This provokes a reactionary movement which sinks philosophy into one of its most profound crises: what is known as *positivism*.

NINETEENTH-CENTURY
PHILOSOPHY

The Triumph over Sensationalism

A history of contemporary philosophy made in the middle years of the twentieth century must place the thinkers of the last century in a new perspective, one which does not coincide with the way in which these figures are usually represented. Indeed, when interpreting the philosophy of the recent past, we must follow two ruling ideas: one, the comprehension of a time which is different from our own, even though not far removed from it; two, the necessity of explaining how our own philosophy derives from the earlier philosophy and how it happens that the earlier epoch has been succeeded by the one in which we live. This necessitates, first of all, an appreciation of the significance of the nineteenth-century philosophers which does not correspond to the one which prevailed at that time. A few obscure thinkers who were misunderstood in their own day are seen today to represent the most substantial and efficacious aspects of the philosophy of the last century. And we note that often what were then the least known parts of their work are now viewed as decisive and even as anticipations of the most profound discoveries of our own epoch.

The nineteenth century is characterized by a certain irregularity with respect to philosophy; actually, nineteenth-century philosophy does not begin until after Hegel's death in 1831. The first third of the nineteenth century and the last third of the eighteenth form a completely separate period dominated by German idealism. A phase of philosophy exhausts itself at Hegel's death, and a deep crisis then overwhelms philosophy and causes it to all but disappear. This is not surprising, because the history of philosophy is discontinuous, and

341

epochs of maximum creative tension are always followed by long years of relaxation, during which the mind does not seem capable of supporting the effort which metaphysics involves. But in the nineteenth century, philosophy is also formally denied, and this is evidence of an extraordinary abhorrence of philosophizing that is at least partially produced by the abuses of the dialectical method which characterize the later phases of the once brilliant German idealism. Men feel an urgent need to concern themselves with the things, with reality itself, to divorce themselves from mental constructions in order to come to terms with reality as such. The European mind of 1830 finds in the individual sciences the model which must be transferred into the realm of philosophy. Physics, biology and history come to represent the exemplary modes of knowledge. This attitude gives rise to *positivism*.

The initial proposition—to concern oneself with reality itself—is irreproachable and constitutes a permanent philosophical imperative. But this is precisely where the problem begins: What is reality? We have seen that philosophy cannot set bounds for itself or define itself extrinsically; rather, its very delimitation supposes a prior question of metaphysics. With excessive haste, the nineteenth century thinks that it can suppress this question, and affirms that reality consists of *sensible facts*. This is the error which invalidates positivism. It would not be going too far to interpret philosophy from Comte to the present as an effort to re-establish that postulate actually, to make itself truly *positive* or, in other words, to discover what authentic reality really is, without using mental constructions or exclusions, in order that it may concern itself faithfully with reality.

Of course, reality is diluted as much by additions as by omissions. What thought superposes on the things changes and falsifies them; but partiality, to take the part as the whole, to believe that *something which is real* is in itself *reality*, does not signify any lesser degree of falsity. Philosophy has repeatedly identified portions or elements of what exists as the sum total of reality, and it has constantly had to exert itself in order to correct this error by incorporating into its vision of reality elements which have been left outside it and which have falsified it by their absence.

However, the error committed at the beginning of the nineteenth century is more serious because it defines reality—it formulates a metaphysical thesis—and at the same time is so unaware of this fact that it denies the possibility of its existence; that is, it does not understand its interpretation of reality as sensible facts for what it is, an interpretation, but takes it to be reality itself. It builds upon this supposition without even being aware of it. Therefore, after positivism, a double problem will confront philosophy: first, philosophy will have to discover the nature of authentic reality, what will later be called the *fundamental reality*, and secondly, it will have to re-establish the necessity for and possibility of metaphysics.

These two tasks are undertaken simultaneously and along parallel paths, but not by means of a speculation on philosophy itself, by virtue of which the validity of metaphysical knowledge is shown, in order later, once this tool has been obtained, to be able to investigate the structure of reality. On the contrary, the very effort of philosophizing will lead to the evidence that positivism was *already* practicing metaphysics at the very moment when it claimed to have eliminated it. Positivism practiced metaphysics without realizing it, that is, in a *not very positive* manner and, therefore, erroneously and faultily. On one hand, the attempt to lead philosophy to true positiveness will oblige thinkers to notice realities which have stubbornly been overlooked: specifically, the realm of ideal objects and the reality of *human life*, with its special modes of being and all their ontological consequences. On the other hand, in order to conceive the above-mentioned realities it will be necessary to use new intellectual tools, and these will give us a new conception of knowledge and of philosophy itself.

Thus our own age finds itself in the situation of having to create a new metaphysics, one which though new is rooted in the entire tradition of the philosophic past. Following the anticipations of a few brilliant thinkers of the nineteenth century, phenomenology, existential philosophy and the philosophy of vital reason have created a method of knowledge and have turned man's attention to the ideal world and the reality of life. Thus the philosophy of our time feels obliged to delve to the roots of the ultimate questions, and in this way acquires its greatest originality.

Intensity returns to philosophic life in France during the first half of the nineteenth century. After the rich epoch of the Enlightenment there appears a group of interesting French thinkers; they are related to the *ideologists* who lived at the end of the seventeenth century and are primarily concerned with problems related to psychology and the origin of ideas. This philosophy, which invokes Condillac's sensationalism as its direct antecedent, initiates a gradual change from this point of view and ends by tackling metaphysical questions; in a real sense this constitutes an important phase in the prehistory of the philosophy of life.

The two principal figures representing this tendency are Pierre

Laromiguière and Joseph Marie Degérando, forerunners of the major thinker of the epoch, Maine de Biran, who later gives rise to the group of spiritualists. Laromiguière (1756–1837) wrote the *Leçons de philosophie*, which are sensationalist in their broad outlines but which nevertheless distinguish between reception and reaction, affirm the activity of the ego as manifested in *attention*, and thus represent a first attempt to supersede pure sensationalism. Degérando (1772–1842), born a generation later, was also a sensationalist; he was influenced by the work of Bacon, Locke and Condillac, but was also well acquainted with German idealism, and this circumstance unsettled his philosophical position. He wrote a long book in four volumes entitled *Des signes et de l'art de penser considérés dans leurs rapports mutuels*, and then the *Histoire comparée des systèmes de philosophie, relativement aux principes des connaissances humaines*, in three volumes. Degérando postulates a *philosophy of experience*; he affirms a dualism of two elements, the *ego* and *contiguous existences*, which are revealed by the fact of resistance. At the same time he attempts to unite rationalism and empiricism; this attitude anticipates eclecticism.

1. Maine de Biran

PHILOSOPHIC SITUATION. The most profound and original of the French philosophers of this time was Maine de Biran (1766–1824). His principal work is the *Essai sur les fondements de la psychologie et sur ses rapports avec l'étude de la nature* (1812); the *Journal, Mémoire sur la décomposition de la pensée* and *Influence de l'habitude sur la faculté de penser* also figure among his most interesting writings. Maine de Biran, who was influenced by Destutt de Tracy and by Laromiguière and who engaged in polemics with Joseph de Maistre and Louis de Bonald, occupies a position somewhat analogous to that of Fichte in Germany. He begins with a sensationalist attitude, is then led to the first rather mature comprehension of human life, and ends up as a theistic and Catholic thinker. Partly because of the originality of his point of view and partly because of his obscure and inconsistent writings, Maine de Biran was misunderstood in his own time, although later French thinkers referred to him as their master. To this day his philosophy is not sufficiently utilized, in spite of efforts made in the present century.

METAPHYSICS. Acting on sensationalist suppositions, Maine de Biran seeks the *primitive fact* on which science must be founded. However, it cannot be *sensation*, because sensation is not even a *fact*. In order to be a fact, a thing must be known, it must exist *for someone*; a fact requires contact between the sensory impression and the *ego*. Consciousness implies a dualism of terms, a coexistence, and this in turn requires a prior *milieu* in which the ego finds itself together with what is known. What is known is always *known jointly*, because to know means *my knowing myself together with* the object. Every fact supposes a dualism of terms which cannot be conceived separately, for one is a function of the other: the ego exists only as it exercises itself when facing an object of resistance. Maine de Biran converts objective concepts into functional concepts; coexistence becomes a dynamical reality, a "doing"—*activity*; the ego and the object of resistance are only elements of that active reality. *

This results in something quite fundamental: *the ego is not a thing*; man constitutes an antithesis to the entire universe; neither is activity a *thing*, nor are its terms, which constitute themselves as terms only when interacting. Maine de Biran understands life as an active tension between an ego and a world which are only elements in the primary reality of activity. The *ego becomes*, it constitutes itself in activity, and thus man can initiate series of free acts and lead a personal, human life. In the thought of Maine de Biran we dimly glimpse an inconsistent and confused vision—badly expressed but nevertheless accurate—of the reality we call *human life*.

2. SPIRITUALISM

THE ECLECTICS. The movement known as French *spiritualism*, which dominated official philosophy for fifty years, took its inspiration from Maine de Biran, but without attaining great profundity, without adopting the most valuable aspects of his thought. The initiator of French spiritualism was Pierre Paul Royer-Collard (1763–1845), an important figure in political doctrinairism, who adopted the teachings of the Scottish school of Thomas Reid and Dugald Stewart. Théodore Jouffroy (1796–1842) was related to this movement. But the most important thinker of the group was Victor Cousin (1792–1867), founder of *eclecticism*, the official philosophy of the Université de France during the reign of Louis Philippe. Cousin was an unoriginal philosopher who tried to reconcile the various systems; his work reveals shifting influences reaching from the Greeks to the German idealists, especially Schelling, and of course the Scottish philosophers and Maine de Biran. Cousin actively stimulated the study of the history of philosophy, which he himself practiced intensively. He published various *Cours d'histoire de la philosophie*, the *Fragments philosophiques*, the *Du vrai, du beau et du bien* and several historical and biographical works, especially studies of the Port-Royal circle.

* Cf. my study "El hombre y Dios en la filosofía de Maine de Biran" in *San Anselmo y el insensato* [*Obras*, IV].

THE TRADITIONALISTS. Another reaction against sensationalism, but with a marked orientation toward social, political and historical problems, appeared in a group of Catholic thinkers whose ties with Rome were strong; this group founded the *ultramontanist* movement, which recognized the Papacy and legitimacy as the bases of social order. These men represented a traditionalist position which mistrusted reason and found the fundamental truths in "belief," of which society is the guardian; in politics they opposed the spirit and doctrines of the French Revolution. The most important thinkers of this circle were Comte Joseph de Maistre (1753–1821) of Savoy, who was Sardinia's ambassador to Russia (*Du Pape*; *Soirées de Saint-Pétersbourg*), and Louis de Bonald (1754–1840), who attempted to systematize traditionalism (*Législation primitive*; *Essai analytique sur les lois naturelles de l'ordre social*). Félicité Robert de Lamennais—who finally left the Church—Jean Baptiste Henri Lacordaire and the Comte de Montalembert (Charles Forbes) were partially connected with this group, but their outlook was more liberal.

The Revolution, which produced this traditionalist reaction, aroused at the same time a movement that was *social* in character; this was led by several French theorists whose social doctrines were utopian imaginings, but not without penetrating ideas on the problem of society. Outstanding here were Saint-Simon (Claude Henri de Rouvroy), François Marie Charles Fourier and Pierre Joseph Proudhon, who at one and the same time stimulated socialistic political currents and the founding of the social sciences.

All these elements are utilized in varying degree by positivism, the most important aspect of nineteenth-century philosophy.

BALMES. The Catalan priest Jaime Luciano Balmes, who was born at Vich in 1810 and died in 1848, represents, together with Sanz del Río, Spain's major contribution to nineteenth-century philosophy; his thought has certain affinities with that of the above-mentioned French theorists. His short life was filled with an intensive activity as politician, journalist and philosopher. His most important works are *El criterio*—a popular logic of common sense—*El protestantismo comparado con el catolicismo*—a rejoinder to François Guizot's *Histoire de la civilisation en Europe*—*Filosofía elemental* and *Filosofía fundamental*.

Balmes, who became familiar with Scholasticism through his training for the priesthood, was able to renew it in a period of great decadence, bringing to it ideas from the Scottish school, on the one hand, and from the systems of Descartes and Leibniz, on the other. Even within the limitations imposed upon his work by the historical circumstances in which he lived and by his early death, his writings still signified a serious and valuable attempt to revive philosophical studies in Spain, and a true reawakening might have been expected as a result. Balmes' view of contemporary philosophy, especially German idealism, is superficial and falls far short of the mark; but he brings many other questions into sharp focus with good sense and frequently with perspicacity.

Outside the strict field of philosophy and very close to the French traditionalists is the work of Juan Donoso Cortés (1809–1853), Spain's ambassador to France. In Paris he came into contact with the Catholic thinkers, who esteemed him highly. His major work is the *Ensayo sobre el catolicismo, el liberalismo y el socialismo*.

Comte's Positivism

LIFE AND WORKS. Auguste Comte was born in 1798 and died in 1857. Although he came from a family that was Catholic, monarchist and conservative, he was quick to adopt an outlook that was inspired by the French Revolution. He collaborated with Saint-Simon (with whom he later broke), and familiarized himself with social problems. He was a student at the École Polytechnique of Paris, and there acquired a solid foundation in mathematics and science. Later he was a tutor at the École, until enmities there caused him to lose the position. While still quite young, he published a series of extremely interesting *Opuscules* on society, and then began the great work in six thick volumes which he called *Cours de philosophie positive*. He next wrote a short general book, the *Discours sur l'esprit positif*, the *Catéchisme positiviste*, and his second basic work, *Système de politique positive, ou Traité de sociologie, instituant la religion de l'Humanité*, in four volumes. The *Cours* was published between 1830 and 1842, and the *Système* between 1851 and 1854.

Comte's life was hard and unhappy. He was unfortunate in his private life and, in spite of his unquestionably brilliant nature and industry, he never achieved the least economic security. In his last years he was supported by his friends and followers, especially those from France and England. Auguste Comte had marks of mental imbalance which sometimes became very much accentuated. At the end of his life Comte fell deeply in love with Clotilde de Vaux, and her death shortly afterward was a loss that helped overwhelm him.

348

1. HISTORY

THE LAW OF THE THREE STATES. According to Comte, knowledge passes through three distinct theoretic states, in the individual as well as in the human species. The *law of the three states*, the basic proposition of positive philosophy, is at once a theory of knowledge and a philosophy of history. These three states are called theological, metaphysical and positive.

The *theological* or fictitious state is provisional and preparatory. In it the mind seeks the *causes and origins of things*, that which is deepest, most distant and inaccessible. There are three distinct phases in this state: *fetishism*, in which objects are personified and attributed magic or divine *power*; *polytheism*, in which personification is withdrawn from material things and transferred to a series of divinities, each of which represents a group of powers: the bodies of water, the rivers, the forests, and so on; and, finally, *monotheism*, the superior phase, in which all these divine powers are united and concentrated in one, called God. As we can see, the designation *theological* for this state is not appropriate; it would be preferable to say religious or perhaps *mythical*. This state, in which the *imagination* predominates, corresponds, Comte says, to *infancy* in Humanity. It is also the primary condition of the mind, that into which the mind falls again and again in all epochs, and only a slow evolution can make the human spirit part with one idea in order to pass on to another. The role of the theological state is historically indispensable.

The *metaphysical* or abstract state is essentially critical and transitional. It is an intermediate stage between the theological and positive states. In it *absolute* knowledge is still sought. Metaphysics tries to explain the nature of beings, their essence, their causes. To do this, however, it resorts, not to supernatural agents, but to abstract *entities*, whence its name *ontology*. The ideas of origin, cause, substance, essence denote something distinct from the things, although *inherent* in them, *closer* to them: the mind, which was striving after the remote, step by step approaches the things. In the previous state the powers were summed up in the concept of God, but here *Nature* is the great general entity which takes the place of God; but this unity is weaker, intellectually as well as socially, and the character of the metaphysical state is, above all, critical and negative, preparatory for the step to the positive state: a kind of crisis of puberty of the human spirit before it reaches the age of manhood.

The *positive* or real state is the *definitive* one. In it imagination is subordinated to *observation*. The human mind relies on the *things*.

Positivism seeks only facts and their laws. Not causes or origins of essences or substances—all this is inaccessible. Positivism relies on the *positive,* on that which is *set forth* or *given*: it is the philosophy of the *datum.* The mind, in a long regression, finally comes to rest face to face with the things. It renounces what it is vain to try to know, and seeks only the laws of phenomena.

RELATIVISM. The positive spirit is *relative.* The study of phenomena is never absolute, but relative to our organization and our situation. The loss or gain of a sense, Comte says, would completely change our world and our knowledge of it. Our ideas are phenomena, not only individual phenomena but also social and collective, and they depend on the conditions of our individual and social existence, and therefore on *history.* Knowledge must incessantly come nearer and nearer to the ideal limit fixed by our necessities. And the goal of knowledge is rational foresight: *voir pour prévoir, prévoir pour pourvoir* (see in order to foresee, foresee in order to provide) is one of Comte's lemmas.

2. SOCIETY

THE SOCIAL CHARACTER OF THE POSITIVE SPIRIT. Comte affirms that ideas govern the world; there is a correlation between what is intellectual and what is social, and the latter depends on the former. The positive spirit must find a new social order to replace the one demolished by critical metaphysics, and must triumph over the crisis of the West. Comte formulates an acute theory concerning spiritual and temporal power. The basis for positive knowledge is the existence of a sufficient social authority. And this reinforces the historical character of positivism; Comte says that the system which explains the past will be master of the future. In this way, by historical continuity and social equilibrium, Comte's political lemma can be realized: *ordre et progrès*; order and progress. And the imperative of Comtean morality—which is an essentially social morality—is to live for one's fellow man: *vivre pour autrui.*

SOCIOLOGY. Comte is the founder of the science of society, which he first called *social physics* and then *sociology.* Comte tries to raise the study of collective Humanity to the positive state, that is, to convert it into a *positive science.* This sociology is, above all, an interpretation of historical reality. In society there governs, also, and principally, the law of the three states, and there are the same number of stages. In one, which lasts until the twelfth century, the *military* dominates. Comte values highly the organizational role that falls to the Catholic Church; in the metaphysical epoch social influence falls to the *lawmakers*; it is the era of the irruption of the middle classes, the passage from military society to economic society; it is a period of transition, critical and dissolvent, revolutionary; Protestantism contributes to this dissolution. Finally, corresponding to the positive state is the *industrial* era, governed by economic interests; in it social order must be re-established, and it must be founded on *intellectual and social* power. The great protagonist of history is Humanity, and Comte's sociology ends by almost deifying it and becoming a *religion*.

THE RELIGION OF HUMANITY. In his last years Comte arrived at ideas which, though eccentric, emerge from the deepest recesses of his thought: for example, the idea of the "religion of Humanity." Humanity is in its totality the *Grand-Être*, the goal of our personal lives; therefore, morality is *altruism*, living for others, for Humanity. And this Great Being must be accorded a cult, first of all private worship, in which man feels at one with his ancestors and descendants, but also public worship. Comte came to imagine the organization of a complete church, with "sacraments," priests, a calendar with feast days devoted to the great figures of Humanity, and so on. The only thing missing in this church is God, and naturally it is for this reason that it has no religious meaning. With this strange idea, which obviously was strongly tinged with madness, Comte expresses very clearly the role he assigns to *spiritual power* in the organization of social life; he seeks his model in the spiritual power par excellence, the Catholic Church, the hierarchy and cult of which are the inspiration for Comte's "religion." And thus the positivist philosopher comes to summarize his thought in a final lemma: *L'Amour pour principe, l'Ordre pour base, et le Progrès pour but* (Love as a principle, Order as a basis, and Progress as a goal). Now we see the full significance of the complete title of Comte's sociology: politics, sociology and the religion of Humanity are inseparably linked together.

3. SCIENCE

THE CLASSIFICATION OF THE SCIENCES. Comte formulated a classification of the sciences which has since had great influence, and which is especially interesting because it throws into relief certain characteristics of his thought. The sciences stand in a determined hierarchic order, as follows:

mathematics-astronomy——physics-chemistry——biology-sociology

This hierarchy has a historical and dogmatic, scientific and logical meaning, says Comte. In the first place, it is the order in which the sciences were developed and, above all, the order in which they attained their positive state. In the second place, the sciences are arranged in decreasing order of generality and increasing order of complexity. In the third place, they are arranged according to their independence: each one has need of those that precede it and is necessary to those that follow it. Finally, they are grouped in three groups of two, with special affinities between them. The life sciences—biology and sociology—are the last to emerge from the theological-metaphysical state. Sociology, especially, is the creation of Comte, who converts it into a true science. Thus, not only is the hierarchy of sciences completed, but the most important discipline within the Comtean scheme of philosophy, defined by its historical and social character, is obtained.

Certain strange omissions will be observed in Comte's classification. It is immediately evident that metaphysics is missing. Positivism considers metaphysics impossible, although, as we have seen, it indulges in it, since Comte elaborates a concrete theory of reality; also missing, naturally, is theology; this scarcely needs an explanation. But in addition, we do not find psychology either; that discipline is treated partly under biology, partly under sociology; Comte considers introspection impossible, and only believes possible experimental psychology, which enters into the sphere of one or the other of the two life sciences, depending on whether the individual or man in his social dimension is being investigated. History and, in general, the *sciences of the spirit* do not appear autonomously in Comte's list, because he was taken with the idea of unity of method, and insisted on always applying the method of the natural sciences, despite his imaginative vision of the role of history.

PHILOSOPHY. What then is philosophy for the positivist? Apparently, it is a reflection upon science. After the sciences are exhausted, there remains no independent object for philosophy but the sciences themselves; philosophy becomes *theory of science*. Thus positive science acquires unity and consciousness of itself. But it is clear that philosophy disappears; and this is what happens in the positivist movement of the nineteenth century, which has very little to do with philosophy.

But this does not occur in Comte's own thought. Aside from what he believes he is accomplishing, there is his actual accomplishment. And we have seen that, in the first place, he has given a philosophy of history (the law of the three states); in the second place, he has given a *metaphysical* theory of reality, conceived in such original and novel terms as that of social being, a historical and *relative* theory; in the third place, he has given a complete philosophical discipline, the science of society—so complete that sociology, in the hands of later sociologists, has never attained the depth of vision that it reached with its founder. This, in short, is the *truest* and most interesting aspect of positivism, the aspect which, despite all appearances and even all positivists, makes it really philosophy.

4. THE SIGNIFICANCE OF POSITIVISM

What attracts most attention in Comte is the importance he attributes to himself at the outset. He is conscious of an enormous, definitive importance which he has for the world, and always begins his books with an air of victory, steeped in the solemnity of an inauguration. Why does Comte have such importance? What does he bear in his hands with such solemnity? Observe how this first grave, almost hieratical gesture is mentally intertwined with the ultimate ceremonies of the *religion* of Humanity. We must seek the thread that goes from the one thing to the other.

Auguste Comte is sure that he is not speaking in his own name; his voice is not his alone: it is the concrete, individualized voice of history; that is why it resounds with such majesty. Comte is, without a doubt, *attuned to his own time*. And that is the important fact. Being attuned to one's own time means being at home in positive philosophy; and positive philosophy is nothing less than the *definitive* state of the human mind. Being attuned to one's own time therefore means having already arrived and not being in the middle of one's journey. This positive science is a discipline of modesty; and this is its virtue. Positive knowledge adheres humbly to the things; it comes to a halt before them, without involvement, without leaping over them to fling itself into a deceptive play of ideas; it no longer seeks *causes*, but only *laws*. And, thanks to this austerity, it attains those laws, and possesses them with precision and with certainty. But it so happens that this situation is not primary; just the contrary: it is the result of the efforts of millennia to restrain the mind, which was dashing off to the farthest distances, and force it to limit itself docilely to the things. These efforts make up all of history; Comte will have to account for all of it in order to understand positivism for what it is, faithfully, without falsifying it, in a *positive* way. And it is nothing but a *result*. Thus we see that the very imperative of positivity also postulates a philosophy of history; and this would be the first aspect of his system: the law of the three states. Positive philosophy is, *ab initio*, something historical.

Time and again Comte returns, in the most explicit manner, to the problem of history, and claims it as the proper domain of positive philosophy. *Tout est relatif; voilà le seul principe absolu* (Everything is relative; that is the only absolute principle)—he had written as early as 1817, when he was still a boy. And in that relativism he finds, nearly thirty years later, the reason for the historical character of positive philosophy, which can explain the *entire* past. This is not a luxury of philosophy, something given to it as an adjunct, but, as Ortega has seen and shown, the essential point in his metaphysics. Perhaps Comte would not have taken account of this, because he did not think he was engaging in metaphysics; but the central importance of this relativism did not escape him. On it is founded positive philosophy's capacity for *progress*, and thus the possibility of changing and improving not only the *condition* of man, but, above all, his *nature*. This is among the weightiest things that can be said, and, for that very reason, I wish to do no more than mention it; a sufficient commentary would lead to problems that cannot even be sketched here.

But I do not wish to conclude without quoting a few words of Comte, lucid and meaningful today, which crystallize his thought: *Today it can be affirmed*—he writes—*that that doctrine which shall have sufficiently explained the past in its totality will inexorably obtain, in consequence of this proof alone, intellectual leadership over the future.*

We see then that beneath his scientific naturalism we find in Comte, as the essential point, a system of thought on historical principles. And this is what gives his philosophy its greatest contemporaneity and fruitfulness. It is completely crisscrossed by the problem which I have attempted to specify, in which its profoundest unity is made evident. And that unity is, precisely, the positive spirit.

Philosophy of Positivist Inspiration

1. THE FRENCH THINKERS

Almost all nineteenth-century philosophy is essentially dominated by positivism and shows its influence in one way or another. The presence of positivism is more vital and constant in France than anywhere else. Here it found a representative who could be called "official" in Maximilien Paul Émile Littré (1801–1881), who in his exposition of Comte's work did not stress its most fruitful and original aspects. Hippolyte Taine (1828–1893) appears within an analogous philosophical milieu; Taine is the author of a witty and superficial book on contemporary French philosophy (*Les philosophes classiques du XIXe siècle en France*), a long book called *De l'intelligence* and numerous studies in history and art. Also in this group is Ernest Renan (1823–1892), an Orientalist and specialist in Semitic philology and the history of religions. One direction of French positivism was especially devoted to sociology, following (with less insight) the path entered upon by Comte. Among these sociologists are Émile Durkheim (1858–1917), whose principal books are *De la division du travail social* (The Division of Labor in Society) and *Les règles de la méthode sociologique* (The Rules of Sociological Method); Gabriel Tarde (1843–1904), author of *Les lois de l'imitation, La logique sociale* and *Les lois sociales*; and Lucien Lévy-Bruhl (1857–1939), a dedicated specialist in studies of ethnography and the sociology of primitive peoples, whose major work is *La mentalité primitive*. Close connection with positivism is also shown by the physician Claude Bernard (1813–1878), author of *Introduction à l'étude de la medecinae expérimentelle* (Introduction to the

Study of Experimental Medicine), who in his later years became involved with metaphysics.

Even though, strictly speaking, they go beyond positivism and partially represent a reaction against it, it is necessary to mention here a group of nineteenth-century French thinkers who were very influential in their day and some of whom prepared the way for the renewal of philosophy achieved by Bergson. These men include: Alfred Fouillée (1838–1912), author of *L'évolutionisme des idées-forces*; Marie Jean Guyau (1854–1888), who had certain affinities with Nietzsche (*La morale d'Épicure, L'irréligion de l'avenir, Esquisse d'une morale sans obligation ni sanction, La morale anglaise contemporaine, L'art au point de vue sociologique*) and whose many ideas were penetrating, though not systematic; Antoine Augustin Cournot (1801–1877), a profound and original thinker not yet thoroughly studied (*Traité de l'enchaîne-ment des idées fondamentales dans les sciences et dans l'histoire; Essai sur les fondements de nos connaissances et sur les caractères de la critique philosophique; Matérialisme, vitalisme, rationalisme; Considérations sur la marche des idées et des événements dans les temps modernes*); Jean Gaspard Félix Ravaisson-Mollien (1813–1900), a continuer of spiritualism and one of the renewers of Aristotelianism in the nineteenth century (*Essai sur la Métaphysique d'Aristote, Rapport sur la philosophie en France au XIXᵉ siècle, Testament philosophique*); and Charles Bernard Renouvier (1815–1903), a neocriticist thinker of great intellectual productivity (*Manuel de philosophie ancienne, Manuel de philosophie moderne, Introduction à la philo-sophie analytique de l'histoire, Uchronie*).

2. English Philosophy

UTILITARIANISM. English positivism is especially concerned with ethical problems, and also with questions of logic. Utilitarian ethics, first developed by Jeremy Bentham (1748–1832) and later most significantly by John Stuart Mill (1806–1873), finds that the goal of our aspirations is pleasure, and that the good is that which is *useful* and gives us pleasure. This is not an egoistic ethics, but is social in character; what it seeks is the *greatest happiness of the greatest number* (*Utilitarianism, On Liberty*). The middle-class, capitalistic and industrial era of the mid-nineteenth century finds an extremely clear expression in utili-tarian ethics. Mill also published an important work on logic: *A System of Logic, Ratiocinative and Inductive*.

EVOLUTIONISM. Also related to positivism and utilitarianism are the English thinkers who develop the concept of evolution, which was French in origin (Turgot, Condorcet, Lamarck) but was given its philosophic formulation by Hegel. Though not himself a philosopher, the biologist Charles Darwin (1809–1882) was extremely influential. His major work, *On the Origin of Species*, was published in 1859–60, but its ideas date from the 1830's and the famous voyage aboard the *Beagle*; this book contained a biological theory of evolution based on the principles of the *struggle for existence* and *adaptation to environment*, with the consequent *natural selection* of the fittest. This doctrine influenced every aspect of nineteenth-century intellectual life and furnished Marx with a basis for his own doctrine.

Herbert Spencer (1820–1903), an engineer who devoted himself to philosophy, adopted the idea of evolution in a different form; he enjoyed an extraordinary popularity in the second half of the century which was then quickly lost. His extremely voluminous output was largely published under the general title of *A System of Synthetic Philosophy*. The various parts are *First Principles* (these are the unknowable and the knowable), *Principles of Biology*, *Principles of Psychology*, *Principles of Sociology* and *Principles of Ethics*. He also wrote, among other works, *The Study of Sociology* and *The Man versus the State*, an expression of liberal political individualism.

According to Spencer, there takes place in the universe an unceasing redistribution of matter and motion, which constitutes evolution when the integration of matter and dissipation of motion prevail, and dissolution when the opposite occurs. This transformation is accompanied by a secondary one, that of the homogeneous into the heterogeneous, and takes place throughout the entire universe and all its domains, from the nebulae to spiritual and social life. The principal cause of evolution is the *instability of the homogeneous*; that which remains quantitatively invariable, as a substratum of all the evolutionary processes, is a power without limits, which Spencer calls *unknowable*. This doctrine, more interesting for its details (for instance, the frequently penetrating sociological observations) than for its feeble metaphysics, dominated European thought for several decades and exerted a profound influence even on Bergson.

3. THE POSITIVIST ERA IN GERMANY

MATERIALISM. As noted earlier, German positivism generally led to materialism and naturalism, which are devoid of philosophic interest. Friedrich Karl Christian Ludwig Büchner, Karl Vogt, Jacob Moleschott, Ernst Heinrich Haeckel and Wilhelm Ostwald are, in general, practitioners of the natural sciences, with unfounded philosophical pretensions, imbued with superficial atheism and materialism and, in short, lacking in true scientific spirit.

358 *Philosophy of Positivist Inspiration*

ATTEMPTS TO SUPERSEDE POSITIVISM. Of greater interest are other, more independent thinkers who bring the popular positivist views of their day into line with the earlier German philosophic tradition or attempt to replace those views. Among these men are Gustav Theodor Fechner (1801–1887), co-founder with Ernst Heinrich Weber of psychophysics, and Wilhelm Wundt (1832–1920), a man of immense knowledge and industry and the most important worker in experimental psychology and the so-called ethnopsychology (*Völkerpsychologie*). Rudolf Hermann Lotze (1817–1881), influenced by Leibniz and the idealists, and Dilthey's predecessor in the Berlin professorship, initiated a reaction against naturalism and worked on the problems of history and esthetics (*Mikrokosmos, System der Philosophie*). Friedrich Adolf Trendelenburg (1802–1872), Dilthey's teacher, was, along with Ravaisson, Gratry and Brentano, the man who reintroduced Aristotelianism to his contemporaries (*Elementa logices Aristotelicae, Logische Untersuchungen*). Gustav Teichmüller (1832–1888), a professor at Dorpat (Estonia) who was influential in Russia, was a perspicacious and learned thinker who wrote important studies of Greek philosophy (*Aristotelische Forschungen, Studien zur Geschichte der Begriffe, Neue Studien zur Geschichte der Begriffe*) and an important book of metaphysics, in which he makes a broad use of the concept of "perspective": *Die wirkliche und die scheinbare Welt: Neue Grundlegung der Metaphysik* (The Real and the Apparent World: New Foundation of Metaphysics). This author is the source of the interpretation of truth in the sense of the Greek ἀλήθεια.

Particularly influential in their day were certain philosophers whose work rapidly lost its popularity: Eduard von Hartmann (1842–1906), who was simultaneously inspired by German idealism and the biological sciences, and whose major work is the *Philosophie des Unbewussten* (Philosophy of the Unconscious); Hans Vaihinger (1852–1933) (*Die Philosophie des Als Ob*), close to pragmatism, who formulated a philosophy of the "as if" (an allusion to Kant's regulative Ideas); and lastly the adherents of the so-called *Empiriokritizismus*—Richard Avenarius (1843–1896): *Kritik der reinen Erfahrung* (Critique of Pure Experience) and Ernst Mach (1838–1916): *Analyse der Empfindungen* (Analysis of Sensations). The titles of their works are clearly indicative of the content.

NEO-KANTIANISM. In the second half of the century Germany is the scene of a philosophic movement which attempts to supersede positivism, although it is in fact conditioned by its spirit. These thinkers saw the salvation of philosophy in the return to Kant, and initiated a revival of Kantianism. We have already seen, when studying Kant, the viewpoint from which the Neo-Kantians consider him.

The first impulse in this direction came from the book by Otto Liebmann (1840–1912) entitled *Kant und die Epigonen* (1865), each chapter of which concluded: "Therefore, it is necessary to return to Kant." Another step in the same direction is marked by Friedrich Albert Lange (1828–1875), author of a famous *History of Materialism*. But the chief representatives of the Neo-Kantian movement are the thinkers of the *Marburg school*: Hermann Cohen (1842–1918), the most important of all, who was the teacher of the young Ortega (*System der Philosophie: Logik der reinen Erkenntnis* [System of Philosophy: Logic of Pure Knowledge], *Ethik des reinen Willens* [Ethics of Pure Will], *Ästhetik des reinen Gefühls* [Esthetics of Pure Feeling]); Paul Natorp (1854–1924), who formulated a Neo-Kantian interpretation of Platonism and made special studies of psychological and pedagogical problems (*Platos Ideenlehre, Kant und die Marburger Schule*); and recently, Ernst Cassirer (1874–1945), a professor in the United States in his last years, who studied the problem of knowledge (*Das Erkenntnisproblem in der Philosophie und Wissenschaft der neueren Zeit* [The Problem of Knowledge], *Substanzbegriff und Funktionsbegriff* [Substance and Function], *Philosophie der symbolischen Formen* [Philosophy of Symbolic Forms], *Phänomenologie der Erkenntnis* [Phenomenology of Knowledge], *Descartes, Leibniz' System*). He also wrote *Philosophy of the Enlightenment* and *Philosophical Anthropology*.

Another important Neo-Kantian group is the so-called *Baden school*, whose most important members are Wilhelm Windelband (1848–1915), a great historian of philosophy (*Einleitung in die Philosophie, Lehrbuch der Geschichte der Philosophie, Präludien*) and Heinrich Rickert (1863–1936), devoted to studies of methodology and epistemology (*Die Grenzen der naturwissenschaftlichen Begriffsbildung, Kulturwissenschaft und Naturwissenschaft, Philosophie des Lebens*).

The Discovery of Life

We now begin to consider the thinkers of the last third of the nine-teenth century. This period, perhaps more clearly than any other, reveals the meaning of the history of philosophy. I will speak of philos-ophers who were, in general, somewhat marginal to the central current of their time. We have seen down what futile paths the thinkers after Comte were led by positivism; therefore, we will find authentic philosophy only in the thinkers who are at variance with the tenor of their age, in those thinkers who go beyond the bounds of the prevailing schools of philosophy. This is true to such an extent that these men either do not seem to be philosophers or else are misunder-stood. However, the foregoing statement must be followed by the observation that such an interpretation of the thought of the end of the nineteenth century is possible only in the twentieth century. Strictly speaking, this thought *came to be* authentic and fruitful *because* it served as a stimulus and precedent for present-day metaphysics; it acquires value only in the light of modern thought. We must collect elements which the last century would have considered most con-temptible and which achieve full actuality only outside themselves, to wit, in the philosophy of recent years. The philosophers I refer to were not, of course, systematic thinkers. In general, they had brilliant intuitions, conjectures, visions; however, although all this amounts to a great deal, it does not, strictly speaking, constitute philosophy. Naturally, philosophy needs *concepts*, but it also requires a *system*. This fragmentary philosophy achieves its reality—Hegel would say its *truth*—in a later phase of philosophy, and in that

360

later stage it constitutes a first step toward an authentic metaphysics.

1. KIERKEGAARD

Søren Kierkegaard (1813–1855) was a Danish thinker whose influence on philosophy, although hardly visible, has been real and lasting. He lived in Copenhagen, tormented by his religious and philosophical problems and influenced, in the negative sense of complete opposition to it, by German idealism. Among Kierkegaard's works we find *The Gospel of Suffering, Either/Or (Enten-Eller)*, the *Philosophical Fragments* and the *Concluding Unscientific Postscript*, one of his most important writings.

Like other thinkers of his time, Kierkegaard appeals to Christianity —in his case, through Protestant theology—in order to understand man's being. He dwells in particular on the concept of *suffering*, which he relates to original sin and in which man feels himself to be alone. This leads Kierkegaard to formulate an *anthropology* shaped by the idea of *existence*; this idea is of very great interest and of considerable philosophical productivity, in spite of its unsystematic character and of the dangerous irrationalism which has made itself felt in certain of Kierkegaard's followers.

Kierkegaard rejects the "eternalization" that Hegelianism introduced into philosophy because that abstract and *sub specie aeternitatis* thought does not take into account *existence*, that is, the very mode of man's being—every man's, even that of the abstract thinker himself. Man is something that is concrete, temporal, in the process of becoming; something which partakes of this mode of being that we call existence because he is a mixture of what is temporal and eternal; something that is submerged in suffering. Motion, which *sub specie aeternitatis* thought denies, is essential to existence. Acting on religious suppositions, Kierkegaard deals with human reality in its strictly individual and personal form, and not in its abstract form, as man in general. He speaks about *my* existence in all its concrete and irreplaceable personal identity. However, this positive aspect of his thought is obscured by his irrationalism. Kierkegaard believes that we cannot conceive of existence and motion, because when we try to conceive of these things they become immovable, eternal and, therefore, abolished. But, since he who thinks, exists, existence and thought are posited at the same time, and existence is the serious topic for philosophy.

Kierkegaard influenced Unamuno considerably, and Heidegger found much of value in his thought. Thus the vital core of Kierkegaard's metaphysics appears in systematic and mature form in the very center of present-day philosophy.

2. Nietzsche

LIFE AND WORKS. Friedrich Nietzsche was born in 1844. He studied classical philology in Bonn and Leipzig and in 1869, when he was twenty-five years old, was named professor of that discipline at Basel. In 1879 he had to give up his position because of ill health, and after that he supported himself independently as a writer. He went insane in 1889 and in 1900, at the close of the nineteenth century, died completely estranged from the world.

Nietzsche is an extremely complex personality; he possessed great artistic talent and is one of the best of the modern German writers. His style, in prose as well as in verse, is passionate, inspired and of great literary beauty. His knowledge of and interest in Greek culture play a large role in his philosophy. However, the central theme of his thought is man, human life, and he is completely preoccupied with history and ethics. Schopenhauer and Richard Wagner influenced him greatly, and perhaps this accentuated his literary and artistic value and broadened his influence, which has been so extensive as to be detrimental to his philosophy and even to preclude a fair evaluation of his work. Indubitably, there is in Nietzsche much more than what the *dilettantism* which took possession of his work and personality at the end of the last century and the beginning of this century has been accustomed to show us. One of the tasks of present-day philosophy is to bring to light the metaphysical content of Friedrich Nietzsche's thought.

Nietzsche's principal works are *Die Geburt der Tragödie* (The Birth of Tragedy), *Unzeitgemässe Betrachtungen* (Inopportune Considerations), *Menschliches, Allzumenschliches* (Human, All Too Human), *Morgenröte* (Dawn), *Also sprach Zarathustra* (Thus Spake Zarathustra), *Jenseits von Gut und Böse* (Beyond Good and Evil), *Zur Genealogie der Moral* (On the Genealogy of Morality), *Der Wille zur Macht* (The Will to Power). The last book was published after his death under a title which the author did not give it and in a form which dilutes its meaning. Recent work by Karl Schlechta has revealed how Nietzsche's works were manipulated in order to give them a racist significance and to relate them to the "totalitarianism" of our century.

THE PRINCIPLE OF DIONYSUS AND THE PRINCIPLE OF APOLLO. An interpretation which Nietzsche makes of Greek thought comes to have great importance in his philosophy. He distinguishes two principles: the principle of Apollo and the principle of Dionysus. Apollo is the symbol of serenity, clarity, moderation, rationalism; he is the Greek *classical* image. On the other hand, Dionysus is the symbol of impulsiveness, excess, uncontrollability, the affirmation of life, eroticism, and orgy as a culmination of the longing to live, to say *Yes!* to life in spite of all its sorrows. Schopenhauer's influence is turned inside out; Nietzsche, instead of negating the will to live, places that will at the center of his thought.

THE ETERNAL RETURN. To a certain extent Nietzsche derives from the positivism of the age; he denies that metaphysics is possible; furthermore, he assumes a loss of faith in God and in the immortality of the soul. However, the life which he affirms and which forever wishes to live longer, which asks for an eternity of happiness, returns time and again. Nietzsche makes use of an idea that derives from Heraclitus in his notion of the "eternal return" (*ewige Wiederkunft*) of the things. After all possible combinations of the elements of the world have been realized, there is an interval of a previously undetermined duration, and then the cycle begins again, and so on, indefinitely. Everything that happens in the world repeats itself in identical fashion time and again. Everything returns eternally, including everything that is evil, miserable and vile. But men can transform the world and themselves by means of a *transmutation of all values* (*Umwertung aller Werte*), and can progress toward becoming supermen. Thus Nietzsche's affirmation of life is not limited to one's accepting and wishing for life only once, but an infinite number of times.

THE SUPERMAN. Nietzsche is opposed to all the equalitarian, humanitarian and democratic trends of his age. He is a champion of mighty personalities. The highest good is life itself, which culminates in the *will to power*. Man must go beyond himself and become something superior to man, just as man is superior to the monkey: this is the theory of the superman. Nietzsche models his superman on unscrupulous and immoral Renaissance personalities who nevertheless had gigantic capacities for life and who were strong, impulsive and energetic. The concept of the superman leads Nietzsche to a new idea of morality.

THE MORALITY OF MASTERS AND THE MORALITY OF SLAVES. Nietzsche is particularly hostile to the Kantian ethics of duty, and also to utilitarian ethics and Christian morality as well. He values only the strong, healthy, impulsive life which has the will to dominate. This represents good, whereas weakness, sickness and failure are evil. Compassion is the greatest evil. Thus Nietzsche distinguishes two types of morality. The morality of the masters is that of powerful individuals of superior vitality; this morality applies only to these superior beings and is based on exigency and on the affirmation of the vital impulses. In contrast, the morality of the slaves is that of weak and miserable people, of degenerates; it is governed by lack of confidence in life and respect for compassion, humility, patience, and the like. Nietzsche says that it is a morality of *resentment*, which opposes everything that is superior and which therefore affirms every form of equalitarianism. Nietzsche attributes this character of *resentment* to Christian morality; however, this is an outright error on his part, arising from his lack of understanding of the meaning of Christianity. Scheler has proved the absolute distance between Christianity and every form of resentment (see Max Scheler: *Ressentiment*). Because of his high regard for energy and power, Nietzsche figures among the thinkers who have most exalted the value of war; war seems to him to be an opportunity for the development of superior values, the spirit of sacrifice, bravery, nobility, and so on. Nietzsche rejects the middle-class nineteenth-century idea of man as an industrious and useful being and affirms the idea of the knight, the courageous and powerful man who vigorously accepts life. All these ideas have a point in common with Christianity, although Nietzsche was not able to see it.

The most important elements of Nietzsche's philosophy are his idea of life and his awareness of the existence of vital values, that is, values which pertain specifically to *human life*. The expression *vital values* contains two of the ideas which come to dominate later philosophy. Nietzsche is a source of the *philosophy of values* and of the *philosophy of life*.

The Return to Traditional Metaphysics

At the same time that the theme of life appears in the philosophy of the nineteenth century, and perhaps even a few years before this happens, the content of philosophy changes and philosophy once again approaches the previous traditional metaphysics which had been interrupted—at least so it seemed—by positivism. This is not just a return to the most immediate form of traditional metaphysics, the German idealist tradition, but rather a return to the traditions of rationalism, Scholasticism and, in particular, Greek philosophy. Because of this, philosophy regains its full dignity and the commencement of a new stage of philosophical productivity becomes possible. This development occurs precisely at the beginning of the present century.

It is not mere coincidence that the thinkers of this tendency were Catholics and, in fact, for the most part priests. The Church, for primarily theological reasons, has kept close to the great metaphysical systems. For a long time—we may say since Suárez—Scholasticism has been practically a dead tradition; to whatever extent it has concerned itself with philosophic questions, it has done so in a "scholastic" spirit in the narrow sense of the word, as a mere exegesis of medieval thought and "refutation of modern errors." Thus it has all too often overlooked the entire history of modern philosophy as if it did not exist, as if it were nothing but a mere error or whim which had incomprehensibly appropriated to itself the popularity once enjoyed by the only true philosophy, that of the Middle Ages, and more specifically Thomism. This conception is absolutely inadmissible, for it has been completely superseded as often as thinkers within the Scholastic tradition have had some knowledge of modern philosophy and of medieval Scholasticism itself. Then it has been seen that the living philosophical continuation of Scholasticism is to be found not so much in the presumptive Neo-Scholastics as in modern philosophy. Descartes and Leibniz are descended from St. Augustine, St. Anselm, St. Thomas, Duns Scotus, Occam and Eckhart, as anyone even moderately acquainted with them knows very well; as, for example, Father Gratry so very fully knew.

Thus, Catholic philosophers had not lost contact with metaphysics. Throughout the nineteenth century, there is a series of attempts to restore maturity to philosophy; this movement culminates in Brentano. At that moment the philosophy of our age is set in motion.

1. THE FIRST ATTEMPTS

BOLZANO. The Austrian philosopher Bernhard Bolzano (1781–1848) lived in the first half of the nineteenth century. He was a Catholic priest, professor of the philosophy of religion at Prague from 1805 to 1820, in which year he was compelled to leave his post. In 1837 he published his major work, *Wissenschaftslehre* (Theory of Science); as far as the "elementary part" of logic is concerned, this book "leaves far behind everything offered by universal literature in the way of systematic essays on logic," according to the opinion of Edmund Husserl, who considered Bolzano "one of the greatest logicians of all time." Bolzano's views were much closer to those of Leibniz than to those of the German idealists who were his contemporaries; he brought a mathematical spirit to the study of logic and the problem of knowledge. In many ways Bolzano anticipated ideas which have proved to be of importance for symbolic and mathematical logic; his theory affirming the character of *being* as independent of the consciousness of spiritual ideal contents deeply influenced Husserl's phenomenology, which, in one of its decisive aspects, is a new championing of *ideal objects*. Bolzano also wrote the *Paradoxien des Unendlichen* (Paradoxes of the Infinite).

ROSMINI AND GIOBERTI. The two Italian philosophers Antonio Rosmini-Serbati (1797–1855) and Vincenzo Gioberti (1801–1852), starting out from very similar positions, also contributed to the reinstatement of metaphysics in the mid-nineteenth century. Both were Catholic priests who took an active part in public life and the political movement in behalf of Italian unity. Rosmini was Sardinia's ambassador to the Pope, Gioberti its premier. Rosmini wrote *Nuovo saggio sull' origine delle idee* (New Essay on the Origin of Ideas), *Principii della scienza morale* (Principles of Moral Science), *Teosofia* (Theosophy) and the *Saggio storico-critico sulle categorie e la dialettica* (Historical and Critical Essay on the Categories and Dialectic). Gioberti's principal works are *Introduzione allo studio della filosofia* (Introduction to the Study of Philosophy), *Degli errori filosofici di Rosmini* (On Rosmini's Philosophical Errors), *Protologia*, *Del buono* (On the Good), *Del bello* (On the Beautiful) and *Teorica del sovrannaturale* (Theory of the Supernatural).

Rosmini seeks the intuition of a "first truth" which is the standard for all other truths, an intelligible form whose union with the intelligence there results the intelligence itself; this is being as such, the primary object of the intelligence. There is a very close connection between these views and those of Malebranche and, consequently, the idea of the vision of the things in God.

Analogously, in Gioberti's thought being is a priori in character; therefore, the human intellect possesses essentially a *direct* knowledge of God, without which it cannot know anything. Something divine appears *directly* to the mind in the created things; it is thus not necessary to prove the existence of God. "The great concept of the Deity," Gioberti says, "has held up to now a more or less secondary place in philosophic doctrines, even in those which, in appearance or in reality, are the most religious.... The speculative sciences have up to now more or less partaken of atheism." In opposition to this, Gioberti's *ideal formula* declares that the ontological principle (God) is the logical and ontological principle at the same time. "All of existence depends upon the Entity, and all knowledge depends upon the intuition of Him.... The concept of the Entity is present in all our thought." One cannot begin philosophy with man, but with God Himself, who posits His own Self; man can recognize His existence, but cannot demonstrate it, because the so-called proofs of the existence of God presuppose "a prior and original *intuition.*"

These Italian thinkers do violence to reality when they overlook the fact that God does not manifest Himself directly, but is hidden and dwells in an *inaccessible light*; therefore, our imperfect knowledge of Him is the true state of the case, and an effort is needed to show His existence, which can be known intellectually only by means of the created things, *per ea quae facta sunt*, as St. Paul says. "No one has ever seen God." The ontologist error was condemned by the Church in 1861 and 1887; it was used to a certain extent by the complex heterodox movement known as *modernism*, which was defined and condemned by the Church in the first years of the present century.

2. GRATRY

Of greater interest and scope is the philosophy of Father Gratry. Auguste Joseph Alphonse Gratry was born at Lille in France in 1805 and died in 1872. He studied at the École Polytechnique and was ordained as a priest; he was a professor at Strasbourg and Paris, and in 1852 founded the Congregation of the Oratory of the Immaculate Conception, a renewal of the Oratory of Jesus to which Malebranche belonged. From 1863 on he was professor of moral theology at the Sorbonne. Gratry's most important works are *La connaissance de l'âme* (The Knowledge of the Soul), *Logique, La morale et la loi de l'histoire* (Morality and the Law of History) and especially *La connaissance de Dieu* (The Knowledge of God), the best philosophical book about God written in a century.

For many years Gratry has been very little known and almost forgotten, especially as a philosopher. His work, which is essentially metaphysical and in which the theme of God is central, could not be understood, strictly speaking, within the positivist environment of his day; his very qualities have been the chief cause of his obscurity. But for precisely this reason he is of the greatest interest to us today. Gratry is clearly aware that the history of philosophy has followed a single course, beginning in Greece and coming down to our own day; thus, in order to expound his personal philosophy, he begins by showing the internal evolution of the problems of philosophy from Plato to rationalism. Secondly, he interprets metaphysics as the essential element of philosophy, in opposition to the opinion current in his time, and takes a decisive step forward along the path of restoring metaphysics. He believes, above all, that the problem of metaphysics is formulated as the continuation of two great questions, which are the ones that philosophy is compelled to cope with today: that of the person and that of God. Lastly, in his *Logic* he expounds, as the principal procedure of reason, a profound theory of induction or dialectic which is very closely related to the phenomenological doctrines of intuition and the knowledge of essences. These are the central themes of Gratry's thought.

If there is a knowledge of God, it is based on an essential aspect of man, just as man's knowledge of the things is based on his contact with them, with their reality. The *knowledge* of God, like all knowledge, is something *derived* from another primary ontological aspect, which is the basis for its *possibility*. The problem of God involves man; since man, essentially, is endowed with a body and exists in a world, the ontology of man takes us back in turn to the ontology of the world in which man finds himself. Thus, all of metaphysics is summed up in the problem of God.

Man, according to Gratry, has three faculties: the primary faculty of *sense* and two derived ones, intelligence and will. Sense is the deeplying part of the person. This sense is threefold: external sense, by means of which I sense the reality of my body and of the world; internal sense, by which I sense myself *and my fellow men*; and divine sense, by which I find God in the depth of my soul, which is the image of Him. This *divine sense* defines man's primary relationship with God, which is *prior to all knowledge and vision*; it is a *fundamental* relationship because the human entity has its basis and its root in God. The soul finds in its own depths a contact with the Deity, and *therein resides its force, which causes it to be.*

God is the root of man, who depends upon Him. God *makes* man *live* and *sustains* him. Therefore, He is the basis of human life; man exists and lives upon his root, *supporting himself* on God. This is the necessary presupposition of all knowledge of the Deity, and it is from this viewpoint that Gratry interprets atheism. The atheist is a man who is devoid of the divine sense; thus, he is *in-sensate* (foolish), *de-ment-ed*. The causes of this estrangement from God are sensuality and pride; through sensuality, man makes the things the center of his existence and turns away from God, while pride makes man consider himself as his own basis. Then the divine sense is extinguished and the heart is darkened, at the same time that the imagination becomes vain, as St. Paul says. Because the soul is rooted in God, it is able to be uprooted; it becomes empty, remaining completely without substance and consistency.

Thus the point of origin of the knowledge of God is the divine sense, the mysterious and obscure contact with God in the depth of the person, which is not knowledge but only a prior condition for the possibility of knowledge. When man conquers his sensuality and pride, he recognizes his insufficiency and can raise himself to God through *similarity* and, especially, through *contrast*. Gratry distinguishes between two procedures of reason: one based on identity, which is the syllogism or deduction, and the other based on the principle of transcendence, which is induction or dialectic. This is the intellectual path by which one reaches God. The result of induction is not contained in the starting point, but goes beyond it; the present datum refers us to *another* one, which is not included in the original point; in order to raise ourselves to the new point we need an inventive impulse (*élan*), which not everyone possesses. The things *induce* us to raise ourselves to God;

this is the fundamental and primary meaning of induction, which is a total movement of the soul.

Father Gratry intuited that, on the one hand, the external world is involved in the deep-lying reality of man, and that, on the other, man, who is not self-sufficient, remains *basically insufficient* even when taken together with the world, because his *basis* in God is still lacking. When he enters within his own depths, man finds, together with contingency, the support which makes him be and live, which *sustains* him; this foundation is not the *world*, which touches us only *superficially*, but God, on whom our *root* rests.

This shows Gratry's great significance for present-day philosophy, since his metaphysics leads us to the latest questions that we have posed and indicates a sure method by which we may deal with them. *

* A detailed study of Gratry's thought and his place in the history of philosophy will be found in my book *La Filosofía del Padre Gratry* [*Obras*, IV].

CONTEMPORARY PHILOSOPHY

Brentano

1. Brentano's Position in the History of Philosophy

Life and works. The Austrian thinker Franz Brentano is extremely important. He was born in Marienberg in 1838 and died in Zürich in 1917. He was a Catholic priest and a professor in Vienna, but later he broke with the Church—without abandoning his profoundly Catholic convictions—and gave up his professorship. Brentano wrote but little, and the greater part of his writings was not published until after his death. Nevertheless, Brentano attracted unusually effective pupils, and his influence, though quiet and inconspicuous, has been immense. Present-day philosophy begins with him; if not its exclusive founder, he is still a major one. Brentano wrote short books, almost pamphlets, of incomparable density and accuracy; and each one has brought about the radical transformation of a philosophical discipline. Brentano and Dilthey together represent the high point of their epoch and constitute the most efficacious and direct antecedent of present-day philosophy. In many respects, Brentano and Dilthey are diametrically opposed; the former is concise, expressive, extremely clear, whereas the latter is diffuse and his thought is unusually vague; Brentano adopts the natural sciences as his model, whereas Dilthey changes everything into history; Dilthey's most direct intellectual antecedents are found in German idealism, whereas Brentano condemns this tradition and, on the contrary, invokes that of Descartes and Leibniz, of St. Thomas and, above all, of Aristotle. Nevertheless, Dilthey and Brentano essentially complement one another, and it is not difficult to see how the philosophy of our time derives from their joint influence.

Brentano's most important works are *Vom Ursprung sittlicher Erkenntnis* (On the Origin of Ethical Knowledge), a brief pamphlet which transformed ethics and led to the value theory; *Die Lehre Jesu und ihre bleibende Bedeutung* (Jesus' Doctrine and Its Permanent Significance); his masterwork *Psychologie vom empirischen Standpunkt* (Psychology from the Empirical Standpoint), from which directly proceeds phenomenology and therefore present-day philosophy in its most rigorous orientation; studies on Aristotle which completely renewed Aristotelianism; several short writings on philosophy and its history, particularly those entitled *Die vier Phasen der Philosophie* (The Four Phases of Philosophy) and *Über die Zukunft der Philosophie* (On the Future of Philosophy); *Kategorienlehre* (Theory of the Categories); *Wahrheit und Evidenz* (Truth and Evidence); and, lastly, an extensive posthumous study: *Vom Dasein Gottes* (On the Existence of God).

BRENTANO'S PHILOSOPHICAL SITUATION. Every philosopher is fixed within a philosophical tradition, and Brentano even more explicitly than most. It is thus necessary to establish his situation in some detail. According to his birth date, he should be a post-Hegelian, immersed in a positivist atmosphere; however, as a Catholic priest he finds himself rooted in a Scholastic and therefore Aristotelian tradition. Brentano has a manifest *congeniality* with Aristotle and St. Thomas—more so with Aristotle, just as that medieval philosopher had with the Greek; after Trendelenburg, Brentano renews Aristotelianism in an epoch in which it had been abandoned; one should not forget that modern philosophy arose as an attempt to displace Aristotle. This Aristotelian element gives exceptional fecundity to Brentano's thought; whenever philosophy has established *real* contact with Aristotle's thought, it has immediately become more precise and serious. Brentano is an example of this, as was Scholasticism in the thirteenth century and, later, Leibniz, and, later still, Hegel. Moreover, Aristotle's close presence is one reason for the indubitable profundity of present-day philosophy. Brentano condemns idealist philosophy from Kant to Hegel; it seems to him to be a *straying* from the true path. It is, according to Brentano, partly—but only partly—true. Brentano adopts the positivist attitude of his time; this attitude was justified to the extent that it asked men to concern themselves with what they encountered without engaging in mental constructions; its serious error lies in the fact that it did not concern itself with what it encountered, but indulged in other, no less groundless constructions. Thus Brentano returns to a point of view in opposition to idealism; he calls his an "empirical viewpoint." Obviously, Brentano is anything but an empiricist; he could be considered such in the sense that Aristotle was an empiricist, but not in the sense that Locke was. Aristotle frequently refers to direct vision without rational deduction; this has been called empiricism, but it has nothing to do with *experience* in the meaning of sensible experience; rather, Aristotle refers to the *noûs*, the noetic vision, by which principles are apprehended directly. We will soon demonstrate the meaning of Brentano's "empiricism," which leads precisely to the total defeat of sensationalist empiricism in its final psychologistic forms.

Brentano establishes a connection between the purest and most authentic root of ancient philosophy and modern philosophy, and from this position he transforms the philosophy of his time. He begins with his vision of two disciplines: psychology and ethics. Let us now consider Brentano's contribution to these disciplines.

2. PSYCHOLOGY

In Brentano's day, psychology consisted of an attempt to change itself into an experimental, positive science; it was an associationist psychology related to English philosophy which attempted to explain everything by means of the associations of ideas, and furthermore to intervene in the other disciplines—for example, in logic, ethics, esthetics—in order to change them in turn into psychology. Brentano's psychology has a completely new character.

PHYSICAL AND PSYCHICAL PHENOMENA. The first essential problem that arises is to differentiate clearly between physical and psychical phenomena. The thinkers of the Middle Ages—Avicenna in particular —knew of a characteristic of psychical phenomena that was forgotten later on; this was what they called *intentional inexistence* (the prefix on the second term means *in*, not negation: *existence in*) or simply *intentionality*. Brentano accepts this characteristic and assigns it an importance and precision that it did not have in Scholasticism.

Intentionality means reference to something that is distinct; in the case of psychical acts, reference to a content, an *object* (this does not mean that the object must be *real*). Thinking is always thinking *of something*; feeling is feeling something; wanting is wanting something; loving or hating is loving or hating something. Thus, every psychical act is directed toward an object; the object may not exist, as when I think of a centaur or of the squared circle or the regular pentahedron; however, both the squared circle and the regular pentahedron exist as *correlatives* of my thought, as objects indicated by my act of imagining or thinking. Brentano says that acts which are not intentional are not psychical acts—for example, the sensation of green, or a stomachache. According to him, sensations are simple non-intentional elements of the psychical (intentional) act that is my *perception* of a green tree; and the psychical act is the *feeling* of discomfort whose intentional object is the stomach-ache.

This idea of intentionality has far-reaching consequences. In the first place, it leads to the reappearance of ideal objects and, among these, to what Husserl will call *meanings*. It also leads to the notion that thought does not exhaust itself, that it is essentially directed toward something distinct from itself. Finally, it gives rise to the belief that man is intentional, ex-centric, and that he points to something distinct from himself. The idea of man as an entity that is "open to the things" is based on this idea of Brentano's.

BRENTANO'S METHOD. What is Brentano's method, the method that he calls "empirical"? To an Englishman, to an associationist psychologist, empiricism would have meant *observation of facts*. The empiricist observes one fact, and another, and then abstracts and generalizes the common factors. Brentano's method is a different kind of empiricism. Let us suppose that I wish to observe a phenomenon: I take *a single case* and see what the essential part of it is, what it consists of, what it cannot exist without. In this way I obtain the *essence* of the phenomenon: then I am able to say, for example, not that psychical acts are *generally* intentional, but that they are *essentially* intentional. Brentano intuits the essence of a phenomenon. This method is refined and perfected by Husserl and becomes phenomenology.

CLASSIFICATION OF PSYCHICAL PHENOMENA. After differentiating the psychical phenomena, Brentano must classify them. Since intentionality is what is essential in them, he classifies them on this basis, according to the various modes of intentional reference. He distinguishes three kinds of acts:

psychical acts $\begin{cases} \textit{representations} \text{ (what have been called "assumptions")} \\ \textit{judgments} \\ \textit{emotions} \text{ (or phenomena of interest, love or volition)} \end{cases}$

Brentano uses the word *representation* very loosely: it is a thought, idea or image. To Brentano, a representation is anything that is *present to the consciousness*. He restates an ancient Scholastic principle which we have already encountered—in Spinoza, for example—and which is known by the name of *Brentano's principle*: "Every psychical act is either a representation or is based on a representation." If I am happy about something, my happiness presupposes a representation of the thing which makes me happy; or if I desire something, of the thing which I desire, and so on. Therefore, there is a first degree of intentionality, which is simple reference to the object represented, and a second degree, in which, *while operating on the basis of a representation*, I take a position on a second intentional act. *Judgment* consists of accepting or rejecting *something* as *true*. Emotion, interest, will or love consists of *one's moving toward something*, that is, of one's appreciating or valuing it, of *one's esteeming it*. This also involves the taking of a position, approval or rejection, but of a different nature. Brentano's ethics derives from this, as does value philosophy later on.

PERCEPTION. In his *Psychology*, Brentano also formulates a theory of perception. He finds two basic modes: *internal* perception (perception of psychical phenomena) and *external* perception (perception of physical phenomena). Internal perception is direct, self-evident and infallible (*adequate*); external perception, on the contrary, is indirect, not self-evident, and subject to error (*inadequate*). Therefore, *internal* perception is the sure criterion of certainty. This idea has been adopted and corrected by Husserl, who believes that all external perceptions and also some internal (empirical) perceptions are inadequate, and that only *phenomenological* perceptions are adequate. In short, it is a question of not making positions of existence; the experiences simply must be described, without taking a position with regard to the existence of anything external to them, for example, of *real* objects.

3. ETHICS

Brentano's ethics is outlined in *Vom Ursprung sittlicher Erkenntnis*, which is the text of a lecture he delivered in Vienna in 1889 entitled "Of the Natural Sanction of the Just and the Moral." Brentano applies to ethics a viewpoint analogous to the one used in his psychology; he calls this viewpoint empirical in the sense that we have seen.

SANCTION. Brentano begins by inquiring about the natural sanction of the just and the moral. If I say that something is good or bad, there must be some basis, some authority or sanction that can verify the goodness or badness of the thing. Brentano rejects the solutions of various earlier philosophers: hedonism, eudaemonism, Kantian morality, and so forth.

Brentano has one ruling point of view: he makes what is true correspond to what is good, and what is logical correspond to what is moral. He says that the ethical imperative is very similar to the logical imperative. What is true is accepted as true in a *judgment*: what is good is accepted as such in an *act of love*. Truth is *believed, affirmed*: goodness is *loved*. Conversely, falsity is *denied*, and evil is *hated*.

THE MORAL CRITERION. What tells me whether a thing is good or bad? The fact that I love or hate it? No. And in logic truth does not depend on whether I affirm or deny something; I may be wrong. A thing is not good because I love it; on the contrary, I love a thing because it is good. But I may be wrong: *error* cannot be restricted to the realm of judgment; a different kind of error is possible in valuation.

Brentano has provisionally transferred us to the sphere of objectivity. That which is good is the object; my reference may be erroneous; my attitude with respect to the things receives its sanction from the things themselves, not from me.

SELF-EVIDENCE. I find myself loving or hating something. I may be wrong. Who can tell me whether the thing is good or bad? Brentano resorts to the parallelism of logic: how does logic provide me with a criterion to know whether I err or not? Brentano distinguishes between *blind judgments* and *self-evident judgments*. I deny many things, and steadfastly affirm and believe in others; but these judgments are more or less obscure, based on faith, authority, custom, and the like. I can believe in such judgments with complete resoluteness, but they do not contain within themselves the basis of their own truth; either they are not true, or else their truth is not a part of them. Such judgments do not contain within themselves the justification of their truth; Brentano calls these blind judgments.

In contrast, there is another class of judgments which Brentano calls *self-evident judgments*. They contain a kind of light which makes it evident that they are true judgments. One does not only believe and affirm them; rather, one *sees* that they are true and completely understands that they cannot be otherwise. I believe that 2 and 2 are 4, not because I have been told so, but because I see that it is so and that it cannot be otherwise. Thus, self-evident judgments are those that contain within themselves the reason for their truth or falsity.

THE JUST LOVE. Let us go back to the problem of ethics, which deals with what is good and what is bad. Brentano says that my loving or hating a thing does not in itself prove that the thing is good or bad. My love or hate must be *just*. Love can be just or unjust, adequate or inadequate. On the other hand, there can be a love that has its own justification within itself. When I love a thing because it is undoubtedly good, then my love is a *just love*. If I love a thing impulsively, confusedly, my love can be either just or unjust. When it is perceived that the thing is good, and why it is good, then the justness of the love becomes manifest. The adequate attitude when confronting a good thing is to love it, and when confronting a bad thing, to hate it. And when a thing is understood as either good or bad, one loves or hates it *by necessity*. One's subsequent conduct is another matter. Brentano recalls the classical verse: *Video meliora proboque, deteriora sequor*. Therefore, ethics is *founded objectively*. And *valuation*, far from being contingent on subjective choice, must adjust to the goodness or badness *of the things*, just as belief must adjust to their truth. Brentano's ethics has given birth to value theory, which contains great internal difficulties, but which represents a major contribution to the objective and hierarchical arrangement of values and therefore to the foundation of ethics and the other estimative disciplines.

4. The Existence of God

Brentano's posthumous book *Vom Dasein Gottes* contains several lectures on the existence of God which were delivered in Würzburg and in Vienna between 1868 and 1891, and a brief treatise dating from 1915 entitled *Gedankengang beim Beweis für das Dasein Gottes* (Outline of a Proof of the Existence of God). In the earlier period, Brentano rejects the ontological proof and affirms four a posteriori proofs: the teleological proof, the proof by motion, the proof by contingency and the psychological proof by the nature of the human soul. Brentano prefers the first two, particularly the teleological proof, to which he gives undreamed-of scientific precision. However, in the 1915 treatise he makes use of the argument by contingency, which is of a purely metaphysical nature.

Brentano first proves the necessity for the existence of the entity, which cannot be absolutely contingent; once the existence of a necessary entity has been proved, he affirms that nothing that comes within our experience, neither physical nor psychical phenomena, is *directly necessary*; therefore, there must be a *transcendent* directly necessary entity.*

Brentano's significance. The core of Brentano's thought is the idea of *self-evidence*. This is the meaning of his "empiricism": the self-evident vision of the essence of the things. This renewed concern with essence represents a return to metaphysics proper; in Brentano, philosophy once again consists of conquering essences, strictly metaphysical knowledge, what philosophy has always been when it has been authentic. On the other hand, Brentano gives us the major elements of present-day philosophy: the assimilation of the entire philosophical tradition, intentionality, the intuition of essences, the idea of value. Dilthey will give us, on his part, historicism. With these elements in hand, the philosophy of our century gets under way.

---

* On the problems associated with this proof, see my study "El problema de Dios en la filosofía de nuestro tiempo" in *San Anselmo y el insensato* [*Obras*, IV].

The Idea of Life

1. DILTHEY

LIFE AND WORKS. Wilhelm Dilthey was born in 1833 and died in 1911. From 1882 on he was a professor at the University of Berlin, where he succeeded Lotze. In the last years of his life he retired from the university and gathered together a small group of pupils at his home. Dilthey's influence has been truly enormous, but belated, inconspicuous and unusual. Dilthey devoted himself especially to historical studies, principally the history of literature and of the other sciences of the spirit; he also was deeply concerned with psychology. His intellectual background was tremendous in scope; he was inspired directly by the German idealists, particularly Schleiermacher, but his development was also shaped by the great rationalists, the medieval philosophers (including the Arabs) and the Greeks. Dilthey's *Introduction to the Sciences of the Spirit* reveals the vast philosophical and historical material that he commanded.

Seemingly, Dilthey's production is little more than this: psychology and history of the spirit. Every time he tried to formulate his philosophy in response to specific publishing requirements, he was only able to supply inadequate sketches. Yet in Dilthey's work there is the inconsistent and always poorly expressed intuition of a new idea: *the idea of life*. One of the two major roots of present-day philosophy is found in Dilthey (the other is in Brentano), but Dilthey's philosophy can only be understood in this way, in its truth, *from the viewpoint* of the now mature philosophy of today. This is the reason

378

for the essential vagueness of Dilthey's thought and style, and for the sparseness and inconspicuousness of his influence.

Dilthey's work consists primarily of sketches or notes, which were partially published after his death. His major book—almost his only book—is the *Einleitung in die Geisteswissenschaften* (Introduction to the Sciences of the Spirit), of which he completed only the first volume.

He also wrote a series of studies grouped under the general title of *Weltanschauung und Analyse des Menschen seit Renaissance und Reformation* (View of the World and Analysis of Man since the Renaissance and the Reformation); another series entitled *Die geistige Welt: Einleitung in die Philosophie des Lebens* (The Spiritual World: Introduction to the Philosophy of Life), in which are to be found the *Ideen über eine beschreibende und zergliedernde Psychologie* (Ideas on a Descriptive and Analytical Psychology) and *Das Wesen der Philosophie* (The Nature of Philosophy); among the writings of his final period is the *Weltanschauungslehre* (Theory of World Views). He also wrote a book called *Das Erlebnis und die Dichtung* (Experience and Poetry).

DILTHEY'S POINT OF VIEW. Hippolyte Taine, Ernest Renan, Wilhelm Wundt, Friedrich Albert Lange and Herbert Spencer belong to the generation prior to Dilthey's, and yet our impression is that they were even farther in the past. They represent that generation of positivist thinkers which begins to feel uncomfortable and reacts against positivism. But strictly speaking, only Dilthey achieves the break with positivism, and even he not completely. Auguste Comte (born in 1798) was three generations earlier: Dilthey—who belonged to the same generation as Brentano, Nietzsche and William James— no longer undergoes Comte's *direct influence*, but only the *residual force* of that influence. The work of Dilthey and the Neo-Kantians is conditioned by their dependence upon positivism in controversial matters.

From Comte's philosophy Dilthey receives two very important ideas, which stimulate his thought in an original and different direction. One idea is that all of earlier philosophy was *partial*, that it did not embrace the whole of reality as it is; the other is that metaphysics is impossible, and that only the positive sciences are a matter of concern. Dilthey attempts to base philosophy "on total, full experience, without truncations: therefore, on entire and complete reality"; on the other hand, he attempts to supersede metaphysics as he understands it, that is, as "absolutism of the intellect": this latter outlook is the tribute he pays to the age he lives in.

Strictly speaking, Dilthey created neither a system, nor a theory of life, nor even a historical doctrine; he did something less and something more: he came into direct contact with the reality of life and, thus, of history. "All men," I have written elsewhere,* apropos of Dilthey, "live within history, but many men do not know this. Others know that their period *will be historical*, but they do not live it as such. Dilthey brought us *historicism*, which is, of course, a doctrine, but first of all a mode of being: *historical consciousness*, with the intellectualist and doctrinal nuances removed from the term 'consciousness.' Today, fully immersed in *this* historicism, we find it very difficult to realize the originality of that discovery. We are conscious of existing within a determined period of time, which is destined to pass away like all other periods, to be superseded by another. We are capable of transporting ourselves into other ages, and we live, naturally, in a world *directly* constituted by temporality. When we study anything whatever, we need to know its date, how it fits into history; otherwise we do not understand it. We think of everything as being enclosed in its historical surroundings; our view of a city, for example, is not the direct view of what the city is *at present*; rather, the city seems to us to be an accumulation of strata of time, a historical 'result,' in which the past survives and the future is in turn betokened. For Dilthey, this is closely related to the skepticism produced by the discrepancies among ideas and systems. The spiritual attitude with which we live excludes everything *definitive*; we do not believe we are settling any problems once and for all; rather, we believe we are supplying answers which are appropriate to our own era, but which are destined to be superseded or corrected in the future. The vision of history in Dilthey is 'an immense field of ruins.' It should be recalled that this was not always the case. There have been long periods in which man has regarded many things as standing apart from time, as being endowed with a certain timeless validity: this is the case with all classical periods. But in less peaceful and settled epochs, especially in those which signified a break with previous norms, the present was declared to be a *new* situation and, at the same time, a *valid* situation, without further qualification. In contrast to history, with its storehouse of errors, the present seemed to be a rectification and elimination of error. Today we feel the peculiar ephemerality of the historical event, but at the same time we feel that the moment in which we live is included in that history. In order to understand any person's name we must add to it the two limiting dates of his life, and when thinking about ourselves we anticipate the still uncertain second date, which is represented by a question mark. Never so much as now has man lived his life as the true reality of *counted days*. And that is history. . . . In our age it is acquiring basic and original

* *Biografía de la Filosofía*, VI, 37 [*Obras*, II].

characteristics hitherto unknown . . . because our age is discovering that what changes is *man himself*. Not only is man within history, not only does he *have* a history, but he *is* history; historicity affects the very being of man." This is Dilthey's point of view.

HUMAN LIFE. Dilthey discovers life in its historical dimension. Of all the different ways in which the nineteenth century came to touch upon that reality which is life, Dilthey's has been the most fruitful. Life is historical in its very substance; history is life itself, from the viewpoint of the totality of mankind. This vital reality is not a "world" of things and persons; it is a complex (*Zusammenhang*, the word Dilthey constantly repeats) of vital *relationships*. Each "thing" is no more than an ingredient of our life, and acquires its meaning within our life. "[A person's] friend is a force which exalts his own existence; each member of his family has a determined place in his life, he understands everything in his environment as life and spirit which have become objectivized there. The bench in front of his door, his house and garden have their essence and their meaning in this objectivity. Thus life creates its own world through the eyes of each individual" (*Theory of World Views*).

The world is always a correlate of the *self*, and the self does not exist without the other term, the *world*. Now, this life appears as a riddle which needs to be *understood*; death, especially, evokes this need, because it is the *incomprehensible*. But life can only be understood *from its own viewpoint*; knowledge cannot look behind the scenes of life. For this reason, in contrast to causal explanation, the method of the natural sciences, Dilthey makes *descriptive understanding* the method of the sciences of the spirit, of the knowledge of life. Since understanding of the life of others, especially in the past, requires an explanation, Dilthey's method is *hermeneutics*. Hence the "descriptive and analytical" psychology which he calls for, in opposition to the explicative psychology of the experimental psychologists, who treat human life as nature.

The structure of human life is a unitary totality, which is determined by the *selfhood of the person*. Every psychical state is a process, but life itself is not; rather, it is a lasting continuity within which occur the processes which pass by, Dilthey says, "in the same way as a fast-moving traveler sees objects disappear behind him which a moment before were in front of him and alongside him, while the totality of the landscape is always preserved." That is, the primary reality is the unity of life, *within* which occur the "things," on the one hand, and, on the other, the psychical "processes." This basic interconnection which is life is characterized by *finality*.

Human life is an original and transcendent unity: it is not a composite of elements; rather, starting out from its unitary reality, the psychical functions are differentiated, but remain united with life in their interconnection. Dilthey says that this fact, which is expressed in its highest degree as the unity of consciousness and the unity of the person, completely distinguishes psychical life from the entire corporeal world. Therefore, Dilthey rejects all forms of psychical fragmentation. Seen in another way, this unity occurs within a milieu. The unity of life is engaged in mutual reaction with the external world.

Life consists in the action of the vital unity upon stimuli, modifying them or adapting them to its conditions by means of voluntary activity. Lastly, transition from one set of members to another within psychical life does not take place by simple causality in the sense of external nature; ideas or representations do not contain a reason sufficient to make them become processes, nor do processes have sufficient reason for their transformation into volitional processes. Dilthey says that one could imagine an entity which would be a mere subject of representations, and which in the midst of the tumult of a battle would be an indifferent and volitionless spectator of its own destruction; or one could imagine that this same entity might follow the struggle raging about it with feelings of fear and alarm, but that nevertheless no defensive movements would proceed from those feelings. The connection that occurs between the elements of psychical life is of a peculiar nature and of a superior type; it proceeds from that primary totality which is human life itself.

Dilthey's analysis of human life, inadequate but extraordinarily perceptive, is the point of departure for present-day metaphysics, and it is constantly necessary to refer back to it.

PHILOSOPHY. "'What is philosophy?' is a question which cannot be answered in accordance with each man's personal taste; rather, the function of philosophy must be empirically discovered in history. It is clear that this history must be understood from the viewpoint of the spiritual vitality from which we ourselves proceed, and in which we live philosophy." These are Dilthey's two guiding ideas: the essence of philosophy can be discovered only in the historical reality of what it actually has been, and history can be understood only from the viewpoint of the life in which it is located. Therefore, Dilthey must make an interpretation of all of history in order to determine the being of philosophy. The two chief traits that are common to all philosophy are *universality* and *autonomy*, or the claim to be universally valid: all other traits are peculiar to individual philosophies.

Dilthey corrects the idea of productive thought which the German idealists found so appealing. Philosophy, Dilthey says, analyzes, but does not produce; it creates nothing; it can only show that which exists. That is, he renews in a truer and more fundamental form the demand of the positivists to hold fast to the things, and not to replace them with mental constructions; this attitude will be shared by phenomenology. Philosophy is the science of the real; that is, of *all* the real, without truncations.

But Dilthey is very far removed from a position of intellectual absolutism. The intelligence is not something isolated and standing apart; rather, it is a *vital function* and has meaning only within the totality which is human life; knowledge of life must be "derived." But in the second place, knowledge does not *exhaust* the real: "In the final analysis reality itself cannot be explained logically, but only understood. In all reality which occurs to us as such there is something ineffable, unknowable." That which is supplied to us, he adds, is irrational.

The basis of systematic philosophy for Dilthey is *autognosis*, consciousness of one's self (*Selbstbesinnung*). From autognosis one proceeds to *hermeneutics*, that is, knowledge of the life of others, the comprehending interpretation of other lives, and thus of history. Lastly, one goes from that point to the knowledge of *nature*. Philosophy proceeds from what is nearest—ourselves—to what is farthest away. Even though absolute systems are not possible—each system contains its own partial truth which, at least in principle, does not exclude the equally partial truth of the other systems—man conceives them and they remain as a constituent fact of human consciousness. Every man has a *Weltanschauung*, an idea or view of the world, which is ultimately rooted not in the intellect, but in *life itself*. These world views, which philosophy at first studies historically, can be reduced to *types* in order that we may know the possible ways of imagining the universe; thus, Ortega (*Guillermo Dilthey y la idea de la vida*) summarizes the four themes of Dilthey's philosophy in this way: (1) history of the evolution of philosophy as a propaedeutic; (2) theory of knowledge; (3) classification of the sciences; (4) theory of world views.

Dilthey calls for a *Critique of Historical Reason*; this is what his *Introduction to the Sciences of the Spirit* claims to be. He hopes to achieve for "the other half of the *globus intellectualis*" what Kant did for the knowledge of nature. This is Dilthey's grand idea: in opposition to the irrationalism reached in the nineteenth century by those who are aware of the failure of "pure reason" when they wish to conceive of life and history, Dilthey champions a new, broader form of reason which does not exclude the historical element. But strictly speaking, he tries only to *apply* reason to history; that is, reason itself. Therefore, he ends by considering the world views as being beyond history, and to that extent he cannot account, that is, *give a reason*, for them. The term *historical reason* in Dilthey does not—cannot—have the scope which we shall see it attain in the philosophy of Ortega.

THE MEANING OF DILTHEY'S PHILOSOPHY. We have seen that in Dilthey's thought two disciplines are indissolubly linked: psychology and history. On the one hand, there is the *analysis of what is human*, especially by means of autognosis: philosophy as a *science of the spirit*. On the other hand, this human reality is history, it is *human life*; this analysis is *philosophy of life* and therefore—to the extent to which this life is that of others and in the past—historical interpretation, *hermeneutics*. Its mode of knowledge is not causal explanation but understanding (*Verständnis*), and its theory constitutes a true critique of historical reason.

We now have several of the ingredients of present-day philosophy; but the group must still be completed. In the first place, there must be a new interpretation of *vital time*, supplied by Henri Bergson; in the second place, after European philosophy has once more re-entered its tradition of metaphysical and systematic thought, the renewal—due to Brentano—of the idea of *intentionality* will stimulate the ripening in Edmund Husserl's philosophy of a new method: *phenomenology*. We shall then have all the elements that constitute the philosophy which is being practiced today: in Germany, *existential philosophy*, especially that of Martin Heidegger; in Spain, Ortega's *metaphysics of vital reason*, which is, moreover, quite different in meaning and in its most profound tendencies; and the doctrines which are derived from one or the other or from both.

2. SIMMEL

LIFE AND WORKS. Georg Simmel, who was born in 1858 and died in 1918, was almost exactly contemporary with Bergson and Husserl. He was a professor at the universities of Strasbourg and Berlin and concerned himself especially with topics related to sociology and history. In spite of some essential faults, Simmel's *Soziologie* is one of the most penetrating attempts to give a firm basis to this discipline. Simmel— one of the most important figures in philosophy in the early years of this century—attempted in his writings to come as close as possible to a direct contact with objects and problems; this gives his works their principal source of attraction and, at the same time, their fruitfulness.

His most important writings are *Kant* (a series of lectures), *Schopen-*

hauer und Nietzsche, Philosophie des Geldes (Philosophy of Money), *Die Probleme der Geschichtsphilosophie* (The Problems of the Philosophy of History), *Grundprobleme der Philosophie* (Fundamental Problems of Philosophy) and *Lebensanschauung* (View of Life); then there are his important *Sociology* and a great many perspicacious essays on *Feminine Culture, Philosophy of Coquetry, Philosophy of Fashion*, and so on.

LIFE AS TRANSCENDENCE. The most profound aspect of Simmel's thought is his conception of life, particularly in the form in which it is expounded in the first chapter of his *Lebensanschauung*. Simmel says that man's position in the world is defined, because at every moment man finds that he is between two limits. Always, everywhere, we *have* limits, and therefore we also *are* limits. There is always a greater and a lesser, a closer to and farther than our *here* and *now* and *thus*; our life appears to be defined by two values which frequently conflict with one another: richness and determination.

But the interesting point is that, although the general limit is necessary to life, any specific, individual limit may be transcended and exceeded. Our actions are similar to those of the chess player; the chess player needs to know with a certain probability the consequences of a move, but the game would be impossible if this prescience were to be extended indefinitely. The limits to human life can be displaced; thus Simmel says paradoxically, "in all senses we are limited, and in no sense are we limited." Every vital action implies both a limitation and the overcoming of a limit. The spirit exceeds itself, transcends itself, and thus appears to be that which is absolutely alive. In this sense, it is possible to say that man is something that ought to be surpassed; man is a limited entity that does not have any limits.

TIME. Simmel begins with a reflection on time in order to achieve a conception of life. The *present* is an unextended *moment*; it is not *time* any more than a point is space. The present is nothing but the coming together of the past and the future, which are themselves, of course, temporal magnitudes, that is, time. However, the past no longer exists, and the future does not yet exist; reality occurs only in the present, and therefore reality is in no sense temporal. "Time does not exist in reality, and reality is not time." But in spite of everything, when life is *lived* subjectively, it is felt to be real in a *temporal* extension. English and Spanish usage do not understand by "present" a mere point, but rather a portion of the past together with a portion of the future, with limits that vary depending on whether we are speaking of the personal, political or historical present.

Life appears to refer to the *future*. This statement can be understood in a rather trivial sense: man always proposes a future end for himself;

however, this end is an immovable point and is separated from the present, and what is most characteristic of the present will's vital penetration (*Hineinleben*) into the future is that *life's present consists of its transcending the present*. There is no real threshold between the present and the future. The future is not a land that we have never trodden upon, separated from the present by a boundary; rather, we live in a frontier region that belongs to the future as much as to the present. "Life is really both past and future." Simmel adds, "Only for life is time real." "Time is the form of consciousness of that which constitutes life itself in its immediate concreteness, and which cannot be enunciated, but only lived; it is life stripped of its contents."

THE ESSENCE OF LIFE. Present life transcends that which is not its presentness, but in such a way that this transcending nevertheless constitutes its presentness. This is the *essence of life*. *Life* is our name for a mode of existence the reality of which is not restricted to the present moment, in which the past and the future are not relegated to irreality; rather, life's peculiar continuity is really maintained beyond this separation; that is, the past really exists by extending into the present, and the present really exists by expanding into the future.

Now then, life occurs only in *individuals*; and this creates a serious problem: life is at the same time unlimited continuity and an ego determined by its limits. Life's transcendence is immanent in it; life's primary phenomenon is that it can exceed itself; in Simmel's phrase, this constitutes "what is absolute in our relativity." Therefore, the principal antinomy is the one that exists between form and continuity; form is individuality, and *life is everywhere individual*.

Simmel relates his conception of life to Schopenhauer's doctrine of the will to live and Nietzsche's doctrine of the will to power; however, he observes that what is decisive is the agreement between the two moments. There are two definitions of life which reciprocally complement each other: life is *more life* and it is *more than life*. This word *more* is no accidental addition. Life is a motion which is always pulling things toward it, attracting things in order to change them into life. Life can exist only because it is *more life*. Death, which according to Simmel resides in life beforehand, is also an aspect of life's transcending itself. Procreation and death both transcend life; one upward and the other downward. Life requires form, and at the same time it requires something more than form.

But life, especially in its creative aspect, also transcends its own contents. It is not only *more life*; it is *more than life*. Life is only a subject's constant transcending of what is foreign to it or the production of what is foreign to it. This does not subjectivize this foreign being; rather, it retains its independence, its "being more than life"; the absoluteness of the *other*, of the *more*, is the formula and condition of life. Life's unity exists in the form of a *dualism*. Thus, in a final clever paradox Simmel can say that life finds its essence and its realization in being *more life* and *more than life*; that is, that life's *positive* element is as such *already* its *comparative* element.

These ideas from Simmel's maturity (his *Lebensanschauung* dates from the year of his death, 1918) signify a brilliant step on the road to the comprehension of the reality of human life.

3. BERGSON

LIFE AND WORKS. With Bergson we leave the nineteenth century and enter the twentieth. Bergson's roots and the first phase of his intellectual development are in the past century; but his life as well as the ultimate significance of his philosophy already belong to our epoch or, more properly speaking, are a typical moment of transition, like the rest of the philosophy of that time: one more step on the road to overcoming positivism in order to return once more to metaphysics.

Henri Bergson was born in Paris in 1859 and died early in January in 1941. He was a professor of philosophy in the Lycées of Angers and Clermont-Ferrand, in the university in the latter city, in the Collège Rollin and in the Lycée Henri IV of Paris; also in the École Normale Supérieure. After 1919, he was professor in the Collège de France, the highest French institution of learning. During his last years, old age forced him to withdraw from public life.

His most important works are his doctoral thesis, *Essai sur les données immédiates de la conscience, Matière et mémoire, Le rire, Durée et simultanéité, L'évolution créatrice*; two collections of essays and lectures: *L'énergie spirituelle* and *La pensée et le mouvant* (which contains his *Introduction à la métaphysique*), and his last book, *Les deux sources de la morale et de la religion*, in which his increasing *rapprochement* with Catholicism was first made public.

SPACE AND TIME. Space and time are usually thought to be comparable and parallel terms—Kant understood them as such. Bergson reacts energetically against this idea, and says that these terms are opposites. Space is an aggregate of points, from any one of which we can pass to any other; time, on the other hand, is irreversible, it has a *direction*, and every moment of time is unsubstitutable, irreplaceable, a true *creation* which cannot be repeated and to which we cannot return. But Bergson's time is not the time of the clock, *spatialized* time, which can be measured and which is represented by a length, but *living time* as it presents itself in its immediate reality to the consciousness: it is what is called *real duration, durée réelle*. Space and time are to each other as matter to memory, as the body to the soul; they correspond to two basically different and even, in a certain sense, opposite intellectual modes of man: thought and intuition.

INTELLECT AND INTUITION. Conceptual thought, which in a narrow sense is called intellect, is the method of scientific knowledge; it moves among the things and tends toward spatialization. In general, science seeks measurement; this process is accomplished either directly through the comparison of length (the meter and the road being measured) or by means of an attempt to reduce other magnitudes to length or to another form of space, for example, to an angle, which can in turn be reduced to length (the clock, the manometer, the dynamometer and the thermometer measure various magnitudes which are in themselves non-spatial by comparing them with the displacement of a needle or the expansion in length of a column of mercury). Thought, which is directed toward science—or toward practical life, the manipulation of *things*—proceeds by means of logic, observation and concepts. Thought tends to discover rigid concepts, which the intellect manages easily. It tends to *solidify everything*. What is more, thought searches for similarities, for things that various individuals have in common; thought generalizes. Intellect is the sphere of that which is inert, at rest, and therefore discontinuous; it is the sphere of matter.

These conditions are different from those required for the apprehension of living reality. Specifically, thought does not apprehend living time, *duration*, the time that I must wait for sugar to dissolve in a glass of water. *Real* motion, such as it is seen from within when I move my arm, is perceived by the intellect as a series of disconnected states of rest, which *are not* motion. Moving one's arm is a *single, continuous, living* motion. Thought schematizes it, fixes it in a concept, stops it; to be precise, it robs it of its fluidity. Only *intuition* is capable of apprehending *real duration*, motion in its true immediacy—in short, life. Intuition can capture mobility, it can comprehend the very process of motion and living time before these things become petrified into concepts. Intellect has application to matter and therefore to science, whereas intuition adapts itself to life. Bergson relates this faculty to *instinct*, that marvelous non-conceptual adaptation to vital problems which animals enjoy.

Bergson says that science and philosophy, which are conceived from a spatial point of view, have hardly known intuition; they have always operated with the categories of conceptual thought, *which is of no use in apprehending life and real time.* Therefore, man finds it very difficult to conceive of these realities; he lacks the appropriate instruments and, what is more, the habit of making use of them. Henri Bergson's philosophy approaches the reality of life with an attitude that differs from the usual one; his attitude is based on mobility itself, on processes that are not yet realized and completed, that are in the very act of being realized. Intuition tries to capture life from within; it does not first kill life, in order to reduce it to a spatialized, conceptual scheme.

"ÉLAN VITAL." The reality of life is dynamic; it is a vital impulse or *élan vital.* This impulse determines an evolution in time; and this evolution is creative, because reality is a living continuity. It is not composed of given elements, and only after reality has been consummated can thought try to compose it with immovable and given elements, as if one could recompose motion from a series of states of repose. This puts Bergson in contact with the philosophy of life, which finds in him one of its clearest and most fecund precursors. However, one must make it clear that Bergson understands life in a *biological* sense rather than in a *biographical* or *historical* sense, and that therefore he does not touch upon the most essential peculiarity of *human* life. Bergson's thought must be completed along these lines if it is to achieve full efficacy. On the other hand, it will also be necessary to overcome the *irrationalism* that menaces every form of intuition. Philosophy is strict knowledge and, therefore, concept and *reason.* Reason will have to conceive of this new object, life, in all its fluidity and mobility; it will be different from scientific and mathematical reason, but it must always be *reason.* Ortega has seen this fully and clearly, and therefore he is careful always to speak of *vital reason.*

4. BLONDEL

Maurice Blondel (1861–1949) is, after Bergson, the most original and interesting figure in contemporary French philosophy. A pupil of Ollé-Laprune, about whom he wrote a work, Blondel represents an aspect within Catholic thought that has been called "pragmatism"— in a very different sense from English and American pragmatism—or "activism" or, better yet, *philosophy of action.* His principal work is a book that is now already quite old, since it dates from 1893: his doctoral thesis entitled *L'Action. Essai d'une critique de la vie et d'une science de la pratique.* After many years during which his activity as a writer was restricted to collaborations in philosophical journals, Blondel published not very long ago three extremely long works: *La pensée, L'Être et les êtres* and a complete revision, in two volumes, of his old thesis *L'Action*, as well as several studies on apologetics and on the Christian spirit in its relationships with philosophy.

Blondel's point of departure is the question whether human life has meaning and man has a destiny. I act without knowing what action is, without having wished to live, without knowing who I am or if I am. And according to what we are told, I am not able at any cost to conquer *nothingness*; rather, I am condemned to life, death and eternity without having known or wished for this. Now then, this problem, which is inevitable, is inevitably solved by man, for good or ill, through his *actions*. Action is man's true, effective answer to the problem of life; therefore, action is necessarily man's first concern.

Action is the most general and most constant fact of my life: Blondel says that action is more than a fact—it is a necessity, since even suicide is an act. We can perform an action only by closing off all other ways and depriving ourselves of everything we could have otherwise known or obtained. Every decision cuts off an infinite number of possible actions. And we cannot desist and suspend action, nor can we delay. If we do not act, something acts in us or outside us, and almost always against us. Blondel says that peace is defeat; action does not tolerate any postponement other than death. Therefore I cannot be guided by my ideas, because complete analysis is not possible to a finite intelligence, and practical life does not tolerate delays: I cannot defer action until I obtain evidence, and all evidence is partial. Furthermore, my decisions usually go beyond my thoughts, and my actions usually go beyond my intentions.

Therefore, we must construct a science of action; it must be integral because every form of thinking and living deliberately implies a complete solution to the problem of existence. Blondel, who of course refers to the religious problem, is opposed to intellectualism and fideism, not in the name of feeling, but in that of action. His criticism of Scholasticism derives from this. Entities are, above all, what they *do*. Philosophy must "prevent thought from idolizing itself, show the insufficiency and natural subordination of speculation, illumine the exigencies and paths of action, prepare and justify the ways of faith." We cannot discuss here the details of this philosophy, the profound and difficult aspects of Blondel's thought; it is sufficient to indicate the viewpoint from which Blondel considers the problem of life.

5. UNAMUNO

LIFE AND WORKS. Miguel de Unamuno, who was born in Bilbao in 1864 and died in Salamanca in 1936, is one of the most important

Spanish thinkers. He cannot be considered a philosopher in the strict sense, and yet he is of extreme interest in the history of philosophy. His work and very personality constitute a philosophic problem in themselves. He wrote copiously in many different genres: poetry, novels and stories, plays, ideological essays. From the viewpoint of philosophy, his most important works are his seven volumes of *Ensayos* (Essays); *La vida de Don Quijote y Sancho* (The Life of Don Quixote and Sancho); *Del sentimiento trágico de la vida* (The Tragic Sense of Life), his most noteworthy book; *La agonía del cristianismo* (The Agony of Christianity); and especially some of his novels and stories: *Paz en la guerra, Niebla, Abel Sánchez, La tía Tula, San Manuel Bueno, mártir* and his poetical narrative *Teresa*.

HIS PROBLEM. Unamuno, who had a keen sense of the problems of philosophy, concentrated his whole intellectual and literary activity on what he called "the one and only question": the personal *immortality* of the individual man, who lives and dies and does not wish to die completely. At a moment of history when the generally accepted sciences did not even touch upon this question, Unamuno, in exasperation, made it the center of his whole life. His religious faith, weak and riddled with doubts ("in the throes of death," to use his expression) did not satisfy him. He thus felt obliged to pose the problem of immortality, which, of course, leads to the problem of *death* and naturally refers back to the problems of *life* and the *person*. But instead of writing philosophical studies, as might have been expected, Unamuno composed essays with little scientific content, poems and especially stories. What is the reason for this unusual literary production?

HIS METHOD. For historical reasons, because he belonged to a particular generation, Unamuno was imbued with the *irrationalism* which I have already mentioned repeatedly. Like Kierkegaard, like William James, like Bergson, he believed that reason does not help us to know life; that when trying to apprehend life in fixed and rigid concepts, reason robs it of its fluidity within time and kills it. Of course, these thinkers were speaking of pure reason, the reason of physics and mathematics. This conviction caused Unamuno to look away from reason and turn toward the *imagination*, which he called "the most substantial faculty." Since it was no longer possible to grasp the reality of life by means of reason, he tried to do it with the imagination, *living* life and *anticipating* the experience of death in *narratives*. Realizing that human life is a happening within time, something told or narrated—in short, history—Unamuno used the story—an original form of story which might be called existential or, better yet, *personal*—

as his method of knowledge. This kind of story constitutes a very fruitful attempt to apprehend human reality directly; it is, to be sure, an inadequate attempt, but one that could serve as the basis for a precise metaphysics, which is not to be found in Unamuno.

Despite his diffuseness and his failure to achieve philosophical fullness, Unamuno was a brilliant prophet who anticipated many important discoveries concerning that reality which is human life; and his findings, incomplete as they are, frequently go beyond all philosophical investigations up to the present. Unamuno is a true precursor of the metaphysics of existence or life, a precursor with a personality of his own. This justifies his inclusion in the history of philosophy, an inclusion which was determined in the final analysis by the fruitfulness of his prophecies, which cannot be studied in detail here. *

* See my book *Miguel de Unamuno* (1943) for a complete study of the philosophical problem posed by Unamuno and his contribution to contemporary philosophy (English translation, Harvard University Press, in press). See also *La Escuela de Madrid* [*Obras*, V].

English-Language Philosophy

As in almost every era, English philosophy presents in our day characteristics that are relatively different from those of Continental philosophy; nevertheless, this does not preclude parallel developments and a long series of reciprocal influences. Moreover, in the last years of the nineteenth century a new factor enters the scene: the United States. Closely related to the British tradition but strongly influenced by the Germans and, to a lesser extent, by the French, the philosophical speculation which begins in America is conditioned by the distinctive social structure of the country and its different perspective on the problems of philosophy. In our century, American thought has in turn influenced British thought; many thinkers of both nations have been active, have taught and have lived on both sides of the Atlantic; thus, a form of English-language philosophy has been created which has various nuances but which presents a common configuration. In the last few decades, this philosophy has begun to influence that of the European Continent, and it is therefore necessary to take into account, if only very concisely, its general meaning and its major phases, since it has become today a decisive component of Western philosophy.

1. Pragmatism

The first important and original sprouting of American thought was pragmatism. Previously the "transcendentalists"—among them Ralph Waldo Emerson (1803–1882) and Henry David Thoreau (1817–1862)—had initiated a reaction against materialism and the prevalence of positivist thinking; this was in New England, in the area of Boston and Cambridge, the site of Harvard University and the first center of intellectual life in America. But America reaches its first philosophical maturity only with the pragmatists. The term "pragmatism" is especially linked with the name of William James; he was the first to use this designation in writing, in 1898; but he had adopted the term from Peirce, who originated the doctrine and had already expounded it twenty years earlier. There has been a great deal of discussion on the relationship between Peirce and James. Forgotten for many years, Peirce has recently aroused lively interest; he has been esteemed much more highly than James, who had enjoyed enormous prestige and was then subjected to severe criticism. There has been discussion of the connection between the two interpretations of pragmatism; it has even been said that "the philosophical movement known as pragmatism is in large part the result of James's having misunderstood Peirce." This is, without doubt, an exaggeration which is due to the belated "discovery" of Peirce and the reaction against the exclusive linking of pragmatism with James and his immediate followers. This is not the place to review the numerous ramifications of the problem; it will be sufficient to indicate the original form in which the doctrine appears in the work of both men and in the subsequent tradition.

PEIRCE. Charles Sanders Peirce (1839–1914), a contemporary of Dilthey, Brentano and Nietzsche, was born in Cambridge, Massachusetts; he taught sporadically at Harvard and Johns Hopkins for several years, and published very little—only articles and reviews of philosophical books, which since his death have been collected into volumes: in 1923 there appeared the volume *Chance, Love and Logic*, edited by Morris R. Cohen; from 1931 on, the eight volumes of *The Collected Papers of Charles Sanders Peirce*, edited by Charles Hartshorne, Paul Weiss and Arthur W. Burks; and finally, another anthology volume, *The Philosophy of Peirce* (or, *The Philosophical Writings of Peirce*), edited by Justus Buchler. One of the most influential of Peirce's writings was the article "How to Make Our Ideas Clear," published in January, 1878; it is the original and basic text of pragmatism. Peirce was able to complete only one book, *The Grand Logic*, which was published as a posthumous work among his collected papers.

Peirce's first readings in philosophy were Friedrich Schiller's *Letters on the Esthetic Education of Man*, Richard Whately's *Logic*, and the *Critique of Pure Reason*, which he learned almost by heart; he also underwent the influence of Scotus and of his own education in mathematics. Peirce's attitude is primarily theoretic: for him philosophy belongs as a "subclass" under the science of discovery, which in turn is a branch of theoretic science. The function of philosophy is to explain and show the unity in the diversity of the universe; philosophy has a twofold point of departure: logic, the relation of signs with their objects, and phenomenology, the raw experience of the objective real world. These two disciplines converge in three basic metaphysical categories which are interrelated in a very complex fashion; these may be called quality, relation and mediation. Peirce's thought, which is quite fragmentary and not very systematic, touched upon numerous problems of the theory of knowledge, logic and metaphysics; but, above all, he proposed to establish a *method*, and that is precisely what pragmatism is.

It is "a method of ascertaining the meaning of hard words and of abstract concepts," or else "a method of ascertaining the meanings . . . of . . . intellectual concepts, that is to say, of those upon the structure of which, arguments concerning objective fact may hinge." More specifically, Peirce proposed to clarify the traditional metaphysical questions and, where possible, to eliminate them as meaningless. This shows that Peirce's pragmatism is, above all, a logical discipline, as opposed to the traditional view of pragmatism derived from a partial and inexact interpretation of the form which it acquired in the work of James. But it should be noted that the "logical" side is not foreign to James, nor the "practical" side to Peirce. For the latter, the function of thought is to produce habits of action; by this path he arrives, laboriously and in frequently obscure and infelicitous formulations, at the idea of pragmatism.

The first expression of pragmatism (in "How to Make Our Ideas Clear") is this: "Consider what effects, that might conceivably have practical bearings, we conceive the object of our conception to have. Then, our conception of these effects is the whole of our conception of the object." A second formula, somewhat lighter and clearer, runs: "In order to ascertain the meaning of an intellectual conception one should consider what practical consequences might conceivably result by necessity from the truth of that conception; and the sum of these consequences will constitute the entire meaning of the conception." Lastly, a third thesis gives greater precision to the meaning of pragmatism in Peirce: "Pragmatism is the principle that every theoretical judgment expressible in a sentence in the indicative mood is a confused form of thought whose only meaning, if it has any, lies in its tendency to enforce a corresponding practical maxim expressible as a conditional sentence having its apodosis in the imperative mood."

In the face of the increasing use of the term "pragmatism" in a sense different from that which he wished to give it, Peirce renounced the use of it and coined the name "pragmaticism" for his own philosophy; this name he judged "ugly enough to be safe from kidnappers." Peirce's work, still not published in its entirety and only partially known and studied, appears today to be very fruitful and valuable.

JAMES. William James (1842–1910), who was of the same generation as Peirce, was born in New York. A professor at Harvard from 1872 on, a physician, a psychologist and a philosopher, he is the most outstanding figure in American philosophy. James, who was an extremely vivid and stimulating writer and lecturer, full of ideas, contributed more than anyone else to the acclimatization of philosophical thought in the United States. His first orientation was toward psychology, a discipline in which he was one of the most fruitful classic researchers; his two books on psychology are both masterpieces, unsurpassed in certain respects; many parts of them are still valid and fertile. His attention was then centered on moral and religious themes and, finally, on metaphysics. His major works are *The Principles of Psychology*, in two volumes, and a more concise and compact treatise, *A Textbook of Psychology*; *The Will to Believe*; *The Varieties of Religious Experience*; *Pragmatism: A New Name for Some Old Ways of Thinking*; *A Pluralistic Universe*; *The Meaning of Truth*; *Some Problems of Philosophy*; and *Essays in Radical Empiricism*.

James's philosophy is one of the attempts undertaken at the close of the nineteenth century to conceive of and understand human life. His psychology represents a penetrating comprehension of the reality of psychical life in its dynamic aspect: the image of the *stream of consciousness* is a revealing one. But this interest in life assumes the form—habitual in his day—of anti-intellectualism and, further, of irrationalism; from Kierkegaard through Oswald Spengler and Unamuno, and including Nietzsche and Bergson, this was the risk run by all analogous movements. With this attitude James takes up the theme of pragmatism. As he understands it, there can *be* no difference that *makes* no difference; we might say that no difference can be indifferent. "The whole function of philosophy," he says, "ought to be to find out what definite difference it will make to you and me, at definite instants of our life, if this world-formula or that world-formula be the true one." This pragmatism, in James's opinion, is not new: its antecedents are found in Socrates and Aristotle, Locke and Berkeley; it is the empirical attitude, but in a more basic and less objectionable form; it means the abandonment of abstraction and insufficiency, of verbal solutions, bad a priori reasoning, rigid principles, closed systems and presumptive absolutes and origins, and a return to concreteness and adequacy, facts, action and power. In contrast to the conception of metaphysics as an enigma that is solved by means of a word or a principle, James asks for the *cash value* of every word; this is not so much a solution as a program for further work and especially an indication of how existing realities may be *changed*. "Theories thus become instruments, not answers to enigmas, in which we can rest." Pragmatism thus understood has no dogmas or doctrines; it is a method that is compatible with various doctrines; it is "the attitude of looking away from first things, principles, 'categories,' supposed necessities; and of looking towards last things, fruits, consequences, facts."

This leads to an idea of truth. James renounces the idea of a harmony between thought and the things, since one could make a judgment about this only by means of thought and the things are accessible only within thought. Ideas, which are part of our experience, are true to the extent that they help us to enter into satisfactory relationships with other parts of our experience. Truth is what "works," what "turns out all right," what "it would be better to believe," in other words, what "*we ought to believe.*" The formulations of this conception of truth are relatively vague and uncertain in James and his followers; the fruitful seed enclosed in this idea is obscured by the irrationalism that threatens it, by the tendency of these philosophers toward a narrow utilitarian interpretation of this "turning out all right" or being successful, a tendency which cuts off an entire decisive group of *vital* acts, such as those of strict intellection; therefore, pragmatism signifies a degradation of the idea of truth, even from its own point of view—that is, from what its point of view would be if one were to take it perfectly seriously.

THE CONTINUERS OF PRAGMATISM. The most important later pragmatists are John Dewey, Ferdinand Canning Scott Schiller and Ralph Barton Perry (1876–1957). John Dewey (1859–1952), who was born in the same year as Husserl and Bergson, was for many years a professor in Columbia University; throughout his long lifetime he was one of the most influential men in the intellectual life of the United States, particularly in the field of education. His most important books are *How We Think, Democracy and Education, Essays in Experimental Logic, Reconstruction in Philosophy, Experience and Nature, A Common Faith, Logic: The Theory of Inquiry, Problems of Man.* Dewey used the word *instrumentalism* to designate his personal version of pragmatism.

F. C. S. Schiller (1864–1937) was born in Altona (near Hamburg),

Germany. He was a professor in Cornell and Oxford and later in California. His principal books are *Humanism* and *Studies in Humanism*. Schiller is also associated with James's philosophy; he considered his own thought, *humanism*, to be a wider form of pragmatism, one that encompassed all philosophical disciplines. Like the earlier pragmatists, Schiller maintained that truth depends on practical consequences; since all intellectual life has as an ultimate goal the individual human entity, all knowledge is subordinate to human nature and its fundamental necessities. Humanism, Schiller says, "is merely the perception that the philosophical problem concerns human beings striving to comprehend a world of human experience by the resources of human minds." Schiller believes that we actually transform the realities by means of our cognitive efforts and that our desires and ideas are therefore real forces in the configuration of the world.

2. Personalism

A second dominant trend in the Anglo-Saxon thought of our time is the movement known as *personalism*. One must note that this term is used in a narrow sense to designate a coherent group or school, particularly in the United States, and in a wider sense to designate many different groups which are united by a common tendency and a spiritual affinity; I use the term here in the wider sense. Personalism's most general feature is its insistence on the reality and value of the person and its attempt to interpret reality from this point of view. Closely related to pragmatism with respect to the problem of logic, opposed to mechanism and *behaviorism* with respect to psychology, and also hostile to a naturalistic interpretation of reality, personalism affirms human freedom and the personal basis of reality, that is, the existence of a personal God. A few idealist thinkers, such as Josiah Royce (1855–1916), are closely related to personalism. Royce, who was born in California and taught in Harvard, wrote *The Spirit of Modern Philosophy*, *Studies in Good and Evil*, *The World and the Individual*, *The Conception of Immortality*, *The Philosophy of Loyalty*. His work has been influential in Europe, partly through the interest of Gabriel Marcel, who wrote a book about him. F. C. S. Schiller's humanism is also closely related to personalism.

The classic form of American personalism is represented by a group of thinkers centered in New England: Borden Parker Bowne (1847–1910), a professor in Boston University (*Metaphysics*, *Philosophy of Theism*, *Theory of Thought and Knowledge*, *Personalism*); Mary Whiton

Calkins (1863–1930) of Wellesley College (*An Introduction to Psychology, The Persistent Problems of Philosophy, The Good Man and the Good*); Edgar Sheffield Brightman (1884–1952), Bowne's successor in Boston University (*The Problem of God, A Philosophy of Religion, An Introduction to Philosophy*). William Ernest Hocking (*b.* 1873) of Harvard is also connected with this group; his principal work is *The Meaning of God in Human Experience*.

3. RECENT TRENDS

SANTAYANA. Jorge Ruiz de Santayana—George Santayana, as he signed his work—was born in Madrid in 1863, grew up in Ávila, was educated in Boston, taught in Harvard, and died in Rome in 1952. Santayana wrote brilliantly in English and was a novelist and essayist; he was not particularly systematic, and has at times been called a realist or naturalist—rather vague denominations—and also a materialist. He left a copious and varied body of work, partly autobiographical, that perhaps culminates in his idea of *animal faith* as a method of approaching reality. His most important books are *The Sense of Beauty; The Life of Reason* (five volumes); *Scepticism and Animal Faith; The Realms of Being* (comprised of four parts: *The Realm of Essence, The Realm of Matter, The Realm of Truth, The Realm of Spirit*); his autobiography consisting of *Persons and Places, The Middle Span*, and *My Host the World*; the novel *The Last Puritan*; and finally, *Dominations and Powers*.

ALEXANDER. Samuel Alexander (1859–1938) was born in Sydney, Australia. He was a professor in Oxford and Manchester, and his thought, which has also been interpreted both as naturalism and as realism, represents one of the grandest metaphysical constructions in contemporary English philosophy. His major work is *Space, Time and Deity*.

WHITEHEAD. Alfred North Whitehead (1861–1947), the most important of the contemporary English philosophers, taught in England (principally mathematics) and after 1924 in the United States (Harvard and Wellesley), where he specialized in philosophy. His mathematical and logical work is of enormous importance, especially his *Principia Mathematica* (written in collaboration with Bertrand Russell). His deep interest in problems of education is evident in a series of works that spans most of his life (*The Aims of Education*); the problem of thought and its forms is another principal theme in his work (*The Function of Reason, Adventures of Ideas, Modes of Thought*); his major work is a book of metaphysics presented as "an essay in cosmology," *Process and Reality* (1929). Whitehead's influence is dominant today, perhaps even more so in the United States than in England.

RUSSELL. Bertrand Russell (*b.* 1872), who has taught in Cambridge, was associated with Whitehead on the great work *Principia Mathematica* and, like Whitehead, is the author of some extremely important contributions to the theory of mathematics and symbolic logic: *The Principles of Mathematics, Introduction to Mathematical Philosophy, An Inquiry into Meaning and Truth.* He is also the author of a book on Leibniz, *Critical Exposition of the Philosophy of Leibnitz*; of *A History of Western Philosophy*; of two books entitled *The Analysis of Mind* and *The Analysis of Matter*; of a general treatise, *An Outline of Philosophy*; of a book on the theory of knowledge, *Human Knowledge*, and of numerous essays and books on education, sociology and politics. He has received the Nobel Prize in Literature (as did Rudolf Christoph Eucken and Henri Bergson before him).

MORE RECENT MOVEMENTS. In England and the United States, these are the decisive thinkers; however, they do not represent the only trends, and the influence of Continental European philosophy is steadily increasing, particularly in America. The Englishman Robin George Collingwood (1889–1943) already belonged to a cosmopolitan Western tradition that was particularly influenced by Italian idealism; this is evident in his two posthumous books *The Idea of Nature* and *The Idea of History*. The same is true to a lesser degree of George Edward Moore (1873–1958), author of *Principia Ethica, Ethics*, and *Philosophical Studies*, who devoted a considerable part of his work to the analysis of which we will speak later; and of Charlie Dunbar Broad (*b.* 1887), who wrote *The Mind and Its Place in Nature, Five Types of Ethical Theory, Ethics and the History of Philosophy.* Both Moore and Broad were professors in Cambridge.

An energetic presentation of European thought is also found in such American thinkers as George Boas (*b.* 1891) and especially Arthur O. Lovejoy (1873–1962), whose most important book is *The Great Chain of Being: A Study in the History of an Idea*, as well as Charles W. Hendel, who studied Rousseau and the English philosophers, and Brand Blanshard (*The Nature of Thought*, and so on), both of Yale, and Philip E. Wheelwright (*The Burning Fountain, Heraclitus, Metaphor and Reality*).

However, the trend which has the most followers in England today is the one which we can call, rather imprecisely, "linguistic analysis," in which almost all present-day British thinkers participate, although to very different extents. The origins of this movement are partly English and partly European, deriving especially from the Vienna

Circle (Moritz Schlick, Hans Reichenbach, Otto Neurath and Rudolf Carnap, who for many years was a professor in the United States). The principal influence was undoubtedly Ludwig Wittgenstein (1889–1951), an Austrian by birth, but for many years a professor in Cambridge. His famous *Tractatus logico-philosophicus* was first published in 1921, and the following year it was republished in the original German, together with an English translation and an introduction by Bertrand Russell. Later, Wittgenstein changed his viewpoints considerably in various articles which were collected after his death in *Philosophische Untersuchungen* (Philosophical Investigations) and other volumes. Among the most interesting contemporary British philosophers are Gilbert Ryle (*The Concept of Mind*), John O. Wisdom (*Other Minds, Philosophy and Psychoanalysis*), C. K. Odgen and I. A. Richards (*The Meaning of Meaning*), John L. Austin (1911–1960; *Sense and Sensibilia, Philosophical Papers*) and Alfred Jules Ayer (*Language, Truth and Logic; The Problem of Knowledge*).

In spite of their great differences, these philosophical groups have some features in common. In Austria as well as in England and the United States, the Vienna Circle cultivated symbolic or mathematical logic, in the same manner as did the Polish logicians of the so-called Warsaw Circle; this trend, a field that is limited but of considerable interest, is perhaps the most valuable one. The work of Łukasiewicz, Alfred Tarski, Carnap, Kurt Gödel and Wittgenstein himself is linked with that of the American logicians Clarence Irving Lewis (*Mind and the World Order*), Alonzo Church, Susanne K. Langer (the author of the interesting book *Philosophy in a New Key*), Willard v. O. Quine (*Mathematical Logic, Methods of Logic, From a Logical Point of View*), Charles W. Morris (*Signs, Language and Behavior*), and so forth. However, aside from this, and by ignoring subtle differences, the positions which these groups take can be summarily characterized in the following way: their general tendency is anti-metaphysical—some consider metaphysics impossible, others think that it is meaningless, that its statements are tautologies or purely "emotive" or without verifiable meaning; they are "empiricists" in a new sense of the word—these movements are sometimes called "logical empiricism" or "logical positivism" or "neopositivism," and sometimes "scientificalism" or "physicalism," and they tend toward the mathematization of thought. In England there has been a dominant belief that the majority of philosophical problems, including philosophical statements, are meaningless and due merely to imperfections of language, which makes it obligatory to undertake a clarification of the questions by means of "linguistic analysis." Naturally, philosophy has undertaken such clarification at all times, but present-day English thought, particularly in Oxford, claims that philosophy *is confined to* such clarification. Many of these thinkers believe that *any* scientific statement can *always* be reduced to a physical statement, that is, one that says that such-and-such an event happened in such-and-such a place at such-and-such a time; in other words, to a pure statement of *fact*. This attitude leads to *behaviorism* or the description of conduct, and in sociology to a social behaviorism.

These positions rest on a rather arbitrary idea of metaphysics that is identified with certain very special forms of it or, rather, with the conception of it that these thinkers invent; on the other hand, many of their affirmations are anything but empirical, and cannot be justified on the basis of their own suppositions. In general, the analysis of "statements" ignores the factor that makes them *philosophical* statements, and this type of thought tends to raise objections rather than practice philosophy. Apart from this, many of these efforts are interesting contributions to the clarification of certain questions.

The increase in relations between Europe and the United States in the last twenty years has been enormous, and is steadily being accelerated. Phenomenology; Heidegger's work; secondarily, that of the existentialists; Ortega's work through numerous translations; the presence of Étienne Gilson and Jacques Maritain—all these contribute to re-establishing the complexity of philosophy in the United States and overcoming the onesidedness of the English influence that held sway for several decades. On the other hand, American thought is becoming more and more well known in Europe. It is to be hoped that the communication between the two sections of Western philosophy, which was broken at the time of the Renaissance and which since then has been evident only in a few discontinuous instances, will be increased. Only in this way can we gain full possession of the Western philosophical tradition.

Husserl's Phenomenology

HUSSERL AND HIS SCHOOL. Edmund Husserl was born in 1859—in the same year as Bergson—and died in 1938. He is Brentano's most important and original pupil. Husserl was a professor in Göttingen and later in Freiburg. He devoted himself to the study of mathematics and, rather late in life, to philosophy. In 1900 he published the first edition of his *Logische Untersuchungen* (Logical Investigations), which renewed and transformed philosophy; in 1913 there appeared the first volume—the only one published during his lifetime—of his *Ideen zu einer reinen Phänomenologie und phänomenologischen Philosophie*) (Ideas for a Pure Phenomenology and Phenomenological Philosophy). His principal works also include *Philosophie als strenge Wissenschaft* (Philosophy as Strict Knowledge, 1911), *Formale und transzendentale Logik* (Formal and Transcendental Logic, 1929) and *Méditations cartésiennes* (1931). His pupil Heidegger published the *Vorlesungen zur Phänomenologie des inneren Zeitbewusstseins* (Lectures for the Phenomenology of the Internal Consciousness of Time). After his death, several essays and the book entitled *Erfahrung und Urteil* (Experience and Judgment, 1939) were published. Much of Husserl's work is still unpublished or in the process of being published, and this precludes an exposition of his last doctrines, particularly with respect to the genealogy of logic. The Husserl Archives in the University of Louvain contain almost 45,000 pages—mostly in shorthand—of unpublished materials. The following works have recently been published: the original text of the *Cartesianische Meditationen; Die Idee der Phänomenologie* of 1907; a new enlarged edition of the first book of the *Ideen* and the second and third books of that work; the important book *Die Krisis der europäischen Wissenschaften und die transzendentale Phänomenologie* (The Crisis of the European Sciences and Transcendental Phenomenology); two volumes of the *Erste Philosophie* (First Philosophy), and most recently, volume IX of the Husserliana series: *Phänomenologische Psychologie* (Phenomenological Psychology).

Husserl derives essentially from Brentano; therefore, his philosophical tradition is the same as Brentano's: Catholic, Scholastic—in short, Greek. We must also note the influence of Bolzano, of the English philosophers—Hume in particular—and most markedly, of Leibniz; and also, of course, the influence of Kantianism. Husserl is also related to Brentano's other pupils, especially to Anton Marty and Alexius Meinong. The phenomenological school, famous for its high standards of scholarship, precision and fecundity, has arisen around the figure of Husserl; its journal, the *Jahrbuch für Philosophie und phänomenologische Forschung* (Yearbook for Philosophy and Phenomenological Investigation), was first published in 1913. The phenomenologists include the most important philosophers of Germany, notably Max Scheler and Heidegger, who represent an original position within phenomenology.

1. IDEAL OBJECTS

PSYCHOLOGISM. Phenomenology makes its appearance just as the twentieth century commences. As we have said, Husserl's *Logical Investigations* was published in 1900; in this work Husserl says he is dealing with "descriptive psychology"; the term *phenomenology* does not yet appear. This book represents a decisive step in the restoration of authentic philosophy.

In order to understand phenomenology, one must locate oneself in the historical framework in which it appears. In 1900 there was no *ruling* philosophy. The idealist tradition had been lost ever since the years in which positivism held sway; philosophical anarchy prevailed. There were only certain trends that opposed metaphysics, which they considered something to be shunned; English-style associationist psychology was dominant. This psychology had infiltrated the philosophical doctrines, contaminating them with *psychologism*. Psychologism is the attitude by which a philosophical discipline is reduced to psychology. For example, the psychologists understand logic to be a *normative* discipline of the psychical acts of thinking. Logic would thus consists of rules on how to think well.

Husserl opposes this psychologism and devotes the first volume of his *Investigations* to combating and overcoming it. If he had not broken with psychologism, he would not have been able to create a philosophy. A minutely detailed controversy was necessary, the fine points of which need not concern us, since psychologism is no longer a problem. Here as well as elsewhere, Husserl's method consists of making descriptions. Husserl agrees that logic deals with ideas, concepts, judgments, and the like, but he does not agree that it is concerned with things of a psychological nature; rather, he says that logic always deals with *ideal* objects. Husserl takes a single case and observes its meaning: for example, the principle of contradiction. According to the psychologists, this principle meant that man could not *conceive* that A is A and not-A. Husserl rejects this view and says that the meaning of the principle is that if A *is* A, it *cannot be* not-A. The principle of contradiction does not refer to the possibility of man's conceiving something, but to the truth of the concept, to the behavior of objects. The principle of contradiction, and likewise all the other principles of logic, have objective validity.

On one hand, psychologism can be skepticism; on the other hand, it tends toward relativism. Skepticism denies that truth can be known; relativism allows that anything can be true, but that truth is *relative*: there is a relativism of individuals and a relativism of the species; truth—the validity of the principles—would be limited to the human species, which cannot conceive that A is A and not-A. Husserl refutes relativism, not only the relativism of individuals, but also that of the species; he says that if the angels understand *A, being* and *truth* to mean the same things we understand them to mean, they must say that A cannot be A and not-A at the same time. It is a question of an a priori and absolute validity that is independent of the psychological conditions of thought. Therefore Husserl calls for, in contraposition to psychologistic logic, a *pure logic of ideal objects*, that is, of the principles of logic, of the pure logical laws and meanings.

PHENOMENOLOGY. Phenomenology is a science of ideal objects. It is therefore an a priori science; furthermore, it is a *universal* science, because it is a science of the *essences* of *experiences*. An experience (*Erlebnis*) is any psychical act; if phenomenology involves the study of all experiences, it must also involve the study of the objects of the experiences, because the experiences are *intentional*, and reference to an object is essential to them. Therefore, phenomenology, which comprises the study of experiences and their intentional objects, is a priori and universal.

IDEAL BEING. Ideal objects are distinguished from real objects by an essential characteristic. Ideal being is *non-temporal*, whereas real being is subject to time, is *hic et nunc*, here and now. The desk as which I am writing is here in the room and, above all, at this moment; but the number three, the circle and the principle of contradiction have a validity apart from time. Therefore, ideal objects are *species*; they do not have the principle of individuation which is the here and now. In Greek, *idea* is that which is *seen*; this is also true of *species* in Latin. Ideal objects are thus species or, using another term, *essences*.

PROBLEMS OF IDEAL BEING. For Husserl, ideal objects are eternal, or rather non-temporal. But it might be asked where they are located. Husserl finds this question meaningless. There are three possible *hypostases*, all of which he rejects:

(1) The *psychological* hypostasis, which would consist in locating ideal objects in the mind; their existence would be mental, they would exist *in my thought*.

(2) The *metaphysical* hypostasis—which is that of Platonism, for example—in which the ideas are entities located in an immaterial place.

(3) The Augustinian or *theological* hypostasis, in which the ideas are located in the mind of God, who is eternally thinking them.

Husserl, sharing the fear of metaphysics which was the inheritance of his era, avoids all semblance of it and says that ideal objects merely have *validity*. This point provoked a controversy over truth between Husserl and Heidegger. Husserl's opinion was that Newton's formula, for example, would be true even if no one had conceived it. Heidegger said that this is meaningless, that the truth of the formula would not exist if there had been no existence to conceive it. If there had been no mind—either human or non-human—to conceive it, there would be heavenly bodies, there would be motion, if you wish, but there would be no *truth* of Newton's formula, nor any other truth. Truth needs someone to conceive it, to discover it (*alétheia*), whether man, angel or God.

2. MEANINGS

WORD, MEANING AND OBJECT. We have seen that phenomenology deals with *meanings*. Let us see how this is to be understood.

Let us think of a word, *table*, for example. We have a number of things here. First of all, a physical, acoustical phenomenon, the *sound* of the word; but this alone is not a word. A physical phenomenon may be a sign: for example, a red cloth is a sign of danger. But this does not suffice, either; to be a sign does not exhaust the being of a word, because expressions may have two functions, one *communicative*, which would encompass the sign-function, and another which is the "solitary life of the soul." I do not make signs to myself in order to understand what I am thinking.

That which makes a word be a word is *meaning* (as early as Aristotle a word was defined as a *phonè semantiké*). What is meaning? Is it located within the word? Obviously not. Different words may have a single meaning (words in different languages, for example). It would then seem that meaning is the *object*; but this is not so, because at times the object *does not exist*, and cannot be the meaning—for example, when I say "a squared circle."

Meanings are *ideal objects*. It is meaning that refers to the object; it intervenes between the word and the object. Meanings consist of references to intentional objects, not necessarily real objects or necessarily ideal, but objects which may be non-existent—for example, if I speak of "a regular pentahedron." This object does not exist; it is neither real nor ideal, but *impossible*, and yet the expression has a meaning which refers to an intentional object. Now, whether the object exists or not is another question which is not of interest here.

INTENTION AND IMPLETION. If I hear or read an expression, I understand it; but there are two very different ways of understanding. One is simple *understanding* of the expression; the other is an intuitive *representation* of meanings. Husserl calls the mere understanding of a meaning *symbolic thought* or *significative intention*. The intuitive representation of meanings he calls *intuitive thought* or *significative impletion* (or "*filling*"). In the first case there is a *mention*, a mere allusion; in the second, an *intuition:* this is an intuition of essences. Phenomenology, which is a descriptive science, describes *essences*, never objects.

Therefore, in order to express anything, a meaning is needed; a meaning is superimposed upon the phenomenon of the expression, and when this meaning is *filled* with content by means of intuition, we have the apprehension of the essence.

3. THE ANALYTIC AND THE SYNTHETIC

WHOLE AND PART. Husserl's third investigation is a study of the whole and its parts; this study is extremely important for the comprehension of phenomenology. The word *whole* suggests something composed of parts. Conversely, *part* suggests a component of a whole.

Husserl distinguishes between *independent* parts (which may exist by themselves, like the leg of a table) and *non-independent* parts (which cannot exist in isolation, like the color or the extension of the table).

Husserl calls the independent parts *pieces* and the non-independent parts *moments*: extension, color, form, and so on.

Within *moments*, two types may be distinguished: (1) color, for example, which is located *in* the table; and (2) the similarity between this table and another one, a similarity which is not located *in* the table. Color is a *trait* of a thing, similarity is a *relationship*.

IMPLICATION AND "CO-PLICATION." Here we run into the problem of what it is that unites the parts. Corporeality does not occur alone, but occurs together with color, extension, and the like. Husserl speaks of two basic types of unions:

(1) We say: all bodies are extended. Corporeality and extension go together. Body *implies* extension; to imply something means to include it; the thing implied is a trait of that which implies it. Among the traits of *body* is that of being *extended*; being a diamond implies being a stone. This is what Kant calls an *analytic judgment*, and is today generally called *implication*.

(2) Ortega gave the name of "co-plication" (*complicación*) to that relationship by which one part is *united* to another but is not contained within it. Color, for example, "*co-plicates*" extension; an unextended color cannot exist. Husserl calls this same relationship "*founding*" (*Fundierung*). Founding may be reversible or irreversible. Trait A and trait B may require each other's presence mutually, or else A may require B, but not conversely. The trait *color* "co-plicates" the trait *extension*, but not the other way around; on the other hand, there is no right without a left, and vice versa. "Co-plication" can thus be either unilateral or bilateral.

ANALYTIC AND SYNTHETIC JUDGMENTS. Husserl speaks of analytic and synthetic judgments with much greater precision than Kant. Analytic judgments are those in which the predicate is implied in the subject. Synthetic judgments are those in which the predicate is not implied in, but added to, the subject. It is obvious that analytic judgments are a priori. But Kant speaks of a priori synthetic judgments. Husserl finds that such judgments are those in which the subject "co-plicates" the predicate; in such judgments there is a "founding" relationship between the subject and the predicate.

4. CONSCIOUSNESS

Phenomenology is a *descriptive science of the essences of pure consciousness*. What is consciousness? Husserl distinguishes three ways of understanding this term:

(1) As the *aggregate* of all *experiences*: the unity of the consciousness.

(2) The way the term is understood when one speaks of *being conscious* of a thing, *taking it into account*. If I see a thing, seeing it is an act of my consciousness (in the first sense); but if I realize that I see it, I am conscious (in the second sense) of having seen it.

(3) Consciousness understood as an *intentional experience*. This is the primary sense of the term.

INTENTIONAL EXPERIENCE. This is a psychical act which consists of more than being an act: it refers to an object. Whether or not the object exists, as an *intentional* object it is something distinct from the psychical act.

A specific intentional experience has two groups of elements: *intentional essence* and *non-intentional contents* (sensations, feelings, and so on); these contents individualize the experiences—for example, the perception of a room from different viewpoints. That which does not differ is the *intentional essence*, which is composed of two elements: *quality* (the characteristic of the act which makes the experience be the experience *of this object* and *in this manner*) and *matter*. If I say "the victor of Jena" and "the vanquished at Waterloo," I have two representations of a single intentional object (Napoleon); but the *matter* is different, since in one case I apprehend Napoleon as the victor and in the other as the vanquished. Let us sum up this explanation diagrammatically:

Intentional experience	intentional essence	quality matter	intentional object
	non-intentional contents	sensations feelings drives	

Husserl distinguishes between the sensory matter, or ὕλη, and the intentional form, or μορφή, and between the intentional act, or *nóesis*, and the objective content to which the act refers, or *nóema*.

PHENOMENOLOGICAL REDUCTION. We have reached the basic aspect of phenomenology, what is called phenomenological ἐποχή (abstention). This consists in taking an experience and "bracketing" it (*Einklammerung*) or "disconnecting" it (*Ausschaltung*).

The root of this is to be found in Husserl's idealism. Idealism had reduced indubitable reality to processes of consciousness. Brentano had said that internal perception is self-evident, adequate and infallible. Husserl follows Brentano's lead, but makes a change. We have a perception; for Husserl, what is indubitable is the perception as such; the perception of a table consists in my apprehending it as existing, as real. It is this, the *belief* that accompanies it, that differentiates perception from other experiences—for example, from a mere representation. But in order not to leave the realm of the indubitable, instead of saying: "I am seeing this table, which exists," I ought to say: "I have an experience, and one of its characteristics is my belief in the existence of the table"; but the belief always figures as a characteristic of the experience. Husserl calls this process of bracketing *phenomenological reduction* or *epokhé*.

These experiences are, after all, mine. And what am I? Phenomenological reduction must also extend to my ego, and the phenomenologist must also "submit" to *epokhé* as a psychophysical subject, as an existential position; all that remains is the *pure ego*, which is not a historical subject in the here and now, but the focus of the experience "rays." This is *pure* or phenomenologically reduced *consciousness*. Thus, we now have the *experiences of pure consciousness*.

But this is not enough. We must take a further step. The phenomenologist carries out phenomenological reduction, and once he is left with experiences he must raise himself to *essences* (eidetic reduction).

ESSENCES. It is impossible to describe any object whatsoever because it has an infinite number of traits. But by means of eidetic reduction one may make the transition from experiences to their essences. What are the essences? Husserl gives a rigorous definition:

The aggregate of all the traits joined together by founding constitutes the essence of the experience.

Let us think of a triangle; I take one trait, its being equilateral; this trait is joined by "co-plication," or "founding," to its being equiangular, and in this way to many other traits; all of them together constitute the essence of the equilateral triangle.

Husserl distinguishes between *definite* and *indefinite* manifolds; in the former, when certain of their elements have been determined, the rest can be rigorously deduced. This is what occurs with mathematical essences: if I determine the traits "polygon with three sides," the entire essence of the triangle can be rigorously deduced from this. One cannot reach the essence of the other kind of manifold so simply or so completely.

5. PHENOMENOLOGY AS A METHOD AND AS AN IDEALIST THESIS

THE COMPLETE DEFINITION. If we gather together the characteristics of phenomenology which we have been discovering, we find that it is a *descriptive eidetic science of the essences of experiences of pure consciousness.* The meaning of this abstruse definition is already transparent to us. We now see why phenomenology is an *a priori* and *universal* science. It is a priori in its fullest sense, because it describes only *essences* (that is, ideal and not empirical objects) of the experiences of a consciousness which is itself not empirical but *pure* and thus also a priori. Phenomenology is *universal* because it is concerned with all experiences, and since experiences refer to their objects, *intentional* objects are encompassed within phenomenological considerations; that is, *all that exists* for the phenomenologist is included.

THE METHOD. This method, which we have explained, leads us to the knowledge of essences, which is traditionally the goal of philosophy. It is a *self-evident* knowledge which is based on *intuition*; this, however, is not a *sensible* but an *eidetic* intuition, that is, an intuition of essences (*eîdos*). From the intuition of a single case I raise myself to the intuition of its essence by means of phenomenological reduction. The example which serves as my basis may be an act of perception or simply an act of imagination; the quality of the act is of no importance to the eidetic intuition.

This phenomenological method is *the method of present-day philosophy.* As a method, phenomenology is a brilliant discovery which opens a free path to philosophy. It is the point of departure from which one necessarily sets out. But it is not just a method: there is a falsity at the very core of phenomenology, and this is its metaphysical significance.

PHENOMENOLOGICAL IDEALISM. Husserl wishes to avoid metaphysics at all costs; this attempt is futile, because philosophy *is metaphysics.* And, in fact, Husserl is indulging in metaphysics when he affirms that pure consciousness is the fundamental reality. Husserl is an idealist; in his work idealism attains its most acute and refined form. But this position is untenable; idealism, in this, its final and most perfect phase, shows its internal contradiction. If we think phenomenology through profoundly, we will leave its domain. This is what the metaphysics of the last few years has done. When phenomenology is fully achieved, it carries us beyond Husserl's thought to other forms in which the original eidetic and descriptive science becomes true philosophy in its fullest and most precise form: metaphysics.

6. PHENOMENOLOGICAL PHILOSOPHY

PHILOSOPHY AS A PRECISE SCIENCE. With regard to the content of philosophy, Husserl renews the old demand of Socrates and Plato, of Descartes and Kant, for the establishment of philosophy as a strict and definitive science. Once again, there is a refusal to attribute ultimate reality to existing philosophy: it is not, Husserl says, that philosophy is an imperfect science, but that it is not yet a science. The two chief obstacles that it encounters in its historical surroundings are *naturalism* —a result of the discovery of nature—which starts out from *thetic* suppositions, from existential "positions," and *historicism*—a result of the discovery of history—which leads to a skeptical attitude of a relativist form. By following these, philosophy becomes *Weltan-schauungsphilosophie*, philosophy of world views, whereas Husserl calls for philosophy as a strict science.

The point of departure, naturally, must be intentionality. All consciousness is "consciousness of," and the study of consciousness, as we have already seen, includes the study of its meanings and its intentional objects. When every existential position is eliminated by means of ἐποχή, we get a *phenomenology* of consciousness. In the psychical realm, understood in this sense, there is no distinction between phenomenon and being; this gives phenomenology a certain "absoluteness," which, of course, excludes all positions or theses. Phenomenological intuition leads to the contemplation of *essences*; essences are something absolutely given, but as essential being (*Wesenssein*), never as existence (*Dasein*).

"Only a really fundamental and systematic phenomenology," Husserl says, "can give us comprehension of the psychical." There-fore, psychology is very closely related to philosophy; this is the kernel of truth that was latent in the erroneous psychologist position: the tendency toward a phenomenological establishment of philosophy.

IDEA OF THE WORLD AND SCIENCE. The great philosophies of the past had a double concern: with science and with the concept of the world. But this situation has changed since the foundation of a "time-less *universitas* of precise sciences"; now, Husserl says, there is a sharp distinction between the concept of the world and science. The "idea" of the former is different for each era; the idea of the latter is timeless ("supratemporal"), and is not limited by any relationship with the spirit of time. Our life goals are of two classes: some are for time, others for eternity; science is concerned with absolute, non-temporal values. One cannot abandon eternity in favor of time. Only science can definitively overcome the necessity which arises from science. Con-cepts of the world may differ among themselves; only science can decide, and its decision, Husserl says, bears the seal of eternity. This science is *one* value among others which are equally justified; it is impersonal, and its quality ought to be the *clarity* which belongs to theory, not the *profundity* proper to wisdom. Our time, Husserl says, bears the promise of a great era, but it is plagued by negative skepticism wearing the mask of positivism; it is necessary to overcome this with a *true positivism*, which will hold fast only to realities, which will take its departure not from philosophies but from the things and problems, and will thus be a science of true principles, of origins, of the ῥιζώματα πάντων. This is the function that can be performed only by the phenomenological apprehension of essences.

TRANSCENDENTAL PHILOSOPHY. To the extent that phenomenology is philosophy and not merely a method, it can be defined as a new kind of transcendental philosophy; it could almost be considered a kind of neo-Cartesianism, a Cartesianism that has been rendered more fundamental and that avoids the deviations with which Descartes marred his own discoveries. In effect, Husserl represents the subtlest and most refined form of that idealism which begins with Descartes.

Husserl demands the *self-evidence* in which the things "themselves" are present. However, there is also a perfect kind of self-evidence, *apodictic self-evidence*, which confers absolute undoubtedness on the order of that possessed by principles. The self-evidence of the world is not apodictic; on the other hand, the *ego cogito* is the ultimate and apodictically certain domain on which all fundamental philosophy must be based. Husserl's return to Descartes' viewpoint, to the principle of the *cogito*, stems from this; however, unlike Descartes, Husserl must not confuse the *ego*, the pure subject of *cogitationes*, with an independent *substantia cogitans*, that is, a human *mens sive animus*. Psychical life is conceived *in the world*; the phenomenological *epokhé* eliminates the existential value of the world, brackets it, and thus focuses its attention on the phenomenologically reduced *transcendental ego*.

PURE SCIENCE OF THE EGO. The *epokhé* isolates a "new and infinite" sphere of existence that is accessible through a new form of experience, transcendental experience. Husserl states—and this is very important —that to every kind of real experience there corresponds something that is purely fictitious, a *quasi experience (Erfahrung als ob)*. An absolutely subjective science thus is originated, and begins provisionally as a pure *science of the ego*; this leads to a transcendental solipsism with which phenomenology will later have to concern itself. Thanks to this peculiar transcendental experience, the *ego* can explicate itself indefinitely and systematically. However, this requires further explanation.

The basic difference between Descartes' position and Husserl's is the idea of *intentionality*. One cannot be content with the simple *ego cogito*, according to which the *ego* becomes a *res* separated from all other reality, as Descartes believed. Since to think is always to think of something, the precise formula is: *ego cogito cogitatum*. Phenomenology does not forget the world: the world remains as the *cogitatum*. The consciousness of the universe is always present (*mitbewusst*); it is the unity of consciousness. The ego of phenomenological meditation can be a spectator of itself, and this "itself" comprises all objectivity that exists for it such as it exists for it. The revelation of the ego through phenomenological analysis thus comprises all intentional objects correlative to the acts, from which every existential position has, of course, been eliminated.

These objects exist and are what they are only as objects of a real or possible consciousness; and, for its part, the *transcendental ego* (or, psychologically speaking, the soul) is what it is only in relation to the intentional objects. The ego apprehends itself as identical to itself. And the basic form of the synthesis of experienced ("lived") acts (each one of which has an experienced duration) is the immanent consciousness of time. It is a characteristic of intentionality that every state of consciousness has an intentional "horizon," which refers to potentialities of consciousness in a continuous *protension*. This horizon defines a "halo" of possibilities that *could be* realized if one were to turn one's perception in another direction. Therefore, indeterminateness is an essential characteristic of the *cogitatum*; it is never definitively given; rather, particularities remain in a state of irresolution.

However, this ego is not an uncharged pole; by virtue of the laws of what Husserl calls *transcendental genesis* (a very important concept which was developed in Husserl's last writings) the ego acquires a new, permanent property with every new kind of act. If I make up my mind, I am already an ego that has made up its mind in a certain way: the act passes, the decision remains. Correlatively, I transform myself when I abjure my decisions and actions. This involves the constitution of a *self*, a permanent *person*, that retains a "style," a personal character. The self constitutes itself for itself in the unity of a *history*. The objects and categories that exist for the self are constituted by virtue of the laws of the genesis. Therefore, eidetic phenomenology, which for Husserl is a "first philosophy," has two phases: the first, *static*, with descriptions and systemizations analogous to those of natural history; the second, *genetic*. This genesis occurs in two forms: active, in which the self participates in a creative way (practical reason), and passive, the principle of which is association. In all these constitutions action is irrational, but Husserl observes that "the *action itself*, with its *irrationality*, is a *structural concept in the system of the concrete 'a priori.'*"

MONADOLOGICAL INTERSUBJECTIVITY. Husserl distinguishes between the self as a mere self-identical pole and substratum of the *habitus*, and the *ego* in its concrete fullness, which he designates by the Leibnizian term *monad*. The monadic *ego* contains the whole of conscious life, both real and potential, and its phenomenological explication coincides with phenomenology in general. However, this solipsism is corrected by the fact that in me, a transcendental *ego*, other *egos*, and thus an "objective world" common to everyone, are transcendentally constituted. Such a world appears, and in it occurs a philosophy common to "all of us," one which we meditate in common, a *Philosophia perennis*.

The *ego* comprises my very being as a monad and the sphere formed by intentionality; in this sphere there is constituted later an *ego*, as it were, *reflected* in my own *ego*, in my monad—that is, a sort of *alter ego*, which is an *analogue*, but at the same time other. Consequently, it is a question of the constitution of the other as *extraneous* within the sphere of my own intentionality. Through its common intentionality, this community of monads constitutes a single world that is the same for all, and this presupposes a "harmony" of the monads.

SPACE AND TIME. My body, which is directly present at every moment, establishes an interrelationship in my sphere: it is given to me in the mode of "here," of *hic*. Every other body—including my neighbor's—is in the mode of *there, illic*. Possible changes in my orientation cause there to be constituted a *spatial* nature, which is in intentional relationship with my body. Anything that is *present, at hand*, can become here, and I can perceive "the same things" *from there* (*illinc*). The *other* seems to me to possess the phenomena that I would have if I were *there*, but his body is given to him in the form of an *absolute here*.

My experiences do not endure; nevertheless, they acquire for me a value of being, of temporal existence, because through re-presentations I return to the original that is no more; these representations are unified in a synthesis accompanied by the self-evident consciousness of *the same thing*. In the case of the ideal objects, Husserl explains their nontemporality as an *omnitemporality*, correlative to the possibility of being produced and reproduced at any moment of time. And the *coexistence* of my self and the other, of my intentional life and that of the other, of my realities and those of the other, presupposes the creation of a *common form of time*.

There can be, then, but one community of monads, comprising all the coexisting monads: a single objective world, or nature. And this world *must* exist if I have within me structures that imply the coexistence of other monads.

THE PROBLEMS OF PHENOMENOLOGICAL PHILOSOPHY. Husserl points

out two stages in phenomenological investigations: a "transcendental esthetic," in a fuller sense than the Kantian, that refers to a noematic a priori of sensible intuition, and a theory of experience of the other (*Einfühlung*). The ultimate origin of all a priori sciences is in a priori and transcendental phenomenology. Husserl says that transcendental phenomenology, systematically and completely developed, is an authentic, concrete, *universal ontology*, which he also calls *concrete logic of being*. Within this there would be, first of all, a solipsist science of the ego, and then an intersubjective phenomenology.

As we have already seen, Husserl, who was shaped by the presuppositions of his age, eliminates metaphysics; however, this elimination is but partly successful. Phenomenology eliminates only *ingenuous* metaphysics, that is, metaphysics that deals with the "absurd things in themselves," and not metaphysics in general. In the interior of the monadic sphere, and as an *ideal possibility*, there reappear for Husserl the problems of contingent reality, death, destiny, the "meaning" of history, and so on. The central problems of philosophy occur within the horizon of the reduced consciousness. Thus there is constituted a system of phenomenological disciplines, the base of which is not the simple axiom *ego cogito*, but a consciousness of oneself, complete, integral and universal, first monadic and then intermonadic. It is first necessary to lose the world through the ἐποχή in order to recover it later in this act of being conscious. This is the final meaning that Husserl gives to phenomenology, which renews the old Delphic precept γνῶθι σεαυτόν (Know thyself) and at the same time St. Augustine's statement: *Noli foras ire, in te redi, in interiore homine habitat veritas* (Do not go outside, return within yourself; truth dwells in the inner man).

The philosophy of Edmund Husserl is one of the three or four great intellectual achievements of our time. Nevertheless, the fecundity and scope of this philosophy are still but little known; this is partly due to accidental reasons, including the not inconsiderable one that the *greater part* of Husserl's work is still unpublished. This material has, however, been saved from the misfortunes of the terrible decade that followed Husserl's death and is preserved at the University of Louvain. In his last published works Husserl begins to deal with new and very serious problems, which lead him to question the very idea of phenomenology and which motivate his final development, known today only in a fragmentary way. It is to be hoped that in the next years there will appear a series of volumes which will give us a new image of Husserl and of the roads beyond phenomenology *sensu stricto* toward which the philosophical thought of our time must direct itself, under Husserl's indisputable—but more or less remote—leadership.*

* For a further discussion, see Ortega, *Apuntes sobre el pensamiento: su teurgia y su demiurgia* (*Obras Completas*, V, pp. 517–19 and 540–42). See also my *Introducción a la Filosofía* (*Reason and Life*), Sections "Phenomenology" (in Chapter IV), "The concept as a function of meaning" (in Chapter V) and "The problem of logic" (in Chapter VII) [*Obras*, II].

Value Theory

It is useful to distinguish value theory (*Werttheorie*) from the "phi-losophy of value" (*Wertphilosophie*) which derives from Rudolf Her-mann Lotze and is represented principally by Wilhelm Windelband and Heinrich Rickert.

The science of judgment or values begins approximately at the turn of the century. Its direct sources are to be found in Brentano's ethics and in phenomenology, which also derives from Brentano. Brentano's immediate pupils—Alexius Meinong and Christian von Ehrenfels, in particular—were the first to concern themselves philosophically with the problem of value. Later, value theory was magnificently developed by two great German thinkers: Max Scheler and Nicolai Hartmann. We must study the characteristics of values before investigating briefly the philosophies of Scheler and Hartmann.

1. THE PROBLEM OF VALUE

THE POINT OF DEPARTURE. In Brentano, "just *love*" was that self-evident love which contains within itself the reason for its justness. It was the love of an object that shows self-evidently that the appropriate attitude with reference to it is to love it. When an object makes us recognize its authentic quality of requiring to be loved, it becomes the *object of just love*. We are only a step away from value theory: I prefer a thing because I see that the thing *has value*, that it is *to be valued*.

Thus, values are something that the things possess and that exercise a strange power over us; they are not limited to being at hand, to being

418

apprehended; rather, values oblige us to *esteem* them, to *value* them. I may perhaps see something that is good and not seek it, yet I cannot help but esteem it. *To see something as good* is already to *esteem* it. This modest, small and intimate act of *esteeming* them is the only thing that values oblige us to do. Thus value is something that the things have which makes us *esteem* them.

But this is not enough. We must raise a second problem. We have seen that there is something which merits and at the same time requires the name of value; but we do not yet know anything about this strange reality. The basic question is: What are values? The answers given to this question have frequently been wrong; value has been confused with other things, and its true nature has remained visible only through the inconsistencies of those erroneous viewpoints.

THE OBJECTIVITY OF VALUE. It has been thought (Meinong) that a thing is of value when it pleases us and, conversely, that when a thing pleases us, it is of value. This would mean that value is subjective, based on the pleasure which a thing produces in me. But it so happens that things please us *because they are good*—or seem good to us, because we find goodness in them. The *cause* of our happiness is goodness apprehended. To be delighted is to be delighted with *something*, and it is not our delight that gives value; rather, it is the other way around: value provokes our delight.

On the other hand, if Meinong's theory were true, only objects that existed would be of value, since they are the only objects that can please us; it turns out, however—as Ehrenfels saw—that we value most that which does not exist: perfect justice, complete knowledge, the health we lack—in short, *ideals*. This obliges Ehrenfels to correct Meinong's theory: the things which have value are not the things which please us, but the things which we find *desirable*. Value is simply the projection of our desire. In this case as in the former, value is subjective; it is something that belongs not to the object, but to the psychical states of the subject. However, both of these theories are incorrect. In the first place, there are certain profoundly unpleasant things which we feel have value: to care for a person who is sick with the plague, to be wounded or die for a noble or worthy cause, and so on. A person may have a more fervent desire to eat than to possess a work of art, or to be rich than to live a just life, and at the same time value a work of art or righteousness much more than food or money. Our valuation of a thing is independent of our delight and desire. It is not in the least subjective; it is objective and is based on the reality of the things.

The words "pleasurable" and "desirable" have a meaning other than that which pleases and that which is desired, a meaning which is of more interest here: that which *deserves* to be desired. This desert or merit is something that the things possess, a dignity which they have in themselves, something independent of my valuation. To value a thing is not to *give* value, but to *recognize* the value which the thing possesses.

VALUES AND GOODS. However, we must now make a distinction between value and the thing which is valued. The things *have* various types and degrees of value. Value is a *quality* of the things, not the things themselves. A painting, a landscape and a woman *have* beauty, but beauty is not any of these things. Things that are valued are called *goods*. Thus, goods are the *bearers of values*, and values are realized or embodied in the goods.

UNREALITY OF VALUE. We say that values are qualities. There are *real* qualities, such as color, form, size, material, and so on, but value is not a real quality. In a painting I find canvas, paints and the depicted forms, all of which are elements of the painting; the painting also possesses beauty, but this is a different type of possession; beauty is an unreal quality; it is not a thing, nor an element of a thing. Besides value, there are other qualities with this characteristic: alikeness, for example. The alikeness between two coins is nothing the coins really possess, so little so that a *single* coin cannot possess alikeness. Alikeness cannot be perceived by the senses; rather, it is observed by means of a comparison which the mind performs; alikeness is seen by means of the intellect. And yet alikeness is perfectly objective, since I cannot say that a table and a book are alike; alikeness is a relationship between things, which is apprehended or recognized by the intellect. The case of value is similar: the mind apprehends value as something objective which impresses itself upon the mind, but something perfectly unreal; value is not *perceived* by means of the senses, nor is it *comprehended*; it is *esteemed*. To apprehend value is, precisely, to esteem it.

CHARACTERISTICS OF VALUE. Values present certain characteristics which clarify even further their objective—their ideally objective—sense. In the first place, they have *polarity*, that is, they are necessarily *positive* or *negative*, in contrast to real things, which have the characteristic of being positive (or, in the extreme case, the characteristic of *privation*). Good is the opposite of bad, beautiful of ugly, and so on. That is, the value "beauty" possesses a positive or negative "charge," as do all the others.

In the second place, there is a hierarchy of values: there are higher and lower ones; elegance is inferior to beauty, beauty to goodness, goodness, in turn, to holiness. There is thus an objective hierarchy of precisely graded values.

In the third place, values possess *matter*, that is, a unique and individual content. Values do not merely exist; they appear with irreducible contents, which one must perceive directly: elegance and holiness are two values with different *matter*, and it would be futile to attempt to reduce one to the other. The reaction of the man who perceives values is different according to their matter: the appropriate reaction to holiness is *reverence*; to goodness, *respect*; to beauty, *pleasure*, and so on.

Therefore, it is possible to classify values with regard to their matter and in accordance with their hierarchy; in every case this classification will follow the double, polar form of positive and negative. Thus, there are values of *utility* (capable/incapable, abundant/ scarce); of *life* (healthy/ill, strong/weak, outstanding/common); of *mind* (true/false, self-evident/probable); of *morality* (good/bad, just/ unjust); of *esthetics* (beautiful/ugly, elegant/inelegant); of *religion* (sacred/profane), and so forth.

PERCEPTION OF AND BLINDNESS TO VALUE. Values may or may not be perceived; every era possesses a sensitivity to certain values and loses it or lacks it with regard to others; certain men are blind to a particular value—for example, to the esthetic value or to the religious value. Values—objective realities—are *discovered*, just as continents and islands are discovered; but at times the sight of them is clouded over and man ceases to feel their strange force. He ceases to esteem them, because he does not perceive them (see Ortega y Gasset: ¿*Qué son los valores?* in *Complete Works*, VI).

BEING AND VALUE. The value theory has insisted, perhaps excessively, on distinguishing value from being. It is said that a value does not *exist*, but that something *has value*; that a value is not an *ens*, but a *valens*. This, however, is dubious, because the question, "What are values?" is meaningful, and we cannot avoid the problem of *being* with the subterfuge of "having value." A careful distinction is made between the good and its value, but one should not forget that Greek metaphysics always said that being, the good and the one accompany one another and are expressed in similar ways. They are, as we have seen, the *transcendentals*. The good of a thing is that which the thing *is*. Being, the good and the one are not *things*, but transcendentals, something that imbues and envelops all things and makes them be, and makes them be *one* and *good*. Thus, it is possible to contemplate the serious problem of the relationship between being and value, which cannot be considered as totally eliminated.

Perhaps this ontological defect has prevented value theory from acquiring greater profundity and importance. A few years ago, it looked as if value philosophy were going to be the important philosophy of our time. Today it is clear that this is not the case. Value theory is now seen to be a closed chapter, one which lacks an ultimate basis. The philosophy of our time has turned its back on value theory and has chosen a more fruitful course by resolutely entering upon the path of metaphysics.

2. SCHELER

LIFE AND WORKS. Max Scheler was born in 1874 and died in 1928. He was a professor at the University of Cologne, and is one of the most important thinkers of our age. His intellectual roots are in the work of Rudolf Christoph Eucken, whose pupil he was, and in that of Bergson, but most of all in Husserl's phenomenology, which he adapts in a personal way. Scheler entered the Catholic Church and in one phase of his life was a true apologist for Catholicism; nevertheless, in his last years he strayed from orthodoxy in the direction of pantheism.

Scheler is a writer of extreme fecundity. His masterpiece is the *Ethics*, the complete title of which is *Der Formalismus in der Ethik und die materiale Wertethik* (Formalism in Ethics and the Material Ethics of Value); in it he criticizes Kant's formalistic ethics and establishes the bases for an ethics of values, with content. He also wrote *Wesen und Formen der Sympathie* (The Nature of Sympathy), a revision of an earlier work; *Das Ressentiment im Aufbau der Moralen* (Resentment in the Structure of Moralities); *Die Stellung des Menschen im Kosmos* (Man's Place in the Cosmos); *Die Wissensformen und die Gesellschaft* (The Forms of Knowledge and Society); and the great work of his Catholic phase: *Vom Ewigen im Menschen* (On the Eternal in Man). Scheler's output was very large, and part of it is not yet published. His studies in *philosophical anthropology* are especially interesting. His book *Vom Ewigen im Menschen* contains two of his best essays: "Reue und Wiedergeburt" (Repentance and Rebirth) and "Vom Wesen der Philosophie" (On the Nature of Philosophy).

SCHELER'S PHILOSOPHY. We cannot enter into a detailed exposition of Scheler's thought. For one thing, it is too complex and copious, and would lead us too far beyond the limits of this survey: Scheler's systematic thought cannot easily be reduced to an essential nucleus from which his many varied ideas can be shown to emanate. For another thing, we are still too close to him to make him a subject of the *history of philosophy* in the strict sense. We can choose either to expound and interpret the content of his philosophy, or else merely to place him in his setting. I shall confine myself completely to the second course of action.

Scheler is a phenomenologist. From its very inception, phenomenology has been an intuitive knowledge of essences. Scheler sets out to win mastery over essences, especially in the areas of man and human life and in the area of value. Scheler's clarity and fruitfulness in this knowledge of essences are remarkable. But knowledge of essences is not enough. Kant had already observed that intuition without a concept is not science, and even though phenomenological intuition is eidetic rather than sensible, philosophy cannot remain content with being a *descriptive* science, not even when it is describing essences; it must be a *system* and its basis must be *metaphysics*. This is Scheler's great failing. His thought, acute and clear as it is, is not strictly metaphysical. Moreover, as a consequence of this, his philosophy is deficient in systematic unity. His brilliant insights illuminate various regions of reality, but he lacks that all-inclusive coherence which philosophic knowledge requires. Philosophic truth must appear in the form of a system in which each truth is sustained by all the others. This system is missing in Scheler.

This makes his thought essentially provisional. His philosophy is like a hothouse where brilliant ideas sprout in confusion, but these ideas lack *roots* from which they can grow and acquire mature significance. After using phenomenology as a knowledge of essences, one must place it in the service of a systematic metaphysics. Scheler did not do this, but he prepared the way for present-day metaphysics. He concentrated his attention on the themes of man and human life: his philosophy was oriented toward a *philosophical anthropology* which he was unable to bring to maturity. When this tendency acquired a systematic basis and became a precise metaphysics, it led to *existential analytics*.

3. HARTMANN

Nicolai Hartmann (1882–1950), a professor at Berlin and later at Göttingen, also represents a phenomenological orientation which is related to Scheler's in its concern with the problems of value. After Scheler's great work on ethics (1913), Hartmann published in 1926 his *Ethics*, an important systemization of the ethics of values. But in addition, Hartmann was intensely occupied with the problems of knowledge and ontology. Therefore we observe in his philosophy its clear intention to be systematic and to become metaphysics.

His most important works besides the above-mentioned *Ethics* are *Platos Logik des Seins* (Plato's Logic of Being), *Grundzüge einer Metaphysik der Erkenntnis* (Fundamental Characteristics of a Metaphysics of

Knowledge), *Das Problem des geistigen Seins* (The Problem of Spiritual Being), *Die Philosophie des deutschen Idealismus* (The Philosophy of German Idealism), *Zur Grundlegung der Ontologie* (Toward a Basis for Ontology), *Möglichkeit und Wirklichkeit* (Possibility and Reality), and *Der Aufbau der realen Welt* (The Structure of the Real World). In 1942 he published "Neue Wege der Ontologie" (New Paths in Ontology), which appeared in a collection of papers entitled *Systematische Philosophie*, which Hartmann himself edited. His last works to appear were *Philosophie der Natur* (Philosophy of Nature), in 1950, and two volumes of short essays, *Kleinere Schriften*.

Heidegger's Existential Philosophy

LIFE AND WORKS. Martin Heidegger, who was born in 1889, is a professor at the University of Freiburg im Breisgau, where he succeeded Husserl after having been a professor at Marburg. He is the most important German philosopher of the present day; in order to find a figure of comparable stature one would have to go back to the great classic thinkers of German philosophy. Heidegger derives directly from phenomenology, and his thought is closely related to that of Husserl and Scheler; but on the other hand, he has ties with the most precise tradition of metaphysics and especially with Aristotle. His doctoral thesis was a study of Duns Scotus. He has written an entire book on the interpretation of Kant as a metaphysician. In his works one observes the constant presence of the great philosophers of the past: the pre-Socratics, Plato, St. Augustine, Descartes, Hegel, Kierkegaard, Dilthey and Bergson, as well as those mentioned above.

Heidegger's thought has great profundity and originality. It also contains great difficulties. Heidegger has created a philosophical terminology that is quite hard to understand, but even harder to translate. In his attempt to express new ideas and to disclose hitherto neglected realities, Heidegger does not eschew a radical reformation of the vocabulary of philosophy, in order to lead us to a clearer intuition of what he wants us to see. For another thing, Heidegger's philosophy is essentially incomplete. Only the first half of his major book has been published; publication of this was followed by a long and almost total silence, by shorter writings, quite different in character and orientation, and by the decision not to publish the second volume. This increases the difficulties of an exposition of his thought, which, strictly speaking, cannot today be carried out with precision and without indulging in conjecture. I shall therefore have to limit myself to indicating Heidegger's point of view and to observing a few major aspects of his metaphysics which will aid in the comprehension of his meaning and in the understanding of his works.

These works are not very extensive. Besides a dissertation on *Die Lehre vom Urteil im Psychologismus* (The Theory of Judgment in Psychologism), the above-mentioned thesis, *Die Kategorien- und Bedeutungslehre des Duns Scotus* (Duns Scotus' Theory of Categories and Meaning) and a lecture on "Der Zeitbegriff in der Geschichtswissenschaft" (The Concept of Time in the Science of History), his major work is the first and only volume of *Sein und Zeit* (Being and Time), published in 1927. In 1929 he published his second book, *Kant und das Problem der Metaphysik* (Kant and the Problem of Metaphysics), a very personal interpretation of the Kantianism of the *Critique of Pure Reason*, understood as a basis for metaphysics. Later in the same year he published two pamphlets, brief but full of content: *Was ist Metaphysik?* (What is Metaphysics?) and *Vom Wesen des Grundes* (On the Nature of Cause). These were followed in 1933 by a speech: "Die Selbstbehauptung der deutschen Universität" (The Self-Affirmation of the German University) and finally, other essays: "Hölderlin und das Wesen der Dichtung" (Hölderlin and the Nature of Poetry)—later included in the volume *Erläuterungen zu Hölderlins Dichtung* (Elucidations of Hölderlin's Poetry)—and "Vom Wesen der Wahrheit" (On the Nature of Truth). In 1947 he published a short book, *Platons Lehre von der Wahrheit. Mit einem Brief über den "Humanismus"* (Plato's Theory of Truth, with a Letter on "Humanism"), in which he opposes certain interpretations of his philosophy, distinguishing his own thought from Jean-Paul Sartre's "existentialism." In 1950 there appeared a volume titled *Holzwege* (Forest Paths), made up of six studies written at different times: "Der Ursprung des Kunstwerkes" (The Origin of the Work of Art), "Die Zeit des Weltbildes" (The Time of the World-Image), "Hegels Begriff der Erfahrung" (Hegel's Concept of Experience), "Nietzsches Wort 'Gott ist tot'" (Nietzsche's Saying, 'God Is Dead'), "Wozu Dichter?" (What Is the Purpose of the Poet?) and "Der Spruch des Anaximander" (Anaximander's Maxim). In 1953 he published the book *Einführung in die Metaphysik* (Introduction to Metaphysics) and, later, various pamphlets and articles: "Georg Trakl"; "Der Feldweg" (The Path in the Fields); ". . . Dichterisch wohnet der Mensch . . ." (Man Lives by Poetry); "Aus der Erfahrung des Denkens" (From the Experience of Thought); "Zur Seinsfrage"

(The Question of Being); "Was ist das—die Philosophie?" (What Is This Thing Philosophy?); and "Hebel—der Hausfreund" (Hebel, the "Friend of the Family"); the recent volumes of essays *Was heisst Denken?* (What Is Meant by Thinking?); *Vorträge und Aufsätze* (Lectures and Essays), which includes, among other essays, "Die Frage nach der Technik" (The Question of Technology); "Überwindung der Metaphysik" (Metaphysics Superseded); "Logos, Moira, Aletheia"; and, finally, *Der Satz vom Grund* (The Principle of Cause), in 1957, and a long, two-volume work, *Nietzsche*, in 1961.

1. THE PROBLEM OF BEING

BEING AND TIME. The problem that Heidegger deals with in his investigation entitled *Sein und Zeit* is *the meaning of being (die Frage nach dem Sinn von Sein)*. He is concerned with not *entities*, but with *being*. Being and nothing else is the subject of his inquiry. And his initial goal is the interpretation of *time* as the possible *horizon* for all intellection of being in general. We must not forget, as others have too frequently forgotten, that Heidegger particularly insists that the fundamental problem is the meaning of being. Everything else anticipates this question and is instrumental in solving it.

BEING AND ENTITY. Heidegger begins by considering the problem of being as it has been dealt with in earlier metaphysics. Ever since Aristotle, being has been understood to be *transcendental*, "that which is most universal of all" (*Metaphysics*, Book III, 4); its universality was understood to be not that of the *genus*, as Plato believed, but a universality based on the unity of *analogy*. However, Heidegger says that this concept of being is not the clearest; on the contrary, it is the most obscure. Being (*Sein*) is not the same as entity (*Seiendes*). Being cannot be defined; but this in itself raises the question of its meaning.

"Being" is the most understandable and self-evident of all concepts. Everyone understands such statements as "the sky *is* blue," "I *am* happy." However, the fact that we understand the everyday use of "being" whereas its meaning and relationship to the entity is obscure to us, indicates that being is an *enigma*. This is why we are obliged to raise the question of the meaning of being. Every ontology, Heidegger says (*Sein und Zeit*), is blind if it does not first sufficiently explain the meaning of *being* and then embrace this explanation as its fundamental theme.

DASEIN AND BEING. Inasmuch as science is an activity carried on by man, it has the mode of being of this entity, man. Heidegger calls this entity *Dasein*. However, he observes that science is not the only mode of being of Dasein, nor even the most immediate. Dasein is understood in its being; the understanding of being is a determination of the being of Dasein. It can therefore be said that Dasein *is* ontological.

The being of Dasein is *Existenz*, existence. Heidegger uses the term *existential* to describe everything relative to the structure of existence. The ontological analytic of the entity Dasein necessitates a prior consideration of existentiality, that is, the mode of being of the entity that *exists*. We already see in this the idea of *being*, and the analytic of Dasein presupposes the prior question of the *meaning of being in general*.

DASEIN AND WORLD. However, in the realm of the sciences, Dasein deals with entities that are not necessarily themselves Dasein. An essential element of Dasein, then, is *being in a world*. Thus, the understanding of the being of Dasein presupposes, in an *equally primary* way, the understanding of the "world" and of the being of the entity that is found within the world. Consequently, the ontologies of the entities that are not themselves Dasein are based on the ontic structure of Dasein. This is why we must look for the *fundamental ontology*, the only one that can give rise to all the others, in the *existential analytic of Dasein* (*existenziale Analytik des Daseins*).

Dasein has a priority over all other entities. It has, in the first place, an *ontic* priority: this entity is determined in its being by existence. Secondly, it has an *ontological* priority: because of its determination as *existence*, Dasein is in itself "*ontological.*" And thirdly, since Dasein is able to comprehend being which is not Dasein, it has an *ontic-ontological* priority: it is the condition for the possibility of all ontologies. Therefore, there is no specific mode of being that Dasein does not comprehend.

THE ANALYTIC OF DASEIN. The analytic of Dasein is not only incomplete; it is also *provisional*. It merely reveals the being of this entity, without interpreting its meaning. Its mission is simply to prepare an opening in the necessary horizon for the primary interpretation of being. Now, the meaning of the being of Dasein is *temporality*. This furnishes us with the *ground* for the understanding of the meaning of being. It is *from the standpoint of time* that Dasein comprehends and interprets being. Time is the horizon for the understanding of being. Therefore, philosophy's first mission is *a primary explanation of time as the horizon for the understanding of being from the standpoint of temporality, as the being of Dasein*.

HEIDEGGER'S METHOD. The method used in connection with the fundamental question concerning being is *phenomenological*. To Heidegger, phenomenology does not involve his subscribing to any "point of view" or "direction," for phenomenology is a *concept of method.* Phenomenology does not describe the "what" of the object of philosophical investigation, but the "how" of this inquiry. Heidegger understands phenomenology as an imperative to go to *the things themselves,* to dispense with all imaginary constructions, chance discoveries and apparent questions.

The word "phenomenology" comes from two Greek words, φαινόμενον (*phainómenon*) and λόγος (*lógos*). The first word derives from *phainesthai,* the middle voice of *phaino,* which means "to place in the light," in clarity, and which comes from the same root as φῶς (*phôs*), light. *Phenomenon* means "that which is shown," that which is placed in the light; therefore, it is not the same as *appearance.* *Lógos* means a saying, *a making manifest* (δηλοῦν); Aristotle explained it as *apophainesthai,* in which we again encounter the root of "phenomenon." And this showing or making manifest is a *discovering,* a making patent, a placing in truth or αλήθεια (*alétheia*). Falsity is, in turn, a *covering up.* This is the meaning of phenomenology: a *mode of access* to the theme of ontology. *Ontology is possible only as phenomenology.*

The meaning of the phenomenological description of Dasein is *interpretation.* Therefore, phenomenology is *hermeneutics.*

PHILOSOPHY. Ontology and phenomenology are not two philosophical disciplines among others. They are two descriptions which characterize philosophy by its *object* and its *method.* Philosophy is *universal phenomenological ontology,* and it begins with the *hermeneutics of Dasein.*

The elaboration of the problems of being comprises two topics, and therefore the investigation is divided into two sections, of which only a part of the first has been published. The outline is as follows:

First part: The analysis of the temporality of Dasein and the explanation of time as the transcendental horizon of the problem of being.

Second part: The foundation for a phenomenological destruction of the history of ontology, guided by the problem of temporality.

This is the meaning of Heidegger's philosophy; it is, in the final analysis, the ancient question concerning *being,* which has still not been answered adequately.

2. THE ANALYSIS OF DASEIN

THE ESSENCE OF DASEIN. The entity whose analysis Heidegger undertakes is every one of us. The being of this entity is always *my own* (*je meines*). The essence of this entity (its *quid,* its *was*) must be understood from the standpoint of its being or existence; however, it is

necessary to interpret this existence in a meaning peculiar to this
entity that is us, and not in the usual sense of that which is present
(*Vorhandensein*). Thus, Heidegger can say: *The "essence" of Dasein
consists in its existence (Das "Wesen" des Daseins liegt in seiner Existenz)*.
Dasein always implies the personal pronoun: "I am," "you are."
Dasein is essentially its own *possibility*; therefore it can "choose itself,"
"win itself," or "lose itself." Thus, it has two modes of being:
authenticity and unauthenticity.

When the characteristics of being refer to Dasein, they are called
existentials, and when they refer to other modes of being they are called
categories. So the entity is a *who* (existence) or a *what* (being present in
the fullest sense). Heidegger observes that the analytic of Dasein is
different from all forms of anthropology, psychology and biology, and
also prior to them. Thus, it is not simply that Heidegger's philosophy
is basically an inquiry into the meaning of being and not about man;
for previous inquiries into the being of Dasein cannot be understood as
anthropology either.

"BEING-IN-THE-WORLD." The determinations of the being of
Dasein have to be seen and understood on the basis of what is called
"being-in-the-world"; this is a *unitary* phenomenon, and therefore it
should not be understood as a complex of the terms in this expression.
In this expression, "in" is not a spatial concept; rather, spatiality is
something that is derived from the primary meaning of "in" and is
based on "being-in-the-world," the basic mode of the being of Dasein.
Nor is knowledge primary, for it is a mode of being of "being-in-the-
world." Knowing the things is one of the possible modes of dealing
with them; however, all modes presuppose the prior and fundamental
situation of Dasein, constitutive of it, which is to be, as a matter of
course, in something that is known chiefly as *world*.

THE WORLD. "Being-in-the-world" (*In-der-Welt-sein*) can be fully
understood only by virtue of a phenomenological consideration of the
world. To begin with, the world is not the *things* (houses, trees, men,
mountains, stars) which exist within the world, and which are
"worldly" (*innerweltlich*). Nor is the world *nature*, an entity which is
found in the world and which can be described in various forms and at
various levels. Not even the ontological interpretation of the being of
these entities refers to the phenomenon "world," which is already
presupposed in these modes of access to objective being.

Ontologically, *world* is a characteristic of Dasein itself. Heidegger
mentions four different ways in which the concept *world* is used:
(1) World as the sum total of the entity that can exist within the world.
(2) World as an ontological term: the being of the entity of which we

are speaking; it sometimes designates a region embracing a multiplicity of entities, as when one speaks of the world of the mathematician. (3) World as that "in which there lives" a factitious Dasein as such. (4) World as the ontologico-existential denomination of *worldliness*.

Man finds himself in a world that is not primarily *present* (*vorhanden*), but *at hand* (*zuhanden*). This is the basis for the things' role as *utensils* (*Zeuge*), a subject which Heidegger has analyzed in depth. Taking this as his point of departure, he has analyzed worldliness and interpreted the Cartesian ontology of the world as *res extensa*, in order ultimately to study the *spatiality* of existence. However, we cannot go into the details of this matter here.

COEXISTENCE. By virtue of the constitutive nature of Dasein, there can be no mere subject without a world; nor can there be one ego isolated from the others. The others *coexist* in "being-in-the-world." The world of Dasein is a *common world* (*Mitwelt*): to *be in* means to *be with* others, and this inherently "worldly" being is *coexistence*. The "who" of this coexistence is not this one or that one; it is not anyone in particular, nor is it everyone together: it is the impersonal, the "they" (*das Man*). An existential characteristic of the "they" is that it is an average term (*Durchschnittlichkeit*). The "they" fulfills Dasein in its everyday life. "The 'they' is an existential and it belongs to the positive constitution of Dasein as a primary phenomenon." And authentic *being itself* is an existential modification of the "they."

EVERYDAY LIFE. On one hand, Dasein is characterized by *facticity*; on the other hand, it is also characterized by *openness* (*Erschlossenheit*), the quality of being essentially open to the things. However, Heidegger distinguishes two different modes of "being-in-the-world." We have, on the one hand, *everydayness* (*Alltäglichkeit*), which is trivial, unauthentic existence. The subject of this trivial existence is the *Man*, the "one," the impersonal "they." Existence becomes trivial—in an unquestionable and necessary manner—in the "they," in the "anyone," and is a decadence or *fall* (*Verfallen*). The *Man* sees itself as fallen and lost in the world. The constitutive mode of existence is to find oneself in a state of *thrownness* (*Geworfenheit*).

AUTHENTIC EXISTENCE. However, Dasein can overcome this everyday triviality and come into its own; then it becomes *eigentliche Existenz* or authentic existence. The mode in which this is found is anguish (*Angst*)—a concept of which Kierkegaard had already made use. This anguish is not due to this or that cause; rather, it is caused by *nothing*; he who is in anguish is in anguish *over nothing*. Thus, it is *nothingness* that reveals itself to us in anguish. And Dasein is seen to be characterized as *Sorge, care,* in its primary meaning of *concern* or *pre-occupation.* Heidegger interprets a Latin fable by Hyginus, according to which Care made man and, in accordance with an edict of Saturn (time), has charge of him while he lives.

TRUTH. The question of the meaning of being is possible only if there is an understanding of being. (This pertains to the mode of being of the entity we call Dasein.) *Being* comes to mean *reality.* This concept raises the question of the existence of the external world, a question that has been decisive in the disputes between realism and idealism; but Heidegger observes that the question of whether there is a world and whether its existence can be proved is meaningless, as it is a question that establishes Dasein as "being-in-the-world." Heidegger distinguishes between *world* as the *where* of being-in (*In-Sein*) and *"world"* as a "worldly" entity. Then the world is essentially *open* (*erschlossen*) with the being of Dasein; and the "world" has also already been discovered with the *openness* of the world.

This result coincides with the thesis of *realism*: the external world really exists. However, Heidegger makes a distinction between his thesis and realism; he does not believe, as does realism, that reality needs to be proved or can be proved. And when *idealism* affirms that being and reality are only "in the consciousness," it affirms that being cannot be explained by the entity: reality is possible only in the understanding of being (*Seinsverständnis*); in other words, for all entities, being is "that which is transcendental"; but if idealism consists of reducing every entity to a subject or consciousness that is indeterminate in its being, then it is just as ingenuous as realism.

The forerunners of present-day philosophy (Maine de Biran, Dilthey) defined reality as *resistance.* However, Heidegger examines this problem in an even more fundamental way. The experience of resistance, discovery by means of the effort of that which resists, is ontologically possible only by virtue of the world's openness. Resistance characterizes the being of the "worldly" entity; but it is based in a prior way on "being-in-the-world," which is open to the things. "Consciousness of reality" is itself a mode of "being-in-the-world." If we wished to take the *cogito sum* as the point of departure of the existential analytic, we would have to interpret the first affirmation, *sum,* to mean: *I am in the world.* However, when Descartes affirms the present reality of the *cogitationes,* he also affirms an ego as a *res cogitans* without a world.

Thus, instead of understanding man as a reality shut up in his own consciousness, the existential analytic sees him as an entity which is *essentially* open to the things and which is defined by its "being-in-the-world"; therefore, as an entity which consists of *transcending* itself. The way was prepared for this conclusion earlier by the discovery of intentionality as a characteristic of psychical acts, a characteristic that naturally affects man's very being. Man transcends himself, points to the things, is open to them. As we have seen, this places the problem of the reality of the external world in a radically new perspective; the external world no longer appears as something "added" to man, but as something that is given along with man.

This is the basis for *truth*. Heidegger reintroduces the ancient, traditional definition of truth as *adaequatio intellectus et rei* (making the mind equal to the thing) in order to prove its inadequacy. Truth is primarily the discovery of being in itself (ἀλήθεια). And this *discovery* is possible only if based on "being-in-the-world." This phenomenon, which is a fundamental and constitutive dimension of Dasein, is the ontological basis for truth, which is therefore seen to be based on the very structure of Dasein. In his essay "Vom Wesen der Wahrheit" (1943), Heidegger locates the essence of truth in *freedom*; freedom is seen as a "letting be" (*Seinlassen*) of the entity; man does not "possess" freedom as a property; rather, freedom, the "existence" man discovers, possesses man; and Heidegger relates this to the historicity of man, the only historical entity.

" *There is* " *truth only in so far as and while there is Dasein*, Heidegger says. The entity is dis-covered and open only when and while there is Dasein. Newton's laws, the principle of contradiction, any truth whatever: all these are true only while *there is* Dasein. Before and afterward there is neither truth nor falsity. Before Newton, his laws were neither true nor false; this does not mean that the entity which these laws discovered did not exist previously, but that the laws turned out to be true through the agency of Newton; by means of these laws the entity discovered became accessible to Dasein, and this is precisely what truth is. Therefore, the existence of "eternal truths" could be demonstrated only if it were proved that there has been and will be Dasein throughout eternity. Thus, every truth is relative to the being of Dasein; this, naturally, does not indicate either psychologism or subjectivism.

But on the other hand, truth coincides with being. "There is" *being*—rather than an *entity*—when there is *truth*. And there is truth only while there is Dasein. Being and truth, Heidegger concludes, "are" equally primary.

DEATH. In Heidegger's philosophy the problem of death appears as an important theme. Dasein is always incomplete, because its conclusion implies at the same time a ceasing to be. It is possible, in a certain sense, to experience the death of one's neighbor. In such a case, the sum of what the neighbor attains in death is a *no longer existing*, in the sense of "no longer being in the world." Death produces the corpse; the *end* of the entity *qua* Dasein is the *beginning* of this entity *qua* present thing. But in spite of everything, the corpse is something more than an inanimate thing, and can be understood only from the viewpoint of life. Death is something peculiar to each and every man: "No one can take some one else's death away from him," Heidegger says.

Death is an essential characteristic of Dasein; but it is not an event within the world. Death for the Dasein is always a "not yet." It is a matter of "coming to one's end," and this is what Heidegger calls literally *being-towards-death* (*Sein-zum-Tode*). This *being-towards-death* is a constituent part of Dasein; and *dying*, from the point of view of its ontological possibility, is based on *Sorge*, care. Death is the most authentic possibility of existence. But the "they," the *Man*, in its trivial everyday existence, tries to hide this fact from itself as much as possible; *they* say: death will surely come but, for the time being, not yet. With this "*but*," Heidegger says, the "they" denies the certainty of death. In this way, the "they" covers up the peculiar feature of the certainty of death: that it is possible at any moment. As soon as a man is born, he is old enough to die; conversely, no one is so old that he does not still have an open future.

Death is the *most proper possibility of Dasein*. In authentic existence, the illusions of the *Man* are overcome, and Dasein is *free* for death. The *state of mind* which permits this acceptance of death as the most proper human possibility is *anguish*. There is not only a *being-towards-death*, but also a *freedom for death* (*Freiheit zum Tode*). This doctrine of Heidegger's bristles with question marks and internal difficulties, which cannot even be alluded to here.

TEMPORALITY. We have seen Dasein characterized as *Sorge*. What, now, is the meaning of this *Sorge*, this *care*? Anguish in the face of death is always a *not yet*; concern is characterized by an *awaiting* (*erwarten*); thus, it is primarily a matter of something in the *future*. And the resoluteness (*Entschlossenheit*) of Dasein is always in a *present*. Lastly, in *Geworfenheit*, "thrownness," the *past*, especially, functions as such. *Temporality* (*Zeitlichkeit*) manifests itself as the sense of authentic *care*, and the primary phenomenon of original and authentic temporality is the *future*. Heidegger subjects temporality and historicity (the latter based on the former) to a profound and far-reaching analysis. He finds that Dasein is essentially linked with time, and this explains the connection between the two central terms of Heidegger's ontology that furnish the title of his major work: *being* and *time*.

This brief outline is not intended as an adequate *exposition* of Heidegger's philosophy, which, at any rate, is perhaps not yet possible today. This philosopher's work is not yet concluded, and furthermore, its interpretation is problematical and controversial. It has been nearly forty years since the first volume of *Being and Time* was published, and the works published by Heidegger since then do not represent a body of doctrine—at least in mature form—comparable to the systematic doctrine in that book. Thus, a question arises over the meaning of Heidegger's philosophy. In his most recent works he has skillfully criticized the too hasty interpretations of his thought. What is of interest here is to show the sense and the position of this metaphysics that is so exceptionally profound, rich and stimulating, but also brimming over with philosophical problems and risks, which are apparent today in the work of those thinkers who with greater or lesser justification claim Heidegger as their teacher and inspirer. I have also tried to offer assistance to those who wish to undertake the very necessary, though difficult, task of reading Heidegger's brilliant work; he is read less frequently and less carefully than may be imagined. Therefore, I deemed it preferable to limit myself principally to the incomplete torso of *Being and Time*, instead of studying in detail his later writings, which would require an enormously painstaking exposition before any clarity could be attained.

3. "EXISTENTIALISM"

In the last few decades, and especially since the end of the Second World War, a highly complex philosophical movement has been greatly developed; this movement, which derives its major ideas from the philosophy of life, is generally referred to under the blanket name of "existentialism," a rather ambiguous and inexact denomination. Some of its representatives are about the same age as Heidegger—for instance, Jaspers, Marcel and Wahl, who belong to the same generation as other, differently oriented thinkers, such as Ortega, Hartmann, Lavelle, Le Senne, Maritain and Gilson. Jaspers, Marcel and Wahl began their philosophy independently of Heidegger, but have undergone his influence; other thinkers have continued his philosophy, developed it, and often denatured it. All these tendencies, very dissimilar in value and fruitfulness, diverging from one another considerably and varying greatly in significance, nevertheless have certain features in common. At one point they seemed to dominate the philosophic scene, at least in Continental Europe and Latin America, but their influence and prestige have slackened in the last few years.

The expression "existentialism" is the one most widely used, and yet many of these philosophers would reject it as a name for their doctrines. In order to establish an approximative classification, it would be possible to distinguish between *existential* philosophy (Heidegger), philosophy *of existence* (Jaspers, Marcel) and *existentialism* (a term which would have to be reserved for Sartre and his followers). All these forms of thought have been inspired, more or less remotely, by Kierkegaard, whose shadow hovers over them. Kierkegaard indicated his aversion to abstract or *sub specie aeterni* thought and called attention to existence: "Abstract thought is *sub specie aeterni*, it makes an abstraction of the particular, of the temporal, of the process of existence, of the anguish of man, who is situated in existence by a combination of the temporal and the eternal." "All logical thought is given in abstract and *sub specie aeterni* language. To think of existence in this way means making an abstraction of the difficulty one finds in thinking the eternal within becoming, which is what we are obliged to do, since whoever thinks is himself located within becoming. Consequently, thinking abstractly is easier than existing (like that which is called a subject)." "God does not think, He creates; God does not exist, He is eternal. Man thinks and exists, and existence separates thought from being, keeps them successively distant from each other." "Subjectivity is truth; subjectivity is reality." These ideas of Kierkegaard are the germ of a great part of the existential doctrines, most directly those of Jaspers and Wahl.

These forms of thought have aroused lively interest. The deeper reason for this, lying beneath any passing fads, is to be found in the fact that these philosophies are abreast of the times; they have stated the true problems of our age, whatever the truth of their solutions may be; they have responded to the desire for concreteness characteristic of all present-day thought; and above all, they have concentrated on the study of that reality which is, under one name or another, human life. I shall attempt to characterize briefly the most important thinkers of this group.

JASPERS. Karl Jaspers, born in Oldenburg in 1883, a professor at Heidelberg and then at Basel, was originally concerned with the sciences; he came to philosophy from psychiatry. His writings are numerous and some are enormously lengthy; the most important are *Allgemeine Psychopathologie* (General Psychopathology), *Psychologie der Weltanschauungen* (Psychology of World Views), *Die geistige Situation der Zeit* (translated as *Man in the Modern Age*), *Philosophie* (1932, three volumes: *Philosophische Weltorientierung* [Philosophical World Orientation], *Existenzerhellung* [Elucidation of Existence], *Metaphysik*), *Vernunft und Existenz* (Reason and Existence), *Nietzsche, Descartes und die Philosophie, Existenzphilosophie, Der philosophische Glaube* (translated as *The Perennial Scope of Philosophy*), *Einführung in die Philosophie* (translated as *Way to Wisdom*), *Vom Ursprung und Ziel der Geschichte* (The Origin and Goal of History), *Rechenschaft und Ausblick* (Accounting and Prospects), *Vernunft und Widervernunft in unserer Zeit* (Reason and Anti-Reason in Our Time), *Von der Wahrheit* (On Truth; the first volume, extremely long, of a *Philosophische Logik*) and *Die grossen Philosophen* (The Great Philosophers). Jaspers has been constantly concerned with ethics and has studied in detail Germany's responsibility in the Second World War, the defense of freedom and the historic problems of our time.

From the psychology of *Weltanschauungen*, or "world views," Jaspers progressed to a philosophy of existence (*Existenzphilosophie*); his philosophy has been characterized by Gabriel Marcel as "an orography of the inner life." It is based on the viewpoint of what Jaspers calls *mögliche Existenz*, or possible existence; that is, the incomplete. The question of being involves and affects the man who asks it; the quest for being is always unachieved, but essential (an echo of Kant's concept of metaphysics as a *Naturanlage*, or natural predisposition; Kant's influence on Jaspers is decisive). For Jaspers, existence is that which is never an object; it must come to grips with itself and with its own transcendence. Jaspers is especially interested in "borderline" or "ultimate" situations (*Grenzsituationen*), which cannot be modified, which belong to *Existenz* but signify the transition to transcendence—the historic determination of existence, death, suffering, struggle, guilt. A major concept in Jaspers' thought is what he calls *das Umgreifende* (that which embraces or involves, "the comprehensive"); it is the being which is not merely subject nor merely object: either the being in itself which surrounds us (world and transcendence) or the being we ourselves are (existence, consciousness, spirit). What we know is *in* the world, it never *is* the world; transcendence in its turn never comes to be the world, but "speaks" through the being in the world. If the world is everything, there is no transcendence; if there is transcendence, it is perhaps indicated by worldly being.

BUBER. Martin Buber (born in Vienna in 1878, died in Jerusalem in 1965) was a Jewish thinker who had close ties with this existentialist thought; his particular interest was in religious themes and Jewish mysticism. He placed special emphasis on subject-object and subject-subject relationships, and particularly on the *I-Thou* relationship. Buber made a great contribution to the theme of man's involvement with his fellows. His most important works are: *Ich und Du* (I and Thou), *Die chassidischen Bücher* (The Hasidic Books),

Zwiesprache: ein Traktat vom dialogischen Leben (Dialogue: a Treatise on Dialogical Life), "Was ist der Mensch?" (What Is Man?) and *Der Mensch und sein Gebild* (Man and His Image).

MARCEL. The first representative of these doctrines in France was Gabriel Marcel (born in 1889). Marcel, who converted to Catholicism in 1929, is a philosopher and playwright; he considers his dramatic works to be an essential part of his philosophical investigations. His most important books are *Journal métaphysique*, *Être et avoir* (Being and Having), *Du refus à l'invocation*, *Homo viator* and especially, *Le mystère de l'être* (The Mystery of Being); among his works for the theater are *Le seuil invisible* (The Invisible Threshold), *Le quatuor en fa dièse* (Quartet in F Sharp), *Un homme de Dieu* (A Man of God), *Le monde cassé* (The Broken World), *Le dard* (The Dart), *Le fanal* (The Lantern), *La soif* (Thirst), *Le signe de la croix* (The Sign of the Cross) and *L'émissaire*.

Marcel is not very systematic; his circuitous thought attempts to adhere to reality, following its meanderings and maintaining the greatest possible authenticity, as well as great fidelity to the things. The beauty of his intellect, his veracity and his lack of frivolity are well known. A religious man who is dominated by respect for reality, he makes a worthy and profound use of his intellectual gifts. He first used the term "existence" in 1914, and his thought has been called "Christian existentialism," but he rejects this name. "There is a plane," Marcel writes, "on which not only is the world meaningless, but on which it is even a contradiction to pose the question of whether it has any meaning; this is the plane of direct existence; it is of necessity the plane of the fortuitous, it is the order of chance."

A decisive distinction for Marcel is the one he makes between *problem* and *mystery*. For him, a problem is something one comes across, which blocks one's path; it is there in its entirety in front of me. A mystery, on the other hand, is something in which I find myself engaged or involved (*engagé*); its essence consists in not being entirely in front of me, as if in that region the difference between "in me" and "facing me" were to lose its meaning. Marcel believes that the problems of philosophy are not properly problems, but rather mysteries in this sense. Marcel uses the concepts of project, vocation, creation and transcendence. To create means to create at a level above one's self; to transcend does not mean to transcend experience, because beyond experience there is nothing, but to have experience of the transcendent. There exists for Marcel an *existential fulcrum*, a standpoint or viewpoint, which is that of man. The problem of the body is stated as the condition of "being incarnate"; this means appearing as this body, without identification or distinction. The body is a manifestation of the nexus which unites me with the world, and I can say, "I am my body." The existential is concerned with being incarnate, the fact of being in the world; and this is a *chez soi*; feeling is not a passive act, but a participation. Marcel has reflected deeply on the human situation, on sacrifice and suicide, on paternity and its relation to the bodily care of the child—hence the possibility of adoptive paternity—and finally on "creative fidelity." Marcel proposes a "concrete philosophy" determined by the "bite of reality," the themes of which are death, suicide, betrayal. The belief in the "thou" is an essential part of this philosophy; being is the site of fidelity, which signifies an enormous compromise and hope as an infinite credit; these ideas, along with faith in personal immortality, are closely linked with love, and are admirably expressed in a line spoken by one of Marcel's characters: *Toi que j'aime, tu ne mourras pas* (You whom I love, you shall not die).

Also of Marcel's generation are Jean Wahl (born 1888), a professor at the Sorbonne and author of *Étude sur le Parménide de Platon, Vers le concret, Études kierkegaardiennes, Petite histoire de "L'existentialisme"* (A Short History of Existentialism) and *Traité de métaphysique*; Louis Lavelle (1883–1951), whose relations with existentialism are much more remote: author of *De l'Être, Traité des valeurs, La dialectique de l'éternel présent*, and so on; and René Le Senne (1883–1954), whose principal books are *Introduction à la philosophie, Le mensonge et le caractère, Obstacle et valeur, Traité de morale générale* and *Traité de caractérologie*. The following generation, also closer to both personalism and spiritualism than to existential thought, is represented by Emmanuel Mounier (1905–1950), founder of the magazine *Esprit* and author of books on politics and of the *Traité du caractère, Introduction aux existentialismes* (Existential Philosophies; an Introduction) and *Le personnalisme*.

SARTRE. The best-known figure in French philosophy in the years following the Second World War is the representative of "existentialism" in the strict sense, Jean-Paul Sartre (born 1905). A *lycée* professor, novelist, playwright, political writer and director of *Les temps modernes*, he studied for some time in Germany, where he was strongly influenced by Husserl's phenomenology and by Heidegger, from both of whom a great part of his ideas are derived. Nevertheless, Heidegger has pointed out the great distance between himself and Sartre; in the last few years, Sartre has come increasingly closer to Marxism. His work is quite extensive; his principal philosophical writings are *L'imagination, Esquisse d'une théorie des émotions* (The Emotions, Outline of a Theory), *L'imaginaire* and *L'être et le néant* (Being and Nothingness; his major work, 1943); after a long silence, he published in 1960 another very long book, *Critique de la raison dialectique*; one should also include his essays "Situations," "Baudelaire," "L'existentialisme est un humanisme" (Existentialism and Humanism), *Saint-Genêt, comédien et martyr,* and so on. In addition, there are his "existentialist" novels *La nausée* (Nausea; 1938), *L'âge de raison* (The Age of Reason), *Le sursis* (The Reprieve) and *La mort dans l'âme* (translated as *Iron in the Soul* and as *Troubled Sleep*); his stories "Le mur" (The Wall), "Les jeux sont faits" (The Chips Are Down) and "L'engrenage" (In the Mesh); his plays *Huis-clos* (No Exit), *Les mouches* (The Flies), *Morts sans sépulture* (translated as *Men Without Shadows*), *La putain respectueuse* (The Respectful Prostitute), *Les mains sales* (translated as *The Red Gloves*), *Le diable et le bon Dieu* (The Devil and the Good Lord), *Nekrassov* and *Les séquestrés d'Altona* (The Condemned of Altona); and an autobiographical book, *Les mots* (The Words).

Sartre began with a phenomenological psychology and moved on to ontology rather belatedly; the subtitle of *L'être et le néant* is "Essai d'ontologie phénoménologique." It is a book of 722 tightly written pages, difficult to read; it uses traditional terminology, which is generally employed with transferred meanings; there are minute analyses, phenomenological descriptions, passages of great literary talent and others where the prose is abstruse and forbidding. The primary meaning of "existentialism" is the priority of existence over essence; this is equivalent to inverting the traditional terms while accepting the old outline of traditional ontology; in a certain sense, one might say that Sartre's philosophy is traditional Scholastic or phenomenological ontology *à rebours,* but without transcending the basic concepts and statements of problems. Therefore, the concepts he uses constantly are being, nothingness, in itself and for itself, for itself and for the other, and so forth. The being of man is interpreted as *pour-soi,* or consciousness, and here he is completely in line with Husserl. "Consciousness," Sartre writes, "is a being for which it is essentially a question of its being in so far as this being implies a being other than itself." "Consciousness is a being for which it is essentially a consciousness of the nothingness of its being." Sartre states the problem in terms of consciousness; in this he is much closer to Husserl than to Heidegger. As for the rest, many of his ideas were formulated by those two philosophers or by Ortega: project, choice (*choix*), "being condemned to be free" (Ortega taught decades earlier that "man is necessarily free," free for anything except for ceasing to be free, but at the same time he saw clearly that even if man always chooses, not everything in his life is an object of choice, neither his surroundings nor his vocation or original project).

Sartre professes what he calls "a consequent atheism," which he bases on extremely feeble and quite unjustifiable reasons; for him, man's basic state of mind when confronting reality is the realization that everything is " too much" (*de trop*)—consequently *nausea*. Man is a passion to found being and constitute the In-itself, the *Ens causa sui*— that is, God. "But the idea of God," Sartre concludes, "is self-contradictory, and we lose ourselves in vain; man is an ineffective passion." In the *Critique de la raison dialectique*, Sartre says that a structural and historical anthropology "trouve sa place à l'intérieur de la philosophie marxiste parce que je considère le marxisme comme l'indépassable philosophie de notre temps et parce que je tiens l'idéologie de l'existence et sa methode 'compréhensive' pour une enclave dans le marxisme lui-même qui l'engendre et la refuse tout à la fois." For Sartre, Marxism is the unavoidable philosophy of our time, and the reason for this is that Marxism has hardly begun to develop and man has not yet been able to overcome the circumstances which engendered it: "loin d'être épuisé, le marxisme est tout jeune encore, presque en enfance: c'est à peine s'il a commencé de se développer. Il reste donc la philosophie de notre temps: il est indépassable parce que les circonstances qui l'ont engendré ne sont pas encore dépassées."

I have quoted this passage from Sartre's work because it exemplifies his habitual manner of reasoning. In recent years, he has been the object of much criticism, and his prestige and influence have declined considerably. Sartre's influence on Simone de Beauvoir, the novelist and author of philosophical studies, has been enormous; and originally the great writer Albert Camus (1913–1960) was close to Sartre in his thinking; however, Camus later broke completely with Marxism. Maurice Merleau-Ponty (1908–1961), who was greatly influenced by the contemporary German philosophers, especially the phenomenologists, is the author of *La structure du comportement*, *Phénoménologie de la perception*, *Les aventures de la dialectique*, *Signes*. Echoes and imitations of these trends have been heard in almost every country of Europe and in Latin America, but in the last few years they have begun to diminish.

Ortega and His Philosophy of Vital Reason

I. ORTEGA'S PERSONALITY

LIFE. José Ortega y Gasset, Spain's most important philosopher, was born in Madrid on May 9, 1883, and died in the same city on October 18, 1955. From 1898 to 1902 he studied for his bachelor's degree in the Faculty of Philosophy and Letters at the University of Madrid, and took his doctorate in 1904 with a thesis on *Los terrores del año mil—Crítica de una leyenda* (The Terrors of the Year 1000—Critique of a Legend). In 1905 he went to Germany and studied at the Universities of Leipzig, Berlin and Marburg; at Marburg, which was philosophically the most important university in Germany at that time, he was a pupil of the great neo-Kantian Hermann Cohen. In 1910 Ortega became professor of metaphysics in the University of Madrid, where he taught until 1936.

Ortega began his activity as a writer in 1902. His collaborations in newspapers and magazines, his books, lectures and publishing efforts decisively influenced Spanish life, and in the last few decades his influence has become increasingly evident outside Spain. In 1923 he founded the *Revista de Occidente* (published until 1936), which, together with its book publishing program, the Biblioteca (still in operation), has kept Spanish-speaking readers fully informed on all intellectual matters. By means of translations and editions Ortega incorporated into Spanish thought the most important parts of European—

442

particularly German—learning and a repertory of classical works; his achievement makes it possible for scholarship in Spain to be the equal of that found in any other country today. A consequence of this effort and especially of Ortega's own philosophical endeavors has been the flourishing of a philosophical school in the full sense of the term; it is known as the *School of Madrid*, and its members include, among others, Manuel García Morente, Fernando Vela, Xavier Zubiri, José Gaos, Luis Recaséns Siches, María Zambrano, Antonio Rodríguez Huéscar, Manuel Granell, José Ferrater Mora, José A. Maravall, Luis Díez del Corral, Alfonso G. Valdecasas, Salvador Lissarrague, Paulino Garagorri, Pedro Laín Entralgo, José Luis Aranguren and the author of this book.

From 1936 on Ortega lived in France, Holland, Argentina, Portugal and Germany, with sojourns in Spain beginning in 1945. These were years in which his thought matured and in which he wrote his most important works. It was also during these years that his writings came to be known outside Spain—writings which now can be read in any of a dozen languages. Ortega always dedicated himself to a meditation on Spain, and all his work is conditioned by his Spanishness; Spanish thought as such is an influential force in the world today because of his efforts. In 1948 he founded in Madrid, with Julián Marías, the Instituto de Humanidades, where he taught and took part in seminars on various topics.

INTELLECTUAL STYLE. Ortega was a great writer. He occupies a secure place among the half-dozen most admirable Spanish prose writers of the century, and truthfully none is superior to him. His literary gifts permitted him to effect a transformation in the language and style of writing, the stamp of which is visible in a great many of our contemporary authors. Ortega created a terminology and a philosophical style in Spanish where previously they did not exist; his technique—the opposite of Heidegger's, for example—consists in rejecting neologisms in general and in restoring to the deeply felt, commonly used expressions of the language, and even to the idioms, their most authentic and original significance, which is often brimming with philosophical meaning or else capable of taking on such meaning. At his hands the metaphor attains, in addition to beauty, a strictly metaphysical value. He used to say, "In philosophy, clarity is courtesy," and in his writings as in his incomparable lectures he achieved maximum transparency for his thought. Ortega carries to an extreme the effort to make himself intelligible, to the point that he quite frequently leads the reader to think that because one has understood him without effort, one does not have to exert oneself to understand him fully. In some of his last writings Ortega arrived at a totally original way of expression, in which fidelity to the spirit of the language is united with absolutely new stylistic procedures, and which corresponds to the form of reason of which his philosophical method consists; this is what I have called the *statement of vital reason.* *

At the same time, Ortega achieved a renewal of certain literary forms. The writing of his works in view of the circumstances in Spain obliged him for many years to publish his thought in articles in newspapers or in essay form; he offered just that amount of philosophy that his readers could effectively absorb at any moment. "It was necessary to seduce readers toward philosophical problems with lyrical methods," he once said. Thus, Ortega wrote articles and essays of a special nature, which constitute some of the most important works of the twentieth century.

Ortega's interest was not limited to strictly philosophical problems; rather, he carried his philosophical point of view to all themes of life: literature, art, politics, history, sociology—all human themes have been dealt with by him. And with respect to an enormous number of questions, one often finds in a page or two by Ortega the illumination one has sought in vain in heavy tomes. However, all his writings, even those that seem furthest removed from philosophy, are linked to a philosophical purpose, and they can be understood fully only in the light of his system. This is because Ortega concerned himself above all with philosophy; and so today, centuries after Suárez, Spain again reckons with an authentic, original and strict metaphysician. By means of his intellectual work and influence, Ortega made philosophy in Spain possible and actual.

WORKS. Ortega's literary production was copious. His *Complete Works*, collected in six volumes, comprise writings published from 1902 to 1943; his later works make up three additional volumes. His most important works are *Meditaciones del Quijote* (Meditations on Quixote), 1914; *El Espectador* (The Spectator) (eight volumes), 1916–1934; *España invertebrada* (Invertebrate Spain), 1921; *El tema de nuestro tiempo* (The Theme of Our Time), 1923; *Las Atlántidas* (The Atlantises), 1924; *La deshumanización del arte e ideas sobre la novela* (The Dehumanization of Art and Ideas on the Novel), 1925; *Kant*, 1924–1929; *La rebelión de las masas* (The Revolt of the Masses), 1930; *Misión de la Universidad* (Mission of the University), 1930; *Guillermo Dilthey y la*

---

* I have given a detailed analysis of this aspect of Ortega's work in my study "Vida y razón en la filosofía de Ortega" in *La Escuela de Madrid; Estudios de filosofía española*, Buenos Aires, 1959 [*Obras*, V]. See also my *Introducción a la Filosofía* [*Obras*, II].

idea de la vida (Wilhelm Dilthey and the Idea of Life), 1933; *En torno a Galileo* (translated into English as *Man and Crisis*), 1933; *Historia como sistema* (History as a System), 1935; *Ensimismamiento y alteración* (Self-absorption and Change), 1939; *Meditación de la técnica* (Meditation on Technique), 1939; *Ideas y creencias* (Ideas and Beliefs), 1940; *Apuntes sobre el pensamiento: su teurgia y su demiurgia* (Notes on Thought: Its Theurgy and Its Demiurgy), 1941; *Estudios sobre el amor* (Studies on Love), 1941; *Del Imperio romano* (On the Roman Empire), 1941; and prefaces to three books: *Historia de la Filosofía* (History of Philosophy) by Emile Bréhier, 1942; *Veinte Años de caza mayor* (Twenty Years of Big-game Hunting) by the Count of Yebes, 1942; and *Aventuras del Capitán Alonso de Contreras*, 1943. His later works include *Papeles sobre Velázquez y Goya* (Papers on Velazquez and Goya), 1950; a preface to *El collar de la Paloma* (known in English as *The Ring of the Dove*) by Ibn Hazm, 1952; *Stücke aus einer "Geburt der Philosophie"* (Pieces from a "Birth of Philosophy"), 1953; *Europäische Kultur und europäische Völker* (European Culture and European People), 1954; *Velázquez*, 1954. The publication of his posthumous writings began in 1957 with his book on sociology, *El hombre y la gente* (Man and People); *¿Qué es filosofía?* (What Is Philosophy?), lectures for a class given in 1929; the extremely important and very long book *La idea de principio en Leibniz y la evolución de la teoría deductiva* (Leibniz' Concept of Principle and the Evolution of the Deductive Theory)—probably the most important of all his works; *Idea del teatro* (Idea of the Theater); the *Meditación del pueblo joven* (Meditation on a Young People); also, a "Preface for Germans" written and published in German in 1934; his first course at the Instituto de Humanidades, *Una interpretación de la Historia universal, Meditación de Europa, Origen y Epílogo de la Filosofía* (Origin and Epilogue of Philosophy); *Vives-Goethe, Pasado y porvenir para el hombre actual* (Past and Future for the Man of Today) and *Unas lecciones de Metafísica*.

Ortega's university lectures are of enormous importance, especially those of 1929 to 1936 and the later ones at the Instituto de Humanidades, which are indispensable for a precise knowledge of his thought. Several have only recently been published. These lectures reveal the systematic connection and integral metaphysical scope of his other published works. In these courses he dealt, above all, with the theme of idealism and its critique, the structure of historical and social life and the metaphysics of vital reason, the first version of Ortega's philosophical system, of which a complete exposition has never been published. Until Ortega's posthumous writings have been completely examined, it will be impossible to write an adequate book on his philosophy; this fact conditions the present exposition which, in spite of my knowledge of the course lectures and of part of Ortega's unpublished work, is of a fragmentary and provisional nature and is meant only to facilitate the approach to Ortega's work itself. *

2. THE GENESIS OF ORTEGA'S PHILOSOPHY

The Critique of Idealism

REALISM AND IDEALISM. Ortega's early formation was neo-Kantian; his years in Marburg gave him a detailed knowledge of Kant, a strict intellectual discipline, an internal vision of an ultimate form of "Scholasticism," and an immersion in the idealist attitude. However, as is evident in his first writings, he quickly reacted in a personal way; a short time later Ortega arrived at positions of his own which, as we shall see, were determined by the conquest of all subjectivism and idealism—without falling back on the old realist thesis: the pressing need for a system and the absolute predominance of metaphysics. These ideas, which passed through an uninterrupted process of development, led him to his system of *metaphysics according to vital reason*, and secondarily represent a decisive critique of idealism.

Realism is an attitude rather than a *thesis*. This attitude presupposes that true reality consists of the things; real being means being for itself, independent of me. However, this apparently quite obvious position which dominated philosophical thought for twenty-two centuries is not beyond criticism. From Descartes to Husserl philosophy maintained a new thesis which corrected and amended the realist thesis: this is what is called idealism.

Descartes discovers that the things are not for sure; that I may be wrong: that there exist such things as dreams and hallucinations, in which I accept as true realities things which are not true realities. The only thing that is certain and beyond doubt is the *ego*. On the other hand, I know nothing of the world of the things except in so far as I am present to them, in so far as *I am a witness* of them. I know of the room because I am in it; if I leave it, does it continue to exist? In the final

* Many specific problems are developed in detail in my above-mentioned study *La Escuela de Madrid* and in *Ortega y tres antípodas* (1950); for the first stage of his intellectual development in particular, see my commentary to the *Meditaciones del Quijote* (Biblioteca de Cultura Básica de la Universidad de Puerto Rico, 1957; 2nd ed., 1966). Although it is not strictly an exposition of Ortega's philosophy, I also refer the reader to my *Introducción a la Filosofía (Reason and Life)*, which is directly based on this philosophy; in this work I make systematic use of the method of vital reason. In addition, a study in depth of this philosophy is to be found in my book *Ortega*, of which Vol. I, *Circunstancia y vocación*, was published in 1960.

analysis, I cannot know that it does. I know only that it exists while I am in it, while it is *with me*. Therefore, the things by themselves, independent of me, are foreign and unknown to me; I do not know anything about them, not even that they exist. Consequently, the things are *for me* or *in me*, they are *ideas of mine*. The table and wall are *things that I perceive*. The fundamental and primary reality is the ego; the things possess a derived and dependent being, based on that of the ego. The ego is the fundamental substance. Descartes says that I can exist without the world, without the things. This is the idealist thesis, which culminated in its most perfect form in Husserl's idealism of pure consciousness, which has already been discussed. Ortega scrupulously opposes this thesis.

THE EGO AND THE THINGS. Idealism is perfectly right in affirming that I can know the things only in so far as I am present to them. The things—at least to the extent that I know them and that it is meaningful to speak of their reality—cannot be independent of me. However, idealism is wrong in affirming the independence of the subject. I cannot speak of the things without me; but neither can I speak of *an ego without the things*. I am never alone; I am always with the things, doing something with them; I cannot be separated from the things, and if they need me, I in turn need them in order to exist. In an equally original and primary way I find myself with my ego and with the things. The true primary reality—the *fundamental reality*—is that of the ego with the things. *I am myself and my circumstance, or surroundings* (*circunstancia*), Ortega wrote as early as 1914, in his first book. And at least in principle this is not a matter of two separable elements—the ego and the things—which are found together by chance; rather, the fundamental reality is this interplay or "business" (*quehacer*) of the ego with the things, which we call *life*. By using the things, man *lives*. This action is the reality in which we originally find ourselves; now it is not a *thing*—either material or spiritual, because the Cartesian *ego* is also a *res*, even though *cogitans*—but an activity, something that we cannot properly say *is*, but that is *done*. *The fundamental reality is our life. And life is made up of what we do and what happens to us. To live is to deal with the world, to direct oneself toward it, to act in it, to concern oneself with it.* Therefore, there is no priority of the things, as the realists believed, nor does the ego have a priority over the things, as the idealists thought. The primary and fundamental reality, of which the ego and the things are but abstract moments, is the dynamic "business" which we call *our life*.

CONSCIOUSNESS. Now we must examine the culminating moment of idealism, idealism in its most refined form: Husserl's phenomenology.

This is not a subjective idealism; he speaks not of the ideas or experiences of an empirical ego, but of the experiences of pure consciousness. In the effort to avoid metaphysics, while at the same time indulging in it, Husserl closes himself up in the *consciousness*.

Nevertheless, it so happens that thought—what we call consciousness—consists in *positing something*. To think is to posit something as true, as existent. Now, phenomenology says that this act of positing is followed by a second act which consists in practicing *epokhé*, in invalidating the first and bracketing it. However, this is neither so clear nor so simple as it appears.

I do not have consciousness of an act while I am experiencing it. I have before me only what is *seen* or what is *thought*; I am not in contact with *seeing* or *thinking*, with what is called *consciousness*. What is involved is: *I with the thing*. I am able to say that I have consciousness when I realize that I *saw* a thing a moment ago but no longer *see* it. When I have consciousness of my experiences, I am not living them, but making them objects of reflection. I am practicing "abstention" upon an object that is the *memory* of my previous vision. I am now experiencing *another* act: the bracketing of my previous act. Nor am I practicing "abstention" in this second act; rather, I am *experiencing* it; I have no consciousness of the second act while experiencing it, either; in it, too, I am *positing*. Thus I can perform phenomenological reduction only upon memories of acts, not upon the experienced or *lived* acts. Pure consciousness, with all its reduced experiences, far from being reality, is merely the result of a mental operation that I perform; that is, it is just the opposite of reality: it is an intellectual construction, a hypothesis. Therefore, phenomenological reduction is impossible.

Act implies *actuality*, the present time, being now; it is pure presentness. *Time* is interposed between the act and its phenomenological reduction—time, which is precisely the form of human life.

Therefore, I do not come into contact with the pure ego, nor with consciousness, nor with reduced experiences; all this is the result of my mental manipulation of my previous acts: precisely the opposite of what is meant by *reality*. It is of the essence of acts that they are experienced simply and that one can reflect upon them only from the vantage point of another act; that is, when they are no longer present and being experienced, but are only in the memory. Phenomenology bears within itself a basically false interpretation of primary reality.

The truth is that I experience acts and that these acts are *intentional*: I see *something*, I think *something*, I want *something*; in short, I have contact with *something*. And I have contact with it in a real and effective way, without any "abstention": *in life*. When we think phenomenology through to its basis, we discover its ultimate erroneous root and we are left outside it, beyond it: we find ourselves not in the consciousness, because, *strictly speaking, there is none*, but in the fundamental reality that is life.

This is Ortega's critique of idealism. He adopts whatever was justified in the idealist thesis, the affirmation of the necessity of the ego as an ingredient of reality, but he corrects the excessiveness of idealism, the affirmation that this ego is the primary reality. Neither the things alone nor the ego alone is the primary reality, but their interplay, the "business" of the ego with the things: in other words, life.

The Stages in the Discovery

It is of interest to consider very briefly the phases through which Ortega's thought passed before he attained the mature form of his philosophy; this will shed light on the meaning of the formulas in which the major theses of his metaphysics are expressed.

I AND MY CIRCUMSTANCE. Ortega's personal viewpoint first appeared in an essay published in 1910 entitled "Adán en el Paraíso" (Adam in Paradise; *Complete Works*, I, 469–498). In the first place, he there employs the term "life" strictly, in the sense of human life, biographical life; in the second place, he stresses man's environment, everything that *surrounds* him, not only directly, but also remotely; not only physically, but also historically and spiritually. Man, Ortega says, is the problem of life, and Ortega understands life as something concrete, incomparable, unique: "Life is individuality." He defines it with greater precision as *coexistence*: "Life is an exchange of substances; therefore, a *living together, coexisting*" (p. 488). He adds: "Adam in Paradise. Who is Adam? Anybody and nobody in particular: life. Where is Paradise? Is it a northern or southern landscape? It does not matter: it is the ubiquitous stage for the immense tragedy of living" (p. 489). Adam in Paradise signifies: myself in the world; and this world, understood properly, is not a thing or a collection of things, but a *stage*, because life is a *tragedy* or drama, something which man performs, something which happens to him along with the things.

In the *Meditaciones del Quijote* (Meditations on Quixote; 1914) there appears in the form of a *concept* the idea that had been expressed as a metaphor in the title "Adam in Paradise": *I am myself and my circumstance*. The reality round about me "forms the other half of my person." And "the reabsorption of his circumstance is man's concrete destiny." Starting with this point of view, Ortega makes an interpretation of what a forest is, avoiding the realist as well as the idealist presupposition; that is, he sets in motion the comprehension of a reality *from the viewpoint of life*. This doctrine culminates in a theory that sees truth as *patency* or unveiling—*alétheia*—civilization as security, and light or clarity as the root of man's constitution (*Complete Works*, I, 322–358).

PERSPECTIVISM. In the same work there also appears the idea that perspective is a constituent ingredient of reality: "The definitive being of the world is neither matter nor soul, nor any determined thing; it is a perspective" (p. 321). This doctrine is found already established as a doctrine (and even endowed with the name *perspectivism*, which Ortega came to prefer after trying other, less intellectualist names) in a paper of 1916, "Verdad y perspectiva" (Truth and Perspective; in *El Espectador*, I; *Complete Works*, II, 15–20). "The individual point of view seems to me to be the only point of view from which we can see the world in its truth." "Reality, precisely because it is reality and is found outside our individual minds, can reach our minds only by multiplying itself into a thousand faces or facets." "Reality can be looked at only from the vantage point which each and every man occupies, by fate, in the universe. Reality and the vantage point are correlates, and just as reality cannot be invented, so the vantage point cannot be feigned." "Every man has a mission of truth. Where my eye is, there is no other; that part of reality which my eye sees is seen by no other. There is no substitute for any of us, we are all necessary." In 1923 he adds, in an even more precise and strict formulation: "*Perspective is one of the components of reality*. Far from being a deformation of reality, it is its organization. A reality which would always turn out to be the same no matter what point it was viewed from is an absurd concept." "This way of thinking leads to a fundamental reformation of philosophy and, what is more important, a reformation of our cosmic sensation." "*Every life is a viewpoint on the universe*." (*El tema de nuestro tiempo* [The Theme of Our Time]; *Complete Works*, III, 199–200).

REASON AND LIFE. Returning again to *Meditaciones del Quijote* (the year 1914 is a decisive one for Ortega's thought) we find in that book the beginnings of a third theme, which is intimately connected with the two preceding ones and which will affect both of them when it reaches its mature formulation: the theme of the relationship between reason and life. "Reason cannot, need not aspire to replace life. This very opposition between reason and life, which is used so much today by those who do not wish to work, is already suspect. As if reason were not a vital and spontaneous function of the same type as sight or touch!" "When we dethrone reason, let us be careful to put it in its proper place" (*Complete Works*, I, 353–354). This idea reappears in a much more precise and rigorous form in *El tema de nuestro tiempo*, where it has become a doctrine of *vital reason: "Reason is only a form and function of life." "Pure reason must yield its domination to vital reason"* (*Complete Works*, III, 178). Later on he says: *"Pure reason must be replaced by a vital reason, in which pure reason can be localized and can acquire fluidity and the power of transformation."* Philosophy needs to set aside its utopian nature, *"preventing that which is a supple and expandable horizon from being ankylosed into a world."* "Well, then: the reduction or conversion of the world into a horizon does not in the least rob it of reality; it merely relates it to the living subject, whose world it is, and endows it with a vital dimension" (pp. 201–202). According to Ortega, the theme of our time is the conversion of pure reason into vital reason: from that point on, his philosophy is the systematic achievement of that task.

3. VITAL REASON

FUNDAMENTAL REALITY. Ortega says time and again that the fundamental reality is our life. But this expression must be understood strictly. *Fundamental* reality does not mean the "sole" reality or the "most important" reality; it merely means what it indicates: the reality which is the *foundation* for all other realities, in which they have their root. The reality of the things or of the ego occurs *in life*, as an aspect of life. "Human life," Ortega writes in *Historia como sistema* (History as a System; *Complete Works*, VI, 13), "is a strange reality, concerning which the first thing that may be said is that it is the fundamental reality, in the sense that we must relate all other realities to it, since the other realities, actual or presumptive, must appear in life in one way or another." Reality as such—as I have written elsewhere*— reality as reality, is constituted within my life; to *be* real means, precisely, to have a basis in my life, and every reality must be related to my life, although *that which* is real may transcend my life in some way. In other words, my life is the presupposition of the very idea and sense of reality, and reality is intelligible only from the standpoint of my life: this means that the term *real* can be understood fundamentally, in its ultimate sense, only within my life. But one should not forget that when we speak of *something real* and derive its aspect of "reality" from my life, the question of the relationship of my life with this "something" remains open; stated in a different way, to say that I am an

---

* *Introducción a la Filosofía*, VII, 66. Cf. also XI, 86.

ingredient of reality does not signify in any way that I am a part or component of the real things or entities; rather, it means that the effective nature of their "reality," understood as the dimension or nature of that which is real, is based on their "existence for me," their "being rooted in my life." Even in the case where *that which* is real is prior, superior and transcendent to my life, independent of it and even —in the case of God—the origin and basis of my life itself, its *reality* as such (if we wish to give some effective meaning to that term and not reduce it to an empty name or an ambiguity) has its *foundation* in the fundamental reality of my life, to which it is "related" in so far as it is "encountered" in it.

VITAL REASON AND HISTORICAL REASON. For centuries, ever since the Greeks, reason has been understood as something which grasps the immutable, the "eternal" essence of the things. Philosophers have sought to consider things *sub specie aeternitatis*, apart from time. This view of reason culminates in the mathematical reason of the seventeenth-century rationalists, which produces the physical sciences, and in Kant's "pure reason." But this mathematical reason, which is so useful in investigating nature, that is, those things which have a fixed being, a ready-made reality, does not work so well in human affairs. The sciences of humanity—sociology, political science, history— appear strangely imperfect in comparison with the marvels of the abstract natural sciences and their corresponding applied sciences. Mathematical reason is incapable of conceiving the changing, *temporal* reality of human life. When dealing with human life, we cannot think *sub specie aeternitatis*, but must think in terms of time.

This self-evident fact, which to a greater or lesser extent has continued to impress itself upon philosophical thought since the nineteenth century, has been the source of the waves of irrationalism that have inundated philosophy during the last hundred years. Ortega, in no way a "rationalist," is opposed to every form of irrationalism. He has written: "For me, reason and theory are synonymous. . . . My ideology does not oppose reason, since it admits of no other mode of theoretic knowledge but reason; it opposes only rationalism" (*Ni vitalismo ni racionalismo* [Neither Vitalism Nor Rationalism]; *Complete Works*, III, 237). The most authentic and primary import of reason is "accounting for [giving a reason for] something"; now, the rationalist does not take into account the irrationality of the materials with which reason deals, and he believes that things behave the way our ideas do. This error essentially mutilates reason and reduces it to something partial and secondary. "All the definitions of reason that made its essential aspect consist of certain special ways of using the intellect were not only too narrow; they sterilized reason, amputating or blunting its decisive dimension. For me, reason, in the true and precise sense, is every intellectual action that puts us in contact with reality, by means of which we meet with the transcendent" (*Historia como sistema; Complete Works*, VI, 46).

In fact, Ortega observes that mathematical reason, pure reason, is only a particular species or form of reason. To understand mathematical reason as reason pure and simple is to take the part for the whole: an error. Alongside mathematical, "eternal" reason, and above it, is *vital reason*. This reason is no less reason than the other kind, just the contrary. As we have seen, Ortega is anything but a "vitalist" with a leaning toward irrationalism. He is speaking of a strict reason that is capable of apprehending the temporal reality of life. Vital reason is *ratio, lógos*, a precise concept. What does it actually consist of?

Vital reason and living are "one and the same thing"; life itself is vital reason, because "to live is to have no other remedy than to reason in the face of one's inexorable circumstance" (*En torno a Galileo; Complete Works*, V, 67). What does this mean? To be alive is already to understand; the primary and fundamental form of intellection is human vital action. To understand something means to relate it to the totality of my life in progress, that is, my life as it is developing, as it is *living*. It is life itself which makes a thing intelligible by placing it in its perspective, by inserting it in its context and making it *function* in that context. *Life is therefore the very organ of comprehension.* Thus, it may be said that *reason is human life*. A human reality becomes intelligible only from the viewpoint of life, when related to that totality in which it is rooted. Only when *life itself functions as reason* are we able to understand something human. Stated with the utmost conciseness, this is what is meant by *vital reason*.

But the horizon of human life is historical; man is defined by the historical level at which it has been his lot to live; what man has been is an essential component of what he is; he is what he is today precisely because he was other things formerly; the realm of human life includes history. Life which functions as *ratio* is historical in its very substance, and history functions in every act of real intellection. Vital reason is by its nature *historical reason*. *

Ortega writes: "It is a question of finding the original and autochthonous reason of history in history itself. Therefore the expression 'historical reason' must be understood with full rigor. Not an extra-

---

* For an extended investigation of the problem of reason, see Chapter V of my *Introducción a la Filosofía*, especially pp. 47–49, from which I have extracted the preceding formulations.

historical reason which appears to fulfill itself in history, but literally, *that which has happened to man, constituting substantive reason*, the revelation of a reality which transcends man's theories and which is man himself at the bottom of his theories. " "Historical reason accepts nothing as a mere fact, but fluidifies every fact into the *fieri* from which it stems: it *sees* how the fact is made" (*Historia como sistema; Complete Works*, VI, 49–50).

It is obvious that this presupposes the elaboration of a series of mental categories and forms capable of grasping historical and vital reality; the mind's habit of thinking *things*, substances in the "Eleatic" sense, as Ortega says, makes it very difficult to arrive at an adequate concept of that which is not a "thing," but an *activity*, temporal life. Ortega asks us to pass beyond the notion of substance and every form of Eleatic thought, so that we can conceive this reality which makes itself. "In order to speak of being-man, we must formulate a non-Eleatic concept of being, just as we have formulated a non-Euclidean geometry. The time has come for the seed sown by Heraclitus to produce its great harvest." Since the vital is always individual and unique, determined by its surroundings, the concepts which apprehend life must be "occasional," such as "I," "you," "this," "that," "here," "now," even (and especially) "life," which is always "the life of each and every man." We are dealing, that is, with concepts that do not always signify *the same thing*; rather, their sense depends, with full rigor, on their *circumstance*. Thus, historical and vital reason is *narrative*; but it presupposes, in its turn, an *analytics* or abstract theory of human life, universal and valid for all life, which becomes filled in each case with circumstantial particularity.

PHILOSOPHY. Man does not consist primarily of *knowing*. Knowing is one of the things that man does; man cannot be defined—as rationalism defined him—by his cognitive dimension. Knowledge occurs in life and must be derived from it. One cannot call knowledge something natural and make it one's point of departure; rather, one must explain *for what reason* and *for what purpose* man knows. There is nothing human in man that is *natural*; everything in him must be derived from his life.

This life is something which we must make. It is thus a problem, insecurity, a *shipwreck*, as Ortega calls it in an expressive metaphor. In this insecurity man seeks a certainty; he needs to *know*, in the primary sense of "to know what to hold fast to." Life is always supported by a system of *beliefs* within which we exist and which we may not even be aware of; when these beliefs fail man, he must do something in order to know what to hold fast to, and this thing that man does, *whatever it may be*, is called *thought*. Then man comes to have *ideas* about the things. Now, not all thought is *knowledge* in the strict sense; knowledge consists of *ascertaining what the things are*, and this presupposes the prior *belief* that the things have a being and that this being is knowable by man. (See *Apuntes sobre el pensamiento* [Notes on Thought]—a brief but decisive study which contains the germ of a transformation of philosophy; *Complete Works*, V, 513–542.)

Knowledge is thus one of the essential ways in which man overcomes uncertainty; by means of knowledge I come to possess not the things—these I already have before me, hence my inquiry—but the *being* of the things. Being is something that *I make*, but it must be clearly understood that I make it *with the things*; being is an interpretation of *reality*, my scheme of holding fast to the things. When I receive knowledge, it is this being of the things—and not the things themselves—that passes into my mind: the being of the mountain, not the mountain itself. Therefore knowledge is a manipulation or, better yet, a "mental construction" (*mentefactura*) of reality, which is deformed or transformed by it; and this is not a deficiency on the part of knowledge, but its essence, and its interest consists precisely in this.

Man never possesses complete knowledge, but neither does he ever completely lack knowledge. His state is one of ignorance or insufficient truth. Man possesses many certainties, but they lack an ultimate basis and some are in contradiction to others. Man needs a basic certainty, a highest authority that can reconcile all antagonisms; this certainty is philosophy. Thus philosophy is the basic truth, the one that does not presuppose other authorities or truths; it must then be the highest authority for all the other particular truths. And therefore it must also be an *autonomous and universal certainty*. This is what makes it different from the sciences, which are partial truths and dependent on prior suppositions. But in addition, philosophy is *its own proof*; it is responsible and is *made by man*, and this distinguishes it from religion, which is based on revelation and therefore comes from God, and from poetry or the experience of life, which are "irresponsible" and do not constitute proof of themselves, even though they are universal. Thus, philosophy is a task or "business" that man, who is lost, carries on in order to attain a basic certainty that can inform him what to hold fast to in life. This explains for what reason and for what purpose man philosophizes.

4. HUMAN LIFE

THE "I" AND THE WORLD. The fundamental reality—that which I find all around me and distinct from all forms of interpretation or theory—is *my life*. And life is what we do and what happens to us. In other words, I find myself with the things, in a determined circumstance or surroundings, having to do something with the things in order to live. Thus I find myself in the midst of life, which is prior to the things and to me; my life is given to me, not as something already made, but as something to be done (*quehacer*). Ortega says that life, in effect, affords much to be done.

The most condensed statement of Ortega's philosophy is the sentence from the *Meditaciones del Quijote* that I quoted earlier: *I am myself and my circumstance* (or surroundings). The things are interpreted as *circum-stantia*, as that which surrounds the " I, " and therefore the things refer to the " I. " Therefore this involves a *world* which is not the sum total of the things, but the *horizon* of totality over the things and separate from them; the things are *in the world*, just as I am; but this world is my world, that is, my circumstance.

To live is to be in the world, to act in it, to be doing something with the things. Thus my circumstance consists of the *other-than-I*, everything that I encounter, *including my body and psyche*. I can be dissatisfied with my body and also with my disposition, intelligence or memory; therefore, these things are received; I find myself with them just as I find myself facing the wall; these realities are the ones that are closest to me, but they are not I. My circumstance, which on the one hand includes even my body and psyche, on the other hand also comprises all of society, that is, all other men, social customs, the entire repertory of beliefs, ideas and opinions that I find in my time; thus it is also my historical circumstance. And since I do not possess reality by itself, and since I make my life essentially *with* my circumstance, I cannot be separated from my circumstance and it and I together make my life whole. This is why Ortega says: I am myself and my circumstance, and if I do not save it, I do not save myself.

This profound analysis leads to a series of important questions, questions dealing with the *who* that is anyone, the " *I* " that makes its life with its circumstance or world—in short, with the major question of the person.

THE VITAL PROJECT. Since life is not something that is ready-made, but something that man must make for himself, man must determine beforehand *what* he is going to be. Ortega says that life is a poetic task, because man must invent what he is going to be. I am a vital program, a project or outline that I intend to carry out and that I have had to conceive in view of my circumstance. I find myself faced with a repertory or keyboard of possibilities and obligations, and I can live only by *choosing* among them. The possibilities are finite, but there are always several of them, and they seem to be many when I project my scheme or vital program upon the pure facilities and difficulties that go to make up my circumstance. Therefore man *cannot live* without a vital project, be it original or unoriginal, worthy or unworthy; for good or ill, man must be the novelist of his own life, he must imagine or invent the character he intends to be; consequently human life is, above all, *pre-tension*.

"Human life," Ortega writes, "is not an entity that changes accidentally; on the contrary, its 'substance' is precisely change, which means that it cannot be thought of Eleatically as substance. Since life is a 'drama' that happens and the 'subject' to whom it happens is not a 'thing' apart and prior to the drama, but a function of it, then the 'substance' is its plot. And if this varies, it means that the variation is 'substantial.' . . . The most disparate forms of being happen to man. To the despair of the intellectualists, *being* is in man mere *happening* and *happening to him*. . . . Man 'goes on being' and 'unbeing' —living. Man continues to accumulate being—the past: he goes on making a being for himself through his dialectical series of experiments. . . . Man is what has happened to him, what he has done. . . . This pilgrim of being, this substantial emigrant, is man. . . . In short, *man has no nature; he has instead . . . history.* Or, what amounts to the same thing: what nature is to the things, history—as *res gestae*—is to man." (*Historia como sistema; Complete Works*, VI, 35–41). But elsewhere: "The being of man is natural and extranatural at the same time, a species of ontological centaur" (*Complete Works*, V, 334); and also: "Human reality has an inexorable structure, which is neither more nor less than cosmic matter" (*Complete Works*, VI, 242).

ETHICS. Not every *activity* is a doing. Certain activities—for example, psychical activities—are pure mechanisms. Strictly speaking, they are not things I do, but things that are done or produced in me: I refer to such activities as imagining, remembering, thinking; at most, what I do is to *begin* to think or imagine, initiate that activity, for whose result I cannot answer. I can *begin* to solve a problem or write a sonnet, but it is not in my hands to find the answer or the appropriate rhymes and metaphors. *Doing* is an activity which *I* perform, *for some reason* and *for some purpose*, and therefore something for which I am responsible.

Well, then, my life is a task to be done, something I must do myself; I have at every moment to decide what I am going to do—and therefore be—at the next moment; I must choose among the possibilities that I encounter, and no one can relieve me of this choice and decision. The problem of *freedom* is thus stated in an entirely new way in Ortega's philosophy. Freedom consists in that compulsory choice among possibilities. "To be free means to lack constitutive identity, to not be ascribed to a determined being, to be able to be other than what one was and to not be able to establish oneself once and for all in any determined being." Man is thus constitutively and necessarily free, but this does not mean that he is completely and forever free. Inasmuch as his life is not ready-made, but something he has to make for himself, man cannot cease to be free; man is *necessarily free*: he does not have the freedom to renounce his freedom.

Since I have to decide what I am going to do at every moment, I need to *justify myself to myself* for doing one thing and not another; life is *responsibility*; in its ultimate substance, it is *moral*. Like all human reality, life admits of *degrees of being*. The things are what they are: a stone is a stone and a horse is a horse; it is meaningless to say that a horse is more or less of a horse; but in contrast, it makes perfect sense to say that a woman is *quite a woman*, or that a man is either *quite* a man or *not much* of a man. Since the being of life is not already and immediately given, it can be realized *fully* or *insufficiently*; it can be *falsified*. When one's life is made from one's own standpoint, when a man is true to the voice which calls him to be a determined thing, and which is therefore known as his *vocation*, his life is *authentic*; when man abandons himself to what is trite and handed down, when he is unfaithful to his intimate and original vocation, he falsifies his life and changes it into *unauthentic* life. Morality consists in authenticity, in bringing life to its maximum reality; to live is *to live more*. Morality consists in each man's realizing his own unique and unsubstitutable destiny.

5. Historical and Social Life

The historicity of human life. Man finds himself living in a particular period of time: at a specific historical level. His life is composed of a peculiar substance, "his time." Whereas a tiger is always the "first tiger," the one who is being a tiger for the first time, man is the *inheritor* of a past, of a series of past human experiences that condition his being and his possibilities. Man *has been* certain concrete things, and *therefore* he can no longer be them and must be other determined things. Individual life is thus already historical; historicity is an essential part of the life of every one of us. Therefore, "in order to understand anything human, be it personal or collective, it is necessary to relate its history. This man, this nation does such and such a thing and is as he or it is *because* previously he or it did this other thing and was this other way. Life only becomes somewhat transparent," Ortega says, "when viewed through *historical reason*. . . . The individual human being does not inaugurate humanity. He immediately encounters in his surroundings other men and the society which they comprise. Hence his humanity, that which begins to develop in him, takes its point of departure from another that has previously developed and reached its culmination; in short, to his humanity there is added an already forged mode of being man, something that he does not have to invent; he need only root himself in it and use it as a starting point for his individual development." (*Historia como sistema; Complete Works*, VI, 40–43).

THE GENERATIONS. History has a precise structure, that of the *generations*. Every man finds a world that is determined by a repertory of beliefs, ideas, usages and problems. Such a form of life possesses a certain stability, it lasts for a certain period of time. Ortega says that it lasts fifteen years. "A generation is a zone of fifteen years during which a certain form of life was prevalent. Thus the generation represents the concrete unit of authentic historical chronology; or, expressed differently, history advances and proceeds by generations. We can now understand the true nature of the affinity between men of a single generation. This affinity derives not so much from them as from their realizing that they are obliged to live in a world that has a determined and unique form." (*Complete Works*, VI, 371).

Generations are determined by a central date and constitute a "zone of dates" of fifteen years—seven years before and seven years after the decisive year. Thus a generation is common to all who were born within this zone of dates. Ortega makes a distinction between *contemporaries*—those who are living at the same time—and *coevals*—those who are of the same age, that is, who belong to the same generation. The *decisive* generations are those in which historical variation is much greater than usual; they govern the over-all structure of historical epochs. In Ortega's hand, the *method of the generations* becomes a tool of exemplary precision in understanding historical reality.*

MAN AND PEOPLE. One of the things we find in the realm of our life is society, social acts—customs, law, the State. These social acts are subscribed to only by men; nothing that deserves to be called *social* is to be found among the other creatures, and the so-called "animal societies" are something very different. Society is thus a fact of human life. However, this raises a serious problem, because human life is

---

* See J. Marías, *El método histórico de las generaciones* (1949) and the chapter entitled "Dinámica de las generaciones" in *La estructura social* (1955).

always *my* life, each man's life, the life of every one of us. It is life on an individual and personal basis, in which the "*I*" finds itself in *surroundings* or a world, without the security of existing in the immediate instant and having always to be doing something in order to assure its existence. Thus, to be precise, what is human is what I do myself, what is personal, what has meaning for me, and therefore what I understand. Therefore, human action presupposes a responsible subject, and life is, in its essence, *solitariness*. On the other hand, what is social does not arise from my solitude, but from my *living jointly* with other men. Thus, society is not life in its primary sense.

By whom are the social acts performed? A man shakes hands because it is what *one* does; a policeman stops traffic because he *is ordered to*. Who is the subject in the social acts? Everybody and nobody in particular; collective humanity, society; in short, *people*.

Therefore, social actions are human and not something else; however, they do not originate with the individual; they are not desired by the individual and frequently they are not even understood by him. To cite a trivial but immediate example, one does not know why one man greets another by shaking hands.

THE INTERINDIVIDUAL AND THE SOCIAL. However, a certain confusion has always prevented sociologists from seeing their problems clearly. They have traditionally contrasted what is individual with what is social or collective: on the one hand, the individual man; on the other, two or more men living jointly, which sociologists have interpreted as collective humanity or society. Ortega establishes an essential distinction which opens the way to a new sociology. There are two very different ways in which men live jointly. One of these is the *interindividual* way, a relationship between two or more individuals *as such*: love, friendship, and so on, are interindividual acts; they are instances of the coexistence of individuals as individuals. What is interindividual does not leave the realm of individual life, life *sensu stricto*. In contrast, the other way is properly *social*; it is impersonal and neither spontaneous nor responsible. Shaking hands, the policeman's stopping traffic, the postman's relationship with the addressee of a letter—these are not original and voluntary acts of individuals as such which individuals *desire* and *understand*. Man merely performs social acts in a mechanical fashion.

CUSTOMS. A *custom* is what we think, say or do because it is what *one* thinks, says or does. Social acts are principally customs. Customs do not ordinarily originate with individuals, but are imposed by society, by *people*. If we do not observe them, society makes reprisals against us (*social* disapproval of the man who does not greet others properly, juridical or *governmental* pressure on the man who crosses the street illegally). Customs are *irrational* and *impersonal*. They are "social or collective life," a very strange form of life that lacks some of life's essential characteristics, something halfway between nature and man, an "almost nature." There is no such thing as a *collective soul*. "Society, collectivity, is the great soulless entity, for it is humanity that has been naturalized, mechanized, almost mineralized." Therefore it is meaningful to call it the social "world." (Remember the problem that the "objective spirit" posed for Hegel.)

Ortega says that these customs permit us to foresee the conduct of individuals whom we do not know, allow us almost to coexist with strangers. Furthermore, they give us the inheritance of the past and bring us abreast of the times; this explains how there can be progress and history: because there is society. Finally, customs, while rendering many aspects of life inflexible and automatic, give man openness for what is most personal and allow him "to create what is new, rational and more perfect."

SOCIETY AND DISSOCIATION. However, one must take note of an extremely important point: if men are sociable, they are also unsociable. That is to say, society is never characterized by stability; it exists as an effort to overcome dissociation and unsociability; it is always problematical. Hence the frightening part of its character, its ties to authority, politics and the State, which "in the final analysis are always violence—in the best of times, to a lesser degree; during social crises, to an awful degree."

One must comprehend collective life as well as individual life because what is collective *happens* to man in his individual life. After studying human life in its originality, by means of the philosophy of vital reason one can approach the two major themes of collective "life": society and history.

This brief sketch of Ortega's philosophy, which cannot begin to include his final statements on the most important themes, is intended merely to demonstrate his extreme originality and importance and to show the direction of his thought. We find that his philosophy is completely rooted in the problem of our time. Step by step, in a meaningful progression, philosophy has led us to the discovery of the reality that is human life. The destiny of the age was to arrive at this point. As early as 1923 Ortega called the task of reducing pure reason to vital reason *the theme of our time*. He did not fail to respond to the inexorable summons of this theme. His last works show the maturity of his thought, the final positions he reached. *Man and People* signifies the authentic foundation of sociology, understood as a theory of social life and therefore rooted in the theory of individual human life, that is, in metaphysics. Ortega's 1929 course, *¿Qué es filosofía?* (What Is Philosophy?), is his first exposition of the essential features of his philosophic system. His book *La idea de principio de Leibniz y la evolución de la teoría deductiva* (Leibniz' Concept of Principle and the Evolution of the Deductive Theory) exhibits a capacity practically unknown up to now for penetrating to the very root of the meaning of Western thought as it is revealed in its history: the Greeks—especially Plato, Aristotle, Euclid, the Skeptics and the Stoics; the Scholastics; the moderns—philosophers, mathematicians and physicists; and the contemporary "existentialists." Ortega's critique shows "the level of our radicalism" and the deeper meaning of the philosophy of vital reason. A detailed exposition of these works—probably Ortega's most important—will have to take into account other writings that are still unpublished; together, they comprise the last phase of his thought. (For more details on this, see my book *Ortega*, of which the first volume has been published.)

6. THE SCHOOL OF MADRID

Ortega's strictly philosophical influence has been so profound that there is no form of thought in the Spanish-speaking world at the present that does not owe some essential part to him; but this influence was exerted more directly and positively upon his personal pupils, especially those who developed their thought in close proximity to him at the University of Madrid or those who were not in his immediate surroundings but who received certain principles and methods of thought from him. At the beginning of this chapter I mentioned the names of some of the thinkers who comprise the so-called School of Madrid; we shall now examine briefly the work of four of them who have made contributions of particular importance to the philosophy of our time. Like other members of the group, their personalities have developed in quite different and independent forms, and this, too, corresponds to the demand for circumstantiality and authenticity that characterizes every nuance of Ortega's thought.

MORENTE. Manuel García Morente (1886–1942) was born at Arjonilla, near Jaén. He studied at Granada and later at Bayonne and Paris, where he was a pupil of Étienne Émile Marie Boutroux and was influenced by Frédéric Rauh and especially Bergson, who was then beginning to dominate French thought. After receiving his degree in philosophy at Paris, Morente completed his studies in Germany

(Berlin, Munich and Marburg) under Cohen, Natorp and Cassirer, the three most important neo-Kantian philosophers. From 1912 on he held the chair in ethics at the University of Madrid, where from 1931 to 1936 he was dean of the Faculty of Philosophy and Letters. Ordained as a priest in 1940, he returned to his professorship and died in Madrid two years later.

Morente was an extremely cultured man and an admirable teacher and translator. In the course of his life his thought followed several paths. He was attracted to the Kantianism of his German teachers, and wrote an admirable exposition of it in his book *La filosofía de Kant*, which used the German philosopher as a point of departure in the past for a speculation concerning the present. Later he became interested in Bergson, whom he made the subject of a short book, *La filosofía de Henri Bergson*. A pupil and friend of Ortega, he attained the most mature phase of his thought in his personal exposition of Ortega's philosophy, with extremely interesting contributions of his own, such as the studies on progress and private life included in his book *Ensayos* (Essays). His most important work, which combines his view of the history of philosophy with his personal orientation, is the published version of a course he gave at the University of Tucumán, Argentina, *Lecciones preliminares de Filosofía*.* After the Civil War and the spiritual crisis that led to his ordination as a priest, Morente published several works which are collected in the volume *Idea de la Hispanidad*, as well as some studies of St. Thomas which, while not fully mature, give an indication of what the final phase of his thought might have been. But this phase was interrupted suddenly by his death.

ZUBIRI. Xavier Zubiri was born in San Sebastián in 1898. He studied philosophy and theology at Madrid, Louvain and Rome, taking his degree in philosophy at Madrid with a thesis entitled *Ensayo de una teoría fenomenológica del juicio* (Essay of a Phenomenological Theory of Judgment) and his degree in theology at Rome. He also pursued scientific and philosophic studies in Germany. In 1926 he became professor of the history of philosophy at the University of Madrid. He was away from Spain from early 1936 until the beginning of the Second World War; he was a professor at the University of Barcelona from 1940 to 1942. Since then he has lived in Madrid, not engaged in official instruction, but giving a series of very influential private courses or short series of lectures since 1945.

Zubiri's specifically philosophical development shows the influence

* A new, considerably abridged and revised edition of this work was published posthumously in Spain under the title *Fundamentos de Filosofía;* the second portion of this work was written by Juan Zaragüeta.

of his three principal teachers: Juan Zaragüeta, Ortega and Heidegger. His theological studies and Zaragüeta's leanings gave Zubiri a profound familiarity with Scholasticism, the mark of which is clearly visible in his thought. Ortega was a decisive factor in his mature development and orientation; Zubiri has written: "We were more than pupils, we were his handiwork, in the sense that he made us think, or at least made us think of things that we had not thought of before and in a form we were not used to.... And we were his handiwork, we who were preparing to be while he was in the process of formation. We received from him then something that no one will be able to receive again: the intellectual irradiation from a thinker in the process of development." Lastly, Zubiri studied with Heidegger at Freiburg from 1929 to 1931, shortly after the publication of *Sein und Zeit*, and the imprint of this instruction has similarly enriched his thought. To this should be added Zubiri's very broad and profound scientific knowledge, ranging from mathematics to neurology, to which he has given extraordinary attention all his life, and his studies of classical and Oriental languages, primarily as aids in the study of the history of religions.

Zubiri's written *œuvre* has been slow in coming and discontinuous, and its volume is still small. His philosophic essays—with the exception of "Sobre el problema de la filosofía" and "Ortega, maestro de filosofía"—were collected in 1944 in the volume *Naturaleza, Historia, Dios* (Nature, History, God). He published nothing else until 1962, when his long study *Sobre la esencia* (On Essence) appeared. In 1963 he published an edited version of a short lecture course, *Cinco lecciones de filosofía*.

Zubiri's historical studies comprise a large part of his work and have extraordinary perspicacity and depth. They are composed in a highly personal manner, as an attempt to seek the roots of his own philosophy; they thus have a relation to the present situation of thought which gives them a strictly philosophical character. This is a well-known quality of the first essays in *Naturaleza, Historia, Dios*—"Nuestra situación intelectual," "¿ Qué es saber ?" and "Ciencia y realidad"—which are an introduction to the consideration of the past—as well as the essays "El acontecer humano: Grecia y la pervivencia del pasado filosófico" (Human Events: Greece and the Survival of Philosophy's Past), "La idea de filosofía en Aristóteles," "Sócrates y la sabiduría griega" (Socrates and Greek Wisdom), and "Hegel y el problema metafísico." A perspective derived much more from theology, though accompanied by the unmistakable presence of current philosophy, is evident in the essay "El ser sobrenatural: Dios y la deificación en la teología paulina" (Supernatural Being: God and Deification in Pauline Theology), perhaps the most illuminating and profound of Zubiri's writings. His last book studies the idea of philosophy through the works of a discontinuous series of thinkers: Aristotle, Kant, Comte, Bergson, Husserl, Dilthey and Heidegger. He has studied the philosophical significance of contemporary physics in the essay "La idea de la naturaleza: la nueva física" (The Idea of Nature: The New Physics).

The most commented on and influential of Zubiri's essays is "En torno al problema de Dios" (Concerning the Problem of God; 1935), which seeks the human dimension from the standpoint of which this problem must be posed. Man is *implanted* in existence or implanted in being; he is supported *a tergo* by something that *makes us be*. This leads to the idea of binding (*religación*): we are *obliged* to exist because we are previously *bound* to that which makes us exist. Existence is not merely *thrown*; it is also *bound* to its root. Man's openness to the things shows that there *are* things; his being bound reveals that there *is* something binding him and that it is the fundamental root of existence. Zubiri calls this *deidad* (deity); the binding which he speaks of poses the intellectual problem of God as fundamental or founding being. From this arise the problems of religion or irreligion, even including atheism, which appear posed in this dimension of binding.

The ideas in the book *Sobre la esencia* were developed over a long period of time in university courses in which Zubiri treated various problems of metaphysics. It is an extremely tightly written and technical book that investigates in great detail and depth a central question of philosophy. Zubiri's purpose is to return to "reality in itself and to ask what is its structural element that we call essence." He uses the concept of structure in a thematic way, basing his argument on the philosophy of Aristotle. Moreover, he criticizes Aristotle's theory of substance, and this critique leads to the concept of *substantivity*, in the discussion of which Zubiri has frequent recourse to Scholastic thought patterns and makes constant use of the intellectual approach of science, physics and even more, biology. A considerable part of the interest of this work is related to the possibilities it offers of understanding biological reality and especially the reality of species. According to Zubiri, essence is an element of a *real* thing, and this element is a primary unit of its traits; on the other hand, this unit is not external, but intrinsic to the thing itself, and a principle on which all the other traits of the thing are based, whether or not they are necessary; essence thus understood, he concludes, is the *truth* of a thing that is within it, the truth of reality. In long analyses he establishes the domain of the "essentiable," "essentiated" reality and the very essence of the real. This complex and difficult book culminates in the exposition of the idea of transcendental order, in which Zubiri criticizes other conceptions of transcendentality and expounds his own. Throughout the book he uses concepts that he had developed in his courses, such as that of "sentient intelligence," which makes man an "animal of realities," defined by this peculiar "habit."

Despite the technicality of his style, his constant use of neologisms and his frequent references to the sciences, Zubiri's courses and writings are full of an unmistakable intellectual passion and a dramatic quality derived from the efforts of an exceptionally profound philosophy to clear a path for itself among its intuitions and unfold them dialectically in order to attain formulas of its own. The volume *Sobre la esencia* is the first of an announced series of "Philosophic Studies"; in these studies Zubiri's enormous knowledge and profound thought will surely be well expressed.

GAOS. José Gaos was born at Gijón in 1900. He was a professor at the universities of Zaragoza and Madrid, and rector of the latter university from 1936 to 1939; since that time he has lived and taught in Mexico. His teachers were Ortega, Morente and Zubiri, with whom he worked closely in the Madrid Faculty of Philosophy and Letters in the years immediately preceding the Civil War. He has devoted a great deal of effort to the translation of philosophic works, especially those of Husserl and Heidegger. He has written numerous studies on Spanish and Latin American thought, on problems in the teaching of philosophy, and on philosophy in the strict sense. His most important books are *Pensamiento de lengua española* (Spanish-language Philosophy), *Filosofía de la filosofía e historia de la filosofía, Dos exclusivas del hombre: la mano y el tiempo* (Two Things Peculiar to Man: The Hand and Time), *Confesiones profesionales, Sobre Ortega y Gasset, Filosofía contemporánea, Discurso de filosofía, Orígenes de la filosofía y de su historia* and *De la filosofía.*

Gaos has always been an admirable teacher; his gift, like Morente's, of instructing and communicating his thought, his clarity of oral expression, his intellectual curiosity, his precision, his wide knowledge and his sense of humor are qualities which have made him, in Spain as in Mexico, a man who has done much to awaken and inspire philosophical vocations, and his influence has been very great. His gifts as a writer, perhaps because of the great bulk of the translations he has completed, are below the level of his brilliant and attractive oral style; therefore, these qualities are especially to be found in those books which are faithful versions of his lectures, such as *Dos exclusivas del hombre*, in which one can discover completely untrammeled the originality, freshness and inspiration of Gaos's thought.

Combined with his vast and precise command of the totality of the philosophic thought of the past, Gaos has received a threefold influence that lends him special forcefulness: that of Ortega, who shaped the very root of Gaos's thought, as he did that of all the thinkers who experienced his direct influence; that of Husserl, whose works he studied with exceptional perceptiveness and insight; and that of Heidegger, perhaps the most apparent influence in the last few years. Gaos, who at times declares that he is nothing more than a professor of philosophy—only when one is truly a "professor" is it possible to develop oneself philosophically—and who makes no attempt to conceal a certain leaning toward skepticism, represents an irreplaceable element in the nascent Spanish philosophy of the present day.

FERRATER. José (Josep) Ferrater Mora belongs to the School of Madrid only indirectly. He was born in Barcelona in 1912, and was a personal pupil of the master professors of that city's university, especially Joaquín Xirau. He emigrated in 1939 and has lived in Cuba, Chile and finally in the United States, where he is a professor at Bryn Mawr. But his philosophic relations to the School of Madrid are very close: Xirau was a pupil of Ortega; Ferrater, referring to Ortega in 1935, spoke of the "filial attitude of one who has absorbed from him, more than ideas, style; more than thoughts, ways of thought." Morente and Zubiri have also exerted considerable influence on Ferrater, and one should not forget the influence of Unamuno and Eugenio (Eugeni) d'Ors upon him.

Ferrater's writings are very copious. Most important is his *Diccionario de Filosofía*, which he has enlarged and perfected in successive editions until it has become a splendid storehouse of philosophical information, abreast of the times, balanced and precise; it is a personal and strictly philosophic presentation of the reality of past and present philosophy. Other books by Ferrater are *Cuatro visiones de la historia universal* (Four Views of Universal History), *Unamuno: bosquejo de una filosofía* (translated as *Unamuno: a Philosophy of Tragedy*), *Ortega y Gasset: etapas de una filosofía* (Ortega y Gasset: an Outline of His Philosophy), *Variaciones sobre el espíritu* (Variations on Spirit), *Cuestiones disputadas*, *La filosofía en el mundo de hoy* (Philosophy Today), *Lógica matemática* (in collaboration with Hugues Leblanc), *El hombre en la encrucijada* (Man at the Crossroads), and *El ser y la muerte* (Being and Death). The last-named book is the one Ferrater considers most representative of his thought; in accordance with a characteristic practice of this author, who likes to go back over his own writings and revise them, it is a new

version of his earlier book *El sentido de la muerte* (The Sense of Death);
its subtitle is "Bosquejo de una filosofía integracionista" (Sketch of an
Integrationist Philosophy). By "integrationism" Ferrater understands "a type of philosophy whose purpose is to construct a bridge
over the gulf that all too often yawns between that thought which
takes as its axis human existence or realities described by analogy to it
and that thought which takes Nature as its axis." He does not want a
mere "leveling" of the doctrines, nor an eclectic selection of elements
from them, nor a "compromise" between their extreme viewpoints;
what he wants is a *bridge* over which one can pass in either direction,
while the respective untenability of each position is preserved. Ferrater, who keeps close watch on everything being done in philosophy
today, in Europe, in the Anglo-Saxon world and even in the Soviet
world, presents this aggregate in a relatively flat, unforeshortened
perspective that is not primarily his own personal one. Outside the
area of philosophy, an analogous attitude may be observed in his
interesting book *Tres mundos: Cataluña, España, Europa* (Three Worlds:
Catalonia, Spain, Europe), written with the tranquillity, keenness and
intelligent irony that characterize all of his intellectual work.

We have followed the entire history of Western philosophy century
by century and stage by stage, from Greece to Ortega and the philosophical group originated by him. God has allowed us to close this
history, as is just, with Spanish names. As we reach this point, philosophy shows us the underlying unity of its meaning, despite all its
differences. At the end we find the entire past present in ourselves.
This is what gives the history of philosophy its seriousness; in it we feel,
in the present, the weight of the entire past. But this ending is not a
conclusion. The history of philosophy comes to a close in the present, but
the present, which is laden with the entire past, bears the future within
itself; the mission of the present consists of setting the future in motion.
Perhaps in the time to come Spain will no longer be outside this
movement, for in Ortega Spain has made philosophy its own.

Bibliography

NOTE TO THE PRESENT EDITION

No title has been added to or deleted from the *Apéndice Bibliográfico* as printed in the twenty-second Spanish edition. This bibliography thus remains, according to the author's wishes, a record of the works he found most useful in writing and revising his book. The translators have added authors' first names and places of publication wherever possible. They have added references to all English translations of works that came to their attention, at the same time deleting references to Spanish translations wherever it was possible to supply the original title or an English translation of a work.

I. DICTIONARIES AND GENERAL HISTORIES OF PHILOSOPHY

Eisler, Rudolf, *Wörterbuch der philosophischen Begriffe und Ausdrücke*, Berlin, 1899.
——— *Philosophen-Lexikon*, Berlin, 1912.
Baldwin, James Mark (ed.), *Dictionary of Philosophy and Psychology*, new ed. (1925, 3 vol. in 4) reprinted New York, 1940–49.
Lalande, André, *Vocabulaire technique et critique de la philosophie*, 4th ed. (2 vol.), Paris, 1932.
Schmidt-Streller, *Philosophisches Wörterbuch*.
Runes, Dagobert David (ed.), *The Dictionary of Philosophy*, New York, 1942.
Ferrater Mora, José, *Diccionario de Filosofía*, 5th ed., Buenos Aires, 1965.
Zaragüeta [Bengoechea], Juan, *Vocabulario filosófico*, Madrid, 1955.
Erdmann, Johann Eduard, *Grundriss der Geschichte der Philosophie*, 3rd ed. (2 vol.), Berlin, 1878.
Windelband, Wilhelm, *Lehrbuch der Geschichte der Philosophie*, 11th ed., Tübingen, 1924; rev. by Heinz Heimsoeth, 1935.
Wundt, W., Oldenberg, H., *et al.*, *Allgemeine Geschichte der Philosophie* (Teil I, Abt. V of *Die Kultur der Gegenwart*), Berlin, 1909.

Baeumler, A. and Schröter, M. (edd.), *Die Grunddisziplinen* (Abt. I of *Handbuch der Philosophie*), Munich, 1934.

Janet-Séailles, *Histoire de la philosophie*, Paris, 1887.

Messer, August, *Geschichte der Philosophie* (3 vol.), Leipzig, 1912–16.

Vorländer, Karl, *Geschichte der Philosophie*, 9th ed. (2 vol.), Hamburg, *c.* 1949–55.

Bréhier, Émile, *Histoire de la philosophie* (2 vol. in 7), Paris, 1926–32. Eng. trans. by Joseph Thomas, *History of Philosophy, Vol. 1: The Hellenic Age*, Chicago, 1963.

Russell, Bertrand, *A History of Western Philosophy*, New York, 1959.

Copleston, Frederick, *A History of Philosophy* (5 vol. published), London, 1946–59.

Rivaud, Albert, *Histoire de la philosophie* (4 vol.), Paris, 1948–62.

Marías, Julián (ed.), *La filosofía en sus textos* (anthology), 2nd ed. (3 vol.), Barcelona, 1960.

II. ON THE ESSENCE OF PHILOSOPHY

Bergson, Henri, *Introduction à la métaphysique*. Eng. trans. by T. E. Hulme, *An Introduction to Metaphysics*, New York, 1912.

Dilthey, Wilhelm, *Das Wesen der Philosophie*, Berlin, 1907. Eng. trans. by Stephen A. Emery and William T. Emery, *The Essence of Philosophy*, Chapel Hill, 1954.

Husserl, Edmund, "Philosophie als strenge Wissenschaft," *Logos*, 1911.

Scheler, Max, "Vom Wesen der Philosophie," in *Vom Ewigen im Menschen*, 1921.

Heidegger, Martin, *Was ist Metaphysik?*, 3rd printing, Bonn, 1931.

Ortega y Gasset, José, *Prólogo a una Historia de la Filosofía* (in Vol. VI of *Obras Completas*), Madrid, 1947.

Zubiri, Xavier, "Sobre el problema de la filosofía," *Revista de Occidente*, Nos. 115 and 118, 1935.

Marías, Julián, *Introducción a la Filosofía*, Madrid, 1947. Eng. trans. by Kenneth S. Reid and Edward Sarmiento, *Reason and Life*, London & New Haven, 1956.

—— *Biografía de la Filosofía*, Buenos Aires, 1954.

—— *Idea de la Metafísica*, Buenos Aires, 1954.

III. GREEK PHILOSOPHY

Sources

Diels, Hermann (ed. & trans.), *Die Fragmente der Vorsokratiker*, 6th ed. (3 vol.), Berlin, 1951–52.

Ritter-Preller, *Historia philosophiae graecae* (1838), 10th ed., Hamburg, 1914.

Arnim, Hans Friedrich August von, *Stoicorum veterum fragmenta* (4 vol.), Leipzig, 1903–24.

Nestle, Wilhelm, (sel., ed. & trans.), *Die Vorsokratiker*, Jena, 1908.

—— *Die Sokratiker.*

—— *Die Nachsokratiker.*

Capelle, Wilhelm, *Die Vorsokratiker*, 1953.

Freeman, Kathleen, *The Pre-Socratic Philosophers*, 2nd ed., Oxford, 1949.

——— *Ancilla to the Pre-Socratic Philosophers* (Eng. trans. of the fragments in Diels), Cambridge, Mass., 1948.

Vogel, C. J. de (ed.), *Greek Philosophy* (3 vol.), Leiden, 1959–63.

General Works

Zeller, Eduard, *Die Philosophie der Griechen* (3 vol. in 6), Leipzig, 1879–92.

Gomperz, Theodor, *Griechische Denker* (3 vol.), Leipzig, 1903–9. Eng. trans. by Laurie Magnus and G. G. Berry, *Greek Thinkers* (4 vol.), London, 1914–31.

Joël, Karl, *Geschichte der antiken Philosophie*, Tübingen, 1921.

Hönigswald, Richard, *Die Philosophie des Altertums*, 1917.

Cassirer, Ernst and Hoffman, E., *Geschichte der antiken Philosophie*, 1925.

Meyer, H., *Geschichte der alten Philosophie*, 1925.

Stenzel, Julius, "Metaphysik des Altertums," in A. Baeumler and M. Schröter (edd.), *Die Grunddisziplinen* (Abt. I of *Handbuch der Philosophie*), Munich, 1934.

Howald, Ernst, *Ethik des Altertums*, Munich, 1934.

Jaeger, Werner Wilhelm, *Paideia*, 3rd ed. (3 vol.), Berlin, 1954–55. Eng. trans. of 2nd German ed. by Gilbert Highet, *Paideia*, 2nd ed. (3 vol.), New York, 1960.

Stace, Walter Terence, *A Critical History of Greek Philosophy*, London, 1920.

Burnet, John, *Early Greek Philosophy* (1892), 4th ed., London, 1930.

——— *Greek Philosophy, I : Thales to Plato*, London, 1914.

Robin, Léon, *La pensée grecque*, new ed., Paris, 1948. Eng. trans. by M. R. Dobie, *Greek Thought and the Origins of the Scientific Spirit*, London and New York, 1928.

Tannery, Paul, *Pour l'histoire de la science hellène*, Paris, 1887.

Schuhl, Pierre Maxime, *Essai sur la formation de la pensée grecque*, 2nd ed., Paris, 1949.

Werner, C., *La philosophie grecque*, Paris, 1938.

Marías, Julián, *Biografía de la Filosofía*, Buenos Aires, 1954.

Monographs

THE PRE-SOCRATICS

Gigon, Olof Alfred, *Der Ursprung der griechischen Philosophie*, Basel, 1945.

Diels, Hermann (ed. & trans.), *Herakleitos von Ephesos*, 2nd ed., Berlin, 1909.

Weerts, Emil, *Heraklit und Herakliteer*, Berlin, 1926.

Reinhardt, Karl, *Parmenides und die Geschichte der griechischen Philosophie*, 1916.

Riezler, Kurt, *Parmenides*, Frankfurt am Main, 1934.

Zubiri, Xavier, *Naturaleza, Historia, Dios*, Madrid, 1944, pp. 216–255.

Bignone, Ettore, *Empedocle*, 1916.

Jaeger, Werner Wilhelm: Eng. trans. by Edward S. Robinson, *The Theology of the Early Greek Philosophers*, Oxford, 1947.

Wheelwright, Philip Ellis, *Heraclitus*, Princeton, 1959.

THE SOPHISTS AND SOCRATES

Gomperz, Heinrich, *Sophistik und Rhetorik*, Leipzig, 1912.
Meunier, Mario, *La légende de Socrate*, 1926.
Kuhn, Helmut, *Sokrates*, Berlin, 1934; reprinted Munich, 1959.
Dawson, Miles Menander, *Ethics of Socrates*, New York, 1924.
Carrill, H. F., *Socrates, or The Emancipation of Mankind*, 1927.
Zubiri, Xavier, "Sócrates y la sabiduría griega," in *Naturaleza, Historia, Dios*, Madrid, 1944.
Tovar, Antonio, *Vida de Sócrates*, Madrid, 1947.
Gigon, Olof Alfred, *Sokrates*, Bern, 1947.

PLATO

Grote, George, *Plato* (4 vol.), London, 1888.
Ritter, Constantin, *Platon*, 1910–23.
Wilamowitz-Moellendorff, Ulrich von, *Platon* (2 vol.), Berlin, 1919; *Platon, sein Leben und seine Werke*, ed. after author's 3rd ed. by Bruno Snell, Berlin, 1948.
Pater, Walter, *Plato and Platonism*, London, 1912.
Natorp, Paul Gerhard, *Platos Ideenlehre*, Leipzig, 1903.
Landsberg, Paul Ludwig; Span. trans., *La Academia platónica*, Madrid, 1926.
Robin, Léon, *Platon*, Paris, 1938.
Moreau, Joseph, *La construction de l'idéalisme platonicien*, Paris, 1938.
Marías, Julián, "Introducción a Platón," in *Fedro* (Span. ed. of Plato's *Phaedrus*), Buenos Aires, 1948.

ARISTOTLE

Brentano, Franz Clemens, *Aristoteles und seine Weltanschauung*, 1911.
Taylor, Alfred Edward, *Aristotle*, reprinted New York, 1955.
Hamelin, Octave, *Le système d'Aristote*, 2nd ed., Paris, 1931.
Siebeck, Hermann, *Aristoteles*, Stuttgart, 1899.
Ross, Sir William David, *Aristotle*, 5th ed., London, 1956.
Jaeger, Werner Wilhelm, *Aristoteles*, 2nd ed., Berlin, 1955. Eng. trans. by Richard Robinson, *Aristotle*, Oxford, 1934.
Bröcker, Walter, *Aristoteles*, 2nd ed., Frankfurt am Main, 1957.
Robin, Léon, *Aristote*, Paris, 1944.
Marías, Julián, Introduction to Span. ed. of Aristotle's *Politics*, Madrid, 1950.
——— Introduction to Span. ed. of Aristotle's *Nicomachean Ethics*, Madrid, 1960.
Allan, Donald James, *The Philosophy of Aristotle*, London and New York, 1957.
Moreau, Joseph, *Aristote et son école*, Paris, 1962.

THE IDEAL OF THE WISE MAN

Guyau, Marie Jean, *La morale d'Épicure*, 1878.
Bignone, Ettore, *Epicuro*, 1920.
Barth, Paul, *Die Stoa*, 6th ed., Stuttgart, 1946.
Marías, Julián, "Introducción a la filosofía estoica," in *Sobre la felicidad* (Span. ed. of Seneca's *De vita beata*), Madrid, 1943.
——— "Marco Aurelio o la exageración," in *San Anselmo y el insensato*, Madrid, 1944.

Bibliography

473

NEOPLATONISM

Simon, Jules, *Histoire de l'école d'Alexandrie* (2 vol.), Paris, 1845.

Vacherot, Étienne, *Histoire critique de l'école d'Alexandrie* (3 vol.), Paris, 1846–51.

Whittaker, Thomas, *The Neo-Platonists*, 2nd ed., Cambridge (Eng.), 1918.

Inge, William Ralph, *The Philosophy of Plotinus*, 3rd ed., London and New York, 1929.

Heinemann, F., *Plotin*, 1921.

Bréhier, Émile, *La philosophie de Plotin*, Paris, 1928. Eng. trans. by Joseph Thomas, *The Philosophy of Plotinus*, Chicago, 1958.

Mehlis, Georg, *Plotin*, Stuttgart, 1924.

IV. CHRISTIANITY

Sources

Migne, Jacques Paul (ed.), *Patrologiae cursus completus. Series Latina* (*P. L.*) (221 vol.), Paris, 1844–64; *Supplementum* in progress since 1958, Paris; Indexes, Rotterdam, 1952. *Series Graeca* (*P. G.*) (161 vol.), Paris, 1857–80; Indexes (2 vol. in 3), Paris, 1928–36.

Rouët de Journel, Marie Joseph (comp.), *Enchiridion Patristicum*, 14th ed., Barcelona, 1946.

General Works

Labriolle, Pierre Champagne de, *Histoire de la littérature latine chrétienne*, 2nd ed., Paris, 1924. Eng. trans. by Herbert Wilson, *History and Literature of Christianity from Tertullian to Boethius*, New York, 1925.

—— *La réaction païenne*, Paris, 1934.

Batiffol, Pierre, *Anciennes littératures chrétiennes. La littérature grecque*, Paris, 1897.

Bardenhewer, Otto, *Geschichte der altkirchlichen Litteratur*, Vol. I, Freiburg im Breisgau, 1952.

Harnack, Adolf von, *Geschichte der altchristlichen Litteratur* (2 vol.), Leipzig, 1893–1904.

—— *Lehrbuch der Dogmengeschichte* (3 vol.), Freiburg im Breisgau, 1888–90. Eng. trans. of 3rd Ger. ed. by Neil Buchanan, *History of Dogma*, reprinted (7 vol. in 4), New York, 1961.

Tixeront, Joseph, *Histoire des dogmes* (3 vol.), Paris, 1905–12.

Puech, Aimé, *Les apologistes grecs du 1er siècle de notre ère*, 1912.

Corbière, *Le christianisme et la fin de la philosophie antique*, 1921.

Faye, Eugène de, *Introduction à l'histoire du gnosticisme*, Paris, 1903.

—— *Gnostiques et gnosticisme*, Paris, 1913.

Newman, H., *Essay on the Development of Christian Doctrine*, 1845.

MacGeffert, A. C., *A History of Christian Thought*, 1932–33.

Marín Sola, J., *La evolución homogénea del dogma católico*, 1923.

Amor Ruibal, A., *Los problemas fundamentales de la filosofía y del dogma* (10 vol.).

Zubiri, Xavier, "El ser sobrenatural: Dios y la deificación en la teología paulina," in *Naturaleza, Historia, Dios*, Madrid, 1944.

Monographs

Prat, *Origène*, Paris, 1907.

474   Bibliography

Faye, Eugène de, *Origène, sa vie, son œuvre, sa pensée* (3 vol.), Paris, 1923–29.
——— *Esquisse de la pensée d'Origène*, 1925. Eng. trans. by Fred Rothwell, *Origen and His Work*, New York, 1929.
Cadiou, *Introduction au système d'Origène*, 1932.
Karrer, Otto, *Augustinus*.
——— *Das religiöse Leben*, 1923.
Portalié, Eugène, "Saint Augustin," in *Dictionnaire de Théologie Catholique* (15 vol. in 27), Paris, 1909–50, col. 2268–2474. Eng. trans. of article by Ralph J. Bastian, *A Guide to the Thought of Saint Augustine*, Chicago, 1960.
Gilson, Étienne Henri, *Introduction à l'étude de Saint Augustin*, 2nd ed., Paris, 1943. Eng. trans. by L. E. M. Lynch, *The Christian Philosophy of Saint Augustine*, New York, 1960.
Troeltsch, Ernst D., *Augustin, die christliche Antike und das Mittelalter*, Munich, 1915.
Eibl, Hans, *Augustin und die Patristik*, Munich, 1923.
Schmaus, *Die psychologische Trinitätslehre des hl. Augustinus*, 1927.
Mausbach, J. *Die Ethik des hl. Augustinus* (2 vol.), 1909.
Przywara, Erich (ed.), *Die Gestalt als Gefüge*, Leipzig, 1934. Eng. trans., *An Augustine Synthesis, arranged by Erich Przywara*, New York, 1945.
Guitton, Jean, *Le temps et l'éternité chez Plotin et Saint Augustin*, Paris, 1933.
Wolfson, Harry Austryn, *The Philosophy of the Church Fathers, Vol. I*, Cambridge, Mass., 1956.
——— *Philo: Foundations of Religious Philosophy in Judaism, Christianity, and Islam* (2 vol.), Cambridge, Mass., 1947.

V. MEDIEVAL PHILOSOPHY

General Works

Huizinga, Johan; Eng. trans., *The Waning of the Middle Ages* (1924), reprinted New York, 1954.
Taylor, Henry Osborn, *The Mediaeval Mind*, 4th ed. (2 vol., 1938), reprinted Cambridge, Mass.
Grabmann, Martin, *Die Geschichte der scholastischen Methode* (2 vol., 1909–11), reprinted Graz, 1957.
——— *Mittelalterliches Geistesleben* (3 vol.), Munich, 1926–56.
——— *Filosofía medieval* (Span. trans., 1928).
——— *Historia de la teología católica* (Span. trans., 1928).
Wulf, Maurice de, *Histoire de la philosophie médiévale*, 6th ed. (2 vol.), Louvain, 1934–36. Eng. trans. of 6th French ed. by Ernest C. Messenger, *History of Mediaeval Philosophy*, 3rd ed. (2 vol.), London, 1935–38.
Gilson, Étienne Henri, *La philosophie au moyen âge*, 2nd ed., Paris, 1952.
——— *L'esprit de la philosophie médiévale*, 2nd ed., Paris, 1944. Eng. trans. by A. C. H. Downes, *The Spirit of Mediaeval Philosophy*, New York, 1936.
——— *History of Christian Philosophy in the Middle Ages*, New York, 1955.
Dempf, Alois, "Die Ethik des Mittelalters," in A. Baeumler and M. Schröter (edd.), *Mensch und Charakter* (Abt. III of *Handbuch der Philosophie*), Munich, 1931.

Dempf, Alois," Metaphysik des Mittelalters, " in A. Baeumler and M. Schröter (edd.), *Die Grunddisziplinen* (Abt. I of *Handbuch der Philosophie*), Munich, 1934.

Munk, Salomon, *Mélanges de philosophie juive et arabe*, Paris, 1859.

Carra de Vaux, Bernard, *La doctrine d'Islam* (2 vol.), Paris, 1909.

Horten, Max Joseph Heinrich, *Die Philosophie des Islam in ihren Beziehungen zu den philosophischen Weltanschauungen des westlichen Orients*, Munich, 1924.

Neumark, David, *Geschichte der jüdischen Philosophie des Mittelalters* (2 vol. in 3), Berlin, 1907–28. *Anhang zum ersten Band*, Berlin, 1913.

Cruz Hernández, Miguel, *Filosofía hispano-musulmana*.

Monographs

Pra, Mario dal, *Scoto Eriugena ed il neoplatonismo medievale*, 1941.

Domet de Vorges, Edmond Charles Eugène, *Saint Anselme*, Paris, 1901.

Koyré, Alexandre, *L'idée de Dieu dans la philosophie de Saint Anselme*, Paris, 1923.

Barth, Karl, *Anselms Beweis der Existenz Gottes*, 1931.

Marías, Julián, *San Anselmo y el insensato*, Madrid, 1944.

Ottaviano, Carmelo, "Riccardo di S. Vittore," *Reale Accademia Nazionale dei Lincei. Atti. Classe di scienze morali, storiche e filologiche*, Ser. 6, Vol. 4, Fasc. 5, 1933, pp. 411–541.

Carra de Vaux, Bernard, *Avicenne*, Paris, 1900.

Cruz Hernández, Miguel, *La metafísica de Avicena*, Madrid, 1949.

Renan, Ernest, *Averroès et l'Averroisme* (1852), Paris, *c.* 1912.

Ṣalibā, Jamīl (Saliba, Djémil) (ed. & trans.), *Étude sur la métaphysique d'Avicenne*, Paris, 1926.

Horten, Max Joseph Heinrich, *Die Metaphysik des Averroes*, Halle an der Saale, 1912.

Asín Palacios, Miguel, *El Islam cristianizado*, Madrid, 1931.

—— *Huellas del Islam*, Madrid, 1944.

Ortega y Gasset, José, "Abenjaldún nos revela el secreto," in *El Espectador*, VIII, Madrid, 1937.

Ibn Khaldûn, *The Muqaddimah. An Introduction to History*, trans. and intr. by Franz Rosenthal (3 vol.), New York, 1958.

Gaos, José, *La filosofía de Maimónides*, 2nd ed., Mexico, 1940.

Gilson, Étienne Henri, *La philosophie de Saint Bonaventure*, Paris, 1924. Eng. trans. by Dom Illtyd Trethowan and F. J. Sheed, *The Philosophy of Saint Bonaventure*, London, 1938.

Baumgartner, Matthias, *Santo Tomás* (Span. trans., Madrid, 1925).

Grabmann, Martin, *Thomas von Aquin*. Eng. trans. by Virgil Michel, *Thomas Aquinas; His Personality and Thought*, New York, 1928.

Sertillanges, Antonin Gilbert, *Saint Thomas d'Aquin* (2 vol.), Paris, 1910.

Maritain, Jacques, *Le docteur angélique*, Paris, 1930. Eng. trans. by J. F. Scanlan, *The Angelic Doctor*, New York, 1931.

Gilson, Étienne Henri, *Le thomisme*, 5th ed., Paris, 1944. Eng. trans. of 3rd French ed. by Edward Bullough, *The Philosophy of St. Thomas Aquinas*, 2nd ed., St. Louis, 1939. Another Eng. trans. by L. K. Shook, *The Christian Philosophy of St. Thomas Aquinas*, New York, 1956.

Meyer, H., *Thomas von Aquin*, 1938.

Manser, Gallus M., *La esencia del tomismo* (Span. trans., Madrid, 1947).

Aguirre, A., *Rogerio Bacon*, Barcelona, 1935.

Carreras y Artau, Tomás and Joaquín, *Historia de la filosofía española : Filosofía cristiana de los siglos XIII al XV*, Madrid, 1939.

Landry, Bernard, *Duns Scot*, 1922.

Gilson, Étienne Henri, *Jean Duns Scot*, Paris, 1952.

Longpré, *La philosophie du b. Duns Scot*, 1924.

Heidegger, Martin, *Die Kategorien- und Bedeutungslehre des Duns Scotus*, Tübingen, 1916.

Harris, Charles Reginald Schiller, *Duns Scotus* (2 vol.), Oxford, 1927.

Abbagnano, Nicola, *Guglielmo di Ockam*, 1931.

Moody, Ernest Addison, *The Logic of William of Ockham*, New York, 1935.

Karrer, Otto (ed.), *Meister Eckehart; das System seiner religiösen Lehre und Lebenswahrheit*, Munich, 1923.

Seeberg, Erich, *Meister Eckhart*, Tübingen, 1934.

Muller-Thym, B. J., *University of Being in M. Eckhart*, 1939.

VI. MODERN PHILOSOPHY

1. GENERAL WORKS

Erdmann, Johann Eduard, *Versuch einer wissenschaftlichen Darstellung der Geschichte der neuern Philosophie* (6 vol.), Riga and Dorpat and Leipzig, 1834–53.

Fischer, Kuno, *Geschichte der neuern Philosophie*, 4th ed. (10 vol.), 1897–1904; 5th ed. (2 vol.), Heidelberg, 1909–12. Eng. trans. of section on Descartes (from 3rd Ger. ed.), *History of Modern Philosophy*, New York, 1887.

Windelband, Wilhelm, *Geschichte der neueren Philosophie*, 7–8th ed. (2 vol.), Leipzig, 1922.

Falckenberg, Richard Friedrich Otto, *Geschichte der neueren Philosophie*, 8th ed., 1927. Eng. trans. of 2nd Ger. ed. by A. C. Armstrong, Jr., *History of Modern Philosophy from Nicolas of Cusa to the Present Time*, 3rd ed. reprinted Calcutta, 1953.

Heimsoeth, Heinz, *La metafísica moderna* (Span. trans., Madrid, 1932).

Litt, Theodor, *La ética moderna* (Span. trans., Madrid, 1933).

Lecky, William Edward Hartpole, *History of the Rise and Influence of the Spirit of Rationalism in Europe*, rev. ed. (2 vol.), New York, 1884.

Cassirer, Ernst, *Das Erkenntnisproblem* (4 vol.), 1906–57; Vol. I–III, Berlin; Vol. IV, Stuttgart. Eng. trans. by William H. Woglom and Charles W. Hendel, *The Problem of Knowledge*, New Haven, 1950.

2. THE RENAISSANCE

General Works

Dilthey, Wilhelm, *Weltanschauung und Analyse des Menschen seit Renaissance und Reformation (Gesammelte Schriften)*, Vol. II, Leipzig.

Burckhardt, Jakob, *Die Cultur der Renaissance in Italien*, 3rd ed. (2 vol.), Leipzig, 1877–78. Eng. trans. by S. G. C. Middlemore, *The Civilization of the Renaissance in Italy*, numerous reprints, of which the currently most economical is New York (2 vol.), 1958.

Heimsoeth, Heinz, *Die sechs grossen Themen der abendländischen Metaphysik*, 3rd ed., Stuttgart, *c.* 1954.

Charbonnel, J. R., *La pensée italienne au XVIe siècle et le courant libertin*, 1917.

Cassirer, Ernst, *Individuum und Kosmos in der Philosophie der Renaissance*, Leipzig, 1927.

Monographs

HUMANISM

Allen, Percy Stafford, *The Age of Erasmus*, Oxford, 1914.

Mann, Margaret, *Érasme et les débuts de la Réforme française, 1517–1536*, Paris, 1934.

Huizinga, Johan: Eng. trans. by F. Hopman, *Erasmus*, New York, 1924.

Bataillon, Marcel, *Érasme et l'Espagne*, Paris, 1937.

Bonilla y San Martín, Adolfo, *Luis Vives y la filosofía del Renacimiento* (3 vol.), Madrid, 1929.

Marañón, Gregorio, *Luis Vives*, Madrid, 1942.

Ortega y Gasset, José, *Vives*, Madrid, 1942.

Estelrich, Joan, *Vives*, Paris, 1942.

NICHOLAS OF CUSA

Vansteenberghe, Edmond, *Le Cardinal Nicolas de Cues*, Paris, 1920.

Rotta, Paolo, "Il Cardinale Nicolò di Cusa," *Università Cattolica del Sacro Cuore, Milano. Pubb. Ser. prima: Scienze filosofiche*, Vol. 12, 1928, pp. i–xvi, 1–448.

Hommes, *Die philosophischen Grundlehren des Nicolaus von Cues*, 1926.

Morin, "Nicolas de Cues," in *Dictionnaire de philosophie et de théologie scolastique*.

Gandillac, Maurice Patronnier de, *La philosophie de Nicolas de Cuse*, 1941.

GIORDANO BRUNO

Berti, Domenico, *Giordano Bruno, sua vita e sue dottrine*, 1880.

Spampanato, Vincenzo, *Vita di Giordano Bruno* (2 vol.), Messina, 1921.

Gentile, Giovanni, *Giordano Bruno e il pensiero del Rinascimento*, 2nd ed., Florence, 1925.

Hönigswald, Richard, *Giordano Bruno* (Span. trans., Madrid, 1925).

MODERN PHYSICS

Prantl, Carl, *Galilei und Kepler als Logiker*, 1875.

Gratry, Auguste Joseph Alphonse, *Logique*, 1855. Eng. trans. by Helen and Milton Singer, *Logic*, La Salle, Ill., 1944.

Snow, Adolph Judah, *Matter and Gravity in Newton's Physical Philosophy*, London, 1926.

Ortega y Gasset, José, "La 'Filosofía de la Historia' de Hegel y la historiología," in Vol. IV of *Obras Completas*, Madrid, 1947.

Zubiri, Xavier, "La nueva física," in *Naturaleza, Historia, Dios*, Madrid, 1944.

Marías, Julián, "Física y metafísica en Newton," in *San Anselmo y el insensato*, Madrid, 1944.

SPANISH SCHOLASTICISM

Solana, Marcial, *Historia de la Filosofía española, siglo XVI* (3 vol.), Madrid, 1940–41.
Getino, Luis G. Alonso, *El Mtro. Fr. Francisco de Vitoria y el renacimiento teológico del siglo XVI*, 3rd ed., 1930.
Mahieu, *François Suarez* (2 vol.), 1921.
Scorraille, R. de, *François Suarez* (2 vol.), 1911.
Recaséns Siches, Luis, *La filosofía del derecho de Francisco Suárez*, 1927.
Conze, R. E., *Der Begriff der Metaphysik bei Franz Suarez*, 1929.
Fichter, Joseph Henry, *Man of Spain, Francis Suarez*, New York, 1940.
Zaragüeta [Bengoechea], Juan, *La filosofía de Suárez y el pensamiento actual*, Madrid, 1941.
Gómez Arboleya, Enrique, *Francisco Suárez, S. I.*, Granada, 1946.
Marías, Julián, " Suárez en la perpectiva de la razón histórica, " in *Ensayos de teoría*, Barcelona, 1954.

3. SEVENTEENTH-CENTURY IDEALISM

DESCARTES

Bordas-Demoulin, Jean Baptiste, *Le Cartésianisme* (2 vol.), Paris, 1843.
Chevalier, Jacques, *Descartes*, Paris, 1921.
Gilson, Étienne Henri, *Études sur le rôle de la pensée médiévale dans la formation du système cartésien*, Paris, 1930.
Koyré, Alexandre, *Descartes und die Scholastik*, 1923.
―――― *Essai sur l'idée de Dieu et les preuves de son existence chez Descartes*, Paris, 1922.
Hamelin, Octave, *Le système de Descartes*, Paris, 1911.
Gouhier, Henri Gaston, *Essais sur Descartes*, Paris, 1937.
―――― *Les premières pensées de Descartes*, Paris, 1958.
Études sur Descartes, pub. by *Revue de métaphysique et de morale*, Paris, 1937.
Jaspers, Karl, *Descartes und die Philosophie*, 3rd ed., Berlin, 1956.
Marías, Julián, " Los dos cartesianismos, " in *Ensayos de teoría*, Barcelona, 1954.
Alquié, Ferdinand, *La découverte métaphysique de l'homme chez Descartes*, Paris, 1950.
Rodis-Lewis, Geneviève, *La morale de Descartes*, Paris, 1957.

CARTESIANISM IN FRANCE

Delbos, Victor, *Étude de la philosophie de Malebranche*, Châtillon s/Seine and Paris, 1924.
Gouhier, Henri Gaston, *La philosophie de Malebranche et son expérience religieuse*, Paris, 1926.
Stieler, Georg, *Nikolaus Malebranche*, Stuttgart, 1925.
Boutroux, Émile, *Pascal*, Paris, 1900.
Strowski, Fortunat Joseph, *Pascal et son temps* (3 vol.), Paris, 1907–8.
Chevalier, Jacques, *Pascal*, Paris, 1922. Eng. trans. by Lilian A. Clare, *Pascal*, New York, 1930.
Jovy, Ernest, *Études pascaliennes*, 1927–28.
Busson, Henri, *La pensée religieuse française de Charron à Pascal*, Paris, 1933.

Guardini, Romano, *Christliches Bewusstsein. Versuche über Pascal*, 3rd ed., Munich, 1956.

SPINOZA

Couchoud, Paul-Louis, *Benoît de Spinoza*, Paris, 1902.
Delbos, Victor, *Le spinozisme*, 2nd ed., Paris, 1926.
Gunn, John Alexander, *Benedict Spinoza*, Melbourne, 1925.
Baensch, O., *et al.* (edd.), *Baruch de Spinoza: Sämtliche philosophische Werke*, 3rd rev. ed. (6 vol. in 2), Leipzig, 1907.
Societas Spinozana, *Septimana Spinozana*, The Hague, 1933.
Sérouya, Henri, *Spinoza, sa vie et sa philosophie*, Paris, 1933.
Dujovne, León, *Spinoza; su vida, su época, su obra, su influencia* (4 vol.), Buenos Aires, 1941–45.

LEIBNIZ

Dilthey, Wilhelm, *Leibniz und sein Zeitalter* (Vol. III of *Gesammelte Schriften*), Leipzig and Berlin, 1927.
Russell, Bertrand, *A Critical Exposition of the Philosophy of Leibniz, with an Appendix of Leading Passages*, 2nd ed., Cambridge, 1937.
Couturat, Louis, *La logique de Leibniz, d'après des documents inédits*, Hildesheim, 1901.
Cassirer, Ernst, *Leibniz' System in seinen wissenschaftlichen Grundlagen*, 2nd ed., Hildesheim, 1962.
Baruzi, J., *Leibniz et l'organisation religieuse de la terre*, Paris, 1907.
Heimsoeth, Heinz, *Die Methode der Erkenntnis bei Descartes und Leibniz* (2 vol.), Giessen, 1912–14.
—— *Leibniz's Weltanschauung*, 1917.
Schmalenbach, Herman, *Leibniz*, 1921.
Kinkel, Walter, *Leibniz*.
Stammler, Gerhard, *Leibniz*, Munich, 1930.
Carr, Herbert Wildon, *Leibniz*, Boston, 1929.
Marías, Julián, annotated Span. ed. of Leibniz' *Discours de métaphysique*, 1942.
Moreau, Joseph, *L'univers Leibnizien*, Paris, 1956.
Ortega y Gasset, José, *La idea de principio en Leibniz y la evolución de la teoría deductiva*, Buenos Aires, 1958.

4. EMPIRICISM

BRITISH PHILOSOPHY

Sorley, William Ritchie, *A History of English Philosophy*, 2nd ed., Cambridge (Eng.), 1937.
Rémusat, Charles de, *Bacon, sa vie, son temps, sa philosophie, et son influence jusqu'à nos jours*, 3rd ed., Paris, 1877.
Wolff, Emil, *Bacon und seine Quellen* (2 vol.), 1910–13.
Spedding, James, *Account of the Life and Times of Francis Bacon* (2 vol.), 1879.
Brochard, Victor, "La philosophie de Bacon," in *Études de philosophie ancienne et de philosophie moderne*, Paris, 1912.

Levi, Adolfo, *Il pensiero di F. Bacone*, 1925.
Hönigswald, Richard, *Hobbes und die Staatsphilosophie*, Munich, 1924.
Meinecke, Friedrich, *Die Idee der Staatsräson in der neueren Geschichte*, Munich, 1924.
Tönnies, Ferdinand, *Thomas Hobbes; Leben und Lehre*, Stuttgart, 1925.
Brandt, Frithiof, *Thomas Hobbes' Mechanical Conception of Nature*. Eng. trans. by Vaughn Maxwell and Annie I. Fausbøll, Copenhagen, 1928.
Laird, John, *Hobbes*, London, 1934.
Polin, Raymond, *Politique et philosophie chez Thomas Hobbes*, Paris, 1953.
Hazard, Paul, *La crise de la conscience européenne (1680–1715)*, Paris, 1935. Eng. trans. by J. Lewis May, *The European Mind, 1680–1715*, London, 1953.
Alexander, Samuel, *Locke*, 1908.
Aaron, Richard Ithamar, *John Locke*, 2nd ed., Oxford, 1955.
O'Connor, Daniel John, *John Locke*, London, 1952. Reprinted New York, 1966.
Petzäll, Åke, *Ethics and Epistemology in John Locke's "Essay Concerning Human Understanding,"* Göteborg, 1937.
Fraser, Alexander Campbell, *Berkeley*, Edinburgh and London, 1881.
Mill, John Stuart, *Berkeley's Life and Writings*, 1871.
Cassirer, Ernst, *Berkeley's System*, 1914.
Luce, Arthur Aston, *Berkeley and Malebranche; a Study in the Origins of Berkeley's Thought*, Oxford, 1934.
Hedenius, Ingemar, *Sensationalism and Theology in Berkeley's Philosophy*. Eng. trans. by Gerda Wingqvist, Uppsala, 1936.
Wild, John Daniel, *George Berkeley; a Study of His Life and Philosophy*, Cambridge (Eng.), 1936.
Warnock, G. J., *Berkeley*, Melbourne and Baltimore, 1953.
Meinong, Alexius, *Hume Studien* (2 vol.), Vienna, 1877–82.
Metz, Rudolf, *David Hume; Leben und Philosophie*, Stuttgart, 1929.
Laing, Bertram Mitchell, *David Hume*, London, 1932.
Laird, John, *Hume's Philosophy of Human Nature*, London, 1932.
Hedenius, Ingemar, *Studies in Hume's Ethics*, Uppsala, 1937.
Maund, Constance, *A Critical Examination of Hume's Epistemology, with Reference to Its Bearing on Modern Problems*, London, 1936.
Jones, Olin McKendree, *Empiricism and Intuitionism in Reid's Common Sense Philosophy*, Princeton, 1927.

THE ENLIGHTENMENT

Cassirer, Ernst, *Die Philosophie der Aufklärung*, Tübingen, 1932. Eng. trans. by Fritz C. A. Koelln and James P. Pettegrove, *The Philosophy of the Enlightenment*, Princeton, 1951.
Hazard, Paul, *La pensée européenne au XVIIIème siècle, de Montesquieu à Lessing* (3 vol. in 2), Paris, 1946. Eng. trans. by J. Lewis May, *European Thought in the 18th Century, from Montesquieu to Lessing*, London, 1954.
Brunetière, Ferdinand, *Études sur le XVIIIe siècle*, Paris, 1911.
Mornet, Daniel, *Les origines intellectuelles de la Révolution Française (1715–1787)*, Paris, 1933.

Desnoiresterres, Gustave [Le Brisoys], *Voltaire et la société au XVIIIe siècle* (8 vol.), Paris, 1867–76.

Lanson, Gustave, *Voltaire*, 2nd ed., Paris, 1910.

Aldington, Richard, *Voltaire*, London, 1925.

Torrey, Norman Lewis, *Voltaire and the English Deists*, New Haven, 1930.

Barckausen, Henri Auguste, *Montesquieu, ses idées et ses œuvres d'après les papiers de la Brède*, Paris, 1907.

Høffding, Harald, *Jean Jacques Rousseau and His Philosophy*. Eng. trans. of 2nd Danish ed. by William Richards and Leo E. Saidla, New Haven and London, 1930.

Wright, Ernest Hunter, *The Meaning of Rousseau*, London, 1929.

Gérin, *J. J. Rousseau*, 1930.

Hendel, Charles William, *Jean-Jacques Rousseau, Moralist* (2 vol.), London, 1934.

Héligon, E., *Condillac*, 1937.

Müller, M., *Essai sur la philosophie de Jean d'Alembert*, 1926.

Delvaille, Jules, *Essai sur l'histoire de l'idée de progrès, jusqu'à la fin du XVIIIe siècle*, Paris, 1910.

Bury, John Bagnell, *The Idea of Progress; an Inquiry into Its Origin and Growth*, London, 1920. Reprinted New York, 1955.

Sée, Henri Eugène, *Les idées politiques en France au XVIIIe siècle*, Paris, 1920.

Dilthey, Wilhelm, *Friedrich der Grosse und die deutsche Aufklärung*.

——— *Das achtzehnte Jahrhundert und die geschichtliche Welt* (Vol. III of *Gesammelte Schriften*), Leipzig and Berlin, 1927.

Croce, Benedetto, *La filosofia di Giambattista Vico* (Vol. 2 of *Saggi filosofici*), 2nd ed., Bari, 1922. Eng. trans. by R. G. Collingwood, *The Philosophy of Giambattista Vico*, London, 1913.

Peters, Richard, *Der Aufbau der Weltgeschichte bei Giambattista Vico*, Stuttgart, 1929.

Giusso, Lorenzo, *La filosofia di Giambattista Vico e l'età barocca*, 1943.

Herr, Richard, *The Eighteenth-Century Revolution in Spain*, Princeton, 1958.

Marías, Julián, *Los Españoles*, Madrid, 1962.

THE FORMATION OF THE MODERN EPOCH

Hazard, Paul, *La crise de la conscience européenne (1680–1715)*, Paris, 1935. Eng. trans. by J. Lewis May, *The European Mind, 1680–1715*, London, 1953.

Sombart, Werner, *Luxus und Kapitalismus*, Munich, 1913. Eng. trans., *Luxury and Capitalism*, New York, 1938.

——— *Krieg und Kapitalismus*, Munich, 1913.

Tawney, Richard Henry, *Religion and the Rise of Capitalism; a Historical Study*, New York, 1926.

Dunning, William Archibald, *A History of Political Theories from Luther to Montesquieu*, New York, 1905.

Weber, Max, *Die protestantische Ethik und der Geist der Kapitalismus*, Tübingen, 1920. Eng. trans. by Talcott Parsons, *The Protestant Ethic and the Spirit of Capitalism*, London, 1930.

Marías, Julián, "La pérdida de Dios," in Vol. IV of *Obras Completas*, Madrid, 1944.

5. GERMAN IDEALISM

KANT

Cohen, Hermann, *Kants Theorie der Erfahrung*, Berlin, 1871.
Ruyssen, Théodore, *Kant*, Paris, 1900.
Cassirer, Ernst, *Kants Leben und Lehre*, 1918.
García Morente, Manuel, *La filosofía de Kant*, Madrid, 1917.
Wundt, Max, *Kant als Metaphysiker*, 1924.
Ortega y Gasset, José, *Kant, 1724–1924; reflexiones de centenario*, Madrid, 1929.
Menzer, Paul, *Kants Lehre von der Entwicklung in Natur und Geschichte*, Berlin, 1911.
Külpe, Oswald, *Immanuel Kant; Darstellung und Würdigung*, 5th ed., Leipzig, 1921.
Heidegger, Martin, *Kant und das Problem der Metaphysik*, Frankfurt am Main, 1934. Eng. trans. by James S. Churchill, *Kant and the Problem of Metaphysics*, Bloomington, 1962.

FICHTE

Lask, Emil, *Fichtes Idealismus und die Geschichte*, Tübingen, 1902.
Léon, Xavier, "La philosophie de Fichte et la conscience contemporaine," in *Revue de metaphysique et de morale*, Paris, 1902.
——— *Fichte et son temps* (2 vol. in 3), Paris, 1922–27.
Medicus, Fritz, *Fichte*, 1911.
——— *Einleitung zu Fichtes Werke*, 1911.
Hartmann, Nicolai, *Die Philosophie des deutschen Idealismus*, 2nd ed., Berlin, 1960.
Heimsoeth, Heinz, *Fichte*, Munich, 1923.
Guéroult, Martial, *L'évolution et la structure de la doctrine de la science chez Fichte*, Paris, 1930.

SCHELLING

Fischer, Kuno, *Schelling*, 1902.
Bréhier, Émile, *Schelling*, Paris, 1912.
Knittermeyer, Hinrich, *Schelling und die romantische Schule*, Munich, 1929.

HEGEL

Dilthey, Wilhelm, *Die Jugendgeschichte Hegels und andere Abhandlungen zur Geschichte des deutschen Idealismus* (Vol. IV of *Gesammelte Schriften*), Leipzig.
Kroner, Richard, *Von Kant bis Hegel* (2 vol.), Tübingen, 1921–24.
Falkenheim, Hugo, *Hegel*, 1911.
Moog, Willy, *Hegel und die hegelsche Schule*, Munich, 1930.
Croce, Benedetto, *Saggio sullo Hegel* (Vol. 3 of *Saggi filosofici*), Bari, 1913. Eng. trans. by Douglas Ainslie, *What Is Living and What Is Dead of the Philosophy of Hegel*, London, 1915.
Gentile, Giovanni, *La riforma della dialettica hegeliana*, 3rd ed., Florence, 1954.
——— *Teoria generale dello spirito come atto puro*, 6th rev. ed., Florence, 1944. Eng. trans. of 3rd ed. by H. Wildon Carr, *The Theory of Mind as Pure Act*, London, 1922.
Cunningham, Gustavus Watts, *Thought and Reality in Hegel's System*, New York, 1910.

Ortega y Gasset, José, "Hegel y América," in Vol. II of *Obras Completas*, Madrid, 1947.

——— "La 'Filosofía de la Historia' de Hegel y la historiología," in Vol. IV of *Obras Completas*, Madrid, 1947.

Zubiri, Xavier, "Hegel y el problema metafísico," in *Naturaleza, Historia, Dios*, Madrid, 1944.

Glockner, Hermann, *Hegel* (2 vol.), Stuttgart, 1929–40.

Hartmann, Nicolai, *Die Philosophie des deutschen Idealismus*, II, 2nd ed., Berlin, 1960.

Steinbüchel, Theodor, *Das Grundproblem der hegelschen Philosophie*, 1933.

THE THOUGHT OF THE ROMANTIC AGE

Dilthey, Wilhelm, *Das Leben Schleiermachers*, 1870.

——— *Das Erlebnis und die Dichtung: Lessing, Goethe, Novalis, Hölderlin*, 13th ed., Stuttgart, 1957.

Mulert, Hermann, *Schleiermacher und die Gegenwart*, Frankfurt am Main, 1934.

Simmel, Georg, *Schopenhauer und Nietzsche. Ein Vortragszyklus*, Leipzig, 1907.

Ruyssen, Théodore, *Schopenhauer*, 1911.

Haase, Heinrich, *Schopenhauer*, Munich, 1926.

Jobit, Pierre, *Les éducateurs de l'Espagne contemporaine. I: Les Krausistes*, Paris, 1936.

López-Morillas, Juan, *El krausismo español*, Mexico, 1956.

Cacho Viu, Vicente, *La Institución Libre de Enseñanza*, Madrid, 1962.

6. NINETEENTH-CENTURY PHILOSOPHY

THE TRIUMPH OVER SENSATIONALISM

Nicolas, A., *Études sur Maine de Biran*, 1858.

Couailhac, Marius, *Maine de Biran*, Paris, 1905.

Michelet, Jules, *Maine de Biran*, Paris, 1906.

Tisserand, Pierre, *L'anthropologie de Maine de Biran*, Paris, 1909.

LaVallette Monbrun, Amable de, *Maine de Biran (1766–1824); essai de biographie historique et psychologique*, Paris, 1914.

Delbos, Victor, "Maine de Biran," in *Figures et doctrines de philosophes*, 2nd ed., Paris, 1926.

Gouhier, Henri Gaston, Introduction to *Œuvres choisies de Maine de Biran*, 1942.

——— *Journal* (of Maine de Biran), edited by Gouhier (3 vol.), Neuchâtel, 1954–57.

Marías, Julián, "El hombre y Dios en la filosofía de Maine de Biran," in Vol. IV of *Obras Completas*, Madrid, 1944.

COMTE'S POSITIVISM

Littré, Emile, *Auguste Comte et la philosophie positive*, Paris, 1863.

Mill, John Stuart, *Auguste Comte and Positivism*, 4th ed., London, 1891.

Lévy-Bruhl, Lucien, *La philosophie d'Auguste Comte*, 1900. Eng. trans. by Frederic Harrison, *The Philosophy of Auguste Comte*, New York, 1903.

Cantecor, G., *Le positivisme*, 1904.
Marcuse, Alexander, *Die Geschichtsphilosophie Auguste Comtes*, Stuttgart, 1932.
Gouhier, Henri Gaston, *La jeunesse d'Auguste Comte et la formation du positivisme* (3 vol.), Paris, 1933–41.
———— *La vie d'Auguste Comte*, Paris, 1931.

PHILOSOPHY OF POSITIVIST INSPIRATION

Taine, Hippolyte Adolphe, *Les philosophes français du XIXᵉ siècle*, Paris, 1857.
Ravaisson-Mollien, Félix, *La philosophie en France au XIXᵉ siècle*, Paris, 1868.
Ferraz, L., *Histoire de la philosophie en France au XIXᵉ siècle* (3 vol.), Paris, 1880–89.
Benrubi, Isaak, *Les sources et les courants de la philosophie contemporaine en France* (2 vol.), Paris, 1933. Eng. trans. by Ernest B. Dicker, *Contemporary Thought of France*, New York, 1926.
Guyau, Marie Jean, *La morale anglaise contemporaine: morale de l'utilité et de l'évolution*, 3rd ed., Paris, 1895.
Muirhead, J. H. (ed.), *Contemporary British Philosophy*, London, 1924.
Saenger, Samuel, *John Stuart Mill. Sein Leben und Lebenswerk*, Stuttgart, 1901.
Britton, Karl, *John Stuart Mill*, London and Baltimore, 1953.

THE DISCOVERY OF LIFE

Lowrie, Walter, *Kierkegaard*, London, 1938.
Høffding, Harald, *Søren Kierkegaard som filosof*, Copenhagen, 1919.
Löwith, Karl, *Kierkegaard und Nietzsche*, Halle an der Saale, 1933.
Bertram, Ernst, *Nietzsche; Versuch einer Mythologie*, 3rd ed., Berlin, 1919.
Pfänder, A., *Nietzsche*, 1911 (Span. trans., Madrid, 1925).
Vetter, August, *Nietzsche*, Munich, 1926.
Jaspers, Karl, *Nietzsche; Einführung in das Verständnis seines Philosophierens*, 3rd ed., Berlin, 1947.
Schlechta, Karl, *Der Fall Nietzsche; Aufsätze und Vorträge*, 2nd ed., Munich, 1959.

THE RETURN TO TRADITIONAL METAPHYSICS

Perraud, Cardinal, *Le Père Gratry, sa vie et ses œuvres*, Paris, 1900.
Braun, L. L., *Gratrys Theorie von der religiösen Erkenntnis*, 1914.
Scheller, E. J., *Grundlagen der Erkenntnislehre bei Gratry*, 1929.
Marías, Julián, "La filosofía del Padre Gratry," in Vol. IV of *Obras Completas*, Madrid, 1944.
———— "La restauración de la metafísica en el problema de Dios y la persona," in Vol. IV of *Obras Completas*, Madrid, 1944.

7. CONTEMPORARY PHILOSOPHY

BRENTANO

Kraus, Oskar, *Brentanos Stellung zur Phänomenologie und Gegenstandstheorie*, 1924.
Rogge, E., *Das Kausalproblem bei Franz Brentano*, 1935.
Cruz Hernández, Miguel, *Francisco Brentano*, Salamanca, 1953.

THE IDEA OF LIFE

Misch, Georg, *Lebensphilosophie und Phänomenologie; eine Auseinandersetzung der dilthey'schen Richtung mit Heidegger und Husserl*, 2nd ed., Leipzig, 1931.
——— Vorbericht to Vol. V of *Diltheys Gesammelte Schriften*, Leipzig, 1923.
Degener, Alfons, *Dilthey und das Problem der Metaphysik*, Bonn and Cologne, 1933.
Ortega y Gasset, José, *Guillermo Dilthey y la idea de la vida*, Madrid, 1934.
Höfer, J., *Vom Leben zur Wahrheit. Katholische Besinnung an der Lebensanschauung Wilhelm Diltheys*, 1936.
Bollnow, Otto Friedrich, *Dilthey; eine Einführung in seine Philosophie*, 2nd ed., Stuttgart, 1955.
Laín Entralgo, Pedro, *Dilthey y el método de la historia*, Madrid, 1942.
Pucciarelli, F., *La esencia de la filosofía*, Buenos Aires, 1944.
Marías, Julián, "Introducción a la filosofía de la vida," in the annotated Span. trans. of Dilthey's *Weltanschauungslehre*, Madrid, 1944.
Hodges, Herbert Arthur, *Wilhelm Dilthey, an Introduction*, London, 1944.
Díaz de Cerio Ruiz, Franco, *Wilhelm Dilthey y el problema del mundo histórico*, Barcelona, 1959.
García Morente, Manuel, *La filosofía de Henri Bergson*, Madrid, 1917.
Zaragüeta [Bengoechea], Juan, *La intuición en la filosofía de Henri Bergson*, Madrid, 1941.
Høffding, Harald, *Henri Bergson's filosofi; karakteristik og kritik*, Copenhagen, 1914.
Chevalier, Jacques, *Bergson*, Paris, 1926. Eng. trans. by Lilian A. Clare, *Henri Bergson*, New York and London, 1928.
LeRoy, Édouard, *Une philosophie nouvelle; Henri Bergson*, Paris, 1912. Eng. trans. by V. Benson, *The New Philosophy of Henri Bergson*, New York, 1913.
Marías, Julián, *Miguel de Unamuno*, Madrid, 1943.
——— *La Escuela de Madrid; estudios de filosofía española*, Buenos Aires, 1959.
Oromí, Miguel, *El pensamiento filosófico de Miguel de Unamuno, filosofía existencial de la inmortalidad*, Madrid, 1943.
Ferrater Mora, José, *Unamuno; bosquejo de una filosofía*, 2nd ed., Buenos Aires, 1957. Eng. trans. by Philip Silver, *Unamuno, a Philosophy of Tragedy*, Berkeley, 1962.
Landsberg, Paul Ludwig, "Reflexiones sobre Unamuno," in *Cruz y Raya*, No. 31, Madrid, 1935.
Serrano Poncela, Segundo, *El pensamiento de Unamuno*, Mexico, 1953.
Calvetti, Carla, *La fenomenologia della credenza in Miguel de Unamuno*, 1955.
Meyer, François, *L'ontologie de Miguel de Unamuno*, Paris, 1955.

ENGLISH-LANGUAGE PHILOSOPHY

Schneider, Herbert Wallace, *A History of American Philosophy*, 2nd ed., New York, 1963.
Moore, Addison Webster, *Pragmatism and Its Critics*, Chicago, 1910.
Pratt, James Bissett, *What Is Pragmatism?*, New York, 1909.
Perry, Ralph Barton, *Present Philosophical Tendencies; a Critical Survey of Naturalism, Idealism, Pragmatism, and Realism; Together with a Synopsis of the Philosophy of William James*, New York, 1912.

Leroux, Emmanuel, *Le pragmatisme américain et anglais; étude historique et critique, suivie d'une bibliographie méthodique*, Paris, 1923.

Hook, Sidney, *The Metaphysics of Pragmatism*, Chicago and London, 1927.

Gallie, W. B., *Peirce and Pragmatism*, Harmondsworth, 1952. Reprinted New York, 1966.

Boutroux, Émile, *William James*. Eng. trans. of 2nd ed. by A. and B. Henderson, New York, 1912.

Knight, Margaret, *William James*, Baltimore, 1950.

Runes, Dagobert David (ed.), *Twentieth Century Philosophy; Living Schools of Thought*, New York, 1943.

Farber, Marvin (ed), *L'activité philosophique contemporaine en France et aux États-Unis* (2 vol.), Paris, 1950. Eng. trans., *Philosophic Thought in France and the United States; Essays Representing Major Trends in Contemporary French and American Philosophy*, Buffalo, 1950.

Schilpp, Paul Arthur (ed.), *The Philosophy of John Dewey*, Evanston and Chicago, 1939.

———— *The Philosophy of George Santayana*, Evanston and Chicago, 1940.

———— *The Philosophy of Alfred North Whitehead*, Evanston and Chicago, 1941.

———— *The Philosophy of Bertrand Russell*, Evanston and Chicago, 1944.

HUSSERL

Celms, Teodors, *El idealismo fenomenológico de Husserl* (Span. trans., Madrid, 1928).

Gaos, José, *La crítica del psicologismo en Husserl*, Zaragoza, 1933.

Zubiri, Xavier, *Ensayo de una idea fenomenológica del juicio*, Madrid, 1927.

Lévinas, Emmanuel, *La théorie de l'intuition dans la phénomenologie de Husserl*, Paris, 1930.

Xirau, Joaquín, *La filosofía de Husserl. Una introducción a la fenomenología*, Buenos Aires, 1940.

Farber, Marvin, *The Foundation of Phenomenology; Edmund Husserl and the Quest for a Rigorous Science of Philosophy*, Cambridge, Mass., 1943.

Spiegelberg, H., *The Phenomenological Movement*, The Hague, 1960.

Roth, Alois, *Edmund Husserls ethische Untersuchungen, dargestellt anhand seiner Vorlesungsmanuskripte*, The Hague, 1960.

VALUE THEORY

Ortega y Gasset, José, *¿ Qué son los valores?*, Madrid, 1923.

———— "Max Scheler; un embriagado de esencias (1874–1928)," in Vol. IV of *Obras Completas*, Madrid, 1947.

Gurwitsch, *Las tendencias actuales de la filosofía alemana* (Span. trans., Madrid, 1935).

Hessen, Johannes, *Wertphilosophie*, 1937.

Lavelle, Louis, *Traité des valeurs*, Paris, 1951.

HEIDEGGER

Jaspers, Karl, *Existenzphilosophie*, 2nd ed., Berlin, 1956.

———— *Vernunft und Existenz : fünf Vorlesungen*, Bremen, 1949. Eng. trans. by William Earle, *Reason and Existence : Five Lectures*, New York, 1955.

Heyse, H., *Idee und Existenz*, 1935.

Bollnow, Otto Friedrich, *Existenzphilosophie*, 4th ed., Stuttgart, 1955.

Delp, A., *Existencia trágica; notas sobre la filosofía de Martin Heidegger*. Span. trans. by J. Iturrioz, Madrid, 1942.

Wagner de Reyna, Alberto, *La ontología fundamental de Heidegger*.

Waelhens, Alphonse de, *La philosophie de Martin Heidegger*, 3rd ed., Louvain, 1948.

García Bacca, J. D., *Nueve grandes filósofos contemporáneos y sus temas*, 1947.

Gaos, José, Introduction to Span. ed. of Heidegger's *Sein und Zeit*, Mexico, 1951.

ORTEGA Y GASSET

García Morente, Manuel, *Ensayos*, Madrid, 1945.

Barja, César, "Ortega y Gasset," in *Literatura española: libros y autores contemporáneos*, Madrid, 1935.

Curtius, Ernst Robert, "Ortega y Gasset," in *Kritische Essays zur europäischen Literatur*, Berne, 1950.

Loeser, Norbert, *Ortega y Gasset en de philosophie van het leven*, 1949.

Marías, Julián, *La Escuela de Madrid; estudios de filosofía española*, Buenos Aires, 1959.

—— *Ortega y tres antípodas*, Buenos Aires, 1950.

—— Commentary to Ortega's *Meditaciones del Quijote*, 2nd ed., Madrid, 1957.

Ferrater Mora, José, *La filosofía de Ortega y Gasset*, Buenos Aires, 1958. Eng. trans., *Ortega y Gasset; an Outline of His Philosophy*, New Haven, 1963.

Garagorri, Paulino, *Ortega, una reforma de la filosofía*, Madrid, 1958.

Gaos, José, *Sobre Ortega y Gasset*, Mexico, 1957.

La Torre (University of Puerto Rico), *Homenaje a Ortega y Gasset*, 1956.

Salmerón, F., *Las mocedades de Ortega y Gasset*, Mexico, 1959.

Niedermayer, Franz, *José Ortega y Gasset*, 1959.

Borel, Jean Paul, *Raison et vie chez Ortega y Gasset*, Chaux-de-Fonds, 1959.

Galen, Gräfin Brigitta von, *Die Kultur- und Gesellschaftsethik José Ortega y Gassets*, Heidelberg, 1959.

Ceplecha, Christian, O.S.B., *The Historical Thought of José Ortega y Gasset*, Washington, 1958.

Walgrave, J. H., *De wijsbegeerte van Ortega y Gasset*, 1959.

Marías, Julián, *Ortega. I: Circunstancia y vocación*, Madrid, 1960.

Díaz de Cerio Ruiz, Franco, *José Ortega y Gasset y la conquista de la conciencia histórica. Mocedad: 1902–1915*, Barcelona, 1961.

García Astrada, Arturo, *El pensamiento de Ortega y Gasset*, Buenos Aires, 1961.

Larraín Acuña, Hernán, *La génesis del pensamiento de Ortega*, Buenos Aires, 1962.

Gaete, Arturo, *El sistema maduro de Ortega*, Buenos Aires, 1962.

Hierro S.-Pescador, José, *El derecho en Ortega*, Madrid, 1965.

Rodríguez Huéscar, Antonio, *Con Ortega y otros escritos*, Madrid, 1965.

Soler Grima, Francisco, *Hacia Ortega*, I, Santiago de Chile, 1965.

Index

Terms appearing in Greek characters in the text are here transliterated and alphabetized according to English order.

CATALOGUE OF DOVER BOOKS

Philosophy, Religion

GUIDE TO PHILOSOPHY, C. E. M. Joad. A modern classic which examines many crucial problems which man has pondered through the ages: Does free will exist? Is there plan in the universe? How do we know and validate our knowledge? Such opposed solutions as subjective idealism and realism, chance and teleology, vitalism and logical positivism, are evaluated and the contributions of the great philosophers from the Greeks to moderns like Russell, Whitehead, and others, are considered in the context of each problem. "The finest introduction," BOSTON TRANSCRIPT. Index. Classified bibliography. 592pp. 5⅜ x 8.
T297 Paperbound **$2.00**

HISTORY OF ANCIENT PHILOSOPHY, W. Windelband. One of the clearest, most accurate comprehensive surveys of Greek and Roman philosophy. Discusses ancient philosophy in general, intellectual life in Greece in the 7th and 6th centuries B.C., Thales, Anaximander, Anaximenes, Heraclitus, the Eleatics, Empedocles, Anaxagoras, Leucippus, the Pythagoreans, the Sophists, Socrates, Democritus (20 pages), Plato (50 pages), Aristotle (70 pages), the Peripatetics, Stoics, Epicureans, Sceptics, Neo-platonists, Christian Apologists, etc. 2nd German edition translated by H. E. Cushman. xv + 393pp. 5⅜ x 8.
T357 Paperbound **$1.85**

ILLUSTRATIONS OF THE HISTORY OF MEDIEVAL THOUGHT AND LEARNING, R. L. Poole. Basic analysis of the thought and lives of the leading philosophers and ecclesiastics from the 8th to the 14th century—Abailard, Ockham, Wycliffe, Marsiglio of Padua, and many other great thinkers who carried the torch of Western culture and learning through the "Dark Ages": political, religious, and metaphysical views. Long a standard work for scholars and one of the best introductions to medieval thought for beginners. Index. 10 Appendices. xiii + 327pp. 5⅜ x 8.
T674 Paperbound **$2.00**

PHILOSOPHY AND CIVILIZATION IN THE MIDDLE AGES, M. de Wulf. This semi-popular survey covers aspects of medieval intellectual life such as religion, philosophy, science, the arts, etc. It also covers feudalism vs. Catholicism, rise of the universities, mendicant orders, monastic centers, and similar topics. Unabridged. Bibliography. Index. viii + 320pp. 5⅜ x 8.
T284 Paperbound **$1.85**

AN INTRODUCTION TO SCHOLASTIC PHILOSOPHY, Prof. M. de Wulf. Formerly entitled SCHOLASTICISM OLD AND NEW, this volume examines the central scholastic tradition from St. Anselm, Albertus Magnus, Thomas Aquinas, up to Suarez in the 17th century. The relation of scholasticism to ancient and medieval philosophy and science in general is clear and easily followed. The second part of the book considers the modern revival of scholasticism, the Louvain position, relations with Kantianism and Positivism. Unabridged. xvi + 271pp. 5⅜ x 8.
T296 Clothbound **$3.50**
T283 Paperbound **$1.75**

A HISTORY OF MODERN PHILOSOPHY, H. Höffding. An exceptionally clear and detailed coverage of western philosophy from the Renaissance to the end of the 19th century. Major and minor men such as Pomponazzi, Bodin, Boehme, Telesius, Bruno, Copernicus, da Vinci, Kepler, Galileo, Bacon, Descartes, Hobbes, Spinoza, Leibniz, Wolff, Locke, Newton, Berkeley, Hume, Erasmus, Montesquieu, Voltaire, Diderot, Rousseau, Lessing, Kant, Herder, Fichte, Schelling, Hegel, Schopenhauer, Comte, Mill, Darwin, Spencer, Hartmann, Lange, and many others, are discussed in terms of theory of knowledge, logic, cosmology, and psychology. Index. 2 volumes, total of 1159pp. 5⅜ x 8.
T117 Vol. 1, Paperbound **$2.25**
T118 Vol. 2, Paperbound **$2.25**

ARISTOTLE, A. E. Taylor. A brilliant, searching non-technical account of Aristotle and his thought written by a foremost Platonist. It covers the life and works of Aristotle; classification of the sciences; logic; first philosophy; matter and form; causes; motion and eternity; God; physics; metaphysics; and similar topics. Bibliography. New Index compiled for this edition. 128pp. 5⅜ x 8.
T280 Paperbound **$1.00**

THE SYSTEM OF THOMAS AQUINAS, M. de Wulf. Leading Neo-Thomist, one of founders of University of Louvain, gives concise exposition to central doctrines of Aquinas, as a means toward determining his value to modern philosophy, religion. Formerly "Medieval Philosophy Illustrated from the System of Thomas Aquinas." Trans. by E. Messenger. Introduction. 151pp. 5⅜ x 8.
T568 Paperbound **$1.25**

LEIBNIZ, H. W. Carr. Most stimulating middle-level coverage of basic philosophical thought of Leibniz. Easily understood discussion, analysis of major works: "Theodicy," "Principles of Nature and Grace," "Monadology"; Leibniz's influence; intellectual growth; correspondence; disputes with Bayle, Malebranche, Newton; importance of his thought today, with reinterpretation in modern terminology. "Power and mastery," London Times. Bibliography. Index. 226pp. 5⅜ x 8.
T624 Paperbound **$1.35**

CATALOGUE OF DOVER BOOKS

THE SENSE OF BEAUTY, G. Santayana. A revelation of the beauty of language as well as an important philosophic treatise, this work studies the "why, when, and how beauty appears, what conditions an object must fulfill to be beautiful, what elements of our nature make us sensible of beauty, and what the relation is between the constitution of the object and the excitement of our susceptibility." "It is doubtful if a better treatment of the subject has since been published," PEABODY JOURNAL. Index. ix + 275pp. 5⅜ x 8.
T238 Paperbound **$1.00**

PROBLEMS OF ETHICS, Moritz Schlick. The renowned leader of the "Vienna Circle" applies the logical positivist approach to a wide variety of ethical problems: the source and means of attaining knowledge, the formal and material characteristics of the good, moral norms and principles, absolute vs. relative values, free will and responsibility, comparative importance of pleasure and suffering as ethical values, etc. Disarmingly simple and straightforward despite complexity of subject. First English translation, authorized by author before his death, of a thirty-year old classic. Translated and with an introduction by David Rynin. Index. Foreword by Prof. George P. Adams. xxi + 209pp. 5⅜ x 8.
T946 Paperbound **$1.60**

AN INTRODUCTION TO EXISTENTIALISM, Robert G. Olson. A new and indispensable guide to one of the major thought systems of our century, the movement that is central to the thinking of some of the most creative figures of the past hundred years. Stresses Heidegger and Sartre, with careful and objective examination of the existentialist position, values—freedom of choice, individual dignity, personal love, creative effort—and answers to the eternal questions of the human condition. Scholarly, unbiased, analytic, unlike most studies of this difficult subject, Prof. Olson's book is aimed at the student of philosophy as well as at the reader with no formal training who is looking for an absorbing, accessible, and thorough introduction to the basic texts. Index. xv + 221pp. 5⅜ x 8½.
T55 Paperbound **$1.65**

SYMBOLIC LOGIC, C. I. Lewis and C. H. Langford. Since first publication in 1932, this has been among most frequently cited works on symbolic logic. Still one of the best introductions both for beginners and for mathematicians, philosophers. First part covers basic topics which easily lend themselves to beginning study. Second part is rigorous, thorough development of logistic method, examination of some of most difficult and abstract aspects of symbolic logic, including modal logic, logical paradoxes, many-valued logic, with Prof. Lewis' own contributions. 2nd revised (corrected) edition. 3 appendixes, one new to this edition. 524pp. 5⅜ x 8.
S170 Paperbound **$2.00**

WHITEHEAD'S PHILOSOPHY OF CIVILIZATION, A. H. Johnson. A leading authority on Alfred North Whitehead synthesizes the great philosopher's thought on civilization, scattered throughout various writings, into unified whole. Analysis of Whitehead's general definition of civilization, his reflections on history and influences on its development, his religion, including his analysis of Christianity, concept of solitariness as first requirement of personal religion, and so on. Other chapters cover views on minority groups, society, civil liberties, education. Also critical comments on Whitehead's philosophy. Written with general reader in mind. A perceptive introduction to important area of the thought of a leading philosopher of our century. Revised index and bibliography. xii + 211pp. 5⅜ x 8½.
T996 Paperbound **$1.50**

WHITEHEAD'S THEORY OF REALITY, A. H. Johnson. Introductory outline of Whitehead's theory of actual entities, the heart of his philosophy of reality, followed by his views on nature of God, philosophy of mind, theory of value (truth, beauty, goodness and their opposites), analyses of other philosophers, attitude toward science. A perspicacious lucid introduction by author of dissertation on Whitehead, written under the subject's supervision at Harvard. Good basic view for beginning students of philosophy and for those who are simply interested in important contemporary ideas. Revised index and bibliography. xiii + 267pp. 5⅜ x 8½.
T989 Paperbound **$2.00**

MIND AND THE WORLD-ORDER, C. I. Lewis. Building upon the work of Peirce, James, and Dewey, Professor Lewis outlines a theory of knowledge in terms of "conceptual pragmatism." Dividing truth into abstract mathematical certainty and empirical truth, the author demonstrates that the traditional understanding of the a priori must be abandoned. Detailed analyses of philosophy, metaphysics, method, the "given" in experience, knowledge of objects, nature of the a priori, experience and order, and many others. Appendices. xiv + 446pp. 5⅜ x 8.
T359 Paperbound **$2.25**

SCEPTICISM AND ANIMAL FAITH, G. Santayana. To eliminate difficulties in the traditional theory of knowledge, Santayana distinguishes between the independent existence of objects and the essence our mind attributes to them. Scepticism is thereby established as a form of belief, and animal faith is shown to be a necessary condition of knowledge. Belief, classical idealism, intuition, memory, symbols, literary psychology, and much more, discussed with unusual clarity and depth. Index. xii + 314pp. 5⅜ x 8.
T235 Clothbound **$3.50**
T236 Paperbound **$1.75**

LANGUAGE AND MYTH, E. Cassirer. Analyzing the non-rational thought processes which go to make up culture, Cassirer demonstrates that beneath both language and myth there lies a dominant unconscious "grammar" of experience whose categories and canons are not those of logical thought. His analyses of seemingly diverse phenomena such as Indian metaphysics, the Melanesian "mana," the Naturphilosophie of Schelling, modern poetry, etc., are profound without being pedantic. Introduction and translation by Susanne Langer. Index. x + 103pp. 5⅜ x 8.
T51 Paperbound **$1.25**

CATALOGUE OF DOVER BOOKS

AN ESSAY CONCERNING HUMAN UNDERSTANDING, John Locke. Edited by A. C. Fraser. Unabridged reprinting of definitive edition; only complete edition of "Essay" in print. Marginal analyses of almost every paragraph; hundreds of footnotes; authoritative 140-page biographical, critical, historical prolegomena. Indexes. 1170pp. 5⅜ x 8.

T530 Vol. 1 (Books 1, 2) Paperbound **$2.50**
T531 Vol. 2 (Books 3, 4) Paperbound **$2.50**
2 volume set **$5.00**

THE PHILOSOPHY OF HISTORY, G. W. F. Hegel. One of the great classics of western thought which reveals Hegel's basic principle: that history is not chance but a rational process, the realization of the Spirit of Freedom. Ranges from the oriental cultures of subjective thought to the classical subjective cultures, to the modern absolute synthesis where spiritual and secular may be reconciled. Translation and introduction by J. Sibree. Introduction by C. Hegel. Special introduction for this edition by Prof. Carl Friedrich. xxxix + 447pp. 5⅜ x 8.

T112 Paperbound **$2.25**

THE PHILOSOPHY OF HEGEL, W. T. Stace. The first detailed analysis of Hegel's thought in English, this is especially valuable since so many of Hegel's works are out of print. Dr. Stace examines Hegel's debt to Greek idealists and the 18th century and then proceeds to a careful description and analysis of Hegel's first principles, categories, reason, dialectic method, his logic, philosophy of nature and spirit, etc. Index. Special 14 x 20 chart of Hegelian system. x + 526pp. 5⅜ x 8.

T254 Paperbound **$2.45**

THE WILL TO BELIEVE and HUMAN IMMORTALITY, W. James. Two complete books bound as one. THE WILL TO BELIEVE discusses the interrelations of belief, will, and intellect in man; chance vs. determinism, free will vs. determinism, free will vs. fate, pluralism vs. monism; the philosophies of Hegel and Spencer, and more. HUMAN IMMORTALITY examines the question of survival after death and develops an unusual and powerful argument for immortality. Two prefaces. Index. Total of 429pp. 5⅜ x 8.

T291 Paperbound **$2.00**

THE WORLD AND THE INDIVIDUAL, Josiah Royce. Only major effort by an American philosopher to interpret nature of things in systematic, comprehensive manner. Royce's formulation of an absolute voluntarism remains one of the original and profound solutions to the problems involved. Part One, Four Historical Conceptions of Being, inquires into first principles, true meaning and place of individuality. Part Two, Nature, Man, and the Moral Order, is application of first principles to problems concerning religion, evil, moral order. Introduction by J. E. Smith, Yale Univ. Index. 1070pp. 5⅜ x 8.

T561 Vol. 1 Paperbound **$2.75**
T562 Vol. 2 Paperbound **$2.75**
Two volume set **$5.50**

THE PHILOSOPHICAL WRITINGS OF PEIRCE, edited by J. Buchler. This book (formerly THE PHILOSOPHY OF PEIRCE) is a carefully integrated exposition of Peirce's complete system composed of selections from his own work. Symbolic logic, scientific method, theory of signs, pragmatism, epistemology, chance, cosmology, ethics, and many other topics are treated by one of the greatest philosophers of modern times. This is the only inexpensive compilation of his key ideas. xvi + 386pp. 5⅜ x 8.

T217 Paperbound **$2.00**

EXPERIENCE AND NATURE, John Dewey. An enlarged, revised edition of the Paul Carus lectures which Dewey delivered in 1925. It covers Dewey's basic formulation of the problem of knowledge, with a full discussion of other systems, and a detailing of his own concepts of the relationship of external world, mind, and knowledge. Starts with a thorough examination of the philosophical method; examines the interrelationship of experience and nature; analyzes experience on basis of empirical naturalism, the formulation of law, role of language and social factors in knowledge; etc. Dewey's treatment of central problems in philosophy is profound but extremely easy to follow. ix + 448pp. 5⅜ x 8.

T471 Paperbound **$2.00**

THE PHILOSOPHICAL WORKS OF DESCARTES. The definitive English edition of all the major philosophical works and letters of René Descartes. All of his revolutionary insights, from his famous "Cogito ergo sum" to his detailed account of contemporary science and his astonishingly fruitful concept that all phenomena of the universe (except mind) could be reduced to clear laws by the use of mathematics. An excellent source for the thought of men like Hobbes, Arnauld, Gassendi, etc., who were Descarte's contemporaries. Translated by E. S. Haldane and G. Ross. Introductory notes. Index. Total of 842pp. 5⅜ x 8.

T71 Vol. 1, Paperbound **$2.00**
T72 Vol. 2, Paperbound **$2.00**

THE CHIEF WORKS OF SPINOZA. An unabridged reprint of the famous Bohn edition containing all of Spinoza's most important works: Vol. I: The Theologico-Political Treatise and the Political Treatise. Vol. II: On The Improvement Of Understanding, The Ethics, Selected Letters. Profound and enduring ideas on God, the universe, pantheism, society, religion, the state, democracy, the mind, emotions, freedom and the nature of man, which influenced Goethe, Hegel, Schelling, Coleridge, Whitehead, and many others. Introduction. 826pp. 5⅜ x 8.

T249 Vol. I, Paperbound **$1.50**
T250 Vol. II, Paperbound **$1.50**

CATALOGUE OF DOVER BOOKS

THE ANALYSIS OF MATTER, Bertrand Russell. A classic which has retained its importance in understanding the relation between modern physical theory and human perception. Logical analysis of physics, prerelativity physics, causality, scientific inference, Weyl's theory, tensors, invariants and physical interpretations, periodicity, and much more is treated with Russell's usual brilliance. "Masterly piece of clear thinking and clear writing," NATION AND ATHENAEUM. "Most thorough treatment of the subject," THE NATION. Introduction. Index. 8 figures. viii + 408pp. 5⅜ x 8. S231 Paperbound **$1.95**

CONCEPTUAL THINKING (A LOGICAL INQUIRY), S. Körner. Discusses origin, use of general concepts on which language is based, and the light they shed on basic philosophical questions. Rigorously examines how different concepts are related; how they are linked to experience; problems in the field of contact between exact logical, mathematical, and scientific concepts, and the inexactness of everyday experience (studied at length). This work elaborates many new approaches to the traditional problems of philosophy—epistemology, value theories, metaphysics, aesthetics, morality. "Rare originality . . . brings a new rigour into philosophical argument," Philosophical Quarterly. New corrected second edition. Index. vii + 301pp. 5⅜ x 8. T516 Paperbound **$1.75**

INTRODUCTION TO SYMBOLIC LOGIC, S. Langer. No special knowledge of math required — probably the clearest book ever written on symbolic logic, suitable for the layman, general scientist, and philosopher. You start with simple symbols and advance to a knowledge of the Boole-Schroeder and Russell-Whitehead systems. Forms, logical structure, classes, the calculus of propositions, logic of the syllogism, etc., are all covered. "One of the clearest and simplest introductions," MATHEMATICS GAZETTE. Second enlarged, revised edition. 368pp. 5⅜ x 8. S164 Paperbound **$1.85**

LANGUAGE, TRUTH AND LOGIC, A. J. Ayer. A clear, careful analysis of the basic ideas of Logical Positivism. Building on the work of Schlick, Russell, Carnap, and the Viennese School, Mr. Ayer develops a detailed exposition of the nature of philosophy, science, and metaphysics; the Self and the World; logic and common sense, and other philosophic concepts. An aid to clarity of thought as well as the first full-length development of Logical Positivism in English. Introduction by Bertrand Russell. Index. 160pp. 5⅜ x 8. T10 Paperbound **$1.25**

ESSAYS IN EXPERIMENTAL LOGIC, J. Dewey. Based upon the theory that knowledge implies a judgment which in turn implies an inquiry, these papers consider the inquiry stage in terms of: the relationship of thought and subject matter, antecedents of thought, data and meanings. 3 papers examine Bertrand Russell's thought, while 2 others discuss pragmatism and a final essay presents a new theory of the logic of values. Index. viii + 444pp. 5⅜ x 8. T73 Paperbound **$2.25**

TRAGIC SENSE OF LIFE, M. de Unamuno. The acknowledged masterpiece of one of Spain's most influential thinkers. Between the despair at the inevitable death of man and all his works and the desire for something better, Unamuno finds that "saving incertitude" that alone can console us. This dynamic appraisal of man's faith in God and in himself has been called "a masterpiece" by the ENCYCLOPAEDIA BRITANNICA. xxx + 332pp. 5⅜ x 8. T257 Paperbound **$2.00**

HISTORY OF DOGMA, A. Harnack. Adolph Harnack, who died in 1930, was perhaps the greatest Church historian of all time. In this epoch-making history, which has never been surpassed in comprehensiveness and wealth of learning, he traces the development of the authoritative Christian doctrinal system from its first crystallization in the 4th century down through the Reformation, including also a brief survey of the later developments through the Infallibility decree of 1870. He reveals the enormous influence of Greek thought on the early Fathers, and discusses such topics as the Apologists, the great councils, Manichaeism, the historical position of Augustine, the medieval opposition to indulgences, the rise of Protestantism, the relations of Luther's doctrines with modern tendencies of thought, and much more. "Monumental work; still the most valuable history of dogma . . . luminous analysis of the problems . . . abounds in suggestion and stimulus and can be neglected by no one who desires to understand the history of thought in this most important field," Dutcher's Guide to Historical Literature. Translated by Neil Buchanan. Index. Unabridged reprint in 4 volumes. Vol I: Beginnings to the Gnostics and Marcion. Vol II & III: 2nd century to the 4th century Fathers. Vol IV & V: 4th century Councils to the Carlovingian Renaissance. Vol VI & VII: Period of Clugny (c. 1000) to the Reformation, and after. Total of cii + 2407pp. 5⅜ x 8.

T904 Vol I Paperbound **$2.50**
T905 Vol II & III Paperbound **$2.75**
T906 Vol IV & V Paperbound **$2.75**
T907 Vol VI & VII Paperbound **$2.75**
The set **$10.75**

THE GUIDE FOR THE PERPLEXED, Maimonides. One of the great philosophical works of all time and a necessity for everyone interested in the philosophy of the Middle Ages in the Jewish, Christian, and Moslem traditions. Maimonides develops a common meeting-point for the Old Testament and the Aristotelian thought which pervaded the medieval world. His ideas and methods predate such scholastics as Aquinas and Scotus and throw light on the entire problem of philosophy or science vs. religion. 2nd revised edition. Complete unabridged Friedländer translation. 55 page introduction to Maimonides's life, period, etc., with an important summary of the GUIDE. Index. lix + 414pp. 5⅜ x 8. T351 Paperbound **$2.00**

Literature, History of Literature

ARISTOTLE'S THEORY OF POETRY AND THE FINE ARTS, edited by S. H. Butcher. The celebrated Butcher translation of this great classic faced, page by page, with the complete Greek text. A 300 page introduction discussing Aristotle's ideas and their influence in the history of thought and literature, and covering art and nature, imitation as an aesthetic form, poetic truth, art and morality, tragedy, comedy, and similar topics. Modern Aristotelian criticism discussed by John Gassner. lxxvi + 421pp. 5⅜ x 8. **T42 Paperbound $2.00**

INTRODUCTIONS TO ENGLISH LITERATURE, edited by B. Dobrée. Goes far beyond ordinary histories, ranging from the 7th century up to 1914 (to the 1940's in some cases.) The first half of each volume is a specific detailed study of historical and economic background of the period and a general survey of poetry and prose, including trends of thought, influences, etc. The second and larger half is devoted to a detailed study of more than 5000 poets, novelists, dramatists; also economists, historians, biographers, religious writers, philosophers, travellers, and scientists of literary stature, with dates, lists of major works and their dates, keypoint critical bibliography, and evaluating comments. The most compendious bibliographic and literary aid within its price range.

Vol. I. THE BEGINNINGS OF ENGLISH LITERATURE TO SKELTON, (1509), W. L. Renwick, H. Orton. 450pp. 5⅛ x 7⅞. **T75 Clothbound $4.50**

Vol. II. THE ENGLISH RENAISSANCE, 1510-1688, V. de Sola Pinto. 381pp. 5⅛ x 7⅞. **T76 Clothbound $4.50**

Vol. III. AUGUSTANS AND ROMANTICS, 1689-1830, H. Dyson, J. Butt. 320pp. 5⅛ x 7⅞. **T77 Clothbound $4.50**

Vol. IV. THE VICTORIANS AND AFTER, 1830-1940's, E. Batho, B. Dobrée. 360pp. 5⅛ x 7⅞. **T78 Clothbound $4.50**

EPIC AND ROMANCE, W. P. Ker. Written by one of the foremost authorities on medieval literature, this is the standard survey of medieval epic and romance. It covers Teutonic epics, Icelandic sagas, Beowulf, French chansons de geste, the Roman de Troie, and many other important works of literature. It is an excellent account for a body of literature whose beauty and value has only recently come to be recognized. Index. xxiv + 398pp. 5⅜ x 8. **T355 Paperbound $2.25**

THE POPULAR BALLAD, F. B. Gummere. Most useful factual introduction; fund of descriptive material; quotes, cites over 260 ballads. Examines, from folkloristic view, structure; choral, ritual elements; meter, diction, fusion; effects of tradition, editors; almost every other aspect of border, riddle, kinship, sea, ribald, supernatural, etc., ballads. Bibliography. 2 indexes. 374pp. 5⅜ x 8. **T548 Paperbound $1.85**

MASTERS OF THE DRAMA, John Gassner. The most comprehensive history of the drama in print, covering drama in every important tradition from the Greeks to the Near East, China, Japan, Medieval Europe, England, Russia, Italy, Spain, Germany, and dozens of other drama producing nations. This unsurpassed reading and reference work encompasses more than 800 dramatists and over 2000 plays, with biographical material, plot summaries, theatre history, etc. "Has no competitors in its field," THEATRE ARTS. "Best of its kind in English," NEW REPUBLIC. Exhaustive 35 page bibliography. 77 photographs and drawings. Deluxe edition with reinforced cloth binding, headbands, stained top. xxii + 890pp. 5⅜ x 8. **T100 Clothbound $6.95**

THE DEVELOPMENT OF DRAMATIC ART, D. C. Stuart. The basic work on the growth of Western drama from primitive beginnings to Eugene O'Neill, covering over 2500 years. Not a mere listing or survey, but a thorough analysis of changes, origins of style, and influences in each period; dramatic conventions, social pressures, choice of material, plot devices, stock situations, etc.; secular and religious works of all nations and epochs. "Generous and thoroughly documented researches," Outlook. "Solid studies of influences and playwrights and periods," London Times. Index. Bibliography. xi + 679pp. 5⅜ x 8. **T693 Paperbound $2.75**

A SOURCE BOOK IN THEATRICAL HISTORY (SOURCES OF THEATRICAL HISTORY), A. M. Nagler. Over 2000 years of actors, directors, designers, critics, and spectators speak for themselves in this potpourri of writings selected from the great and formative periods of western drama. On-the-spot descriptions of masks, costumes, makeup, rehearsals, special effects, acting methods, backstage squabbles, theatres, etc. Contemporary glimpses of Molière rehearsing his company, an exhortation to a Roman audience to buy refreshments and keep quiet, Goethe's rules for actors, Belasco telling of $6500 he spent building a river, Restoration actors being told to avoid "lewd, obscene, or indecent postures," and much more. Each selection has an introduction by Prof. Nagler. This extraordinary, lively collection is ideal as a source of otherwise difficult to obtain material, as well as a fine book for browsing. Over 80 illustrations. 10 diagrams. xxiii + 611pp. 5⅜ x 8. **T515 Paperbound $3.00**

CATALOGUE OF DOVER BOOKS

WORLD DRAMA, B. H. Clark. The dramatic creativity of a score of ages and eras — all in two handy compact volumes. Over ⅓ of this material is unavailable in any other current edition! 46 plays from Ancient Greece, Rome, Medieval Europe, France, Germany, Italy, England, Russia, Scandinavia, India, China, Japan, etc. — including classic authors like Aeschylus, Sophocles, Euripides, Aristophanes, Plautus, Marlowe, Jonson, Farquhar, Goldsmith, Cervantes, Molière, Dumas, Goethe, Schiller, Ibsen, and many others. This creative collection avoids hackneyed material and includes only completely first-rate works which are relatively little known or difficult to obtain. "The most comprehensive collection of important plays from all literature available in English," SAT. REV. OF LITERATURE. Introduction. Reading lists. 2 volumes. 1364pp. 5⅜ x 8.
Vol. 1, T57 Paperbound **$2.50**
Vol. 2, T59 Paperbound **$2.50**

MASTERPIECES OF THE RUSSIAN DRAMA, edited with introduction by G. R. Noyes. This only comprehensive anthology of Russian drama ever published in English offers complete texts, in 1st-rate modern translations, of 12 plays covering 200 years. Vol. 1: "The Young Hopeful," Fonvisin; "Wit Works Woe," Griboyedov; "The Inspector General," Gogol; "A Month in the Country," Turgenev; "The Poor Bride," Ostrovsky; "A Bitter Fate," Pisemsky. Vol. 2: "The Death of Ivan the Terrible," Alexey Tolstoy "The Power of Darkness," Lev Tolstoy; "The Lower Depths," Gorky; "The Cherry Orchard," Chekhov; "Professor Storitsyn," Andreyev; "Mystery Bouffe," Mayakovsky. Bibliography. Total of 902pp. 5⅜ x 8.
Vol. 1 T647 Paperbound **$2.25**
Vol. 2 T648 Paperbound **$2.00**

EUGENE O'NEILL: THE MAN AND HIS PLAYS, B. H. Clark. Introduction to O'Neill's life and work. Clark analyzes each play from the early THE WEB to the recently produced MOON FOR THE MISBEGOTTEN and THE ICEMAN COMETH revealing the environmental and dramatic influences necessary for a complete understanding of these important works. Bibliography. Appendices. Index. ix + 182pp. 5⅜ x 8. T379 Paperbound **$1.35**

THE HEART OF THOREAU'S JOURNALS, edited by O. Shepard. The best general selection from Thoreau's voluminous (and rare) journals. This intimate record of thoughts and observations reveals the full Thoreau and his intellectual development more accurately than any of his published works: self-conflict between the scientific observer and the poet, reflections on transcendental philosophy, involvement in the tragedies of neighbors and national causes, etc. New preface, notes, introductions. xii + 228pp. 5⅜ x 8. T741 Paperbound **$1.50**

H. D. THOREAU: A WRITER'S JOURNAL, edited by L. Stapleton. A unique new selection from the Journals concentrating on Thoreau's growth as a conscious literary artist, the ideals and purposes of his art. Most of the material has never before appeared outside of the complete 14-volume edition. Contains vital insights on Thoreau's projected book on Concord, thoughts on the nature of men and government, indignation with slavery, sources of inspiration, goals in life. Index. xxxiii + 234pp. 5⅜ x 8. T678 Paperbound **$1.65**

THE HEART OF EMERSON'S JOURNALS, edited by Bliss Perry. Best of these revealing Journals, originally 10 volumes, presented in a one volume edition. Talks with Channing, Hawthorne, Thoreau, and Bronson Alcott; impressions of Webster, Everett, John Brown, and Lincoln; records of moments of sudden understanding, vision, and solitary ecstasy. "The essays do not reveal the power of Emerson's mind . . . as do these hasty and informal writings," N.Y. Times. Preface by Bliss Perry. Index. xiii + 357pp. 5⅜ x 8. T477 Paperbound **$1.85**

FOUNDERS OF THE MIDDLE AGES, E. K. Rand. This is the best non-technical discussion of the transformation of Latin pagan culture into medieval civilization. Covering such figures as Tertullian, Gregory, Jerome, Boethius, Augustine, the Neoplatonists, and many other literary men, educators, classicists, and humanists, this book is a storehouse of information presented clearly and simply for the intelligent non-specialist. "Thoughtful, beautifully written," AMERICAN HISTORICAL REVIEW. "Extraordinarily accurate," Richard McKeon, THE NATION. ix + 365pp. 5⅜ x 8. T369 Paperbound **$2.00**

PLAY-MAKING: A MANUAL OF CRAFTSMANSHIP, William Archer. With an extensive, new introduction by John Gassner, Yale Univ. The permanently essential requirements of solid play construction are set down in clear, practical language: theme, exposition, foreshadowing, tension, obligatory scene, peripety, dialogue, character, psychology, other topics. This book has been one of the most influential elements in the modern theatre, and almost everything said on the subject since is contained explicitly or implicitly within its covers. Bibliography. Index. xlii + 277pp. 5⅜ x 8. T651 Paperbound **$1.75**

HAMBURG DRAMATURGY, G. E. Lessing. One of the most brilliant of German playwrights of the eighteenth-century age of criticism analyzes the complex of theory and tradition that constitutes the world of theater. These 104 essays on aesthetic theory helped demolish the regime of French classicism, opening the door to psychological and social realism, romanticism. Subjects include the original functions of tragedy; drama as the rational world; the meaning of pity and fear, pity and fear as means for purgation and other Aristotelian concepts; genius and creative force; interdependence of poet's language and actor's interpretation; truth and authenticity; etc. A basic and enlightening study for anyone interested in aesthetics and ideas, from the philosopher to the theatergoer. Introduction by Prof. Victor Lange. xxii + 265pp. 4½ x 6⅜. T32 Paperbound **$1.45**

Books Explaining Science and Mathematics

WHAT IS SCIENCE?, N. Campbell. The role of experiment and measurement, the function of mathematics, the nature of scientific laws, the difference between laws and theories, the limitations of science, and many similarly provocative topics are treated clearly and without technicalities by an eminent scientist. "Still an excellent intro- duction to scientific philosophy," H. Margenau in PHYSICS TODAY. "A first-rate primer . . . deserves a wide audience," SCIENTIFIC AMERICAN. 192pp. 5⅜ x 8.   S43 Paperbound **$1.25**

THE NATURE OF PHYSICAL THEORY, P. W. Bridgman. A Nobel Laureate's clear, non-technical lectures on difficulties and paradoxes connected with frontier research on the physical sciences. Concerned with such central concepts as thought, logic, mathematics, relativity, probability, wave mechanics, etc. he analyzes the contributions of such men as Newton, Einstein, Bohr, Heisenberg, and many others. "Lucid and entertaining . . . recommended to anyone who wants to get some insight into current philosophies of science," THE NEW PHILOSOPHY. Index. xi + 138pp. 5⅜ x 8.   S33 Paperbound **$1.25**

EXPERIMENT AND THEORY IN PHYSICS, Max Born. A Nobel Laureate examines the nature of experiment and theory in theoretical physics and analyzes the advances made by the great physicists of our day: Heisenberg, Einstein, Bohr, Planck, Dirac, and others. The actual process of creation is detailed step-by-step by one who participated. A fine examination of the scientific method at work. 44pp. 5⅜ x 8.   S308 Paperbound **75¢**

THE PSYCHOLOGY OF INVENTION IN THE MATHEMATICAL FIELD, J. Hadamard. The reports of such men as Descartes, Pascal, Einstein, Poincaré, and others are considered in this investi- gation of the method of idea-creation in mathematics and other sciences and the thinking process in general. How do ideas originate? What is the role of the unconscious? What is Poincaré's forgetting hypothesis? are some of the fascinating questions treated. A penetrating analysis of Einstein's thought processes concludes the book. xiii + 145pp. 5⅜ x 8.   T107 Paperbound **$1.25**

THE NATURE OF LIGHT AND COLOUR IN THE OPEN AIR, M. Minnaert. Why are shadows some- times blue, sometimes green, or other colors depending on the light and surroundings? What causes mirages? Why do multiple suns and moons appear in the sky? Professor Minnaert explains these unusual phenomena and hundreds of others in simple, easy-to-understand terms based on optical laws and the properties of light and color. No mathematics is required but artists, scientists, students, and everyone fascinated by these "tricks" of nature will find thousands of useful and amazing pieces of information. Hundreds of observational experiments are suggested which require no special equipment. 200 illustrations; 42 photos. xvi + 362pp. 5⅜ x 8.   T196 Paperbound **$2.00**

*MATHEMATICS IN ACTION, O. G. Sutton. Everyone with a command of high school algebra will find this book one of the finest possible introductions to the application of mathematics to physical theory. Ballistics, numerical analysis, waves and wavelike phenomena, Fourier series, group concepts, fluid flow and aerodynamics, statistical measures, and meteorology are dis- cussed with unusual clarity. Some calculus and differential equations theory is developed by the author for the reader's help in the more difficult sections. 88 figures. Index. viii + 236pp. 5⅜ x 8.   T440 Clothbound **$3.50**

SOAP-BUBBLES: THEIR COLOURS AND THE FORCES THAT MOULD THEM, C. V. Boys. For continuing popularity and validity as scientific primer, few books can match this volume of easily- followed experiments, explanations. Lucid exposition of complexities of liquid films, surfac tension and related phenomena, bubbles' reaction to heat, motion, music, magnetic fields. Experiments with capillary attraction, soap bubbles on frames, composite bubbles, liquid cylinders and jets, bubbles other than soap, etc. Wonderful introduction to scientific method, natural laws that have many ramifications in areas of modern physics. Only com- plete edition in print. New Introduction by S. Z. Lewin, New York University. 83 illustra- tions; 1 full-page color plate. xii + 190pp. 5⅜ x 8½.   T542 Paperbound **95¢**

CATALOGUE OF DOVER BOOKS

THE STORY OF X-RAYS FROM RÖNTGEN TO ISOTOPES, A. R. Bleich, M.D. This book, by a member of the American College of Radiology, gives the scientific explanation of x-rays, their applications in medicine, industry and art, and their danger (and that of atmospheric radiation) to the individual and the species. You learn how radiation therapy is applied against cancer, how x-rays diagnose heart disease and other ailments, how they are used to examine mummies for information on diseases of early societies, and industrial materials for hidden weaknesses. 54 illustrations show x-rays of flowers, bones, stomach, gears with flaws, etc. 1st publication. Index. xix + 186pp. 5⅜ x 8. **T622 Paperbound $1.35**

SPINNING TOPS AND GYROSCOPIC MOTION, John Perry. A classic elementary text of the dynamics of rotation — the behavior and use of rotating bodies such as gyroscopes and tops. In simple, everyday English you are shown how quasi-rigidity is induced in discs of paper, smoke rings, chains, etc., by rapid motions; why a gyrostat falls and why a top rises; precession; how the earth's motion affects climate; and many other phenomena. Appendix on practical use of gyroscopes. 62 figures. 128pp. 5⅜ x 8. **T416 Paperbound $1.00**

SNOW CRYSTALS, W. A. Bentley, M. J. Humphreys. For almost 50 years W. A. Bentley photographed snow flakes in his laboratory in Jericho, Vermont; in 1931 the American Meteorological Society gathered together the best of his work, some 2400 photographs of snow flakes, plus a few ice flowers, windowpane frosts, dew, frozen rain, and other ice formations. Pictures were selected for beauty and scientific value. A very valuable work to anyone in meteorology, cryology; most interesting to layman; extremely useful for artist who wants beautiful, crystalline designs. All copyright free. Unabridged reprint of 1931 edition. 2453 illustrations. 227pp. 8 x 10½. **T287 Paperbound $3.00**

A DOVER SCIENCE SAMPLER, edited by George Barkin. A collection of brief, non-technical passages from 44 Dover Books Explaining Science for the enjoyment of the science-minded browser. Includes work of Bertrand Russell, Poincaré, Laplace, Max Born, Galileo, Newton; material on physics, mathematics, metallurgy, anatomy, astronomy, chemistry, etc. You will be fascinated by Martin Gardner's analysis of the sincere pseudo-scientist, Moritz's account of Newton's absentmindedness, Bernard's examples of human vivisection, etc. Illustrations from the Diderot Pictorial Encyclopedia and De Re Metallica. 64 pages. **FREE**

THE STORY OF ATOMIC THEORY AND ATOMIC ENERGY, J. G. Feinberg. A broader approach to subject of nuclear energy and its cultural implications than any other similar source. Very readable, informal, completely non-technical text. Begins with first atomic theory, 600 B.C. and carries you through the work of Mendelejeff, Röntgen, Madame Curie, to Einstein's equation and the A-bomb. New chapter goes through thermonuclear fission, binding energy, other events up to 1959. Radioactive decay and radiation hazards, future benefits, work of Bohr, moderns, hundreds more topics. "Deserves special mention . . . not only authoritative but thoroughly popular in the best sense of the word," Saturday Review. Formerly, "The Atom Story." Expanded with new chapter. Three appendixes. Index. 34 illustrations. vii + 243pp. 5⅜ x 8. **T625 Paperbound $1.60**

THE STRANGE STORY OF THE QUANTUM, AN ACCOUNT FOR THE GENERAL READER OF THE GROWTH OF IDEAS UNDERLYING OUR PRESENT ATOMIC KNOWLEDGE, B. Hoffmann. Presents lucidly and expertly, with barest amount of mathematics, the problems and theories which led to modern quantum physics. Dr. Hoffmann begins with the closing years of the 19th century, when certain trifling discrepancies were noticed, and with illuminating analogies and examples takes you through the brilliant concepts of Planck, Einstein, Pauli, Broglie, Bohr, Schroedinger, Heisenberg, Dirac, Sommerfeld, Feynman, etc. This edition includes a new, long postscript carrying the story through 1958. "Of the books attempting an account of the history and contents of our modern atomic physics which have come to my attention, this is the best," H. Margenau, Yale University, in "American Journal of Physics." 32 tables and line illustrations. Index. 275pp. 5⅜ x 8. **T518 Paperbound $1.50**

SPACE AND TIME, E. Borel. Written by a versatile mathematician of world renown with his customary lucidity and precision, this introduction to relativity for the layman presents scores of examples, analogies, and illustrations that open up new ways of thinking about space and time. It covers abstract geometry and geographical maps, continuity and topology, the propagation of light, the special theory of relativity, the general theory of relativity, theoretical researches, and much more. Mathematical notes. 2 Indexes. 4 Appendices. 15 figures. xvi + 243pp. 5⅜ x 8. **T592 Paperbound $1.45**

FROM EUCLID TO EDDINGTON: A STUDY OF THE CONCEPTIONS OF THE EXTERNAL WORLD, Sir Edmund Whittaker. A foremost British scientist traces the development of theories of natural philosophy from the western rediscovery of Euclid to Eddington, Einstein, Dirac, etc. The inadequacy of classical physics is contrasted with present day attempts to understand the physical world through relativity, non-Euclidean geometry, space curvature, wave mechanics, etc. 5 major divisions of examination: Space; Time and Movement; the Concepts of Classical Physics; the Concepts of Quantum Mechanics; the Eddington Universe. 212pp. 5⅜ x 8. **T491 Paperbound $1.35**

CATALOGUE OF DOVER BOOKS

*THE EVOLUTION OF SCIENTIFIC THOUGHT FROM NEWTON TO EINSTEIN, A. d'Abro. A detailed account of the evolution of classical physics into modern relativistic theory and the concomitant changes in scientific methodology. The breakdown of classical physics in the face of non-Euclidean geometry and the electromagnetic equations is carefully discussed and then an exhaustive analysis of Einstein's special and general theories of relativity and their implications is given. Newton, Riemann, Weyl, Lorentz, Planck, Maxwell, and many others are considered. A non-technical explanation of space, time, electromagnetic waves, etc. as understood today. "Model of semi-popular exposition," NEW REPUBLIC. 21 diagrams. 482pp. 5⅜ x 8.
T2 Paperbound **$2.25**

EINSTEIN'S THEORY OF RELATIVITY, Max Born. Nobel Laureate explains Einstein's special and general theories of relativity, beginning with a thorough review of classical physics in simple, non-technical language. Exposition of Einstein's work discusses concept of simultaneity, kinematics, relativity of arbitrary motions, the space-time continuum, geometry of curved surfaces, etc., steering middle course between vague popularizations and complex scientific presentations. 1962 edition revised by author takes into account latest findings, predictions of theory and implications for cosmology, indicates what is being sought in unified field theory. Mathematics very elementary, illustrative diagrams and experiments informative but simple. Revised 1962 edition. Revised by Max Born, assisted by Gunther Leibfried and Walter Biem. Index. 143 illustrations. vii + 376pp. 5⅜ x 8.
S769 Paperbound **$2.00**

PHILOSOPHY AND THE PHYSICISTS, L. Susan Stebbing. A philosopher examines the philosophical aspects of modern science, in terms of a lively critical attack on the ideas of Jeans and Eddington. Such basic questions are treated as the task of science, causality, determinism, probability, consciousness, the relation of the world of physics to the world of everyday experience. The author probes the concepts of man's smallness before an inscrutable universe, the tendency to idealize mathematical construction, unpredictability theorems and human freedom, the supposed opposition between 19th century determinism and modern science, and many others. Introduces many thought-stimulating ideas about the implications of modern physical concepts. xvi + 295pp. 5⅜ x 8.
T480 Paperbound **$1.65**

THE RESTLESS UNIVERSE, Max Born. A remarkably lucid account by a Nobel Laureate of recent theories of wave mechanics, behavior of gases, electrons and ions, waves and particles, electronic structure of the atom, nuclear physics, and similar topics. "Much more thorough and deeper than most attempts . . . easy and delightful," CHEMICAL AND ENGINEERING NEWS. Special feature: 7 animated sequences of 60 figures each showing such phenomena as gas molecules in motion, the scattering of alpha particles, etc. 11 full-page plates of photographs. Total of nearly 600 illustrations. 351pp. 6⅛ x 9¼.
T412 Paperbound **$2.00**

THE COMMON SENSE OF THE EXACT SCIENCES, W. K. Clifford. For 70 years a guide to the basic concepts of scientific and mathematical thought. Acclaimed by scientists and laymen alike, it offers a wonderful insight into concepts such as the extension of meaning of symbols, characteristics of surface boundaries, properties of plane figures, measurement of quantities, vectors, the nature of position, bending of space, motion, mass and force, and many others. Prefaces by Bertrand Russell and Karl Pearson. Critical introduction by James Newman. 130 figures. 249pp. 5⅜ x 8.
T61 Paperbound **$1.60**

MATTER AND LIGHT, THE NEW PHYSICS, Louis de Broglie. Non-technical explanations by a Nobel Laureate of electro-magnetic theory, relativity, matter, light and radiation, wave mechanics, quantum physics, philosophy of science, and similar topics. This is one of the simplest yet most accurate introductions to the work of men like Planck, Einstein, Bohr, and others. Only 2 of the 21 chapters require a knowledge of mathematics. 300pp. 5⅜ x 8.
T35 Paperbound **$1.85**

SCIENCE, THEORY AND MAN, Erwin Schrödinger. This is a complete and unabridged reissue of SCIENCE AND THE HUMAN TEMPERAMENT plus an additional essay: "What Is an Elementary Particle?" Nobel Laureate Schrödinger discusses such topics as nature of scientific method, the nature of science, chance and determinism, science and society, conceptual models for physical entities, elementary particles and wave mechanics. Presentation is popular and may be followed by most people with little or no scientific training. "Fine practical preparation for a time when laws of nature, human institutions . . . are undergoing a critical examination without parallel," Waldemar Kaempffert, N. Y. TIMES. 192pp. 5⅜ x 8.
T428 Paperbound **$1.35**

CONCERNING THE NATURE OF THINGS, Sir William Bragg. The Nobel Laureate physicist in his Royal Institute Christmas Lectures explains such diverse phenomena as the formation of crystals, how uranium is transmuted to lead, the way X-rays work, why a spinning ball travels in a curved path, the reason why bubbles bounce from each other, and many other scientific topics that are seldom explained in simple terms. No scientific background needed—book is easy enough that any intelligent adult or youngster can understand it. Unabridged. 32pp. of photos; 57 figures. xii + 232pp. 5⅜ x 8.
T31 Paperbound **$1.35**

*THE RISE OF THE NEW PHYSICS (formerly THE DECLINE OF MECHANISM), A. d'Abro. This authoritative and comprehensive 2 volume exposition is unique in scientific publishing. Written for intelligent readers not familiar with higher mathematics, it is the only thorough explanation in non-technical language of modern mathematical-physical theory. Combining both history and exposition, it ranges from classical Newtonian concepts up through the electronic theories of Dirac and Heisenberg, the statistical mechanics of Fermi, and Einstein's relativity theories. "A must for anyone doing serious study in the physical sciences," J. OF FRANKLIN INST. 97 illustrations. 991pp. 2 volumes.
T3 Vol. 1, Paperbound **$2.25**
T4 Vol. 2, Paperbound **$2.25**

CATALOGUE OF DOVER BOOKS

SCIENCE AND HYPOTHESIS, Henri Poincaré. Creative psychology in science. How such concepts as number, magnitude, space, force, classical mechanics were developed and how the modern scientist uses them in his thought. Hypothesis in physics, theories of modern physics. Introduction by Sir James Larmor. "Few mathematicians have had the breadth of vision of Poincaré, and none is his superior in the gift of clear exposition," E. T. Bell. Index. 272pp. 5⅜ x 8.
S221 Paperbound **$1.35**

THE VALUE OF SCIENCE, Henri Poincaré. Many of the most mature ideas of the "last scientific universalist" conveyed with charm and vigor for both the beginning student and the advanced worker. Discusses the nature of scientific truth, whether order is innate in the universe or imposed upon it by man, logical thought versus intuition (relating to mathematics through the works of Weierstrass, Lie, Klein, Riemann), time and space (relativity, psychological time, simultaneity), Hertz's concept of force, interrelationship of mathematical physics to pure math, values within disciplines of Maxwell, Carnot, Mayer, Newton, Lorentz, etc. Index. iii + 147pp. 5⅜ x 8.
S469 Paperbound **$1.35**

THE SKY AND ITS MYSTERIES, E. A. Beet. One of the most lucid books on the mysteries of the universe; covers history of astronomy from earliest observations to modern theories of expanding universe, source of stellar energy, birth of planets, origin of moon craters, possibilities of life on other planets. Discusses effects of sunspots on weather; distance, age of stars; methods and tools of astronomers; much more. Expert and fascinating. "Eminently readable book," London Times. Bibliography. Over 50 diagrams, 12 full-page plates. Fold-out star map. Introduction. Index. 238pp. 5¼ x 7½.
T627 Clothbound **$3.50**

OUT OF THE SKY: AN INTRODUCTION TO METEORITICS, H. H. Nininger. A non-technical yet comprehensive introduction to the young science of meteoritics: all aspects of the arrival of cosmic matter on our planet from outer space and the reaction and alteration of this matter in the terrestrial environment. Essential facts and major theories presented by one of the world's leading experts. Covers ancient reports of meteors; modern systematic investigations; fireball clusters; meteorite showers; tektites; planetoidal encounters; etc. 52 full-page plates with over 175 photographs. 22 figures. Bibliography and references. Index. viii + 336pp. 5⅜ x 8.
T519 Paperbound **$1.85**

THE REALM OF THE NEBULAE, E. Hubble. One of great astronomers of our day records his formulation of concept of "island universes." Covers velocity-distance relationship; classification, nature, distances, general types of nebulae; cosmological theories. A fine introduction to modern theories for layman. No math needed. New introduction by A. Sandage. 55 illustrations, photos. Index. iv + 201pp. 5⅜ x 8.
S455 Paperbound **$1.50**

AN ELEMENTARY SURVEY OF CELESTIAL MECHANICS, Y. Ryabov. Elementary exposition of gravitational theory and celestial mechanics. Historical introduction and coverage of basic principles, including: the ecliptic, the orbital plane, the 2- and 3-body problems, the discovery of Neptune, planetary rotation, the length of the day, the shapes of galaxies, satellites (detailed treatment of Sputnik I), etc. First American reprinting of successful Russian popular exposition. Follow actual methods of astrophysicists with only high school math! Appendix. 58 figures. 165pp. 5⅜ x 8.
T756 Paperbound **$1.25**

GREAT IDEAS AND THEORIES OF MODERN COSMOLOGY, Jagjit Singh. Companion volume to author's popular "Great Ideas of Modern Mathematics" (Dover, $1.55). The best non-technical survey of post-Einstein attempts to answer perhaps unanswerable questions of origin, age of Universe, possibility of life on other worlds, etc. Fundamental theories of cosmology and cosmogony recounted, explained, evaluated in light of most recent data: Einstein's concepts of relativity, space-time; Milne's a priori world-system; astrophysical theories of Jeans, Eddington, Hoyle's "continuous creation;" contributions of dozens more scientists. A faithful, comprehensive critical summary of complex material presented in an extremely well-written text intended for laymen. Original publication. Index. xii + 276pp. 5⅜ x 8½.
T925 Paperbound **$1.85**

BASIC ELECTRICITY, Bureau of Naval Personnel. Very thorough, easily followed course in basic electricity for beginner, layman, or intermediate student. Begins with simplest definitions, presents coordinated, systematic coverage of basic theory and application: conductors, insulators, static electricity, magnetism, production of voltage, Ohm's law, direct current series and parallel circuits, wiring techniques, electromagnetism, alternating current, capacitance and inductance, measuring instruments, etc.; application to electrical machines such as alternating and direct current generators, motors, transformers, magnetic magnifiers, etc. Each chapter contains problems to test progress; answers at rear. No math needed beyond algebra. Appendices on signs, formulas, etc. 345 illustrations. 448pp. 7½ x 10.
S973 Paperbound **$3.00**

ELEMENTARY METALLURGY AND METALLOGRAPHY, A. M. Shrager. An introduction to common metals and alloys; stress is upon steel and iron, but other metals and alloys also covered. All aspects of production, processing, working of metals. Designed for student who wishes to enter metallurgy, for bright high school or college beginner, layman who wants background on extremely important industry. Questions, at ends of chapters, many microphotographs, glossary. Greatly revised 1961 edition. 195 illustrations, tables. ix + 389pp. 5⅜ x 8.
S138 Paperbound **$2.25**

CATALOGUE OF DOVER BOOKS

BRIDGES AND THEIR BUILDERS, D. B. Steinman & S. R. Watson. Engineers, historians, and every person who has ever been fascinated by great spans will find this book an endless source of information and interest. Greek and Roman structures, Medieval bridges, modern classics such as the Brooklyn Bridge, and the latest developments in the science are retold by one of the world's leading authorities on bridge design and construction. BRIDGES AND THEIR BUILDERS is the only comprehensive and accurate semi-popular history of these important measures of progress in print. New, greatly revised, enlarged edition. 23 photos; 26 line-drawings. Index. xvii + 401pp. 5⅜ x 8. T431 Paperbound **$2.00**

FAMOUS BRIDGES OF THE WORLD, D. B. Steinman. An up-to-the-minute new edition of a book that explains the fascinating drama of how the world's great bridges came to be built. The author, designer of the famed Mackinac bridge, discusses bridges from all periods and all parts of the world, explaining their various types of construction, and describing the problems their builders faced. Although primarily for youngsters, this cannot fail to interest readers of all ages. 48 illustrations in the text. 23 photographs. 99pp. 6⅛ x 9¼. T161 Paperbound **$1.00**

HOW DO YOU USE A SLIDE RULE? by A. A. Merrill. A step-by-step explanation of the slide rule that presents the fundamental rules clearly enough for the non-mathematician to understand. Unlike most instruction manuals, this work concentrates on the two most important operations: multiplication and division. 10 easy lessons, each with a clear drawing, for the reader who has difficulty following other expositions. 1st publication. Index. 2 Appendices. 10 illustrations. 78 problems, all with answers. vi + 36 pp. 6⅛ x 9¼. T62 Paperbound **60¢**

HOW TO CALCULATE QUICKLY, H. Sticker. A tried and true method for increasing your "number sense" — the ability to see relationships between numbers and groups of numbers. Addition, subtraction, multiplication, division, fractions, and other topics are treated through techniques not generally taught in schools: left to right multiplication, division by inspection, etc. This is not a collection of tricks which work only on special numbers, but a detailed well-planned course, consisting of over 9,000 problems that you can work in spare moments. It is excellent for anyone who is inconvenienced by slow computational skills. 5 or 10 minutes of this book daily will double or triple your calculation speed. 9,000 problems, answers. 256pp. 5⅜ x 8. T295 Paperbound **$1.00**

MATHEMATICAL FUN, GAMES AND PUZZLES, Jack Frohlichstein. A valuable service for parents of children who have trouble with math, for teachers in need of a supplement to regular upper elementary and junior high math texts (each section is graded—easy, average, difficult —for ready adaptation to different levels of ability), and for just anyone who would like to develop basic skills in an informal and entertaining manner. The author combines ten years of experience as a junior high school math teacher with a method that uses puzzles and games to introduce the basic ideas and operations of arithmetic. Stress on everyday uses of math: banking, stock market, personal budgets, insurance, taxes. Intellectually stimulating and practical, too. 418 problems and diversions with answers. Bibliography. 120 illustrations. xix + 306pp. 5⅝ x 8½. T789 Paperbound **$1.75**

GREAT IDEAS OF MODERN MATHEMATICS: THEIR NATURE AND USE, Jagjit Singh. Reader with only high school math will understand main mathematical ideas of modern physics, astronomy, genetics, psychology, evolution, etc. better than many who use them as tools, but comprehend little of their basic structure. Author uses his wide knowledge of non-mathematical fields in brilliant exposition of differential equations, matrices, group theory, logic, statistics, problems of mathematical foundations, imaginary numbers, vectors, etc. Original publication. 2 appendixes. 2 indexes. 65 illustr. 322pp. 5⅜ x 8. S587 Paperbound **$1.75**

THE UNIVERSE OF LIGHT, W. Bragg. Sir William Bragg, Nobel Laureate and great modern physicist, is also well known for his powers of clear exposition. Here he analyzes all aspects of light for the layman: lenses, reflection, refraction, the optics of vision, x-rays, the photoelectric effect, etc. He tells you what causes the color of spectra, rainbows, and soap bubbles, how magic mirrors work, and much more. Dozens of simple experiments are described. Preface. Index. 199 line drawings and photographs, including 2 full-page color plates. x + 283pp. 5⅜ x 8. T538 Paperbound **$1.85**

*INTRODUCTION TO SYMBOLIC LOGIC AND ITS APPLICATIONS, Rudolph Carnap. One of the clearest, most comprehensive, and rigorous introductions to modern symbolic logic, by perhaps its greatest living master. Not merely elementary theory, but demonstrated applications in mathematics, physics, and biology. Symbolic languages of various degrees of complexity are analyzed, and one constructed. "A creation of the rank of a masterpiece," Zentralblatt für Mathematik und Ihre Grenzgebiete. Over 300 exercises. 5 figures. Bibliography. Index. xvi + 241pp. 5⅜ x 8. S453 Paperbound **$1.85**

*HIGHER MATHEMATICS FOR STUDENTS OF CHEMISTRY AND PHYSICS, J. W. Mellor. Not abstract, but practical, drawing its problems from familiar laboratory material, this book covers theory and application of differential calculus, analytic geometry, functions with singularities, integral calculus, infinite series, solution of numerical equations, differential equations, Fourier's theorem and extensions, probability and the theory of errors, calculus of variations, determinants, etc. "If the reader is not familiar with this book, it will repay him to examine it," CHEM. & ENGINEERING NEWS. 800 problems. 189 figures. 2 appendices; 30 tables of integrals, probability functions, etc. Bibliography. xxi + 641pp. 5⅜ x 8. S193 Paperbound **$2.50**

CATALOGUE OF DOVER BOOKS

THE FOURTH DIMENSION SIMPLY EXPLAINED, edited by Henry P. Manning. Originally written as entries in contest sponsored by "Scientific American," then published in book form, these 22 essays present easily understood explanations of how the fourth dimension may be studied, the relationship of non-Euclidean geometry to the fourth dimension, analogies to three-dimensional space, some fourth-dimensional absurdities and curiosities, possible measurements and forms in the fourth dimension. In general, a thorough coverage of many of the simpler properties of fourth-dimensional space. Multi-points of view on many of the most important aspects are valuable aid to comprehension. Introduction by Dr. Henry P. Manning gives proper emphasis to points in essays, more advanced account of fourth-dimensional geometry. 82 figures. 251pp. 5⅜ x 8.   T711 Paperbound **$1.35**

TRIGONOMETRY REFRESHER FOR TECHNICAL MEN, A. A. Klaf. A modern question and answer text on plane and spherical trigonometry. Part I covers plane trigonometry: angles, quadrants, trigonometrical functions, graphical representation, interpolation, equations, logarithms, solution of triangles, slide rules, etc. Part II discusses applications to navigation, surveying, elasticity, architecture, and engineering. Small angles, periodic functions, vectors, polar coordinates, De Moivre's theorem, fully covered. Part III is devoted to spherical trigonometry and the solution of spherical triangles, with applications to terrestrial and astronomical problems. Special time-savers for numerical calculation. 913 questions answered for you! 1738 problems; answers to odd numbers. 494 figures. 14 pages of functions, formulae. Index. x + 629pp. 5⅜ x 8.   T371 Paperbound **$2.00**

CALCULUS REFRESHER FOR TECHNICAL MEN. A. A. Klaf. Not an ordinary textbook but a unique refresher for engineers, technicians, and students. An examination of the most important aspects of differential and integral calculus by means of 756 key questions. Part I covers simple differential calculus: constants, variables, functions, increments, derivatives, logarithms, curvature, etc. Part II treats fundamental concepts of integration: inspection, substitution, transformation, reduction, areas and volumes, mean value, successive and partial integration, double and triple integration. Stresses practical aspects! A 50 page section gives applications to civil and nautical engineering, electricity, stress and strain, elasticity, industrial engineering, and similar fields. 756 questions answered. 556 problems; solutions to odd numbers. 36 pages of constants, formulae. Index. v + 431pp. 5⅜ x 8.   T370 Paperbound **$2.00**

PROBABILITIES AND LIFE, Emile Borel. One of the leading French mathematicians of the last 100 years makes use of certain results of mathematics of probabilities and explains a number of problems that for the most part, are related to everyday living or to illness and death: computation of life expectancy tables, chances of recovery from various diseases, probabilities of job accidents, weather predictions, games of chance, and so on. Emphasis on results not processes, though some indication is made of mathematical proofs. Simple in style, free of technical terminology, limited in scope to everyday situations, it is comprehensible to laymen, fine reading for beginning students of probability. New English translation. Index. Appendix. vi + 87pp. 5⅜ x 8½.   T121 Paperbound **$1.00**

POPULAR SCIENTIFIC LECTURES, Hermann von Helmholtz. 7 lucid expositions by a preeminent scientific mind: "The Physiological Causes of Harmony in Music," "On the Relation of Optics to Painting," "On the Conservation of Force," "On the Interaction of Natural Forces," "On Goethe's Scientific Researches" into theory of color, "On the Origin and Significance of Geometric Axioms," "On Recent Progress in the Theory of Vision." Written with simplicity of expression, stripped of technicalities, these are easy to understand and delightful reading for anyone interested in science or looking for an introduction to serious study of acoustics or optics. Introduction by Professor Morris Kline, Director, Division of Electromagnetic Research, New York University, contains astute, impartial evaluations. Selected from "Popular Lectures on Scientific Subjects," 1st and 2nd series. xii + 286pp. 5⅜ x 8½.   T799 Paperbound **$1.45**

SCIENCE AND METHOD, Henri Poincaré. Procedure of scientific discovery, methodology, experiment, idea-germination—the intellectual processes by which discoveries come into being. Most significant and most interesting aspects of development, application of ideas. Chapters cover selection of facts, chance, mathematical reasoning, mathematics, and logic; Whitehead, Russell, Cantor; the new mechanics, etc. 288pp. 5⅜ x 8.   S222 Paperbound **$1.50**

HEAT AND ITS WORKINGS, Morton Mott-Smith, Ph.D. An unusual book; to our knowledge the only middle-level survey of this important area of science. Explains clearly such important concepts as physiological sensation of heat and Weber's law, measurement of heat, evolution of thermometer, nature of heat, expansion and contraction of solids, Boyle's law, specific heat. BTU's and calories, evaporation, Andrews's isothermals, radiation, the relation of heat to light, many more topics inseparable from other aspects of physics. A wide, non-mathematical yet thorough explanation of basic ideas, theories, phenomena for laymen and beginning scientists illustrated by experiences of daily life. Bibliography. 50 illustrations. x + 165pp. 5⅜ x 8½.   T978 Paperbound **$1.00**

CATALOGUE OF DOVER BOOKS

Orientalia

ORIENTAL RELIGIONS IN ROMAN PAGANISM, F. Cumont. A study of the cultural meeting of east and west in the Early Roman Empire. It covers the most important eastern religions of the time from their first appearance in Rome, 204 B.C., when the Great Mother of the Gods was first brought over from Syria. The ecstatic cults of Syria and Phrygia — Cybele, Attis, Adonis, their orgies and mutilatory rites; the mysteries of Egypt — Serapis, Isis, Osiris, the dualism of Persia, the elevation of cosmic evil to equal stature with the deity, Mithra; worship of Hermes Trismegistus; Ishtar, Astarte; the magic of the ancient Near East, etc. Introduction. 55pp. of notes; extensive bibliography. Index. xxiv + 298pp. 5⅜ x 8.
T321 Paperbound **$2.00**

THE MYSTERIES OF MITHRA, F. Cumont. The definitive coverage of a great ideological struggle between the west and the orient in the first centuries of the Christian era. The origin of Mithraism, a Persian mystery religion, and its association with the Roman army is discussed in detail. Then utilizing fragmentary monuments and texts, in one of the greatest feats of scholarly detection, Dr. Cumont reconstructs the mystery teachings and secret doctrines, the hidden organization and cult of Mithra. Mithraic art is discussed, analyzed, and depicted in 70 illustrations. 239pp. 5⅜ x 8.
T323 Paperbound **$2.00**

CHRISTIAN AND ORIENTAL PHILOSOPHY OF ART, A. K. Coomaraswamy. A unique fusion of philosopher, orientalist, art historian, and linguist, the author discusses such matters as: the true function of aesthetics in art, the importance of symbolism, intellectual and philosophic backgrounds, the role of traditional culture in enriching art, common factors in all great art, the nature of medieval art, the nature of folklore, the beauty of mathematics, and similar topics. 2 illustrations. Bibliography. 148pp. 5⅜ x 8.
T378 Paperbound **$1.50**

TRANSFORMATION OF NATURE IN ART, A. K. Coomaraswamy. Unabridged reissue of a basic work upon Asiatic religious art and philosophy of religion. The theory of religious art in Asia and Medieval Europe (exemplified by Meister Eckhart) is analyzed and developed. Detailed consideration is given to Indian mediaeval aesthetic manuals, symbolic language in philosophy, the origin and use of images in India, and many other fascinating and little known topics. Glossaries of Sanskrit and Chinese terms. Bibliography. 41pp. of notes. 245pp. 5⅜ x 8.
T368 Paperbound **$1.75**

BUDDHIST LOGIC, F.Th. Stcherbatsky. A study of an important part of Buddhism usually ignored by other books on the subject: the Mahayana buddhistic logic of the school of Dignaga and his followers. First vol. devoted to history of Indian logic with Central Asian continuations, detailed exposition of Dignaga system, including theory of knowledge, the sensible world (causation, perception, ultimate reality) and mental world (judgment, inference, logical fallacies, the syllogism), reality of external world, and negation (law of contradiction, universals, dialectic). Vol. II contains translation of Dharmakirti's Nyayabindu with Dharmamottara's commentary. Appendices cover translations of Tibetan treatises on logic, Hindu attacks on Buddhist logic, etc. The basic work, one of the products of the great St. Petersburg school of Indian studies. Written clearly and with an awareness of Western philosophy and logic; meant for the Asian specialist and for the general reader with only a minimum of background. Vol. I, xii + 559pp. Vol. II, viii + 468pp. 5⅜ x 8½.
T955 Vol. I Paperbound **$2.50**
T956 Vol. II Paperbound **$2.50**
The set **$5.00**

THE TEXTS OF TAOISM. The first inexpensive edition of the complete James Legge translations of the Tao Te King and the writings of Chinese mystic Chuang Tse. Also contains several shorter treatises: the T'ai Shang Tractate of Actions and Their Retributions; the King Kang King, or Classic of Purity; the Yin Fu King, or Classic of the Harmony of the Seen and Unseen; the Yu Shu King, or Classic of the Pivot of Jade; and the Hsia Yung King, or Classic of the Directory for a Day. While there are other translations of the Tao Te King, this is the only translation of Chuang Tse and much of other material. Extensive introduction discusses differences between Taoism, Buddhism, Confucianism; authenticity and arrangement of Tao Te King and writings of Chuang Tse; the meaning of the Tao and basic tenets of Taoism; historical accounts of Lao-tse and followers; other pertinent matters. Clarifying notes incorporated into text. Originally published as Volumes 39, 40 of SACRED BOOKS OF THE EAST series, this has long been recognized as an indispensible collection. Sinologists, philosophers, historians of religion will of course be interested and anyone with an elementary course in Oriental religion or philosophy will understand and profit from these writings. Index. Appendix analyzing thought of Chuang Tse. Vol. I, xxiii + 396pp. Vol. II, viii + 340pp. 5⅜ x 8½.
T990 Vol. I Paperbound **$2.25**
T991 Vol. II Paperbound **$2.25**

CATALOGUE OF DOVER BOOKS

EPOCHS OF CHINESE AND JAPANESE ART, Ernest T. Fenollosa. Although this classic of art history was written before the archeological discovery of Shang and Chou civilizations, it is still in many respects the finest detailed study of Chinese and Japanese art available in English. It is very wide in range, covering sculpture, carving, painting, metal work, ceramics, textiles, graphic arts and other areas, and it considers both religious and secular art, including the Japanese woodcut. Its greatest strength, however, lies in its extremely full, detailed, insight-laden discussion of historical and cultural background, and in its analysis of the religious and philosophical implications of art works. It is also a brilliant stylistic achievement, written with enthusiasm and verve, which can be enjoyed and read with profit by both the Orientalist and the general reader who is interested in art. Index. Glossary of proper names. 242 illustrations. Total of 704 pages. 5⅜ x 8½.

T364-5 Two vol. set, paperbound **$5.00**

THE VEDANTA SUTRAS OF BADARAYANA WITH COMMENTARY BY SANKARACHARYA. The definitive translation of the consummation, foremost interpretation of Upanishads. Originally part of SACRED BOOKS OF THE EAST, this two-volume translation includes exhaustive commentary and exegesis by Sankara; 128-page introduction by translator, Prof. Thibaut, that discusses background, scope and purpose of the sutras, value and importance of Sankara's interpretation; copious footnotes providing further explanations. Every serious student of Indian religion or thought, philosophers, historians of religion should read these clear, accurate translations of documents central to development of important thought systems in the East. Unabridged republication of Volumes 34, 38 of the Sacred Books of the East. Translated by George Thibault. General index, index of quotations and of Sanskrit. Vol. I, cxxv + 448pp. Vol. II, iv + 506pp. 5⅜ x 8½.

T994 Vol. I Paperbound **$2.00**
T995 Vol. II Paperbound **$2.00**

THE UPANISHADS. The Max Müller translation of the twelve classical Upanishads available for the first time in an inexpensive format: Chandogya, Kena, Aitareya aranyaka and upanishad, Kaushitaki, Isa, Katha, Mundaka, Taittiriyaka Brhadaranyaka, Svetarasvatara. Prasna — all of the classical Upanishads of the Vedanta school—and the Maitriyana Upanishad. Originally volumes 1, 15 of SACRED BOOKS OF THE EAST series, this is still the most scholarly translation. Prof. Müller, probably most important Sanskritologist of nineteenth century, provided invaluable introduction that acquaints readers with history of Upanishad translations, age and chronology of texts, etc. and a preface that discusses their value to Western readers. Heavily annotated. Stimulating reading for anyone with even only a basic course background in Oriental philosophy, religion, necessary to all Indologists, philosophers, religious historians. Transliteration and pronunciation guide. Vol. I, ciii + 320pp. Vol. II, liii + 350pp.

T992 Vol. I Paperbound **$2.25**
T993 Vol. II Paperbound **$2.25**
The set **$4.50**

Prices subject to change without notice.

Dover publishes books on art, music, philosophy, literature, languages, history, social sciences, psychology, handcrafts, orientalia, puzzles and entertainments, chess, pets and gardens, books explaining science, intermediate and higher mathematics, mathematical physics, engineering, biological sciences, earth sciences, classics of science, etc. Write to:

Dept. catrr.
Dover Publications, Inc.
180 Varick Street, N. Y. 14, N. Y.